INTRODUCTION TO BANKING

Barbara Casu
University of Wales, Bangor

Claudia Girardone
University of Essex

Philip Molyneux
The University of Wales, Bangor

 Prentice Hall
FINANCIAL TIMES

An imprint of **Pearson Education**
Harlow, England • London • New York • Boston • San Francisco • Toronto • Sydney • Singapore • Hong Kong
Tokyo • Seoul • Taipei • New Delhi • Cape Town • Madrid • Mexico City • Amsterdam • Munich • Paris • Milan

Pearson Education Limited

Edinburgh Gate
Harlow
Essex CM20 2JE
England

and Associated Companies throughout the world

Visit us on the World Wide Web at:
www.pearsoned.co.uk

First published 2006

ISBN-10 0-273-69302-6
ISBN-13 978-0-273-69302-4

British Library Cataloguing-in-Publication Data
A catalogue record for this book is available from the British Library

Library of Congress Cataloging-in-Publication Data
A catalog record of this book is available from the Library of Congress

10 9 8 7 6 5 4 3 2 1
10 09 08 07 06

Typeset in 9/12pt Stone Serif by 30
Printed and bound by Ashford Colour Press Ltd., Gosport

The publisher's policy is to use paper manufactured from sustainable forests.

Contents

Part 1 INTRODUCTION TO BANKING

Chapter 1 What is special about banks?   3

Chapter 2 Banking activities and current issues in banking   20

Part 2 CENTRAL BANKING AND BANK REGULATION

Part 4 COMPARATIVE BANKING MARKETS

List of figures

List of tables

List of boxes

Preface

It is well enough that people of the nation do not understand our banking and monetary system, for if they did, I believe there would be a revolution before tomorrow morning. Henry Ford

The aim of this textbook is to provide a comprehensive introduction to theoretical and applied issues relating to the global banking industry. Despite the fears of Henry Ford, we do not think reading this book will cause a revolution but we do hope it will at least provide you with an enjoyable and interesting insight into the business of banking.

A major motivation for writing this text has been to fill a gap in the market. For a number of years we have all taught banking courses and we have become aware of students' frustration about the lack of a comprehensive yet accessible textbook that deals with a broad spectrum of introductory banking issues. Most introductory texts that cover banking issues tend to be broad-based, focusing on economics and finance and these (in our view) do not provide sufficient coverage of the theoretical and institutional detail that is essential for an accurate understanding of critical banking issues. While there are textbooks that provide such coverage targeted at advanced undergraduates and the postgraduate market, there is no text that has comprehensive coverage of such issues for those new to the study of banking. In addition, many textbooks that cover banking as part of broadly based money and banking courses tend to pay only limited attention to international experiences. As such, we have written this text to provide (we hope) an essential teaching and learning resource for anyone who has to deliver introductory lectures to undergraduates as well as teaching more advanced postgraduate and professional banking courses.

The banking industry has experienced marked changes in recent years as deregulation has allowed banking firms to diversify into the broad financial services area. Commercial banks have become full service financial firms, offering a range of non-traditional financial services including insurance, securities business, pensions and the like. Many banks are even dropping the word 'Bank' from their titles to emphasise their much broader role in the provision of financial services to households and corporations. In addition, various trends such as industry consolidation, securitisation and disintermediation are having a significant effect resulting in a smaller number of major players operating in credit, capital and money markets businesses that increasingly overlap. As banking systems open up, many institutions are also pursuing international strategies, so the traditional focus on banking as a mainly domestic business is changing. This rapidly evolving environment poses both threats and opportunities to both bank managers and owners. The former have to be increasingly aware of both domestic and international developments in the management process and in particular be aware of the various risk–return tradeoffs in all areas of a bank's activities. Capital needs to be managed effectively, in order to adhere to minimum regulatory requirements and also to generate returns in excess of the cost of capital to boost shareholders' returns. The market pressure on banks to generate good returns for shareholders has been a key element of bank strategy in recent years – bankers have been forced to cut costs, boost revenues (mainly through fee and commission income sources) and to manage their capital resources much more efficiently. These are just some of the important issues that are explained in this book.

The text is organised into four main parts:

 ## Part 1 Introduction to banking

Chapter 1 What is special about banks?
Chapter 2 Banking activities and current issues in banking
Chapter 3 Types of banking
Chapter 4 International banking

This part of the text provides an introduction to the nature of financial intermediation, covering the main reasons proposed as to why banks exist, and focusing on key issues such as adverse selection, moral hazard and delegated monitoring. The section also covers the information production, liquidity transformation and consumption smoothing role of banks as well as various other issues relating to the bank intermediation process. We then go on to provide a detailed account of the main services provided by banks and highlight current developments including consolidation, conglomeration and other trends. As the financial sectors in many countries comprise a wide range of different types of banking firms, these are then explained covering commercial banks, mutual banks, investment banks and private banks, as well as different forms of banking activity such as universal versus specialist banking and also 'interest free' Islamic banking. Given the increasing role of banks on the global scene, the final part of this section looks at the main features of international banking, highlighting the reasons why banks locate overseas or conduct international activity. We also outline the main services provided by international banks covering payments, credit, money and capital markets activity, highlighting the role of the Euromarkets – Eurobonds and Eurocurrency activity and also syndicated lending.

The main aim of Part 1 is to familiarise students with the reasons banks exist, the main services they offer, recent trends impacting on business areas, different types of banking firms and the differences between domestic and international banking business. This section provides the reader with the relevant knowledge of global banking business and should also heighten awareness of contemporary banking issues that put the following sections into context.

 ## Part 2 Central banking and bank regulation

Chapter 5 Theory of central banking
Chapter 6 Central banks in practice
Chapter 7 Bank regulation and supervision

As the banking system is the main conduit of monetary policy, it is important that students of banking are aware of the main functions of a central bank, its monetary policy role and its other functions. Part 2 deals first with the theory of central banking, outlining the role and functions of central banks, as well as the rationale for their existence. We also discuss the conduct of monetary policy, distinguishing between instruments, targets and goals, as well as the benefits of central bank independence. We then move on to discuss how the Bank of England, European Central Bank and US Federal Reserve conduct monetary policy, and the role of banks in this process. The final section focuses on bank regulation and supervision. We discuss the pivotal role played by banks in the economy to understand the rationale for regulation, and outline the aims and objectives of regulation and different types of regulation. Regulations governing UK, European and international banks are also discussed in the context of recent EU legislative developments and the new Basle II capital adequacy regime.

By the end of Part 2 students should be aware of the pivotal role played by monetary policy and supervisory regulation and its impact on the banking sector (and economy as a whole). The reader should be familiar with the rationale for central banking, the main tools and instruments of monetary policy and how various major central banks undertake their operations. Students should be familiar with the reasons banks are so heavily regulated and why having adequate solvency and liquidity are critical to maintain a safe and sound banking system. In particular, readers should understand the important role played by capital in the banking sector as well as with the Basle I and the new Basle II accords. Also there should be awareness of how bank regulation is implemented at the EU level – particularly in the context of how Basle capital recommendations are introduced into EU national law.

 ## Part 3 Issues in bank management

Chapter 8 Banks' balance sheet and income structure
Chapter 9 Managing banks on- and off- the balance sheet
Chapter 10 Banking risks
Chapter 11 Banking risks management

Part 3 of the text is organised to provide a detailed insight into the financial features of banking firms. The first section focuses on the balance sheet and income features of both commercial and investment banks, highlighting the main differences between the two types of institutions. Substantial attention to detail is paid to the components of the financial statements of these types of banks. In addition, we outline the role of traditional ratio analysis for evaluating bank performance and asset quality and also consider a relatively new performance indicator relating to shareholder value creation. The remainder of the section provides a detailed introduction to bank financial management issues, covering asset and liability management, capital management, liquidity management and off-balance sheet management. The important role played by derivative instruments in off-balance sheet business is introduced, together with a discussion of loan sales and securitisation. We then go on to discuss the various forms of risks faced by banks (including credit, interest rate, foreign exchange, market, operational and other risk types). The final chapter in Part 3 introduces a number of key approaches to bank risk management.

By the end of Part 3 students should be familiar with the main components of banks' balance sheets and income statements, be aware of off-balance sheet activity and should be able to analyse bank performance and other issues using traditional ratio analysis. In addition, they should have an insight into how banks manage their on- and off-balance sheet positions and be familiar with the main risks faced in banking operations. After this section they should be familiar with the main risk management approaches undertaken in banking.

 ## Part 4 Comparative banking markets

Chapter 12 UK banking
Chapter 13 European banking
Chapter 14 Banking in the new EU Member States
Chapter 15 Banking in the United States
Chapter 16 Banking in Japan
Chapter 17 Banking in emerging and transition economies

Part 4 focuses on the features of various banking systems, highlighting the main institutional features of these systems (types of banks, non-bank deposit firms, role of other financial firms) as well as various structural trends (number of banks, branches, M&A activity, market concentration and such like) and regulatory developments. We have tried to cover systems that (we hope) will be of interest to as wide an audience as possible, covering: the United Kingdom, the United States, Europe, Japan and various emerging and transition banking markets. It is interesting to note that similar trends are apparent in most of these systems, namely, a decline in the number of banks, consolidation and concentration, the increased role of foreign banks, the broadening of banks' business into other financial services areas, greater disintermediation and the ongoing and omnipresent role of regulatory change. However, the heterogeneity of different systems is highlighted by the strong performance of UK and US banks in recent years compared to the very poor performance of Japanese banks; the role of state ownership in many emerging markets; restrictions in banking activity in various systems and so on. Part 4 provides a detailed insight into various banking systems which we hope will be of interest and also of practical use for anyone wishing to be aware of banking sector features and developments across the globe.

By the end of Part 4 students should be familiar with the institutional features of the banking/financial systems of the UK, US, Europe, Japan and various emerging markets and transition economies. They should be aware of how the institutional features of the different banking systems are changing and the trends that are common to all systems. A full understanding of these characteristics will provide students with the relevant framework to analyse and discuss the structural and performance features of these (and other) banking systems.

We have written this book to provide an introductory grounding to the theory and practice of banking which we hope will serve as a useful guide for anyone studying banking subjects at an introductory level and for those who are perhaps considering a career in the banking/financial services industry. We hope you enjoy reading it, and we encourage correspondence regarding any omissions or any recommendations regarding improvement of the content.

Acknowledgements

This text could never have been completed without the direct and indirect help and support of a wide range of individuals. First and foremost we must acknowledge the role of our students in helping to develop our course and lecture material which has been a critical element in encouraging us to write this text. In addition, numerous discussions with fellow banking researchers and professionals have also helped us greatly. Particular thanks must go to members of the European Association of Banking and Finance Professors (known as the 'Wolpertinger Club') who have emphasised the need for a comprehensive introductory book on banking issues – we hope this book goes some way towards meeting this objective.

In compiling this textbook we would like to acknowledge the comments and discussions provided by various individuals with whom we have undertaken collaborative banking research in the past. In addition, thanks to the many colleagues who have discussed teaching and other matters relating to the study of banking, as well as to those who have given us valuable feedback on the text, including outside referees. While there are too many persons to thank individually, special thanks go to:

Yener Altunbas, University of Wales Bangor, UK
Mario Anolli, Università Cattolica del Sacro Cuore, Milan, Italy
Razak Bakouche, University of Wales Bangor, UK
Elena Beccalli, London School of Economics, UK
Harald Benink, Erasmus University, Rotterdam, Netherlands
Allen N. Berger, Federal Reserve Board, US
Göran Bergendahl, Göteborg University, Sweden
Cesare Bisoni, Università degli Studi di Modena e Reggio Emilia, Italy
Vittorio Boscia, Università di Lecce, Italy
Philip Bourke, University College Dublin, Republic of Ireland
Frans Brinkhuis, Amsterdamse Academie, Netherlands
Santiago Carbó, Universidad de Granada, Spain
Francesco Cesarini, Università Cattolica del Sacro Cuore, Milan, Italy
Shanti Chakravarty, University of Wales Bangor, UK
Georgios Chortareas, University of Essex, UK
Jerry Coakley, University of Essex, UK
Leigh Drake, Nottingham University, UK
Leo van Eerden, Vrije Universiteit Amsterdam, Netherlands
Stewart Falconer, Napier University, Edinburgh, UK
Joe Falzon, University of Malta, Malta
Franco Fiordelisi, Università Roma Tre, Italy
Blaise Gadanecz, Bank for International Settlements, Switzerland
Alicia García-Herrero, Banco de España, Spain
Ted Gardener, University of Wales Bangor, UK
John Goddard, University of Wales Bangor, UK

Elisabetta Gualandri, Università degli Studi di Modena e Reggio Emilia, Italy
Shelagh Heffernan, City University, London, UK
Barry Howcroft, Loughborough University, UK
David B. Humphrey, Florida State University, US
Munawar Iqbal, Islamic Development Bank, Saudi Arabia
Stephen James, Teesside Business School, University of Teesside, Middlesbrough, UK
Alper Kara, University of Wales Bangor, UK
Ray Kinsella, University College Dublin, Republic of Ireland
Mario La Torre, Università di Roma "La Sapienza", Italy
Sándor Ligeti, Budapest University of Economic Sciences, Hungary
Ted Lindblom,Göteborg University, Sweden
Rene Van der Linden, Amsterdamse Academie, Netherlands
David Llewellyn, Loughborough University, UK
David Maude, (previously with Bank of England and McKinsey & Co)
Ximo Maudos, University of Valencia & IVIE, Spain
David Marquez, European Central Bank, Frankfurt
Donal McKillop, The Queen's University of Belfast, Northern Ireland, UK
Víctor Méndez, Universidad de Oviedo, Spain
Joël Métais, Université de Paris-Dauphine, France
Ewa Miklaszewska, University of Krakow, Poland
Elisabetta Montanaro, Università degli Studi di Siena, Italy
Neil B. Murphy, Virginia Commonwealth University, Richmond, US
Hassan Naqvi, London School of Economics, UK
Laura Nieri, Università G. D'Annunzio, Pescara, Italy
Hacer Saduman Okumus, Istanbul Commerce University, Turkey
Bob Sedgwick, School of Business and Finance, Sheffield Hallam University, UK
Fazeer Sheik-Rahim, University of Mauritius, Réduit, Mauritius
Anna Omarini, Università Luigi Bocconi, Italy
Marco Onado, Università Luigi Bocconi, Italy
Lars Oxelheim, Lund University, Sweden
José Manuel Pastor, University of Valencia & IVIE, Spain
Arturo Patarnello, Università Milano Bicocca, Italy
Francisco Pérez, University of Valencia & IVIE, Spain
Paulo Soares de Pinho, Universidade Nova de Lisboa, Portugal
Giovanni Battista Pittaluga, Università degli Studi di Genova, Italy
Daniele A. Previati, Università Roma Tre, Italy
Javier Quesada, University of Valencia & IVIE, Spain
Francisco Rodríguez, Universidad de Granada, Spain
John Thornton, International Monetary Fund, US
Neil Tomkin, Cass Business School, City University, London, UK
Mario Tonveronachi, Università degli Studi di Siena, Italy
Paul Turner, Department of Economics, Loughborough University, UK
Rudi Vander Vennet, Ghent University, Belgium
Eleuterio Vallelado, Universidad de Valladolid, Spain
Paul Walker, Middlesex University Business School, London, UK
Robert Webb, Caledonian Business School, Glasgow Caledonian University, UK
Jonathan Williams, University of Wales Bangor, UK
John Wilson, University of St Andrews, Scotland, UK

Finally, thanks also to our families for the encouragement and support in accommodating our academic foibles and helping us to complete a large project of this kind.

Barbara Casu thanks Martin, who has been forced to read her draft chapters and could now sit an exam of 'Introduction to Banking' as successfully as our best students. Thank you for helping with editing and computer problems and for being generally very supportive.

Claudia Girardone thanks Marc for his support and inspiration while writing this text (lately his golf skills have improved as he could not see much of me at weekends!). She would also like to thank her Mum, for patiently reproducing a number of tables.

Philip Molyneux's children (while generally preferring to play computer games, draw Japanese cartoons, study chemistry and English literature!, do modern dance, surf and so on) have at least had the courtesy to find time to make a few positive comments and Del has been her usual supportive self.

Barbara Casu (The University of Wales, Bangor)
Claudia Girardone (University of Essex)
Phil Molyneux (The University of Wales, Bangor)

Publisher's acknowledgements

We are grateful to the following for permission to reproduce copyright material:

Building Societies Association for an extract from their web site http://www.bsa.org.uk; HMSO for an extract from 'Memorandum of Understanding between HM Treasury'; Thomson Learning for an extract from *Banking Management*, 4th edn, by Koch, © 2000, reprinted with permission of South-Western, a division of Thomson Learning; and Bank of England for an extract from 'Banking concentration in the UK', by A. Logan, published in the *Financial Stability Review* June 2004.

Table 2.4 from *Payment and Securities Settlement System in the EU*, Blue Book (ECB, 2004), reprinted by permission of the publisher; Table 2.5 from *Statistics on Payment and Settlement Systems in Selected Countries*, BIS (Committee on Payment and Settlement Systems of the Group of Ten Countries, 2004), reprinted by permission of the Bank for International Settlement; Table 3.2 from *Euromoney*, January 2005, reprinted with permission from *Euromoney*; Table 3.4 from *Thirty Years of Islamic Banking*, Macmillan (Iqbal, M. and Molyneux, P. 2005), reprinted by permission of the publisher; Figure 5.5 from *Monetary Policy Frameworks in a Global Context*, Routledge (Mahadeva, I. and Sterne, G., eds, 2000); Table 13.2 and Table 13.3 from *Report on EU Banking Structure* (ECB, 2004); Table 15.3 and Table 15.4 from *Fortune*, by permission of Fortune; Table 17.2 from *BIS Seventy-fifth Annual Report*, BIS (2005), reprinted by permission of the Bank for International Settlement.

We are grateful to the Financial Times Limited for permission to reprint the following material:

'Learning by doing, not by revolution', © *Financial Times*, 8 October 2004; 'Will investment banks sustain their explosive advance?', © *Financial Times*, 27 January 2005; 'Joining Europe's mainstream', © *Financial Times*, 29 November 2004; 'A brief jargon buster', © *Financial Times*, 29 November 2004; 'Keeping pace with effective results', © *Financial Times*, 27 January 2005; 'Hopes of mergers revive on continent', © *Financial Times*, 8 October 2004; 'Top bankers are back on the trail of the super-rich', © *Financial Times*, 27 January 2005; 'Retail sector gives bankers cause to cheer', © *Financial Times*, 16 May 2005; 'Mergers are sign of return to confidence', © *Financial Times*, 27 June 2005; 'Reform of banks is a priority', © *Financial Times*, 27 July 2005; Table 9.1 © *Financial Times*, 23 September 2005.

In some instances we have been unable to trace the owners of copyright material, and we would appreciate any information that would enable us to do so.

List of abbreviations and acronyms

$bn	Billions of United States dollars
£mil	Millions of Great Britain pounds
2-BCD	EU Second Banking Co-ordination Directive
ABS	Asset-backed security
ACH	Automated clearing house
AES	Advanced execution services
AIM	Alternative investment market
ALCO	Asset and Liability Committee
ALM	Asset–liability management
APACS	Association for Payment Clearing Services
APT	Arbitrage pricing theory
ATM	Automated teller machine
B2B	Business-to-business
BA-CA	Bank Austria Creditanstalt
BBA	British Bankers Association
BACS	Banks Automated Clearing System
BBVA	Banco Bilbao Vizcaya
BCBS	Basle Committee on Banking Supervision
BCCSs	Bill and Cheque Clearing Systems
BCD	Banking Co-ordination Directive
BIS	Bank for International Settlement
BOJ-NET	Bank of Japan Financial Network System
BSC	Banking Supervision Committee
BVCA	British Venture Capital Association
C&CC	Cheque and Clearing Company
C/I	Cost–Income ratio
CAD	EU Capital Adequacy Directive
CAGR	Compound Annual Growth Rate
CAMEL	Capital, asset, management, earnings, liquidity
CAMELS	Capital, asset, management, earnings, liquidity, sensitivity to risk
CAPM	Capital asset pricing model
CCB	China Construction Bank
CCBM	Correspondent Central Banking Model
CCBS	Centre for Central Banking Studies
CCCL	Cheque and Credit Clearing Company Limited
CD	Certificate of deposit
CDO	Collateralised debt obligation
CDS	Credit default swaps
CEBS	Committee of European Banking Supervisors
CEECs	Central and Eastern European countries

CEIOPS	Committee of European Insurance and Occupational Pensions Supervisors
CESR	Committee of European Securities Regulators
CHAPS	Clearing House Automated Payments System
CHIPS	Clearing House Interbank Payments System
CI	Credit institution
CIBC	Canadian Imperial Bank of Commerce
CLS	Continuous linked settlement
CML	Council of Mortgage Lenders
CP	Commercial Paper
CRAM	Country Risk Assessment Model
CRIS	Control Risks Information Services
CSFB	Credit Suisse First Boston
DG	Duration gap
DMO	Debt Management Office
DTI	Deposit-taking institution
EBC	European Banking Committee
EBRD	European Bank for Reconstruction and Development
EBT	Electronic Benefits Payment
ECB	European Central Bank
ECOFIN Council	The Economic and Financial Affairs Council
EDI	Electronic data interchange
EDP	Excessive deficit procedure
EEA	European Economic Area
EFN	European forecasting network
EFTPOS	Electronic fund transfer at point of sale
EI	Exposure indicator
EIOPC	European Insurance and Occupational Pensions Committee
EIU	Economist Intelligence Unit
EL	Expected loss
EM	Equity multiplier
EMI	European Monetary Institute
EMS	European Monetary System
ERM	Exchange Rate Mechanism
ERM II	Exchange Rate Mechanism II
ESC	European Securities Committee
ESCB	European System of Central Banks
ESF	European Securitisation Forum
EU	European Union
EURIBOR	Euro Interbank Offered Rate
Euroarea	EU Member States that have adopted the Euro
Euroland	Another term for EU Member States that have adopted the Euro
Eurozone	EU Member States that have adopted the Euro
EVA	Economic Value Added
EVCA	European Venture Capital Association
F Gap	Financing Gap
FCC	Financial Conglomerates Committee
FDI	Foreign Direct Investment
FDIC	Federal Deposit Insurance Corporation

FED	Federal Reserve Bank
FEDNET	Federal Reserve's national communications network
FFIEC	Federal Financial Institutions Examination Council
FICC	Fixed Income, Currencies and Commodities Department
FOMC	Federal Open Market Committee
FR	Federal Reserve
FRA	Forward rate agreement
FRN	Floating rate note
FRS	Federal Reserve System
FSA	Financial Services Authority
FSAP	Financial Services Action Plan
FSCS	Financial Services Compensation Scheme
FSMA	Financial Services and Markets Act 2000
FXYCS	Foreign Exchange Yen Clearing System
GCC	Gulf Co-operation Council
GDP	Gross Domestic Product
GNI	Gross National Income
HICP	Harmonised Index of Consumer Prices
HNWI	High Net Worth Individual
IBF	International Banking Facility
ICICI	Industrial Credit and Investment Corporation of India
ICRG	International Country Risk Guide
IFC	International Finance Corporation
IFRS	International Financial Reporting Standards
IMM	International Money Market
IPO	Initial Public Offering
IRB	Internal ratings-based (approach)
IRS	Interest rate swap
ISA	Individual savings accounts
ISD	Investment Services Directive
ISP	Internet service provider
IT	Information technology
KYC	Know Your Customer
L gap	Liquidity gap
L/C	Letter of credit
LBS RMS	London Business School Risk Measurement Service
LGE	Loss Given that Extent
LIBOR	London Interbank Offer Rate
LIFFE	London International Financial Futures Exchange
LOLR	Lender of Last Resort
M gap	Maturity gap
M&A	Merger and Acquisition
M1	Narrow money
M2	Intermediate money
M3	Broad money
MBBG	Major British Banking Groups
MBS	Mortgage Backed Securities
MCOB	Mortgage Conduct of Business
MEW	Mortgage Equity Withdrawal
MFI	Monetary financial institution

MHFG	Mizuho Financial Group
MMF	Money market funds
MNC	Multinational company
MPC	Monetary Policy Committee
MRO	Main Refinancing Operation
MTFG	Mitsubishi Tokyo Financial Group
MUFJ	Mitsubishi UFJ Financial Group
MVE	Market value of equity
NCB	National central bank
NCUA	National Credit Union Administration
NDTI	Non-deposit-taking institutions
NIF	Note Issuance Facilities
NII	Net interest income
NIM	Net interest margin
NIM-8	Five central and Eastern European countries and three Baltic States
NMS	New Member State
NPL	Non-performing loan
OBS	Off-balance sheet
OCC	Office of the Comptroller of the Currency
OCH	Overseas Clearing House
OECD	Organisation for Economic Co-operation and Development
OIE	Overseas Investment Exchange
OIS	Overnight index swap
OMO	Open market operation
OTC	Over-the-counter
OTS	Office of Thrift Supervision
PC	Personal computer
PE	Probability of Loss Event
PLL	Provision for loan losses
POEA	Premium Over Earning Assets
PWC	Price Waterhouse Coopers
RAPM	Risk adjusted performance measurement
RAR	Risk–asset ratio
RAROC	Risk adjusted return on capital
RBI	Reserve Bank of India
RBSG	Royal Bank of Scotland Group
REPO	Repurchase agreement
RMB	Renminbi (People's Currency)
ROA	Return on assets
ROCH	Recognised overseas clearing house
ROE	Return on equity
ROIE	Recognised Overseas Investment Exchange
RPI	Retail Price Index
RPIX	Retail Price Index (excluding Mortgage Interest Payments)
RTGS	Real Time Gross Settlement
RWA	Risk-weighted asset
S&Ls	Savings and loans
S&LA	Savings and loans association
S&P	Standard & Poor's

SDRs	Special Drawing Rights
SEPA	Single Euro Payments Area
SME	Small and medium-sized enterprises
SMFG	Sumitomo Mitsui Financial Group
SMP	Single Market Programme
SPV	Special purpose vehicle
SUERF	Société Universitaire Européenne de Recherches Financières
SWIFT	Society for Worldwide Interbank Financial Telecommunication
TARGET	Trans-European Automated Real-time Gross settlement Express Transfer
T-bills	Treasury bills
T-bonds	Treasury bonds
TBTF	Too Big To Fail
UCITS Directive	Undertaking for Collective Investment in Transferable Securities
VaR	Value at risk
WSE	Warsaw Stock Exchange
WTO	World Trade Organisation
YTM	Yield to maturity
Zengin System	Zengin Data Telecommunication System
AT	Austria
BE	Belgium
CY	Cyprus
CZ	Czech Republic
DE	Germany
DK	Denmark
EE	Estonia
ES	Spain
FI	Finland
FR	France
GR	Greece
HU	Hungary
IE	Ireland
IT	Italy
LT	Lithuania
LU	Luxembourg
LV	Latvia
MT	Malta
NL	Netherland
PL	Poland
PT	Portugal
SE	Sweden
SI	Slovenia
SK	Slovakia
UK	United Kingdom
US	United States (of America)

Part 1

INTRODUCTION TO BANKING

Chapter 1

What is special about banks?

Learning objectives

- To understand the role of financial intermediaries in the economy
- To understand lenders' and borrowers' different requirements and how banks can help to bridge such differences
- To understand how financial intermediaries reduce transaction, information and search costs
- To analyse the theories of financial intermediation

1.1 Introduction

The first question one may ask when reading this book is 'What is so special about banks?' This chapter aims to offer some insights into the nature of the banking business and what makes banks 'special'. A bank is a financial intermediary that offers loans and deposits, and payment services. Nowadays banks also offer a wide range of additional services, but it is these functions that constitute banks' distinguishing features. Because banks play such an important role in channelling funds from savers to borrowers, in this chapter we use the concepts of 'bank' and 'financial intermediary' almost as synonyms as we review the role of banks and their main functions: size transformation; maturity transformation and risk transformation. The difference between banks and other financial intermediaries is introduced in Chapter 2. The second part of this chapter gives an overview of some important concepts in information economics as they apply to banking. The final sections present five theories to explain why banking exists and the benefits of financial intermediation.

1.2 The nature of financial intermediation

To understand how banks work, it is necessary to understand the role of financial intermediaries in an economy. This will help us to answer the question about why we need banks. Financial intermediaries and financial markets' main role is to provide a mechanism by which funds are transferred and allocated to their most productive opportunities.

A bank is a financial intermediary whose *core* activity is to provide loans to borrowers and to collect deposits from savers. In other words they act as *intermediaries* between borrowers and savers, as illustrated in Figure 1.1.

By carrying out the intermediation function banks collect surplus funds from savers and allocate them to those (both people and companies) with a deficit of funds (borrowers). In doing so, they channel funds from savers to borrowers thereby increasing economic efficiency by promoting a better allocation of resources.

Arguably, savers and borrowers do not need banks to intermediate their funds: in **direct finance**, as shown in Figure 1.2, borrowers obtain funds directly from lenders in financial markets.

A **financial claim** is a claim to the payment of a future sum of money and/or a periodic payment of money. More generally, a financial claim carries an obligation on the issuer to pay interest periodically and to redeem the claim at a stated value in one of three ways:

Figure 1.1 The intermediation function

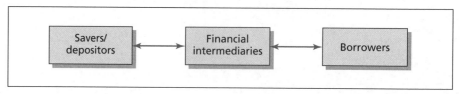

Figure 1.2 **Direct finance**

1) on demand;
2) after giving a stated period of notice;
3) on a definite date or within a range of dates.

Financial claims are generated whenever an act of borrowing takes place. Borrowing occurs whenever an economic unit's (individuals, households, companies, government bodies, etc.) total expenditure exceeds its total receipts. Therefore borrowers are generally referred to as **deficit units** and lenders are known as **surplus units**. Financial claims can take the form of any **financial asset**, such as money, bank deposit accounts, bonds, shares, loans, life insurance policies, etc. The lender of funds holds the borrower's financial claim and is said to hold a financial asset. The issuer of the claim (borrower) is said to have a **financial liability**.

The borrowing–lending process illustrated in Figure 1.2 does not require the existence of financial intermediaries. However, two types of barriers can be identified to the direct financing process:

1) the difficulty and expense of matching the complex needs of individual borrowers and lenders;
2) the incompatibility of the financial needs of borrowers and lenders.

Lenders are looking for safety and liquidity. Borrowers may find it difficult to promise either.

Lenders' requirements:
- The *minimisation of risk*. This includes the minimisation of the risk of default (the borrower not meeting its repayment obligations) and the risk of the assets dropping in value.
- The *minimisation of cost*. Lenders aim to minimise their costs.
- *Liquidity*. Lenders value the ease of converting a financial claim into cash without loss of capital value; therefore they prefer holding assets that are more easily converted into cash. One reason for this is the lack of knowledge of future events, which results in lenders preferring short-term lending to long-term.

Borrowers' requirements:
- Funds *at* a particular specified date.
- Funds *for* a specific period of time; preferably *long-term* (think of the case of a company borrowing to purchase capital equipment which will only achieve positive returns in the longer term or of an individual borrowing to purchase a house).
- Funds at the *lowest possible cost*.

In summary, the majority of lenders want to lend their assets for short periods of time and for the highest possible return. In contrast the majority of borrowers demand liabilities that are cheap and for long periods.

Financial intermediaries can bridge the gap between borrowers and lenders and reconcile their often incompatible needs and objectives. They do so by offering suppliers of funds safety and liquidity by using funds deposited for loans and investments. Financial intermediaries help minimise the costs associated with direct lending – particularly **transactions costs** and those derived from **information asymmetries** (these concepts will be analysed in more detail in Section 1.4).

Transactions costs relate to the costs of searching for a counterparty to a financial transaction;[1] the costs of obtaining information about them; the costs of negotiating the contract; the costs of monitoring the borrowers; and the eventual enforcements costs should the borrower not fulfil its commitments. In addition to transaction costs, lenders are also faced with the problems caused by asymmetric information. These problems arise because one party has better information than the counterparty. In this context, the borrower has better information about the investment (in terms of risk and returns of the project) than the lender. Information asymmetries create problems in all stages of the lending process.

Transaction costs and information asymmetries are examples of market failures; that is, they act as obstacles to the efficient functioning of financial markets. One solution is the creation of organised financial markets. However, transaction costs and information asymmetries, though reduced, still remain. Another solution is the emergence of financial intermediaries. Organised financial markets and financial intermediaries co-exist in most economies; the flow of funds from units in surplus to unit in deficit in the context of direct and **indirect finance** are illustrated in Figure 1.3.

Figure 1.3 Direct and indirect finance

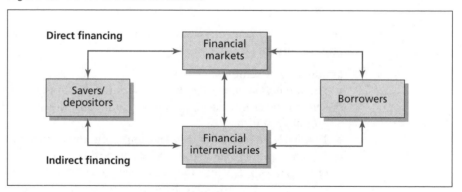

Having discussed the advantages of financial intermediation over direct finance, it is necessary to point out that financial intermediaries create additional costs for borrowers and lenders who use their services. Therefore, in order to be able to state that intermediated finance is more advantageous than direct finance, it is necessary that the benefits of such activity outweigh the costs associated with intermediation.

---

[1] Transaction costs can be defined as the costs of running the economic system (Coase, 1937). In particular, it is common to distinguish between co-ordination costs (e.g., costs of search and negotiation) and motivation costs (e.g., costs due to asymmetric information and imperfect commitment). Transaction costs can be measured in time and money spent in carrying out a financial transaction.

The role of financial intermediation has now become more complex as intermediaries perform additional roles, such as brokerage services (i.e., buying and selling stocks and bonds for clients) and securitisation (i.e., the pooling and re-packaging of illiquid financial assets into marketable securities) thus creating an extra layer of intermediation, as illustrated in Figure 1.4. When financial intermediaries hold claims issued by other financial intermediaries, then an extra layer of financial intermediation is created. Nowadays, given the increased complexity of credit flows, it is not uncommon to have more than two layers of intermediation.

Figure 1.4 **Modern financial intermediation**

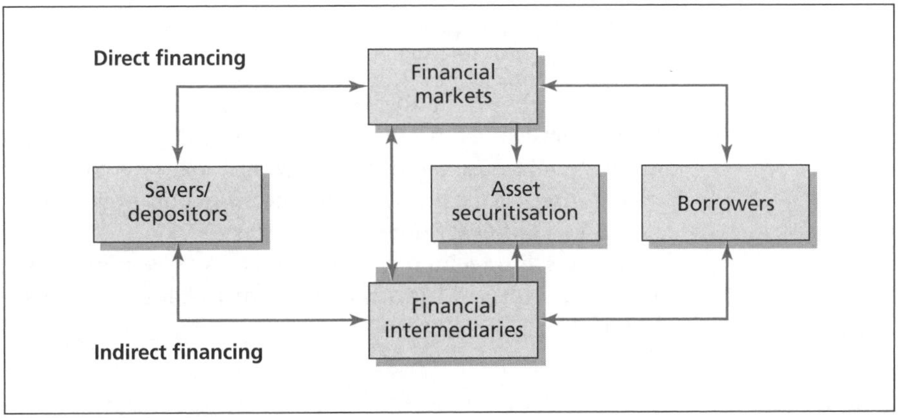

1.3 **The role of banks**

To understand fully the advantages of the intermediation process, it is necessary to analyse what banks do and how they do it. We have seen that the main function of banks is to collect funds (deposits) from units in surplus and lend funds (loans) to units in deficit. Deposits typically have the characteristics of being small-size, low-risk and high-liquidity. Loans are of larger-size, higher-risk and illiquid. Banks bridge the gap between the needs of lenders and borrowers by performing a transformation function:

a) size transformation;
b) maturity transformation;
c) risk transformation.

a) Size transformation

Generally, savers/depositors are willing to lend smaller amounts of money than the amounts required by borrowers. For example, think about the difference between your savings account and the money you would need to buy a house! Banks collect funds from savers in the form of small-size deposits and repackage them into larger size loans. Banks perform this size transformation function exploiting **economies of scale** associated with the lending/borrowing function, because they have access to a larger number of depositors than any individual borrower (see Section 1.4.2).

b) Maturity transformation

Banks transform funds lent for a short period of time into medium- and long-term loans. For example, they convert demand deposits (i.e. funds deposited that can be withdrawn on demand) into 25-year residential mortgages. Banks' liabilities (i.e., the funds collected from savers) are mainly repayable on demand or at relatively short notice. On the other hand, banks' assets (funds lent to borrowers) are normally repayable in the medium to long term. Banks are said to be 'borrowing short and lending long' and in this process they are said to 'mismatch' their assets and liabilities. This mismatch can create problems in terms of **liquidity risk**, which is the risk of not having enough liquid funds to meet one's liabilities.

c) Risk transformation

Individual borrowers carry a risk of default (known as credit risk) that is the risk that they might not be able to repay the amount of money they borrowed. Savers, on the other hand, wish to minimise risk and prefer their money to be safe. Banks are able to minimise the risk of individual loans by diversifying their investments, pooling risks, screening and monitoring borrowers and holding capital and reserves as a buffer for unexpected losses.

The tools and techniques used by banks to perform these transformations and to minimise the risks inherent with such transformations will be illustrated in Chapter 11.

1.4 Information economies

As discussed earlier, banks provide an important source of external funds used to finance business and other activities. One of the main features of banks is that they reduce transaction costs by exploiting scale and scope economies and often they owe their extra profits to superior information. Sections 1.4.1 and 1.4.2 look into information economies as they apply to the banking industry.

1.4.1 Transaction costs

Banks traditionally differ from other financial intermediaries for two main reasons: (1) bank liabilities (i.e., deposits) are accepted as a means of exchange; and (2) banks are the only intermediaries that can vary the level of deposits and can create and destroy credit. Modern views on financial intermediation indicate as a crucial function of financial intermediaries the transformation of primary securities issued by firms (deficit units) into secondary securities that are more attractive to surplus units.

In this context, financial intermediation can be explained in terms of reduction of transaction costs: secondary securities will be less risky, more convenient and more liquid than primary securities, because banks benefit from economies of scale in transaction technologies and are able to carry out a rational diversification of risks. This allows them to offer lower loan rates relative to direct financing. However, most bank assets are illiquid (non-negotiable) and this can be explained by issues relating to asymmetric information (see Section 1.4.3).

1.4.2 Economies of scale and economies of scope

Financial intermediaries reduce transaction, information and search costs mainly by exploiting economies of scale. By increasing the volume of transactions, the cost per unit of transaction decreases. Moreover, by focusing on growing in size, financial intermediaries are able to draw standardised contracts and monitor customers so that they enforce these contracts. They also train high-quality staff to assist in the process of finding and monitoring suitable units in deficit (borrowers). It would be very difficult, time-consuming and costly for an individual to do so.

Financial intermediaries can reduce risks by 'pooling', or aggregating, individual risks so that in normal circumstances, surplus units will be depositing money as deficit units make withdrawals. This enables banks, for instance, to collect relatively liquid deposits and invest most of them in long-term assets. Another way to look at this situation is that large groups of depositors are able to obtain liquidity from the banks while investing savings in illiquid but more profitable investments (Diamond and Dybvig, 1983).

Economies of scope refer to a situation where the joint costs of producing two complementary outputs are less than the combined costs of producing the two outputs separately. Let us consider two outputs, Q_1 and Q_2 and their separate costs, $C(Q_1)$ and $C(Q_2)$. If the joint cost of producing the two outputs is expressed by $C(Q_1,Q_2)$, then economies of scope are said to exist if:

$$C(Q_1,Q_2) < C(Q_1) + C(Q_2) \tag{1.1}$$

This may arise when the production processes of both outputs share some common inputs, including both capital (for example, the actual building the bank occupies) and labour (such as bank management). Consider, for example, the economies derived from the joint supply of both banking and insurance services. A bank might sell both mortgages and life insurance policies that go with them, therefore creating cross-selling opportunities for the bank (for more details on bancassurance, see Section 3.2.1). However, the literature indicates that economies of scope are difficult to identify and measure.

1.4.3 Asymmetric information

Information is at the heart of all financial transactions and contracts. Three problems are relevant:

- not everyone has the same information;
- everyone has less than perfect information, and
- some parties to a transaction have 'inside' information which is not made available to both sides of the transaction.

Such 'asymmetric' information can make it difficult for two parties to do business together, and this is why regulations are introduced to help reduce mismatches in information.

Transactions involving asymmetric (or private) information are everywhere. A government selling a bond does not know what buyers are prepared to pay; a bank does not know how likely a borrower is to repay; a firm that sells a life insurance policy does not know the precise health of the purchaser (even though they have a good idea); an investor that buys an equity in Nokia does not know the full details about the company's operations and future prospects. These types of informational asymmetries can distort both firm's and user's incentives that result in significant inefficiencies.

Information is at the centre of all financial transactions and contracts. Decisions are made beforehand (*ex ante*) on the basis of less than complete information and sometimes with counterparties who have superior information with the potential for exploitation. In any financial system, information is not symmetrically distributed across all agents, which implies that different agents have different information sets. Put another way, full and complete information is not uniformly available to all interested parties. In addition, not all parties have the same ability to utilise the information that is available to them. In particular, parties have more information about themselves (including their intentions and abilities) than do others. The problem arises because information is not a free good and the acquisition of information is not a costless activity. If either were the case, there would never be a problem of asymmetric information.

Asymmetric information, and the problems this gives rise to, are central to financial arrangements and the way financial institutions behave to limit and manage risk. Information asymmetries, or the imperfect distribution of information among parties, can generate **adverse selection** and **moral hazard** problems as explained in Section 1.4.3.1. Another type of information asymmetry relates to the **agency costs** between the **principal** (e.g. bank) and **agent** (e.g. borrower). These issues are analysed in Section 1.4.3.2.

1.4.3.1 Adverse selection and moral hazard

One problem that often arises from asymmetric information is adverse selection. The better informed economic agent has a natural incentive to exploit his informational advantage. Those who are uninformed should anticipate their informational handicap and behave accordingly. It is the interaction between the inclination of the informed to strategically manipulate and the anticipation of such manipulation by the uninformed that results in distortion away from the 'first best' (the economic outcome in a setting where all are equally well informed). Adverse selection is a problem at the search/verification stage of the transaction (*ex ante*); it is sometimes referred to as the 'lemon' problem (Akerlof, 1970). In his famous study entitled 'Market for Lemons', George Akerlof explains the consequences of asymmetric information in a situation where the buyer, and not the seller, does not know the quality of the commodity being exchanged. In this context, the vendor is aware that they are the only one knowing the true characteristics of the commodities and can exaggerate the quality. Conversely, the buyer can form an opinion on the quality of the commodities only after buying the commodity (i.e., *ex post*). Akerlof demonstrates that if there are a relatively high number of bad commodities in the market, the market will function poorly, if at all. A common example of this phenomenon is in the second-hand car market; here the sellers know whether or not their car is a lemon (a bad car) but the buyers cannot make that judgement without running the car. Given that buyers cannot tell the quality of any car, all cars of the same type will sell at the same price, regardless of whether they are lemons or not. The risk of purchasing a lemon will lower the price buyers are prepared to pay for a car, and because second-hand prices are low, people with non-lemon cars will have little incentive to put them on the market. One possible solution to the adverse selection problem is to offer a warranty, as it would be viewed as a signal of quality. Hence '**signalling**' refers to actions of the 'informed party' in an adverse selection problem. On the other hand the action undertaken by the less informed party to determine the information possessed by informed party is called '**screening**' (for example, the action taken by an insurance company to gather information about the health history of potential customers).[2]

Economic transactions often involve people with different information. In the context of financial markets, for example, those who buy insurance or take out bank loans are likely to have a better idea of the risks they face than the insurance company or bank. As such, it is often those who face the bigger risks who are more likely to want to buy insurance and those with the riskiest business proposals who are more likely to seek bank loans and therefore are more likely to be selected. Adverse selection in financial markets results in firms attracting the wrong type of clients; this in turn pushes up insurance premiums and loan rates to the detriment of lower-risk customers. Financial firms such as banks and insurers, therefore, seek to screen out/monitor such customers by assessing their risk profile and adjusting insurance premiums and loan rates to reflect the risks of individual clients.

In banking, adverse selection can occur typically as a result of loan pricing. As shown in Figure 1.5, the relationship between the return the bank can expect from a certain loan and the loan price is increasing and positive up to a certain point (for example an interest rate of 12 per cent). Any prices above that level (shaded area in the figure) will decrease the expected return for the bank because of adverse selection: only the most risky borrowers (i.e., those with a low probability of repayment, such as speculators) will be ready to accept a loan at a very high price.

Another issue relating to information asymmetries is moral hazard (or hidden action). Superior information may enable one party to work against the interests of another. In general, moral hazard arises when a contract or financial arrangement creates incentives for parties to behave against the interest of others. For example, moral hazard is the risk that the borrower might engage in activities that are undesirable from the lender's point of view because they make it less likely that the loan will be repaid and thus harm the interest of the lender. A classic example is the use of funds originally borrowed for a 'safe' investment project (a car

Figure 1.5 Adverse selection in loan pricing

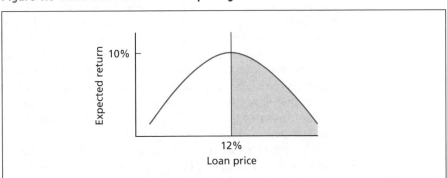

_____

[2] In 2001 the Nobel Prize for economics was awarded to three economists 'for their analyses of markets with asymmetric information': G.A. Akerlof, A.M. Spence and J.E. Stiglitz.

purchase, a home improvement) which are then gambled in a high-risk project (for example, invested in a 'get rich quick' scheme). Thus for a bank, moral hazard occurs after the loan has been granted (*ex post*) and is associated with the monitoring and enforcement stages. Those that obtain some form of insurance may take greater risks than they would do without it because they know they are protected, so the insurer may get larger claims than expected. Examples of moral hazard in banking relate to: deposit insurance and the lender-of-last-resort function of the central bank (see Chapter 7).

Monitoring is required whenever there are the problems of moral hazard and adverse selection. A standard example often given is the case of bank loans where lenders screen out excessively high risks, and regularly monitor the performance of the borrowers by obtaining various types of financial information – for example companies are often required to submit periodic reports detailing the performance of their business. In addition, for loans to large companies, there are 'rating' agencies (like Standard & Poor's, Moody's) that provide information on firm performance and credit ratings, that is an estimate of the amount of credit that can be extended to a company or person without undue risk (See Table 4.1 Credit risk ratings – Moody's and Standard & Poor's). Banks also send inspectors to firms to monitor their progress. However, it is particularly difficult for consumers/investors to monitor financial firms to see how they are performing and what they are doing with their deposits or investments. This is one reason why we have regulators to monitor financial firm behaviour.

1.4.3.2 Principal–agent problems

Financial transactions often create principal–agent problems of one sort or another. This is also related to the problem of incentive structures in that the central issue is how a principal is able to rely on the agent acting in the interests of the principal employing him rather than his own selfish interest and against those of the principal. The problem arises because the agent often has superior information and expertise (which may be the reason the principal employs them). The agent can choose his or her behaviour after the contract has been established, and because of this the agent is often able to conceal the outcome of a contract. Agency problems also arise because the agent cannot be efficiently or costlessly monitored. Unless these problems can be solved, the agency costs involved can act as a serious deterrent to financial contracting with resultant losses. The challenge is to create financial contracts or arrangements that align the interests of the principal and the agent.

A typical example of principal–agent problem refers to a situation of separation of ownership and control in a firm. Managers in control (the *agents*) may act in their own interest rather than in the interest of shareholders (the *principals*) because the managers have less incentive to maximise profits than shareholders.[3] A firm acting in the interest of the shareholders has an incentive to undertake investments that benefit the shareholders at the expense of creditors. However, as observed by Jensen and Meckling (1976) the assumption that managers act in the best interest of the shareholders is questionable. As an agent of the shareholders, the manager can do many things that may not be in the best interest of the shareholders. For example,

---

[3] Note that shareholders in the US are referred to as stockholders. Also it is useful to remember that equity or ordinary shares in the UK are referred to as common stock in the United States.

managers may select low-risk investment projects with a view toward protecting their positions and reputations! To summarise, the principal (the shareholder) is unable to completely control the agent's behaviour. If it were possible to costlessly observe the agent's action, there would be no moral hazard. It is obvious that the principal anticipates the agent's behaviour. Therefore, the principal attempts to design a contract that aligns the agent's incentives with his own.

The example above shows that principal–agency issues are inextricably linked to information asymmetry and moral hazard. The behaviour of contracting parties (counterparties) needs to be monitored after a contract has been agreed to ensure that information asymmetries are not exploited by one party against the interest of the other, and also because frequently a fiduciary relationship (a relationship of trust and confidence) is created by a financial contract. In both cases, parties need to be monitored to ensure that their behaviour is consistent with both their interests. A special characteristic of many financial contracts is that the value (for example: the future returns on an investment; the amount of loan repayments to a bank – some of which may suffer from default; returns on long-term savings products) cannot be observed or verified at the point of purchase, and that the post-contract behaviour of a counterparty determines the ultimate value of the contract. This also creates a need for monitoring. In addition, monitoring is needed because many financial contracts are long-term in nature and information acquired before a contract is agreed may become irrelevant during the course of the contract as circumstances and conditions change. Above all, the value of a contract or financial product cannot be ascertained with certainty at the point the contract is made or the product is purchased. This often distinguishes financial contracts from other economic contracts such as purchases of goods. While the need for monitoring is accepted, it is an expensive activity and parties involved need to balance the costs and benefits of such monitoring.

As the cost of monitoring principal–agent relationships can be expensive and difficult for the market to resolve, public regulatory agencies help perform this task – for instance they monitor financial service firms to minimise conflicts between principals (financial firms) and agents (customers).

1.4.3.3 The free-rider problem

One general solution to information problems is for those involved in financial transactions to invest in information. However, this is not a costless activity and free-rider problems may emerge as, in some cases, no one party can appropriate the full value of the costly information acquired.

Free-rider problems occur when people who do not pay for information take advantage of the information that other people have paid for. For example: you purchase information that tells you which firms are good and which are bad. You believe the purchase is worthwhile because you can buy securities of good firms that are undervalued so you will gain extra profits. But free-rider investors see that you are buying certain securities and will want to buy the same.

Governments could produce information to help investors distinguish good from bad firms and provide it to the public free of charge. The main drawback is that this action may be politically difficult. Moreover it never completely eliminates the problem. By encouraging bank lending, a bank can profit from the information it produces by making private loans (i.e., avoiding free-rider problems).

1.4.3.4 Relationship and transaction banking

In credit markets one way to overcome agency and adverse selection problems, is for the parties to enter a *relational contract*. Relational contracts are informal agreements between the bank and the borrowers sustained by the value of future relationships. Modern financial intermediation theory has emphasised the role of banks as relationship lenders: this is when banks invest in developing close and long-term relationships with their customers. Such relations improve the information flow between the bank and the borrower and thus are beneficial to both parties. If the customer has a 'history' (e.g., they have borrowed previously from the bank over a long period of time), then the bank's screening and monitoring costs will be much lower compared with the cost associated with new customers. On the other hand, borrowers will find it easier to get future loans at (relatively) low rates of interest.[4]

Recent literature (see Boot, 2000 and Boot and Thakor, 2000) has indicated that relationship banking can be sustained under high competitive pressures. In other words, the informational savings derived from relationship lending can be considered as a primary source of competitive advantage for existing banks over new market participants; this is because by drawing relational contracts, banks can 'isolate' themselves from competition from other banks and/or non-bank financial intermediaries.

Our discussion above seems to suggest that the creation of strong links between banks and companies might be beneficial to both businesses. Indeed in bank-based systems such as Japan and Germany, banks hold equity stakes in companies they lend to and banks in turn have members on the Board of Directors of these companies. In Anglo-Saxon countries (such as the United States and the United Kingdom) such arrangements are typically not allowed.

In recent years, the intense disintermediation process that has characterised the financial and banking markets, coupled with the increasingly common *transaction banking*, has started to challenge the importance of banks as relationship lenders. Transaction banking involves a pure funding transaction where the bank essentially acts as a 'broker'; an example is that of a mortgage loan made by a bank and then sold on to an investor in the form of a security. This process is known as securitisation and it is explained in more detail in Section 9.6. It is obvious that in transaction banking there is no relationship between the parties and no flexibility in the contract terms.

1.5 Why do banks exist? Theories of financial intermediation

There are five theories that explain why financial intermediation (banking) exists. These theories relate to: delegated monitoring; information production; liquidity transformation; consumption smoothing; and the role of banks as a commitment mechanism.

---

[4] It has been observed (e.g., Heffernan, 2005, p. 7) that in the presence of relationship banking there could be more scope for borrower opportunism.

1.5.1 Financial intermediation and delegated monitoring

One of the main theories put forward as an explanation for the existence of banking relates to the role of banks as 'monitors' of borrowers. Since monitoring credit risk (likelihood that borrowers default) is costly, it is efficient for surplus units (depositors) to delegate the task of monitoring to specialised agents such as banks. Banks have expertise and economies of scale in processing information on the risks of borrowers and, as depositors would find it costly to undertake this activity, they delegate responsibility to the banks.

One of the most relevant studies explaining why banks exist on the basis of contract theory is by Diamond (1984), according to whom **delegated monitoring** on behalf of small lenders provides the raison d'être of banking:

> An intermediary (such as a bank) is delegated the task of costly monitoring of loan contracts written with firms who borrow from it. It has a gross cost advantage in collecting this information because the alternative is either duplication of effort if each lender monitors directly or a free-rider problem in which case no lender monitors. Financial intermediation theories are generally based on some cost advantage for the intermediary. Schumpeter assigned such a *delegated monitoring* role to banks.
>
> Diamond (1984, p. 393)

Diamond's study investigates the determinants of delegation costs and develops a theoretical model in which a financial intermediary (typically a bank or an insurance company) has net cost savings relative to direct lending and borrowing. Diamond's approach is essentially developed around two interconnected factors:

1) diversification among different investment projects; this is crucial in explaining why there is a benefit from delegating monitoring to an intermediary that is not monitored by its depositors; and
2) the size of the delegated intermediary that can finance a large number of borrowers.

Since usually diversification will increase with the number of bank loans, larger delegated intermediaries will generate higher economies of scale in monitoring and this will allow for greater portfolio diversification than any individual lender could achieve.

One issue that arises, however, relates to who is 'monitoring the monitor'. Surplus units (depositors) can reduce monitoring expense if the costs of monitoring the intermediary are lower than the costs of surplus units lending direct to borrowers and therefore directly incurring the monitoring costs. As a financial intermediary increases in size, it can commit to offer deposit facilities to surplus units only if the intermediary is undertaking the appropriate monitoring activity.

1.5.2 Information production

If information about possible investment opportunities is not free, then economic agents may find it worthwhile to produce such information. For instance surplus units could incur substantial search costs if they were to seek out borrowers directly. If there were no banks, then there would be duplication of information production costs as surplus units would individually incur considerable expense in seeking out the relevant information before they committed funds to a borrower. An alternative is to have a smaller number of specialist agents (banks) that choose to produce the same information.

Banks have economies of scale and other expertise in processing information relating to deficit units – this information may be obtained upon first contact with borrowers but in reality is more likely to be learned over time through repeated dealings with the borrower. As banks build up this information (e.g., the knowledge of credit risk associated with different types of borrowers – 'customer relationships') they become experts in processing this information. As such they have an information advantage and depositors are willing to place funds with a bank knowing that these will be directed to the appropriate borrowers without the former having to incur information costs.

1.5.3 Liquidity transformation

Banks provide financial or secondary claims to surplus units (depositors) that often have superior liquidity features compared to direct claims (like equity or bonds). Banks' deposits can be viewed as contracts that offer high liquidity and low risk that are held on the liabilities side of a bank's balance sheets. These are financed by relatively illiquid and higher risk assets (e.g., loans) on the assets side of the bank's balance sheet. It should be clear that banks can hold liabilities and assets of different liquidity features on both sides of their balance sheet through diversification of their portfolios. In contrast, surplus units (depositors) hold relatively undiversified portfolios (e.g., deposits typically have the same liquidity and risk features). The better banks are at diversifying their balance sheets, the less likely it is that they will default on meeting deposit obligations.

1.5.4 Consumption smoothing

The three aforementioned theories are usually cited as the main reasons why financial intermediaries (typically banks) exist. However, recent studies have suggested that banks perform a major function as consumption smoothers. Namely, banks are institutions that enable economic agents to smooth consumption by offering insurance against shocks to a consumer's consumption path. The argument goes that economic agents have uncertain preferences about their expenditure and this creates a demand for liquid assets. Financial intermediaries in general, and banks in particular, provide these assets via lending and this helps smooth consumption patterns for individuals.

1.5.5 Commitment mechanisms

Another theory that has recently developed aims to provide a reason as to why illiquid bank assets (loans) are financed by demand deposits that allow consumers to arrive and demand liquidation of those illiquid assets. It is argued that bank deposits (demand deposits) have evolved as a necessary device to discipline bankers. To control the risk-taking propensity of banks, demand deposits have evolved because changes in the supply and demand of these instruments will be reflected in financing costs and this disciplines or commits banks to behave prudently (ensuring banks hold sufficient liquidity and capital resources).

1.6 The benefits of financial intermediation

Financial intermediation, as noted previously, is the process of channelling funds between those who wish to lend or invest and those who wish to borrow or require investment funds. Financial intermediaries act as principals, creating new financial assets and liabilities.

A wide range of financial institutions are engaged in financial intermediation, including banks, insurance and pension firms, securities houses and others. Many of the services offered by financial institutions also include both intermediation and non-intermediation activities (e.g., payment services, fund management services and so on).

An important distinguishing characteristic of financial intermediation is that new financial assets and liabilities are created. In the case of a bank deposit, the nature of the claims and liabilities created is usually straightforward. The depositor has a claim for a given amount of money, perhaps to be repaid on demand, while the bank has a matching liability to repay a given amount of money. If the bank on-lends deposits it has a claim against the borrower for a given amount of money, to be repaid (with interest) at a given point in time in the future. The borrower, naturally, has a liability to repay that sum of money with interest on the specified date.

The significance of financial intermediation within the financial system is best appreciated in terms of the benefits that it generates. These benefits accrue to *ultimate lenders (surplus units)*, to *ultimate borrowers (deficit units)* and to *society as a whole*.

1.6.1 The benefits to ultimate lenders (surplus units)

These may be summarised as follows:

- *Greater liquidity* is generally achieved by lending to a financial intermediary rather than directly to an ultimate borrower.
- *Less risk is involved*, due to the pooling of risk inherent with financial intermediation, the improved risk assessment that intermediaries are able to undertake and the portfolio diversification that can frequently be achieved. This reduction in risk may be reflected in guaranteed interest rates on deposits with a financial intermediary.
- *Marketable securities* may be issued as the counterpart to deposits with a financial intermediary. For example, a certificate of deposit (CD) is a type of time deposit where the bank issues a certificate that a deposit has been made (this is particularly common in the US). The certificate of deposit can then be sold in the market whenever an individual/firm needs cash. Hence depositors, instead of waiting until maturity of the securities, may sell them in the market to regain the cash. This clearly enhances the liquidity of the depositors' funds (in the broadest sense).

- *Transaction costs* associated with the lending process are likely to be reduced significantly, especially where straightforward deposit facilities are utilised.
- The *lending decision is simplified*, since there are fewer lending opportunities to financial intermediaries than there are ultimate borrowers. In addition, the assessment of the opportunities for lending to intermediaries is generally a simpler procedure than the assessment of the opportunities for lending to ultimate borrowers.

1.6.2   The benefits to ultimate borrowers (deficit units)

These may be summarised as follows:

- Loans will generally be available for *a longer time period* from financial intermediaries than from the ultimate lenders.
- Financial intermediaries will generally be prepared to grant loans of *larger amounts* than will ultimate lenders.
- Using financial intermediaries will generally involve *lower transaction costs* than would be incurred if borrowers had to approach ultimate lenders directly.
- The *interest rate* will generally be *lower* when borrowing from financial intermediaries, compared with borrowing directly from ultimate lenders. As we have seen, financial intermediaries, through the minimisation of information costs and the diversification of risk, can actually reduce the cost of intermediation.
- When borrowing from financial intermediaries, there is a greater likelihood that loans will be *available when required*.

1.6.3   The benefits to society as a whole

Financial intermediation is not only beneficial to borrowers and lenders, but it is considered likely to:

- Cause *a more efficient utilisation of funds within an economy*, since the evaluation of lending opportunities will be improved.
- Cause a *higher level of borrowing and lending to be undertaken*, due to the lower risks and costs associated with lending to financial intermediaries.
- Cause an *improvement in the availability of funds to higher-risk ventures*, due to the capability of financial intermediaries to absorb such risk. High-risk ventures are widely considered to be important for creating the basis of future prosperity for an economy.

1.7   Conclusions

This chapter has analysed the key features of financial intermediation. Banks, as other financial intermediaries, play a pivotal role in the economy, channelling funds from units in surplus to units in deficit. They reconcile the different needs of borrowers and lenders by transforming small-size, low-risk and highly liquid deposits into loans which are of larger size, higher risk and illiquid (transformation function). We discussed the main reasons banks have advantages in the intermediation process relating to matching the needs of ultimate lenders (depositors) and borrowers. In particular, we explored the concepts of transaction costs, economies of scale and economies of scope. The relevance of information costs and the notion of information asymmetries were also introduced. These are costs due to imperfect distribution of information among parties and can be defined as situations in which one or more of the parties to a transaction does not have all or part of the relevant information needed to tell whether the terms of the contract are mutually acceptable and/or are being met. Situations of this kind give rise to adverse selection and moral hazard problems; another type of information asymmetry relates to the agency costs between the principal (bank) and agent (borrower). The reasons for the existence of banks are then related to five theories that relate to: delegated monitoring; information production; liquidity transformation; consumption smoothing; and the role of banks as a commitment mechanism. The chapter concludes with an overview of the main benefits of financial intermediation.

Key terms

Financial claim	Economies of scope
Financial asset	Information asymmetries
Financial liability	Adverse selection
Direct finance	Moral hazard
Indirect finance	Signalling
Deficit units	Screening
Surplus units	Agency costs
Transactions costs	Principal–agent problems
Economies of scale	Delegated monitoring
Liquidity risk	

Key reading

Akerlof, G.A. (1970) 'The Market for 'Lemons': Quality Uncertainty and the Market Mechanism' *Quarterly Journal of Economics*, **84** (8), 488–500.

Coase, R. (1937) 'The Nature of the Firm' *Economica*, **4**, 386–405.

Diamond, D.W. (1984) 'Financial intermediation and delegated monitoring' *Review of Economics Studies*, **51** (3), 393–414.

Revision questions and problems

1 What is the role of financial intermediaries in an economy?
2 What is special about banks?
3 How do lenders' and borrowers' requirements differ? How can financial intermediaries bridge the gap between them?
4 Explain how banks can lower transaction costs.
5 Explain the relevance of information asymmetries in the intermediation process.
6 How do adverse selection and moral hazard affect the bank lending function? How can banks minimise such problems?
7 How are banks affected by agency problems?
8 Describe the main theories put forward to explain the existence of financial intermediaries.

Chapter 2

Banking activities and current issues in banking

Learning objectives

- To understand what modern banks do
- To describe the main services offered by banks
- To understand the importance of the payment system
- To understand the main forces of change in the banking industry
- To identify the main trends derived from the forces of change

2.1 Introduction

This chapter offers some insights into the nature of the banking business; it reviews the main services offered by banks (loans and deposits, and payment services) as well as a wide range of additional services, such as insurance and investment services. In this context, special attention is given to the significant changes in payment systems with an extensive discussion on the major instruments and services that modern banks provide to their customers from plastic money to e-banking.

The second part of the chapter describes the main forces that generate change in the banking sector, such as the deregulation and re-regulation processes, competitive pressures, financial innovation and technology. Finally, the chapter highlights the main trends resulting from these forces of change, for example conglomeration and globalisation.

2.2 What do banks do?

We have seen in Chapter 1 that financial intermediaries channel funds from units in surplus to units in deficit. In order to better understand how banks work, we need to examine their assets and liabilities. Table 2.1 summarises a typical bank balance sheet (details of banks' balance sheet and income structure are presented in Chapter 8).

Table 2.1 **A simplified bank balance sheet**

Liabilities	Assets
Customer deposits	Cash
Equity	Liquid assets
	Loans
	Other investments
	Fixed assets
Total	**Total**

For banks, the main source of funding is customer deposits (reported on the liabilities side of the balance sheet); this funding is then invested in loans, other investments and fixed assets (such as buildings for the branch network), and it is reported on the assets side of the balance sheet. The difference between total assets and total liabilities is the bank capital (equity). Banks make profits by charging an interest rate on their loans that is higher than the one they pay to depositors.

As with other companies, banks can raise funds by issuing bonds and equity (shares), and saving from past profits (retained earnings). However, the bulk of their money comes from deposits (see Section 8.2); it is this ability to collect deposits from the public that distinguishes banks from other financial institutions, as explained in Section 2.3.

2.3   Banks and other financial institutions

Banks are **deposit-taking institutions** (DTIs) and are also known as *monetary financial institutions* (MFIs). Monetary financial institutions play a major role in a country's economy as their deposit liabilities form a major part of a country's money supply and are therefore very relevant to governments and Central Banks for the transmission of monetary policy (see Chapter 5). Banks' deposits function as money; as a consequence, an expansion of bank deposits results in an increase in the stock of money circulating in an economy (see Box 2.1). All other things being equal, the money supply, that is the total amount of money in the economy, will increase.

Box 2.1   How banks create money: the credit multiplier

In order to understand how banks create money we illustrate a simple model of the **credit multiplier** based on the assumption that modern banks keep only a fraction of the money that is deposited by the public. This fraction is kept as reserves and will allow the bank to face possible requests of withdrawals. Suppose that there is only one bank in the financial system and suppose that there is a mandatory reserve of 10 per cent. This means that banks will have to put aside as reserves 10 per cent of their total deposits. The balance sheet of this bank over three time periods is illustrated in Table 2.2.

Table 2.2 **The case of a single bank under a 10 per cent reserve ratio (£mil)**

		Initial period (a)	Intermediate period (b): increase deposits by £50,000	Final period (c): adjust reserve ratio
Liabilities:	Deposits	50	50.05	50.05
Assets:	Reserves	5	5.05	5.005
	Loans	45	45	45.045
Reserve ratio		10%	10.1%	10%

In the initial position (a) we assume that the bank has £50 million-worth of deposits and is adhering to a 10 per cent reserve ratio. That is, for every £10 it receives in deposits, it keeps £1 in cash and can invest the other £9 as loans. In this case the bank's £50 million-worth of deposits are broken down into £5 million cash and £45 million loans. Position (b) shows the effect of an increase in deposits by £50,000. Initially, this extra £50,000 of deposits is kept as reserves. However, as the bank earns no money by simply holding excess reserves, it will wish to reduce it back to 10 per cent. In position (c) the bank returns to the initial 10 per cent reserve holding as required by the reserve ratio. At the same time, the bank will increase its loans by £45,000. In this example, the credit multiplier is defined as the ratio of change in deposits to the change in level of reserves:

$$\text{Credit multiplier} = \frac{\Delta\ Deposits}{\Delta\ Reserves} = \frac{50.05 - 50}{5.005 - 5} = \frac{0.05}{0.005} = 10$$

▶

where:

Δ Deposits = the change in the level of deposits

Δ Reserves = the change in the level of reserves.

The credit multiplier is the same as the reciprocal of the reserve ratio (i.e. 1/0.10 =10).

Considering that most banking systems operate with more than one bank, we can assume that if bank A gets a £50,000 increase in its deposit, 10 per cent will be kept as reserves and the remaining £45,000 will be lent out and will find its way to another bank. Let us suppose that such an amount is lent to an individual who deposits it in bank B. In turn, bank B will hold 10 per cent in cash (£4,500) and invest the rest, which finds its way to bank C. As illustrated in Table 2.3 at each stage the growth in deposits is exactly 90 per cent of what it was at the previous stage.

Table 2.3 **The banking system under a 10 per cent reserve ratio (£,000)**

	Δ Deposits	Δ Loans	Δ Reserves
Bank A	50.00	45.00	5.00
Bank B	45.00	40.50	4.50
Bank C	40.50	36.45	4.05
Bank D	36.45	32.81	3.64
Bank E	32.81	29.53	3.28
–	–	–	–
Total all banks	500.00	500.00	50.00

The sum of the additional deposit created in a system with n banks can also be represented as:

$$50 + (50 \times 0.9) + (50 \times 0.9^2) + (50 \times 0.9^3) + (50 \times 0.9^4) + ... + (50 \times 0.9^n)$$

This geometric series will sum to $\dfrac{50}{(1 - 0.9)} = 500$

Since the deposit multiplier equals the reciprocal of the required reserve ratio (1/0.1), then following an injection of £50,000 of cash in the system (i.e., new deposits), the process will end (achieve equilibrium) when an additional £500,000 of deposits has been created. It should be noted that this multiple deposit creation process acts also in reverse, i.e., multiple deposit contraction.

The credit multiplier explained above has several drawbacks. As with most theories, the assumptions behind this simple model are not very realistic. The creation of deposits is much less 'mechanical' in reality than the model indicates and decisions by depositors to increase their holdings in currency or of banks to hold excess reserves will result in a smaller expansion of deposits than the simple model predicts. Further, there are leakages from the system: for example, money flows abroad; people hold money as cash or buy government bonds rather than bank deposits. These considerations, however, should not deter from the logic of the process, which is: bank deposits 'create' money.

The monetary function of bank deposits is often seen as one of the main reasons why deposit-taking institutions (DTIs) are subjected to heavier regulation and supervision than their **non-deposit-taking institution** (NDTI) counterparts (such as insurance companies, pension funds, investment companies, finance houses and so on).

Figure 2.1 Classification of financial intermediaries in the UK

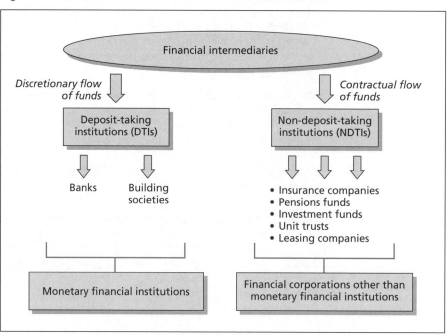

One further feature that distinguishes monetary financial institutions from other financial corporations lies in the nature of financial contracts: deposit holdings are said to be *discretionary*, in the sense that savers can make discretionary decisions concerning how much money to hold and for how long. Depositors are free to decide the frequency and amount of their transactions. On the other hand, holding assets from other financial institutions requires a contract which specifies the amount and frequency of the flow of funds. For example, the monthly contributions to a pension fund or to an insurance provider are normally fixed and pre-determined. Therefore the flow of funds in and out of other financial intermediaries is described as *contractual*.

Figure 2.1 illustrates the classification of financial institutions in the UK. However, it is important to keep in mind that there is no unique, universally accepted classification of financial intermediaries. Furthermore, distinctions are becoming blurred. As we will see later on in this chapter, regulation; financial conglomeration; advances in information technology and financial innovation; increased competition; and globalisation have all contributed to change the industry in recent years.

All countries have regulations that define what banking business is. For example, in all EU countries banks have been permitted to perform a broad array of financial services activity since the early 1990s and since 1999 both US and Japanese banks are also allowed to operate as full service financial firms. A good example of the breadth of financial activities that banks can undertake is given by the UK's Financial Services and Markets Act 2000 which defines the range of activities that banks can engage in, including:

● Accepting deposits
● Issuing e-money (or digital money) i.e., electronic money used on the internet
● Implementing or carrying out contracts of insurance as principal

- Dealing in investments (as principal or agent)
- Managing investments
- Advising on investments
- Safeguarding and administering investments
- Arranging deals in investments and arranging regulated mortgage activities
- Advising on regulated mortgage contracts
- Entering into and administering a regulated mortgage contract
- Establishing and managing collective investment schemes (for example investment funds and mutual funds)
- Establishing and managing pension schemes

In recent years, conglomeration has become a major trend in financial markets, emerging as a leading strategy of banks. This process has been driven by technological progress, international consolidation of markets and deregulation of geographical or product restrictions (see Section 2.6.2). In the EU, financial conglomeration was encouraged by the Second Banking Directive (1989), which allowed banks to operate as **universal banks**: enabling them to engage, directly or through subsidiaries, in other financial activities, such as financial instruments, factoring, leasing and investment banking. In the US, the passing of the Gramm-Leach-Bliley Act in 1999 removed the many restrictions imposed by the Glass-Steagall Act of 1933. Since 1999 US commercial banks can undertake a broad range of financial services, including investment banking and insurance activities. Similar reforms have taken place in Japan since 1999. As banks nowadays are diversified financial services firms, when we think about banks, we should now think more about the particular type of financial activity carried out by a specialist division of a large corporation rather then the activity of an individual firm.

 ## 2.4 Banking services

Modern banks offer a wide range of financial services, including:

- Payment services
- Deposit and lending services
- Investment, pensions and insurance services
- E-banking

The following sections offer an overview of such services.

2.4.1 Payment services

An important service offered by banks is that they offer facilities that enable customers to make payments. A **payment system** can be defined as any organised arrangement for transferring value between its participants. Heffernan (2005) defines the payment systems as a by-product of the intermediation process, as it facilitates the transfer of ownership of claims in the financial sector. These payment flows reflect a variety of transactions: for goods and services as well as financial assets. Some of these transactions involve high-value transfers, typically between financial institutions. However, the highest number of transactions relates to transfers between individuals and/or companies. If any of these circulation systems failed, the functioning of large and important parts of the economy would be affected. Banks play a major role in the provision of payment services.

For personal customers the main types of payments are made by writing cheques from their current accounts (known as 'checking accounts' in the United States) or via debit or credit card payments. In addition, various other payment services are provided including giro (or credit transfers) and automated payments such as direct debits and standing orders. Payments services can be either paper-based or electronic and an efficient payments system forms the basis of a well-functioning financial system. In most countries the retail payments systems are owned and run by the main banks. Note that the importance of different types of cashless payments varies from country to country as will be illustrated in Table 2.4.

- **Cheques** are widely used as a means of payment for goods and services. If individual A buys goods and gives a cheque to individual B, it is up to B to pay the cheque into their own bank account. Individual B's bank then initiates the request to debit individual A's account. Individual A's bank authorises (clears) the cheque and a transfer of assets (settlement) then takes place. Cheque payments are known as debit transfers because they are written requests to debit the payee's account.
- **Credit transfers** (or Bank Giro Credits) are payment where the customer instructs their bank to transfer funds directly to the beneficiary's bank account. Consumers use bank giro transfer payments to pay invoices or to send payment in advance for products ordered.
- **Standing orders** are instructions from the customer (account holder) to the bank to pay a fixed amount at regular intervals into the account of another individual or company. The bank has the responsibility for remembering to make these payments. Only the account holder can change the standing order instructions.
- **Direct debits** are originated by the supplier that supplied the goods/service and the customer has to sign the direct debit. The direct debit instructions are usually of a variable amount and the times at which debiting takes place can also be either fixed or variable (although usually fixed). If a payment is missed, the supplier can request the missed payment on a number of occasions. If the payments are continually missed over a period of time, the customer's bank will cancel the direct debit. Many retail customers pay utility bills (electricity, gas, water bills) in this way.
- **Plastic cards** include credit cards, debit cards, cheque guarantee cards, travel and entertainment cards, shop cards and 'smart' or 'chip' cards. Technically, plastic cards do not act themselves as a payment mechanism – they help to identify the customers and assist in creating either a paper or electronic payment.
    - **Credit cards** provide holders with a pre-arranged credit limit to use for purchases at retail stores and other outlets. The retailer pays the credit card company a commission on every sale made via credit cards and the consumer obtains free credit if the bill is paid off before a certain date. If the bill is not fully paid off then it attracts interest. Visa and MasterCard are the two most important bank-owned credit card organisations. Credit cards have become an increasingly important source of consumer lending particularly in the UK and US. For example, in 1971 there was only one type of credit card (Barclaycard) available in the UK and by 2003 there were around 1,300. The

largest five UK banks accounted for 64.1 per cent of the market. The amount of money owed on credit cards in the UK has increased exponentially from £32m, in 1971, to over £49bn by 2003.[1]

- **Debit cards** are issued directly by banks and allow customers to withdraw money from their accounts. They can also be used to obtain cash and other information when used through automated teller machines (ATMs).
- **Cheque guarantee cards** were first introduced because of retailers' reluctance to accept personal cheques. Typically, when paying by cheque further identi-fication of the payer is provided by presentation of the cheque guarantee card and details from the card will be written on the cheque in order to guarantee payment. Most of these types of cards also act as debit cards.
- **Travel and entertainment cards (or charge cards)** provide payment facili-ties and allow repayment to be deferred until the end of the month, but they do not provide interest-free credit. Unlike credit cards, all bills have to be repaid at the end of the month and no rollover is allowed. Typically, unpaid balances are charged at a higher interest rate than for credit cards, to discour-age late payment. The most widely used charge cards include American Express and Diners Club.
- **Smart, memory or chip cards** are cards that incorporate a microprocessor or a memory chip. The microprocessor cards can add, delete and otherwise manipulate information on the card and can undertake a variety of functions and store a range of information. Memory-chip cards (for example, pre-paid phone cards) can only undertake a pre-defined operation. There are over 20 million smart cards issued by banks in Europe that perform various functions although the main characteristic of the microprocessor technology is that it provides extra security features for card payment, although various schemes offer store value cards for small transactions.

Note that the importance of different types of cashless payments varies from coun-try to country as illustrated in Table 2.4 – for example in the European Union cheques are more widely used in Britain and France compared with elsewhere. (Also remember that businesses as well as consumers use these payment services.) Table 2.5 illustrates the usage of plastic cards in various countries; it highlights the widespread use of credit cards, shows that cheque guarantee cards are widely used in the UK and Switzerland and notes that smart cards (listed as cards with e-money functions) are relatively commonplace in Belgium, the Netherlands, Singapore and Switzerland.

2.4.2 Deposit and lending services

In addition to payment services personal banking includes the offer of a broad range of **deposit and lending services**. These are summarised as follows:

- **Current or checking accounts** that typically pay no (or low) rates of interest and are used mainly for payments. Banks offer a broad range of current accounts tailored to various market segments and with various other services attached.

[1] See the UK government's white paper on 'The Consumer Credit Market in the Twenty-first Century', Department of Trade and Industry, 2003. Available at http://www.dti.gov.uk/ccp/topics1/pdf1/creditwp.pdf.

Table 2.4 Use of cashless payments (number of transactions per inhabitant)

	Cheques					Payments by credit and debit cards					Direct debits				
	1998	1999	2000	2001	2002	1998	1999	2000	2001	2002	1998	1999	2000	2001	2002
Belgium	9	8	7	6	3	34	39	45	51	58	12	14	16	17	16
Denmark	13	11	10	9	8	68	74	79	87	94	21	23	24	26	27
Germany[1,2]	6	5	5	4	2	12	15	20	22	24	51	53	56	57	54
Greece[3,4]	1.6	1.6	1.6	1.6	1.5	na	na	5	5	4	na	0.3	0.3	0.6	1.0
Spain[5]	6	5	5	4	4	10	12	13	15	25	21	25	29	29	29
France	80	74	74	71	75	43	48	54	60	67	26	29	32	34	36
Ireland	34	42	32	23	19	4	19	22	30	35	11	13	13	13	9
Italy	11	12	10	10	9	6	8	10	13	16	6	9	10	11	12
Luxembourg	2.1	1.7	1.6	1.2	0.9	47	52	58	64	73	4	5	6	8	10
The Netherlands[4]	3	2	1	0.3	na	41	47	53	62	69	46	50	53	55	58
Austria[6]	3	2	1	1	1	8	10	13	17	22	27	29	33	34	43
Portugal[7]	28	28	27	27	25	31	39	47	55	60	7	10	11	12	12
Finland[4]	0.4	0.2	0.2	0.2	0.2	58	63	71	79	94	6	8	8	9	10
Sweden	0.5	0.5	0.2	0.2	0.1	24	29	36	45	65	8	10	10	11	13
United Kingdom	51	49	46	43	40	50	58	65	72	79	30	32	34	36	39
EU[8]	26	25	24	22	23	26	30	34	39	45	28	30	32	33	33
Euro area[8,9]	23	22	21	19	20	21	24	28	32	37	28	30	33	33	33

[1] Payments by credit cards from 2000 onwards, the figure includes retailer card transactions.

[2] Direct debits: debit card transactions are not included under this item but are shown under 'Payments by credit and debit cards'.

[3] All cheques for which the acquiring bank is different from the issuing bank.

[4] The figures for payments by credit and debit cards include payments by cards with a delayed debit function.

[5] This table does not include data relating to bills of exchange, traveller's cheques and other documents.

[6] Credit cards does not include delayed debit cards (charge cards): credit transfers and direct debits do not include items initiated by banks; these items are not available.

[7] This table does not include data related to bills of exchange.

[8] Total excluding countries for which data are not available.

[9] Following its entry into the Euro area, the figures for 2001 onwards include Greece.

[10] na = not available.

Source: European Central Bank (ECB) (2004a) *Payment and securities settlement systems in the EU,* Blue Book, April, Table 12, p. 19.

Table 2.5 Number of plastic cards

	Cards with a cash function		Cards with a debit function		Cards with a credit function		Cards with a debit function issued by retailers		Cards with an e-money function		Cards with a cheque guarantee function	
	2002	2003	2002	2003	2002	2003	2002	2003	2002	2003	2002	2003
Belgium	1,442.6	1,505.6	1,306.5	1,322.9	294.2	298.5	158.1	115.9	800.7	n.a.	n.a.	n.a.
Canada[1]	n.a.	n.a.	n.a.	n.a.	1,653.4	1,671.4	n.a.	n.a.	2.4	n.a.	n.a.	n.a.
France[2]	741.5	775.0	683.5	722.0	n.a.	n.a.	n.a.	n.a.	13.7	20.7	n.a.	n.a.
Germany	1,447.5	1,420.3	1,135.5	1,096.9	384.4	393.5	n.a.	n.a.	758.9	761.2	n.a.	n.a.
Italy	476.6	503.3	458.5	484.4	374.9	441.1	n.a.	n.a.	5.3	11.5	n.a.	n.a.
Japan[3]	2,603.4	2,631.2	n.a.	n.a.	1,919.3	1,990.3	n.a.	n.a.	n.a.	n.a.	n.a.	n.a.
The Netherlands[4]	1,634.9	1,649.7	1,337.6	1,335.8	315.8	350.9	n.a.	n.a.	1,071.3	1,083.4	n.a.	n.a.
Singapore[5]	1,417.6	1,386.1	1,417.6	1,386.1	773.2	835.1	n.a.	n.a.	2,343.8	2,751.0	n.a.	n.a.
Sweden[4]	535.6	578.4	548.3	622.2	376.0	409.2	n.a.	n.a.	54.9	n.a.	n.a.	n.a.
Switzerland	1,233.3	1,255.2	789.6	802.2	453.9	453.6	n.a.	n.a.	502.8	525.2	789.6	802.2
United Kingdom	2,399.9	2,663.3	1,003.6	1,058.7	1,065.8	1,200.2	n.a.	n.a.	n.a.	n.a.	1,031.9	947.5
United States	2,999.6	n.a.	903.5	n.a.	4,361.1	n.a.	39.6	n.a.	n.a.	n.a.	n.a.	n.a.

Note: A card which has several functions is considered in each relevant column (for example, a eurocheque card which can be used to withdraw cash, to make payments and to guarantee a cheques is counted under each of these items). For this reason, the figures should not be added together.
na = not available.

[1] Data on cards with a credit function as at 31 October.
[2] Figures for cards with a credit function are not provided.
[3] Data on cards with a cash function are as at end-March of the following year. Data on cards with a credit function include cards with a delayed debit function and are as at end-March of the current year.
[4] Data on cards with a credit function include cards with a delayed debit function.
[5] Data on cards with a cash and/or debit function are based on a survey of selected local and foreign banks.

Source: Bank for International Settlement (BIS) (2004a) 'Statistics on Payment and Settlement Systems in Selected Countries', Prepared by the Committee on Payment and Settlement Systems of the Group of Ten Countries, October, Table 9, p. 84.

- **Time or savings deposits** that involve depositing funds for a set period of time for a pre-determined or variable rate of interest. Banks offer an extensive range of such savings products, from standard fixed term and fixed deposit rate to variable term with variable rates. All banks offer deposit facilities that have features that are a combination of time and current accounts whereby customers can withdraw their funds instantly or at short notice. Typically deposits that can be withdrawn on demand pay lower rates than those deposited in the bank for a set period.

- **Consumer loans and mortgages** are commonly offered by banks to their retail customers. Consumer loans can be *unsecured* (that is no collateral is requested; such loans are usually up to a certain amount of money and for a short to medium time period: for example, in the UK unsecured loans are up to £25,000 and repaid over five years) or *secured on property* (typically from £20,000 to £100,000 and repaid over ten years in the UK) and interest rates are mainly variable (but can be fixed). In addition bank's of course offer an extensive array of mortgage products for the purchase of property. The main types of UK mortgages (that typically extend for 20–25 years) include: *variable rate* (interest payments vary relative to a benchmark rate such as the bank's standard lending rate or those determined by outside bodies such as the Bank of England's base rate or LIBOR); *fixed rate* (rates are fixed for a set period, usually 2–5 years, and then revert to variable rate); *capped* (rates vary but a cap is placed on the maximum rate paid over a specified period); *discount mortgages* (where rates vary but are discounted at a few percentages below a benchmark rate over a period – e.g., 1 per cent discount to the base rate over the first two years); and *cashback mortgages* (where those taking out the mortgage receive a single lump sum or cashback generally based on the value of the loan). Mortgages can also be obtained in foreign currency, for the purchase of overseas properties, and also for 'buy-to-let' property.

In addition to deposit and lending services many banks have diversified into a broader range of areas offering a 'one-stop' facility to meet all retail customer financial needs. This includes the offer of an extensive array of investment products, pensions, insurance and other services.

2.4.3 Investment, pensions and insurance services

- **Investment products** offered to retail customers include various securities-related products including mutual funds (known as unit trusts in the UK), investment in company stocks and various other securities-related products (such as savings bonds). In reality there is a strong overlap between savings and investments products and many banks advertise these services together.

- **Pensions and insurance services** are nowadays widely offered by many banks. Pension services provide retirement income (in the form of annuities) to those contributing to pension plans. Contributions paid into the pension fund are invested in long-term investments with the individual making contributions receiving a pension on retirement. The pension services offered via banks are known as private pensions to distinguish them from public pensions offered by the state. Usually there are tax advantages associated with pensions contributions as most governments wish to encourage individuals to save for their retirement. Insurance products protect individuals (policyholders) from various adverse events. Policyholders pay regular premiums and the insurer promises compensation if the specific insured event occurs. There are two main types of insurance – life insurance and general (or property and casualty) insurance. The latter is insurance that does not involve death as the main risk. It includes home, travel, medical, auto and various other types of insurance. Banks offer both life and non-life insurance products with the latter mainly being travel, property, mortgage repayment and other types of protection. In the UK, there has also been substantial growth in income protection insurance (insurance that replaces earnings if individuals are unable to work) and critical illness insurance (that covers medical costs and/or income).

Other services offered to retail customers include financial advisory services, safe-keeping facilities and foreign exchange services.

2.4.4 E-banking

A number of innovative financial products have been developed in recent years, taking advantage of rapid technological progress and financial market development. Transactions made using these innovative products are accounting for an increasing proportion of the volume and value of domestic and cross-border retail payments. Mainly, we can refer to two categories of payment products:

- **E-money** includes reloadable electronic money instruments in the form of stored value cards and electronic tokens stored in computer memory.
- **Remote payments** are payment instruments that allow (remote) access to a customer's account.

Figure 2.2 exemplifies the role of **e-banking** in the world of business conducted through electronic networks.

Figure 2.2 **A definition of e-banking**

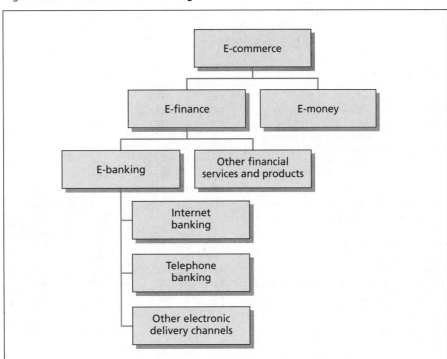

E-banking is now regarded as part of an overall distribution strategy particularly in retail banking, and it is offered by all major banks. Overall, banks' involvement in remote banking can be summarised as follows:

- Major institutions offer 'traditional' remote banking services (ATMs and telephone banking) and have started to offer a growing number of on-line PC banking and internet banking services.
- Some small-sized specialised banks operate without branches exclusively via remote banking channels. In most cases these banks are subsidiaries of existing banking groups (for example in the UK the virtual bank 'First Direct' is part of the HSBC group and the bank 'Smile' is part of the Co-operative Bank).
- Innovative new institutions are setting up business on the internet, also covering traditional banking activities. This activity is often promoted by large to medium-sized banks (see Box 2.2).

The intensity with which banks have promoted various remote banking 'models' differs significantly from one country to another. Table 2.6 shows the type of banking services currently offered via traditional branches and remote channels. However, it is necessary to keep in mind that the specific services may vary considerably from one country to another.

Even though electronic banking, in the form of ATMs and telephone banking, is not a new phenomenon, it is only with the increased usage of the internet that the number of banks offering services and customers using online banking services has increased substantially. However, as highlighted in Table 2.6, online banking is still predominantly used for rather simple and standardised retail products and

Table 2.6 Banking services offered via branches and remote channels

Services	Branches	ATMs	Telephone person-to-person	Telephone tone or voice-activated	PC banking on-line PC banking	PC banking Internet banking
Cash withdrawals	YES	YES	NO	NO	NO	NO
Loading of prepaid cards	NO	YES	YES	YES	YES	YES
Loading of e-money	NO	NO	NO[1]	NO[1]	YES	YES
General information on bank products and market developments	YES	YES	YES	YES	YES	YES
Account balance information	YES	YES	YES	YES	YES	YES
Money transfer	YES	YES	YES	YES	YES	YES
Direct debits and standing orders	YES	YES	YES	YES	YES	YES
Credit and debit card requests	YES	YES	YES	NO	YES	YES
New cheque books orders	YES	YES	YES	YES	YES	YES
Investment advice	YES	NO	YES	NO	YES[2]	YES[2]
Securities transactions	YES	NO	YES	NO	YES	YES
Loans (standardised)	YES	NO	YES	NO	YES	NO[3]
Deposits business	YES	YES	YES	NO	YES	YES
Non-standardised banking transactions	YES	NO	NO	NO	NO	NO[3]
Insurance products	YES	NO	YES	NO	YES	YES

[1] Not usually.
[2] For standard products.
[3] Not yet.

Source: Adapted from European Central Bank (1999).

services. Although most internet strategies have been developed especially for the retail segment, some banks have also developed services to target the corporate segment as well. Box 2.2 illustrates an example of online banking and financial services for large companies.

As with the foreign exchange market, it seems likely that multinational companies (MNCs) and other international firms will make increasing use of such internet services to manage their finances. Finally, despite the growing trend towards more and more banking and financial services being offered online, some researchers have cast doubts on the overall profitability of internet banking (see Box 2.3).

Box 2.2 **New online banking and financial services delivery channels for large companies**

Multinational companies and large banks are both seeking to capitalise on the opportunities provided by the growth in e-business by developing their corporate internet banking business. The desire to provide one-stop, lower-cost solutions for international corporate clients is a major factor driving these developments, as is the perceived demand for such services. Anecdotal evidence suggests that there are over 500 fully functioning internet sites providing international (wholesale) banking services of various kinds to the corporate sector. These activities mainly focus on the markets of the United States, Canada, western Europe and Australia.

Compared to retail banking, the development of internet wholesale banking has been relatively slow. This is largely due to the complexity of the business. Typically, banks have dealt with the needs of their larger corporate customers by directing business through relationship managers. These managers deal with the specific wholesale needs of individual clients, including:

● commercial lending;
● cash management services;
● trade and foreign exchange services;
● investment management and trust services; and
● payments processing.

While international banking has traditionally had the most electronic links to its customers, this has been mainly on a product-by-product basis.

With the growth of e-business, traditional corporate relationships outside the banking industry are changing radically. Value chains are being re-configured, trading communities (e-marketplaces) are being created and numerous purchasing and other internet portals are being established. New business-to-business (B2B) relationships are forcing global banks to consider ways of changing their wholesale banking operations so as to embrace many of these

developments. It also means that international corporate clients now expect global banks to offer multiproduct, web-based platforms. For example, a confidential survey by Greenwich Associates of 8,000 US middle-market corporations found that only 21 per cent purchased wholesale banking products online. The reasons cited for the limited use of such services related to concerns about website functionality, security and internet service provider (ISP) reliability. The same survey, however, noted that over two-thirds of the companies said they would use wholesale internet banking services if 'they provided the benefits they felt that the internet could provide'. These benefits relate to safe electronic bill presentment/payment, an integrated source for company-related information and remote access via wireless devices.

A major strategic challenge for banks is to develop wholesale internet services which will allow corporate users to obtain information and initiate seamless transactions for multiple products and services. Large banks also need to continue to develop their web offerings if they are to become the main portals for corporate banking services. As B2B e-commerce grows, clients will increasingly seek a broad array of services (such as wireless access, transaction processing, various customised services, information products and multibank access). Banks will need to provide these if they are to be successful in the web-based wholesale banking business.

An important issue for the development of web-based banking services for international firms is how these should be positioned in the new e-marketplaces. Developing the appropriate portal strategy is critical in this respect. As online markets expand, reaching and retaining wholesale clients continues to pose new challenges. In particular, the creation of new e-marketplaces allows non-bank intermediaries to position themselves along the value chain that

▶

exists between a bank and its corporate customer. Corporate banking portals allow companies to evaluate the prices of various wholesale banking services, thereby distancing traditional banks from their clients. The major risk banks face is that developments in B2B e-commerce could result in their acting as mainly payments processors while other companies pick up the higher-value business.

Aware of the opportunities and threats afforded by the new environment many large banks are hastening the development of wholesale internet banking portals. The advantages associated with developing a proprietary internet portal dedicated to wholesale banking include:

- more effective communication with clients;
- reduced risk of competitors accessing the bank's client base;
- greater revenues from cross-selling and customised solutions;
- internet access and content that can be managed, tailored and packaged for different client segments; and
- the opportunity to develop client relationships and loyalty.

However, it is by no means certain which type of wholesale internet banking strategy will be successful. Consequently, banks have adopted a variety of approaches to develop their online corporate banking services for their larger clients.

Various banks have created their own e-marketplaces by forming bilateral links with their international corporate clients or by joining marketplaces where important corporate relationships are dominant. The services on offer relate mainly to payment processing. Some have also positioned themselves in new e-markets, providing treasury services or niche operations.

Others have grouped together to reap the benefits of market power and provide broader wholesale banking services across their various product ranges. For example, through the service provider IntraLinks.com, Chase Manhattan, other banks and third parties negotiate and establish terms for large syndicated loans. IntraLinks.com now claims to account for around 90 per cent of the syndicated loan information services market.

Various banks have also developed client connectivity sites that allow the bank to position their offerings within a larger context of services that may be attractive to clients.

Despite the recent activity in establishing an online presence, the number of internet portals devoted to international corporate banking still remains relatively small and the range of services on offer fairly limited. However, some analysts forecast significant growth in the number and range of wholesale portals.

One area of online wholesale banking which has registered major growth in recent years has been that of foreign exchange. Banks have been quick to set up foreign exchange trading platforms because of the threat posed by others in setting up dealing facilities. With approximately 88 per cent of foreign exchange trading currently being processed manually (compared to 67 per cent of equity trades), the opportunities afforded by the automation of foreign exchange trading appear substantial. Foreign exchange is the single largest wholesale market, with around 1.5 trillion dollars' worth of foreign exchange traded daily.

The automation of foreign exchange trading allows for a reduction in transaction costs and provides banks with access to a broader client base. The standard procedure for currency trading begins with a corporate treasurer calling a trader at a bank and being quoted a price based on the size of the deal and other relationship considerations. The treasurer may then contact a few other banks to source the best deal. When an order is placed, the trader documents the features of the deal and inputs the relevant details to undertake the foreign exchange trade on behalf of the corporate client. This system, however, is flawed as:

- only relatively large companies qualify for such trading relationships, with a large number of still large firms denied similar access to the foreign exchange market;
- prices are not transparent, in that they are not immediately obvious to the buyer and may have a large spread, depending on the range of banks approached; and
- manual processes limit the number of deals traders can handle and may result in delays in transaction processing.

Given these limitations, banks and other companies have sought to develop foreign exchange internet portals that are geared towards creating more efficient and transparent mechanisms for companies undertaking foreign exchange trades. The new mechanisms provide quotes from a number of institutions where prices tend towards a consensus, thus reassuring corporate treasurers and other users that the rates they are being offered are close to the rates that global banks charge each other. Greater trans-

▶

parency should help to attract more corporate customers. In addition, automated sites can process multiple, parallel trades from existing customers, as well as new business from smaller companies which have not hitherto had access to such services. Table 2.7 lists the major foreign exchange trading sites that are currently operational.

The foreign exchange trading sites fall into three main categories:

- sites that allow companies to trade only with participating banks with which they have existing relationships (e.g., FXall);
- multi bank sites that allow companies to trade with any bank providing foreign exchange services (Currenex); and
- non-bank trading sites owned by foreign exchange trading firms (such as Cognotec).

Many analysts believe that online foreign exchange sites are likely to gain the lion's share of the market in the near future. Such systems are expected to streamline the trading process by allowing international firms access to a range of dealers through a single point of entry. In addition, the liquidity and market leadership provided by the sites with major bank backing are likely to be the most successful as these will provide greater price transparency, lower spreads and faster order execution than is currently available offline or through sites provided by single global banks.

In addition to the development of foreign exchange trading sites, various other internet sites have sought to introduce services for the trading of other international related products and services. Most of these have been developed by non-banks and seek to provide more price-transparent and efficient markets through a variety of capital and money

Table 2.7 Foreign exchange online trading sites

Company	Ownership	Products
FX Connect	State Street	FX Connect provides real-time, fully interactive foreign exchange trade execution with multiple counterparties, 24 hours a day.
Cognotec	Independent	Foreign exchange; Auto Deal Life; Auto Deal Direct.
Currenex	Independent (25 participating banks)	Low-cost technology provider of foreign exchange and money market trading solutions for global financial institutions, funds, corporations and other market participants. Through private branded systems as well as a global electronic communications network of FX price makers, prime brokers and intermediaries, Currenex supports real-time, auditable, online trading around the clock in all currencies.
FXall	Dealer consortium (Bank of America, HSBC, JP Morgan, Goldman Sachs)	FXall is an electronic trading platform offering customers foreign currency trade execution, access to research, and straight through processing. With an increasing number of leading global banks providing liquidity, FXall is designed to aid corporate treasurers, money managers, hedge funds, central banks and other institutional clients.
GAIN Capital	Independent	Provider of foreign exchange services, including direct-access trading and asset management. Services clients from more than 80 countries around the globe, including fund managers and individual traders.
Volbroker	Bank Consortium – Citibank, Deutsche Bank, Goldman Sachs, JP Morgan, Royal Bank of Scotland and UBS	Currency options; inter-dealer.

▶

market instruments. While global banks appear to be focusing on developing their online foreign exchange and payment services, new operators appear to have stolen the lead in developing sites relating to fixed income, derivatives and commercial paper trading. The rapid introduction of such services is a reflection of the anticipated demand for online wholesale trading. Table 2.8 lists some of the sites that aim to meet this expected growth in demand for online trading services.

Table 2.8 Online trading sites for international firms – fixed income, commercial paper and derivatives

Company	Ownership	Products
GlobalLink.com	State Street	Fixed income and interest rate derivatives, strategic analysis and trading.
Blackbird.com	Independent and strategic alliance with Chicago Mercantile Exchange	Over the Counter (OTC) derivatives (inter-dealer). Connects 80 financial institutions worldwide, trades 2 million instruments in six currencies.
Tradebonds.com	Independent	Online bond trading. Provides execution and support covering corporate, municipal, US Treasury, agency, mortgage-backed securities and money market instruments.
CPmarket.com	Independent	Electronic platform for institutional investors to execute transactions directly with issuers of commercial paper, certificates of deposit, time deposits and money market fund providers.
SwapsWire.com	Dealer consortium (23 institutions)	Online dealer facilities for Interest Rate Swaps (IRS), Forward Rate Agreements (FRAs), Overnight Index Swaps (OIS), Interest Rate Caps and Floors, Interest Rate Swaptions, and Credit Default Swaps (CDS) in nine currencies.
TradeWeb.com	Independent	Fixed income products including US treasuries, commercial paper, European government bonds, mortgage-backed securities (MBS), Pfandbriefe/ covered bonds, Euro supra-nationals/ agencies, agency discount notes and Euro commercial paper.

Box 2.3 Is internet banking profitable?

Recent studies by the European Central Bank seem to cast some doubt on the profitability of internet banking. Some banks, they reckon, have overestimated the potential for internet banking, possibly as a result of overconfidence in the so-called 'new economy'. Advertising expenses and initial investments are high, while the number of new accounts may not develop as expected. Customers' habits are difficult to change. Further, concerns about security seem to be restraining the expansion of e-banking. As a result, quite a number of European internet banking and brokering projects are facing serious difficulties or have even been abandoned. Internet banking can lead to a reduction in operational costs since it requires a smaller workforce and no physical branch network. On the other hand, if a strategy of very competitive pricing is used to gain market share, profitability may be threatened. Nevertheless, e-banking continues to have strong potential to help banks reduce their costs and operate more efficiently. European banks seem to be well aware of this potential, as expenditure on e-banking is expected to continue to increase in both retail and wholesale areas.

2.5 Current issues in banking

This part outlines the general trends that have characterised the banking sector in most advanced economies over the last twenty years or so. Many of these trends are still ongoing today and for some emerging and developing countries they have just begun to occur. We first describe the main forces that generate change in the banking sector, such as the deregulation and re-regulation processes, competitive pressures, financial innovation and technological change. We then highlight the main trends resulting from these forces of change, in particular conglomeration and globalisation.

2.5.1 Structural and conduct deregulation

Financial deregulation essentially consists of removing controls and rules that in the past have protected financial institutions, especially banks. **Structural deregulation**, more generally, refers to the opening up, or liberalisation, of financial markets to allow institutions to compete more freely. Specifically, this process encompasses structure and conduct rules deregulation (such as the removal of branch restrictions and credit ceilings, respectively).

In Europe, the benefits of a deregulated market were first identified by Cecchini's 1988 study on the costs of 'non-Europe', that confirmed the importance of deregulating financial sectors within the move towards creating a single European market for goods, services and capital. Cecchini estimated that up to one-third of the total gains from deregulating all economic sectors during the first six years after 1992 would come directly and/or indirectly from deregulating financial services. However, in Europe deregulation was boosted mainly by the need to improve competitive viability of the sector.

> Deregulation is typically undertaken to improve the performance of the industry being deregulated. If efficiency is raised, the improvement in resource allocation will benefit society and may lead to price reductions and/or service expansion for consumers if competition is sufficient. However, in many cases deregulation is initiated less by a desire to benefit consumers than by a need to improve the competitive viability of the industry [...] One such example [...] is the harmonisation and unification of banking markets in Europe – removing restrictions that have limited the ability of banks in one country from aggressively entering markets in other countries [...].
>
> Berger and Humphrey (1997, p. 190)

There is no doubt that the deregulation process has helped in the ending of 'repressed' banking systems and is most likely one of the major contributors to Europe's single market programme (Dermine, 2002). Furthermore, the wide liberalisation and harmonisation processes at the EU level have contributed in creating a business environment where operational efficiency and technology implementation play key roles in shaping banks' strategies. Hunter *et al.* (2000) identify three joint effects of deregulation and technology. First, the loosening of banking laws coupled with the advantages of technology (in terms of potential economies of scale and other efficiencies) has encouraged the consolidation process. As a result the number of banks has shrunk virtually everywhere. Second, the introduction of new technologies in a deregulated context intensified competition and improved banks' ability to adjust prices and terms of financial products. Finally, the barriers between bank and non-bank financial institutions disappeared, allowing, for example, the rise of universal banking activity. Major structural deregulation has come a little later in the United States and Japan as witnessed by the repeal of the Glass-Steagall Act in 1999 (via the Gramm-Leach-Bliley Act of 1999 that now allows for the establishment of financial services holding companies that can undertake commercial and investment banking as well as insurance activity) as well as the 'Big-bang' reforms in Japan (also in 1999) that also widen the activities of banks' permissible business.

2.5.2 Supervisory re-regulation

One consequence of the process of deregulation has been the increased perceived riskiness of the banking business. Banks rapidly adapted their portfolios and strategies to the new environment and their financial activities increasingly took place outside the traditional bank regulatory framework.

In such a context, even strongly market-oriented systems needed to strengthen supervision. This was considered to be an important element in improving the safety and soundness of the overall financial sector. **Re-regulation** can therefore be defined as the process of implementing new rules, restrictions and controls in response to market participants' efforts to circumvent existing regulations. Alternatively, it can be viewed as a response to minimise any potential adverse effects associated with excessive competition brought about through structural deregulation. Capital adequacy convergence will become a central issue in the need to help level the 'playing fields' on which international banks compete. This has occurred in the context of a gradual shift from direct forms of control, often at the full discretion of regulatory authorities, to more indirect and objective types of controls.

The process of supervisory re-regulation has been shaped by global pressures. The first efforts to encourage convergence towards common approaches and standards at the international level were initiated by the Basle Committee on Banking Supervision in the 1970s. Since then capital adequacy standards and associated risk regulation have been important policy issues and fundamental components of bank prudential re-regulation. For example, at the EU level the two complementary measures to the Second Banking Directive (Own Funds and Solvency Ratio Directives) dealing with capital adequacy can be considered examples of supervisory prudential re-regulation. The rules implementing Basle II (see Chapter 7) are also examples of supervisory re-regulation.

2.5.3 Competition

Before the deregulation process, in most countries, banks were characterised by relatively high levels of government controls and restrictions that inhibited competition and maintained a protected banking environment. For instance, interest rate restrictions and capital controls were widespread, and branching restrictions existed in many countries. The main purpose of these controls was to ensure stability in the system and prevent banking crises.

In the United States for example, the 1933 Glass-Steagall Act forbade banks from underwriting equities and other corporate securities. Typically, commercial banks undertook traditional banking business, namely deposit taking and lending; deposit prices were regulated and there were maximum rates that banks could charge on loans. In Europe there was a similar setting and in most countries government controls and regulatory restrictions limited the competitive environment.

This close supervision of the banking sector dominated structural control, which in turn aimed at ensuring the sound functioning of the market and a better allocation of resources. There is no doubt that **competitive pressures** on banks have increased as a result of structural deregulation and liberalisation of the sector. In most advanced economies banks now are free to set the prices for their services (loans, deposits and other products such as insurance) and they compete with other banks (domestic and foreign) as well as non-bank financial intermediaries.

Technological advances and innovations in the payment systems have helped to reduce the barriers to cross-border trade in banking services, thereby also promoting greater competition. These fundamental forces of change are discussed below.

2.5.4 Financial innovation and the adoption of new technologies

The definition of 'innovation' includes both the concept of invention (the ongoing research and development function) and diffusion (or adoption) of new products, services or ideas.

Financial innovation, like innovation elsewhere in business, is an ongoing process whereby private parties experiment to try to differentiate their product and services, responding to both sudden and gradual changes in the economy. Financial innovation can be defined as the act of creating and then popularising new financial instruments as well as new financial technologies, institutions and markets. Specifically, we can distinguish:

- **Financial system/institutional innovations**. Such innovations can affect the financial sector as a whole; they relate to business structures, to the establishment of new types of financial intermediaries, or to changes in the legal and supervisory framework.
- **Process innovations**. These include the introduction of new business processes leading to increased efficiency, market expansion, etc.
- **Product innovations**. Such innovations include the introduction of new credit, deposit, insurance, leasing, hire purchase, derivatives and other financial products. Product innovations are introduced to respond better to changes in market demand or to improve efficiency.

In a recent study, Frame and White (2002) define a financial innovation as a new product (e.g., adjustable rate mortgages) or service (e.g., online security trading), a novel organisational form (e.g., virtual banks), or new processes (e.g., credit scoring) that reduce costs or risks or that improve quality.

Progress in information technology affects all aspects of banking and can be regarded as one of the main driving forces generating change in the sector. Rapid innovation contributes to the dynamic efficiency of the financial sector, which ultimately affects the overall growth of the economy.

Technology reduces significantly the costs of information management (i.e., collection, storage, processing and transmission) and information asymmetries in financial transactions. It can be used as an important strategic tool for banks to safeguard long-term competitiveness, cost-efficiency and improve their profitability. On the customers' side, technological innovation introduces automated channels (e.g., remote banking) that allow the provision of banking services without face-to-face contact between the bank employee and the customer.

In terms of products and services supplied to customers, the most typical innovations in modern banking concern the payment systems and include the use of a wide range of automated channels for supplying and delivering various banking services and activities. Common examples include developments in the use of: debit and credit cards, standing orders and direct debits, automatic teller machines (ATMs) and EFTPOS (electronic funds transfer at the point-of-sale) terminals, internet and PC banking, telephone/mobile banking and digital TV banking.

Innovation has also resulted in the widespread use of new financial instruments like derivative products. Introduced initially to reduce risk through hedging, derivatives like swaps, options and futures are in fact often used for speculative purposes thereby often exposing banks to excessively high risks. This is because they include contingent claims that represent a financial exposure across markets. Moreover, as these types of transactions do not appear on the bank's balance sheet they are often referred to as 'off-balance sheet' (OBS) business.[2]

Within banking institutions, technology allows for the use of computer software and databases for the management of information. As pointed out by Hunter *et al.* (2000) the term 'technological change' can refer not only to changes in machines, computer hardware and software, but also to changes in the way that work is organised. Moreover, technology has allowed banks to adopt various segmentation strategies whereby profitable customers are given a wider range of products and less profitable customers are moved towards lower-cost commoditized services. Furthermore, one of the main current trends for global banks is financial innovation in risk management where sophisticated approaches have developed such as the use of credit derivatives and securitisation. Such complex financial instruments are used as part of the banking business as well as end-products for customers.

The widespread use of technology is not without risks (ECB, 1999). Strategically, banks run the risk of investing in IT resources that could quickly become outdated. Legal risk is related to the uncertainty surrounding the applicable laws and regulations on a number of aspects relating to technology (e.g., the legal status of remote banking, validity and proof of transactions, the respect of customers' privacy). However, innovation can and does arise from efforts to circumvent regulation (Frame and White, 2002). Another issue relates to the increase in operational risk (that is the risk associated with the potential of systems failure) as banks may tend not to upgrade their systems of internal control to cope with the new operational environment (see Molyneux and Shamroukh, 1999). Finally, the possibility of systemic risk may increase since technology increasingly links banks to each other through alliances and joint ventures, standardisation and the possibility of using similar software and hardware. As a consequence, technological developments in banking also have important consequences for prudential regulation and supervision (on operational risk and Basle II see Chapter 7).

---

[2] See Section 9.5 for more detail on OBS business.

2.6 Responses to the forces of change

This section highlights banks' main responses to the abovementioned forces of change. In particular we will focus on the conglomeration process (through mergers and acquisitions) and the processes of internationalisation and globalisation.

2.6.1 Mergers and Acquisitions

Mergers and Acquisitions (M&As) are changing the structure of many banking sectors. They are not a force of change in themselves, but rather a response to the forces of change and to changes in market structures.

M&As refer to the combining of two or more entities into one new entity. They are often explained by the equation that one plus one equals more than two, because a common motive is to increase the value of the new entity. Although the terms 'mergers' and 'acquisitions' are sometimes used interchangeably to refer to the combination of two (or more) separate enterprises, they have slightly different connotations:

- A **merger** is when two, usually similarly sized, banks agree to go forward as a new single bank rather than remain separately owned and operated.
- An **acquisition** is when a bank takes over another one and clearly becomes the new owner. Acquisitions are also known as takeovers and they normally occur when big institutions buy smaller ones.

Some of the most common motives for M&As include the following:

- *Economies of scale* are achieved by creating a combined institution of larger size capable of achieving lower unit costs of producing financial services. The financial services industry is an information and distribution intensive industry with high fixed costs implying relatively high potential for economies of scale and cost cutting. These can be achieved for instance, through consolidation of the credit department and branch delivery system.
- *Economies of scope* can generate cost savings from delivering services jointly through the same organisation rather than through specialised providers. Economies of scope can arise internally, through joint production and marketing or externally, through joint consumption. For instance, there are potential scope economies available if both banking and insurance products are supplied by the same institutions.
- *Eliminating inefficiencies.* Poor management may leave banks with unexploited opportunities to cut costs and increase sales and earnings. Such banks are natural targets for being taken over by other institutions with more efficient management. Cost efficiency can be considerably improved by takeovers in which relatively more efficient banks acquire relatively less efficient banks and increase the efficiency of the target bank after the operation.

Other motives can include increasing *market power*, for instance through removal of a competitor and political power enhancement; and *diversification* of product lines and improvement of marketing and distribution. These potential gains will likely produce higher margins and improve the profitability and value of the combined institutions.

In the European banking sector the recent wave of M&As has brought about significant structural changes[3] (see also Chapter 13). In the United States M&As have dramatically transformed the banking sector: over the period 1980–2003 the number of banking institutions halved from about 16,000 to about 8,000; and the asset share of the ten largest commercial banks rose from 22 per cent to 46 per cent (Pilloff, 2004). Table 2.9 shows the assets, deposits and branches of the fifty largest US bank mergers that took place between 1994 and 2003. As reported by Pilloff, over the ten-year period there have been 3,517 mergers that involved the acquisition of about $3.1 trillion in assets. Most deals (about 75 per cent) involved the purchase of a commercial banking organisation by another commercial banking organisation and concerned relatively small institutions. However, the few acquisitions of very large banks accounted for a significant share of the assets, deposits and branches acquired over the period so they were responsible for the major changes derived from consolidation in the industry.

Recent trends indicate that mergers among foreign banks and cross-border mergers are becoming increasingly common. Table 2.10 summarises the different dimensions of the M&As covered by industry sector and country with specific reference to the EU market.

There have been many domestic M&As over the last 15 years in the European Union (see Chapter 13) that have consolidated national banking markets. As concerns international conglomeration, in June 2005 Unicredit, Italy's largest bank announced the takeover of HVB Group, Germany's second biggest bank. EU banks have also expanded in Latin America, Turkey and China: Latin America attracted expansion from the major Spanish banks; whereas the financial crisis that occurred in Turkey in the late 1990s created buying opportunities for British, French and Greek banks. Some of the major Dutch, British, French and German banks have increased their foothold in the United States. In fact, the most important transactions involving EU banks outside the European Economic Area (EEA) in terms of deal value were acquisitions in the United States by ABN-AMRO, Deutsche Bank and HSBC (see Table 2.9). The entrance of China into the World Trade Organisation (WTO) and the forthcoming opening of the Chinese financial markets have increased the interest of some European as well as US banks in making Chinese bank acquisitions. Indeed, China is a very attractive market for foreign banks because it has well over $1 trillion in household savings, almost all of it *'lying fallow in four sprawling and dysfunctional state banks'*.[4]

2.6.2 Conglomeration

Consolidation in the global banking industry has resulted in the emergence of financial conglomerates that conduct an extensive range of businesses with a group structure. In the European Union, **financial conglomeration** was encouraged by the Second Banking Directive (1989) which enabled banks to operate as universal banks offering the full range of financial services including commercial

---

[3] A report prepared by the Banking Supervision Committee (BSC) reports the results of an analysis of M&As involving European banks see ECB (2000).
[4] *The Economist* (2003). 'Banking in China: strings attached', 6 March.

Table 2.9 Fifty largest US banks' M&As (1994–2003)

Target rank	Acquirer	Target	Target Year acquired	Assets	Deposits	Number of offices
1	NationsBank Corporation	BankAmerica Corporation	1998	201,576	129,723	1,960
2	Norwest Corporation	Wells Fargo & Company	1998	96,316	70,875	1,459
3	Bank One Corporation	First Chicago NBD Corporation	1998	90,700	53,578	648
4	Firstar Corporation	U.S. Bancorp	2001	85,402	53,289	1,053
5	Chase Manhattan Corporation	J.P. Morgan & Company, Inc.	2000	73,832	4,676	3
6	Chemical Banking Corporation	Chase Manhattan Corporation	1996	71,913	35,815	349
7	First Union Corporation	Wachovia Corporation	2001	70,022	41,538	786
8	Wells Fargo & Company	First Interstate Bancorp	1996	59,187	48,510	1,130
9	Fleet Financial Group, Inc.	BankBoston Corporation	1999	50,722	34,648	451
10	Citigroup, Inc.	Golden State Bancorp, Inc.	2002	50,680	22,978	357
11	Washington Mutual, Inc.	Ahmanson & Company (H.F.)	1998	50,291	37,611	416
12	First Chicago Corporation	NBD Bancorp, Inc.	1995	46,606	29,735	611
13	NationsBank Corporation	Barnett Banks, Inc.	1998	44,066	34,450	670
14	First Union Corporation	CoreStates Financial Corporation	1998	43,967	32,201	575
15	NationsBank Corporation	Boatmen's Bancshares, Inc.	1997	43,034	30,933	607
16	Washington Mutual, Inc.	Great Western Financial Corporation	1997	41,010	27,572	416
17	FleetBoston Financial Corporation	Summit Bancorp	2001	39,925	26,200	493
18	Deutsche Bank AG	Bankers Trust Corporation	1999	39,465	27,558	3
19	Firstar Corporation	Mercantile Bancorporation, Inc.	1999	35,448	23,795	453
20	First Union Corporation	First Fidelity Bancorporation	1996	35,405	27,803	688
21	Fleet Financial Group, Inc.	Shawmut National Corporation	1995	34.220	22.443	362
22	Golden State Bancorp, Inc.	First Nationwide Holdings, Inc.	1998	33,987	15,102	229
23	First Bank System, Inc.	U.S. Bancorp	1997	33,383	25,549	631
24	HSBC Holdings, Plc	Republic New York Corporation	1999	31,848	13,588	92
25	Washington Mutual, Inc.	Dime Bancorp, Inc.	2002	27,971	13,467	129
26	Fleet Financial Group, Inc.	National Westminister Bancorp	1996	27,279	18,143	315
27	KeyCorp	Society Corporation	1994	27,245	17,646	459
28	SunTrust Banks, Inc.	Crestar Financial Corporation	1998	25,524	17,970	372
29	Fifth Third Bancorp	Old Kent Financial Corporation	2001	24,243	16,791	300
30	Star Banc Corporation	Firstar Holdings Corporation	1998	22,511	15,024	248
31	AmSouth Bancorporation	First American Corporation	1999	22,215	14,074	376
32	Wells Fargo & Company	First Security Corporation	2000	21,395	12,773	332
33	Washington Mutual, Inc.	Keystone Holdings, Inc.	1996	21,382	12,793	159
34	National City Corporation	First of America Bank Corporation	1998	20,821	15,966	504
35	Washington Mutual, Inc.	Bank United Corporation	2001	18,647	8,392	158
36	BankAmerica Corporation	Continental Bank Corporation	1994	17,375	8,771	1
37	ABN AMRO Holding NV	Standard Federal Banorporation	1997	15,757	10,932	181
38	CoreStates Financial Corporation	Meridian Bancorp, Inc.	1996	15,264	12,498	351
39	M&T Bank Corporation	Allfirst Financial, Inc.	2003	15,064	11,516	267
40	Citigroup, Inc.	European American Bank	2001	14,971	10,125	99
41	MacAndrews and Forbes Holdings	First Nationwide Bank, FSB	1994	14,927	9,796	205
42	MacAndrews and Forbes Holdings	Cal Fed Bancorp, Inc.	1997	14,192	8,882	128
43	National City Corporation	Integra Financial Corporation	1996	14,019	10,310	253
44	PNC Financial Services Group	Midlantic Corporation	1995	13,507	10,894	310
45	ABN AMRO Holding HV	Michigan National Corporation	2001	11,746	8,270	188
46	Royal Bank of Canada	Centura Banks, Inc.	2001	11,657	7,748	251
47	BankBoston Corporation	BayBanks, Inc.	1996	11,627	10,254	242
48	First Union Corporation	Signet Banking Corporation	1997	11,289	8,219	237
49	Southern National Corporation	BB&T Financial Corporation	1995	11,126	8,184	298
50	BB&T Corporation	First Virginia Banks, Inc.	2003	10,998	9,449	361

Note: Values in million US $.
Source: Pilloff (2004).
http://www.federalreserve.gov/pubs/staffstudies/2000-present/ss176.pdf.

Table 2.10 **M&As: industry, sector and country dimensions**

	Domestic banks' M&As	International banks' M&As
Between credit institutions	M&As involving credit institutions located in the same country	M&As involving credit institutions located in different countries, one of which is an EU country
	Domestic conglomeration	International conglomeration
Across sectors	M&As between credit institutions and insurance companies and/or other financial institutions all located in the same country	M&As involving credit institutions located in a EU country with insurance companies and/or other financial institutions located abroad (either within or outside the EU)

Source: Adapted from ECB (2000).

banking, investment banking, insurance and other services. In United States, the passing of the Gramm-Leach-Bliley Act of 1999 enabled banks to establish financial holding companies that can now engage in a full range of financial services (as did the 'Big-bang' reforms in Japan) (see Chapters 15 and 16 for more details on US and Japanese developments).

Financial conglomerates are defined as a group of enterprises, formed by different types of financial institutions, operating in different sectors of the financial industry. Group organisational structure is believed to bring about, on the one hand the possibility of exploiting greater cost economies and, on the other hand the capacity of the group to isolate risk from its different activities. On the revenue side, the ability of financial conglomerates to distribute a full range of banking, securities and insurance services may increase their earning potential and lead to a more stable profit stream. Customers may value a bundled supply of financial services more than separate offers for reasons of transactions and information costs. On the other hand, it is argued that such structures may have drawbacks, such as conflicts of interest and concentration of power.[5] The process of conglomeration is mainly bank-driven, as banks have been actively expanding into other areas, in particular asset management.

Similar to, but different from, conglomeration is the establishment of jointly owned enterprises offering specialised financial services. In some European countries, for example, savings banks and co-operative banks have set up such jointly owned enterprises that provide asset management, stockbroking and settlement activities as well as insurance, all of which are sold to or distributed by the member institutions of the sector. An example would be the jointly owned investment management firm of the savings bank sector in a country. In economic terms, such jointly owned enterprises provide equal opportunities of marketing and servicing as financial conglomerates. The development of such enterprises as well as co-operation agreements is common, in countries such as Austria and Germany. According to the ECB (2000), domestic conglomeration has been driven by banks; and banks are mainly expanding into asset management and the business of investment services in general.

---

[5] Casu and Girardone (2004).

2.6.3 Globalisation

The structural changes in the financial system and banking sectors, brought about by the process of financial liberalisation, have allowed an increase in the overall level of competition. Globally, many nations have removed regulatory barriers to international banking. At the same time, growth in international activities and trade of multinational corporations has increased the demand for services from financial institutions that operate cross-border. This trend towards globalisation is occurring in most private sectors of the economy. As companies and individuals requiring financial services are becoming more globally oriented, they demand appropriate financial services.

It follows that **globalisation** can be defined as the evolution of markets and institutions such that geographic boundaries do not limit financial transactions. It is obvious that there are economic, political and cultural aspects of globalisation. In this context, we refer primarily to the situation where geographic barriers to trade and financial markets activity have been eliminated and this has allowed a gradual intensification in the interconnections and integration between financial markets and financial institutions throughout the world. The globalisation phenomenon refers to the emergence of a broadly integrated, international but practically single market in finance: in short, the so-called 'global village' concept.

Globalisation and internationalisation are highly interrelated. This is because globalisation is changing the world economy as a result of increased international trade and cultural exchange. Hence in our context, internationalisation generally refers to the rapid growth in international business of banks (e.g., growth in multinational banking, see Section 4.7 on the increasing role of foreign banks in domestic banking systems) and can be considered as an essential condition for globalisation.

Therefore we can define '*global banks*' as the institutions with the widest reach, that is, either though subsidiaries or branches they provide services in several world countries and have a presence in all continents. '*International banks*' are institutions that provide cross-border services, but operate in too few countries, or are relatively too small, to be defined as global. Such banks are also referred to as '*regional banks*' (Berger *et al.*, 2003). Finally, a '*local bank*' is an institution providing services only in the country where it is headquartered.

2.6.4 Other responses to the forces of change

Other important responses to the forces of change described above are: disintermediation, growth in OBS activities and securitisation.

Disintermediation is the process whereby economic units bypass banks and other financial institutions in order to invest their funds directly in the financial markets. Disintermediation is often associated with relatively good market transparency and is mostly present in strongly market-oriented systems such as those found in the United States and Britain. Another important response to the forces of change is the growth in **off-balance sheet (OBS) activities** and particularly derivative products. Modern banks do a considerable amount of OBS business; typically these activities refer to promises or commitments of the bank to undertake

Box 2.4   Focus on globalisation

The banking industry still appears far from being globally integrated. A recent study by Berger *et al.* (2003) finds that in industrialised countries the foreign share of bank assets remains at or below 10 per cent. In a frictionless banking market with no barriers to integration, commercial customers will select the bank that provides the price, quality and mix of services that will best facilitate their business operations. Berger *et al.* (2003) define two potentially important criteria for a foreign affiliate's choice of bank: the bank's *nationality* and *reach*. *Bank nationality* refers to the country in which the bank is headquartered. Some companies might value banking services that require a detailed knowledge of the country in which they operate (*host-based expertise*). Banks headquartered in the nation that hosts the affiliate will likely have an advantage in offering these services. Other companies might value a bank that offers 'home-based expertise' – that is, an understanding of the home market of the affiliate's parent. Banks from third countries (that is, from neither the host nor the home country) may not have host-based or home-based expertise, but they might still competitively offer services in other dimensions valued by company. *Bank reach* refers to the size and geographic scope of the bank. Some companies may value a large, global bank that can offer a broad range of financial services, expertise within many foreign markets, superior risk diversification and the ability to facilitate large deals. Other companies may prefer the advantages of a smaller bank that offers services in only a local area because such a bank is more likely to establish a close relationship with the customer and provide customised services. In the absence of barriers, the extent of integration in the banking industry will depend on how customers value different banking services and the extent to which banks of a given nationality and reach can provide those services. Essentially, if customers place a high value on global services and have little value for host-based or home-based expertise, then we might expect to see an integrated banking industry, perhaps with a few global banks dominating markets around the world. Conversely, if customers value host-based expertise and place less value on global services, then we should observe limited banking industry integration. Thus, depending on the services valued by bank customers, we could have a world with extensive integration or one with little integration. Berger *et al.* (2003) argue that foreign banking organisations may be at significant competitive disadvantages in providing the price, quality and mix of services that best suit bank customers, and that such disadvantages may limit the integration of the banking industry. Overall, the findings suggest that domestic banks possess some competitive advantages that may significantly limit the global integration of the banking industry.

certain types of business in the future; one simple example of OBS activity is overdrafts facilities. Other common OBS items include derivatives transactions (e.g., futures, options and swaps), underwriting business and various other commitments and guarantees. Finally, **securitisation** refers to the process whereby loans and other financial assets (e.g., mortgages) are pooled together for sale as securities to investors (see Section 9.6).

2.7 Conclusions

Deregulation and financial liberalisation, in addition to technological developments, have changed the environment in which banks are operating. Further, internationalisation and globalisation has affected the operations of financial institutions in general and of banks in particular.

As a result of structural deregulation many banks now compete with non-banking financial intermediaries and in previously inaccessible domestic and foreign markets. The erosion of demarcation lines between the various types of financial institutions has caused the distinctions between different types of banks (and other financial sector institutions) to become blurred, creating greater homogeneity between the services and products offered.

In response to these pressures, banks have attempted to adopt strategies aimed at improving efficiency, in order to expand their output and increase the range of services offered. Many banks have been forced to increase in size, either through mergers or through internally generated growth, in order to compete. The trend towards consolidation, through M&A activities and conglomeration, can be interpreted as a response to increasing pressures to realise potential scale and scope economies, and also to reduce labour and other costs in an attempt to eliminate inefficiencies. Many banks now offer a wider range of products and services, and conduct much of their business off-the balance sheet. The pursuit of financial innovation has also led to the wider use of more sophisticated financial instruments, including swaps and options.

The future of banking will likely be shaped in large part by the environment (regulatory, technological and competitive) in which it operates. The general macroeconomic conditions and demographic factors will probably also have an effect. Economic stability will ensure low bank failure rates and strong profit growth for banks, while demographic trends (the aging of the population and the continued entry of immigrants) could in some countries change savings demand and investment patterns.

Globalisation is expected to increase competition in most areas of financial services, and it may also be able to realise economies of scale and scope. At the same time, it will keep opening up new markets for banks, particularly in trading, asset management and investment banking activities. In particular, the rapid integration of the wholesale and capital markets, as well as large-value payment systems, will produce more and new kinds of linkages among banks.

This means that even if banks remain nationally based, they will be subject to international market developments and national tendencies will increasingly be influenced by international developments. Hence new regulatory structures will likely be necessary as banks become bigger in size and more exposed to risks originating from abroad, as well as risks to global financial stability.

Deposit-taking institution	E-money/e-banking
Non-deposit-taking institution	Remote payments
Credit multiplier	Financial/structural deregulation
Universal bank	Re-regulation
Payment system	Competitive pressures
Cheques	Financial innovation
Credit transfers	Financial conglomeration
Standing order	Globalisation/internationalisation
Direct debit	Mergers and Acquisitions (M&As)
Plastic cards	Disintermediation
Deposit and lending services	OBS activities
Investment, pensions and insurance services	Securitisation

Key reading

Bank for International Settlements (2004a) 'Statistics on payment and settlement systems in selected countries', Committee on Payment and Settlement Systems Publication No.60, Basle: BIS, http://www.bis.org/publ/cpss60.htm.

Berger, A.N., Dai, Q., Ongena, S. and Smith, D.C. (2003) 'To what extent will the banking industry be globalized? A study of bank nationality and reach in 20 European nations', *Journal of Banking & Finance*, **27**, (3), March 2003, 383–415.

Pilloff, S.J. (2004) 'Bank merger activity in the United States 1994–2003', Staff Study 176, Board of Governors of the Federal Reserve System, May, http://www.federalreserve.gov/pubs/staffstudies/2000-present/ss176.pdf.

Revision questions and problems

1 What is a deposit-taking institution?
2 Define a payment system.
3 Describe the main characteristics of different types of plastic cards.
4 What is e-banking?
5 What are the main forces that generate trends in the banking sector?
6 Outline the differences between deregulation and re-regulation of the banking sector.
7 What are the most common motives for M&As?
8 Define the disintermediation process.

Chapter 3

Types of banking

Learning objectives

- To distinguish between traditional and modern banking
- To understand the differences between commercial and investment banking
- To describe the main features of mutuality
- To understand the differences between private and corporate banking
- To outline the main aspects of Islamic banking

3.1 Introduction

This chapter outlines the main types of firms that undertake banking business and describes the main features of commercial and investment banking. The first part of the chapter describes the recent trend towards the development of financial service conglomerates and the widespread acceptance of the universal banking model. We then go on to outline the main types of banks engaged in commercial banking activity and also focus on the products and services offered to personal (including private banking) and corporate banking customers. Discussion on corporate banking services is split between services offered to small companies and corporate and investment banking products offered to mid-sized and large companies. Finally, we briefly highlight the main aspects of investment banking business and end by looking at some aspects of non-interest-based Islamic banking. A major theme throughout the chapter is the increasing blurring of distinctions between particular areas of banking and financial services provision, and the focus on customer relationships and meeting the increasingly complex and diverse needs of clients.

3.2 Traditional versus modern banking

Banking business has experienced substantial change over the last 30 years or so as banks have transformed their operations from relatively narrow activities to full service financial firms. Traditionally, banks' main business consisted of taking deposits and making loans and the majority of their income was derived from lending business. Net interest margins (the difference between interest revenues from lending minus the interest cost on deposits) was the main driver of bank profitability. In such an environment banks sought to maximise interest margins and control operating costs (staff and other costs) in order to boost profits. Banks strategically focused on lending and deposit gathering as their main objectives.

Up until the 1990s many banking markets were highly regulated and competition was restricted. In Britain banks were restricted from doing various securities and investment banking business up until 1986 when various reforms allowed commercial banks to acquire stockbroking firms. In continental Europe, branching restrictions were in place in Spain and Italy until 1992 and banks were also limited in terms of the types of business they could conduct. The implementation of the EU's 1988 Second Banking Directive in 1992 established a formal definition of what constituted banking business throughout Europe and this introduced the so-called universal banking model. Under the **universal banking** model, banking business is broadly defined to include all aspects of financial service activity – including securities operations, insurance, pensions, leasing and so on. This meant that from 1992 onwards banks throughout the European Union could undertake a broad range of financial services activity.

A similar trend has also occurred in the United States. For example, there were nationwide branching restrictions in place until the passing of the Riegle-Neal Interstate Banking and Branching Efficiency Act in 1994 which allowed national banks to operate branches across state lines after 1 June 1997. Also the Gramm-

Leach-Bliley Act in November 1999 allowed commercial banks to undertake securities and insurance business thus establishing the possibility of universal banking activity for US banks. Similar legislation was also enacted in Japan in 1999.

The type of business banks can undertake, therefore, has expanded dramatically. As detailed in Chapter 2, in addition to deregulation various other factors have also had an impact on banking business globally. Capital restrictions that limited the free flow of funds across national boundaries gradually disappeared throughout the 1980s facilitating the growth of international operations. The role of state-owned banks in Europe and elsewhere has declined as a result of privatisation and various balance sheet restrictions (known as portfolio restrictions) have also been lowered or abolished allowing banks greater freedom in the financial management of their activities. These global trends have also been complemented by advances in technology that have revolutionised back-office processing and front-office delivery of financial services to customers. The general improvements in communication technology and the subsequent decline in costs allow dissemination of information throughout a widespread organisation, making it practical to operate in geographically diversified markets. Lower communication costs also increase the role of competitive forces, as physically distant financial service providers become increasingly relevant as competitors.

Technology has also continued to blur the lines of specialisation among financial intermediaries. The development of the internet and other computing technology, for example, has enabled insurance companies to offer banking services online (such as the online bank Egg owned by Prudential in Britain) and has also promoted asset securitisation particularly in the United States (where standardised packages of loans are moved off banks' balance sheets and sold to investors, resulting in intermediation of similar assets across different types of intermediaries). Advances in computing power also allow investment banks and other financial service firms to offer accounts with characteristics similar to bank accounts. Technological developments, therefore, have generally facilitated growth in the range of financial services available and heightened the competitive environment.

It can be seen that banking business has changed dramatically from an activity characterised by limited competition and a relatively restricted product offering to a much more competitive and diverse activity. These differences are highlighted in Table 3.1.

Table 3.1 shows that the nature of banking business has changed from being relatively restricted and uncompetitive to a much more dynamic activity. Banks are now regarded as full service financial firms – and many banks have even dropped the word 'bank' from their name in their promotional material, such as 'Barclays' in Britain and JP Morgan Chase in the United States. The transformation of banks into full service financial institutions has been motivated by the strategic objective of banks to be able to meet as broad a range of customer financial service demands as possible. The increase in products and services that can be sold to customers helps strengthen client relationships and (so long as customers value the services being provided) should boost returns to the bank over the longer term.

In an increasingly competitive environment banks have sought to diversify their earnings – complementing interest revenues from lending activity with fee and commission income from selling non-traditional banking products such as insurance. The greater emphasis on building client relationships means that banks have had to become much more demand-oriented, focusing on meeting the needs of a more diverse and financially sophisticated client base.

Table 3.1 Traditional versus modern banking

Traditional banking	Modern banking
Products and services: LIMITED • Loans • Deposits	Products and services: UNIVERSAL • Loans • Deposits • Insurance • Securities/investment banking • Pensions • Other financial services
Income sources: • Net interest income	Income sources: • Net interest income • Fee and commission income
Competitive environment: • Restricted	Competitive environment: • High competition
Strategic Focus: • Assets size and growth	Strategic focus: • Returns to shareholders • Creating shareholder value (generating Return-on-equity, ROE, greater than the cost of capital)
Customer focus: • Supply led	Customer focus: • Demand led • Creating value for customers

Banks have also had to pay much greater attention to the performance of their operations and in particular to rewarding their owners (shareholders). Traditionally, when banking markets were relatively restricted and uncompetitive there was less pressure on banks to generate high profits in order to boost their stock prices and keep shareholders happy. Typically, banks focused on strategies based on asset growth – in other words they sought to become larger as this was viewed as the main indicator of commercial success. Nowadays, bank strategy focuses on creating value for shareholders (the bank's owners) and strategies based solely on asset growth are no longer deemed appropriate. The main reason for this shift in emphasis is because demands from shareholders have increased as has banks' demand for capital. In banking, capital is a resource available to the bank that it uses to protect itself against potential losses and to finance acquisition or expansion. A commercial bank's balance sheet comprises assets (e.g., loans, securities and fixed assets) and liabilities (mainly deposits) plus capital (e.g., shareholders' equity plus retained profits and various other items). The regulators set minimum capital requirements (e.g., Basle ratios) so banks have sufficient resources to bear losses incurred from bad loans or from other activity. As such, banks need to generate sufficient performance for their equity to increase in value in order to attract new shareholders as well as keeping established shareholders. Senior managers therefore prioritise strategies that seek to increase the overall value of the bank (reflected in the share value of the bank and its overall market capitalisation). In modern banking, strategies that are expected to boosts banks stock prices are therefore prioritised.

3.2.1   Universal banking and the bancassurance trend

A key feature of the deregulation trend is that it has allowed banks to compete in areas of the financial services industry that up until recently were prohibited. While the universal banking model has been an integral feature of European banking since the early 1990s, it has been a more recent development in the United States and Japan. One area that deserves particular attention regarding the adoption of the universal banking model has been the increased role of commercial banks in the insurance area (see Genetay and Molyneux, 1998). While it is relatively early to fully assess these developments in the United States and Japan (as the systems only allowed for banks to do insurance business from late 1999), the experiences of European banks provide a neat example of how the combination of banking and insurance business has developed. The combination of banking and insurance is known as '**bancassurance**' or 'allfinanz'.

Bancassurance is a French term used to define the distribution of insurance products through a bank's distribution channels. Bancassurance – also known as allfinanz – describes a package of financial services that can fulfil both banking and insurance needs at the same time. A high street bank, for example, might sell both mortgages and life insurance policies to go with them (so that if the person taking out the mortgage dies then the life insurance will pay up to cover the outstanding mortgage).

Since the 1980s, the trend towards bancassurance has been steadily increasing. Some of the reasons put forward to explain such a trend are:

● Cross-selling opportunities for banks (scope economies).
● Non-interest income boosted at a time of decreasing interest margins.
● Risk diversification.
● Banks converting into full service financial firms (deregulation).

Until the 1980s, banks in many countries sold insurance guarantees that were a direct extension of their banking business. For example, credit insurance on consumer loans was common in France. Banks were also selling buildings insurance and home/contents insurance for property purchase funded by mortgages.

During the 1980s major developments occurred, particularly in France, where banks started offering capitalisation products (for example endowment products). However, despite the existence of an insurance component, it was a support factor to the savings objectives of these products. The 1990s brought greater customer orientation in the financial sector and banks in several EU countries attempted to exploit better the synergies between banking and insurance.

In 2004, bancassurers in Europe had an approximate 35 per cent share of the life insurance market. Nowadays, the term 'bancassurance' encompasses a variety of structure and business models. The development of each model has largely occurred on a country-by-country basis as the models are tailored to the individual market structures and traditions.[1] In broad terms, bancassurance models can be divided between 'distribution alliances' and 'conglomerates'.

As shown in Figure 3.1 the 'conglomerate' model goes beyond the traditional bancassurance model of 'distribution alliances' which involves simply cross-selling of insurance products to banking customers, as it involves retaining the customers

---

[1] Comité Européen des Assurances (2003).

Figure 3.1 **Bancassurance models**

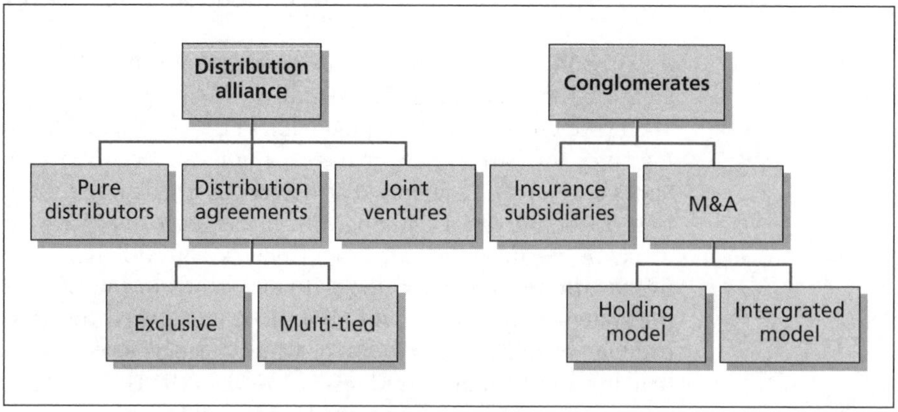

within the banking system and capturing the economic value added, that is a measure of the bank's financial performance, rather than simply acting as a sales desk on behalf of the insurance company. The conglomerate model is where a bank has its own wholly owned subsidiary to sell insurance through its branches whereas the distribution channel is where the bank sells an insurance firm's products for a fee.

In practice the use of 'conglomerate' and 'distribution alliance' models is influenced by the role of the banking sector in the particular country. In countries such as Italy, France, Spain and Britain, where banks are trusted and visited regularly, the 'conglomerate' model is likely to be preferred. In France, bancassurance represented 61 per cent of life and pensions market premium income at the end of 2002. In general, most of the major European markets have seen a rapid rise in the market share of bancassurance for sales of life assurance and pensions products in recent years. However, it is important to note that, because of the complexity of the bancassurance models and different implementation in EU countries, the figures may understate real sales levels. This holds true particularly for sales that are made through 'Distribution Alliances', which may lead to some understatement of the share of bancassurance, particularly in the United Kingdom.[2]

3.3 Retail or personal banking

Retail or **personal banking** relates to financial services provided to consumers and is usually small-scale in nature. Typically, all large banks offer a broad range of personal banking services including payments services (current account with cheque facilities, credit transfers, standing orders, direct debits and plastic cards), savings, loans, mortgages, insurance, pensions and other services (these services have been reviewed in Section 2.4).

A variety of different types of banks offer personal banking services. These include:

---

[2] Comité Européen des Assurances (2003).

- Commercial banks;
- Savings banks;
- Co-operative banks;
- Building societies;
- Credit unions; and
- Finance houses

3.3.1   Commercial banks

Commercial banks are the major financial intermediary in any economy. They are the main providers of credit to the household and corporate sector and operate the payments mechanism. Commercial banks are typically joint stock companies and may be either publicly listed on the stock exchange or privately owned.

Commercial banks deal with both retail and corporate customers, have well-diversified deposit and lending books and generally offer a full range of financial services. The largest banks in most countries are commercial banks and they include household names such as Citibank, HSBC, Deutsche Bank and Barclays.

While commercial banking refers to institutions whose main business is deposit-taking and lending it should always be remembered that the largest commercial banks also engage in investment banking, insurance and other financial services areas. They are also the key operators in most countries' retail banking markets.

3.3.2   Savings banks

Savings banks are similar in many respects to commercial banks although their main difference (typically) relates to their ownership features – savings banks have traditionally had mutual ownership, being owned by their 'members' or 'shareholders' who are the depositors or borrowers. The main types of savings banks in the United States are the so-called Savings and Loans Association (S&Ls or thrifts), which traditionally were mainly financed by household deposits and lent retail mortgages. Their business is more diversified nowadays as they offer a wider range of small firm corporate loans, credit cards and other facilities. Originally the US S&Ls were mainly mutual in ownership but now many have become listed. They represent the second largest deposit-taking group of financial institutions in the United States: there were 1,332 S&Ls in March 2005 with assets of $1.7 trillion. Savings banks are also important in various other countries. In Germany, for instance, they account for more than 50 per cent of the retail banking market and are the major players in household finance.

The German savings banks are public institutions owned by Federal or local governments who underwrite potential losses.[3] Savings banks are also important in Spain – and these also have quasi public ownership. Note that in Britain LloydsTSB was created by the merger of Lloyds Bank and Trustee Savings Bank (TSB), and the latter converted from a type of mutual status to a publicly listed bank before merg-

---

[3] Various state guarantees that enabled the German central savings banks, the *Landesbanken*, to obtain low cost (AAA rated) purchased funds, are being withdrawn after EU recommendations about unfair competitive practice, and this will also affect the financing cost of the whole sector.

ing with Lloyds. As such, savings banks nowadays do not play a significant role in the UK banking market.

It should be noted that savings banks (in Europe and elsewhere) adhere to the principal of mutuality and pursue objectives relating to the social and economic development of the region or locality in which they operate. Unlike commercial banks they may pursue strategic objectives other than maximising shareholder wealth or profits. Typically their business focuses on retail customers and small businesses, but as some have become very large (especially in Germany and Spain) they closely resemble commercial banks in their service and product offering.

3.3.3 Co-operative banks

Another type of institution similar in many respect to savings banks are the **co-operative banks**. These originally had mutual ownership and typically offered retail and small business banking services. A recent trend has been for large numbers of small co-operative banks to group (or consolidate) to form a much larger institution – examples of which include Rabobank in the Netherlands and Credit Agricole in France – both of these are now listed and have publicly traded stock. In Britain the Cooperative Bank also is publicly listed.

3.3.4 Building societies

Another type of financial institution offering personal banking services prevalent in the United Kingdom and various other countries (such as Australia and South Africa) are known as **building societies**. These are very similar to savings and co-operative banks as they have mutual ownership and focus primarily on retail deposit-taking and mortgage lending.

As noted by the UK Building Society Association:

> A building society is a mutual institution. This means that most people, who have a savings account, or a mortgage, are members and have certain rights to vote and receive information, as well as to attend and speak at meetings. Each member has one vote, regardless of how much money they have invested or borrowed or how many accounts they may have. Each building society has a board of directors who direct the affairs of the society and who are responsible for setting its strategy. Building societies are different from banks, which are companies (normally listed on the stock market) and are therefore owned by, and run for, their shareholders. Societies have no external shareholders requiring dividends, and are not companies. This normally enables them to run on lower costs and offer cheaper mortgages and better rates of interest on savings than their competitors.
>
> Building Societies Association (2005) website http://www.bsa.org.uk.

Chapter 12 provides more detail on the UK building society sector and shows that the number of these fell substantially during the 1990s as the largest converted from mutual to publicly listed companies and therefore became banks.

3.3.5 Credit unions

Credit unions are another type of mutual deposit institution that is growing in importance in some countries (especially in the United States and Ireland). These are non-profit institutions that are owned by their members. Member deposits are used to offer loans to the members. Many staff are part-time and they are usually regulated differently from banks. In the United States there were 9,058 as of March 2005 with 82 million members with deposits exceeding $520 billion and loans of over $355 billion.[4]

3.3.6 Finance houses

Finance companies provide finance to individuals (and also companies) by making consumer, commercial and other types of loans. They differ from banks because they typically do not take deposits and raise funds by issuing money market (such as commercial paper) and capital market instruments (stocks and bonds). In the United Kingdom these are sometimes referred to as hire purchase firms, although their main types of business are retail lending and (in Britain and continental Europe) leasing activity. All major retail firms and motor companies have their own finance house subsidiaries – for example General Motors' finance house used to fund car purchase is known as GMAC Financial Services. A distinction is usually made between sales finance institutions (loans made by a retailer or car firm to fund purchases); personal credit institutions (that make loans to 'non-prime' or high-risk customers who usually cannot obtain bank credit) and business credit finance houses that use factoring (purchasing accounts receivables) and leasing to finance business activity.

The largest finance houses in Britain are subsidiaries of the major banks and they are significant operators in the unsecured consumer loan business. For instance, finance houses provided £68.4 billion of new finance to the consumer sector in 2004 and this represented nearly 30% of all unsecured lending in the United Kingdom. Around £18 billion of finance was related to car purchase and finance houses 'financed at least 50 per cent of all new car registrations in the United Kingdom in 2004'.[5]

3.4 Private banking

So far we have discussed personal banking business outlining the various services on offer and the main types of financial institutions undertaking such activity. Another area of banking closely related to personal banking that has grown substantially over the last decade or so is known as **private banking**.

---

[4] Also see Ferguson and McKillop (1997) for a comprehensive analysis of the credit union industry.
[5] See the consumer finance section of the UK's Finance and Leasing Association website at http://www.fla.org.uk for more details.

Private banking concerns the high-quality provision of a range of financial and related services to wealthy clients, principally individuals and their families. Typically, the services on offer combine retail banking products such as payment and account facilities plus a wide range of up-market investment-related services. Market segmentation and the offering of high quality service provision forms the essence of private banking and key components include:

● tailoring services to individual client requirements;
● anticipation of client needs;
● long-term relationship orientation;
● personal contact;
● discretion.

The market for private banking services has been targeted by many large banks because of the growing wealth of individuals and the relative profitability of private banking business. The CapGemini Merrill Lynch Wealth Report (2005)[6] highlights various features of the market for high net worth individuals (HNWIs):

● 8.3 million people globally each hold at least US$1million in financial assets;
● HNWIs' wealth totalled US$30.8 trillion, an 8.2 per cent gain over 2003;
● Wealth generation was driven by fast-paced Gross Domestic Product (GDP) performance and moderate market capitalisation growth;
● HNWIs' wealth and population growth in North America outpaced those in Europe for the first time since 2001;
● Singapore, South Africa, Hong Kong, and Australia witnessed the highest growth in HNWI numbers; and
● HNWIs' financial wealth is expected to reach US$42.2 trillion by 2009, growing at an annual rate of 6.5 per cent.

An important feature of the private banking market relates to client segmentation. The bottom end of the market is referred to as the 'mass affluent' segment – typically individuals who have up to $100,000 of investable assets. The top end of the market are often referred to as 'ultra HNWIs' with over $50 million in investable assets and in-between lie HNWI's ($500,000 to $5 million) and very high HNWIs ($5 million to $50 million). The level of service and the range of products on offer increases with the wealth of the respective client.

Table 3.2 shows a listing of major private banks taken from a Euromoney (2005) ranking. It can be seen that major Swiss banks such as UBS and Credit Suisse are represented – this is not surprising as Switzerland is the global capital of offshore private banking business (where HNWIs have their investments managed by banks outside their home country). In addition, other large commercial banks have substantial private banking operations including HSBC, Deutsche Bank and Barclays.

The table also shows that the top US investment banks such as JPMorgan, Goldman Sachs and Merrill Lynch also rank highly in private banking as do some lesser-known Swiss banks (such as Pictet & Cie and Lombard Odier Darier Hentsch).

---

[6] CapGemini Merrill Lynch Wealth Report (2005).

Table 3.2 **Best global private banks**

1	UBS	13	MeesPierson
2	Citigroup Private Bank	14	Rothschild
3	Credit Suisse Private Banking	15	Morgan Stanley
4	HSBC Private Bank	16	Société Générale Private Banking
5	JPMorgan Private Bank	17	ING Private Banking
6	Goldman Sachs	18	Lombard Odier Darier Hentsch
7	Pictet & Cie	19	Barclays
8	Deutsche Bank, Private Wealth Management	20	Union Bancaire Privée
9	Merrill Lynch	21	Julius Baer
10	ABN Amro Private Banking	22	Nordea
11	Coutts & Co	23	Royal Bank of Canada
12	BNP Paribas Private Bank	24 =	Carnegie
		24 =	LCF Edmond de Rothschild

Source: Euromoney (2005) January.

3.5 Corporate banking

Corporate banking relates to banking services provided to companies although typically the term refers to services provided to relatively large firms. For example, Barclays refers to its activities with firms as 'business banking' and distinguishes between three size categories – firms with turnover up to £1 million, £1 million to £10 million and greater than £10 million. Services offered to the latter, namely the largest firms, are referred to as corporate banking services. Note that this distinction is not clear-cut and some banks do not explicitly distinguish between 'business banking' and 'corporate banking' although one should be aware that the term 'corporate banking' is used mainly to refer to services provided to relatively large firms whereas business banking may relate to a wide range of activity ranging from financial services provided to small start-up firms as well as larger companies.

Banking services provided to small and medium-sized firms are in many respects similar to personal banking services and the range of financial products and services on offer increases and grows in complexity the larger the company. Below we highlight the main banking services used by different sizes of firms.

3.5.1 Banking services used by small firms

There are four main types of banking service on offer to small firms:

1) Payment services;
2) Debt finance;
3) Equity finance;
4) Special financing.

3.5.1.1 Payment services

As noted earlier, banks play a pivotal role in the payments system. They provide clearing services to businesses and individuals making sure that current account transactions are processed smoothly; issue credit and debit cards that enable

customers to make payments and offer instant access to cash through their automated teller machines (ATMs) and branch networks. In many respects the payments
services on offer to small firms are similar to retail customers'. The former are provided with business current accounts that give firms access to current accounts that
provide a broad range of payment services. In the United Kingdom these include:

- Cash and cheque deposit facilities;
- Cheque writing facilities;
- Access to the CCCL (Cheque and Credit Clearing Company Limited) that deals
  with paper-based payments and processes the majority of cheques and paper-
  based credits;
- Access to BACS Limited (Banks Automated Clearing System), an automated
  clearing house responsible for clearing of electronic payments between bank
  accounts; processing direct debits, direct credits and standing orders;
- Access to CHAPS Clearing Company (Clearing House Automated Payments
  System) that provides electronic same day transfer of high-value payments.
  (Small firms, however, rarely use CHAPS as transaction costs are prohibitively
  expensive. In 1998 the average value of a CHAPS transaction was £2.3 million,
  compared to £552 for BACS and £636 for CCCL).

These are core payment services for which there are no substitutes. The supply of
payment services to small firms is dominated by the main UK banks and these also
control the wholesale networks for many transaction services.

One of the critical features of the payments system relates to small firm access
to cash and the ability to make payments in cash and cheque form. Like retail customers, small firms use their business current accounts via the branch network to
make cash and cheque payments into their current accounts. They also use the
ATM network to obtain cash. In terms of the types of payments made by small
firms in the United Kingdom, cheques and automated transactions such as direct
debits and standing orders predominate. Cash and plastic card payments only
account for around 5 per cent of the volume of business payments made in Britain.

3.5.1.2 Debt finance for small firms

The access to external finance is a critical success ingredient in the development of
any business and to this extent small firms are no different from their larger counterparts. Traditional bank loan and overdraft finance are the main sources of
external finance for small firms, although one should bear in mind that many
small firms rely on internal funding to finance their operations. With regards to
lending to small firms, features can obviously vary from country to country – in
the United Kingdom, for instance the majority of bank lending is at variable rates
of interest (as opposed to fixed rate lending) and in the case of term lending, typically has a maturity of more than five years.

The other main sources of external finance include:

- **Asset-based finance** – this includes both **hire purchase** and **leasing**. These two
  types of financial services are generally grouped together but they are two distinct types of product. Hire purchase agreements result in the purchaser of the
  goods building up ownership over a pre-determined period. On final payment
  the goods belong to the individual or firm making the payments. Leasing products are similar, but the legal ownership of the good remains with the lessor. For

example, a lease is an agreement where the owner (lessor) conveys to the user (lessee) the right to use equipment (e.g. vehicles) in return for a number of specified payments over an agreed period of time. Unlike a bank loan, a lease is an asset-based financing product with the equipment leased usually the only collateral for the transaction. Typically a firm will be offered a leasing agreement that covers not only the equipment costs but also the delivery, installation, servicing and insurance.

- **Factoring and invoice discounting** – **factoring** is the purchase by the factor and sale by the company of its book debts on a continuing basis, usually for immediate cash. The factor then manages the sales ledger and the collection of accounts under terms agreed by the seller. The factor may assume the credit risk for accounts (the likelihood that sales invoices will not be paid) within agreed limits (this is known as *non-recourse factoring*), or this risk may remain with the seller (*factoring with recourse*). (It is best to think of a factoring firm as a company's debt collector. The factor takes on responsibility for recovering payments on sales made.) **Invoice discounting** is similar to factoring but here the sales accounting functions are retained by the seller.
- **Shareholders and partners** – these are individuals who provide their own personal finance to the firm and this confers ownership rights.
- **Trade credit** – credit given to firms by trading partners allowing the former to delay payment.
- **Venture capital** – long-term external equity provided by **venture capital** firms. The venture capitalist is an equity partner who places greater emphasis on the final capital gain (dependent on the market value of the company). According to the British Venture Capital Association (BVCA) (http://www.bvca.co.uk/) investments typically last for three to seven years. In addition to finance, the venture capital firm (or individual) will provide expertise, experience and contacts to help develop the business.
- **Other sources** – this category includes a broad variety of alternative finance sources that ranges from credit card borrowing, loans from private individuals conferring no ownership (e.g., a loan from a member of a family); various government grants for small business, and so on.

3.5.1.3 Equity finance for small firms

Most small firms rely on bank- and asset-based financing for their external financing and few access either public or private equity finance. **Private equity finance** can be distinguished according to two main types: formal and informal. Formal equity finance is available from various sources including banks, special investment schemes, and private equity and venture capital firms. The informal market refers to private financing by so-called *'business angels'* – wealthy individuals who invest in small unquoted companies. According to the Bank of England[7] the term private equity is increasingly being used in the United Kingdom instead of venture capital, where the latter typically refers to higher-risk start-up capital investments. It is estimated that under 5 per cent of small firm external finance is from some form of venture capital funding.

---

[7] Bank of England (2001)

All the main UK banks offer a range of equity products to small firms although there are differences in their willingness to undertake direct equity investments. For instance, HSBC has operated a network of HSBC Enterprise Funds mainly aimed at making investments in the £5,000 to £250,000 range. In addition, the same bank operates HSBC Ventures specialising in equity investments of between £250,000 and £1 million. All the other main banks offer some form of private equity investment services although these tend to be geared to larger firms or those in certain sectors – such as high-tech start-ups. It is interesting to note that the British Bankers Association (BBA)[8] provides a section of its website dedicated to offering information on small firm financing. It also provides links to those wishing to know about equity investments to the British Venture Capital Association (BVCA)[9] and the National Business Angel Network. The Business Angel Network is supported by Barclays, HSBC, LloydsTSB and the Royal Bank of Scotland/NatWest along with the London Stock Exchange and the Corporation of London.

In addition to bank equity finance and that provided by business angels, Britain has the largest formal venture capital market in the world outside the United States. According to the European Venture Capital Association (EVCA),[10] UK venture capital firms invested some €19 billion in 2004 – over half of all European venture capital funding.

However, one should not forget that there are a number of public equity markets that provide funding for small firms with strong growth potential. In the United Kingdom the main public equity market is the Official List of the London Stock Exchange. Smaller firms are categorised in the FTSE Small Cap (market capitalisation of £65 million to £400 million) or FTSE Fledgling (market capitalisation of less than £65 million) indices. There is also a small market index that combines the FTSE Fledgling, Small Cap and TechMark[11] indices.

While access to the Official List is (in most cases) limited to medium-sized firms, fast-growth firms seeking a UK stock market listing are most likely to access the Alternative Investment Market (AIM). This is the second tier of the stock market and it has less onerous admission and trading requirements than the Official List.

Other sources of public equity finance in the UK include OFEX, an off-market trading facility provided by JP Jenkins Limited that has lower requirements than the AIM and provides seed capital to firms that may be contemplating an AIM or Official Listing in the future.

3.5.1.4 Special financing

In addition to all the above mentioned means of finance available to small firms, many countries have a range of government initiatives that seek to promote entrepreneurship and the development of the small firm sector. Britain is no exception, and there are a plethora of various initiatives aimed at promoting the development of the small firm sector.

Such recent schemes in the UK include initiatives geared to:

---

[8] See http://www.bba.org.uk.
[9] See http:// www.bvca.co.uk.
[10] See http://www.evca.com.
[11] TechMark was launched in November 1999 as the London Stock Exchange's index for innovative technology companies.

- Financing small businesses in economically deprived areas;
- Financing technology-based small firms; and
- Financing ethnic minority firms.

In addition to these the government also offers a wide range of fiscal advantages aimed at stimulating small firm growth, and especially start-ups.

3.5.2 Banking services for mid-market and large (multinational) corporate clients

The mid-market and multinational corporate sector is served by a variety of financial service firms including mainly commercial banks, investment banks and asset finance firms. These firms offer a broad range of services at varying levels of sophistication. The core banking products and services typically focus on the following range of needs:

1) Cash management and transaction services.
2) Credit and other debt financing facilities – loans, overdrafts, syndicated loans, commercial paper, bonds and other facilities.
3) Commitments and guarantees.
4) Foreign exchange and interest rate-related transactions.
5) Securities underwriting and fund management services.

At the bottom end of the middle-market sector companies generally require the services provided to the small firm sector but as they become larger they increasingly require a broader array of more sophisticated products.

3.5.2.1 Cash management and transaction services

An important area where larger company banking services differ from small firms is in the provision of cash management and transaction services. Cash management services have grown mainly as a result of: (a) corporate recognition that excess cash balances result in a significant opportunity cost due to lost or foregone interest, and (b) firms needing to know their cash or working capital position on a real-time basis. These services include:

- *Controlled disbursement accounts.* These current (or chequing) accounts are debited early each day so that firms get an up-to-date insight into their net cash positions.
- *Account reconciliation services.* A current account feature that provides a record of the firm's cheques that have been paid by the bank.
- *Wholesale lockbox facilities* whereby a centralised collection service for corporate payments is used to reduce the delay in cheque payment and receipt (i.e., clearing).
- *Funds concentration.* Redirects funds from accounts in a large number of different banks or branches to a few centralised accounts at one bank.
- *Electronic funds transfer.* Includes overnight wholesale payments via a variety of different mechanisms depending on the country in which the bank is based. In Britain, overnight wholesale payments are made through CHAPS and automated payment of payrolls or dividends by automated clearing houses (such as BACS). In the United States overnight wholesale payments are made through Clearing House Interbank Payments System (CHIPS) and Fedwire, and automated payroll

payments through various automated clearing houses. International banks also conduct automated transmission of payments messages by the Society for Worldwide Interbank Financial Telecommunication (SWIFT), an international electronic message service owned and operated by US and European banks that instructs banks to make various wholesale payments.

- *Cheque deposit services.* Encoding, endorsing, microfilming and handling cheques for customers.
- *Electronic sending of letters of credit.* Allows corporate clients to access bank computers to initiate letters of credit.
- *Treasury management software.* Allows efficient management of multiple currency portfolios for trading and investment services.
- *Computerised pension fund services.*
- *Online corporate advisory and risk management services.*
- *Electronic data interchange (EDI).* An advanced application of electronic messaging that allows businesses to transfer and transact invoices, purchase orders, shipping notices and so on automatically, using banks as clearinghouses.

3.5.2.2   Credit and other debt financing

Large companies often have to decide whether they are going to raise funds in the domestic or foreign currency. For instance, they may raise finance in a foreign currency in order to offset a net receivable position in that foreign currency. For example, consider a UK company that has net receivables in Euro (€). If it requires short-term finance it can borrow Euro and convert them into pounds for which it needs funds. The net receivables in Euro will then be used to pay off the loan. In this particular example, foreign currency financing reduces the company's exposure to exchange rate fluctuations. This strategy, of course, is attractive if the interest rate of the foreign currency loan is low. The main point to emphasise is that both short- and longer-term borrowings, whether they relate to standard loan facilities or the issue of short- or longer-term debt instruments, can be denominated in either local or foreign currency.

Short-term financing

All companies have to raise short-term finance (for under one year) periodically and in most cases this is usually provided by banks. Typically, small firms will arrange extended overdraft facilities or negotiate term loans to meet short-term financing needs. In contrast larger firms can negotiate credit lines with a number of banks so they are not dependent on one sole supplier of funds. Bank credit, of one form or another, may be denominated in the domestic currency of the firm or in a foreign currency. Large firms can also raise short-term funds in the capital markets by issuing various types of short-term paper. The arrangement of bank credit lines, overdraft facilities and the issue of short-term funding instruments are the responsibilities of the Treasury function.

Commercial paper

Large firms have access to various markets for short-term finance through the issuance of tradable instruments. One method that has been increasingly used by large firms to raise short-term finance has been through the issue of commercial paper (CP). Dealers issue this paper without the backing of an underwriting syndicate, so a selling price is not guaranteed to the issuers. Maturities can be tailored to the investor's preferences. Dealers make a secondary market in commercial paper by offering to buy the paper before maturity. The US commercial paper market is the largest in the world and is the main way (outside bank credit) that large US firms raise short-term finance. Commercial paper issues denominated in currency outside the country of issue (such as a Yen or Eurocommercial paper issue made in London) are known as Eurocommercial paper. (Note that this is not to be confused with the new European currency – a Euro CP issue can be denominated in any currency as long as the issue of the paper is made outside of the country or area of issue of the currency.) Commercial paper issues are often preferred to bank credit especially when large firms have better credit ratings than banks and this means that the former can borrow on cheaper terms. As only a handful of international banks have the highest credit rating (for example, AAA given by Standard & Poor's credit rating agency) this means that many large firms – such as General Motors and Coca-Cola – are perceived as being more creditworthy than the banks with which they do business. As such these firms can issue short-term financial instruments at finer terms than their relationship banks.

Euronotes

Euronotes are another type of instrument that large firms can issue to raise short-term funds. They are unsecured debt securities with interest rates based on interbank rates (mainly LIBOR – the London Inter Bank Offered Rate is the rate banks charge for lending wholesale funds to one another). These instruments typically have one-, three- or six-month maturities although they are often rolled-over as a form of medium-term financing. In the case of Euronotes, commercial banks usually underwrite the issue of these instruments guaranteeing an issue price. Banks and other companies purchase these as part of their investment portfolios.

Repurchase agreements (repos)

In addition to the aforementioned types of short-term financing there are numerous other types of financing techniques that companies can use to raise short-term finance. Recently, many large firms have developed their repo (repurchase agreement) activities. A repo deal involves pledging collateral (usually government bonds or some low-risk instrument) in return for short-term wholesale funds. At a set date, the funds will be repaid and the collateral 'released'. There are various types of repurchase agreements that involve varying agreements concerning the sale and buy-back of wholesale funds backed by various types of collateral agreements. A main attraction of this type of business is that it allows companies to raise short-term funds at wholesale rates by pledging longer-term financial assets. (It is a technique widely used by banks to facilitate liquidity in the money market.)

Long-term financing

Companies also have to raise long-term finance (for over one year) in order to finance long-term investments. Large companies have access to a broad array of credit facilities including overdraft and both secured and unsecured lending facilities. For large lending requirements companies can borrow via the syndicated lending market. In addition, the largest companies can also issue bonds[12] – either domestic or Eurobonds.

---

[12] For a brief introduction to the bond market, see Appendix A1.

Syndicated lending

Syndicated loans are a special category of loans in which an arranger, or group of arrangers, forms a group of creditors on the basis of a mandate to finance the company (or government) borrower. The main corporate borrowers in the syndicated loan market tend to be the largest multinational firms. Large firms typically chose this type of loan primarily because the required loan size is too great to be obtained from one bank (see also Section 4.6.1.3).

Eurobonds

Eurobonds are defined as securities that are issued, and largely sold, outside the domestic market of the currency in which they are denominated. Eurobonds are similar in many respects to domestic corporate bonds consisting of largely fixed-rate, floating-rate and equity-related debt (convertibles) with maturities usually around 10–15 years. Unlike domestic corporate bonds (that are denominated in the home currency and issued in the home market), the Eurobond market is subject to lower regulation and is instead effectively self-regulated by the Association of International Bond Dealers. The 'Euro' prefix in the term Eurobond simply indicates that the bonds are sold outside the countries in whose currencies they are denominated.

Eurobonds are issued by multinational firms, large domestic companies, sovereign governments, state firms and other international institutions.

3.5.2.3 Commitments and guarantees

Commitments relate to services where a bank commits to provide funds to a company at a later date for which it receives a fee. Such services include unused overdraft facilities and the provision of credit lines. Banks also provide facilities that enable companies to raise funds by issuing marketable short-term instruments such as commercial paper, Euronotes and (for longer maturities) medium-term notes. In the United States many large companies issue commercial paper to raise short-term funds and these facilities are almost always backed-up by a line of credit from a bank. In other words, the bank has a commitment to provide credit in case the issuance of commercial paper is not successful.

Guarantees relate to where a bank has underwritten the obligations of a third party and currently stands behind the risk of the transaction. Default by a counterparty on whose behalf a guarantee has been written may cause an immediate loss to the bank. Examples include such things as a standby letter of credit. This is an obligation on behalf of the bank to provide credit if needed under certain legally pre-arranged circumstances. Commercial letters of credit are widely used in financing international trade. This is a letter of credit guaranteeing payment by a bank in favour of an exporter against presentation of shipping and other trade documents. In other words it is a guarantee from the importers' bank ensuring that payment for the goods can be made.

3.5.2.4 Foreign exchange and interest rate services offered to large firms

Banks can offer their corporate clients a variety of tools to manage their foreign exchange and interest rate risk. These instruments, broadly referred to as derivatives (also see Chapter 9), involve transactions such as:

- *Forward foreign exchange transactions* – which are contracts to pay and receive specified amounts of one currency for another at a future date at a pre-determined exchange rate. Default by one party before maturity exposes the other to an exchange risk.
- *Currency futures* – these are contracts traded on exchanges for the delivery of a standardised amount of foreign currency at some future date. The price for the contract is agreed on the purchase or selling date. As with forward contracts, gains or losses are incurred as a result of subsequent currency fluctuations.
- *Currency options* – these allow the holder of the contract to exchange (or equally to choose not to exchange) a specific amount of one currency for another at a predetermined rate during some period in the future. For a company buying an option the risk lies in the ability of the counterparty not to default on the agreement (credit risk). For the bank writing the option the risk lies in its exposure to movements in the exchange rate between the two currencies (a market risk).
- *Interest rate options* – these are similar to currency options. The buyer has the right (but not the obligation) to lock into a pre-determined interest rate during some period in the future. The writer of the option (typically a bank) is exposed to interest rate movements, the buyer to counterparty default.
- *Interest rate caps and collars* – a bank (or other lender) guarantees the maximum rate (cap) or maximum and minimum rate (collar) on variable rate loans.
- *Interest rate and currency swaps* – in a currency swap two parties contract to exchange cash flows (of equal net present value) of specific assets or liabilities that are expressed in different currencies. In the so-called 'plain vanilla' interest rate swap two parties contract to exchange interest service payments (and sometimes principal service payments) on the same amount of indebtedness of the same maturity and with the same payment dates. One party provides fixed interest rate payments in return for variable rate payments from the other, and vice versa.

Note that many companies engage in **risk management** with the use of such financial instruments provided via their banks. Companies can also go direct to the market to hedge various interest rate and exchange rate positions. Companies engaged in substantial international trade have greater need to hedge their foreign currency positions and therefore make wider use of currency-related options, futures and forward transactions.

3.5.2.5 Securities underwriting and fund management services

As companies become larger they increasingly seek funding direct from the capital market and as such they require banks to arrange and underwrite equity and bond issues. **Securities underwriting** had traditionally been the preserve of investment banks (or so-called merchant banks in the United Kingdom) but during the 1990s universal banking became the 'norm' and now nearly all large commercial banks have an investment banking operation that underwrites issues.

In the case of securities underwriting, the underwriter undertakes to take up the whole or a pre-agreed part of a capital market issue (equity or bonds) at a pre-determined price. The main risk is that the underwriter will be unable to place the paper at the issue price.

Banks also can provide their corporate clients with **asset management** services, not only to manage a company's own investments but also to manage the pension funds of the firm's employees. The main investment banks are leaders in institutional fund management – this refers to the management of pension, insurance, corporate and other large-scale investments.

A major attraction for banks to provide services like commitments, guarantees, foreign exchange and interest rate-related transactions, securities underwriting and fund management services are that they are all fee-based and off-balance sheet (see Chapter 9). All the services listed above earn banks commissions and fees. In addition, they do not relate to any asset (e.g., a loan or investment) that has to be booked on the bank's balance sheet – hence the term 'off-balance sheet'.

As the above suggests, the range of products and services offered has grown rapidly over the last twenty years or so, as indicated in Figure 3.2. This increase in products can partially be explained by the growing overlap of commercial and investment banking services on offer to medium-sized and larger companies.

Figure 3.2 Large corporate banking product set

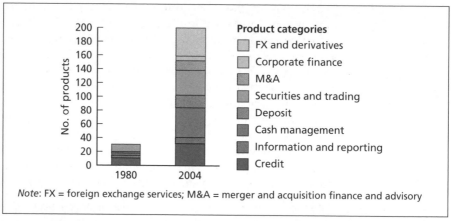

Note: FX = foreign exchange services; M&A = merger and acquisition finance and advisory

Source: Authors' estimates.

3.6 Investment banking

The previous sections provide an overview of the main banking services offered to companies – some of which are similar to those provided to retail customers but on a larger scale. However, we have also briefly discussed a range of services – such as securities underwriting (including the issue of commercial paper, Eurobonds and other securities) that may be less familiar. These activities have traditionally been undertaken by **investment banks** (or the investment bank subsidiaries of commercial banks) and relate generally to large-scale or wholesale financing activities. Investment banks mainly deal with companies and other large institutions and they typically do not deal with retail customers – apart from the provision of upmarket private banking services as noted earlier.

While we have already briefly outlined various investment banking products and services available to the corporate sector it is best at this stage to explain the main features of investment banking activity to show how it differs from commercial banking.

The main role of investment banks is to help companies and governments raise funds in the capital market either through the issue of stock (otherwise referred to as equity or shares) or debt (bonds). Their main business relates to issuing new debt and equity that they arrange on behalf of clients as well as providing corporate advisory services on mergers and acquisitions (M&As) and other types of corporate restructuring. Typically, their activities cover the following areas:

● financial advisory (M&A advice);
● underwriting of securities issues (guaranteeing a price that the new equity or bond issue will sell for);
● trading and investing in securities on behalf of the bank or for clients. This activity can include trading and investments in a wide range of financial instruments including bonds, equities and derivatives products;
● *Asset management* – managing wholesale investments (such as pension funds for corporate clients) as well as providing investment advisory services to wealthy individuals (private banking) and institutions;
● *Other securities services* – brokerage, financing services and securities lending.

Note that sometimes financial advisory and underwriting is referred to as investment banking to distinguish this from trading and other securities-related business. It is also important to remember that investment banks do not hold retail deposits and their liabilities are mainly securities and short-term wholesale financing. Table 3.3 lists the top global investment banks based on fee earnings for 2004. US investment banks predominate although one should be aware that traditionally the main US investment banks (who tended to dominate global investment banking) were the so-called 'bulge bracket' firms including – Goldman Sachs, Merrill Lynch, Morgan Stanley. Because legislation (Glass-Steagall Act of 1933) prohibited commercial banks from doing investment banking business the market was dominated by the specialist investment banks. However, since 1999 and the abandonment of Glass-Steagall, US commercial banks have acquired investment banks (Citigroup now includes the investment bank Salomon Brothers and the brokerage firm Smith Barney; and the commercial bank Chase is now linked up to JP Morgan). This means that banks such as Citigroup and JPMorgan Chase offer both commercial and investment banking services. As explained earlier, intermediaries that undertake a wide range of financial services business (such as commercial and investment banking, insurance, pensions, and so on) are referred to as universal banks. Universal

Table 3.3 Bloomberg 20 top investment banks by fees (2004)

Company	Total fees ($ billion)	Company	Total fees ($ billion)
Citigroup (US)	3.70	ABN Amro Bank (Netherlands)	0.90
Goldman Sachs (US)	3.60	Nomura Securities (Japan)	0.70
Morgan Stanley (US)	3.30	RBC Capital Markets (Canada)	0.70
JP Morgan Chase (US)	3.00	HSBC (UK)	0.70
Merrill Lynch (US)	2.70	Rothschild (UK)	0.60
UBS (Switzerland)	2.40	Daiwa Securities (Japan)	0.60
Credit Suisse (Switzerland)	2.10	Lazard (UK/US)	0.50
Deutsche Bank (Germany)	1.80	Wachovia (US)	0.50
Lehman Brothers (US)	1.60	Bear Stearns (US)	0.40
Bank of America (US)	1.00	BNP Paribas (France)	0.40

Source: Adapted from http://www.Bloomberg.com.

banking is common practice in Europe and one can also see from Table 3.3 that a variety of European commercial banks do substantial investment banking business.

The main difference between commercial banking and investment banking is that the former refers to deposit and lending business while the latter relates to securities underwriting and other security-related business. Banks such as HSBC or Deutsche Bank are referred to as commercial banks because their main business is deposit- and lending-related – although they both have substantial investment banking operations. Goldman Sachs and Morgan Stanley are known as investment banks because securities-related activity constitutes the bulk of their banking operations even though they also take wholesale deposits and lend.

In terms of services offered to large companies, commercial banks typically provide cash management, payments and credit facilities whereas investment banks arrange other types of financing through the issue of equity and debt to finance company expansion. They also offer an extensive array of other securities-related services including risk management products (such as interest rate and foreign exchange derivatives) and also advice on company M&A activity as well as other company restructuring. In recent years, however, these distinctions have become blurred as large commercial banks have either acquired or expanded their investment banking services to meet the increasing demands of corporate clients. Also the growth in global stock market activity has encouraged many commercial banks to develop asset management and private banking operations to deal with the growing demand for securities-related services from both institutional investors and wealthy private clients.

3.7 Universal versus specialist banking

As commercial banks increasingly undertake investment banking (as well as insurance and other financial activity) this has led to a debate as to the benefits of universal compared to **specialist banking**. The major activity of many financial institutions is the provision of financial intermediation services, i.e., the channelling of funds between lenders and borrowers, and the creation of new financial assets and liabilities in the process. However, it should be recognised that financial institutions may provide a wide range of other services including:

- trading in financial assets on behalf of their customers, i.e., acting as brokers or agents for clients;
- trading in financial assets for their own accounts, i.e., acting as proprietary dealers;
- helping to create financial assets for their customers and then selling these assets to others in the market, for example underwriting and issuing new shares;
- providing investment advice to personal customers or business advice to firms on mergers and takeovers;
- fund management, for example managing the whole or part of a pension fund; and
- insurance services.

In fact, the largest financial institutions nowadays offer a plethora of products and services incorporating all the finance types undertaken by different sorts of financial institutions. This is a reflection of the universal banking trend where large financial firms benefit (or at least attempt to benefit) from scale, scope and other economies associated with the production and distribution of a wide range of products and services. In other words, large banks have transformed themselves into full service financial firms offering a complete spectrum of personal and corporate banking services. The aim is to cross-sell many different products and services to customers through the product lifecycle.

For the personal banking customer, the typical product lifecycle is:

● Juniors (under 18 years of age) – offer basic deposit and payment services.
● Young adults (around 18 to say 25 years of age) – offer payment and limited credit facilities including student loans, travel insurance, property insurance, credit and debit card facilities.
● Adult/Young families (no children) – extend unsecured credit facilities, offer mortgages for house purchases, cross-sell house and related insurance, car insurance, encourage savings by offering savings and investment products to cover possible future costs associated with having a family;
● Young families with children – offer a wider range of mortgage options and credit facilities, sell protection products such as life insurance, critical illness insurance (e.g., 'what would happen if one of you became ill or died – how would your children be supported?, etc.). Cross-sell savings and investment products (e.g. 'how will you fund your child's education? etc).
● Middle-aged families (children left home) – sell pensions, savings and investment products (e.g., 'what will you live off when you retire?'), and so on

It can be seen that the financial requirements of personal banking customers span an extensive array of banking-, securities-, pensions- and insurance-related areas. The aim of banks is to cross-sell such an array of products and services to meet customer needs and also to generate more fee and commission income. A similar example for the product cycle of companies would show a reliance on commercial banking credit and payment facilities while the firm is small and as it grows a broader array of corporate and investment banking services would be demanded.

Given these aspects of the financial services industry it is hardly surprising that there has been a trend towards the creation of large financial services conglomerates and the acceptance of universal banking practice in many countries.

3.8 Islamic banking

So far this chapter has focused entirely on Western-based or conventional interest-based banking business. However, it would remiss of us not to mention the relatively recent development of **Islamic banking** business that is occurring in various parts of the world and is based on non-interest principles. Islamic *Shariah* law prohibits the payment of *riba* or interest but does encourage entrepreneurial activity. As such, banks that wish to offer Islamic banking services have to develop products and services that do not charge or pay interest. Their solution is to offer various profit-sharing-related products whereby depositors share in the risk of the bank's lending. Depositors earn a return (instead of interest) and borrowers repay loans based on the profits generated from the project on which the loan is lent.

An example of a commonly used profit-sharing arrangement in Islamic banking is known as *Musharakah*, which is an arrangement where a bank and a borrower establish a joint commercial enterprise and all contribute capital as well as labour and management as a general rule. The profit of the enterprise is shared among the partners in agreed proportions while the loss will have to be shared in strict proportion of capital contributions. The basic rules governing the *Musharakah* contract include:

- The profit of the enterprise can be distributed in any proportion by mutual consent. However, it is not permissible to fix a lump sum profit for anyone.
- In case of loss, it has to be shared strictly in proportion to the capital contributions.
- As a general rule all partners contribute both capital and management. However, it is possible for any partner to be exempted from contributing labour/management. In that case, the share of profit of the sleeping partner has to be a strict proportion of his capital contribution.
- The liability of all the partners is unlimited.

There are a wide variety of Islamic banking products and services based on various profit sharing and other forms of arrangements that enable financial intermediation without the use of interest. Globally there are around 100 Islamic banks and financial institutions working in the private sector, excluding those in the three countries, namely, Pakistan, Iran and Sudan, which have declared their intention to convert their entire banking sector to Islamic banking. The geographical distribution of these Islamic banks is given in Table 3.4, which shows that the largest number of Islamic banks is in the Gulf Cooperation Council (GCC) countries followed by other Middle Eastern countries.

In addition to the development of Islamic banking practices in parts of the world where the Islamic faith is an integral feature of the socio-economic make-up of the population, there has also been a growing interest from Western banks in developing such services for their customers. HSBC, for instance, was the first to offer an Islamic mortgage to its UK customers and Lloyds TSB has followed suit by introducing a similar product in March 2005, details of which are summarised in Box 3.1.

Table 3.4 Islamic banks by regions (2002)

Region	Number of institutions	Percentage
South and South East Asia	18	18.56
GCC	42	43.30
Other Middle Eastern countries	14	14.43
Africa	9	9.28
Rest of the world	14	14.43
Total	97	100

Note: GCC = Gulf Co-operation Council countries (Saudi Arabia, Bahrain, Kuwait, Oman, Qatar, and the United Arab Emirates)

Source: M. Iqbal and P. Molyneux (2005) *Thirty Years of Islamic Banking*. London: Macmillan, Table 4.5, p. 57.

Box 3.1	Lloyds TSB's Islamic mortgage product

On 21 March 2005 Lloyds TSB launched its debut *Shariah*-compliant Islamic home finance scheme at five branches in London, Luton and Birmingham, all cities with large Muslim populations.

Lloyds TSB, one of the top three banking groups in the UK, instead of developing its own standalone Islamic mortgage product, is utilising and co-branding a product off-the-shelf, the *Alburaq* Home Financing Scheme which is based on the pioneering diminishing *Musharakah* contract (a declining equity participation scheme between buyer and lender), which was pioneered last year by ABC International Bank and Bristol & West, a subsidiary of the Bank of Ireland Group in London. The Lloyds TSB scheme will be initially test-marketed by selected branches of the High Street bank. The added value which Lloyds TSB brings, stresses a spokesman, is our bespoke service elements. We only offer Islamic home finance from a single provider. According to Sheikh Nizam Yaquby, 'the diminishing *Musharaka* offers the most viable solution for housing finance. This particular contract has been successfully implemented by mortgage providers in the US, the UK and Pakistan.'

Under this mode, the financial institution and client jointly purchase the house. The ownership of the house is split between the bank and the customer; and it is agreed that the customer will purchase the share of the bank in the house gradually, thus increasing his own share until all the share of the bank is purchased by him thus making him the sole owner of the asset after a specified period. But during the financing period, the bank's share is leased to the customer who pays rent for using the bank's share in the asset. The Alburaq home financing scheme, which typically has a tenor of up to 25 years, offers two payment options to the customer. In the first option, the rent is fixed for an initial period of six months, and is then reviewed every six months. In the second option, the rent is fixed for two years, and is then reviewed every six months.

Source: Adapted from http://www.arabnews.com.

3.9 Conclusions

This chapter outlines the main types of banking business undertaken globally. The main focus has been on commercial and investment banking activities although the last part of the chapter briefly highlighted some features of non-interest Islamic banking practices. A major feature of banking business has been the blurring distinction between different types of banking business and the emergence of full financial service conglomerates that offer an extensive array of retail, corporate and investment banking products. Many banks also offer insurance, pensions and other non-banking financial services. Even traditional Western banks nowadays offer various Islamic banking products and services to meet the needs of their customers.

This change in the features of banking business simply reflects the desire of banks to meet the ever increasing and divergent needs of their customers – both personal and corporate. It also reflects the trend to diversify earnings supplementing traditional commercial banking interest income with fee- and commission-based revenues from other sources. The ultimate aim is to offer clients a spectrum of products and services that strengthen customer relationships and provide services that clients value.

Key terms

Universal banking	Invoice discounting
Traditional banking	Venture capital
Modern banking	Private equity finance
Bancassurance	Commercial paper
Retail or personal banking	Euronotes
Commercial banks	Repos
Savings banks	Syndicated loans
Co-operative banks	Eurobonds
Building societies	Commitments and guarantees
Credit unions	Risk management
Finance houses	Securities underwriting
Private banking	Asset management
Corporate banking	Investment banking
Leasing	Specialist banking
Hire purchase	Islamic banking
Factoring	

Key reading

CapGemini Merrill Lynch (2005) *World Wealth Report*. USA: Merrill Lynch, Pierce, Fanner & Smith Incorporated. http://www.merrilllynch.com/media/48237.pdf.

Iqbal, M. and Molyneux, P. (2005) *Thirty Years of Islamic Banking*. London: Macmillan.

Revision questions and problems

1 In what ways does traditional banking differ from modern banking?

2 What is bancassurance?

3 Explain the main characteristics of the different types of banks that offer personal (retail) banking services.

4 What are the primary features of private banking?

5 What are the main features of corporate banking?

6 What are venture capitalists? To what extent are they similar to private equity finance?

7 What are the typical services offered by banks to the large (multinational) corporate sector? Distinguish between short- and long-term financing.

8 What services do investment banks typically offer to customers?

9 What are the benefits of universal banking compared to specialist banking?

10 What distinguishes Islamic banking from Western banking?

Chapter 4

International banking

Learning objectives

- To outline the main features of international banking

- To describe the history of international banking

- To understand the reasons for the growth of international banking

- To understand the main theories on the rationale for international banking

- To describe the most common international banking products and services

4.1 Introduction

The growth in foreign bank activity and international banking in general has been a major factor of financial system development. This chapter provides an insight into the main characteristics of international banking and highlights its diverse and dynamic features. The first part of the chapter defines what we mean by international banking, provides a brief history and then discusses the range of products and services offered by international banks. Here the focus is on banking services provided to large corporations – namely treasury management services, credit, debt and equity financing as well as trade finance and various risk management products. The chapter concludes by discussing features of country risk evaluation and notes the growing presence of foreign bank activity in a global setting.

4.2 What is international banking?

International banking refers to business undertaken by banks across national borders and/or activities that involve the use of different currencies. A more precise definition of international banking is provided by Lewis and Davis (1987, p. 221) who classify international banking into two main types of activity – **traditional foreign banking** and **Eurocurrency banking**. Traditional foreign banking involves transactions with non-residents in domestic currency that facilitates trade finance and other international transactions. Eurocurrency banking involves banks undertaking wholesale (large-scale) foreign exchange transactions (loans and deposits) with both residents and non-residents.

The definition above suggests that international banks are involved with financing trade, transacting foreign exchange business and making wholesale (large) short-term Eurocurrency loans and deposits.

While banks engaged in international banking are typically involved in this type of activity, the definition is rather broad and does not really take account of the fact that many banks have operations in various countries. Traditional foreign banking and Eurocurrency banking, for instance, do not require that banks have a physical presence in a foreign country – such activity can be conducted within a single country. For example, UK banks can undertake domestic currency transactions with customers in Hong Kong without any physical presence in the latter. Similarly, wholesale Eurodollar loans (wholesale loans denominated in US dollars) can be made between banks based in London without any of these banks needing a physical presence in the United States.

In order to account for the fact that many banks have physical operations in various countries a distinction is made between multinational and international banking. **Multinational banking** refers to banks having some element of ownership and control of banking operations outside their home market. The main feature of multinational banking is that it requires some form of **foreign direct investment** (FDI) by banks in overseas markets reflecting a physical presence. (As one can guess, the definition comes from the literature on multinational enterprises and FDI.)

One should note that international banking and multinational banking are terms that are used interchangeably to refer to banks that have global activities. For the purpose of this chapter we will use international banking as it is a more commonly used term, although one needs to be aware that the following sections discuss international activities of banks in their broadest sense.

4.3 A brief history of international banking

The origins of international banking date back over 4,000 years, when various civilisations used letters of credit and bills of exchange issued across sovereign boundaries to finance trade. The history of banks having a physical presence outside their home country is more recent, widely acknowledged as starting in the fifteenth century when Florentine bankers (notably the Medici family) established subsidiaries or foreign branches in other jurisdictions to help finance trade, scientific, military, artistic and other endeavours. From the fourteenth to the sixteenth centuries, Florence was regarded as the scientific and cultural capital of the Western world and the city gave birth to the Renaissance and modern European art. It has been argued that commercial and artistic developments were inextricably linked by a change in social attitudes that emphasised the creation of wealth and conspicuous consumption. This not only prompted the development of regional banking business but also encouraged international activity because financing requirements could not be met locally.[1]

The modern era of international banking can be viewed as occurring in two distinct phases. The first phase commenced with the rise of colonialism during the nineteenth century and continued into the twentieth century. The second phase of international bank expansion was linked to the growth of US multinational firms and the changing financial regulatory landscape from the late 1950s and early 1960s onwards:

● **Colonial banking**. British banks opened branches in their Australian, Caribbean and North American colonies in the 1830s. Further expansion took place starting from the 1850s onwards and by the end of the century British banks had operations in South Africa, Latin America, India and parts of Asia as well as in the Middle East and some European countries. Other colonial powers also expanded their banking activities in the latter part of the nineteenth century, particularly Belgian, French and German banks that set up operations in Latin America, Africa and China as well as in London. One noticeable difference between the British banks and their European counterparts was that the former established 'colonial banks', otherwise known as 'British overseas banks' or 'Anglo foreign banks' that only provided services outside Britain. In contrast the European banks undertook both domestic and foreign activity, often via the acquisition of banks or through the establishment of subsidiaries. In other words, European bank expansion overseas was more similar to the type of activity conducted nowadays – domestic banks acquiring foreign operations or setting up

---

[1] Banca Monte dei Paschi di Siena, the oldest bank in the world, was founded in 1472. Also see Parks (2005) for an excellent insight into the role of the Medici family in banking, art and other matters in fifteenth-century Florence.

subsidiaries through which business could be undertaken whereas British banks were specifically set up to do banking only in the colonies. It should be noted that various Japanese and Canadian banks also developed international activities in the latter part of the nineteenth and early twentieth centuries.

● **Modern international banking.** The expansion of banks overseas during the first half of the twentieth century was somewhat limited due to the decline of the British and other colonial empires, economic uncertainty brought about by the world wars, and the changing political landscape in many countries that sought to establish their own banking systems by restricting (even nationalising) foreign banks. It was not until the emergence of the United States as a major economic power and the growth of their multinational companies that the second wave of international banking activity took place. This occurred from the late 1950s and early 1960s onwards, when US banks began to expand overseas to meet the financial requirements of multinational firms, as well as to take advantage of cheaper financing outside the home market. US banks were subject to limits on how much interest they could pay on deposits (known as Regulation Q) and also had to maintain onerous reserve requirements. They found that by establishing subsidiaries outside the United States (typically in London) these operations were not subject to home regulations – so US banks could pay more interest on dollar deposits and could do more dollar lending at finer terms via their overseas subsidiaries as these were not subject to the home regulations. US banks were attracted to London because substantial dollar deposits were located there – some say that this was because the anti-communist sentiment in the United States (characterised by the so-called 'McCarthy witch hunts' from 1947 to 1954) encouraged the Russian, Chinese and other governments to move large-scale dollar funds out of New York to London as they thought these might be frozen. In any event, US banks flocked to London and, to a lesser extent, other major financial centres (e.g., Paris) during the 1960s. This was the birth of the **Eurocurrency markets** – markets where wholesale foreign currency deposits and lending takes place. US banks continued to dominate international banking during the 1970s, although from the late 1970s and throughout the 1980s Japanese banks replaced them as the major international lenders (reflecting the growth of Japanese multinational companies over the period). The 1990s witnessed a decline in the relative importance of Japanese banks on the international scene due to problems in their home market, and their position was replaced by European banks that have expanded their international operations as a result of various factors (including the creation of the European Union's single market).

4.4 Why do banks go overseas?

An extensive body of literature has examined the rationale for the expansion of companies overseas. This literature spans the economics literature on the determinants of foreign direct investment (FDI), studies on the strategic behaviour of firms as well as empirical evidence on the performance and efficiency advantages of international companies. Many of the theories applicable to the overseas expansion of non-financial firms can be applied to banks.

The main theories describing the motives for overseas expansion relate to:

1) Factor price differentials and trade barriers.
2) Arbitrage and the cost of capital.
3) Ownership advantages.
4) Diversification of earnings.
5) Excess managerial capacity.
6) Location and the product lifecycle.

These theories are briefly discussed below.

4.4.1   Factor prices and trade barrier theories

The theoretical and empirical literature on the determinants of FDI focuses on two main motives for overseas expansion – factor price differentials and trade barriers that inhibit exports. The former, known as **vertical FDI**, suggests that overseas activity occurs so that firms can take advantage of international factor price differences. Headquarter services require substantial physical and human capital inputs whereas production is mainly manual labour intensive. Companies become multinational when they establish production in lower manual labour cost countries and headquarters where skilled labour costs are low. The alternative motivation for the existence of multinationals relates to trade barriers that make exporting costly. Where trade costs are high the firm establishes in countries to access markets and this is referred to as **horizontal FDI**.

One can see that these two main motives for FDI derive from study of the real sector. In the case of banking, evidence would seem to suggest that horizontal FDI is likely to be a much more important motive for cross-border activity than vertical FDI. For instance, the strategic reasons for banks to establish multinational operations are most likely to be based on advantages associated with 'internalising' informational advantages as opposed to trading at arm's length. Because it is difficult to find efficient markets for long-distance transactions in some areas of banking (such as retail banking, lending to small firms, specific credits to companies operating in different regulatory and economic environments) investment overseas is likely to be an important feature of the industry.

Regulations governing many areas of business are also country-specific and act as substantial trade barriers. This means that in many areas of business (and particularly in banking) it may be difficult to undertake cross-border activity without a physical presence within a country. For example, differences in tax treatments, consumer protection legislation, marketing rules, definition of products and so on, mean that the cross-border selling of many financial services products and services is problematic unless the bank has a physical presence in the market in which it wishes to sell its products. Box 4.1 highlights how trade barriers impact on banks' decisions to locate overseas.

4.4.2   Arbitrage and the cost of capital

One of the main theories explaining the overseas investment decision of firms relates to the **arbitrage** activities of firms, in that companies that raise their finance in strong currency markets can borrow relatively cheaply and they can invest their

Box 4.1   Trade barriers and banking

Many jurisdictions prohibit the sale of financial services without establishment – a bank must have a physical presence before it can enter the market. These barriers may be less onerous when banks operate in areas that have a more international dimension such as investment and international banking, although it is noticeable that even the world's largest investment banks typically have extensive physical market presence in many countries. In general, domestic regulations dictate that banks must have a physical presence in the country before they can access various markets – this, therefore, acts as a substantial trade barrier facilitating both cross-border establishment as well as M&A activity. Bringing together informational advantages associated with having a market presence plus the barriers brought about by domestic financial services regulation means that cross-border activity in banking can mainly be characterised by horizontal FDI.

proceeds in markets where currencies are weak and firms can be acquired relatively cheaply. For a simple example, the substantial 20–30 per cent depreciation of the US dollar against the Euro and British sterling during 2003 meant that European investors could acquire US banks 20–30 per cent more cheaply than they could do previously. All other things being equal, this means that overseas banks can be purchased cheaper due to currency depreciation and the overall returns from the acquired firm will be boosted – as return on capital will obviously be higher. (The theoretical argument is the same as the reason European holidaymakers flock to destinations with relatively weak currencies and may be deterred from visiting destinations with strong currencies.)

More formally, the **cost of capital** argument focuses on the cost of raising finance (see Chapter 8, Section 8.4.3 for more details). At any one time, some currencies are relatively strong whereas others are weak. Investors require a lower return or interest rate for securities issued in the stronger currency. As such, firms that issue securities in strong currencies require a lower cost of capital (it is cheaper for them to borrow via the issue of equity or debt instruments). Subsequently, these firms can acquire overseas assets at higher prices than local firms who issue securities in local currencies, and still appear to be buying foreign firms relatively cheaply. So if the Euro is strong compared with the dollar, Euro-based firms can raise funds for acquisition more cheaply than their US counterparts, and therefore can acquire stakes or outbid them to make purchases, say in the US market.

While cost of capital arguments have been put forward as the main reason for the acquisition of US banks by their UK and European counterparts from the late 1990s to 2005, this theory cannot really explain the following:

- why some firms invest overseas in markets which have the same currency;
- why there is cross-investment between firms from the same currency, for instance, why UK firms invest in the United States and why US firms invest in the United Kingdom; or
- why firms incur substantial costs in setting up new operations overseas instead of just making an acquisition.

As a consequence, various other theories have been proposed to explain overseas expansion of banks (and other firms).

4.4.3 Ownership advantages

Given the limitations of the cost of capital argument, attention has been placed on identifying why foreign banks seek to operate overseas when they seem to have various disadvantages compared to domestic/indigenous banks.

Typically, the main disadvantages for foreign banks entering overseas markets can be identified as:

- Indigenous banks are likely to be better informed regarding the demand features of the local markets as well as the legal and institutional framework under which business is conducted. Foreign banks, therefore, can only acquire this expertise at a cost.
- Foreign banks have to incur costs associated with operating at a distance and these include such things as management, regulatory and other costs.

Given that these disadvantages are likely to be evident, the argument goes that banks that locate overseas must have some type of compensating advantages that enable them to compete with indigenous firms on equal terms – these are in general referred to as **ownership advantages**.

These so-called 'ownership advantages', which may be related to technological expertise, marketing know-how, production efficiency, managerial expertise, innovative product capability, and so on, must be easily transferable within the bank and the skills and other 'ownership advantages' diffused effectively throughout the organisation.

The concept of 'ownership advantages' is a rather broad concept. It is by no means clear how long it takes banks to build such advantages, whether such advantages relate mainly to innovative products and services, or whether they emanate mainly through the operation of more efficient organisational or production processes. There is also little evidence on the costs associated with developing such advantages. However, the fact that banks do expand into markets where they at first appear to have an inherent disadvantage compared with incumbent firms, means that they must have some form of advantage compared with domestic operators.

4.4.4 Diversification of earnings

An obvious motive for foreign expansion relates to the aim of management to diversify business activity. This theory states that the investment decisions of banks stem from a conscious effort by managers to diversify earnings and therefore reduce risk. By expanding into different markets, banks expose their operations to the risk and return profile of specific business areas. If a German bank believes the prospects for retail banking in the United States are more attractive than retail banking in its home market then it makes sense to consider expansion in the United States. This will diversify earnings and make the German bank less exposed to its home market.

Diversification of bank earnings and risk reduction can be brought about by expansion into foreign markets and risk will be reduced the less correlated earnings in the foreign country are to those in the home market. You should be aware that finance theory tells us that investors wish to construct diversified portfolios of shares so that all their investments are not exposed to the same adverse shocks – hence they construct portfolios by choosing an array of investments looking for low correlations between the price movements of the stock in order to maximise diversification benefits to yield a given expected return and risk (for more details see Appendix A2). This principle is the same for banks (and other firms) when they consider expanding overseas. Also remember that banks can diversify by doing similar business activity in different countries and also by expanding into new areas (such as insurance, mutual funds, investment management, investment banking, and so on) both at home and abroad.

4.4.5　Theory of excess managerial capacity

Another theory of foreign investment relates to the desire of companies to use up **excess managerial capacity**. A bank may require the use of certain managerial and other resources that can be only fully utilised when they achieve a certain size. For instance, if a firm has a highly specialised management team it may not get the best use of this team if it only focuses on business in one particular geographical market. Companies can extend their scale of operations by expanding overseas and into new markets and these managerial resources will be more efficiently utilised.

4.4.6　Location and the product lifecycle

In addition to the theories mentioned above another school of thought focuses on location theories that are linked to the **product lifecycle**. Here the focus is on the nature of the product (or services) produced and the changing demand and production cost features of the product in different markets.

The product lifecycle has three main stages:

1) innovative or new product;
2) maturing product;
3) standardised product.

The **innovative (or new product) stage** is when a good or service is produced to meet a new consumer demand or when a new technology enables the creation of innovative goods. Typically, these new demands are first met by banks located in mature and well-established markets – also generally those with higher GDP per capita income. In the first instance, the product may not be standardised and communication between the production process and selling arm of the company needs to be close and frequent as the product establishes a market presence. As the communication costs increase with distance the new product is likely to be produced and sold in the home market before any international expansion is considered.

As the bank gains from 'learning by doing' and the most efficient forms of production, distribution and selling are identified, the product becomes more standardised. This is known as the **mature product stage**. Customers are more aware of the product's features and also are likely to become more price-sensitive (demand for the product in the home market becomes more elastic). As the market expands, the producer is likely to benefit from scale economies so production costs fall. When the product or service reaches maturity and foreign customers become aware of the new good then demand is likely to grow (especially from those in relatively more prosperous overseas markets). Usually, investment is initially likely to take place in high-income countries that have demand features similar to the home market although where the costs of producing and operating locally exceed those of exporting. This pattern of **production diffusion** whereby innovative products are first produced and sold in prosperous economies then trickle down to (relatively) less wealthy markets characterises overseas expansion in the mature product stage. This feature is common to many retail financial services, such as credit cards, that originated in the United States in the 1960s, spread to Europe in the 1970s and 1980s and in the 1990s became commonplace in many developing countries.

The final stage of the product lifecycle is that of the **standardised product** where the product is uniform and undifferentiated and competition between producers is based solely on price. In this case knowledge about foreign markets is not important and the main issue for the producer is to find the lowest cost of production. In this stage of the product lifecycle, production is transferred to the lowest cost country so the firm can maintain competitive advantage.

4.4.7 Other theories on the rationale for international banking

While there are a host of theories explaining why international banking exists no one theory seems adequately to explain all types of foreign expansion. Banks may wish to simultaneously diversify their income streams and also find the lowest cost production base. Many banks and other financial firms have developed services with strong brand images through effective differentiation strategies, but they may still wish to charge relatively high prices and also produce at the lowest cost.

In fact, if one reviews the literature on the motives for foreign expansion, it can be seen that all the theories come up with some form of explanation that tries to determine why banks seek to produce and sell their own products and services through foreign operations rather than exporting from the home market. Other theories concerning the rationale for international banking relate to:

- **Firm-specific advantages.** Some banks have advantages (whether financial, based on distribution and production expertise, selling experience, etc.) that make foreign expansion more amenable. Size often confers such advantages as large banks typically have a wide array of financing sources, may benefit from scale and scope economies and have more expert management and systems that make foreign expansion easier. They also are more likely to have the relevant financial resources to undertake large-scale overseas activity.
- **Location advantages.** There may be a variety of attractions associated with overseas location that the aforementioned theories do not cover. We mentioned a couple of location advantages when we talked about the product lifecycle above, but other location benefits relate to a variety of production, distribution and selling attributes of the product or service in question. For instance, banks like to group together in financial centres (as in London, New York and Tokyo) to benefit from the close proximity of the foreign exchange market and other Eurocurrency activities. The liquidity of London's foreign exchange market (the largest in the world) attracts foreign banks and other service firms (such as accountants, lawyers, consulting firms, and so on) because of the business available.

Overall, one has a broad range of theories to choose from in explaining the rationale for foreign bank expansion. In reality, one can probably pick a variety of different theories to explain the motives for foreign expansion and the choice of explanations are likely to vary on a case-by-case basis.

4.4.8 **Practice of bank expansion in foreign markets**

Complementing the theories noted above, one can identify a host of strategic reasons for banks wishing to establish foreign operations. These are outlined as follows:

- **Customer-seeking strategies**. Banks seek to undertake overseas expansion in order to obtain new customers or to follow established clients. The reason banks are more likely to seek new customers through foreign establishment (either through M&A activity or establishing new operations themselves) relates to the barriers associated with the cross-border selling of products and services without a physical presence. Typically, this view suggests that the decision to invest overseas is associated with the higher costs involved with meeting clients' needs from a distance as opposed to investment in the foreign market. The rush of banks into the Chinese market (with a customer base equivalent to 22 per cent of the world's population) is a good example of how the world's largest firms have been motivated by the commercial opportunities afforded by an underdeveloped retail and commercial banking market.

- **Obtaining a foothold strategy**. Foreign expansion can be motivated by the desire to establish a presence in order to test the market. Information can be obtained by making experimental foreign investment and over time banks can decide on whether to expand or contract their activities. For instance, various US and European investment banks have made relatively modest acquisitions of securities firms in the Japanese market in order to see if they can develop their private banking business.

- **Follow the leader strategy**. When a large bank undertakes investment in a foreign market it may well encourage others to follow. There is anecdotal evidence that various multinational firms (including large banks) emulate their competitors' cross-border strategies regarding investment decisions in major markets. Some form of herd instinct seems apparent vis-à-vis the recent rush of many banks and other large firms into the Chinese and other Asian economies. The recent move of commercial and investment banks acquiring asset management firms across Europe and the United States, as well as Spanish bank expansion in Latin America, are two examples of the herd instinct in international banking activity.

- **Customer-following strategies**. It has been argued that banks in their home markets have information advantages associated with their on-going client relationships. The nature of these relationships put these firms in a privileged position to follow their customers abroad. If a bank's major corporate customer enters a new market, it may wish to obtain its banking services locally and this is likely to encourage foreign expansion. Customer-following strategies are common in banking – big firms need big banks so they can meet their growing financing needs. The capital markets, of course, can meet certain financing requirements of large firms – especially when markets are buoyant. When capital markets become less accommodating then companies turn to their banks. In other words, when companies become larger and industries more concentrated, the banking industry will follow suit.

- **Performance and efficiency advantages.** The most obvious reason justifying foreign expansion is that it adds to overall firm performance and shareholder value. That is, returns generated from cross-border operations will add to group returns, boosting profits and ultimately increasing the bank stock price for its shareholders. Given that a major strategic objective of banks is to generate sufficient risk-adjusted returns to their owners, one would expect that there is evidence to suggest that foreign operations add value in some way. Cross-border expansion can therefore be expected to add value to the bank by improving operating costs and/or increasing market power in setting prices.

- **Managerial motives.** International banking activity may, of course, be motivated by managerial motives rather than the objective of maximising profits and shareholder value. Entrenched managers may make international investment decisions based on their own preferences for pay, power, job security, risk aversion, and so on. In general, international expansion may either strengthen or weaken the hands of entrenched managers directly by affecting the market for corporate control or governance, or indirectly by changing the market power of the firm. Put simply, managers may seek to expand internationally so they control larger firms – salaries and benefits being higher in bigger firms/banks. Managers may wish to expand in order to make their companies less prone to hostile takeovers, or they may believe that geographical diversification helps improve their own managerial prospects but this may not necessarily be the same as increasing the share price or profits of the bank.

- **Government motives.** It could be argued that a major factor that has motivated the growth of international banking activity has been deregulation aimed at fostering more competitive, innovative and open markets. The deregulation of many over-protected banking markets has had the effect of encouraging foreign bank entry and this, in theory at least, should boost competition and encourage domestic banks to become more efficient. For example, one of the main objectives of the EU's Single Market Programme has been to reduce barriers to trade in banking and financial services across all member countries in order to encourage foreign bank expansion.

 4.5 Types of bank entry into foreign markets

When undertaking business in foreign markets banks have a number of choices regarding the structure of their activities. The choice of structure depends on a broad range of considerations including the amount of investment the bank wishes to undertake, tax issues, and other factors. The five main types of structure that banks can choose include:

1) correspondent banking;
2) representative office;
3) branch office;
4) agency;
5) subsidiary.

4.5.1 Correspondent banking

The lowest level of exposure to the foreign market can be achieved through a **correspondent banking** relationship. This simply involves using a bank located in the overseas market to provide services to a foreign bank. Typically banks will use correspondent banks to do business in markets where they have no physical presence and as such these types of services are widely used by smaller banks. Box 4.2 illustrates the correspondent banking services provide by one of Canada's largest banks – the Canadian Imperial Bank of Commerce (CIBC).

It can be seen that the sort of services offered via a correspondent banking relationship relate mainly to the offer of payment and other transaction services as well as various trade credit facilities. Correspondent banks such as CIBC earn a fee from the foreign banks for providing these services. It should be clear that foreign banks only have a minimal exposure to foreign markets via correspondent banking relationships.

4.5.2 Representative office

Banks can obtain slightly greater exposure to a foreign market via a **representative office**. Representative offices are usually small and they cannot provide banking business – that is they cannot take deposits or make loans. Representative offices are used to prospect for new business and they usually only act as marketing offices for parent banks. Typically a bank will set up a representative office in risky markets as the cost of running such small offices is negligible and they can easily be closed if commercial prospects are not good.

4.5.3 Branch office

Establishing a **branch office** usually indicates a higher level of commitment to the foreign market compared with the representative office. A branch is a key part of the parent bank and acts as a legal and functional part of the parent's head office. In many respects a foreign branch is similar to a domestic branch although the former is likely to have more autonomy in making commercial decisions tailored to the specific features of the foreign market. Branches can perform all the functions that are allowed by the banking authorities of the host country, namely taking loans and making deposits, as well as selling other types of products and services.

Branches are the most common form of foreign bank expansion as the costs are less than establishing a wholly owned subsidiary and they enable banks to conduct a full range of business activity.

Figure 4.1 shows the type of foreign bank structure in the United States at December 2004. Of the 476 foreign banks operating in the United States, 231 had branch operations with assets amounting to $1,130 billion followed by 67 subsidiaries with assets of some $398 billion. In addition, the United States hosted 130 representative offices and 45 agencies. The latter held over $22.8 billion of assets. Foreign banks accounted for 18.1 per cent of total US banking sector assets, 15.3 per cent of deposits and 10.5 per cent of lending in the United States. With regard to lending, foreign banks tend to focus on company lending – reflected by the fact that their share of total business loans stood at 21.5 per cent by December 2004.

Box 4.2   **Canadian Imperial Bank of Commerce (CIBC) correspondent banking services**

CIBC is a leader in payment processing, and is a major provider of funds transfer services for correspondent banks globally. CIBC's main correspondent banking services include:

a) Current account services, including multicurrency accounts, a full range of statements, and pooling services.
b) Payment services in all major currencies to any bank or other beneficiary, anywhere in Canada or through our subsidiaries in the Caribbean. These include: treasury settlement, cash settlement of securities, customer transfers to beneficiaries in Canada, disbursements, international bulk payments and pension payments.
c) Cash letter clearing services, including clean collections.
d) Documentary business such as letters of credit, documentary collections and guarantees.

Customer service teams are specialists in the investigation of client account activities, including payments, cash letters, collections, compensation claims, mail and pension payments, drafts and money orders.

CIBC delivers account and wire payment services reliably and efficiently and has made the bank a valued partner to banks throughout the world. In addition CIBC has strengths in related areas such as trade finance and institutional trust and custody services.

CIBC has established strong clearing relationships with a multitude of banks around the globe. It has been providing correspondent banking services to foreign banks for nearly a century.

Source: Adapted from http://www.cibc.com/ca/correspondent-banking.

Figure 4.1 **Number of foreign banks in the US by organisational type (December 2004)**

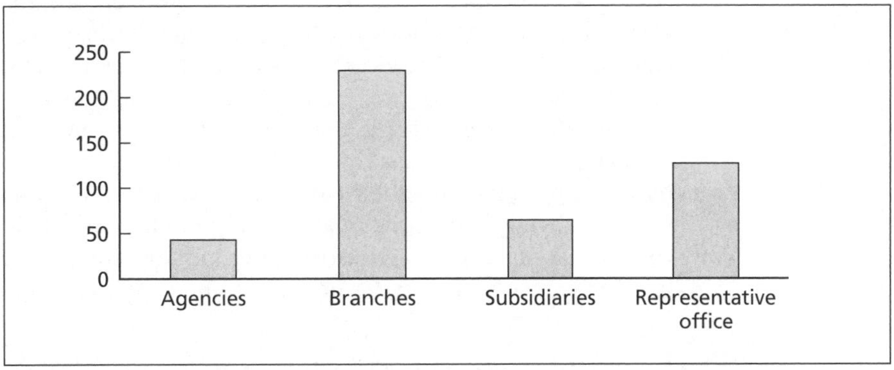

Source: Compiled from Federal Reserve Structure and Share Data for US Offices of Foreign Banks data, December 2004.

4.5.4   Agency

Agencies are similar to branches in that they form an integral part of the parent bank. They lie somewhere between branches and representative offices as they can do less than the former and more than the latter. For example, in the United States a foreign bank agency cannot take deposits but is allowed to lend.

4.5.5   Subsidiary

A **subsidiary** is a separate legal entity from the parent bank, has its own capital and is organised and regulated according to the laws of the host country. Where branches and agencies expose the whole capital of the parent bank to risk from overseas activity, the risk exposure of a subsidiary is limited by its own capital exposure. (Of course, if a foreign bank subsidiary faced difficulties the regulators would expect the parent bank to provide support – although legally they do not have to do this given that subsidiaries have separate corporate identities.)

Subsidiaries may be the result of acquisition or organic start-ups – they also tend to be costly as the business has to be capitalised separately from the parent. One main advantage of having a subsidiary is that it generally signals a stronger commitment to do business in a country compared with other forms of entry and reflects the foreign companies' more positive assessment of future prospects for the market. In addition, subsidiaries are usually allowed to undertake a broad range of banking business subject to the rules and regulations of the host country. For example, prior to 1999 US commercial banks were prohibited from undertaking full-scale investment banking business in their home market so many of the largest banks established subsidiaries overseas where they could undertake this type of business.

4.6   International banking services

Section 4.5 described the different forms of bank entry into foreign markets and from this it should be clear that banks can offer a wide range of different types of banking and financial services via their international operations. One of the difficulties in describing types of international banking activity relates to its diversity. Traditionally the role of banks in providing services to multinational companies has been emphasised as the main feature of international banking, but as many banks have expanded overseas their customer provision now spans the full spectrum of services ranging from niche retail banking products to wholesale investment and commercial banking activity. Bearing this in mind, the following sections focus on banking products and services provided to international business.

4.6.1   Products and services to international business

All international businesses are served by a variety of financial service firms including mainly commercial banks, investment banks and asset finance firms. The core banking products and services are similar (but not exclusively) to those offered to large corporate clients, which were reviewed in Section 3.5.2. These typically focus on the following range of needs:

1) money transmission and cash management;
2) credit facilities – loans, overdrafts, standby lines of credit and other facilities;
3) syndicated loans (only available to large companies and multinational firms);
4) debt finance via bond issuance (only available to large companies and multinational firms);
5) other debt finance including asset-backed financing;
6) domestic and international equity (the latter typically only available to large companies and multinational firms);
7) securities underwriting and fund management services;
8) risk management and information management services; and
9) foreign exchange transactions and trade finance.

4.6.1.1 Money transmission and cash management

An important area where firms conducting international activities differ from smaller domestic-oriented firms is in the provision of **cash management and transaction services**, as they have to deal with remittances and payments in both the domestic and foreign currency. Although many companies may not be large enough to have well-developed treasury activities they are likely to have more advanced cash management systems than their domestic counterparts. The cash management function in firms has developed mainly as a result of:

a) corporate recognition that excess cash balances result in a significant opportunity cost due to lost or foregone interest;
b) the firm's need to know its cash or working capital position on a real-time basis; and
c) the need for foreign currency flows of cash to be managed effectively in order to minimise possible exchange rate risk.

The extent to which such services are used obviously depends on the scale of the firm's activities and the extent of its international operations. The largest companies will have treasury functions that resemble small banks conducting this type of business, whereas mid-sized companies are likely to have a limited array of cash management activities.

4.6.1.2 Credit facilities – loans, overdrafts, standby lines of credit and other facilities

Firms of all sizes have a broad array of bank **credit facilities** available for use in financing their operations. These range from standard loan facilities that may be fixed or floating rate, secured or unsecured, and can have short- to long-term maturities. In many respects these types of loan facilities are not really any different from consumer loans apart from their size. Companies also, of course, have access to on-going overdraft facilities to meet short-term financing needs.

In addition to these standard products, larger companies will have access to Eurocurrency markets. The Eurocurrency market is essentially a high-volume, low-risk borrowing and depositing market. The main segment of the market is the interbank market where a relatively small number of large commercial banks undertake deposit and lending activities. Other important participants include companies and governments who use the market to fund short-term deficits and invest short-term surpluses. Various other financial institutions, such as investment banks, also use the market to fund large-scale holdings of securities through pledging these in repurchase (repo) agreements. Unlike banks, which issue certificates of deposit (CD), large non-financial companies can fund their short-term deficits by issuing commercial paper (CP) or by discounting trade receivables in the form of banker's acceptances. These are techniques used for raising short-term wholesale funds denominated in a currency other than the home currency. For instance, a UK multinational company (MNC) may issue $5 million of commercial paper to raise short-term finance or can simply borrow in the interbank market – the latter is a dollar Eurocurrency loan. (Similarly, the UK firm may have access to dollar funds and place, say, a $5 million deposit with a bank – this is known as a Eurocurrency deposit.) Access to the Eurocurrency markets is mainly the preserve of banks and large international companies. Box 4.3 provides a snapshot of recent non-bank activity in the Eurocurrency markets highlighting the short-term foreign currency financing of international enterprises.

In addition to standard loan products, banks will also provide their corporate clients with various commitments and guarantees (see Section 3.5.2).

4.6.1.3 Syndicated loans

In a **syndicated loan,** two or more banks (members of the syndicate) agree jointly to make a loan to a borrower. Every syndicate member has a separate claim on the borrower, although there is only a single loan agreement contract. One or several lenders will typically act as an arranger or lead manager, instructed by the borrower to bring together the consortium of banks prepared to lend money at a given set of terms. Corporate borrowers usually have their relationship banks at the core of the syndicate and they may bring in other institutions according to the size, complexity and the pricing of the loan as well as the desire of the firm to extend the range of its banking relationships. Pricing of the loan is set at a margin above the interbank rate (usually LIBOR) and fees are also paid by the borrower to the syndicate for arranging the loan.

Syndicated loans may take the form of:

- term loans – where the loan amount is specified for a set time;
- revolving credit facilities – where part of the loan can be drawn down, repaid and then redrawn depending on the borrowers discretion;
- standby letters of credit – where the credit facility is arranged to enhance the credit risk of the borrower; and
- single- or multi-currency loans.

Box 4.4 briefly notes global telecom firm's involvement in the syndicated loan market.

Typically, access to the syndicated loans market is restricted to only the largest firms as the smallest loans typically exceed $50 million. The main advantages of this form of borrowing are:

- arranging a syndicated loan is less costly, in terms of set-up fees, compared with a bond issuance;
- borrowers can achieve lower spreads than they might have to pay to individual banks if they intended to borrow through a series of bilateral bank borrowing;

Box 4.3   Short-term Eurocurrency lending to non-banks loan customers stagnate in the third quarter of 2003

Following a comparatively large increase in the third quarter, loans to non-bank borrowers stagnated in the fourth. Total claims on non-banks were up by $37 billion, less than two thirds of which actually took the form of new loans.

However, this rather modest aggregate growth masks some relatively large underlying movements. In particular, total claims in US dollars rose by $35 billion, despite a notable contraction in claims by banks in the United States, while euro-denominated claims declined for the first time since the introduction of the euro.

Banks in the reporting area seemed to have halted their tentative advance in international lending to corporate and other non-bank private sector borrowers in the fourth quarter. A resumption of Japanese banks' investment in US Treasury and other debt securities vis-à-vis the United States accounted for a large part of the $35 billion overall increase in US dollar-denominated claims.

Moreover, the BIS consolidated data indicate that portfolio shifts towards the non-bank private sector, while apparent in several euro area countries in the third quarter, remained stable vis-à-vis this sector for most banking systems in the fourth. Although US banks did raise their exposure to this sector, $16 billion of their $26 billion in new international claims flowed to such borrowers in the United Kingdom, offshore centres (primarily the Cayman Islands) and Luxembourg, suggesting that increased credit ties with non-bank financials was responsible.

Overall, activity involving offshore and other major financial centres, either as lenders or borrowers, remained significant in the fourth quarter. Banks in off-shore centres accounted for a rise in lending to non-bank borrowers in the United States, extending $40.5 billion in loans, which possibly reflected the funding of affiliated securities houses and hedge fund activity. At the same time, banks in the United States reduced loans to non-bank borrowers in offshore centres by $22 billion; excluding this move, loans to these borrowers in offshore centres rose by $3.6 billion, mainly as a result of credit from banks in the United Kingdom and the euro area. Claims on non-bank customers in other major financial centres also increased. Banks in the reporting area, primarily in the euro area and the United States, directed $19 billion in new loans to non-banks in the United Kingdom. Similarly, banks in the United Kingdom and the euro area channelled $12 billion to non-banks in Luxembourg.

Source: BIS (2004b) *74th Annual Report (1st April 2003 – 31 March 2004)* Basle: BIS.

- syndication can also provide a more flexible funding structure which guarantees the availability of funds in the currency of their choice;
- it widens a company's circle of lenders through syndicates that include foreign banks;
- a syndication provides the borrower with a stable source of funds which is of particular value in the event that other capital markets (such as the bond market) are subject to disruption;
- syndication allows borrowers to raise larger sums than they would be able to obtain through either the bond or equity markets under a time constraint;
- the facilities can be arranged quickly and discreetly which may be of value for certain transactions such as takeovers; and

---

Box 4.4 **Multinational telecoms' funding of 3-G licences and syndicated lending**

A recent example of how international firms rely on banks for their funding relates to the telecom industry's financing of its 3-G (third generation) mobile telephony licences. Since 1999, European and other governments raised billions by auctioning these licences to the world's largest telecom firms, and the latter have been burdened by inordinate levels of debt ever since. In fact, global telecoms' share prices have been depressed since 2000 after the realisation that they paid too much for these licences. The money that was raised to pay for these licences was predominantly funded by the syndicated loans market.

The syndicated loans market is best known for funding the financial requirements of less-developed countries and comes to prominence when a country defaults or has difficulties in making loan repayments on its debt. Famous cases include the Mexican default in 1982 and more recently Argentina's near default at the end of 2001. Although much is said about groups of banks (syndicates) lending to developing countries and the problems of Third World Debt, much less is made of syndicated lending to developed countries and large firms – although this constitutes the bulk of the market. The main point is that in the scramble to raise billions of dollars to finance the 3-G licences, the world's largest telecoms firms had to resort to this market in addition to more traditional bank financing. Various commentators have noted that the largest Swedish banks are now heavily exposed to the sector as a result of their financing Nokia's, Ericsson's and other telecoms' bids.

Another reason why the international telecoms firms resorted to raising finance via the syndicated loan market was because of the relatively depressed nature of the international corporate bond and equity markets over this period. In general, in periods of buoyant capital markets large firms will raise funds in the capital markets, as it is cheaper than borrowing from banks. When markets turn down then banks become an alternative (sometimes the only) source of finance. This is why the banking system is sometimes referred to as the 'lender-of-last resort' to big companies.

- commitments to lend can be cancelled relatively easily compared to borrowing via securities markets where such actions could have an adverse impact on investor confidence.

Syndicated credits are priced according to the perceived credit risk of the borrower – this is the risk that a borrower may default. This is translated into a margin (or spread) over LIBOR or some other interbank benchmark rate. Higher credit risks, therefore, pay larger margins above LIBOR for their syndicated loans. Pricing is in 100ths of a per cent, known as basis points. For instance, a top class AAA borrower may pay only 50 basis points (0.5 per cent interest) over LIBOR, where a high-risk borrower may pay 300 basis points (3 per cent) above LIBOR. Pricing obviously varies according to the type of borrower, purpose of loan, whether the loan is secured or not and other factors. Typically, the size of the margin increases with credit risk. Around 35 per cent of syndicated loans are given a credit risk weighting by the credit rating agencies. The scheme used by Standard & Poor's and Moody's to assess credit risk is shown in Table 4.1. Triple-A rated loans have the

Table 4.1 **Credit risk ratings – Moody's and Standard & Poor's**

Moody's	S&P	Quality of issue
Aaa	AAA	Highest quality. Very small risk of default.
Aa	AA	High quality. Small risk of default.
A	A	High-medium quality. Strong attributes, but potentially vulnerable.
Baa	BBB	Medium quality. Currently adequate, but potentially unreliable.
Ba	BB	Some speculative element. Long-run prospects questionable.
B	B	Able to pay currently, but at risk of default in the future.
Caa	CCC	Poor quality. Clear danger of default.
Ca	CC	High speculative quality. May be in default.
C	C	Lowest rated. Poor prospects of repayment.
D	–	In default.

lowest margins and pricing increases as one moves down the credit risk spectrum. Loans that have a credit rating less than BBB are regarded as speculative, making these types of credit most costly. Note, however, that in reality the majority (around 60 per cent) of syndicated credits are not rated, while only 5 per cent or so are 'high-risk' or speculative grade. The majority of issues do not need to be rated as lenders go on the established credit ratings of companies and other borrowers in the bond market as a guide to the parties' credit risk.

In addition to the spread over LIBOR, the borrower also has to pay a variety of fees. The arranger and other members of the lead management team generally earn some upfront fee for putting the deal together – this is known as a *praecipium* or *arrangement fee*. The underwriters similarly earn an *underwriting fee* for guaranteeing the availability of funds. Other participants (those on at least the manager or co-manager level) may also expect to receive a *participation fee* for agreeing to join the facility. The actual size of the fee generally varies with the size of the commitment. The most junior syndicate members typically only earn the spread over LIBOR or over a comparable market reference rate.

Once the credit is established, and as long as it is not drawn, the syndicate members often receive a *commitment or facility fee* (to compensate for the cost of regulatory capital that needs to be set aside against the commitment) again proportional to the size of the commitments. As soon as the facility is drawn, the borrower may have to pay a *utilisation fee*. This is paid for instance if the company draws more than a pre-agreed proportion of the facility – for example, it may be agreed that if the borrower draws more than 50 per cent of a facility it will have to pay its lenders an additional five basis points utilisation fee on top of the margin. The agent bank typically earns an *agency fee*, usually payable annually to cover the costs of administering the loan. Loans sometimes also include penalty clauses whereby the borrower agrees to pay a pre-payment fee or otherwise compensate lenders in the event that it reimburses its debt prior to the specified term.

4.6.1.4 **Debt finance via bond issuance**

In addition to the credit facilities mentioned above, large companies can also raise funds in the capital markets by issuing debt instruments known as **bonds**.[2] Bonds

---

[2] For an introduction to bonds and bond markets, see Appendix A1.

are simply contracts between a lender and borrower by which the borrower promises to repay a loan with interest. Typically, bonds are traded in the market after issue so their price and yields vary. Bonds can take on various features and a classification of bond types depends on the issuer, priority, coupon rate and redemption features as shown in Figure 4.2.

Large companies as well as governments and international organisations all issue bonds to raise medium- to long-term finance. The most important feature relating to a bond is the credit quality of the issuer – typically governments (especially in the developed world) are believed to be lower risk than firms and so their bonds pay lower interest than those of commercial concerns. However, since some of the world's largest companies have better credit ratings than some fragile economies, this means that the former can raise bond finance cheaper than the latter. Nearly all bond issuers have to be credit rated in order to assess their ability to make interest (and ultimately principal) payments for their bond financing. The credit rating process is the same as that outlined for syndicated credits and shown in Table 4.1.

There are many types of corporate bonds that a firm can issue. It can raise funds in its home market (and currency) by issuing domestic bonds, or it may wish to issue an international bond the main types of which include:

● **Eurobonds** – any bond that is denominated in a currency other than that of the country in which it is issued. Bonds in the Eurobond market are classified according to the currency in which they are denominated. So, for example, a Eurobond denominated in US dollars issued in Japan (or anywhere outside the US) would be known as a Eurodollar bond.
● **Foreign bonds** – denominated in the currency of the country into which a foreign entity issues the bond. For instance a yen-denominated bond issued in Japan by a US firm is (a foreign bond) known as a Samurai bond. Similarly, a UK firm issuing a dollar bond in the US is known as a Yankee bond, and a French firm issuing a sterling bond in the UK is known as a Bulldog bond.

Figure 4.2 Bond features

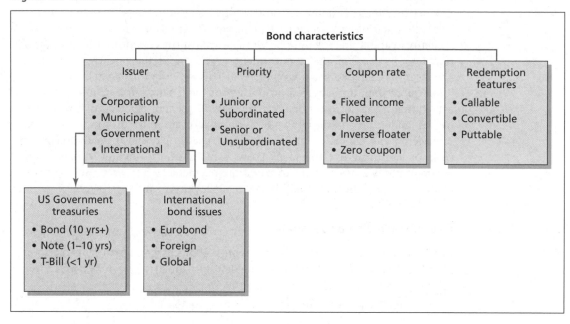

● **Global bonds** – can be issued in both foreign and Eurobond markets. In general, a global bond is similar to a Eurobond but it can be offered within the country whose currency is used to denominate the bond. For example, a global bond denominated in dollars could be sold either in the US or any other country through the Eurobond market.

Companies have therefore a broad range of bond types with which they can raise debt finance. In addition to the creditworthiness of the borrower, bonds are characterised by their priority, coupon rate and redemption features.

The *priority* of the bond relates to the holder of the bond's repayment standing in the event that the issuer defaults on payments. Bonds that are classified as senior debt (otherwise known as unsubordinated debt) means that the holders of such bonds are first in line to receive payment if the company defaults and payment is to be made from a liquidation of assets. In contrast, junior (or subordinated) bond-holders would receive payment after senior bond investors – as such this form of debt is more risky and commands a higher premium than senior debt.

Companies can choose a variety of types of interest payments, or coupons, to pay on their bonds. The traditional (or *plain vanilla*) bond just pays a fixed rate semi-annual coupon over the life of the bond and the last payment will include both the final coupon payment and the repayment of principal (which is the par value of the bond). In addition, the coupon can be set at a floating rate, usually relating to LIBOR or some other variable market rate.

Both bond investors and issuers are exposed to interest rate risk since they are locked into either receiving or paying a set coupon rate over a specified period of time. For this reason, various types of bonds offer additional redemption features in order to minimise these risks. For example, there are *callable bonds* that give the issuer the right but not the obligation to redeem their issue of bonds before the bond's maturity date. In this case the issuer of the bond has to pay the bondholders a premium to compensate the holder for the fact that the bond may be redeemed before maturity. For *American callable bonds* the bond can be redeemed at any date (after a set period) whereas *European callable bonds* can only be redeemed on dates specified by the issuer. Typically, an issuer will redeem its bonds when current interest rates are lower than that being paid on its bonds – so the firm could redeem its bonds and make a new issue at a lower coupon rate. There are also *puttable bonds* that give holders the right to sell back the bonds to the issuer at a predetermined price and date.

Another type of bond is the *convertible bond* that gives holders the right but not the obligation to convert their bonds into a predetermined number of shares at a set date before maturity.

4.6.1.5 Other debt finance including asset-backed financing

The access to external finance is a critical success ingredient in the development of any business. Traditional bank loan and overdraft finance are the main sources of external finance for relatively small firms that conduct international business, whereas bond and syndicated loans form a major feature of multinational financing. In addition to these sources of debt finance, all firms (irrespective of size) have access to other forms of debt finance that can involve both domestic and/or international relationships and they include:

- asset-based finance; and
- factoring and invoice discounting.

As introduced in Section 3.5.1, **asset-based finance** encompasses both leasing and hire purchase and the main difference between them is that in the former the asset remains the property of the leasing company at the end of the contract, whereas in the case of hire purchase the firm making payments obtains ownership. More formally, a lease is an agreement where the owner conveys to the user the right to use equipment and (say) vehicles in return for a number of specified payments over an agreed period of time. Unlike a bank loan a lease is an asset-based financing product with the equipment leased usually the only collateral security for the transaction. Typically a company will be offered a **leasing** agreement that covers not only the equipment costs but also the delivery, installation, servicing and insurance.

There are two main kinds of leases used by companies:

- **Capital or lease finance** – a standard finance lease is defined as one which transfers substantially all the risks and rewards inherent in the ownership of the asset to the lessee (the lessee is the user of the leased asset). The risks include any loss in value of the asset value through such things as obsolescence, unsatisfactory performance, wear and tear, and so on. Under the terms of a finance lease, the lessor (the person who rents land or property to a lessee) usually receives lease payments amounting to the full cost of the leased asset, together with a return on the finance that has been provided. This means that the lessor is not exposed to any financial risks associated with the residual value of the asset. Under a finance lease there is no statutory obligation to have a purchase option over the leased asset.
- **Operating lease** – is any lease other than a finance lease. As such operating leases embrace a broad range of different types of lease in which a substantial proportion of risks and rewards associated with ownership of the asset remain with the lessor. Operating leases have two main features. First, they have a non-cancellable lease period that is much shorter than the life of the asset. Second, the lessee has little or no interest in the residual value of the asset at the end of the lease. The residual guarantees from the proceeds of the sale of the asset – which is a hallmark of many finance leases (think about car finance leases) – are absent in the case of standard operating leases. Again there is no statutory obligation to have a purchase option over the leased asset.

Hire purchase differs from lease contracts in that customers pay for the cost of the asset, together with the financing charges, over the hire period and take legal title on the equipment at the time of final payment (or there may be a nominal purchase option fee at the end of the payment period). For tax and accounting purposes the customer in a hire purchase agreement is treated as the owner from the outset and this allows them to claim capital allowances for taxation purposes and they can also report the asset on the company's balance sheet.

The main attractions of leasing are as follows:

- As the bank/finance company holds title to the asset while repayments remain outstanding, and the asset belongs to the bank/finance company should the company go bankrupt, the bank or finance company has some assurance that payments will be maintained by the customer (even if this relates to the return of the asset being financed).

- Bank overdraft or loan facilities may not be available of the size required to finance outright purchase of the asset. A lease agreement provides up-front finance for the whole cost of the asset subject to one advance or rental. More important though, a lease once obtained will provide guaranteed continuity of credit over the agreed hire period. In contrast, an overdraft facility can be withdrawn at short notice.
- Companies are able to avoid tying up their working capital by using leasing agreements.
- There may be certain tax advantages associated with lease finance compared with outright purchase of assets and this is a more important consideration for 'Big-ticket' lease deals (as in such things as aircraft and computer systems leasing).

The main disadvantages of lease finance relate to the typically higher costs compared with traditional bank funding and the fact that the firm does not own the asset, thereby reducing the value of company fixed assets.

Other sources of finance for companies are through the use of **factoring** and **invoice discounting services**. As illustrated in Section 3.5.1, factoring is a lending product that enables a company to collect money on credit sales. The factor purchases the company's invoice debts for cash, but at a discount, and subsequently seeks repayment from the original purchaser of the company's goods or services. Factoring involves the factor managing the sales ledger of a company whereas invoice discounting is a narrower service where the discounting firm collects sales receipts but the firm still manages its ledger.

Factors and invoice discounters charge for providing an advance to the company and this is usually around 80 per cent of the total value of the invoices. When the factor/invoice discounter receives the invoice payments they release the 20 per cent residual to the client, less charges. The main charges are: an *administration charge*, sometimes called a service or commission charge; and a *discounting* or *finance charge* (i.e., interest). Factors make administration charges for collecting debt contained in invoices and for credit management/sales ledger on behalf of clients. In the United Kingdom, they typically charge around 1–3 per cent of invoice values. As already mentioned, invoice discounters also advance funds against clients' invoices, but unlike factors, they do not provide administration services. A factor or discounter may have recourse to the client when a customer of that client refuses to pay an invoice that has been factored – this is known as *recourse factoring*. If there is no recourse then the service is known as *non-recourse factoring*. In the latter case, the factor will charge the client for insurance against bad debt.

4.6.1.6 Domestic and international equity

Once they get to a certain size, companies have the choice of diversifying their sources of external finance by accessing the capital market. We have already noted that the largest firms can issue bonds and raise funds in the syndicated loans market, but before they can access these markets it is more than likely that they have become publicly listed on their domestic stock exchanges and raised equity finance through the issue of shares (or stock as it is known in the United States). The next step maybe to consider a listing in a foreign market – known as a **Euroequity** issue. However, most firms are not known well enough overseas to attract foreign investors so they may first try a Eurobond issue where the market is for professional investors and if this is a success they may progress to a cross-listing of their shares on another stock exchange.

There has been a substantial growth in the cross-listing of shares during the 1990s and the US market has been a popular destination for such listings. In particular, European and Asian companies are keen to seek out US investors by listing not only in their home market but also in the United States. The main rationale is that a foreign listing provides the company with access to a more liquid capital market and a cheaper source of funding. There is also substantial prestige associated with obtaining a foreign listing on a major international stock market like the London and New York exchanges. Firms also seek to cross-list to diversify their source of funding and to tap new investor segments – such as various institutional investors that may not be prevalent in home markets. A cross-listing of equity in another market may also establish a secondary market for shares used to acquire other firms in the host market and such shares can also be used to compensate local management and employees in foreign subsidiaries.

4.6.1.7 Securities underwriting, fund management services, risk management and information management services

In addition to the financial services already mentioned, international banks also provide a variety of sophisticated services that complement traditional credit and debt finance facilities. These services are numerous but they can be broadly grouped into three main categories: guarantees; foreign exchange- and interest rate-related transactions; securities underwriting and fund management services (the main features of such services have been illustrated in Section 3.5.2).

4.6.1.8 Foreign exchange transactions and trade finance

Firms involved in international trading activity can rely on the banking system to provide various forms of trade finance that help facilitate the import and export of goods. The three main types of trade finance relate to the provision of **letters of credit, forfaiting** and **countertrade**.

Letters of credit

A letter of credit is a legal banking agreement that allows importers to offer secure terms to exporters (see also Section 9.5.5). Letters of credit have been used for centuries in international trading transactions. The letter of credit from a bank guarantees to the seller that if various documents are presented, the bank will pay the seller the amount due. It is simply an undertaking given by the issuing bank on behalf of the buyer to pay a seller a specific amount of money on presentation of specified documents representing the supply of goods within certain time limits. These documents must conform to terms and conditions set out in the letter of credit and documents must be presented at a specified place.

Such an agreement offers security to the seller as an assurance of payment from an international bank, on the condition that the terms of the letter of credit are complied with. In addition, a seller can also raise extra finance using the letter of credit as collateral if necessary.

The attraction from the buyer's perspective is that they do not have to pay cash up front to a foreign country before receiving the documents of title to the goods purchased. This is obviously helpful when the buyer is unfamiliar with suppliers overseas. In addition, a letter of credit protects the buyer's interests as the bank will only pay the supplier if specific documents are presented. Payment will be given if

Table 4.2 **Letters of credit**

Step 1	Buyer and seller agree terms, including means of transport, period of credit offered, latest date of shipment and other relevant terms to be used.
Step 2	Then the buyer applies to the bank for a letter of credit to be issued.
Step 3	The bank evaluates the buyer's credit rating, and may require a cash cover and/or a reduction of other lending limits.
Step 4	The issuing bank will issue a letter of credit. This will be sent to the advising bank by airmail, telex or SWIFT.
Step 5	The advising bank will establish authenticity of the letter of credit using signature books or test codes, then informs the seller (beneficiary).
Step 6	The advising bank may confirm the letter of credit, i.e., add its own payment undertaking.
Step 7	The seller should check that the letter of credit matches the commercial agreement, and that the terms and conditions can be satisfied in good time.
Step 8	If there is anything that may cause a problem, an amendment should be requested.
Step 9	The seller ships the goods and gathers together all the documents asked for in the letter of credit, such as the invoice and transport document.
Step 10	Before presenting the documents to the bank, the seller should check them for discrepancies against the letter of credit, and correct the documents where necessary.
Step 11	The documents are presented to a bank, often the advising bank.
Step 12	The advising bank checks the documents against the letter of credit. If the documents are compliant, the bank pays the seller and forwards the documents to the issuing bank.
Step 13	The issuing bank will also check the documents. If they are in order the issuing bank will reimburse the seller's bank immediately.
Step 14	The issuing bank debits the buyer and releases the documents (including transport document), so that the buyer can claim the goods from the carrier.

Notes:
[1] The letter of credit refers to documents representing the goods – not the goods themselves.
[2] Banks are not in the business of examining goods on behalf of their customers.
[3] Typically the documents requested will include a commercial invoice, a transport document such as a bill of lading or airway bill, an insurance document and many others.

these documents comply with the terms and conditions set out in the letter of credit. The buyer can also include safeguards into the letter of credit such as inspection of the goods, quality control and set production and delivery times. Table 4.2 sets out the main features of a standard letter of credit agreement.

An *irrevocable letter of credit* provides a guarantee by the issuing bank in the event that all terms and conditions are met by the buyer. A *revocable letter of credit*, in contrast, can be cancelled or altered by the buyer after it has been issued by the buyer's bank.

Forfaiting

In a forfaiting transaction, the exporter agrees to surrender the rights to claim for payment of goods or services delivered to an importer under a contract of sale, in return for a cash payment from a forfaiting bank. The forfaiting bank takes over the exporter's debt and assumes the full risk of payment by the importer. The exporter is thereby freed from any financial risk in the transaction and is liable only for the quality and reliability of the goods and services provided. The buyer's obligation is usually supported by a local bank guarantee and can in certain cases be guaranteed by the government. As in the case of letters of credit, the documentation requirements are relatively straightforward. This requires evidence of the underlying transaction, copies of shipping documents and confirmations from the bank guaranteeing the transaction. Forfaiting transactions can be on a fixed or floating interest rate basis. The exporter will receive the funds upon presentation of all the relevant documents, shortly after shipment of goods, and payment will usually be made in the form of a letter of credit.

Countertrade

Countertrade is a general term used to cover a variety of commercial mechanisms for reciprocal trade. Simple barter is probably the oldest and best-known example, however, other techniques such as switch-trading, buy-back, counter-purchase and offset have developed to meet the requirements of a more integrated global world economy. The main types of countertrade include:

- *simple barter* – direct exchange of physical goods between two parties;
- *switch-trading* – involves transferring use of bilateral balances from one country to another. For instance, an export from the United States to Libya will be paid for with a dollar amount paid into an account at a bank in Libya. This in turn can only be used to buy goods from Libya. The original US exporter may buy unrelated goods from Libya or may sell the dollars at a discount to a 'switch-trader' who buys Libyan goods for sale elsewhere;
- *buy-back* – this is an agreement where the exporter of plant or equipment agrees to take payment in the form of future production from the plant;
- *counter-purchase* – involves an initial export whereby the exporter receives 'payment' in goods unrelated to what the exporter manufactures;
- *offset* – refers to the requirement of importing countries that their purchase price be offset in some way by the seller, this can include requirements to source production locally, to transfer technology or to increase imports from the importing country.

There are a wide range of countertrade mechanisms that aim to facilitate trade in goods. This type of activity is usually more prevalent in countries that limit FDI and are subject to greater political risk.

4.6.2 'New' credit products and securitisation

The growing corporate emphasis on capital market financing is also driving the development of a wider range of **'new' credit products** (see also Section 9.6). For instance, corporate debt is widely traded in the United States, either as bonds, syndicated loans or securitised assets – loans that are bundled together and sold as a security in the market. In the United States a broad array of loans are being securitised, including corporate loans, mortgages, credit card receivables, computer leases, and so on. The growth in credit derivatives business has also helped boost the market for tradable corporate credit products. Credit derivatives are tradable instruments that can be used to manage credit risk – the likelihood of default. The growth of such business means that nowadays around 50 per cent of all credits to US firms are tradable. This contrasts with the situation in Europe, where less than 20 per cent of credits are tradable.

While the European corporate bond market is under-developed compared with that in the United States, analysts predict that it will grow rapidly over the next five years. As companies seek to use a range of debt products it is most likely that many will choose tradable debt financing from the onset with high-yield corporate debt being the fastest growing segment.

As developments in these segments of the credit product market enhance liquidity this should facilitate the **securitisation** trend. While Europe has witnessed some high-profile bank loan securitisations (mainly in the form of Collateralised Debt Obligations, CDOs[3]) it is expected that the restructuring of banks' and large companies' balance sheets will continue at a faster pace, thus boosting the securitisation trend. Traditionally the bulk of loan securitisations in Europe were related to bank mortgage loans or top-end AAA corporate loans (see Table 4.1). Triple AAA loans are those of the highest credit quality assigned by the credit rating agencies; loans rated below BBB are regarded as high-yield or 'junk' issues. The growth of a deeper and more liquid market for corporate credit will therefore help the securitisation of lower-grade credits. Securitisation in Europe has traditionally been limited by the lack of quoted companies, poor disclosure standards and various other factors. Nevertheless, it seems likely that these obstacles will be overcome by the development of viable vehicles for securitising smaller credit issues and the growing investor demand for such products.

The securitisation trend in both the United States and Europe is also likely to be reinforced further by e-issuance and e-trading platforms that will extend beyond the primary equity markets and fixed income trading already undertaken by many global as well as investment banks. At present, a handful of firms are attempting to develop online standards for a wide range of government and corporate bond secondary markets. In the United States firms such as TradeWeb and Deal Composer are developing such services, as are their European counterparts – such as EuroMTS.

In addition to a wider range of tradable credit products, many companies will also seek to use more tax efficient means of asset financing to fund their business including leasing and factoring/forfaiting. Traditionally, this type of business in the United States has been provided by specialist firms – such as GE Capital, whereas in Europe the main asset finance firms are owned by large banks. As more companies aggressively manage their balance sheets and identify the tax and other accounting advantages associated with alternative asset financing structures they are likely to increasingly require specialist services in this area. While businesses such as aircraft and computer leasing have been around for some time it is envisaged that a wider array of super-specialist asset finance firms may emerge, or may be developed by global banks, to deal with the financing needs of specific

---

[3] CDOs are securitisations of packages of corporate bonds, loans and credit default swaps. They typically comprise of between 50 and 150 underlying securities, so the spread of risk or 'granularity' is less than, for example, mortgage securitisations. Balance sheet CDOs are created by banks from assets already on their books, although banks increasingly acquire assets in the market to create a CDO, sometimes to meet the requirements of a particular investor. The risk of default is usually insured with a specialist insurance firm to achieve a higher credit rating for the different tranches (parts) of the CDO. Depending on the underlying assets, CDOs are also known as collateralised bond or loan obligations.

industries or market segments. Various European global banks have suggested that they may re-direct their asset finance business towards the medium-sized corporate sector to complement their traditional lending business.

Overall, global credit markets are expected to witness major changes over the next few years. Following the US model, Europe is likely to experience rapid growth in the corporate bond, syndicated lending, credit derivatives and loan securitisation business. Much more of this activity will relate to non-investment-grade or 'middle-market' company businesses, many of which have modest international activities. In addition, traditional bank credit will also be substituted with asset finance that better matches corporate client needs and risk profiles.

4.7 Increasing role of foreign banks in domestic banking systems

Over recent years there has been a substantial growth of foreign bank activity in many banking markets. The increased presence of foreign banks reflects the global liberalisation of financial systems that has encouraged new entry plus the desire of banks to seek out new sources of profit internationally. The growth of new markets in China, southeast Asia and in the transition economies of eastern Europe has prompted a wave of foreign bank expansion. In addition, as non-financial companies seek to source production and distribution facilities in a global marketplace this has also encouraged banks to follow suit. Banks not only operate in many different countries but they also do locate various parts of their operations in various parts of the world – call and IT centres in India being a noticeable example.

Table 4.3 shows the structural features of banking systems throughout the world and highlights the importance of foreign banks in domestic systems. It can be seen that in various countries such as New Zealand, Luxembourg and Bostwana nearly all the banks are foreign – for example in New Zealand foreign banks (mainly Australian) control over 99 per cent of the domestic banking system. In the United Kingdom foreign banks account for slightly below 53 per cent of total banking sector assets.

Much of the foreign bank activity undertaking in domestic banking systems relates to traditional commercial banking business, namely deposit and loans business. (For instance, in Chapter 14 we note that foreign banks operating in the new EU Member States of central and eastern Europe mainly operate in the domestic retail market and compete head-on with domestic operators.)

Remember that at the start of this chapter we explained that international banking relates to banks doing business across borders and/or with foreign currencies and that this can encompass all types of banking activity – retail banking, corporate banking, investment banking, and so on. The focus of most of this chapter has been on banks providing international banking services to large firms as the products and services on offer tend to be different from those provided to domestic retail and small firm customers. However, one should always be aware that international banking (despite generally being commonly viewed as banking relationships with large multinational companies) also includes retail and other commercial banking business in foreign markets and that these activities barely differ from domestic retail operations.

Table 4.3 **Structure of banking systems around the world**

Country	Bank assets/ GDP	Rank	% of bank assets – government-owned	Rank	% of bank assets – foreign-owned	Rank	% of bank assets in top 3 banks	Rank	Net interest margin as % of total assets	Rank
High-income countries										
Australia	145.27	19	0.00	39	17.10	27	62.95	14	2.41	24
Belgium	315.12	6	0.00	40	24.10	23	57.39	21	1.15	7
Canada	153.84	14	0.00	42	6.10	41	55.32	23	1.76	15
Cyprus	76.27	33	3.30	35	10.90	34	78.00	7	1.60	12
Denmark	121.41	22	0.00	43	3.70	51	73.56	8	1.86	16
Finland	75.25	34	21.90	18	7.80	38	97.17	1	1.56	11
France	146.8	17	8.70	28	11.60	32	42.43	37	1.08	6
Germany	313.29	7	42.00	9	4.20	49	17.66	52	1.19	8
Greece	100.21	25	13.00	24	5.00	44	59.20	16	2.48	27
Israel	146.67	18	45.60	5	10.70	35	72.10	10	2.18	19
Italy	150.46	16	17.00	22	5.00	45	37.10	42	1.93	17
Japan	164.13	12	1.15	38	5.90	42	22.66	49	1.32	10
Korea	97.7	26	29.70	15	0.00	54	39.20	41	2.10	18
Luxembourg	3,423.18	1	5.03	33	94.97	3	17.06	54	0.36	3
Netherlands	357.6	5	5.90	32	3.80	50	79.00	6	1.60	13
New Zealand	153.82	15	0.00	48	99.00	1	58.99	17	2.42	25
Portugal	238.29	9	20.80	19	11.70	31	34.20	45	1.60	14
Singapore	801.86	2	0.00	50	50.00	8	17.20	53		
Slovenia	66.13	37	39.60	10	4.60	48	51.41	27	4.04	40
Spain	155.75	13	0.00	52	11.00	33	43.99	35	2.23	22
Sweden	128.91	20	0.00	53	1.80	52	68.99	12	1.30	9
Switzerland	538.9	3	15.00	23	8.50	36	67.06	13	0.85	5
United Kingdom	311.08	8	0.00	54	52.60	7	16.20	55	2.20	21
United States	65.85	38	0.00	55	4.70	47	21.48	50	3.35	36
Average	343.66		11.20		18.95		49.60		1.85	
Upper-middle income countries										
Argentina	54.24	45	30.00	14	49.00	9	29.80	46	4.90	43
Botswana	28.92	50	2.39	37	97.61	2	91.80	3	5.20	44
Brazil	55.17	43	51.50	4	16.70	28	44.70	33	5.30	45
Chile	96.58	27	11.70	26	32.00	18	41.24	39	3.82	37
Czech Republic	124.9	21	19.00	21	26.00	21	46.26	32	2.65	28
Estonia	59.33	41	0.00	44	85.00	4	92.40	2	3.90	38
Lithuania	26.88	52	44.00	7	48.00	10	72.90	9	0.13	2
Malaysia	166.07	11	0.00	46	18.00	26	41.26	38	2.20	20
Mauritius	96.15	28	0.00	47	25.80	22	80.70	5	3.17	34
Mexico	30.48	49	25.00	16	19.90	24	49.52	28	5.55	46
Panama	385.68	4	11.56	27	38.33	14	28.30	47	2.30	23
Poland	54.45	44	43.70	8	26.40	20	39.70	40	4.04	39
Saudi Arabia	92.81	29	0.00	49	0.00	55	58.00	19	2.90	31
Venezuela	6.03	55	4.87	34	33.72	16	44.27	34	13.20	53
Average	91.26		17.41		36.89		54.35		4.23	
Lower-middle-income countries										
Bolivia	65.61	39	0.00	41	42.30	12	49.00	30	5.60	47
El Salvador	62.39	40	7.00	31	12.50	30	58.20	18	4.89	42
Guatemala	27.65	51	7.61	29	4.93	46	25.67	48	6.12	48
Jamaica	74.34	35	56.00	3	44.00	11	89.90	4	6.90	51
Jordan	213.92	10	0.00	45	68.00	5	52.70	26	2.90	30
Morocco	88.74	32	23.90	17	18.78	25	48.12	31	3.33	35
Peru	36.35	47	2.50	36	40.40	13	59.90	15	4.80	41

Country	Bank assets/ GDP	Rank	% of bank assets – government-owned	Rank	% of bank assets – foreign-owned	Rank	% of bank assets in top 3 banks	Rank	Net interest margin as % of total assets	Rank
Lower-middle-income countries continued										
Philippines	90.78	30	12.12	25	12.79	29	19.36	51	3.08	33
Romania	25.49	53	70.00	2	8.00	37	57.58	20	6.71	50
South Africa	89.78	31	0.00	51	5.20	43	57.34	22	2.93	32
Thailand	116.85	23	30.67	12	7.16	39	53.56	24	0.54	4
Turkey	67.35	36	35.00	11	66.30	6	35.06	43	6.51	49
Average	79.94		20.40		27.53		50.53		4.53	
Lower-income countries										
India	47.55	46	80.00	1	0.00	53	34.60	44	2.78	29
Indonesia	100.79	24	44.00	6	7.00	40	52.80	25	-3.84	1
Kenya	56.06	42	30.60	13	29.40	19	43.40	36	7.50	52
Moldova	25.29	54	7.05	30	33.37	17	49.30	29	17.91	54
Nepal	32.02	48	20.00	20	35.00	15	69.21	11	2.44	26
Average	52.34		36.33		20.95		49.86		5.36	

Note: Income groups are based on the World Bank country classification of economies as of April 2003. The economies are grouped according to 2001 gross national income (GNI) per capita. The groups are defined as: low-income, $745 or less; lower-middle income, $746–$2,975; upper-middle income, $2,976–$9,205; and high-income, $9,206 or more.

Source: Adapted from Barth, J.R., Caprio, G. and Nolle, D.E. (2004), 'Comparative International Characteristics of Banking', Office of the Comptroller of the Currency, *Economic and Policy Analysis Working Paper* 2004–01, (OCC: Washington DC) pp. 60–1.

 ## 4.8 Conclusions

This chapter provides an insight to the reasons for banks undertaking international business, and highlights the evolution of foreign bank activity. It can be seen that a major feature of international banking is to provide commercial and investment banking and other services to global companies as well as to undertake a range of commercial banking and other activities in overseas markets. In terms of the products and services offered to large international companies, banks provide payments and treasury management services and also facilitate access to international financing either in the short term via the Eurocurrency markets or over the longer term via bond, equity and syndicated lending markets. Foreign bank presence can take various forms and the range of services on offer can vary markedly from bank to bank. It is important to remember that international banking activity nowadays spans the full spectrum of the financial services industry and incorporates a wide range of players. Foreign banks are present in nearly every country and their importance is generally increasing, as is the sophistication of their operations and products on offer. The risks associated with international banking are complex and varied. One should always remember that changes in the economic and political stability of a country can have a significant impact on overseas operations. This type of risk is known as **country risk** and is discussed later (in Section 10.7). Banks (as well as other firms that have international operations) need to manage their exposure to country risk effectively in order to achieve the appropriate diversification benefits as well as the required risk-adjusted returns from their overseas activities.

Key terms

Traditional foreign banking	Correspondent banking
Eurocurrency banking	Representative office
Multinational banking	Branches, agencies and subsidiaries
Foreign Direct Investment (FDI)	Cash management and transaction services
Colonial banking	Credit facilities
Modern international banking	Syndicated loan
Vertical FDI	Bonds
Horizontal FDI	Leasing and hire services
Arbitrage	Asset-based finance
Cost of capital	Factoring and invoice discounting services
Ownership advantage	Euroequity
Excess managerial capacity	Letters of credit
Product lifecycle	Forfaiting
Innovative (or new product) stage	Countertrade
Mature product stage	New credit products
Production diffusion	Securitisation
Standardised products	
Firm-specific advantages	
Location advantages	

Key reading

Barth, J.R, Caprio, G. and Nolle, D.E. (2004) 'Comparative International Characteristics of Banking', *Economic and Policy Analysis Working Paper*, 2004–01, Washington DC: Office of the Comptroller of the Currency.

BIS (2004b) *74th Annual Report (1 April 2003–31 March 2004)*, Basle:BIS.

Lewis, M.K. and Davis, K.T. (1997) *Domestic versus International Banking*. London: Philip Allan.

Revision questions and problems

1 In what ways does traditional foreign banking differ from Eurocurrency banking?

2 Why do banks go overseas? What are the main theories on the rationale for international banking?

3 Explain the main strategic reasons why banks may wish to establish foreign operations.

4 What do correspondent banking relationships involve?

5 Explain why banks engage in syndicated loans. Use information from the most recent BIS annual report to illustrate your answer.

6 Outline the main type of bonds that an international banking institution can issue.

7 What is a Euroequity issue?

8 In what way(s) can the banking sector provide trade finance that helps facilitate the import and export of goods for firms involved in international trading?

Part 2

CENTRAL BANKING AND BANK REGULATION

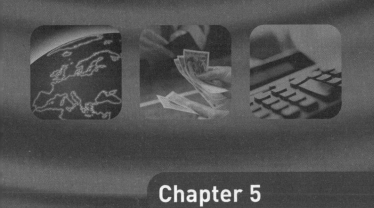

Chapter 5

Theory of central banking

Learning objectives

- To understand the crucial role of central banks in the financial sector
- To describe the main functions of the central bank
- To understand the monetary policy functions of central banks
- To understand the arguments put forward by the free banking theorists
- To discuss the arguments for and against an independent central bank

5.1 Introduction

The core functions of central banks in any countries are: to manage **monetary policy** with the aim of achieving **price stability**; to prevent liquidity crises, situations of money market disorders and financial crises; and to ensure the smooth functioning of the payments system. This chapter explores these issues and focuses in particular on the conduct of monetary policy, distinguishing between instruments, targets and goals. Furthermore, it examines some basic concepts as they relate to central banking theory. Specifically, the chapter investigates the following fundamental areas:

● What are the monetary policy functions of a central bank?
● Why do banks need a central bank? and
● Should central banks be independent from government?

The chapter presents an introduction to these topics. The specific functions, organisation and roles of the Bank of England, the European Central Bank and the US Federal Reserve System are described in Chapter 6.

5.2 What are the main functions of a central bank?

A central bank can generally be defined as a financial institution responsible for overseeing the monetary system for a nation, or a group of nations, with the goal of fostering economic growth without inflation.

The main functions of a central bank can be listed as follows:

1) The central bank controls the issue of notes and coins (legal tender). Usually, the central bank will have a monopoly of the issue, although this is not essential as long as the central bank has power to restrict the amount of private issues of notes and coins.
2) It has the power to control the amount of credit-money created by banks. In other words, it has the power to control, by either direct or indirect means, the money supply.
3) A central bank should also have some control over non-bank financial intermediaries that provide credit.
4) Encompassing both parts 2 and 3, the central bank should effectively use the relevant tools and instruments of monetary policy in order to control:
   a) credit expansion;
   b) liquidity; and
   c) the money supply of an economy.
5) The central bank should oversee the financial sector in order to prevent crises and act as a **lender-of-last-resort** in order to protect depositors, prevent widespread panic withdrawal, and otherwise prevent the damage to the economy caused by the collapse of financial institutions.
6) A central bank acts as the government's banker. It holds the government's bank account and performs certain traditional banking operations for the government, such as deposits and lending. In its capacity as banker to the government it can manage and administer the country's national debt.

7) The central bank also acts as the official agent to the government in dealing with all its gold and foreign exchange matters. The government's reserves of gold and foreign exchange are held at the central bank. A central bank, at times, intervenes in the foreign exchange markets at the behest of the government in order to influence the exchange value of the domestic currency.

Table 5.1 presents a comparison between the main tasks performed by the US central bank, known as the Federal Reserve System (FRS) and the Euroarea European System of Central Banks (ESCB) headed by the European Central Bank based in Frankfurt (more details will be given in Chapter 6).

Table 5.1 Tasks of the Federal Reserve System and the European System of Central Banks

	FRS	ESCB
Define and implement monetary policy	Yes	Yes
Issue banknotes	Yes	Yes
Conduct foreign exchange operations	Yes	Yes
Hold and manage official reserves	Yes	Yes
Act as the fiscal agent for the government	Yes	NCBs*
Promote stability of financial system	Yes	Yes
Supervise and regulate banks	Yes	Some NCBs*
Implement consumer protection laws	Yes	Some NCBs*
Promote the smooth operation of the payments system	Yes	Yes
Collect statistical information	Yes	Yes
Participate in international monetary institutions	Yes	Yes

* NCBs refers to national central banks of the Eurosystem.

Source: Pollard (2003), p. 18.

It is possible to note that there are no marked differences between the two systems: for example both the FRS and the ESCB are the sole issuers of banknotes for their respective economies; and they are responsible for maintaining the stability of the banking system. However, the ESCB has no direct role in banking supervision as responsibility for supervision in the Euroarea is determined by the national central banks or other government agencies.

5.3 **How does monetary policy work?**

There are five major forms of economic policy (or, more strictly macroeconomic policy) conducted by governments that are of relevance. These are: monetary policy; **fiscal policy; exchange rate policy; prices and incomes policy;** and **national debt management policy.**

● **Monetary policy** is concerned with the actions taken by central banks to influence the availability and cost of money and credit by controlling some measure (or measures) of the money supply and/or the level and structure of interest rates.[1]

---

[1] See also Appendix A1.

- **Fiscal policy** relates to changes in the level and structure of government spending and taxation designed to influence the economy. As all government expenditure must be financed, these decisions also, by definition, determine the extent of public sector borrowing or debt repayment. An expansionary fiscal policy means higher government spending relative to taxation. The effect of these policies would be to encourage more spending and boost the economy. Conversely, a contractionary fiscal policy means raising taxes and cutting spending.
- **Exchange rate policy** involves the targeting of a particular value of a country's currency exchange rate thereby influencing the flows within the balance of payments. In some countries it may be used in conjunction with other measures such as exchange controls, import tariffs and quotas.[2]
- A **prices and incomes policy** is intended to influence the inflation rate by means of either statutory or voluntary restrictions upon increases in wages, dividends and/or prices.
- **National debt management policy** is concerned with the manipulation of the outstanding stock of government debt instruments held by the domestic private sector with the objective of influencing the level and structure of interest rates and/or the availability of reserve assets to the banking system.

In this section we focus on what monetary policy involves. However, it must be remembered that any one policy mentioned above will normally form part of a policy package, and that the way in which that policy is employed will be dependent upon the other components of that package. Box 5.1 provides essential background reading for this section on the concept and functions of **money**.

---

[2] Note that exchange controls, tariffs and quotas are restricted or forbidden under a number of trade agreements (such as those implemented by the EU and the World Trade Organisation).

| Box 5.1 | **The concept and functions of money and monetary aggregates** |

In general money is represented by the coins and notes that we use in our daily lives; it is the commodity readily acceptable by all people wishing to undertake transactions. It is also a mean of expressing a value for any kind of goods or service. For economists, money is referred to as 'money supply' and includes anything that is accepted in payment for goods and services or in the repayment of debts. In an economic system money serves four main functions: 1) medium of exchange; 2) unit of account; 3) store of value; and 4) standard of deferred payment.

1) **Medium of exchange** is probably the main function of money. If barter were the only type of trade possible, there would be many situations in which people would not be able to obtain the goods and services that they wanted most. The advantage of the use of money is that it provides the owner with generalised purchasing power. The use of money gives the owner flexibility over the type and quantities of goods they buy, the time and place of their purchases, and the parties with whom they choose to deal. A critical characteristic of a medium of exchange is that it be acceptable as such. It must be readily exchangeable for other things. It is usual for the government to designate certain coins or paper currency as the medium of exchange.

2) If money is acceptable as a medium of exchange it almost certainly comes to act as a **unit of account** by which the prices of all commodities can be defined and then compared. This, of course, simplifies the task of deciding how we wish to divide our income between widely disparate items. For this reason it is sometimes said that money acts as a measure of value, and this is true if value is taken to mean both price and worth, the latter being a much more subjective concept.

3) Money is also a liquid **store of value** in that it provides individuals with a means of holding and accumulating their wealth in a form which can, at any time, be converted immediately into goods and

services. When a person holds money as a store of value they are effectively treating it as a substitute to holding alternative forms of financial assets such as bonds or deposit accounts. The holder of money therefore foregoes the payment of an explicit yield in return for the acceptance of an implicit yield in the form of convenience and certainty.

4) Money can also act as a **standard of deferred payment**. Due to this function it is possible to undertake a number of transactions in the present and actually settle the account (or bill) at some time in the future, e.g., buy now and pay later. The sale and production of goods is made easier by money performing this function since goods and services can be acquired prior to payment being made. Because money acts as a standard of deferred payment the acquisition of labour, raw materials and other goods and services can be acquired and the various parties involved will know the sums involved and payments to be made at a future date. Although this particular function of money is not essential for lending, borrowing and production to take place, it certainly makes such activities easier. Money's function as a standard for deferred payment may be questioned in times of high inflation where the real value of money declines rapidly. In such situations the debtor would benefit from a deferred payment. However, the meaning of the function of money as a standard for deferred payment is that it permits commercial lending to take place. A borrower can agree that if a lender supplies him with ten units of money today, he will pay back eleven units in (say) three months' time. The charging of interest has become possible.

The formal definition of what constitutes money is summarised by central banks definitions of what they call **monetary aggregates**. In the UK for example, official estimates of the money supply have been published since 1966. The earliest definition of the money supply was a broad one covering notes and coin held by UK non-banks and deposits (in both sterling and foreign currency) held by UK residents with banks in the United Kingdom. From 1970 onwards, this definition has been amended and supplemented on a number of occasions, reflecting developments in the financial system and policy. Common practice amongst central banks is to construct monetary aggregates from a list of monetary assets by adding together those that are considered to be likely sources of monetary services. The monetary aggregates play a role in the formulation of the monetary policy. In the UK, **M0** is the narrowest measure of money stock and **M4** the broadest.

M0	=	Sterling notes and coin in circulation
	+	banks' operational deposits with the Bank of England
M4	=	Notes and coin held by the private sector in sterling
	+	Private sector £ non-interest bearing sight bank deposits
	+	Private sector £ interest-bearing sight and time bank deposits
	+	Private sector holdings of £ certificates of deposit
	+	Private sector holdings of building society shares and deposits and £ certificates of deposit
	+	Building society holdings of bank deposits and bank certificates of deposit and notes and coin.

Note that sight deposits include funds that can be converted immediately and without restrictions into cash (see also Chapter 2); time deposits are funds that are invested at a bank for a fixed period of time and that the investor cannot access until the end of an agreed period (e.g., 30- and 60-day savings accounts). Certificates of deposit (CD) are negotiable certificates confirming that a (usually large) deposit has been made for a specified period of time with a bank.

M4 can be analysed either in terms of its components – cash and deposits – or of its asset counterparts, which represent the other side of the banks' and building societies' balance sheets (and must, as an accounting identity, sum to the same). These counterparts include banks' and building societies' lending to the private sector and their transactions with the public sector and with overseas residents.

The European Central Bank's definition of monetary aggregates is slightly different from the Bank of England's detailed above. In line with international practice, the Eurosystem has defined a narrow aggregate (M1), an 'intermediate' aggregate (M2) and a broad aggregate (M3). These aggregates differ with regard to the degree of 'moneyness' of the assets included. These are defined as:

● **Narrow money (M1)** includes currency (i.e., bank notes and coins), as well as balances which can immediately be converted into currency or used for cashless payments (i.e., overnight deposits).
● **Intermediate money (M2)** comprises narrow money (M1) and deposits with a maturity of up to two years and deposits redeemable at a period of notice of up to three months. The definition of M2

▶

reflects the particular interest in analysing and monitoring a monetary aggregate that, in addition to currency, consists of deposits which are liquid.

- **Broad money (M3)** comprises M2 and marketable instruments issued by the MFI sector. Certain money market instruments, in particular money market fund (MMF) shares/units and repurchase agreements are included in this aggregate. A high degree of liquidity and price certainty make these

instruments close substitutes for deposits. As a result of their inclusion, M3 is less affected by substitution between various liquid asset categories than narrower definitions of money, and is therefore more stable.

Sources: Adapted from Bank of England (1999); and from 'The ECB's definition of Euroarea monetary aggregates' http://www.ecb.int/stats/money/aggregates/aggr/html/hist.en.html.

Monetary policy relates to the control of some measure (or measures) of the money supply and/or the level and structure of interest rates. In recent years, much greater emphasis has been placed on monetary policy within a government's policy package. This is because a broad consensus has emerged that suggests that price stability is an essential pre-condition for achieving the central economic objective of high and stable levels of growth and employment. Monetary policy is viewed as the preferred policy choice for influencing prices.

Although traditionally the choice of monetary policy over fiscal policy as the main policy tool was viewed as a matter of ideological choice, nowadays it is seen more as a pragmatic solution. As it is widely recognised that high and variable inflation harms long-term growth and employment, policymakers have tended to focus on those policies that appear to be most successful in dampening inflationary pressures. Price stability, therefore, has become a key element of economic strategy, and monetary policy is widely accepted as the most appropriate type of policy to influence prices and price expectations.

The preference for using monetary policy over other types of policy relates to two main factors – the role of the monetary authorities (central banks) as sole issuers of banknotes and bank reserves (known as the monetary base) and the long-run neutrality of money (see below).

The central bank is the monopoly supplier of the monetary base and as a consequence can determine the conditions at which banks borrow from the central bank. The central bank can influence liquidity in the short-term money markets and so can determine the conditions at which banks buy and sell short-term wholesale funds. By influencing short-term money market rates, the central bank influences the price of liquidity in the financial system and this ultimately can impact on various economic variables such as output or prices.

In the long run a change in the quantity of money in the economy will be reflected in a change in the general level of prices but it will have no permanent influence on real variables such as the level of (real) output or unemployment. This is known as the *long-run neutrality of money*. The argument goes that real income or the level of employment are, in the long term, determined solely by real factors, such as technology, population growth or the preferences of economic agents. Inflation is therefore solely a monetary phenomenon.

As a consequence in the long run:

- A central bank can only contribute to raising the growth potential of the economy by maintaining an environment of stable prices.
- Economic growth cannot be increased through monetary expansion (increased money supply) or by keeping short-term interest rates at levels inconsistent with price stability.

In the past it has been noted that long periods of high inflation are usually related to high monetary growth. While various other factors (such as variations in aggregate demand, technological changes or commodity price shocks) can influence price developments over the short period, over time these influences can be offset by a change in monetary policy.

5.4 Monetary policy functions of a central bank

The most important function of any central bank is to undertake monetary control operations. Typically, these operations aim to administer the amount of money (money supply) in the economy and differ according to the monetary policy objectives they intend to achieve. These latter are determined by the government's overall macroeconomic policies (see Box 5.2).

Box 5.2 Monetary policy objectives

Monetary policy is one of the main policy tools used to influence interest rates, inflation and credit availability through changes in the supply of money (or liquidity) available in the economy. It is important to recognise that monetary policy constitutes only one element of an economic policy package and can be combined with a variety of other types of policy (e.g., fiscal policy) to achieve stated economic objectives. Historically, monetary policy has, to a certain extent, been subservient to fiscal and other policies involved in managing the macroeconomy, but nowadays it can be regarded as the main policy tool used to achieve various stated economic policy objectives (or goals).

The main objectives of economic (and monetary) policy include:

- **High employment** – often cited as a major goal of economic policy. Having a high level of unemployment results in the economy having idle resources that result in lower levels of production and income, lower growth and possible social unrest. However, this does not necessarily mean that zero unemployment is a preferred policy goal. A certain level of unemployment is often felt to be necessary for the efficient operation of a dynamic economy. It will take people a period of time to switch between jobs, or to retrain for new jobs, and so on – so even near full employment there maybe people switching jobs who are temporarily out of work. This is known as *frictional unemployment*. In addition, unemployment may be a consequence of mismatch in skills between workers and what employers want – known as *structural unemployment*. (Typically, although structural unemployment is undesirable monetary policy cannot alleviate this type of unemployment). The goal of high employment, therefore, does not aim to achieve zero unemployment but seeks to obtain a level above zero that is consistent with matching the demand and supply of labour. This level is known as the *natural rate of unemployment*. (Note, however, that there is much debate as to what is the appropriate natural level of unemployment – usually a figure of around 4 per cent is cited as the appropriate level.)

- **Price stability** – considered an essential objective of economic policy, given the general wish to avoid the costs associated with inflation. Price stability is viewed as desirable because a rising price level creates uncertainty in the economy and this can adversely affect economic growth. Many economists (but by no means all) argue that low inflation is a necessary prerequisite for achieving sustainable economic growth.

- **Stable economic growth** – provides for the increases over time in the living standards of the population. The goal of steady economic growth is closely related to that of high employment because firms are more likely to invest when unemployment is low – when unemployment is high and firms have idle production they are unlikely to want to invest in building more plants and factories. The rate of economic growth should be at least comparable to the rates experienced by similar nations.

▶

- **Interest rate stability** – a desirable economic objective because volatility in interest rates creates uncertainty about the future and this can adversely impact on business and consumer investment decisions (such as the purchase of a house). Expected higher interest rate levels deter investment because they reduce the present value of future cash flows to investors and increase the cost of finance for borrowers.
- **Financial market stability** – also an important objective of the monetary authorities. A collapse of financial markets can have major adverse effects on an economy. The US Wall Street Crash in 1929 resulted in a fall of manufacturing output by 50 per cent and an increase in unemployment to 25 to 30 per cent of the US work force by 1932. (Over 11,000 banks closed over this period.) Such major crises may be rare, but they do highlight the serious consequences of financial crises. A less dramatic but more recent example of how policymakers view the adverse effects of a crisis in financial markets relates to the case of the US-based hedge fund Long-Term Capital Management. In September 1998 the US Federal Reserve organised a rescue of Long-Term Capital Management, a very large and prominent hedge fund on the brink of failure. The monetary authorities intervened because they were concerned about the serious consequences for world financial markets if they allowed the hedge fund to fail. Note that financial market stability is influenced by stability of interest rates because increases in interest rates can lead to a decrease in the value of bonds and other investments resulting in losses in the holders of such securities.

- **Stability in foreign exchange markets** – has become a policy goal of increasing importance especially in the light of greater international trade in goods, services and capital. A rise in the value of a currency makes exports more expensive (an increase in the value of sterling relative to the dollar means that consumers in the United States have to pay more for UK goods), whereas a decline in the value of a currency leads to domestic inflation (if sterling declines relative to the dollar, US goods sold in the United Kingdom become more expensive). Extreme adverse movements in a currency can therefore have a severe impact on exporting industries and can also have serious inflationary consequences if the economy is open and relatively dependent on imported goods. Ensuring the stability of foreign exchange markets is therefore seen as an appropriate goal of economic policy.

At first glance it may appear that all these policy objectives are consistent with one another, however conflicts do arise. The objective of price stability can conflict with the objectives of interest rate stability and full employment (at least in the short-run) because as an economy grows and unemployment declines, this may result in inflationary pressures forcing up interest rates. If the monetary authorities do not let interest rates increase this could fuel inflationary pressures, yet if they do increase rates then unemployment may occur. These sorts of conflicts create difficulties for the authorities in conducting monetary and other macroeconomic policy.

Typically, the most important long-term monetary target of a central bank is price stability that implies low and stable inflation levels. As shown in Figure 5.1 such a long-term goal can only be attained by setting short-term *operational targets*. Operational targets are usually necessary to achieve a particular level of interest rates, commercial banks' reserves or exchange rates. Often they are complemented by *intermediate targets* such as a certain level of long-term interest rates or broad money growth (monetary aggregates). In choosing the intermediate targets, policymakers should take into account the stability of money demand and the controllability of the monetary aggregate. The chosen target should also be a good indicator of the effect of the monetary policy decision on the price stability target. Broad aggregates normally show higher stability and display better indicator properties than narrow aggregates. In contrast, in the short term narrow aggregates are easier to control via official interest rates than broad aggregates. Although central banks cannot use monetary policy instruments directly to affect intermediate targets, they can use them to affect operating targets, such as reserve money and short-term interest rates, which influence movements in intermediate variables.

Figure 5.1 Monetary policy instruments, targets and goals

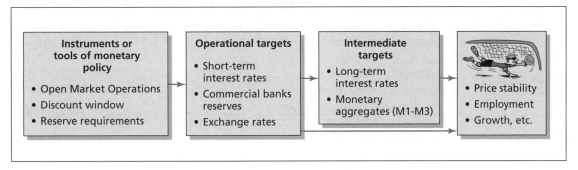

Let us now focus on the tools or instruments of monetary policy. In the past, it was common for central banks to exercise direct controls on bank operations by setting limits either to the quantity of deposits and credits (e.g., ceilings on the growth of bank deposits and loans), or to their prices (by setting maximum bank lending or deposit rates). More recently, as a result of the significant financial liberalisation process aimed at achieving an efficient allocation of financial resources in the economy, there has been a movement away from direct monetary controls towards indirect ones (Gray *et al.*, 2002).

Indirect instruments influence the behaviour of financial institutions by affecting initially the central banks' own balance sheet. In particular the central bank will control the price or volume of the supply of its own liabilities (reserve money) that in turn may affect interest rates more widely and the quantity of money and credit in the whole banking system.

To understand how a central bank can direct and control the money supply through indirect instruments it is essential to first evaluate the role and importance that the different classes of assets and liabilities detailed in its balance sheet have for monetary policy.

As any other bank, the central bank has to produce a financial statement each year (for more details on banks' accounts see Chapter 8) and the items contained in its balance sheet do not differ substantially from those of commercial banks.

As an example, Box 5.3 reports selected balance sheet data for the Bank of England as published on February 2004.

If we focus on the asset side, it is possible to see that the two most significant assets of the Bank of England are debt securities (approximately 54 per cent of total assets) and loans and advances (38 per cent). On the liability side, debt securities are again the largest proportion (41 per cent), followed by deposits by central banks (34 per cent) and deposits by banks and building societies (15 per cent).

As shown in Figure 5.2, the indirect instruments used by central banks in monetary operations are generally classified into the following:

● **Open market operations** (OMOs);
● **discount windows** (also known as 'standing facilities'); and
● **reserve requirements**.

Box 5.3	Balance sheet, Bank of England as at 29 February 2004

	(£m)
Assets	
Cash	5
Items in course of collection	305
Balance with the European Central Bank	86
Loans and advances to banks, the money market and customers (38%)	**5,891**
Debt securities (54%)	**8,343**
Equity shares and participating interest	29
Shares in group undertakings	18
Tangible fixed assets	208
Prepayments, accrued income and other assets	628
Total assets (100%)	**15,513**
Liabilities	
Deposits by central banks (34%)	**4,684**
Deposits by banks and building societies (15%)	**2,059**
Customer accounts	1,027
Debt securities in issue (41%)	**5,739**
Other liabilities	444
Total liabilities (100%)	**13,953**
Capital	15
Revaluation reserves	158
Profit and loss account	1,387
Shareholder's funds	*1,560*
Total liabilities and capital	**15,513**

Note: Figures may not add due to rounding.
Source: Adapted from Bank of England (2004) Annual Report. http://www.bankofengland.co.uk/annualreport/2004accounts.pdf.

5.4.1 Debt securities and open market operations

Debt securities are mainly represented by Treasury securities (i.e., government debt) that central banks use in open market operations. These operations are the most important tools by which central banks can influence the amount of money in the economy.

Although the practical features of open market operations may vary from country to country, the principles are the same: the central bank operates in the market and purchases or sells government debt to the non-bank private sector. In general, if the central bank sells government debt the money supply falls (all other things being equal) because money is taken out of bank accounts and other sources to purchase government securities. This leads to an increase in short-term interest rates. If the government purchases (buys-back) government debt this results in an injection of money into the system and short-term interest rates fall. As a result, the central bank can influence the portfolio of assets held by the private sector.

This will influence the level of liquidity within the financial system and will also affect the level and structure of interest rates.

The main attractions of using open market operations to influence short-term interest rates are as follows:

- they are initiated by the monetary authorities who have complete control over the volume of transactions;
- open market operations are flexible and precise – they can be used for major or minor changes to the amount of liquidity in the system;
- they can easily be reversed;
- open market operations can be undertaken quickly.

Figure 5.2　Open market operations

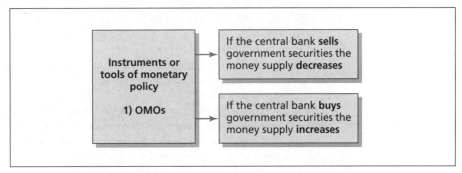

Open market operations are the most commonly used indirect instruments of monetary policy in developed economies. One of the main reasons for the widespread use of open market operations relates to their flexibility in terms of both the frequency of use and scale (i.e., quantity) of activity. These factors are viewed as essential if the central bank wishes to fine-tune its monetary policy. In addition, OMOs have the advantage of not imposing a tax on the banking system.

In the United Kingdom, the Bank of England's open-market operations involve buying and selling of securities and the use of 'repo' agreements. Box 5.4 illustrates this process (and for more details, see http://www.bankofengland.co.uk).

5.4.2 Loans to banks and the discount window

The second most important monetary policy tool of a central bank is the so-called 'discount window' (in the United Kingdom this tool is often referred to as 'standing facilities'). It is an instrument that allows eligible banking institutions to borrow money from the central bank, usually to meet short-term liquidity needs. As shown in Box 5.3, discount loans to banks account for a relatively large proportion of a central bank's total assets (about 40 per cent).[3]

By changing the discount rate, that is, the interest rate that monetary authorities are prepared to lend to the banking system, the central bank can control the supply of money in the system. If, for example the central bank is increasing the discount rate, it will be more expensive for banks to borrow from the central bank so they will borrow less thereby causing the money supply to decline. Vice versa,

---

[3] Note that lending by the central bank is usually collateralised.

Box 5.4 **Bank of England and the official repo rate**

The Bank of England's Monetary Policy Committee reviews the interest rate decision the first Thursday of every month, reviewing the so-called *repo rate*. In the United Kingdom, the official repo rate determines the price at which the Bank of England is prepared to engage in repo transactions with the private sector. Repo transactions are effectively sale and repurchase agreements relating to financial assets. For example, the Bank of England may engage in gilt repo transactions, whereby the Bank purchases gilt-edged securities from private sector counterparties with a legally binding commitment that the securities will be repurchased by the counterparties at a pre-determined price and date. Gilt repos are, in effect, cash loans with the gilt-edged securities used as collateral. Alternatively, the Bank may make outright purchases of bills in cases where there is a shortage of liquidity within the financial system. Bill purchases will take place at a discount rate equal to the ruling repo rate. The Bank is able to engineer a shortage of liquidity in order to force the market to raise funds from it at its repo rate. This action then has a knock-on effect throughout the whole structure of interest rates within the economy since the repo rate is representative of the marginal cost of funds to the banking system as a whole.

Bank of England open-market operations involve the buying and selling of securities and the use of repo agreements. The aim is to influence interest rates on instruments with up to 14 days to maturity, and hence, through the money market structure, short-term rates of interest in general. The level of short-term interest rates is felt to have an important influence on the demand for loans, and hence on the growth of credit creation within the economy. Open-market operations may also affect the reserve bases of banks and building societies, and hence the ability of those institutions to lend. Subject to meeting the overriding monetary policy requirements, the Bank's operations are intended to help the banking system manage its liquidity effectively. One of the advantages of changes in the repo rate and the use of open-market operations over other methods of monetary control is that they impinge upon financial institutions in general rather than on banking institutions in particular. While the initial impact is centred upon the Bank of England's counterparties in the repo and discount markets, the effects will quickly filter through to affect all institutions as the interest rates prevailing in the markets change.

Figure 5.3 **Discount window**

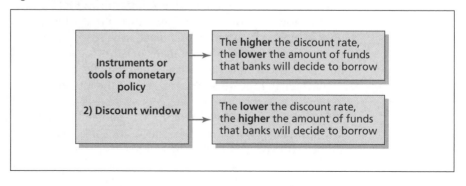

if the central bank is decreasing the discount rate, it will be cheaper for banks to borrow from it so they will borrow more money (see Figure 5.3).

Manipulation of the discount rate can therefore influence short-term rates in the market. For instance, the Eurozone's discount rate is known as a 'marginal lending facility', which offers overnight credit to banks from the Eurosystem.

In the United States, when the Federal Reserve System was established (see Chapter 6), lending reserve funds through the discount window was intended to be the most important instrument of central banking operations but it was soon replaced by open market operations. Indeed, today banks are discouraged from using this type of borrowing. For more details on this particular issue, see http://www.frbdiscountwindow.org/

Direct lending to banks can also occur through the central bank's lender-of-last-resort (LOLR) function. By acting as a lender-of-last-resort the central bank provides liquidity support directly to individual financial institutions if they cannot obtain finance from other sources. Therefore it can help to prevent financial panics. Some drawbacks of this function are discussed in Section 5.5.

5.4.3   Reserve requirements

Banks need to hold a quantity of reserve assets for prudential purposes. If a bank falls to its minimum desired level of reserve assets it will have to turn away requests for loans or else seek to acquire additional reserve assets from which to expand its lending. The result in either case will generally be a rise in interest rates that will serve to reduce the demand for loans.

The purpose of any officially imposed reserve requirements is effectively to duplicate this process. If the authorities impose a reserve requirement in excess of the institutions' own desired level of reserves (or else reduce the availability of reserve assets) the consequence will be that the institutions involved will have to curtail their lending and/or acquire additional reserve assets. This will result in higher interest rates and a reduced demand for loans that, in turn, will curb the rate of growth of the money supply.

By changing the fraction of deposits that banks are obliged to keep as reserves, the central bank can control the money supply. This fraction is generally expressed in percentage terms and thus is called the *required reserve ratio*: the higher the required reserve ratio, the lower the amount of funds available to the banks. Vice versa, the lower the reserve ratio required by the monetary authorities, the higher the amount of funds available to the banks for alternative investments (Figure 5.4).

Figure 5.4 **Reserve requirements**

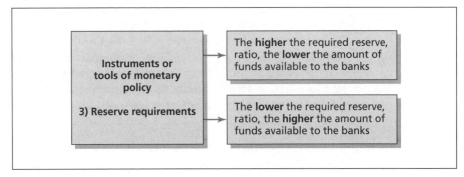

The advantage of reserve requirements as a monetary policy tool is that they affect all banks equally and can have a strong influence on the money supply. However, the latter can also be a disadvantage, as it is difficult for the authorities to make small changes in money supply using this tool. Another drawback is that a call for greater reserves can cause liquidity problems for banks that do not have excess reserves.[4] If the authorities regularly make decisions about changing reserve requirements it can cause problems for the liquidity management of banks. In general, an increase in reserve requirements affects banks' ability to make loans and reduces potential bank profits because the central bank pays no interest on reserves.

In some countries, such as in the United States, Japan and Eurozone, central banks use reserve requirements now and again as a monetary policy tool. However, in reality they are rarely used compared with OMOs and the discount window. In fact, various central banks (such as those in Switzerland, New Zealand and Australia) have eliminated them entirely. The main reason for this is that the application of reserve ratios discriminates against banks (as other financial firms do not have to hold reserves at the central bank). Also many banks nowadays have internal resources well in excess of minimum reserve requirements and so any call to increase reserves from the authorities can easily be achieved without affecting bank behaviour in a significant fashion.

In the United Kingdom, compulsory reserve requirements were used during most of the post-war period but were abandoned as a monetary policy tool in the late 1970s especially as a result of the processes of deregulation and innovation. There is, however, a compulsory *cash ratio deposit* (not used for monetary policy purposes) determined by the Bank of England that amounts to 0.15 per cent of all UK-based banks' and building societies' eligible liabilities. Note in Box 5.3 that the central bank's accounts reveal a relatively large percentage of liabilities consisting of banks' deposits (15 per cent). These are actually assets of the banks that hold them and represent the reserves that banks can demand from the central bank at any time.

Reserve requirements are often referred to as **instruments of portfolio constraint**. It means that they may be imposed by the authorities on the portfolio structure of financial institutions, with the purpose of influencing credit creation and, possibly, the type of lending taking place. Other instruments of portfolio constraint that are potentially available for use include: special deposits, moral suasion and direct controls.

5.4.4 Other instruments of portfolio constraint

5.4.4.1 Special deposits

In the United Kingdom, special deposits are deposits that the Bank of England may require from certain banking institutions. These deposits, equal to a specified proportion of certain elements of bank's deposit liabilities, are then 'frozen' at the Bank of England and may not be used as part of the reserve asset base for lending purposes. While they are particularly discriminatory as regards the institutions to which they apply, they do have a very rapid impact upon the ability of these institutions to create credit and are useful for drawing off any excess reserve assets within the system. At present, they are not used for monetary policy purposes.

---

[4] 'Excess reserves' can be defined as additional reserves that banks decide to hold over the present mandatory requirements.

During the 1970s the Bank of England used a scheme known as 'supplementary special deposits'. These were deposits that banking institutions had to make at the Bank of England if the growth rate of some interest-bearing deposit liabilities exceeded an upper limit set by the Bank. The Bank of England operated this mechanism, referred to as the 'corset', on a periodic basis between 1973 and 1980. Institutions exceeding the specified growth rate for liabilities were required to make supplementary special deposits with the Bank on a scale dependent upon the extent of the overshoot. Supplementary special deposits could not be used as part of the reserve asset base by banks, and they attracted no interest payment. The main objective of special deposits is to remove excess liquidity from the system if bank deposit growth (and therefore loan growth) is increasing too rapidly.

5.4.4.2 Moral suasion

Moral suasion refers to the range of informal requests and pressure that the authorities may exert over banking institutions. The extent to which this is a real power of the authorities relative to direct controls is open to question, since much of the pressure that the authorities would exert involves the institutions having to take actions that might not be in the bank's commercial interests. However, the position and potential power of the authorities probably provides them with some scope to use moral suasion, which may perhaps be utilised most effectively in the context of establishing lending priorities rather than absolute limits to credit creation.

5.4.4.3 Direct controls

Direct controls involve the authorities issuing directives in order to attain particular intermediate targets. For example, the monetary authorities might impose controls on interest rates payable on deposits, may limit the volume of credit creation or direct banks to prioritise lending according to various types of customer. Although these direct controls have the benefits of speed of implementation and precision, they are discriminating towards the institutions involved and are likely to lead to disintermediation as both potential borrowers and potential lenders seek to pursue their own commercial interests. Their use, therefore, is perhaps best reserved for short-term requirements not least since their effectiveness will tend to decline the longer they are applied. Such controls, however, are widely used in many developing countries where the authorities may force banks to (say) lend a certain percentage of loan-book to 'priority sectors'.

5.4.4.4 The decline in use of portfolio constraints

In contrast to market intervention instruments (OMOs and the discount window), instruments of portfolio constraint tend to have a narrow and therefore distorting impact. Although in principle they could be applied to a wide range of financial institutions, in the past in Britain and the United States they have been applied only to banking institutions. The result of this is that banks have, in effect, been discriminated against. It should also be noted that disintermediation has often occurred as potential borrowers have sought alternative sources of funds, from outside of the monetary control regime.

As we noted in the case of reserve requirements, there has generally been a decline in the use of portfolio constraints as a tool of monetary policy in the world's largest economies (although they are prevalent in many developing countries).

Portfolio constraints are less widely used in the developed world for the following reasons:

- Deregulation and increasing competition in the provision of financial services and products traditionally offered by banks have broadened considerably the number and type of institutions that would need to be brought within the control regime. Defining and implementing effective portfolio constraints would be difficult and open to controversy.
- Disintermediation, primarily involving large companies, has undermined portfolio constraints. By contrast, the use of market intervention (interest rates) allows the authorities to influence all relevant parts of the financial system, with monetary control coming via the price of credit.
- Throughout the 1950s, 1960s and 1970s, when portfolio constraints were used extensively, most countries maintained a system of foreign currency exchange control. This restriction on the movement of funds to and from abroad prevented borrowers from seeking finance from overseas when domestic monetary policy was restrictive. These exchange controls had the effect of supporting the portfolio constraints but (for many countries) they now no longer exist, with the result that domestic borrowers have much greater scope to seek funds from overseas.
- Portfolio constraints are regarded as inimical to competition because they place restrictions, of one kind or another, on the business freedom and growth of banks and other intermediaries falling within the constraints. Also, markets are distorted and economic efficiency tends to be undermined.

5.5 Why do banks need a central bank?

The banking sectors of most countries have a pyramid structure where a central bank is at the apex and the ordinary banking institutions are at the base of the pyramid. Central banks can also be thought of as 'super-banks', at the centre of the financial system, responsible for both 'macro' functions, such as monetary policy decisions; and 'micro' functions, including the lender-of-last resort (LOLR) assistance of the banking sector. Over time the role and functions of central banks have developed and evolved, as has the environment in which banks operate.

Liberalisation, financial innovation and technology have contributed to major changes in the operating environment (see Chapter 2, Section 2.5). Many banks have converted their status to private institutions – that by definition are demand or customer-driven – while the global riskiness and uncertainty of the sector has significantly increased. The next section focuses on the LOLR function of central banks and is followed by an introduction to the free-banking theories.

5.5.1 The lender-of-last-resort (LOLR) function of the central bank

In this section we focus on the LOLR function of a central bank that is often subject to controversial debates and criticisms because it implies direct intervention of the monetary authorities in the banking markets.

In its role as a LOLR, the central bank will provide reserves to a bank (or banks) experiencing serious financial problems due to either a sudden withdrawal of funds by depositors or to a situation where the bank has embarked on highly risky operations and thus cannot find liquidity anywhere else (i.e., no other institutions will lend to a bank considered near collapse). Technically, this important function of central banks derives from the discount window tool that, as illustrated in section 5.4.2, is one of the instruments used to influence reserves and money supply in the banking sector. However, central banks operate under different frameworks in conducting the LOLR activities. These differences can reflect various country-specific factors such as public policy objectives, historical experience or other elements.

It is clear that the central bank will extend credit to an illiquid bank to prevent its failure only in exceptional situations and in doing so it also carries out a 'macro' function by preventing potential financial panics. However, the central bank cannot guarantee the solvency of every banking institution in a country. (On the relationship between liquidity and solvency see Box 5.5). This is because it would encourage bankers to undertake undue risk and operate imprudently, especially if banks knew that they would always be bailed out (by taxpayers' money) were they to become insolvent. In other words, the security of the LOLR function could induce or increase moral hazard in banks' behaviour.

One of the most famous examples of the direct support given by the Bank of England to the banking sector was offered in 1973/74 where the Bank organised help for 26 fringe (or secondary) banks facing severe liquidity problems. In the United States, famous examples of the FED acting as a LOLR include the rescue effort of two troubled banks: Franklin National in 1974 and Continental Illinois National Bank in 1984.

5.5.2 The free-banking hypothesis

The presence of a central bank acting as a 'super-bank' has been investigated by the so-called 'free-banking school'. **Free banking** theorists argue that regulation should be left to the market. Therefore, they object to a single central bank being given the 'privilege' – or monopoly – in issuing banknotes.

Similarly, a number of researchers in the field argue that the possibility for modern banks of 'refinancing' at the central bank is not in line with the current developments of a banking market that is increasingly driven by the objective of shareholders' wealth maximisation. In particular, they claim that in market-based economies the availability of the LOLR function of the central bank is detrimental to the good functioning and efficiency of the banking system as a whole because it may give rise to distortions and misallocation of resources.

In the words of Dowd (1996a, pp. 35–6):

> Once the government intervenes in the economy, the banking system becomes weaker and inefficient; the currency becomes debauched, and so on. The banking system becomes weak because the government preys on it, or because it sets up a system of deposit insurance or lender of last resort that undermines the banks' own incentives to maintain their financial health...

This argument begs the question: could the market function efficiently without a central bank? Yes, according to the laissez-faire economists whose main ambitions are: to prohibit government 'predation' on the financial system; to abolish all rules distorting the free functioning of the financial sector, including capital adequacy

Box 5.5   Relationship between liquidity and solvency

As we noted earlier, the liquidity of a bank relates to its ability to meet short-term obligations (expected and unexpected) when they fall due. For example, banks can predict with a certain degree of accuracy how much cash they need to hold to meet such things as payment of utility bills (electricity, water bills), rent on buildings and (under normal market conditions) deposit withdrawals. In addition to these expected calls on liquidity banks also have to hold a cushion above this amount to meet unexpected liquidity requirements and this is why liquidity risk management is a key feature of banking business (see Section 11.6).

Solvency is the ability of a bank ultimately to meet all its obligations. This means that the value of assets has to be greater than liabilities – the difference between the two being the bank's capital. If some assets go bad (e.g., loans are not repaid) then the bank must make charges against the loan portfolio (loan loss provisions) that are paid for from retained profits. As long as profits are sufficient to cover these provisions, the level of bank capital and its capital adequacy ratio (the Basle risk-weighted capital–asset ratio) remains unchanged. However, when profits do not cover provisions, then losses will have to be written out of capital (the amount of capital the bank has declines) or alternatively, shareholders will be asked to provide additional capital to restore the capital ratio to the required level.

The liquidity and solvency position of a bank are related because a severe liquidity shortfall can ultimately result in a solvency problem. For example, a continuous liquidity shortage could lead a bank to tighten its lending policy, for instance, by not renewing short-term revolving lines of credit. This would force borrowers to repay their loans earlier than expected and those unable to do so will default on their loan payments. In turn, the quality of the loan portfolio will deteriorate, requiring additional loan loss provisions. If the bank does not have sufficient provisions then the losses will be written out of capital resources thus reducing the solvency of the bank. In general, if a bank is unable to meet its liquidity requirements it will first attempt to obtain support through the LOLR facility by borrowing from the central bank. However, if this option is not available then the bank will have to consider bearing the losses from its capital resources thus reducing the bank's capital position.

A liquidity crisis can quickly change into a solvency crisis. For example, if a bank has actual (or even perceived) liquidity difficulties, and this becomes known to other banks, then the latter will withdraw their wholesale interbank deposits from the bank, leading to a wholesale deposit run, which may then spread to retail deposit withdrawals. In this case the bank will not be able to meet its short-term obligations and will have to resort to using capital resources to bear any losses. Ultimately the bank may not have sufficient capital resources to meet these losses, resulting in insolvency.

In the case of an individual bank failure, the decision as to whether a bank is illiquid or insolvent is a critical judgement that the regulators have to make in order to decide whether to support a troubled bank or to let it fail. For example, if a small bank is facing financial difficulties the regulator has to decide whether this is a result of a short-term liquidity problem or a longer-term solvency issue. If the authorities decide the problems are caused by liquidity problems they are more likely to offer support through the lender-of-last-resort facility (providing new liquidity to the bank to help it get through its liquidity problem). If the bank is deemed to have a solvency problem then the authorities are more likely to consider letting the bank go bankrupt or organising some form of rescue. In theory regulators should consider supporting banks with a liquidity problem but not with a solvency problem – although we know in reality that this is not always the case (See for example, Section 16.6 that examines the support of technically insolvent Japanese banks by the authorities.) Another point to note is that regulators have a very difficult task in deciding whether a bank that is in trouble is either illiquid or insolvent as often a decision has to be made very quickly as to whether liquidity support is to be provided or not. Often regulators have to decide in a matter of days the liquidity and solvency position of a troubled bank and they will also have to take into consideration whether a decision not to provide liquidity will result in failure and serious systemic repercussions. In general, the relationship between liquidity and solvency is at the heart of bank regulation and is a critical feature of the bank supervisory process.

regulation; and to eliminate deposit insurance and the lender-of-last-resort function. The free-banking school theorists argue that depositors would adapt to the competitive nature of the banking sector and accept that they would lose funds if their bank failed. However, bank managers would want to keep depositors' confidence for the usual reasons that if investors had any doubts about the safety of their bank, they would react by withdrawing their money. As a result bank managers would be willing to maintain adequate capital as well as other measures necessary to reassure depositors. This process would ensure an acceptable level of safety and soundness of the banking sector (see also Dowd, 1996a).

An interesting theoretical explanation for the existence of central banks is given by Charles Goodhart (1989). He highlights three possible reasons that might lead banks to prefer to form interbank organisations (a banking club) to which to delegate certain functions. First, the transaction and monitoring costs for interbank loans would be reduced if the central bank arranged them centrally. Second, banks would be obliged to hold a sort of 'socially optimum' amount of reserves that most probably would not keep otherwise. Finally, they would mitigate potential negative externalities derived by bank contagion effects.

In Goodhart's view central banks are needed for two main reasons. First, because banks provide two essential functions: they operate the payment systems and undertake portfolio management services. These are considered to be 'public goods' and hence need to be preserved; on the other hand, bankers themselves have an economic interest in protecting the reputation of the banking sector as a whole and in keeping the confidence of investors. A central bank aims to prevent the collapse of the banking sector that could arise from information problems, abuses by bankers and excessive risk taking.

However, Goodhart's argument challenges the conventional view that the joint provision of payments' services together with portfolio management functions of banks exposes the monetary system to contagious failure, which a central bank should prevent. Instead, the author maintains that it is the special nature of banks' assets, largely non-marketable, fixed nominal-value loans of uncertain true worth that makes them more vulnerable than other non-banking firms.

While there is debate about the merits and demerits of central banks it is a fact that there is a central bank in virtually every country in the world. One of the major current issues is whether central banks should be given independence from governments, and if so, to what extent.

5.6 Should central banks be independent?

In recent years there has been a significant trend towards **central bank independence** in many countries and the issue has generated substantial debate all over the world. Theoretical studies seem to suggest that central bank independence is important because it can help produce a better monetary policy. For example, an extensive body of literature predicts that the more independent a central bank, the lower the inflation rate in an economy.

Central bank independence can be defined as independence from political influence and pressures in the conduct of its functions, in particular monetary policy. It is possible to distinguish two types of independence: *goal independence*, that is, the ability of the central bank to set its own goals for monetary policy (e.g., low inflation, high production levels); and *instrument independence*, that is, the ability of the central bank to independently set the instruments of monetary policy to achieve these goals (for example, see Mishkin, 2000).

It is common for a central bank to have instrument independence without goal independence; however, it is rare to find a central bank that has goal independence without having instrument independence. In the United Kingdom, for example, the Bank of England is currently granted instrument independence and practises what is known as *inflation targeting*. This means that it is the government that decides to target the inflation rate (currently (2005) set at 2 per cent) and the Bank is allowed to independently choose the policies that will help to achieve that goal. Such a situation is only acceptable in a democracy because the Bank is not elected and thus goals should only be set by an elected government.

While central bank independence indicates autonomy from political influence and pressures in the conduct of its functions (in particular monetary policy), dependence implies subordination to the government. In this latter case, there is a risk that the government may 'manipulate' monetary policy for economic and political reasons. It should be noted, however, that all independent central banks have their governors chosen by the government; this suggests that to some extent central banks can never be entirely independent.

In a recent survey of 93 world central banks, central bankers defined independence in many different ways, as shown in Figure 5.5.

Figure 5.5 shows that central banks tend to feel more independent when they have instrument independence and the ability to formulate policy (45 per cent) while only 22 per cent of respondents mentioned the ability to set targets, objectives and goals.

It is possible to distinguish between the case 'for' and the case 'against' independence. In general terms there are mainly political and economic reasons in support of central bank independence. Moreover, there is a principal–agent problem between the public (the principal) and the central bank and the government (the agents). The agents may have incentives to act against the interest of the public. According to the supporters of central bank independence it is the government in particular that has a strong incentive to act in its own interest. Only an

Figure 5.5 How central bankers define independence

* The responses are the authors' categorisation of answers to the questions 'How would you define central bank independence?' There were 60 usable responses (23 from industrialised economies and 37 from developing and transitional economies). Respondents cited an average of 2.9 categories in industrialised economies and 2.2 in developing and transitional economies.

Source: Mahadeva and Sterne (2000, p. 111).

independent central bank operating outside the day-to-day business of politics can be considered a guarantor of long-term economic stability.

5.7 Conclusions

A central bank's main function is to undertake monetary control operations and thus to administer the amount of money in the economy given the specific monetary policy objectives set by the government. Modern central banks tend to use *indirect instruments*, or tools, in the conduct of their monetary policy and can generally choose between: (1) open market operations; (2) the discount window; and (3) reserve requirements. OMOs are at present the most popular instruments used by central banks as they are tax-free (in that they do not place specific constraints on banks' operations) and flexible (in terms of their frequency of use and scale of activity). In particular, the main attractions for using open market operations to influence short-term interest rates are as follows: they are initiated by the monetary authorities who have complete control over the volume of transactions; they are flexible and precise – they can be used for major or minor changes in the amount of liquidity in the system; they can easily be reversed; and finally they can be undertaken quickly.

While the role and core functions of central banks around the world keep evolving to adapt to the transformations in the operating environment, one school of thought, the free-banking school, has questioned whether central banks are needed. In essence, free bankers doubt the effectiveness of central banks in a demand-oriented banking market that is increasingly driven by the profit maximisation culture. In particular, they criticise the use of the LOLR function and central bank's monopoly in issuing banknotes. Against this viewpoint, C. Goodhart confirms the need for a central bank using his theory of banking 'clubs'. He emphasises that banks are especially vulnerable to crises due to the special nature of their assets, which are largely non-marketable.

Today there is a trend in both developed and developing countries towards the increased independence of central banks from political pressure. Typically, a central bank will be conferred instrument independence but not goal independence; this means that the central bank can independently set the instruments of monetary policy to achieve the macroeconomic goals determined by the government of the day.

Key terms

Monetary policy	Open market operations
Fiscal policy	Discount window
Exchange rate policy	Reserve requirement
Prices and incomes policy	Instruments of portfolio constraint
National debt management policy	Lender-of-last-resort
Money	Free banking
Monetary aggregates	Central bank independence
Price stability	

Key reading Dowd, K. (1996) *Competition and Finance: A New Interpretation of Financial and Monetary Economics*. London: Macmillan.

Goodhart, C.A.E. (1989) 'Why do banks need a central bank', chapter 8, pp. 176–93, in *Money, Information and Uncertainty*, 2nd edn. London: Macmillan.

Mishkin, F. (2000) 'What should central banks do?', *Federal Reserve Bank of St Louis Review*, November–December.

Revision questions and problems

1 What are the five major forms of economic policy?

2. What is money and what are the monetary aggregates?

3 Outline the differences between monetary policy tools, instruments and goals.

4 Why are OMOs the most popular monetary policy tool?

5 Explain the meaning and limitations of the 'instruments of portfolio constraint'.

6 What is the lender-of-last resort function? Why is it controversial?

7 What are the main arguments put forward by the free-banking theorists?

8 What are the arguments for and against an independent central bank?

Chapter 6

Central banks in practice

Learning objectives

- To describe the functions and role of the Bank of England, the European Central Bank and the Federal Reserve System

- To describe the organisational structure and corporate governance of the Bank of England, the ECB and the Federal Reserve System

- To understand the relationship between the ECB and the national central banks

- To understand the role of monetary policy in practice

6.1 Introduction

This chapter investigates the functions, structure and role of central bank operations. In particular, Section 6.2 focuses on the Bank of England; Section 6.3 on the **European Central Bank**; and finally, Section 6.4 investigates the US Federal Reserve System. We start by focusing on the structure and functions of these central banks, which are among the most important central banks in the world. We then look at the decision-making process within these organisations and finally discuss some of the most relevant operational changes.

6.2 The Bank of England

The Bank of England is the central bank of the United Kingdom. As we discussed in Chapter 5, a central bank is ultimately responsible for the organisation of its country's official financial policies, including the monetary policy, and acts as banker to the government and general overseer of the whole financial system.

The origins of the Bank of England can be traced back to 1694 when it received its charter as a joint stock company. The Bank, in fact, was established in order to improve the fund-raising capability of the British government. It was not until the Bank Charter Act of 1844, however, that the Bank of England obtained full central bank status. The 1844 Act ultimately led to a monopoly for the Bank in the production of notes and coins in the United Kingdom.

During the nineteenth century the Bank of England consolidated its position as overseer of the British banking system by standing ready to purchase bills of exchange issued by other commercial banks, if the need arose. This lender-of-last-resort function helped maintain public confidence and credibility in the banking system. In fact, during the nineteenth century the Bank of England found itself performing many of the functions that are today thought commonplace for a central bank: the main issuer of bank notes and coins; lender-of-last-resort; banker to the government and to other domestic banks; and guardian of the nation's official reserves. As well as providing banking services to its customers, the Bank of England manages the United Kingdom's foreign exchange and gold reserves and the government's stock register. The latter is a register of government securities (gilts).

It must be remembered, however, that although the Bank of England has performed these functions (as well as undertaking a larger role in the financial management of the economy) it still remained a private joint stock company, operating for a profit. The Bank of England Act of 1 March 1946 nationalised the Bank and the state acquired all of the Bank's capital. In 1997 the government gave the Bank operational independence to set monetary policy and statutory responsibilities for the stability of the financial system as a whole (see Box 6.1).

6.2.1 Constitution of the Bank

The Bank of England is a public corporation with a fundamental role with regard to the objectives of maintaining a stable and efficient monetary and financial framework. Like other nationalised organisations, the actual degree of operational

> ### Box 6.1   The Bank of England – 300 years of history
>
> - Established 1694 (The Royal Charter)
> - 1734 the Bank moved to Threadneedle Street, London, its current premises
> - 1781 renewal of the Bank's Charter – The Banker's Bank
> - 1844 Bank Charter Act – the Bank took on the role of Lender-of-Last-Resort
> - 1946 Bank of England Act – the Bank was nationalised and formally recognised as a Central Bank
> - Until 1997 the Bank was statutorily subordinate to the Treasury
> - 1998 Bank of England Act – the Bank was granted operational independence

freedom has always been rather limited. In May 1997 the Treasury proposed a number of institutional and operational changes to the Bank of England that were set out in the **Bank of England Act 1998** (1 June).

For the first time, the Bank of England was given operational independence in setting interest rates that became the responsibility of the newly created **Monetary Policy Committee (MPC)** working within the Bank.

However, the legislation provides that, in extreme circumstances and if the national interest demands it, the government will have the power to give instructions to the Bank on interest rates for a limited period.

Furthermore, in the 1998 Act, the regulation of the banking sector was taken away from the Bank and given to a newly established 'super' regulator called the **Financial Services Authority (FSA)**. Finally, as a result of these changes, the Bank's functions for the national debt management passed to the newly created UK **Debt Management Office (DMO)** that is legally and constitutionally part of HM Treasury.

In October 1997, the Bank, Her Majesty's Treasury and the FSA signed a **'Memorandum of Understanding'** which made provisions for the establishment of a high-level standing committee which meets regularly and provides a forum where the three organisations can develop a common position on financial stability issues. The main features of this Memorandum of Understanding are shown in Box 6.2.

6.2.2   Organisational structure of the Bank of England

The organisational structure of the Bank of England has changed remarkably as a result of the 1998 Bank of England Act. Currently the Bank's activities are divided into three main areas: monetary analysis and statistics; market operations; and financial stability. There are also a number of other divisions; for example, the Bank has a division responsible for European matters (the Co-ordination Division for Europe) and a Centre for Central Banking Studies whose main activity is to offer teaching and technical assistance to other central banks.

The Bank of England is currently managed by a Court of Directors, which comprises the governor, two deputy governors and 16 directors. The directors are all non-executive. Governors are appointed for five years and the directors for three years. Under the 1998 Act, the responsibilities of the Court are to manage the Bank's affairs, other than the formulation of monetary policy, which is the respon-

Box 6.2   Memorandum of Understanding between HM Treasury, the Bank of England and the FSA

This Memorandum of Understanding establishes a framework for co-operation between HM Treasury, the Bank of England and the FSA in the field of financial stability. It sets out the role of each institution, and explains how they will work together towards the common objective of financial stability. The division of responsibilities is based on four guiding principles:

1) *Clear accountability*. Each institution must be accountable for its actions, so each must have unambiguous and well-defined responsibilities;
2) *Transparency*. Parliament, the markets and the public must know who is responsible for what
3) *No duplication*. Each institution must have a clearly defined role, to avoid second guessing, inefficiency and the duplication of effort. This will help ensure proper accountability
4) *Regular information exchange*. This will help each institution to discharge its responsibilities as efficiently and effectively as possible.

The Bank's responsibilities

The Bank will be responsible for the overall stability of the financial system as a whole; which will involve:

i) Stability of the monetary system. The Bank will monitor this, as part of its monetary policy functions. It will act daily in the markets, to deal with day to day fluctuations in liquidity;
ii) Financial system infrastructure, in particular payments systems at home and abroad. As the bankers' bank, the Bank will stand at the heart of the system. It will fall to the Bank to advise the Chancellor, and answer for its advice, on any major problem inherent in the payments systems. The Bank will also be closely involved in developing and improving the infrastructure, and strengthening the system to help reduce systemic risk;
iii) Broad overview of the system as a whole. The Bank will be uniquely placed to do this: it will be responsible for monetary stability, and will have high level representation at the institution responsible for financial regulation Through its involvement in the payments systems it may be the first to spot potential problems. The Bank will be able to advise on the implications for financial stability of developments in the domestic and international markets and payments systems; and

it will assess the impact on monetary conditions of events in the financial sector;
iv) Being able in exceptional circumstances to undertake official financial operations, in order to limit the risk of problems in or affecting particular institutions spreading to other parts of the financial system;
v) The efficiency and effectiveness of the financial sector, with particular regard to international competitiveness. The Bank will continue to play its leading role in promoting the City.

The FSA's responsibilities

The FSA is responsible for:

i) The authorisation and prudential supervision of banks, building societies, investment firms, insurance companies and friendly societies;
ii) The supervision of financial markets and of clearing and settlement systems;
iii) The conduct of operations in response to problem cases affecting firms, markets and clearing and settlements systems within its responsibilities;
iv) Regulatory policy. The FSA will advise on the regulatory implication for firms, markets and clearing systems of developments in domestic and international markets and of initiatives, both domestic and international, such as EC directives.

The Treasury's responsibilities

The Treasury is responsible for the overall institutional structure of regulation, and the legislation which governs it. It has no operational responsibility for the activities of the FSA and the Bank, and will not be involved in them. But there are a variety of circumstances where the FSA and the Bank will need to alert the Treasury about possible problems: for example, where a serious problem arises, which could cause wider economic disruption; where there is or could be a need for a support operation; where diplomatic or foreign relations problems might arise; where a problem might suggest the need for a change in the law; or where a case is likely to lead to questions to Ministers in Parliament. This list is not exhaustive, and there will be other relevant situations. In each case it will be for the FSA and the Bank to decide whether the Treasury needs to be alerted.

Source: Memorandum Of Understanding Between HM Treasury, The Bank of England And The FSA – Bank of England Act, 1998.

sibility of the MPC (see Section 6.2.3.1). This includes determining the Bank's objectives and strategy and aiming to ensure the effective discharge of the Bank's functions and the most efficient use of the Bank's resources.

The Court of Directors determines the Bank's core purposes that should be in line with the Bank's overall objectives and strategy. According to the latest statement approved by the Court in May 2004, the core purposes of the Bank of England are essentially twofold: monetary stability and financial stability. In working towards its core purposes, the Bank is organised into three main operational areas:

1) Monetary Analysis and Statistics;
2) Market Operations; and
3) Financial Stability

supported by a central services area.

1) Monetary Analysis and Statistics

In carrying out its monetary policy responsibilities the Bank needs to use economic analysis including projections of future developments in the United Kingdom and internationally. The division produces a number of publications, in particular the *Quarterly Bulletin* and the *Inflation Report*, the latter being particularly useful for the aims of the MPC since it provides an assessment of prospects for inflation (generally over two years) relative to the inflation target.

2) Markets

The Market Operations area at the Bank of England can be divided into three main divisions:

1) *Sterling Markets Division*: that conducts the operations needed to meet the interest rate target set by the MPC while maintaining liquidity in the system (for more details on open market operations see Chapter 5);
2) *Foreign Exchange Division*: responsible for operations in the foreign exchange market and for the management of HM Treasury's foreign exchange reserves;
3) *Risk Management Division*: responsible for measuring, monitoring and managing risks associated with the Bank's financial operations.

3) Financial Stability Division

As its name suggests, the Financial Stability Division is mainly responsible for identifying the most relevant threats and risks to the stability of the UK financial system. The division is involved in studies that assess issues relating to the structure, functions and operations of both domestic and overseas markets. It makes policy proposals and encourages changes that can increase the safety and soundness of the whole international system. The area contributes to the monetary policy process and publishes the *Financial Stability Review*.

Other divisions and functions of the Bank of England include:

- **Banking services:** a) services to the government and other customers (e.g., central banks and other financial institutions) are provided by the *Customer Banking Division*; b) note issue is managed by the *Notes Division*; c) the *Market Services Division* operates the Real Time Gross Settlements (RTGS) system through which payments relating to the major UK payments and securities settlement systems are settled; d) the *Registrar's Department* maintains the principal registers of hold-ings and other stocks for the government.

● **Co-ordination Division for Europe:** This division represents the Bank of England at the EU level and is in charge of co-ordinating plans for a possible future adoption of the Euro in Britain.

● **Central services:** Essentially the services provided by the Central Services divi-sion are carried out to ensure the reputation of the Bank is maintained. Support functions given by these divisions include: finance, IT, property, personnel, press, governors' private offices and public relations, the investment unit, legal services and the newly created Business Continuity division.

● **Internal audit:** The Internal Audit division works independently and reports directly to senior staff in the Bank on issues relating to the adequacy of systems of internal controls and the effectiveness of risk management and governance processes.

● **Centre for Central Banking Studies (CCBS):** The centre carries out research on practical issues relating to central banking and provides training and advisory services. Its main objectives are 'to foster monetary and financial stability world-wide, to promote the Bank's core purposes, and to provide opportunities for Bank of England staff to obtain broader perspectives on their own areas of expertise' (CCBS prospectus).

Figure 6.1 illustrates the divisional structure at the Bank of England.

Figure 6.1 Managing the Bank of England

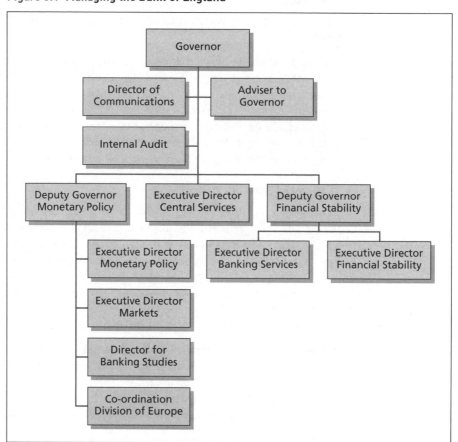

6.2.3 Objectives and functions of the Bank of England

The main objectives of the Bank of England can be summarised as follows:

- maintaining the integrity and value of the currency;
- maintaining the stability of the financial system, both domestic and international; and
- seeking to ensure the effectiveness of the United Kingdom's financial services industry.

Given the aforementioned objectives, the core functions are: to implement monetary policy, ensure the stability of the financial system and act as a lender-of-last-resort.

6.2.3.1 Core purpose of monetary stability and the role of the Monetary Policy Committee

The first core purpose of the Bank is to ensure monetary stability by maintaining stable prices and confidence in the currency. *Price stability* is met by influencing the price of money, i.e., by changing the level of short-term nominal interest rates (on the difference between nominal and real rates see Appendix A1). Decisions are taken by the MPC that aim to meet the government's annual inflation target (at the end of 2005 this stood at 2 per cent). With regard to *confidence in the currency*, the Bank is also responsible for safeguarding the value of the currency.

Monetary Policy Committee and the objective of monetary stability

The Bank's MPC is made up by the governor, the two deputy governors, the Bank's chief economist, the executive director for market operations and four external members appointed directly by the Chancellor. The MPC meets every month and decides on the level of short-term interest rates (4.5 per cent in January 2006). Once the MPC decides that it is to change short-term interest rates, the Bank can engage in open market operations via the repo market (as discussed in Chapter 5). Another way for the Bank to influence the supply of money is by choosing the interest rate at which it will provide the cash that the banking system as a whole needs at the end of each settlement day to achieve balance.

It is important to highlight that all monetary authorities are concerned about the level of interest rates and they conduct open market operations or manipulate reserves in order to influence short-term rates. Clearly the main goals of macroeconomic policy – high employment, growth, financial system stability and so on – benefit from a low and stable interest rate environment. The point to emphasise is that while for example in the United States the authorities explicitly target short-term interest rates as a major policy tool, the Bank of England focuses primarily on an inflation target.

A clear and stable inflation target is the most relevant way of making the objectives of monetary policy credible, thus ensuring inflation expectations are consistent with price stability. In the United Kingdom intermediate targets, such as monetary aggregates, have had an uncertain relationship with the main goal of maintaining price stability. This is why the Bank of England nowadays uses inflation targets as the main feature of its monetary policy. Box 6.3 provides a summary of the evolution of inflation targeting as the mainstay of UK monetary policy.

Box 6.3   Inflation targeting in the United Kingdom

The adoption of formal inflation targets in 1992 marked an important break with the past. The other key date is 1997, when the Bank of England was granted operational independence; the institutional framework then put in place entrenched and enhanced the credibility of inflation targeting and has been widely admired. Moreover, in the UK, as in many other inflation targeting countries, a track record of success, built up over more than a decade, has progressively reinforced the credibility of these targets. As a result, people and firms have increasingly come to expect inflation to stay close to the official target – a belief which itself helps to keep it there.

The institutional framework is set out in some detail in the 1998 Bank of England Act. The Bank of England is required to set interest rates so as 'to maintain price stability and subject to that to support the economic policy of HM Government, including its objectives for growth and employment'. The government is required to specify what its economic objectives are, including what is meant by price stability. The remit of the MPC must be set out in writing at least annually and it must be published.

The remit has always had important elements of flexibility. For example, while the MPC is directed to aim for the target 'at all times' and to treat deviations from target symmetrically, it is not expected to react mechanically. Instead, if inflation deviates from target by more than 1%, the governor is required to write to the Chancellor explaining the circumstances and setting out what action the MPC considers necessary to return to target. No letter has been written so far, but only because circumstances have not warranted it.

Performance over the six years since the Bank became independent has been impressive. Against the target of 2.5% for Retail Price Index (excluding Mortgage Interest Payments) (RPIX) which ran from 1997 until December 2003, average inflation was 2.4%. For 68 out of the 79 months, inflation was within 0.5 per cent of the target – below it for 42 months, above it for 30, and on target for the remaining seven. Notwithstanding the stock market crash and the slowdown in world activity, the UK economy has continued to grow steadily and employment has remained strong.

On a longer-term view, the decade of inflation targeting since 1992 looks remarkably stable by post-war standards. The recent slowdown has been exceptionally mild compared with all previous slowdowns since the beginning of the 1970s, and since 1992 growth in both real GDP and consumer spending has also been significantly less volatile, with 46 quarters of positive growth, and no significant downturn in consumption since mid-1994.

Of course, better monetary policy and low inflation are only part of this story. It matters that monetary policy has been supported by fiscal discipline. Just as important are the many labour and product market reforms that, over a long period of time, have given the UK a more flexible and competitive economy, which is capable of adapting quickly to sudden change without prolonged periods of unemployment and under-utilised capacity.

Source: Adapted from speech given by Rachel Lomax, Deputy Governor of The Bank of England. See Bank of England (2005a).

6.2.3.2 Core purpose of financial stability and the function of lender-of-last-resort

The Bank of England is responsible for maintaining the stability of the UK financial system. This role is linked to the objectives of ensuring the *safety and soundness* of the financial system and this implies important interrelated issues, including:

- the development of a robust financial sector;
- safe and efficient payment and settlement arrangements;
- an appropriate legal regime;
- effective disclosure requirements;
- sound principles for prudential regulation;
- monitoring current developments in domestic and international financial systems; and the
- efficient means of financial crisis management.

The Bank has the important responsibility of supporting and promoting a competitive and efficient financial centre in Britain. Most importantly the Bank is expected to act in such a way as to minimise potential threats to the whole financial sector. In exceptional circumstances, the Bank may act as the lender-of-last-resort (LOLR). However, since 1997 the supervision function of the UK banking sector has been transferred to the FSA that essentially acts as a 'super-regulator' (see Box 6.4).

The Bank of England as lender-of-last-resort

The Bank of England has acted as lender-of-last resort for the banking system for over a century. This means that the Bank stands ready to supply funds to the banking sector if liquidity or (much worse) solvency problems arise (on the distinction between liquidity and solvency see Box 5.5 in the previous chapter).

Box 6.4 **The Financial Services Authority and the objective of financial stability**

Since 1997 the banking supervision function has been transferred from the Bank of England to a 'super-regulator': the Financial Services Authority (FSA). The FSA is an independent non-governmental body that was given statutory powers by the Financial Services and Markets Act 2000. According to the 2000 Act, the FSA regulates the financial services industry and has four main objectives:

1) maintaining market confidence;
2) promoting public understanding of the financial system;
3) the protection of consumers; and
4) fighting financial crime.

The FSA also aims to maintain efficient, orderly and clean financial markets and help retail consumers achieve a fair deal. So while the Bank of England has had responsibility for the stability of the financial system as a whole, the FSA supervises individual banks and other financial organisations including recognised financial exchanges such as the London Stock Exchange.

The FSA works closely with the HM Treasury and the Financial Stability area of the Bank through the Joint Standing Committee established in 1997.

However, this does not mean that the Bank guarantees the solvency of every banking institution in the United Kingdom. Rather, the situation is that the Bank stands ready to accommodate shortages of cash in the banking sector, perhaps resulting from the non-bank private sector or from an unusually large net flow of funds from private bank accounts to the government's accounts at the Bank of England. This view adopts a short-term view of the lender-of-last-resort. It is argued that the Bank, in its role as lender-of-last-resort, is not prepared to guarantee the solvency of every banking institution because this would encourage bankers to take undue risks and operate imprudently (i.e., increase moral hazard, see Chapter 7), especially if banks knew that they would be bailed out (by taxpayers' money) if they became insolvent. In other words, the Bank may lend money to a troubled institution to avoid a possible systemic crisis that may arise as a result of the bank failing. However, this 'safety net' is not meant to protect individual institutions or their managers and shareholders. Rather, it exists only to protect the stability of the financial sector as a whole.

6.3 The European Central Bank (ECB)

Established on 1 June 1998 and based in Frankfurt, Germany, the European Central Bank, is one of the world's youngest central banks. It is the central bank for Europe's single currency, the Euro. The legal basis for the ECB is the Treaty establishing the European Community and the statute of the **European System of Central Banks** (ESCB) and of the European Central Bank. The statute established both the ECB and the European System of Central Banks as from 1 June 1998. According to its statute, the ECB's primary objective is price stability in the Euroarea, thus it is responsible for monitoring inflation levels and maintaining the purchasing power of the common currency.

The *Euroarea* currently comprises twelve EU Member States that have replaced their national currencies by 1 July 2002: Austria, Belgium, Finland, France, Germany, Greece, Ireland, Italy, Luxembourg, Netherlands, Spain and Portugal. Denmark and the United Kingdom negotiated an 'opt-out' protocol to the EU Treaty, granting them the option of joining the Euroarea or not. Sweden initially did not meet the necessary conditions for entry and in September 2003 rejected the Euro in a national referendum. On 1 May 2004 ten new Member States joined the European Union – the Czech Republic, Estonia, Cyprus, Latvia, Lithuania, Hungary, Malta, Poland, Slovakia and Slovenia (see Box 6.5). These countries have diverse socio-economic backgrounds and are at various stages of economic and financial sector development. However, they all aim to eventually adopt the Euro but only when (according to the European Central Bank) they fulfil certain economic criteria, namely, a high degree of price stability, a sound fiscal situation, stable exchange rates and converged long-term interest rates. (Note that the current Euroarea members had to fulfil the same criteria.) As of January 2006 none of the ten countries had adopted the Euro. Slovenia, Estonia and Lithuania plan to be the first to join in 2007, followed by Latvia (in 2008) and Cyprus (by 2008) and Slovakia (in 2009). Poland, the Czech Republic and Hungary have stated that they aim to adopt the Euro in around 2010 while Malta has not yet said when it will be ready to convert to the single currency (see also Chapter 14).

Box 6.5 The single currency and EU enlargement

On 1 May 2004, the Czech Republic, Estonia, Cyprus, Latvia, Lithuania, Hungary, Malta, Poland, Slovakia and Slovenia joined the European Union.

Since the enlargement took place, the governors of the central banks of the new EU countries have become members of the general council of the ECB. The New Member States central banks' experts are also members of the committees of the ESCB. However, they will not join the main decision-making body – the governing council – until they adopt the Euro.

New Member States will not automatically adopt the Euro; they will do so when they fulfil the 'Maastricht convergence criteria'. The 10 new EU countries do not have a right to opt-out of the single currency like the one exercised by the UK and Denmark.

There is no pre-determined timetable for the new countries to join the single currency. They will adopt the Euro only when they fulfil certain economic criteria, namely, a high degree of price stability, a sound fiscal situation, stable exchange rates and converged long-term interest rates.

Figure 6.2 **EU enlargement**

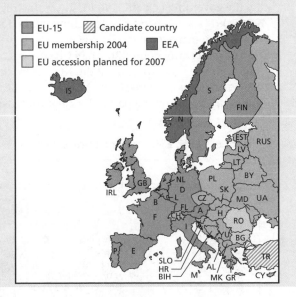

The origin of the ECB can be traced back to the recent history of the Economic and Monetary Union (see also Chapter 13). In 1994 the EMI (European Monetary Institute) was created; the EMI was the precursor to the ECB. On 25 May 1998 the governments of the then 11 participating Member States appointed the president, the vice-president and the four other members of the Executive Board of the ECB. Their appointment took effect from 1 June 1998 and marked the establishment of the ECB.[1]

---

[1] See http://www.ecb.int/about/emu.htm.

The ECB and the **National Central Banks** (NCBs) of all EU Member States, regardless of whether they have adopted the Euro or not, constitute the European System of Central Banks or ESCB. As shown in Figure 6.3, the **Eurosystem** instead comprises the ECB and the NCBs of those countries that have adopted the Euro.

The term Eurosystem was chosen by the governing council of the ECB to describe the arrangements by which the ESCB carries out its tasks within the Euroarea. As long as there are EU Member States that have not yet adopted the Euro, this distinction between the Eurosystem and the ESCB will need to be made.

The National Central Banks of the new EU countries are now members of the general council of the ECB but they will not join the main decision-making body – the governing council – until they adopt the Euro.

6.3.1 Organisational structure of the Bank

There are three main decision-making bodies of the ECB: the executive board, the governing council and the general council.

The **executive board** consists of the president of the ECB, the vice-president and four other members, appointed by the heads of state or government of the Euroarea countries. It is responsible for implementing monetary policy, as defined by the governing council, and for giving instructions to the national central banks (NCBs). It also prepares the governing council meetings and is responsible for the day-to-day management of the ECB.

The **governing council** of the ECB consists of the six members of the executive board plus the governors of all the NCBs from the 12 Euroarea countries. The council's main responsibilities are: 1) to adopt the guidelines and take the decisions necessary to ensure the performance of the tasks entrusted to the Eurosystem; and

Figure 6.3 ECB, ESCB and the Eurosystem

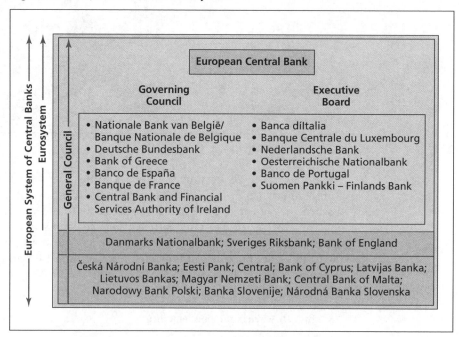

2) to formulate monetary policy for the Euroarea, including key interest rates and reserves. The statute (article 7)[2] establishes independence from political interference of the ECB and ESCB in the carrying out of their tasks and duties.

The **general council** is the ECB's third decision-making body. It comprises the ECB's president and the vice-president and the governors of the national central banks of all 25 EU member states. The general council contributes to the ECB's advisory and co-ordination work and helps prepare for the future enlargement of the Euroarea.

6.3.2 Core functions of the ECB

The functions of the ECB (and of the ESCB) are specified in the statute that is a protocol attached to the 1992 Treaty on the European Union: 'The primary objective of the ESCB shall be to maintain price stability.' Moreover, 'without prejudice to the objective of price stability, the ESCB shall support the general economic policies in the Community with a view to contributing to the achievement of the objectives of the Community as laid down in Article 2' (Treaty Article 105.1). Article 2 on the Treaty on European Union states the objectives of the Union as being a high level of employment and sustainable and non-inflationary growth.

More specifically, according to the Treaty establishing the European Union (article 105.2), the basic tasks of the ECB are to:

1) define and implement monetary policy for the Euroarea;
2) conduct foreign exchange operations;
3) hold and manage the official foreign reserves of the Euroarea countries (portfolio management); and
4) promote the smooth operation of payment systems.

6.3.2.1 Monetary policy

By July 2002, 12 out of 15 EU countries, namely Austria, Belgium, Finland, France, Germany, Greece, Ireland, Italy, Luxembourg, Netherlands, Portugal and Spain, had replaced their national currencies with the Euro. Responsibility for monetary policy within the Eurozone was transferred to the ECB working with the national central banks of the Eurozone member states. This grouping of institutions, as noted above, is known as the Eurosystem.

The primary objective of the Eurosystem, as defined by statute, is to maintain price stability. Without prejudice to this objective, the Eurosystem is expected to support the general economic policies of the EU. It is also required to operate in accordance with open-market economy principles, emphasising free competition and an efficient allocation of resources. A successful monetary policy by the ECB contributes positively to the achievement of the objectives of high economic growth, employment and price stability in Europe.

The ECB uses three main monetary policy tools:

● Open market operations – normally in the form of repo transactions or secured loans. The most important instrument is the so-called reverse transaction (applicable

---

[2] See the 1/6/2004 Protocol on the Statute of the European System of Central Banks and of the European Central Bank http://www.ecb.int/ecb/legal/pdf/en_statute.pdf.

on the basis of repurchase agreements or collaterised loans) used via its main refinancing operations (MROs). For example the interest rate on the MRO stood at 2 per cent in June 2005).

- Standing facilities – used to provide or to absorb overnight liquidity in the markets.
- A minimum reserve requirement – applied to selected financial institutions.

Moreover, in order to achieve its primary objectives, the ECB sets its monetary policy instruments on the basis of a strategy comprising two 'pillars':

- The first relates to monetary analysis and in particular focuses on the close monitoring of the growth rate of a broad monetary aggregate (M3) relative to an announced medium-term target growth rate.
- The second focuses on broad economic analysis and encompasses an assessment of inflationary pressures based on a range of indicators such as economic growth, the Euro exchange rate, business and consumer surveys and Eurozone fiscal policies.

The strategy of the ECB includes a definition of price stability equal to a year-on-year increase in the HICP (Harmonised Index of Consumer Prices) for the Euroarea of 2 per cent.[3] In addition, it includes an analytical framework for the assessment of the risks to price stability that is based on the aforementioned two pillars of economic and monetary analysis. The decision of what type of monetary policy has to be undertaken is made by the governing council, as shown in Figure 6.4.

It has been argued that the ECB may not have given enough weight to the monetary implications of the transition of Eurozone economies to the use of a single currency and the effect of a single set of interest rates throughout the Eurozone. A particular problem has been the weakness of the German economy relative to the economies of some other members of the Eurozone that have experienced higher growth, employment rates and inflation in recent years. This causes problems for setting monetary policy in the Eurozone as the ECB has to accommodate the diverse features of macroeconomic performance of all member countries when setting policy. For example, Ireland's booming economy would probably have benefited more from a tighter monetary policy stance (hence dampening inflationary pressures) than the expansionary policy conducted by the ECB that has been geared to boosting sluggish economic performance in Germany, France and Italy. Until various structural adjustments in Eurozone markets can be completed, particularly in respect of freer market competition and the flexibility of labour markets, the ECB still faces major challenges in implementing a 'one-size-fits-all' monetary policy in the Eurozone.

The ECB places considerable emphasis on intermediate targeting of monetary aggregates, particularly M3, its broad measure of money, for the Eurozone. In setting a so-called *reference value* for broad monetary growth, the governing council of the ECB has taken account mainly of price stability, i.e., inflation below 2 per cent, and of a growth rate of 2–2.5 per cent per annum for real Gross Domestic Product

---

[3] From the time of its inception until May 2003, the ECB defined its statutory requirement to maintain price stability as keeping the rate of inflation at less than 2 per cent p.a. This chosen objective was not only regarded as having been excessively harsh when global inflationary pressures were low, but also it may be thought to have lacked the flexibility that would have been offered by the use of an inflation target band. In May 2003 the ECB effectively announced a loosening of its policy regime by indicating that henceforth it would seek to maintain the rate of inflation within the Eurozone *close to* 2 per cent p.a. over the medium term.

Figure 6.4 The stability-oriented monetary policy strategy of the ECB

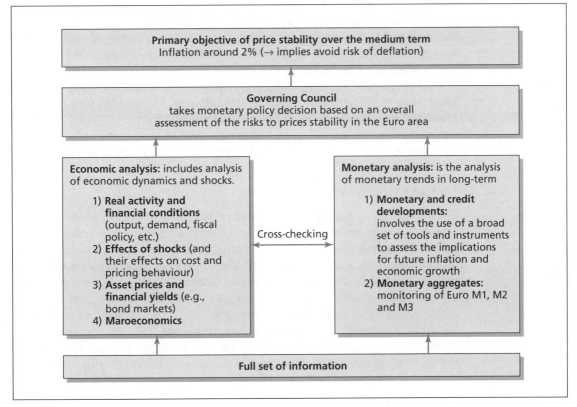

Source: Adapted from http://www.ecb.int.

(GDP). Furthermore, the medium-term decline in the velocity of money (the ratio between the nominal GDP and nominal M3) is considered to lie in the approximate range of 0.5–1 per cent each year. Based on these considerations, the governing council decided to set the first reference value for monetary growth at 4.5 per cent.

The use of what is effectively an intermediate target for a broad monetary aggregate (the 'quantitative reference rate' for the growth of M3) by the ECB has been increasingly questioned. The reported overshooting of this target variable undoubtedly contributed to pressure for restrictive monetary policy and could ultimately undermine the credibility of monetary policy and confidence in the monetary authorities. This may have been a factor in the ECB's decision to announce that it would put less emphasis on the M3 money supply measure, and would look more towards indicators of the real Eurozone economy in setting its policy.

Another controversial issue relates to the extent and nature of democratic control over the ECB and its openness and accountability for its actions. Quite simply, it may be argued that the ECB has been given the power to determine its own inflation objective without recourse to the democratically elected governments of the Eurozone countries, and on the basis of only limited disclosure of the underlying monetary policy decision-making processes. This is not to question the importance of independence from political pressure in respect of the implementation of policy once the objectives have been set.

To be fair, the criticisms that may be made of the ECB should not be allowed to disguise its widely acknowledged achievements. The establishment of the Eurozone and the practical aspects of launching a new currency have occurred with far fewer problems than might have been feared. The objective of price stability within the Eurozone has been broadly achieved, although the 2 per cent target has been periodically overshot.

Finally, it is worth noting that EU governments have recently signed an agreement known as the *Stability and Growth Pact* (see Box 6.6) that aims to limit individual member states' fiscal policies and public financing regimes. The 'pact' was adopted mainly on the grounds that fiscal policies may conflict with the inflation objective, or may cause the economic performance of member states to diverge.

6.3.2.2 Foreign exchange operations

The second most important basic task of the ECB is the conduct of foreign exchange operations and this includes: 1) foreign exchange interventions; and 2) operations such as the sale of foreign currency interest income and so-called commercial transactions. At present (2005) the Eurosystem may decide, if and when needed, to conduct foreign exchange interventions either on its own (unilateral interventions) or within the framework of co-ordinated intervention involving other central banks (concerted interventions). Interventions may also take place within the framework of the **exchange rate mechanism** (ERM II). The ERM II is an arrangement in which a fixed exchange rate is established between the euro and the national currency of each participant in the mechanism (see also Chapter 14).

6.3.2.3 Portfolio management

The ECB owns, manages and is responsible for the risk management of three portfolios: 1) the *foreign reserves portfolio*, that ensures that the ECB has sufficient liquidity to conduct its foreign exchange operations; 2) the *own funds portfolio*, that provides the ECB with a reserve to meet possible losses; and finally 3) the *pension fund portfolio*, that represents the assets invested by the ECB and its staff in the ECB's retirement plan. While trying to achieve the best possible portfolio returns the ECB strictly separates portfolio management activities from other ECB activities. The ECB is responsible for the monitoring and management of the financial risks incurred either directly or by the NCBs of the Eurosystem acting on behalf of the ECB.

6.3.2.4 Payment system

The ECB, together with the Eurosystem, aims to achieve a smooth and prudent operation of payment and settlement systems. This is considered essential for a sound currency and the conduct of monetary policy; for guaranteeing the effective functioning of financial markets; and to ensure stability of the banking and financial sectors.

More specifically, the Eurosystem fulfils its task by:

- providing payment and securities settlement facilities: the Eurosystem runs a settlement system for large-value payments in Euro (called TARGET, Trans-European Automated Real-time Gross settlement Express Transfer system). It

Box 6.6	The EU's Stability and Growth Pact

The EU's Stability and Growth Pact was formally adopted by resolution of the European Council in June 1997, and it focuses upon the strengthening of the surveillance and co-ordination of economic policies within EU Member States. A major purpose of these arrangements is to contribute to the credibility of the Eurozone's monetary policy in pursuit of price stability. Technically, Member States have committed themselves to achieving budgetary positions 'close to balance or in surplus' in the medium term. They are allowed to deal with normal cyclical fluctuations in their economies, but are expected to keep general government deficits to less than 3 per cent of gross domestic product. Within this framework, countries within the Eurozone are required to submit stability programmes to the EU Council and the European Commission, while EU Member States outside the Eurozone have to submit convergence programmes.

Since 1997 the French and German governments have regularly breached the terms of the Stability Pact leading to accusations from smaller EU countries that big economies are in some way politically favoured. The flouting of the public spending conditions eventually led to a revision of the rules. Heads of state and government agreed at an EU summit on 22–23 March 2005 to reform of the Stability and Growth Pact. Under the revised Stability and Growth Pact, Member States must still keep their public deficits under a 3 per cent deficit/GDP ratio and their debts under a 60 per cent debt/GDP ratio. However, the pact's rules have been made more 'flexible' across a range of areas. For example, Member States will avoid an excessive deficit procedure (EDP) if they experience any negative growth at all (previously –2 per cent), can draw on more 'relevant factors' to avoid an EDP and will have longer deadlines if they do move into a deficit position greater than the stipulated minimum. The European Central Bank has noted its concerns about the new arrangements, suggesting that they weaken fiscal discipline as illustrated in Figure 6.5.

Figure 6.5 ECB and the revised Stability and Growth Pact

PRESS RELEASE

21 March 2005 – Statement of the Governing Council on the ECOFIN Council's report on Improving the implementation of the Stability and Growth Pact.*

The Governing Council of the ECB is seriously concerned about the proposed changes to the Stability and Growth Pact. It must be avoided that changes in the corrective arm undermine confidence in the fiscal framework of the European Union and the sustainability of public finances in the euro area Member States. As regards the preventative arm of the Pact, the Governing Council also takes note of some proposed changes which are in line with its possible strengthening.

Sound fiscal policies and a monetary policy geared to price stability are fundamental for the success of Economic and Monetary Union. They are prerequisites for macroeconomic stability, growth and cohesion in the euro area. It is imperative that Member States, the European Commission and the Council of the European Union implement the revised framework in a rigorous and consistent manner conducive to prudent fiscal policies.

More than ever, in the present circumstances, it is essential that all parties concerned fulfil their respective responsibilities. The public and the markets can trust that the Governing Council remains firmly comitted to deliver on its mandate of maintaining price stability.

* The ECOFIN Council is one of the oldest configurations of the EU Council. It is composed of the Economics and Finance Ministers of the Member States, as well as Budget Ministers when budgetary issues are discussed. The ECOFIN Council covers EU policy in a number of areas including: economic policy coordination, economic surveilance, monitoring of Member States' budgetary policy and public finances, the Euro (legal, practical and international aspects), financial markets and the capital movements and economc relations with third countires.

Source: ECB (2005a).

also provides a mechanism for the cross-border use of collateral (CCBM, Correspondent Central Banking Model);[4]

- overseeing the Euro payment and settlement systems: the Eurosystem sets standards to ensure the soundness and efficiency of systems handling Euro transactions. It also assesses the continuous compliance of Euro payment and settlement systems with these standards;
- setting standards for securities clearing and settlement systems;
- ensuring an integrated regulatory and oversight framework for securities settlement systems (e.g., in the framework of the co-operation between the European System of Central Banks and the Committee of European Securities Regulators (ESCB–CESR));
- acting as a catalyst for change: the Eurosystem promotes efficiency in payment systems and the adaptation of the infrastructure to the needs of the single Euro payments area (SEPA). It also promotes an efficient securities market by encouraging the removal of barriers towards integration.

6.3.2.5 Other functions of the ECB

In addition to the core functions discussed above, the ECB carries out a number of other activities including:

- *banknotes*: the ECB has exclusive right to authorise issuance of banknotes;
- *statistics*: the ECB collects financial statistics in co-operation with the NCBs;
- *financial stability and supervision*: the Eurosystem acts in a way that contributes to the broad aim of financial stability; and
- *international and European co-operation*: the ECB ensure that co-operation with relevant EU and international institutions is maintained.

According to article 15 of its statute, to retain legitimacy as an independent central bank, the ECB must be accountable to democratic institutions and the general public. Accordingly, the ECB is required to publish quarterly reports on the activities of the Eurosystem as well as a consolidated Weekly Financial Statement. In addition, it has to produce an annual report on its activities and on the monetary policy of the previous and the current year. The annual report has to be addressed to the European Parliament, the European Council and the European Commission.

6.4 Federal Reserve Bank

The **Federal Reserve** (or the Fed), the central bank of the United States of America, was founded by Congress in 1913, with the signing of the Federal Reserve Act. It was created to provide the nation with '*a safer, more flexible, and more stable monetary and financial system*'.[5]

---

[4] The TARGET is used for the settlement of central bank operations, large-value Euro interbank transfers as well as other Euro payments. It provides real-time processing and settlement in central bank money. The CCBM ensures that all assets eligible for use either in monetary policy operations or to obtain intraday liquidity in TARGET are available to all its counterparties – regardless of where in the Euro area the assets or the counterparty are situated.

[5] See http://www.federalreserve.gov.

As the United States' central bank, the Federal Reserve derives its authority from the US Congress. It is considered an independent central bank because its decisions do not have to be ratified by the president or anyone else in government, it does not receive funding from Congress, and the terms of the members of the **Board of Governors** span multiple presidential and congressional terms. However, the Federal Reserve is subject to oversight by Congress, which periodically reviews its activities and can alter its responsibilities by statute. Also, the Federal Reserve must work within the framework of the overall objectives of economic and financial policy established by the government. Therefore, the Federal Reserve can be more accurately described as 'independent within the government'.

6.4.1 Organisational structure of the Fed

The Fed is a Federal System, composed of a central governmental agency, the Board of Governors, in Washington, DC, and 12 regional Federal Reserve Banks, located in major cities throughout the United States.[6] These components share responsibility for supervising and regulating certain financial institutions and activities; for providing banking services to depository institutions and to the federal government; and for ensuring that consumers receive adequate information and fair treatment in their business with the banking system.

A major element of the System is the **Federal Open Market Committee (FOMC)**, which is made up of the members of the Board of Governors, the president of the Federal Reserve Bank of New York, and presidents of four other Federal Reserve Banks, who serve on a rotating basis. The FOMC oversees open market operations, which is the main tool used by the Federal Reserve to influence money market conditions and the growth of money and credit.

The structure of the Federal Reserve System includes the following entities:

- Board of Governors
- Federal Reserve Banks
- Federal Open Market Committee
- Board of Directors
- Member Banks.

6.4.2 The Board of Governors

The Board of Governors of the Federal Reserve System was established as a federal government agency. The Board comprises seven members, appointed by the president and confirmed by the Senate to serve 14-year terms of office. The appointments are staggered so that one term expires on 31 January of each even-numbered year. To avoid political interference, governors may serve only one full term. The president designates, and the Senate confirms, two members of the Board to be chairman and vice-chairman, for four-year terms. Each of the 12 Federal Reserve Districts can select only one member of the Board of Governors. It is a duty of the President of the United States to ensure that there is a fair representation of regional interests and the interests of various sectors of the public.

---

[6] The 12 regional Federal Reserve Banks include: Federal Reserve Banks of Atlanta, Boston, Chicago, Cleveland, Dallas, Kansas City, Minneapolis, New York, Philadelphia, Richmond, St Louis and San Francisco. See 6.4.3 for more details.

The primary responsibility of the Board members is the formulation of monetary policy. The seven Board members constitute a majority of the 12-member FOMC, the group that makes the key decisions affecting the cost and availability of money and credit in the economy. The board sets reserve requirements and shares the responsibility with the Reserve Banks for discount rate policy. These two functions plus open market operations constitute the main monetary policy tools of the Federal Reserve System.

In addition to monetary policy responsibilities, the Federal Reserve Board has regulatory and supervisory responsibilities over banks that are members of the system, bank holding companies and international banking facilities[7] in the United States. (See Chapter 15 for more detail on regulation of the US banking system.) The Board also sets margin requirements, to prevent excess use of credit for purchasing or carrying securities. In addition, the Board plays a key role in assuring the smooth functioning and continued development of the nation's payments system.

The chairman of the Board advises the President of the United States on economic policy and may represent the United States in negotiation with other countries on economic matters. The current (2006) chairman of the Fed is Mr Ben Bernanke. Table 6.1 reports the previous chairmen since 1913.

6.4.3 The Federal Reserve Banks

Each of the 12 Federal Reserve Districts has a Federal Reserve Bank: Boston, New York, Philadelphia, Cleveland, Richmond, Atlanta, Chicago, St Louis, Minneapolis, Kansas City, Dallas, and San Francisco. Federal Reserve Banks operate under the general supervision of the Board of Governors in Washington. Each bank has a nine-member board of directors that oversees its operations. All reserve banks,

Table 6.1 **Chairmen of the Fed since 1913**

Chairmen	Dates of term
Charles S. Hamlin	Aug. 10, 1914–Aug. 9, 1916
W.P.G. Harding	Aug. 10, 1916–Aug. 9, 1922
Daniel R. Crissinger	May 1, 1923–Sept. 15, 1927
Roy A. Young	Oct. 4, 1927–Aug. 31, 1930
Eugene Meyer	Sept. 16, 1930–May 10, 1933
Eugene R. Black	May 19, 1933–Aug. 15, 1934
Marriner S. Eccles	Nov. 15, 1934–Jan. 31, 1948
Thomas B. McCabe	Apr. 15, 1948–Mar. 31, 1951
Wm. McC. Martin, Jr	Apr. 2, 1951–Jan. 31, 1970
Arthur F. Burns	Feb. 1, 1970-Jan. 31, 1978
G. William Miller	Mar. 8, 1978–Aug. 6, 1979
Paul A. Volcker	Aug. 6, 1979–Aug. 11, 1987
Alan Greenspan	Aug. 11, 1987–Jan. 31, 2006
Ben Bernanke	Feb. 1, 2006 – present

---

[7] International banking facilities (IBFs) enable depository institutions in the United States to offer deposit and loan services to foreign residents and institutions free of Federal Reserve System reserve requirements, as well as some state and local taxes on income. IBFs permit US banks to use their domestic US offices to offer foreign customers deposit and loan services which formerly could be provided competitively only from foreign offices.

except those in Boston and Philadelphia, have branches that help them carry out their work. There are 25 branches in all.

Five of the twelve presidents of the Federal Reserve Banks serve as members of the FOMC. The president of the Federal Reserve Bank of New York serves on a continuous basis; the other presidents serve one-year terms on a rotating basis. Each Federal Reserve Bank has a research staff to gather and analyse a wide range of economic data and to interpret conditions and developments in the economy to assist the FOMC in the formulation and implementation of monetary policy.

In terms of monetary policy, the boards of directors of the Federal Reserve Banks can initiate changes in the discount rate. Such changes must be approved by the Board of Governors.

6.4.4 The Federal Open Market Committee (FOMC)

The FOMC is composed of the seven members of the Board of Governors and five Reserve Bank presidents. Each year one member is elected to the committee by the boards of directors of Reserve Banks in each of the following groups: 1) Boston, Philadelphia and Richmond; 2) Cleveland and Chicago; 3) Atlanta, St Louis and Dallas; and 4) Minneapolis, Kansas City and San Francisco. The president of the New York Fed is a permanent voting member of the FOMC, and the presidents of the other Reserve Banks serve one-year terms as voting members on a rotation that is set by law.

By statute, the FOMC determines its own organisation; it elects its chairman and vice chairman and selects staff officers to serve on the committee. Traditionally, the Chairman of the Board of Governors is elected chairman and the president of the Federal Reserve Bank of New York is elected vice-chairman.

By law, the FOMC must meet at least four to eight times each year in Washington, DC. At each regularly scheduled meeting, the committee reviews economic and financial conditions and decides on the monetary policy to be carried out to meet its long-term goals of price stability and sustainable economic growth.

Before each meeting of the FOMC, written reports on past and prospective economic and financial developments are prepared and sent to committee members and to non-member Reserve Bank presidents. At the meeting itself, staff officers present oral reports on the current and prospective business situation, on conditions in financial markets, and on international financial developments. After these reports, the committee members and other Reserve Bank presidents turn to policy. Typically, each participant expresses his or her own views on the state of the economy and prospects for the future and on the appropriate direction for monetary policy. However, the monetary policy decisions are based on national, rather than local economic conditions. At the meeting, economic developments, as well as the economic forecasts and conditions in the banking system, foreign exchange markets, and financial markets are discussed. The committee must reach a consensus regarding the appropriate course for policy, which is incorporated in a directive to the Federal Reserve Bank of New York – the bank that executes transactions for the System Open Market Account. The directive sets forth the committee's objectives for long-run growth of certain key monetary and credit aggregates.

Open market operations as directed by the FOMC are the major tool used to influence the total amount of money and credit available in the economy. The

Federal Reserve attempts to provide enough reserves to encourage expansion of money and credit in keeping with the goals of price stability and sustainable growth in economic activity.

6.4.5   The Board of Directors

Reserve Bank boards of directors are divided into three classes of three persons each. Class A directors represent the member commercial banks in the district, and most are bankers. Class B and class C directors are selected to represent the public. Class A and class B directors are elected by member banks in the district, while class C directors are appointed by the System's Board of Governors in Washington. All directors serve three-year terms.

Directors cannot be members of Congress, and class B and class C directors cannot be officers, directors or employees of a bank. Because a Reserve Bank directorship is a form of public service, directors are also expected to avoid participation in political activities.

The responsibilities of directors are broad, ranging from the supervision of the Reserve Bank (assigned by the Federal Reserve Act) to making recommendations on monetary policy. Directors review their Reserve Bank's budget and expenditures. They are also responsible for the internal audit programme of the Bank.

The Federal Reserve Act also requires directors to set the bank's discount rate every two weeks, subject to approval by the Board of Governors in Washington. Directors bring to the Federal Reserve a regional perspective, an independent assessment of the business outlook, and judgement and advice on the credit conditions of the districts they represent.

6.4.6   The Member Banks

All national banks (i.e., banks chartered by the Office of the Comptroller) are required to be members of the Federal Reserve System. Banks chartered by states are not required to be members, but they can be if they so choose.[8] While many large state banks have become Fed members, most state banks have chosen not to join. Member banks must subscribe to stock in their regional Federal Reserve Bank in an amount equal to 3 per cent of their capital and surplus. They receive a 6 per cent annual dividend on their stock and may vote for class A and class B directors of the Reserve Bank. However, the stock does not carry with it the control and financial interest that is normal for the common stock of a for-profit organisation. It offers no opportunity for capital gain and may not be sold or pledged as collateral for loans. The stock is merely a legal obligation that goes along with membership.

---

[8] The US banking system is a 'dual banking system'. This refers to the fact that both state and federal governments issue bank charters (licences). The Office of the Comptroller of the Currency (OCC) charters national banks; the state banking departments charter state banks. As a consequence, in US banking 'National' or 'State' in a bank's name has nothing to do with where it operates; it refers to the kind of charter the bank has. The charter is an institution's primary regulator; the Comptroller of the Currency supervises approximately 3,191 national banks. State bank supervisors oversee about 7,524 commercial banks. See Chapter 15 for more details on bank licensing and regulation in the United States.

6.4.7 Functions of the Fed

Today the Federal Reserve's duties fall into four general areas: 1) conducting the nation's monetary policy; 2) supervising and regulating banking institutions and protecting the credit rights of consumers; 3) maintaining the stability of the financial system; and 4) providing certain financial services to the US government, the public, financial institutions and foreign official institutions.[9]

The Fed's mission is: '*to promote sustainable growth, high levels of employment, stability of prices*'. Typically, macroeconomic policy in the US (as in the UK and the Eurozone) emphasises economic policy packages where monetary policy is pre-dominant. This is because price stability is viewed as an essential pre-condition for achieving the main economic objective of high and stable levels of growth and employment.

6.4.7.1 Monetary policy

Monetary policy in the United States (as in the United Kingdom) was dominated by targeting monetary aggregates in the second half of the 1970s and the early 1980s. This was based on the view that if the authorities could target the growth of (some measure of) money supply in the economy it could contain inflationary pressures. In the United States for instance, targeted growth rates of various money measures were used (e.g., M1 – cash and notes + bank checking accounts and M2 – M1+ savings accounts and money market funds) with growth ranges being of the order of 3–6 per cent for the former and 4–7 per cent for the latter. In the United States, M3 (mainly reserves + bank deposits) is nowadays the most widely used broad measure of money. However, these are no longer used as major intermediate targets of monetary policy because since the mid-1980s the empirical relationship between monetary supply (aggregate) growth and inflation has been found to be weak at best.

To carry out monetary policy, the Federal Reserve employs three tools:

- open market operations;
- the discount rate;
- reserve requirements.

Open market operations refer to the purchases and/or sales of US Treasury and Federal Agency securities. These purchases and sales of US Treasury and Federal Agency securities largely determine the federal funds rate – the interest rate at which depository institutions lend balances at the Federal Reserve to other depository institutions overnight. The federal funds rate, in turn, affects monetary and financial conditions, which ultimately influence employment, output, and the overall level of prices. Decisions regarding open market operations are taken by the FOMC. The **discount rate** is the interest rate charged to commercial banks and other depository institutions on loans they receive from their regional Federal Reserve Bank's lending facility; the discount window. **Reserve requirements** are the amount of funds that a depository institution must hold in reserve against specified deposit liabilities. Depository institutions must hold reserves in the form of vault cash or deposits with Federal Reserve Banks. The Board of Governors of the Federal Reserve System is responsible for the discount rate and reserve requirements.

---

[9] Federal Reserve System (2005a).

Box 6.7   US Federal Reserve's interest rate target

Table 6.2 Intended federal funds rate; change and level, June 2004 to May 2005

Date	Change (basis points)		Level (per cent)
	Increase	Decrease	
2005			
May 3	25	–	3.00
March 22	25	–	2.75
February 2	25	–	2.50
2004			
December 14	25	–	2.25
November 10	25	–	2.00
September 21	25	–	1.75
August 10	25	–	1.50
June 30	25	–	1.25

Source: US Federal Reserve Bank (2005), http://www.federal reserve.gov/fomc/fundsrate.htm

During the 1980s, the focus gradually shifted toward attaining a specified level of the federal funds rate, a process that was largely complete by the end of the decade. Beginning in 1994, the FOMC began announcing changes in its policy stance, and in 1995 it began to explicitly state its target level for the federal funds rate. Since February 2000, the statement issued by the FOMC shortly after each of its meetings usually has also included the Committee's assessment of the risks to the attainment of its long-term goals of price stability and sustainable economic growth.

Since the early 1990s, the United States has targeted its federal funds rate as its primary tool of monetary policy. Box 6.7 briefly notes this main feature of US monetary policy.

6.4.7.2 Supervision and regulation

The Federal Reserve Board is responsible for implementing the Federal Reserve Act, which established the Federal Reserve System, and a number of other laws relating to a range of banking and financial activities. As a consequence, the Federal Reserve Board has regulation and supervision responsibilities over banks. This includes monitoring banks that are members of the system, international banking facilities in the United States, foreign activities of member banks, and the US activities of foreign-owned banks. The Fed also needs to ensure that banks act in the public's interest.

However, the Fed is only one of several government agencies that share responsibility for ensuring the safety and soundness of the US banking system.[10] (Chapter 15 discusses the role of the Fed and other agencies that regulate the US banking system.)

6.4.7.3 Financial stability

The Fed's goals with respect to supervision and regulation include promoting the safety and soundness of the banking system, fostering stability in financial markets, ensuring compliance with applicable laws and regulations, and encouraging banking institutions to responsibly meet the financial needs of their communities.

---

[10] The role of the Fed as supervisor and regulator was recently redefined under the Gramm-Leach-Bliley (GLB) Act in November 1999 (see http://banking.senate.gov/conf/). See Chapter 15 for more details.

6.4.7.4 Services to the US government

The Fed serves as a bank, not only for other banks, but also for the federal government. The government maintains accounts at the Fed, and makes its payments by writing cheques against these accounts or by transferring funds from the account electronically. The Fed helps the government borrow funds that it needs. It processes the vast majority of bids that individuals and institutions make to buy securities at the Treasury's weekly, monthly and quarterly auctions. The Fed also issues and redeems US Savings Bonds for the federal government.

Other services provided by the Reserve Banks include: clearing cheques drawn on the Treasury's account; acting as fiscal agents for the government (i.e, the Reserve Banks sell, service and redeem Treasury securities). Furthermore, the Fed is responsible for issuing (and withdrawing) currency and coins from circulation.

6.5 Performance of central banks: a comparison

One of the main functions of any central bank is to undertake monetary control operations in order to achieve its policy targets. Typically, these operations differ in relation to the monetary policy objectives they intend to achieve (see Chapter 5). These latter are determined by the government's overall macroeconomic policies and include: price stability, stable economic growth and high employment. In addition, these goals benefit from a low and stable interest rate environment. As noted earlier in this chapter, monetary authorities conduct open market operations or manipulate reserves in order to influence short-term rates. Moreover, central banks have different approaches to monetary policy. In the United States, for instance the authorities explicitly target short-term interest rates while in the United Kingdom and the Euroarea, central banks have adopted inflation targeting as a major policy tool.

Since the early 1990s the primary tool of monetary policy of the Fed has been the targeting of federal funds rate (see Box 6.7). In particular, by undertaking open-market operations the Fed affects the interest rate, that is, the rate charged by one depository institution on an overnight sale of immediately available funds (balances at the Federal Reserve) to another depository institution; the rate may vary from depository institution to depository institution and from day to day. We noted in this chapter that target federal funds rate is set by the FOMC. As shown in Table 6.3, the US economic policies have generally been successful in achieving a relatively good inflationary performance although the Fed does not target it explicitly as in the case of the Bank of England and the ECB.

In the United Kingdom the Bank of England focuses primarily on an inflation target. Table 6.3 shows that over the last six years the MPC has been relatively successful in achieving and maintaining a rate of inflation for the United Kingdom within the target band set for it by the government (currently (2005) 2 per cent p.a.). Nonetheless, the MPC's repo rate decisions have sometimes been criticised as a result of the adverse effects that interest rate changes have had for some parts of the economy, such as, for instance, the manufacturing sector, particularly in respect of its international trading position. In other words, while the monetary policy objective is achieved, some parts of the economy may suffer, if, for instance, an interest rate rise causes exchange rates to rise thus making exports more difficult.

Table 6.3 **Interest rates and inflation (targets and actual)**

	BOE			ECB			Fed operational target		
Year	Repo rate	Inflation		MROs: min bid rate	Inflation		Federal Reserves rate	Inflation	
	Actual[a]	Target	Actual	Actual[a]	Target	Actual	Actual	Target[f]	Actual
1998	7.25%	2.5%	1.6%	n.a.	n.a.	n.a.	5.44%	n.a.	1.6%
1999	6.00%	2.5%	1.3%	3.00%	<2%	1.1%	5.12%	n.a.	2.7%
2000	5.75%	2.5%	0.8%	3.00%	<2%	2.1%	5.64%	n.a.	3.4%
2001	6.00%	2.5%	1.2%	4.75%	<2%	2.3%	6.35%	n.a.	1.6%
2002	4.00%	2.5%	1.3%	3.25%	<2%	2.3%	1.48%	n.a.	2.4%
2003	4.00%	2.5%[b]	1.4%	2.75%	<2%[d]	2.1%	1.18%	n.a.	1.9%
2004	3.75%	2.0%	1.3%	2.00%	<2%	2.1%	1.38%	n.a.	3.3%
2005	4.75%	2.0%	1.9%[c]	2.00%	<2%	2.2%[e]	2.29%	n.a.	3.2%[g]

[a] January data.
[b] The change in the inflation target was formally decided by the Chancellor on 10 December 2003 (see http://www.hm-treasury.gov.uk/media//CD101/lettertogovofbofepbr03.pdf)
[c] January to July 2005 only.
[d] In 2003 the governing council clarified that the ECB aims at maintaining the inflation rate below but close to 2 per cent over the medium term.
[e] As at July 2005.
[f] The FED does not target a specific numerical reference value for inflation.
[g] Relative to July 2004.

From its inception until May 2003, the ECB pursued an inflation rate objective within the Eurozone of *less than* 2 per cent p.a. One of the drawbacks of this policy was that the use of a maximum target rate for inflation, instead of a target band or a minimum level (as operated by the Bank of England), could build in deflationary bias to policy decisions and may militate against discretionary easing of policy at appropriate times during the economic cycle. In May 2003 the ECB announced a loosening of its policy regime by indicating it would seek to maintain the rate of inflation *close* to 2 per cent p.a. over the medium term. However, the ECB's approach still differs substantially from that taken in the United Kingdom where the government specifies and may alter the inflation target band. In addition the Bank of England's MPC must publish minutes of meetings and reports providing insight into the decision-making process.

The ECB focuses on a broader range of intermediate targets including monetary aggregates. In particular one of the main pillars of the ECB's monetary policy strategy is the monitoring of the growth rate of M3, a broad monetary aggregate. The reported overshooting of this target, shown clearly in Figure 6.6, and the increased concern over the possible repercussions on the credibility of the Bank's monetary policy have most probably been a factor in the ECB's decision to announce that it would put less emphasis on the M3 money supply measure, and would look more towards indicators of the real Eurozone economy in setting its policy.

Another important criticism of the ECB refers to the implications of using a single set of interest rates for the Eurozone (the minimum bid rate for the main refinancing operations or MROs, see Table 6.3): for some countries, Germany probably being the best example, this has resulted in a relatively lower growth and

Figure 6.6 **EU area: M3 growth January 1999–July 2005**

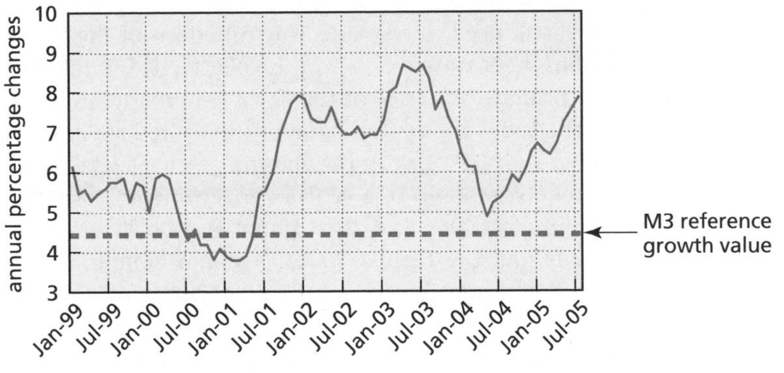

Source: ECB (2005).
http://stats.ecb.int/stats/download/bsi_m3contrib/bsi_m3contrib/bsi_m3contrib.pdf.

higher unemployment rates. Until necessary structural adjustments in Eurozone markets can be completed, particularly in respect of free-market competition and the flexibility of labour markets, it may be argued that it would be wise to allow appropriate accommodation in the one-size-fits-all monetary policy of the Eurozone. This is especially so given the importance of the German economy on the world stage.

It must also be recognised that monetary policy is only one (albeit important) part of the economic policy framework within the Eurozone. Of particular significance to the operation of monetary policy is the EU's *Stability and Growth Pact* (see Box 6.6). This pact was necessary because it would be inappropriate to allow individual Member States to pursue fiscal policies and public financing regimes that may conflict with the inflation objective, or which may cause the economic performance of member states to diverge.

6.6 Conclusions

The Bank of England is the central bank for the United Kingdom. It was established in 1694 and it is one of the world's oldest central banks. Its operational structure was reformed in 1997. The Bank of England Act (1998) set forth a series of changes, including the definition of responsibilities of the Bank, the FSA and HM Treasury. Following the Act, the Bank of England was given operational independence in setting interest rates. The monetary policy function of the Bank is carried out by the MPC. This is responsible for setting short-term interest rates. The main objectives of the Bank of England are: to maintain the integrity and value of the currency; to maintain the stability of the financial system; and to ensure the effectiveness of the UK financial services.

The ECB was established in 1998 and it is one of the world's youngest central banks. It is the central bank for all the countries that have adopted the single currency, the Euro. The ECB and the NCBs of all EU Member States, regardless of whether they have adopted the Euro or not, constitute the European System of

Central Banks or ESCB. The ECB and the NCBs of those countries that have adopted the Euro form the Eurosystem. As long as there are EU Member States that have not yet adopted the euro, this distinction between the Eurosystem and the ESCB will need to be made. The functions of the ECB (and of the ESCB) are specified in the Statute that is a protocol attached to the Treaty on the European Union. The primary objective of the ESCB is to maintain price stability.

The Fed is the central bank of the United States of America and was founded by Congress in 1913, with the signing of the Federal Reserve Act. The Fed is a Federal System, composed of a central, governmental agency, the Board of Governors, in Washington, DC, and 12 regional Federal Reserve Banks, located in major cities throughout the United States. A major component of the System is the FOMC, which is responsible for conducting open market operations. The Fed explicitly targets short-term interest rates as its major tool of monetary policy, whereas the Bank of England and the ECB place a greater emphasis on inflation-targeting.

Key terms		
Bank of England Act 1998		**Eurosystem**
Monetary Policy Committee (MPC)		**National Central Banks (NCBs)**
Financial Services Authority (FSA)		**Exchange rate mechanism**
Debt Management Office (DMO)		**Federal Reserve Bank (Fed)**
Memorandum of Understanding		**Board of Governors**
European Central Bank (ECB)		**Federal Open Market Committee (FOMC)**
European System of Central Banks (ESCB)		

Key reading		
Bank of England	http://www.bankofengland.co.uk
European Central Bank	http://www.ecb.int
Federal Reserve Bank	http://www.Federalreserve.gov

Revision questions and problems

1 What are the main functions and objectives of the Bank of England?

2 How does the Bank of England meet its objective of price stability?

3 Describe the relationship between the ECB and the NCBs of EU Member States.

4 What does the term *Eurosystem* refer to?

5 What are the core functions of the European Central Bank?

6 Describe the operational structure of the Federal Reserve Bank.

7 What is the role of the FOMC?

8 What are the core functions of the Federal Reserve Bank? How do they differ from those of the Bank of England and of the European Central Bank?

Appendix 6.1 The NCBs of the EU (the European System of Central Banks – ESCB)

Austria, Oesterreichische Nationalbank — http://www.oenb.at/

Belgium*, Banque Nationale de Belgique — http://www.bnb.be/

Cyprus, Central Bank of Cyprus — http://www.centralbank.gov.cy/

Czech Republic, Ceská Národní Banka — http://www.cnb.cz/

Denmark, Danmarks Nationalbank — http://www.nationalbanken.dk/

Estonia, Eesti Pank — http://www.bankofestonia.info/

Finland, Suomen Pankki — http://www.bof.fi/

France*, Banque de France — http://www.banque-france.fr/

Germany*, Deutsche Bundesbank — http://www.bundesbank.de/

Greece, Bank of Greece — http://www.bankofgreece.gr/

Hungary, Magyar Nemzeti Bank — http://www.mnb.hu/

Ireland, Central Bank of Ireland — http://www.centralbank.ie/

Italy*, Banca d'Italia — http://www.bancaditalia.it/

Latvia, Latvijas Banka — http://www.bank.lv/

Lithuania, Lietuvos Bankas — http://www.lbank.lt/

Luxembourg, Banque Centrale du Luxembourg — http://www.bcl.lu/

Malta, Central Bank of Malta — http://www.centralbankmalta.com/

Netherlands*, De Nederlandsche Bank — http://www.dnb.nl/

Poland, Narodowy Bank Polski — http://www.nbp.pl/

Portugal, Banco de Portugal — http://www.bportugal.pt/

Slovakia, Národná Banka Slovenska — http://www.nbs.sk/

Slovenia, Banka Slovenije — http://www.bsi.si/

Spain, Banco de España — http://www.bde.es/

Sweden*, Sveriges Riksbank — http://www.riksbank.se/

United Kingdom*, Bank of England — http://www.bankofengland.co.uk/

* means that the country is in the G10

Chapter 7

Bank regulation and supervision

Learning objectives

- To understand the rationale for financial regulation
- To appreciate different types of regulation
- To understand the limitation and costs of regulation
- To understand the causes for regulatory reform
- To introduce the regulation of the UK and EU financial sectors
- To understand bank capital regulation

7.1 Introduction

The regulation of financial markets in general and of banking institutions in particular is considered a controversial issue. The financial sector is one of the most heavily regulated sectors in the economy and banking is by far the most heavily regulated industry. In Chapter 1 we presented some of the reasons why banks are considered 'special'; outlined the existence of market imperfections (such as information asymmetries, moral hazard and adverse selection) and noted how the existence of banks can help minimise such problems. In this chapter we note the pivotal role played by banks in the economy to understand the rationale for regulation (Section 7.2). We will discuss the aims and objectives of regulation, the different types of regulation (Section 7.3) and the possible reasons behind regulatory failure (Section 7.4). Section 7.5 reviews the causes of regulatory reform. This chapter will also review the regulation of the UK banking and financial system (Section 7.6), with particular focus on the role of the Financial Services Authority (FSA), the UK single regulator. Many of the national rules and regulations that govern European banks stem from international policy initiatives, such as the Basle Capital Adequacy Accord (reviewed in Section 7.7), and EU regulation that is considered in Section 7.8.

Before we discuss the rationale for regulation it is useful to introduce various terms that are often used to describe the regulatory environment. **Regulation** relates to the setting of specific rules of behaviour that firms have to abide by – these may be set through legislation (laws) or be stipulated by the relevant regulatory agency (for instance, the Financial Services Authority in the UK). **Monitoring** of these regulations refers to the process whereby the relevant authority assesses financial firms to evaluate whether these rules are being obeyed. **Supervision** is a broader term used to refer to the general oversight of the behaviour of financial firms. In practice one should note that these terms are often used interchangeably in general discussion of the regulatory environment.

7.2 The rationale for regulation

Financial systems are prone to periods of instability. In recent years, a number of financial crises around the world (South-east Asia, Latin America and Russia) have brought about a large number of bank failures. Some argue that this suggests a case for more effective regulation and supervision. Others attribute many of these crises to the failure of regulation. Advocates of the so-called '*free banking*' argue that the financial sector would work better without regulation, supervision and central banking.[1] In the absence of government regulation, they argue, banks would have greater incentives to prevent failures.

However, the financial services industry is a politically sensitive one and largely relies on public confidence. Because of the nature of their activities (illiquid assets

---

[1] See section 5.5.2 for more discussion on free banking and note the works of Dowd (1996a,b); Benston and Kaufman (1996).

and short-term liabilities), banks are more prone to troubles than other firms. Further, because of the interconnectedness of banks, the failure of one institution can immediately affect others.

This is known as **bank contagion** and may lead to **bank runs**. Banking systems are vulnerable to **systemic risk**, which is the risk that problems in one bank will spread through the whole sector.

Bank runs occur when a large number of depositors, fearing that their bank is unsound and about to fail, try to withdraw their savings within a short period of time. A bank run starts when the public begins to suspect that a bank may become insolvent. This creates a problem because banks keep only a small fraction of deposits in cash; they lend out the majority of deposits to borrowers or use the funds to purchase other interest-bearing assets. When a bank is faced with a sudden increase in withdrawals, it needs to increase its liquidity to meet depositors' demands. Banks reserves may not be sufficient to cover the withdrawals and banks may be forced to sell their assets. Banks assets (loans) are highly illiquid in the absence of a secondary market and if banks have financial difficulties they may be forced to sell loans at a loss (known as 'fire-sale' prices in the United States) in order to obtain liquidity. However, excessive losses made on such loan sales can make the bank insolvent and bring about bank failure.

Bank loans are highly illiquid because of information asymmetries: it is very difficult for a potential buyer to evaluate customer-specific information on the basis of which the loan was agreed. The very nature of banks' contracts can turn an illiquidity problem (lack of short-term cash) into insolvency (where a bank is unable to meet its obligations – or to put this differently – when the value of its assets is less than its liabilities).

In summary, regulation is needed to ensure consumers' confidence in the financial sector. According to Llewellyn (1999) the main reasons for financial sector regulation are:

● to ensure systemic stability;
● to provide smaller, retail clients with protection; and
● to protect consumers against monopolistic exploitation.

Systemic stability is one of the main reasons for regulation, as the social costs of bank failure are greater than the private costs. The second concern is with consumer protection. In financial markets '*caveat emptor*' (a Latin phrase meaning 'Let the buyer beware') is not considered adequate, as financial contracts are often complex and opaque. The costs of acquiring information are high, particularly for small, retail customers. Consumer protection is a particularly sensitive issue if customers face the loss of their lifetime savings. Finally, regulation serves the purpose of protecting consumers against the abuse of monopoly power in product pricing.

7.3 Types of regulation

It is possible to identify 3 different types of regulation:

1) Systemic regulation;
2) Prudential regulation;
3) Conduct of business regulation.

7.3.1 Systemic regulation

Charles Goodhart *et al.* (1998) define systemic regulation as regulation concerned mainly with the safety and soundness of the financial system. Under this heading we refer to all public policy regulation designed to minimise the risk of bank runs that goes under the name of the **government safety net**. In particular, this safety net encompasses two main features – **deposit insurance** arrangements and the **lender-of-last-resort** function.

- *Deposit insurance* is a guarantee that all or part of the amount deposited by savers in a bank will be paid in the event that a bank fails. The guarantee may be either explicitly given in law or regulation, offered privately without government backing or may be inferred implicitly from the verbal promises and/or past actions of the authorities. In recent years, many nations have adopted or are considering a system of explicit or formal deposit insurance. In the United States, the Federal Deposit Insurance Corporation (FDIC) guarantees that depositors are paid in full for the first $100,000 they have deposited in the event of a bank failure.

  In the United Kingdom, new deposit protection arrangements were introduced in 2001. The body responsible for administering this new scheme is known as the Financial Services Compensation Scheme (FSCS), which was set up under the Financial Services and Markets Act 2000 (FSMA).[2] The FSCS covers business conducted by firms authorised by the Financial Services Authority (FSA). Payments under the scheme are limited to 100 per cent of the first £2,000 of a depositor's total deposits with the bank and 90 per cent of the next £33,000, resulting in a maximum payment of £31,700. Most depositors, including individuals and small firms, are covered.[3]

- *The lender-of-last-resort* (LOLR) function is one of the main functions of a central bank. The central bank, or other central institution, will provide funds to banks that are in financial difficulty and are not able to access any other credit channel. A more detailed discussion of the functions of central banks was presented in Chapter 5. Through the LOLR mechanism, the authorities can provide liquidity to the banking sector at times of crises.

7.3.2 Prudential and conduct of business regulation

Prudential regulation is mainly concerned with consumer protection. It relates to the monitoring and supervision of financial institutions, with particular attention paid to asset quality and capital adequacy. The case for prudential regulation is that consumers are not in a position to judge the safety and soundness of financial institutions due to imperfect consumer information and agency problems associated with the nature of the intermediation business. In the United Kingdom prudential regulation is undertaken by the FSA and aims to ensure that the firms it regulates are financially sound. This includes specifying standards covering risk management and other related requirements. Bank capital regulation is discussed in Section 7.8.

---

[2] The regulatory structure of the UK financial services is reviewed in Part 3.
[3] More information on the Financial Services Compensation Scheme (FSCS) can be found at http://www.fscs.org.uk/.

Conduct of business regulation focuses on how banks and other financial institutions conduct their business. This kind of regulation relates to information disclosure, fair business practices, competence, honesty and integrity of financial institutions and their employees. Overall, it focuses on establishing rules and guidelines to reduce the likelihood that:

- consumers receive bad advice (possible agency problem);
- supplying institutions become insolvent before contracts mature;
- contracts turn out to be different from what the customer was anticipating;
- fraud and misrepresentation takes place;
- employees of financial intermediaries and financial advisors act incompetently.

7.4 Limitations of regulation

So far, we have highlighted the case for financial regulation, which depends mainly on various market imperfections and failures (information asymmetries, agency problems, etc.), which, in the absence of regulation, would produce sub-optimal results and reduce consumer welfare. As a consequence, the purpose of regulation should be limited to correcting for identified market imperfections and failures. There are, however, a number of arguments against regulation.

Regulatory arrangements, in particular the 'safety net' arrangements create **moral hazard**. The concept of moral hazard was introduced in Chapter 1. Deposit insurance and the LOLR can cause people to be less careful than they would be other-wise. For example, with 100 per cent deposit insurance, depositors will not be concerned about the behaviour of their bank. Similarly, the belief that the LOLR will eventually bail out troubled banks may encourage institutions to take greater risks in lending. Box 7.1 illustrates these concepts. Other examples of the moral hazard caused by the government safety net are known as the **too big to fail** (TBTF) and the **too important to fail** (TITF) cases. Because the failure of a large (or strategically important) bank poses significant risks to other financial institutions and to the financial system as a whole, policymakers may respond by protecting bank creditors from all or some of the losses they otherwise would face. If managers of large (or important) banks believe that they will be bailed out by the authorities (with taxpayers' money) if they get into financial difficulty then this increases the moral hazard incentives for big banks, resulting in banks taking on even greater risks and expecting an eventual bail out.

Banks may also benefit from regulatory **forbearance**. Regulatory forbearance (or renegotiation) is an example of time inconsistency. Time inconsistency refers to the problem that it may not be optimal *ex-post* (after an event occurs) to implement regulations that were optimal *ex-ante* (before the event occurred). When financial intermediaries are in trouble, there may be pressures not to apply existing regulations, for example, to impose higher capital or liquidity requirements. This is because it could worsen the institution's problems. If the bank was allowed to fail, this could drain the deposit insurance fund. Furthermore, publicity surrounding a bank facing difficulties may worry the public; who may be induced to withdraw their savings, thereby aggravating the bank's problems (with a possible domino effect on other institutions leading to further bank failures). Also, there

Box 7.1   Moral hazard and government safety net arrangements

Financial regulation and supervision are needed because moral hazard can be associated with government safety net arrangements that are designed to protect the banking and financial system. For example, banks that face liquidity problems and cannot borrow from other banks in the market may approach the regulators to act as a 'lender-of-last-resort' in order to provide emergency liquidity assistance. This, in principle, seems a good thing as the authorities have a mechanism for providing liquidity to the banking system at times of crises. However, the moral hazard arises in that if banks all believe they have access to the 'lender-of-last-resort' they may be inclined to take on excessive risks knowing that in the event of trouble they will be bailed out by the authorities (in other words, the taxpayer, as these are public funds being used). To mitigate this moral hazard problem the authorities need to establish a regulatory framework that assures access to the lender-of-last-resort facility is by no means guaranteed for banks. Linked to this is the *Too Big Too Fail* argument whereby the largest banks are viewed as being too big to be allowed to fail and therefore they must have guaranteed access to the lender-of-last-resort – which could cause moral hazard problems. No financial regulatory authority will ever provide guaranteed access to the lender-of-last-resort financing, although history does tell us that (for systemic and other reasons) large banks are likely to be bailed out more than small banks. In years gone by when the Bank of England regulated the UK banking system they referred to the *too important to fail* view arguing that size by itself was not the relevant criteria for bailing out troubled banks – rather the significance or importance of banks in specific markets and the expected scale/impact of potential failure should be the main criteria in providing support. This was used as a justification for helping to save the troubled but small Johnson Matthey bank in 1984 as it played a key role in the London gold market. Similar moral hazard issues relate to the design of appropriate deposit insurance and other investment (and insurance) compensation schemes. As noted earlier, if deposit insurance is too generous it creates incentives for banks to take on more risk as they know their customers' deposits will be protected in the event of a bank failure. Similar arguments can be put forward for other compensation schemes. Financial regulations need to be designed to reduce such possible moral hazards occurring; it is important to note that regulation can never eliminate all information asymmetries, but it can (and should) be formulated in order to minimise the potential adverse effects of such market failures.

might be political costs associated with enforcing regulations and therefore an incentive to delay action. There are some benefits of forbearance. First, not publicising the bank's problems may help avoiding systemic risk caused by bank runs. In addition, the bank may be worth more as a 'going concern', that is, remaining in operation rather than going out of business and liquidating its assets. To stay operational, a bank must be able to generate enough resources. As we have seen, banks assets are highly illiquid and therefore their sale might not generate enough cash to satisfy creditors.

There are, however, costs associated with forbearance. First, it may cause moral hazard: forbearance in one case may lead to expectations of similar behaviour in future cases, causing other financial institutions to observe regulations less carefully. Furthermore, regulators and regulated firms may become locked into an ever-worsening spiral, resulting in a loss of public confidence in how banks and the financial system in general are being regulated.

Regulation can create problems of **agency capture**; that is the regulatory process can be 'captured' by producers (in this case by banks and other financial institutions) and used in their own interest rather than in the interests of consumers. For example, some have argued that the new Basle Capital Accord has had too much input from banking sector participants and large banks in particular. The new capital rules allow the largest banks to use their own internal models for assessing risk and capital adequacy positions – which are likely to lead to the biggest banks holding less capital for regulatory purposes. The fact that major banks have had a strong say in devising regulations that govern their own operations is a possible indicator of agency capture.

Regulation is a costly business and the **costs of compliance** with the regulatory process will be passed on to consumers, resulting in higher costs of financial services and possibly less intermediation business. In addition, regulatory costs may act as a barrier to entry in the market and this may consolidate monopoly positions. The notion of incremental compliance costs is set out in Alfon and Andrews (1999), p. 16 as follows:

> Compliance costs are the costs to firms and individuals of those activities required by regulators that would not have been undertaken in the absence of regulation. Thus the term 'compliance costs' as used here refers to the incremental costs of compliance caused by regulation, not to the total cost of activities that happen to contribute to regulatory compliance. Examples of compliance costs include the costs of any additional systems, training, management time and capital required by the regulator.

However, none of these criticisms is enough to reject financial regulation. Regulation is always about making judgements and considering trade-offs between costs and benefits. While it is important to recognise the limitations of regulation, a well-designed regulatory framework is necessary to ensure consumers' confidence in the financial sector.

Although there are costs involved, there is also evidence that consumers and other users demand appropriate regulation: public pressure to introduce regulations may derive from the view that market solutions to regulations do not provide users with the appropriate reassurance that they are being protected appropriately.

Table 7.1 **Bank regulation: key concepts**

Objectives	Reasons	Rationale	Costs
Sustain systemic stability	Key position of banks in the financial system	Market imperfections and failures	Moral hazard
Maintain the safety and soundness of financial institutions	Consumer demand	Potential systemic problems	Agency capture
Protect consumers		Monitoring of financial firms	Compliance costs Costs of entry/exit
		Ensuring consumers' confidence	Control over products/ activities/prices

7.5 Causes of regulatory reform

During recent years, the scope and complexity of financial regulation has tended to grow almost continually. This has been partially in response to public reaction to financial scandals and the consequent political pressures generated. Other factors that have had an impact on regulatory reform are the internationalisation and globalisation trends. The increased international activity of financial firms means that foreign institutions play an increasing role in many domestic financial sectors. Throughout the world financial liberalisation has provided a passport for banks to offer services cross-border. The increased presence of foreign financial firms raises issues relating to how they should be regulated. The main issue relates to who is ultimately responsible if a foreign bank faces difficulties in an overseas market – should it be the host or home country regulator? Generally, for large complex banks the host regulator will supervise foreign subsidiary activity but it is the home country that is ultimately responsible if the bank faces difficulties. In addition to the issue of regulatory responsibility, the internationalisation trend has also encouraged much greater debate about convergence of rules – in order to ensure that banks operate under similar regulations in different jurisdictions. In Europe, for instance, there is an ongoing debate under the EU Financial Services Action Plan (FSAP) concerning the most effective regulatory framework. It has been argued that minimal harmonisation (regulation based on minimum standards) allows for greater flexibility in implementing legislation and is likely to result in (or sustain) more uneven competitive playing fields than if one chooses maximum harmonisation. Harmonisation should always result in some form of convergence in national rules and at the same time should increase actual and potential competition (as well as the safety of the system) if it is to be effective. There is clear consensus that a strong commitment to on-going harmonisation of supervisory standards across the EU financial services industry is needed; many commentators recognise the need for greater co-operation between supervisory authorities and improved relations between supervisory authorities, market participants and consumers.

Another factor affecting regulatory reform – and closely linked to the internationalisation trend – is the globalisation phenomenon. The growth in international activities and trade of multinational corporations has increased the demand for services from financial institutions that operate cross-border and therefore financial firms continue to expand their international presence. This means that various financial firms operate globally (e.g., HSBC, Citibank, Goldman Sachs, Morgan Stanley). As a result, banks are increasingly exposed to risks originating from abroad, and risks to financial stability are less and less confined to national borders. This calls, at the minimum, for greater regulatory oversight and co-ordination between national regulators. Further, consolidation in the global banking industry has resulted in the emergence of financial conglomerates that conduct an extensive range of businesses with a group structure. In the EU, financial conglomeration was encouraged by the Second Banking Directive (1989) which enabled banks to operate as universal banks: that is to engage, directly or through subsidiaries, in other financial activities, such as financial instruments, insurance, factoring, leasing and investment banking. The formation of financial conglomerates is forcing regulators to re-think the way in which the financial sector should be supervised. Table 7.2 shows the range of financial business that banks are permitted to undertake in various countries. Note that Table 7.2 has not been updated

Table 7.2 Permissible banking activities and ownership in high income countries[a]

Country	Securities activities	Insurance activities	Real estate activities	Index of activities restrictiveness[b]	Bank ownership of non-financial firms	Non-financial firm ownership of banks	Overall restrictiveness[b]
Australia	Unrestricted	Permitted	Restricted	6	Permitted	Restricted	11
Belgium	Permitted	Permitted	Restricted	7	Permitted	Permitted	11
Canada	Unrestricted	Permitted	Unrestricted	4	Restricted	Restricted	10
Cyprus	Permitted	Permitted	Unrestricted	5	Restricted	Restricted	11
Denmark	Unrestricted	Permitted	Permitted	5	Restricted	Permitted	10
Finland	Unrestricted	Restricted	Unrestricted	5	Permitted	Unrestricted	8
France	Unrestricted	Permitted	Unrestricted	4	Permitted	Unrestricted	7
Germany	Unrestricted	Unrestricted	Unrestricted	3	Permitted	Unrestricted	6
Greece	Permitted	Restricted	Permitted	7	Permitted	Permitted	11
Israel	Permitted	Prohibited	Prohibited	10	Restricted	Permitted	15
Italy	Unrestricted	Permitted	Prohibited	7	Restricted	Restricted	13
Japan	Restricted	Prohibited	Restricted	10	Restricted	Restricted	16
Korea	Permitted	Permitted	Permitted	6	Restricted	Restricted	12
Luxembourg	Unrestricted	Permitted	Unrestricted	4	Permitted	Restricted	9
Netherlands	Unrestricted	Permitted	Unrestricted	4	Permitted	Unrestricted	7
N. Zealand	Unrestricted	Unrestricted	Unrestricted	3	Unrestricted	Unrestricted	5
Portugal	Unrestricted	Permitted	Restricted	6	Restricted	Unrestricted	10
Singapore	Unrestricted	Permitted	Restricted	6	Permitted	Permitted	10
Slovenia	Permitted	Permitted	Permitted	6	Restricted	Permitted	11
Spain	Unrestricted	Permitted	Restricted	6	Unrestricted	Permitted	9
Sweden	Unrestricted	Permitted	Restricted	6	Restricted	Unrestricted	10
Switzerland	Unrestricted	Unrestricted	Unrestricted	3	Permitted	Unrestricted	6
UK	Unrestricted	Permitted	Unrestricted	4	Unrestricted	Unrestricted	6
USA[c]	Restricted	Restricted	Restricted	9	Restricted	Restricted	15

Notes:
[a] Countries ranked from less to most restrictive.
[b] A higher number indicates greater restrictiveness.
[c] US data is pre-Gramm-Leach-Bliley Act (1999).

Securities: the ability of banks to engage in the business of securities underwriting, brokering, dealing, and all aspects of the mutual funds industry. *Insurance*: the ability of banks to engage in insurance underwriting and selling. *Real estate*: the ability of banks to engage in real estate investment, development and management.

Activities
Unrestricted = a full range of activities can be conducted in the bank (takes an index value of 1). *Permitted* = a full range of activities can be conducted, but some or all must be conducted in subsidiaries (takes an index value of 2). *Restricted* = less than a full range of activities can be conducted in the bank or subsidiaries (takes an index value of 3). *Prohibited* = the activity cannot be conducted in either the bank or subsidiaries (takes an index value of 4).

Mixing banking and commerce, bank ownership of non-financial firms
Unrestricted = a bank may own 100 per cent of the equity in a non-financial firm. *Permitted* = a bank may own 100 per cent of the equity in a non-financial firm, but ownership is limited based on a bank's equity capital. *Restricted* = a bank can only acquire less than 100 per cent of the equity in a non-financial firm. *Prohibited* = a bank cannot acquire any equity investment in a non-financial firm.

Mixing banking and commerce, non-financial firm ownership of banks
Unrestricted = a non-financial firm may own 100 per cent of the equity in a bank. *Permitted* = unrestricted, but need prior authorisation or approval. *Restricted* = limits are placed on ownership, such as a maximum percentage of a bank's capital or shares. *Prohibited* = no equity investment in a bank is allowed.

Source: Adapted from Barth, J.R., Caprio, G. and Nolle, D.E. (2004) 'Comparative International Comparisons of Banking', *Economic and Policy Analysis Working Paper*, 2004–01, Washington DC, Office of the Comptroller of the Currency, pp. 64–6.

to include developments in the United States and that since the passing of the Gramm-Leach-Bliley Act in 1999 banks, insurance companies, securities firms, and other financial institutions can operate under common ownership and offer their customers a complete range of financial services.

In addition to the aforementioned factors various other forces can have a marked impact on the regulatory environment. Major financial crises can have a big impact on regulatory changes, mainly because the occurrence of a crisis is an indication that regulation in place prior to the difficulties was not sufficient.

Another factor that can change regulations is **financial innovation**. As new financial products and services emerge and gain in market significance, there are often calls for new regulation – for instance the US Federal Reserve in early 2005 called for greater regulation of **hedge funds** (which are private investment funds that trade and invest in various assets such as securities, commodities, currency and derivatives on behalf of their clients) due to their rapid growth and potentially destabilising activity. Similar examples can be given regarding the regulation of derivatives activity and other financial instruments. One of the reasons financial innovations tend to attract regulatory attention is that often the innovations are due to regulatory avoidance. In other words, financial firms and markets create new products not only to meet new demands but also to circumvent regulations. For example, the growth of off-balance sheet activities (derivatives trading, securities underwriting, foreign exchange trading, and so on) during the first half of the 1980s can be explained by the fact that this business was not subject to capital regulations in contrast to on-balance sheet business. Similarly, the flow of US dollars to the United Kingdom during the 1960s and the start of the dollar Eurobond market has been explained mainly because restrictive regulations in the United States (reserve requirements, limits on deposit rates – Regulation Q, and other limits on United States domestic bond issues) that encouraged dollars to flow to London and borrowers to raise dollar debt finance by issuing Eurobonds. Firms innovate to get around regulations and the regulators are always one step behind the market – this is known as the *regulatory dialectic*.

7.6 Financial regulation in the United Kingdom

The regulatory environment in the UK banking and financial services industry has changed dramatically since the mid-1980s. In general, new legislation has covered three main areas. First, a range of regulatory changes have been sought to reduce demarcation lines between different types of financial service firms (especially between banks and building societies) as well as commercial and investment banking business. Second, the UK has also implemented various pieces of EU legislation into domestic banking law facilitating the introduction of the single banking licence and harmonising prudential regulation for both commercial banks and investment firms. Finally, the most recent legislation laid down in the Financial Services and Markets Act 2001 has been put in place to transfer regulatory responsibility for the whole financial system to a 'super-regulator' – the Financial Services Authority – in the light of the Labour government's decision to make the Bank of England independent for monetary policy purposes. The major regulatory developments as well as other significant events are shown in Table 7.3.

The United Kingdom's current regulatory framework has been shaped by three main changes, following the election of the Labour government in 1997. The first was the creation of a single regulatory authority, the Financial Services Authority (FSA). The second was the granting of independence to the Bank of England in the conduct of monetary policy in the new Bank of England Act. Finally, the Financial Services and Markets Act (FSMA) came into force on 1 December 2001, making substantial changes to the regulatory structure.

Table 7.3 Major changes in the UK regulatory environment 1986–2006

Date	Regulatory event	Effects on banks/building societies
1986	**Big Bang:** London Stock Exchange abolishes fixed minimum commissions and single capacity trading.	Commercial banks can purchase stockbroking firms.
1986	**Building Societies Act** (came into effect in January 1997): Increased potential for commercial lending, by allowing building societies to provide other services relating to house purchase and finance. Provisions made for building societies to convert from mutual to corporate status. Limits imposed on wholesale funding. Building societies are not able to obtain more than 20 per cent of their funding from money market sources (although this could be raised to 40 per cent by statutory instrument). Building Societies Commission created to supervise building societies.	Lending limits: Class 1 lending 90% of assets. Class 2 and 3 combined 10%. Class 3 lending, 5% of assets. Class 1: advances secured on first mortgage to owner-occupiers of residential property. Class 2: non-class 1, wholly secured loans. Class 3: unsecured loans, interests in estate agencies, broking and other subsidiary activities.
1987	**1987 Banking Act**	Banking Act strengthened the Bank of England's regulatory powers. New legislation created a single category of authorisation, requiring institutions to be able to satisfy 'fit and proper' tests. The deposit protection fund was increased to protect 75% of retail deposits up to a maximum of £20,000.
January 1988	**Building societies' wholesale funding limit:** The wholesale funding limit was raised to its maximum ceiling of 40%. The unsecured lending limit per capita also increased, from £5,000 to £10,000.	Some societies had difficulties competing in the mortgage market with the 20% limit. This problem was overcome by increasing the limit to 40%.
1989	**EU Second Banking Co-ordination Directive:** Council of European Communities adopted 2-BCD.	Main effect of the 2-BCD was to give a passport to a bank authorised in one Member State to open a branch/do business in another Member State without further authorisation.
1990–93	**Building society lending limits:** Over the period 1990–93, limits on Class 2 and Class 3 lending combined increased from 10 to 17.5 to 20 to 25%. Over the period 1990–93, limits on Class 3 lending increased from 5 to 7.5 to 10 to 15%.	Building societies able to take on more unsecured lending.
1992	**EU Second Consolidated Supervision Directive** (implemented in 1993): Replaces the Consolidated Supervision Directive of 1983.	Extends the range of institutions subject to requirement of consolidated supervision and extends the range of activities covered by consolidated supervision

Table 7.3 **Continued**

Date	Regulatory event	Effects on banks/building societies
1993	**Large exposures:** Implementation in the UK of the EU Directive on the monitoring and control of large exposures of credit institutions.	
April 1995	**EU Capital Adequacy Directive (CAD)** introduced: Amended in December 1995.	Sets minimum capital requirements for market risks in the trading books of banks and investment firms.
July 1995	**Deposit protection scheme:** The Credit Institutions (Protection of Depositors) Regulations amended in the UK Deposit Protection Scheme to meet the requirements of the EU Deposit Guarantee Schemes Directives.	The main change to the level and scope of protection provided was an increase in the maximum level of protection for an individual depositor from 75% of £20,000 to 90% of £20,000 (or ECU 22,222 if higher). This brought the scheme into line with the Building Societies Investor Protection Scheme.
1996	Introduction of **gilt repo market.**	
1996	**Real Time Gross Settlement** (RTGS) (a system for large-value funds transfers) went live.	
1996	**Investment Services Directive** introduced	Purpose was to provide a single European 'passport' to investment firms and make changes in access to regulated markets.
1996	**Sterling Liquidity:** New system for measuring sterling liquidity was introduced for the large UK banks.	Prior to this, most banks in the UK were supervised on the 'mismatch' approach, whereby assets and liabilities are allocated on the maturity ladder and limits are set on the size of the mismatch in various time bands. This approach was less suitable for very large banks whose balance sheets were characterised by highly diversified retail deposit bases. For large banks it is more suitable to hold an adequate stock of liquid assets.
1996	**CAD-2:** Amendment to the Capital Adequacy Directive – due to be implemented end 1998 in the UK.	Provision made for banks to use a measurement system for market risks similar to that in CAD, but also to use their own internal Value-at-Risk (VaR) models as the determinant of supervisory capital for market risks (including commodities).
1997	**Chancellor announces Bank of England independence:** Supervisory responsibilities transferred to the Financial Services Authority.	
1997	**Building Societies Act**	Extends building societies' powers to compete with the banks.
1998	**Bank of England Act**	Legally establishes monetary policy independence for the Bank of England.
February 2000	**Cruickshank Report** into Competition in Banking	Recommends reform of the payments system through the establishment of a new licensing/ regulatory body to be known as PayCom. Refers bank services to the SMEs (small and medium-sized enterprises) sector to the Competition Commission under a complex monopoly reference.

▶

Table 7.3 Continued

Date	Regulatory event	Effects on banks/building societies
2001	**UK Financial Services and Markets Act (FSMA)**	On 1 December 2001 the FSMA replaced not only the Financial Services Act 1986 but also the Insurance Companies Act 1982 and the Banking Act 1987. The FSMA consolidated and substantially replaced the law on financial services regulation in the UK.
		The Financial Services Authority (FSA) assumed the responsibilities of nine former regulators (Bank of England Supervision & Surveillance Division, Insurance Directorate of DTI, Lloyd's of London, Building Societies Commission, Friendly Societies Commission, Register of Friendly Societies, Securities & Futures Authority, Personal Investment Authority and the Investment Management Regulatory Organisation) to create what is known as a 'super-regulator.'
		The FSA has also taken over the role as the UK Listing Authority from the Stock Exchange. In 2005 the FSA became the regulator of mortgage lending and the general insurance regulator. The FSA has power under the Unfair Terms in Consumer Contracts Act, regulates Lloyd's Insurance market, and has taken over from the Treasury in dealing with recognised overseas investment exchanges.
2002	**UK Competition Commission Report** into the Supply of Banking Services by Clearing Banks to small and medium-sized Enterprises (SMEs). (This followed on from the recommendations of the Cruickshank Inquiry in 2000.)	The report recommended a number of measures to apply to all the eight main clearing groups to reduce barriers to entry and expansion in the SME banking area. Primary among these were measures to ensure fast error-free switching of accounts regarded as crucial to a more competitive market. In addition, it was recommended that measures should be taken to limit bundling of services, improve information and transparency and to examine the scope for sharing of branches.
		The report also concluded that the four largest clearing groups – Barclays, HSBC, Lloyds TSB and RBSG – were charging excessive prices (including interest forgone on non-interest-bearing current accounts) and therefore making excessive profits, in England and Wales, of about £725 million a year over the last three years with adverse effects on SMEs or their customers. For the most part, the report found no such excessive prices in Scotland or Northern Ireland. The commission recommended that the four largest clearing groups be required to pay interest on current accounts in England and Wales at Bank of England base rate less 2.5%. The four largest clearing groups should be allowed alternatively to offer SMEs accounts that are free of money transmission charges, as applies in the personal sector; or to offer SMEs a choice between the two options.

Table 7.3 **Continued**

Date	Regulatory event	Effects on banks/building societies
1999–2005	**EU Financial Services Action Plan (FSAP)**	In May 1999 the European Commission initiated the Financial Services Action Plan (FSAP). This sets down a range of regulatory actions for the period 1999–2005 aimed at creating a single market for financial services.
		Regulations agreed at the EC level have to be implemented into the UK (and other EU) countries' regulatory frameworks.
		The FSAP has been established so that the European financial system will be capable of fully benefiting from the advantages that the introduction of the Euro offers in addition to guaranteeing the stability and competitiveness of the financial sector.
		The decision to move to a common system for financial reporting for EU-listed companies has been one of the boldest and most significant steps under the FSAP. For the first time, European investors will be able to compare 'like with like' when reading annual accounts.
		In the UK, companies listed on the stock exchange have had to provide financial reports compiled using international accounting standard since January 2005.
		The European Commission has issued a directive (in 2005) stipulating how Basle II should be applied to EU member state banks.
		Other FSAP initiatives relate to improved corporate governance and company law throughout the EU.[1]
1999–2006	**Basle II Capital Adequacy Accord**	On 3 June, 1999, the Basle Committee on Banking Supervision formally launched proposals for a new capital adequacy framework (Basle II). The original 1988 Accord established an international standard around a capital ratio of 8%.
		The new accord's main aim is to introduce a more comprehensive and risk-sensitive treatment of banking risks to ensure that regulatory capital bears a closer relationship to credit and other risks.[2]

Notes:
[1] For a detailed overview of the 42 FSAP initiatives see http://europa.eu.int/comm/internal_market/en/finances/actionplan/index.htm.
[2] See the Bank for International Settlements website for more information on Basle II, http://www.bis.org/publ/bcbsca.htm.

Source: Adapted from Bowen, A., Hogarth, G. and Pain, D. (1998), 'The recent evolution of the UK banking industry and some implications for financial stability', Appendix 1 pp.. 293–4, in *The Monetary and Regulatory Implications of Changes in the Banking Industry*, BIS Conference Papers, Vol. 7. March 1999, pp. 251–94, and authors' own updates.

The regulation of the UK financial sector has also been influenced by EU banking and investment directives. More details on EU regulation can be found in Chapter 13.

7.6.1 The UK Financial Services Authority (FSA)

The FSA is an independent non-governmental body, it is a limited company financed by levies on the industry. The FSA is accountable to Treasury ministers and to Parliament. The overall FSA policy is set out by the board, which consist of the chairman, three executive directors and eleven non-executive directors, all appointed by the Treasury. The FSA exercises its statutory powers under the Financial Services and Markets Act (FSMA). The FSMA assign the FSA four main objectives:[4]

- to maintain confidence in the UK financial system;
- to promote public understanding of the financial system;
- to secure an appropriate degree of protection for consumers while recognising their own responsibilities (the *caveat emptor* clause);
- to reduce the scope for financial crime.

The FSA takes a radically different approach to regulation from that of its predecessors, its goal being 'to maintain efficient, orderly and clean financial markets and help retail consumers achieve a fair deal'. This new approach is founded on a risk-based approach to the regulation of all financial business that integrates and simplifies the different approaches adopted by the predecessor regulators.

The FSA has taken on a series of new responsibilities not previously covered by regulatory organisations. These regulatory responsibilities relate to:

- **Lloyd's insurance market.** The FSA has responsibility for regulating the Lloyd's insurance market. (Lloyd's is the world's leading specialist insurance market.[5])
- **The code of market conduct.** This is part of the new regime for tackling market abuse.
- **Unfair terms in consumer contracts.** The FSA has powers to take action to address terms in financial services consumer contracts that are unfair.
- **Recognised overseas investment exchanges.** The FSA has taken over from the Treasury responsibility for applications from, and supervision of, recognised overseas investment exchanges (ROIEs) and recognised overseas clearing houses (ROCHs).[6]
- **Regulation of certain aspects of mortgage lending.** Mortgage lenders will have to be authorised by the FSA and so have to meet the threshold conditions set out in the FSMA. Many lenders are already authorised as banks or building societies. The FSA assumed its powers to regulate mortgages with effect from 31 October 2004, when its Mortgage Conduct of Business (MCOB) rules came into effect.

---

[4] For further detail, see 'Introduction to the Financial Services Authority' http://www.fsa.gov.uk/pubs/other/fsa_intro.pdf.

[5] Lloyd's is not an insurance company but a society of members, both corporate and individual, who underwrite in syndicates on whose behalf professional underwriters accept risk. Supporting capital is provided by investment institutions, specialist investors, international insurance companies and individuals.

[6] For overseas investment exchanges (OIEs) and overseas clearing houses (OCHs) recognition confers them an exemption from the need to be authorised to carry on regulated activities in the United Kingdom. In order to be recognised, OIEs and OCHs must comply with the recognition requirements laid down in the Financial Services and Markets Act 2000 (Recognition Requirements for Investment Exchanges and Clearing Houses) Regulations 2001.

Figure 7.1 **Main responsibilities of the FSA**

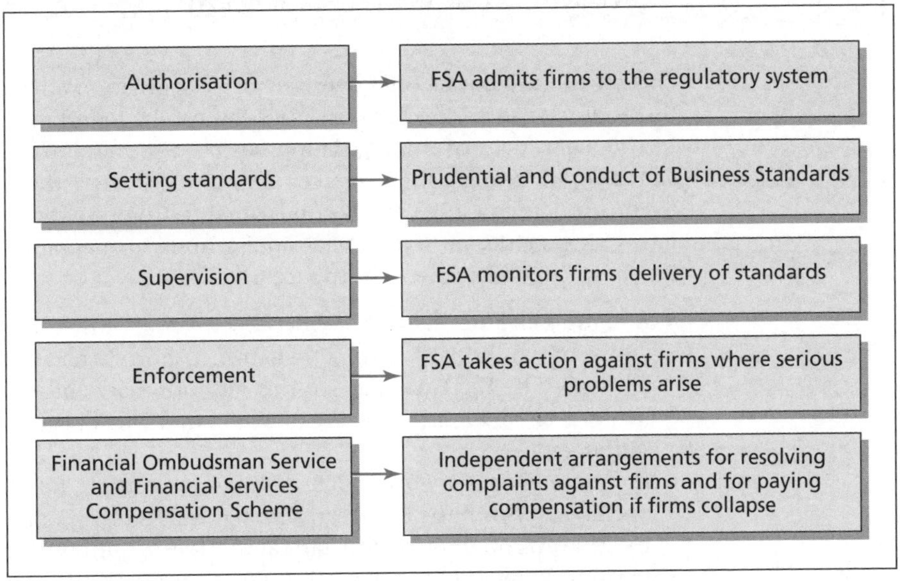

Authorisation	→	FSA admits firms to the regulatory system
Setting standards	→	Prudential and Conduct of Business Standards
Supervision	→	FSA monitors firms delivery of standards
Enforcement	→	FSA takes action against firms where serious problems arise
Financial Ombudsman Service and Financial Services Compensation Scheme	→	Independent arrangements for resolving complaints against firms and for paying compensation if firms collapse

Source: Adapted from 'Introduction to the Financial Services Authority' http://fsa.gov.uk/pubs/other/fsa_intro.pdf.

● **Supervision of credit unions.** Under the new regulatory framework (which came into effect in July 2002), credit union members will benefit from similar consumer protection arrangements as exist for bank and building society customers (participation in the Financial Ombudsman Scheme and the Financial Services Compensation Scheme). This will make credit unions more attractive to consumers.

When introduced in 1997, the single regulator for the whole of the UK financial industry was a radical new concept. Since then, countries like Japan, Korea, Germany, Sweden, the Netherlands and others have followed the unified model. The main arguments in favour of the creation of a single 'super-regulator' for the financial sector are as follows:

● the blurring of distinctions between services offered by different institutions;
● the increasing presence of financial conglomerates; and
● the possibility of exploiting economies of scale in regulation and monitoring.

Critics, on the other hand, question whether a single regulator can balance the conflicting demands of prudential and conduct of business regulation. They also fear that central banks and regulatory authorities might fail to co-operate closely enough over systemic threats. Finally, they point to the cost of excessive legislation.

Although it is relatively early to assess fully the success of single regulators, preliminary reports from the UK FSA are encouraging. However, world-wide experience is mixed. As pointed out by Barth, Caprio and Levine (2001), a crucial aspect in the success of the new regulatory structure is the political environment in which the 'super-regulator' exists and the level of independence it commands. Whereas the unified supervision model has a lot to offer in developed countries; in the developing world, where financial markets are still dominated by banks, depriving central banks of their supervisory powers may not be conducive to stability.

7.7 EU financial sector legislation

This section provides a brief overview of EU legislation affecting the banking and financial services sector. Further discussion can be found in Chapter 13.

The main focus of this legislation has been to harmonise rules and regulation aimed at promoting a single market in financial services throughout the European Union. In January 1993 the Second Banking Co-ordination Directive came into force. This legislation had crucial implications for banking activities within the European Union because it introduced:

- A *single European banking license* which ensures that EU-incorporated banks which are authorised within their own country's regulations (e.g., UK banks authorised by the Financial Services Authority) are automatically recognised as banks in any part of the European Union by virtue of their home country recognition; and
- *Home country supervisors* which are now responsible for the supervision of all operations within the European Union of banks incorporated in the home country. However, the local monetary authorities retain exclusive responsibility for measures imposed upon banks in respect of monetary policy. In addition, host countries have primary responsibility for the supervision of liquidity and risk.

Consequently, a bank that is authorised within the United Kingdom by the Financial Services Authority is now able to set up branches in any other EU Member State. Also, it is allowed to provide a wide range of cross-border banking services without the need for separate authorisation by the authorities of the host country.

Clearly, it is necessary for *harmonised* banking authorisation regulations to exist in the various EU countries if there is to be mutual recognition of each other's banks. Therefore, the Second Banking Co-ordination Directive sets out:

- Minimum levels of capital required before authorisation can be granted.
- Supervisory requirements in relation to major shareholders and banks' participation in the non-banking sector.
- Accounting and internal control requirements.

In December 1990, the Bank of England implemented the *Solvency Ratio Directive* (relating to credit risk and capital ratios) and the *Own Funds Directive* (defining capital for supervisory purposes). On 1 January 1996 the EU *Capital Adequacy Directive* became effective, setting out minimum capital requirements for market risks in the trading books of banks and investment firms. The Financial Services Authority has now implemented an up-dated version of this directive, which is compatible with the amendments to the *Basle Accord*, implemented at the same time.

In addition to the abovementioned directives, which are of direct relevance to banking activities, there are several other directives relevant to the broader context of banks' business operations. Examples are the:

- *Capital Liberalisation Directive* – aims to make illegal the imposition of exchange controls on movements of capital within the European Union.
- *Admissions Directive* – harmonises requirements for a company to have its shares listed on any EU Stock Exchange.
- *UCITS Directive* (Undertaking for Collective Investment in Transferable Securities) – relates to investments such as mutual funds (in the United

Kingdom open-ended mutual funds are known as unit trusts, whereas closed-end funds are known as investment trusts).

- *Investment Services Directive*, which provides a single EU 'passport' for investment firms. Authorised firms in each EU country are given appropriate access to the markets of other EU countries, upon the basis of mutual recognition of authorisation. *Conglomerates Directive* – harmonises rules and regulations for the supervision of financial conglomerates (typically firms that combine banking, insurance, pensions, securities and other financial activities).
- *Pensions Directive* – harmonises rules and regulations for the supervision of pensions business.

Other EU legislation adopted, either fully implemented or being implemented in the United Kingdom (at the time of writing in 2005) includes directives on: company prospectuses (relating to share issues); treatment of collateral in wholesale financial transactions; insurance mediation services; distance marketing and on-market abuse (insider trading and such like). Legislation that is currently being finalised includes: the Investment Services Directive (ISD) which sets the legislative framework for investment firms and securities markets in the EU, providing for a single passport for investment services; Transparency Directive aimed at reducing informational asymmetries in capital markets; Solvency 2 aimed at introducing harmonised solvency rules for insurance firms; and directives on cross-border payments and re-insurance business.

A recent major EU initiative has been its Financial Services Action Plan. The plan was endorsed by the European Council in Lisbon in March 2000, and set out 42 measures that were planned to be adopted by 2005 with the objective of promoting a single market in EU financial services.[7] The ultimate aim is to promote a more competitive and dynamic financial services industry with better regulation and this will feed through into enhanced economic growth. Consumers of financial products should obtain lower prices, and producers of such services will benefit from lower costs.

A further challenge will arise with the implementation of the so called Lamfalussy Procedure, which is briefly explained in Box 7.2.

Box 7.2   The Lamfalussy procedure

In July 2000 the French Presidency of the EU initiated the appointment of a Committee of Wise Men chaired by Alexandre Lamfalussy, with the task of drafting proposals for improving the effectiveness of the EU's securities market regulatory process. In February 2001, the Wise Men's report proposed a new four-level legislative process, where significant powers are delegated to implementing committees. The procedure, now known as the Lamfalussy procedure, aims to simplify and speed up the complex and lengthy regular EU legislative process by means of a four-level approach. It was extended to the entire EU financial sector in December 2002.

▶

---

[7] See Appendix 13.1 for details of all the 42 measures set-out in the Financial Services Action Plan.

According to the Lamfalussy procedure, the EU institutions adopt framework legislation under the auspices of the Commission (*level one*). The Commission then prepares the detailed technical implementing measures with the help of four specialist committees (*level two*). These are the European Banking Committee (EBC), the European Securities Committee (ESC), the European Insurance and Occupational Pensions Committee (EIOPC) and the Financial Conglomerates Committee (FCC) for supervisory issues relating to cross-sector groups. They decide on implementing measures put forward by the Commission. In developing the implementing measures, the Commission is again advised by committees of experts at the *third level* of the Lamfalussy procedure. These are the *Committee of European Banking Supervisors (CEBS)*, the Committee of European Securities Regulators (CESR) and the Committee of European Insurance and Occupational Pensions Supervisors (CEIOPS). The Banking Supervision committee also includes representatives from the national central banks. Apart from

Figure 7.2 The Lamfalussy Procedure

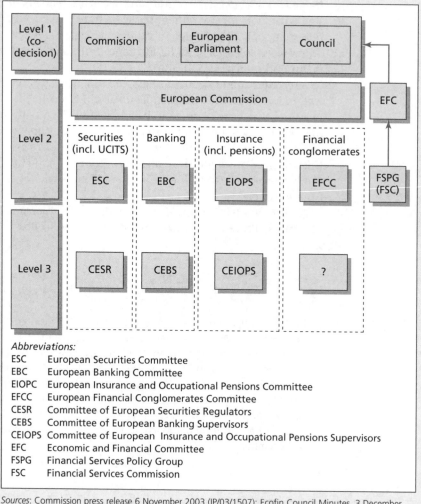

Abbreviations:
ESC   European Securities Committee
EBC   European Banking Committee
EIOPC   European Insurance and Occupational Pensions Committee
EFCC   European Financial Conglomerates Committee
CESR   Committee of European Securities Regulators
CEBS   Committee of European Banking Supervisors
CEIOPS Committee of European Insurance and Occupational Pensions Supervisors
EFC   Economic and Financial Committee
FSPG   Financial Services Policy Group
FSC   Financial Services Commission

Sources: Commission press release 6 November 2003 (IP/03/1507); Ecofin Council Minutes, 3 December 2002, 14368/02.

advising and assisting the Commission in the development of technical imple-menting measures, the committees of experts also deal with the exchange of supervisory information, the consistent implementation of European legal acts and the harmonisation of supervisory practices in the European market for finan-cial services. At the *final level*, the Commission – in close co-operation with the member states, the regulatory authorities involved in level three and the private sector – checks that Community law is applied consistently. The Lamfalussy proce-dure is illustrated in Figure 7.2.

7.8 Bank capital regulation

The role of capital in the financial sector, and for banks in particular, is a central element of regulation. A bank's capital may be defined as the value of its net assets (i.e., total assets minus total liabilities). In practice, this capital is the sum of the bank's paid-up share capital and its accumulated capital reserves. A bank's capital is vital for the protection of its depositors, and hence for the maintenance of gen-eral confidence in its operations, and the underpinning of its longer-term stability and growth.

The role of capital in banking can be illustrated by a simple balance sheet dia-gram as shown below where Bank Greedy has assets of £55 billion and £5 billion of capital. The bank has £54 billion in loans and £50 billion held in deposits.

A) Bank Greedy balance sheet

Liabilities (£)		Assets (£)	
Capital	5 billion	Cash and liquid assets	1 billion
Deposits	50 billion	Loans	54 billion
Total	55 billion	Total	55 billion

Now let us assume that the bank has made some risky loans and £4 billion-worth of loans go bad. The bank believes they will never be repaid (the bank cannot recover these loans). Bank Greedy has to take a 'hit' and the losses can be borne by the capital cushion. As shown below in B) assets shrink by £4 billion and capital falls to £1 billion.

B) Bank Greedy balance sheet after £4 billion loans go bad

Liabilities (£)		Assets (£)	
Capital	1 billion	Cash and liquid assets	1 billion
Deposits	50 billion	Loans	50 billion
Total	51 billion	Total	51 billion

In this case Bank Greedy can bear the loss of £4 billion as it has sufficient capital to cover these losses. Note that we assume that cash and liquid assets remain at £1 billion.

If, however, the losses exceed £5 billion then Bank Greedy does not have enough capital to cover these losses and it cannot meet depositor obligations. See what happens if instead of a £4 billion loss Bank Greedy has £7 billion loans go bad. This is shown in C:

C) Bank Greedy balance sheet after £7 billion loans go bad

Liabilities (£)		Assets (£)	
Capital	0 billion	Cash and liquid assets	1 billion
Deposits	48 billion	Loans	47 billion
Total	48 billion	Total	48 billion

It can be seen that Bank Greedy has used all its £5 billion capital to cover these losses and deposits of £2 billion have also had to be used to make up the shortfall – this means that the bank cannot repay all its depositors as the value of deposits have fallen from the original £50 billion to £48 billion – in theory the bank would have to tell its depositors that it had some bad news and unfortunately some will not be able to withdraw their deposits (or that all depositors will bear a loss). Of course, in reality this does not happen as the bank is insolvent (bust).

The main point to stress is that any losses incurred by a bank – whether these are caused by bad loans, securities trading, the failure of a subsidiary, fraudulent activity or whatever, have to be met out of its capital – as deposits have to be protected at all costs in order to maintain confidence in the bank, as well as the banking system overall. This is why bank regulators spend so much time and energy focusing on the capital adequacy of banks.

The adequacy of any given amount of capital not only depends upon the absolute volume of assets to be covered, but is also affected by the quality of those assets. The more risky the assets, the greater must be the cushion of capital funds, all other things being equal, in order to maintain a given level of capital adequacy.

For a number of years, the Bank of England specified for each UK bank individually a minimum required ratio of capital to risk-weighted assets. If the actual ratio were to fall below this 'trigger' ratio, the Bank of England would be likely to intervene in the bank's activities. This regulatory capital ratio was set to take account of the Bank of England's assessment of the bank's managerial capacity with regard to its risk position, its profitability and its overall prospects. In addition, it was expected that, in normal circumstances, each bank would maintain a 'target' capital ratio that included a margin over the value of its trigger ratio. The UK banking sector regulator, previously the Bank of England, and now the Financial Services Authority, has modified this approach in the light of evolving international standards. Moves on an international level to harmonise the capital adequacy ratios of banks in different countries have led to a more rigorously defined framework for capital adequacy in the UK. The Committee on Banking Regulations and Supervisory Practices of the Bank for International Settlements (BIS) put forward a framework in July 1988 for the harmonisation of standards of capital adequacy. The objective of this framework was to strengthen the world's banking system and place it in a better position to withstand any future problems in world financial markets. In addition, the requirements are intended to provide a more equal basis for competition between banks in different countries and to remove the incentive for banks to relocate activities to other countries in order to take advantage of relatively lax regulatory requirements.

7.8.1 The 1988 Basle Capital Accord

The Basle Committee on Banking Supervision[8] was created at the end of 1974 and was charged by the Group of Ten (or G-10, the largest ten industrialised countries in the world: Belgium, Canada, France, Germany, Italy, Japan, Netherlands, Sweden, the United Kingdom and the United States), plus Luxembourg and Switzerland, central bank governors to seek a common approach among its members towards measuring **capital adequacy** and the prescription of minimum capital standards. In July 1988, the Basle Committee on Banking Supervision introduced its 1988 Capital Accord (the Accord). The majority of the world's leading central banks undertook to implement the Basle Accord by the end of 1992. (The EU implemented almost all of the features of the Basle Accord into EU, and therefore Member States', law by the end of 1992.) This Accord is now known as 'Basle I'.

The Accord reflected the culmination of the committee work on international convergence of capital adequacy and is based on a risk–asset ratio (RAR) approach (see Box 7.3 below). The committee stated that: 'a weighted risk ratio in which capital is related to different categories of asset and off-balance sheet exposure, weighted according to broad categories of relative riskiness, is the preferred method for assessing the capital adequacy of banks' (BIS, 1988, paragraph 9).

The original 1988 Capital Accord established an international standard around a capital ratio of 8 per cent and focused on risks associated with lending (credit risks) thereby ignoring other types of risk. The Basle definition of capital is made up of two elements: Tier 1 ('core capital') and Tier 2 ('supplemental capital'). Bank total capital is the sum between Tiers 1 and 2 ('capital base'). Specifically, the elements of capital according to the 'International Convergence of Capital Measurement and Capital Standards' are:

Tier 1 a) Ordinary paid-up share capital/common stock
       b) Disclosed reserves

Tier 2 a) Undisclosed reserves
       b) Asset revaluation reserves
       c) General provisions/general loan loss reserves
       d) Hybrid (debt/equity) capital instruments
       e) Subordinated term debt

More details on the definitions of capital elements can be found in Box 7.3. The sum of Tier 1 and Tier 2 elements is eligible for inclusion in the capital base, subject to various limits described in the 1988 Basle report.

The general framework for capital adequacy risk-weighted assets can be summarised as follows. There are four risk classes in the weighted-risk system that reflects credit risk exposure:

a) No risk: 0% (e.g., cash or equivalents)
b) Low risk: 20% (e.g., short-term claims maturing in a year or less)
c) Moderate risk: 50% (e.g., mortgages)
d) Standard risk: 100% (e.g., commercial loans)

---

[8] The Basle Committee is the Committee of Central Banks and Bank Supervisors from the major industrialised countries that meets every three months at the BIS (Bank for International Settlements) in Basle, Switzerland. Note the French spelling of the name of the Swiss city is Basle (whereas the German spelling is Basel). Both forms are commonly used.

> ### Box 7.3 Details of capital elements (established 1988 and applied in 1992)
>
> **Tier 1 (core capital)** = common stockholders' equity + non-cumulative perpetual preferred stock + any surplus + minority interest in the equity accounts of consolidated subsidiaries – goodwill and other intangibles (deduction is carried out only if some conditions are met).
>
> REQUIRED TIER 1 CORE CAPITAL IS EQUAL TO RISK WEIGHT × 4% OF WEIGHTED RISK ASSETS.
>
> **Tier 2 (supplementary capital)** = allowance for losses on loans and leases (reserves) + cumulative perpetual, long-term and convertible preferred stock + perpetual debt and other hybrid debt/equity instruments + intermediate-term preferred stock and term subordinated debt. The total of Tier 2 is limited to 100% of Tier 1. Other limitations are specified in the 1992 revised guidelines.
>
> **Deductions** from total capital (Tier 1 + Tier 2) consist of investments in unconsolidated banking and financial subsidiaries, reciprocal holdings of capital securities, and other deductions (such as other subsidiaries or joint ventures) as determined by supervisory authorities with handling on a case-by-case basis or as a matter of policy after formal rule making.
>
> REQUIRED TOTAL CAPITAL (TIER 1 + TIER 2 – DEDUCTIONS) IS EQUAL TO RISK WEIGHT × 8% OF WEIGHTED RISK ASSETS

> ### Box 7.4 RAR (risk–asset ratio) approach
>
> The RAR is a relatively simple approach that sets out to appraise capital adequacy on the basis of banks' relative riskiness. Banks' assets are divided by the supervisory authorities into a number of equivalent risk classes. Different 'risk-weights' are assigned to each of the equivalent risk classes of assets. Total weighted-risk assets are calculated as follows:
>
> 1) $W = \Sigma\, a_i r_i$ where $A = \Sigma\, a_i$ and
> 2) $RAR = C/W$ where W = total weighted assets
> RAR = risk–asset ratio
> A = bank total assets
> a_i = risk classes of assets
> r_i = risk-weights
> C = capital as defined by the supervisory authorities
>
> Moreover, conversion factors were set for calculating credit-equivalent amounts for off-balance sheet (OBS) items.
>
> a) 0% (e.g., unused portion of loan commitments),
> b) 20% (e.g., commercial letters of credit)
> c) 50% (e.g., revolving underwriting facilities)
> d) 100% (e.g., standby letters of credit)

Essentially, the capital adequacy scheme is based on a four-step approach:

1) Classify assets into one of four risk categories described above;
2) Convert OBS commitments and guarantees on their on-balance sheet 'credit-equivalent' values and classify them in the appropriate risk category;
3) Multiply the £ amount of assets in each risk category by the appropriate risk-weight; this equals 'risk-weighted assets';
4) Multiply 'risk-weighted assets' by the minimum capital percentages, either 4% for Tier 1 capital or 8% for total capital for a bank to be adequately capitalised.

For example: take a bank with the following assets:

- Cash: £100m (0% risk weighting)
- Loans to other banks: £500m (20% risk weighting)
- Mortgage loans to owner-occupiers: £800m (50% risk weighting)
- Commercial loans: 100% (£1,500m)

Its minimum capital ratio under Basle I can be calculated as follows:

> Total Risk-Weighted Assets (RWA)
> = (£100m × 0) + (£500m × 0.2) + (£800m × 0.5) + (£1500m × 1)
> = £0 + £100m + £400m + £1500m
> = £2000m

Minimum capital requirement is 8% of £2000m = £160 million of which at least 50% needs to be held in the form of Equity (Tier 1) capital.

If the RAR calculated by the bank falls below the minimum ratio stipulated by the regulatory authorities then this obviously indicates the institution has inadequate capital. A summary of the minimum capital adequacy requirements is given below. Box 7.5 shows how to distinguish well-capitalised banks from those that are undercapitalised.

The Basle Accord was generally regarded as a step forward in the regulation of bank capital adequacy. It involved international agreement and it became the basis for most nations' capital regulations for all banks. Nevertheless, almost immediately debate began as to its efficiency and effectiveness. Questions were raised on capital ratios appearing to lack economic foundation, risk-weights not accurately reflecting the risk associated with assets (e.g., the riskiness of loans) and the lack of recognition of asset portfolio diversification. It should also be noted that many nations chose to set capital adequacy ratios somewhat higher than the Accord's minimum, reflecting their own assessment of the risk associated with individual banks' activities.

7.8.2 The 1996 amendments to the 1988 Accord

The original capital Accord focused on risks arising from the lending activity of banks thereby ignoring other types of risks (for an overview see Chapter 10). A proposal for changing the original Accord to include capital charges for market risks

---

Box 7.5   Five capital-adequacy categories of banks

1) Well-capitalised:
Total capital to risk-weighted assets 10%
Tier 1 capital to risk-weighted assets 6%
Tier 1 capital to total assets 5%

2) Adequately capitalised (fulfilling minimum requirements):
Total capital to risk-weighted assets 8%
Tier 1 capital to risk-weighted assets 4%
Tier 1 capital to total assets 4%

3) Undercapitalised:
Fails to meet one or more of the capital minimums for an adequately capitalised bank

4) Significantly undercapitalised:
Total capital to risk-weighted assets <6%
Tier 1 capital to risk-weighted assets <3%
Tier 1 capital to total assets <3%

5) Critically undercapitalised:
[(Common equity capital + perpetual preferred stock – Intangible assets)/total assets] = < 2%

---

incurred by banks was issued by the Basle Committee in April 1995. The objective was to provide 'an explicit capital cushion for the price risks to which banks are exposed, particularly those arising from trading activities'. The Basle Committee defined market risk as:[9]

> the risk of losses in on- and off-balance-sheet positions arising from movements in market prices.

In particular, the risks covered by the proposed framework were: a) the bank's trading book position in debt, equity instruments and related off-balance sheet contracts, and b) commodity and foreign exchange positions held by the bank. The amendments to the Accord to incorporate market (trading) risk resulted in the inclusion of an 'ancillary' or Tier 3 capital to support trading book activities. Moreover, a significant innovation in the market risk requirements consisted in the opportunity given to banks to use their internal risk-assessment models (see Chapter 11 for more details) for measuring the riskiness of their trading portfolios.

Overall, these regulatory changes in the minimum capital required for market risk came into force in 1996, and represented a significant step forward for the committee in strengthening the soundness and stability of the international banking and financial systems.

---

[9] See Chapter 10 for a definition of banking risks.

The new Capital Accord (Basle II)

In response to the criticisms of the original Accord, a number of changes were made. On 3 June 1999, the Basle Committee on Banking Supervision formally launched proposals for a new capital adequacy framework (which was to become known as Basle II). The first version of the proposed Accord received strong criticism from bankers and academics, which prompted the committee to make substantial changes to the new framework. A consultative document was published in April 2003 and agreement on the new Accord was reached in May 2004. Central bank governors and the heads of bank supervisory authorities in the Group of Ten (G10) countries endorsed the publication of the *International Convergence of Capital Measurement and Capital Standards: a Revised Framework.*[10]

The new Accord's main aim is to introduce a more comprehensive and risk-sensitive treatment of banking risks to ensure that regulatory capital bears a closer relationship to credit risk. In particular, the setting of minimum capital requirements will be based on an update of the current risk-weighting approach including the use of banks' internal risk ratings and external credit risk assessments. The New Basle Capital Accord has undergone an extensive review and the Basle Committee envisions implementation by the end of 2006.[11]

Basle II is built on three main pillars. *Pillar 1* deals with the quantification of new capital charges and relies heavily on banks' internal risk-weighting models and on external rating agencies. *Pillar 2* defines the supervisory review process and *Pillar 3* focuses on market discipline, imposing greater disclosure standards on banks in order to increase transparency.

Pillar 1

The first pillar seeks to amend the old rules by introducing risk weightings that are more closely linked to borrower's credit standing. The existing risk-weighting classification requires credit institutions (banks) and investment firms to hold at least 8 per cent of their assets as capital. Assets are adjusted using a risk-weighting formula, allowing loans judged to be less risky to be backed by less capital. However, this method has been criticised on the grounds that the original Accord's risk-weighting categories are too crude, so much so that they bear little relationship to the actual likelihood of default. For instance, unsecured loans to large companies and sole traders are counted as bearing the same 100 per cent risk. This means banks have to hold the same amount of capital for regulatory purposes for these types of loans even if the former are viewed as being substantially less risky than the latter. In consequence, banks have tended to migrate towards riskier loans, which command higher interest rates while requiring the same level of capital backing.

The new Basle proposals refine the old methodology, to reflect with greater precision the varying underlying risks against which banks are required to hold capital. The new Accord does not propose changes to the current definition of capital or the minimum requirement of 8 per cent capital to risk-weighted assets. The proposal mainly

---

[10] The full text of the new Accord can be found on the BIS website: http://www.bis.org/publ/bcbs107.htm (see also Basle Committee on Banking Supervision (2004a)).
[11] See Basle Committee on Banking Supervision (1999, 2000, 2001a), Morgan Stanley (2001) and Karacadag and Taylor (2000) for discussion on the expected impact of Basle II. For more recent analysis see the BIS website and the coverage of impact studies.

affects how banking risks (credit risk, which is risk of a borrower's default; operational risk, which is the risk associated with the potential for systems failure; and market risk, which is the risk that the value of investments will decrease due to movements in market prices) are going to be measured.[12] Methods for measuring credit risk are more complex than in the current Accord, a measure for operational risk has been explicitly proposed, while the measure of market risk remains unchanged.

The biggest changes relate to the calculation of capital backing for credit risk. Under Basle II, banks will be able to choose between what is known as the 'standardised approach' and the Internal Ratings-based (IRB) approach. In the standardised approach the new Accord defines risk weights within broad categories of sovereigns, banks and companies, by reference to an external credit assessment firm (credit rating agency) subject to strict standards. Under IRB, banks are allowed to use their internal credit risk assessments subject to strict methodological and disclosure requirements.

Together with changes to the risk-weighting scheme (Pillar 1), the proposed Accord rests on two other 'pillars', namely improved supervision and enhanced market discipline. These are intended to act as a lever to strengthen the safety and soundness of the banking system.

Pillar 2

The supervisory review process aims to ensure that a bank's capital adequacy position is consistent with its overall risk profile. To this end, bank regulators must be able to make qualitative judgements on the ability of each bank to measure and manage its own risks. The US Federal Reserve has recently supported the idea that bank examiners should evaluate capital management processes on a continuous basis, but also contends that supervisors should establish explicit capital adequacy goals after assessing the potential risks to the institution concerned. Supervisors should also have the ability to require banks to hold capital in excess of minimum regulatory requirements. The Basle Committee's discussions with regulators from outside the G10 area emphasised the need for higher capital requirements for weaker or riskier institutions. This is already the practice in some countries; for instance, some financial sector regulators in the G10 require various banks to hold capital equivalent to more than 20 per cent of their assets. Such a review process is likely to require a substantial increase in supervisory resources in many countries, where the regulatory systems are currently geared only towards adhering to standard quantitative guidelines.

Pillar 3

The third pillar seeks to enhance effective market discipline facilitated by introducing high disclosure standards with regard to bank capital. This requires banks to provide more reliable and timely information enabling market participants to make better risk assessments.

Taken together, Pillar 1 provides the rules for quantifying risk sensitivity and the minimum capital charges associated with these risks. This is balanced by the supervisory judgements available under Pillar 2 and market disclosure rules of Pillar 3. Ultimately, the new Accord seeks to create a more comprehensive and flexible regulatory framework, without sacrificing the safety and soundness achieved by the Basle I Accord. Figure 7.3 summarises the main features of the New Basle Accord.

---

[12] See Chapter 11 for details on the measurement and management of banking risks.

Figure 7.3 **The Basle II Accord**

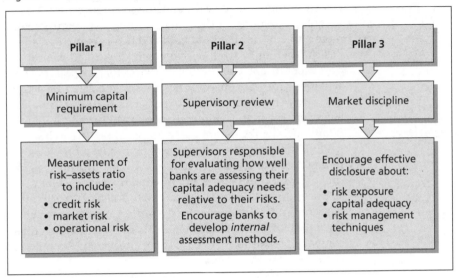

It is difficult to be definitive about the likely strategic impact of Basle II. Peterson (2001) argues that some of the biggest winners and losers under the Basle II proposals are comparatively easy to identify; we summarise these in Table 7.4 and discuss them below.

Table 7.4 **Potential winners and losers under Basle II**

Winners	*Losers*
• Large prudent banks	• Weak OECD credits
• Retail banks	• High-yield loan market
• Highly credit-rated corporations	• Credit derivatives
• Asset-backed market	• Repos markets
• Multilateral development banks	• Asset management
• High-yield bond market	
• Mortgage banks	
• OECD outsiders	

Big, prudent banks should see a reduction in their regulatory capital. This will result in the ability of those banks to use and exploit the IRB approach using their internal models to arrive at capital requirements for risk-management purposes. In the short-term, however, they will have to meet the costs of upgrading their internal systems and technology. Compliance (and related disclosure) costs are also likely to be significant. Bigger and more sophisticated banks are likely to benefit, while the smaller and less sophisticated banks will lose.

Some of the biggest winners from the abolition of the old (Basle I) risk-weighting bands are relatively creditworthy countries that are not members of the OECD. Risk-weightings under the standardised approach will fall from 100 per cent to either 20 per cent or 0 per cent. Banks based in these countries will also be better off. Similarly, highly rated companies (all risk-weighted at 100 per cent under Basle I) will also benefit from a much lower risk-weighting. As a result, banks will have an increased incentive to lend to these companies.

All asset-backed securities (ABSs) were risk-weighted at 100 per cent under Basle I whereas under the Basle II standardised approach, asset-backed bonds will be risk-weighted according to their credit rating. This should make higher quality ABSs more attractive for banks to hold and this may increase the respective demand.

Top-rated multilateral development banks (i.e., institutions that provide financial support and professional advice for economic and social development activities in developing countries, such as the Asian Development Bank) have their asset weightings cut from 20 per cent to 0 per cent under the standardised approach. For high-yield bonds, banks will have to hold more capital under Basle II (although banks are not big investors in high-yield bonds). However, since bank lending to less creditworthy borrowers will be more heavily penalised under Basle II, these companies may be pushed into the junk bond market, thereby increasing the supply of funds and depth of bond markets generally.

Under Basle II, the weakest corporate and bank credits attract a weighting of 150 per cent (under the standardised approach), but unrated entities only attract a 100 per cent (albeit minimum) weight. This apparent preferential treatment of unrated companies seems likely to have some impact. For example, some companies might choose to remain unrated.

Initial views were that retail banks may be among the losers. Nevertheless, their capital treatment and the continuing calibration of retail banking credit risks seem to have reduced (if not reversed) this potential. Banks engaged in substantial mortgage business look likely to benefit due to the lower charge on secured retail lending. Problems also include the new operational risk charge and the increased costs of compliance.

Initial concerns were raised that the capital treatment of credit derivatives may adversely affect liquidity in the market for credit default swaps and it has also been argued that there will be damaging consequences for repo market participants. Finally, concerns have also been expressed about the possible impact on asset management, and in particular how the new operational risk capital charge will apply to the asset management operations of banks.

7.8.4 Costs of implementing Basle II

There have been various concerns expressed about the complexity and costs of Basle II. It has been suggested that Basle II will markedly increase the cost of regulation through adding increased layers of complexity. The cost of developing and implementing new risk-management systems will be considerable and this could lead to effective barriers to entry. The estimates of the costs to market participants associated with implementing Basle II vary:

- According to a survey of 30 banks (average assets: US$100m) undertaken by Standard & Poor's Risk Solutions in March 2004, costs of compliance ranged between US$1m and US$100m.
- A source quoted in *The Economist* (2004a) estimates that implementation of the new rules will amount to 0.05% of assets – or somewhere ranging between $100 and $200 million for the largest banks.
- A study by PriceWaterhouse Coopers (PWC) research group for the European Commission suggested that the application of capital requirements may cost European banks €20–30 billion between 2002 and 2006; the study also noted that the top investment banks (that are likely to implement the most sophisticated approaches) would have to commit between €80 and €150 million.

- Mercer Oliver Wyman (a consulting firm) has estimated that the cost for large banks is of the order of £100m to £200m or five basis points of their asset base. This cost is likely to fall substantially as specialist expertise is accumulated and the current demand for Basle II implementation technology and staff abates.

Looking at these (and other) estimates of the cost of implementation it appears that the consensus calculation is around 0.05% (five basis points) of total assets – noting that it is likely to be lower for small banks that implement less complex approaches.

As far as we are aware there are no estimates concerning the costs to regulatory authorities with regard to implementing the new regulations. While there are clearly substantial costs associated with regulators having to change from rules-based regulation to a process based on supervision it is very difficult to quantify the expenses that will be incurred. Costs will obviously be higher in countries where there are more banks (most noticeably Germany) and where these are large and internationally active (for instance, the United Kingdom).

Finally, while the above covers the costs to market participants and (briefly regulatory authorities) it would be remiss of us not to note the potential indirect costs associated with the effects of Basle II. There is a growing literature on the potential pro-cyclical effects of Basle II that suggest that the new rules may exacerbate downturns in the business cycle. For instance, as credit risk increases in a recession, capital requirements are likely to rise, inducing credit rationing. It has also been suggested that these effects may be accentuated by the introduction of 'fair value' accounting by banks (where banks have to report market-value information as opposed to historic cost financial data) – which commences in Europe within the adoption of international accounting guidelines IAS39 (from the start of January 2005).

7.8.5 Basle II, EU Capital Adequacy Directive and implementation

An important issue to be aware of is the link between the Basle Accord and EU legislation. Basle II proposals will need to be implemented into law. In the case of Europe, this means that EU legislators have to agree to equivalent/similar legislation, which will then be implemented into Member State law.

The current European legislation on capital adequacy (originally known as the Solvency Ratio Directive of 1989 – now incorporated in the Codified Banking Directive of 2000) was based on the Basle I Accord. This applies to all banks and investment firms in the EU.

As noted by the EU, 'in order to maximise consistency between the EU legislation and the international framework, the European Commission and EU members of the Basle Committee have had as a primary objective ensuring the suitability of Basle II for application in the EU Single Market'. This means that Basle II will be implemented into EU law but various changes will be made to suit the specifics of the European financial system.

The EU Capital Adequacy Directive (CAD) is the legislation that is based on Basle II and will be applied to all banks and investment firms. However, there are some EU changes to the Basle II recommendations, such as:

- rules on partial use which would allow less complex institutions to make use of the more sophisticated methodologies for some of their portfolios while using the simpler methodologies for others;

- tailoring of the new operational risk requirements in their application to low- and medium-risk investment firms;
- specific rules on how the applications of cross-border groups for approval to use the more sophisticated methodologies should be handled; and
- lower capital requirements for banks' 'venture capital' business, which is key for the financing of small start-up companies in some Member States.

Basle II applies on a consolidated basis to internationally active banks, whereas the new EU capital requirements will be applied on a consolidated and individual basis to all credit institutions and investment firms. In the United States it is expected that only a relatively small number (around 20) of large, internationally active banks would be required to adopt Basle II and these would implement the most advanced approaches for determining their risk-based capital requirements. Other banks could apply to be treated under the new rules. In Japan the implementation of Basle II appears much less advanced than in the United States and Europe. It seems likely, however, that the Japanese authorities will adopt an approach similar to that of the United States.

Box 7.6   Basle II: learning by doing, not by revolution   FT

Fast forward to January 2008. The global economy is in a mild recession. Bad news for banks, as the level of bad loans is likely to rise. Oh, and some rogue trader has managed to run up $500m in foreign exchange losses for his bank following a series of unauthorised trades.

Such a double whammy is among the scenarios that the new Basle II capital adequacy framework should deal with. So will the financial services sector be a safer place, for depositors, shareholders and regulators?

In fact, it already is. For all the tortuous years of negotiations leading up to the final Basle II consultation draft of July 2004, banks have already made huge strides in improving their risk-management systems.

Basle II seeks to relate the amount of regulatory capital that banks hold more closely to the risks they actually take. The current system uses the blunt instrument of fixed percentages, with limited regard to the relative riskiness of a particular corporate loan or other assets.

The bulk of the discussions between banks and regulators over the last four years has been on the relative risk-weightings of different asset classes, the so-called Pillar 1 of the new accord. The impacts are also broadly understood. The lowering of capital requirements for retail products such as residential mortgages is expected to encourage banks to shift more capital towards consumer finance operations, at the expense of investment banking and structured finance products such as securitisation.

But the other two 'pillars' of Basle II have garnered less attention, with their promises of improved disclosure by banks and more intense supervision by regulators. This is where the focus of banks' work and investment is expected to be over the next two years. 'I think Pillar 2 and Pillar 3 are quite ground breaking', says Kim Olson, managing director at Fitch Ratings, the credit-rating agency. 'It is a window into what the risk profile [of a bank actually] is.'

But while banks are being asked to provide far more information about their asset portfolios, analysts believe that most have to make up a lot of ground to meet both the minimum disclosure requirements in financial reports and presentations and make them comparable between institutions. 'There are very few examples of great disclosure,' comments Ms Olson.

Banks such as Barclays and Deutsche have led the way in providing parallel financial reports, which include both capital ratios based on the current rules and on their own internal assessments of the capital they need to hold. 'But it's still modest compared with what Basle II will require,' says Tom Garside, managing director at Mercer Oliver Wyman, a consultancy. 'The main complaint is that there is too much disclosure [required]', says Mr Garside, citing gripes among bankers that the rules 'will add 75 pages' to an annual report.

The use of internal risk management systems is central to Basle II. Banks can opt to use either a 'standardised' approach, in which their capital requirement will continue to be set by their national regulator, or an approved internal ratings system, based on their own experience of the performance of their assets.

The first comes into force at the end of 2006, with the advanced level applied a year later.

▶

Most large European banks are expected to opt for the internal system. This is more expensive because it requires the gathering and processing of much more data – usually five years of history for a particular asset class. However, the more precise measurement of actual risks is expected to lead to a lower capital charge compared with the standard approach, making it an attractive option because it will allow banks to pursue a competitive advantage over rivals through the more efficient use of capital.

The lure of an internal system – in spite of the more onerous disclosure requirements – is particularly strong for European institutions. US regulators have already said they plan to apply Basle II to only the ten most 'internationally active' banks, and some countries such as China and India do not plan to adopt the new rules at all, or at least not in the same timescale.

The European Parliament is working on legislation that will apply the rules to all banks, from Deutsche and HSBC to the smallest lender.

The broad application of Basle II in Europe has created concerns that there will not be an international 'level playing field', but the enhanced role of regulators in applying the new rules also places a greater burden on national authorities to monitor their own institutions in a manner consistent with their peers' approach.

But with risk management turning into more of a science than an art, there is intense competition for staff between banks, regulators and financial analysts. 'The feeling [among banks] is that the regulators are completely swamped,' says Mr Garside.

Basle II has provided banks with a huge incentive to improve their risk-management systems. It aims to provide regulators and financial analysts with better information to assess their relative performance.

The challenge will be to find the right people and tools to harness the new framework, amid intense competition for staff among banks, firms and regulators.

Source: Financial Times (2004) 'European Banking Survey 2004', 8 October, by Doug Cameron.

7.9 Conclusions

In this chapter we have reviewed the issue of financial regulation, with specific focus on the regulation of the UK and EU banking sectors. The chapter began with a review of the rationale for regulation, introducing the reader to different types of regulation. The limitations of regulation were also analysed, in particular the moral hazard issue connected with the government safety net arrangements such as deposit insurance and the lender-of-last-resort function. The chapter also focused on the Basle Capital Accord and the effort of the Basle Committee to provide common regulatory standards for internationally active banks.

Key terms

Regulation	Moral hazard
Monitoring	Too big to fail/Too important to fail
Supervision	Forbearance
Contagion	Agency capture
Bank runs	Compliance costs
Systemic risk	Hedge funds
Government safety net	Financial innovation
Deposit insurance	Capital adequacy
Lender-of-last-resort	

Key reading Bank for International Settlements (2004a) 'Basle II: International Convergence of Capital Measurement and Capital Standards: a Revised Framework', http://www.bis.org/publ/bcbs107.htm.

Barth, J.R., Caprio, G. and Levine, R.E. (2001) 'Bank Regulation and Supervision: What Works Best?' *World Bank Policy Research Working Paper*, No. 2725, http://www.nber.org/papers/w9323.pdf.

Goodhart, C.A.E., Hartmann, P., Llewellyn, D., Rojas-Suarez, L. and Weisbrod, S. (1998) *Financial Regulation. Why, How and Where Now?* London: Routledge.

Llewellyn, D. (1999) 'The Economic Rationale for Financial Regulation', *FSA, Occasional Papers Series, No.1*, http://www.fsa.gov.uk/pubs/occpapers/op01.pdf.

Revision questions and problems

1 Is there a rationale for the regulation of financial intermediaries and financial markets?

2 What is a bank run?

3 What are the main types of financial regulation?

4 Why are the 'safety net' arrangements said to increase moral hazard in financial markets?

5 What are the main limitations of financial regulation?

6 What is regulatory forbearance? Describe the main costs and benefits of engaging in forbearance.

7 What are the main drivers of regulatory reforms?

8 Describe the UK regulatory environment.

9 Describe the main EU regulation impacting on the banking and financial sector.

10 Illustrate the main features of the Basle Capital Accords.

Part 3

ISSUES IN BANK MANAGEMENT

Chapter 8

Banks' balance sheet and income structure

Learning objectives

- To understand the importance of banks' financial statements
- To identify the main assets and liabilities of commercial and investment banks
- To understand the sources of revenue for commercial and investment banks
- To understand the importance of economic capital
- To describe the concept of shareholder value creation and the cost of equity capital
- To become familiar with the most commonly used bank financial ratios

8.1 Introduction

Traditionally, the business of banks is to intermediate funds between surplus units and deficit units thereby linking depositors with borrowers. Banks also provide pooling of risk, liquidity services and undertake delegated monitoring. Financial intermediaries can be classified according to their different **balance sheet** structures. For deposit-taking institutions, the main source of funding (customer deposits) are reported on the liabilities side of the balance sheet, while the allocation of these funds (cash, loans, investments, and fixed assets) is detailed on the assets side. Banks' profits are derived from the **income statement (profit and loss account)**, a document that reports data on costs and revenues and measures bank performance over two balance sheet periods. This chapter focuses on understanding commercial and investment banks' financial statements and describes the main characteristics of their balance sheet and income statements. The last part of the chapter investigates the most common bank financial ratios such as **return-on-assets**, **return-on-equity** and the **cost–income** ratio.

8.2 Retail banks' balance sheet structure

The **balance sheet** is a financial statement of the wealth of a business or other organisation on a given date. This is usually at the end of the financial year. For commercial banks the balance sheet lists all the stock values of sources and uses of banks' funds. Banks' funds come from:

a) the general public (retail deposits);
b) companies (small, medium, and large corporate deposits);
c) other banks (interbank deposits);
d) equity issues (share issues, conferring ownership rights on holders);
e) debt issues (bond issues and loans); and
f) saving past profits (retained earnings).

The above is generally classified as banks' **liabilities** (debt) and **capital** (equity). These funds are then transformed into financial and, to a lesser extent, real **assets**:

a) cash;
b) liquid assets (securities);
c) short-term money market instruments such as Treasury bills, which banks can sell (liquidate) quickly if they have a cash shortage;
d) loans;
e) other investments; and
f) fixed assets (branch network, computers, premises).

Table 8.1 summarises the assets and liabilities in a simplified commercial bank balance sheet.

Banks liabilities (e.g., retail deposits) tend to have shorter maturities than assets (e.g., mortgage loans). This mismatch derives from the different requirements of depositors and borrowers: typically the majority of depositors want to lend their assets for short periods of time and for the highest possible return. In contrast, the majority of borrowers require loans that are cheap and for long periods. The asset

Table 8.1 **Simplified commercial bank balance sheet**

Assets	Liabilities
Cash	Deposits: retail
Liquid assets	Deposits: wholesale
Loans	
Other investments	Equity
Fixed assets	Other capital terms
Total assets	**Total liabilities and equity**

transformation function of banks is derived from these characteristics. To recap, banks have the primary function of being asset transformers because they intermediate between depositors and borrowers by changing the characteristics of their liabilities as they move from one side of the balance sheet to the other. Capital (see also Section 8.2.1.3 below) is sometimes referred to as equity capital or net worth and is equal to the difference between assets and liabilities.

8.2.1 Assets and liabilities of commercial banks: main components

The balance sheet provides information about the bank's financial position at the end of the accounting period. It comprises three principal components: a) the assets the bank controls; b) the liabilities the bank is obliged to meet; and c) the equity interests of the bank's owners.

Tables 8.2 and 8.3 exhibit the combined balance sheet for UK banks as reported by the Bank of England. The tables aggregate assets and liabilities of all financial institutions recognised by the Bank of England as UK banks for statistical purposes.

8.2.1.1 The assets side

On the asset side, banks store a relatively small amount (about 0.5 per cent of total assets in 2004) of cash in the form of *notes and coins* to meet daily commitments. To ensure their liquidity, banks are also required to hold assets with the Bank of England in the form of *cash ratio deposits*. In the United Kingdom, according to the current regulation, both banks and building societies with average eligible liabilities of £500 million or more are required to hold non-operational, non-interest-bearing deposits with the Bank of 0.15 per cent. Banks can also keep *other balances with the Bank of England* (i.e., other than cash ratio deposits); these deposits give the central bank a source of income.

In case of cash shortage, banks can ask for a loan in the interbank market. The interbank market constitutes an important portion of the money markets and it is the place where banks meet each day to exchange liquidity. Therefore, the item *market loans* in the asset side of a bank balance sheet includes wholesale loans that are typically very short-term (i.e., overnight or 'call' loans), very liquid (they allow banks to lend money and call them back at short notice) and characterised by large volumes (typically >£1 million).

Bankers' acceptances are negotiable time drafts, or bills of exchange, that have been accepted by a bank that, by accepting, assumes the obligation to pay the holder of the draft the face amount of the instrument on the maturity date specified. They are used primarily to finance the export, import, shipment or storage of goods. *Acceptances granted* comprise a claim on the party whose bill the banks have accepted, except for bills both accepted and discounted by the same bank that are included as lending (unless subsequently rediscounted).

Another important source of liquidity is provided by *bills*. As shown in Table 8.2, the main bills held by banks are *Treasury bills* (or *T-bills*) that are essentially a form of short-term government borrowing; *bank bills* (usually eligible for rediscounting at the Bank of England) and other short-term bills including *local government bills* and *public corporation bills*.

Further liquidity is provided by the item *claims under sale and repurchase agreements*. This item comprises cash claims arising from the purchase of securities for a finite period with a commitment to re-sell.

By far the most important item on the asset side, *advances*, includes all balances with, and lending to, customers not included elsewhere. Despite the dramatic changes that have characterised the banking sector over the last two decades (see Chapter 2) loans are still the primary earning assets of banks, and account for a relatively large proportion of total assets. As reported in Table 8.2, in 2004 loans were the largest items on the balance sheet: sterling advances held on the asset side of banks in the United Kingdom totalled £1,204.1 billion, which was over 57 per cent of total sterling assets. Typically, UK banks lend to individuals, financial and non-financial firms. The major categories of loans are: *commercial loans* (such as short-term loans to businesses); *consumer loans* (for example: overdrafts and credit card loans); *mortgage lending* and *real estate loans* (such as long-term loans to finance commercial real estate such as office buildings).

The next item on the asset side of the balance sheet is *investments*. These include all longer-term securities beneficially owned by the reporting institution and include securities that the reporting institution has sold for a finite period, but with a commitment to repurchase (i.e., repos), but exclude securities that have been bought for a finite period, but with a commitment to resell (i.e., reverse repos). Securities are defined as marketable or potentially marketable income-yielding instruments including bonds, floating rate notes (FRNs), preference shares and other debt instruments, but excluding certificates of deposit and commercial paper that are shown as market loans.

The remaining non-deposit assets include:

- *Items in suspense and collection* that include, for example, debit balances awaiting transfer to customers' accounts and balances awaiting settlement of securities transactions. Collections comprise cheques drawn, and in course of collection, on other UK banks and building societies.
- *Accrued amounts receivable* are gross amounts receivable, but have not yet been received, and include interest and other revenues.
- *Other assets* include holdings of gold bullion and gold coin, other commodities, together with land, premises, plant and equipment and other physical assets owned, or recorded as such, including assets leased out under operating leases. Assets leased out under finance leases are included as loans.
- *Eligible banks' total sterling acceptances* comprise all bills accepted by a reporting institution whose bills are eligible for rediscount at the Bank of England including those that the reporting institution has itself discounted.

Finally, in 2004 UK banks had about £2,603 billion in foreign currency assets (e.g., foreign currency loans) of which approximately 44 per cent were Euro-denominated. As shown in Table 8.2, foreign currency assets and liabilities account for a significant proportion of total bank assets.

Table 8.2 **Bank of England aggregate assets of UK banks (end-year 2004, £000million amounts)**

Assets	£000 mil end-year 2004	% over total sterling assets
Notes and coins	10.6	0.5
With UK central bank	**1.9**	**0.1**
– Cash ratio deposit	1.8	0.1
– Other	0.1	0.0
Market loans	**511.8**	**24.3**
– UK banks	342.7	16.3
– UK banks' CDs, etc.	59.5	2.8
– UK banks commercial paper	0.1	0.0
– UK building societies, CDs, etc., and deposits	7.2	0.3
– Non-residents	102.3	4.9
Acceptances granted	**1.4**	**0.1**
– UK building societies	0.0	0.0
– UK public sector	0.0	0.0
– Other UK residents	1.3	0.1
– Non-residents	0.1	0.0
Bills	**16.8**	**0.8**
– Treasury bills	14.5	0.7
– UK bank bills	0.6	0.0
– UK building societies	0.0	0.0
– Other UK	1.0	0.0
– Non-residents	0.7	0.0
Claims under sale and repurchase agreements	**262.9**	**12.5**
– Of which British government securities	116.7	5.5
– UK banks	64.4	3.1
– UK building societies	0.3	0.0
– UK public sector	10.8	0.5
– Other UK residents	50.4	2.4
– Non-residents	20.5	1.0
Advances	**1,204.1**	**57.1**
– UK public sector	6.1	0.3
– Other UK residents	1,159.5	55.0
– Non-residents	38.4	1.8
Investments	**159.6**	**7.6**
– British government securities	-4.2	-0.2
– Other UK public sector	0.3	0.0
– UK banks	34.7	1.6
– UK building societies	1.9	0.1
– Other UK residents	100.9	4.8
– Non-residents	26.0	1.2
Items in suspense and collection	22.1	1.0
Accrued amounts receivable	20.0	0.9
Other assets	12.9	0.6
TOTAL STERLING ASSETS	**2,107.3**	**100.0**
Total foreign currency assets	2,603.6	
– Of which total Euro assets	1,155.8	
TOTAL ASSETS	**4,710.9**	

Note: Figures may not add due to rounding.

Source: Bank of England, Monetary and Financial Statistics Interactive database and authors' calculations.

8.2.1.2 **The liability side**

On the liabilities side, as illustrated in Table 8.3, the first item reported is *notes out-standing* and *cash-loaded cards*. This includes all notes and cash held by banks, including the sterling notes issued by Scottish and Northern Ireland banks and cash-loaded cards issued by banks (these are electronic cards, smart cards, etc.).

The largest proportion of bank liabilities is in the form of deposits that are typically made by individuals and firms, including deposits by other UK banks. The majority of deposits are represented by sight and time deposits, as shown in Figure 8.1.

Sight deposits comprise those deposits where the entire balance is accessible with-out penalty, either on demand or by close of business on the day following the one on which the deposit was made. *Time deposits* comprise all other deposits and they include for example 30- and 60-day savings bank deposits and ISA deposits.[1]

As shown in Figure 8.1, deposits also include acceptances granted, liabilities under sale and repurchase agreements and certificates of deposit.

Acceptances granted represent the banks' liabilities to the owners of bills. *Liabilities under sale and repurchase agreements* comprise cash receipts arising from the sale of securities or other assets that the bank has sold temporarily with a commitment to repurchase. The bulk of a bank's liabilities under sale and repurchase agreements are British government securities, accounting for 46 per cent of the total.

CD and other short-term paper issued: certificates of deposits (CD) are certificates given to depositors in return for a (wholesale) deposit. The holder of the CD receives interest at a fixed or floating rate. CD are short-term securities and are re-saleable in the market. This item also contains promissory notes issued by the reporting institutions, unsubordinated capital market instruments (except deben-tures and secured loan stocks) of any maturity and subordinated loan stocks with

Figure 8.1 Breakdown of UK banks' sterling deposits, end-year 2004

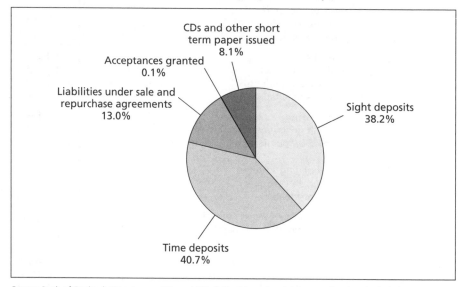

Source: Bank of England, Monetary and Financial Statistics Interactive database and authors' calculations.

---

[1] ISAs (Individual Savings Accounts) were introduced in the United Kingdom in 1999. These are tax-free savings and investment accounts that can be used to save cash, or invest in stocks and shares.

maturity of five years or less. Other subordinated loan stocks and debentures are
included in capital and other funds (see below for the details on the capital item).
The remaining non-deposit liabilities, as reported in Table 8.3, include:

● *Items in suspense and transmission*, such as balances awaiting settlement of securities transactions, standing orders and credit transfers debited to customers'
accounts, and other items for which the corresponding payment has not yet
been made by the reporting institution.
● *Net derivatives*, which comprise the overall net derivatives position of contracts
that are included within the trading and banking books of the reporting institutions (see Section 9.5 for more details).

Table 8.3 **Bank of England aggregate liabilities of UK banks (end-year 2004, £000
million amounts)**

Liabilities	£000 mil end-year 2004	% over total sterling liabilities
Notes outstanding and cash-loaded cards	4.3	0.2
Sight Deposits	**757.5**	**35.9**
– UK banks	109.9	5.2
– UK building societies	1.7	0.1
– UK public sector	6.6	0.3
– Other UK residents	566.8	26.8
– Non-residents	72.5	3.4
Time deposits	**807.5**	**38.2**
– UK banks	230.7	10.9
– UK building societies	4.0	0.2
– UK public sector	10.9	0.5
– Other UK residents	321.9	15.2
– Of which Tessa	0.0	0.0
– Of which SAYE	2.3	0.1
– Of which cash ISAs	60.3	2.9
– Non-residents	177.4	8.4
Liabilities under sale and repurchase agreements	**258.5**	**12.2**
– of which British govt securities	109.7	5.2
– UK banks	86.9	4.1
– UK building societies	0.1	0.0
– UK public sector	0.1	0.0
– Other UK residents	35.0	1.7
– Non-residents	26.7	1.3
Acceptances granted	**1.4**	**0.1**
CDs and other short term paper issued	**160.2**	**7.6**
TOTAL STERLING DEPOSITS	**1,812.8**	**85.9%**
Sterling items in suspense and transmission	17.9	0.8
Net derivatives	−15.5	−0.7
Accrued amounts payable	26.3	1.2
Sterling capital and other internal funds	265.4	12.6
TOTAL STERLING LIABILITIES	**2,111.3**	**100.0**
Total foreign currency liabilities	2,599.6	
Of which total Euro liabilities	1,098.1	
TOTAL LIABILITIES	4,710.9	

Note: Note: Figures may not add due to rounding.

Source: Bank of England, Monetary and Financial Statistics Interactive database and authors' calculations.

- *Accrued amounts payable*, which are gross amounts payable that have not yet been paid or credited to accounts.
- *Capital and other internal funds*, which consist primarily of shareholders' funds, reserves and long-term debt.

Finally, Table 8.3 shows that in 2004 UK banks had about £2,600 billion in foreign currency liabilities (e.g., foreign currency sight and time deposits) of which approximately 43 per cent were Euro-denominated.

Tables 8.4 and 8.5 illustrate the end-year 2004 consolidated financial data for a major UK bank, Barclays.

Figures 8.2 and 8.3 illustrate the breakdown of the major components of Barclays' assets and liabilities. Focusing on the asset side, about 64 per cent of Barclays' assets derive from loans of which 23 per cent are banking and trading loans to other banks while the vast majority consist of loans to retail customers (77 per cent). The banking group holds a substantial portfolio of debt security investments that corresponds to about 24 per cent of total assets.

The most significant item on the liability side is deposits (66 per cent of the total), of which 34 per cent is from banks and the remaining portion is from retail clients. Only 14 per cent of total liabilities are represented by short- and long-term debt securities (e.g., commercial paper, CDs and bonds).

Figure 8.3 also reports details on shareholders' capital (see Section 8.2.1.3) and the memorandum items. Note that these items do not sum up to the total balance sheet but include details on off-balance sheet contingent commitments (these latter will be explained in Section 9.5).

Table 8.4 **Barclays' assets, end-year 2004 (£m)**

Assets		
Cash and balances at central banks		1,753
Items in course of collection from other banks		1,772
Treasury bills and other eligible bills		6,658
Loans and advances to banks – banking	24,986	
– trading	50,145	
		75,131
Loans and advances to customers – banking	189,847	
– trading	65,099	
		254,946
Debt securities		127,428
Equity shares		12,166
Interests in joint ventures – share of gross assets	147	
– share of gross liabilities	−119	
		28
Interests in associated undertakings		381
Intangible fixed assets		4,295
Tangible fixed assets		1,921
Others assets		22,154
Prepayments and accrued income		5,078
Retail life-funds assets attributable to policyholders		8,378
Total assets		**522,089**

Source: http://www.investorrelations.barclays.co.uk.

Table 8.5 **Barclays' liabilities, end-year 2004 (£m)**

Liabilities			
Deposits by banks	– banking	74,211	
	– trading	36,813	
			111,024
Customer accounts	– banking	171,963	
	– trading	45,755	
			217,718
Debt securities in issue			67,806
Items in course of collection due to other banks			1,205
Other liabilities			76,565
Accruals and deferred income			6,582
Provisions for liabilities and charges – deferred tax			738
Provisions for liabilities and charges – other			467
Dividend			1,011
Subordinated liabilities:			
Undated loan capital – non-convertible			6,149
Dated loan capital – convertible to preference shares		15	
– non-convertible		6,113	
			6,128
Total liabilities			**495,393**
Minority interests (including non-equity interests)			901
Shareholders' funds – equity			17,417
Retail life – fund liabilities to policyholders			8,378
TOTAL LIABILITIES AND SHAREHOLDERS' FUNDS			**522,089**
Memorandum items			
Contingent liabilities:			
Acceptances and endorsements		303	
Guarantees and assets pledged as collateral security		30,011	
Other contingent liabilities		8,245	
			38,559
Commitments – standby facilities, credit lines and other			134,051

Source: http://www.investorrelations.barclays.co.uk.

Figure 8.2 **Barclays' assets, end-year 2004 (£m)**

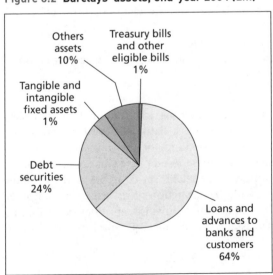

Source: Barclays (2004) Annual Report.

Figure 8.3 **Barclays' liabilities, end-year 2004 (£m)**

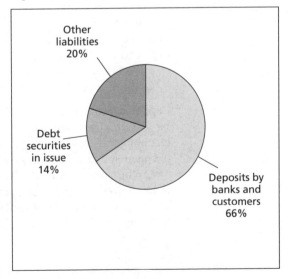

Source: Barclays (2004) Annual Report.

8.2.1.3 **Banks' equity capital**

Defined as the value of assets minus the value of liabilities the **capital** (or 'net worth' or 'equity capital') represents the ownership interest in a firm.

> **Capital = Assets – Liabilities**

Bank capital and liabilities represent the specific sources of funds (see Figure 8.3). However, compared to manufacturing firms typically banks are highly leveraged and thus hold a lower proportion of equity to assets (see Box 8.1). If a relatively small amount of loans are not repaid, this can seriously affect the level of equity and leave the bank technically insolvent. This is because if loans are not repaid then losses have to be borne by the capital cushion that banks hold to protect against such losses. The greater the level of capital relative to the losses incurred then the greater protection the bank will have. If losses exceed the level of capital then a bank will become technically insolvent because even if it could liquidate all its assets there would not be sufficient funds to cover deposits. In such circumstances, the need to ensure depositors' confidence (a major issue for the banking sector) may result in one of the following:

1) other banks can engage in a rescue package to pump new capital into the troubled bank; or
2) the authorities can decide to rescue the troubled bank using taxpayers money. The potential repercussions on the whole banking sector are such that regulatory authorities monitor bank behaviour and try to ensure that banks have adequate capital[2] and that they are run in a safe and sound manner (see also Section 7.8).

In general, the primary function of capital is to reduce the risk of failure by providing protection against operating and any other losses. It does this in five ways by:

1) providing a cushion for firms to absorb unanticipated losses with enough margin to inspire confidence and enable the bank to remain solvent;
2) protecting uninsured depositors (depositors not protected by a deposit insurance scheme that covers small depositors) in the event of insolvency and liquidation;
3) protecting bank insurance funds and taxpayers;
4) providing ready access to financial markets and thus guarding against liquidity problems caused by deposit outflows; and
5) limiting risk taking.

Capital is also needed to acquire plant and other real investments that are necessary to provide financial services. For example, a bank will need capital for its technological investments, branching network and for the management of the payment systems. A bank can also use its capital resources to finance acquisitions.

Capital and risk are strictly connected. Generally speaking, more risk requires more capital so capital adequacy should be a function of risk exposure, all other things being equal. Today banks are exposed to many different financial risks; this is because their activities are increasingly taking place in markets that can be

---

[2] Adequate capital corresponds to the 'C' in the CAMEL structure that includes also 'A' that is good Assets; 'M', competent Management; 'E', good Earnings; and 'L', sufficient Liquidity.

Box 8.1	Typical capital structure of a manufacturing firm versus a retail bank

Manufacturing firm	%	Bank	%
Assets		**Assets**	
Short-term assets	55	Short-term assets	70
Fixed assets	45	Long-term and fixed assets	30
Total assets	100	Total assets	100
Liabilities		**Liabilities**	
Short-term liabilities	25	Short-term liabilities	75
Long-term debt	30	Long-term debt	17
Shareholders' equity	45	Shareholders' equity	8
Total liabilities	100	Total liabilities	100

The debt/equity ratio (or financial leverage) of the manufacturing firm is 55/45= 1.22 and the debt/equity ratio of the bank is 92/8=11.5.

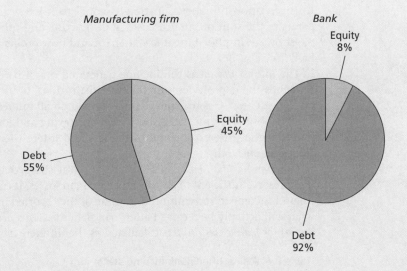

The structure of the balance sheet is extremely important for all firms. It is obvious that the way it is leveraged affects the value of the firm; it is an objective for financial managers to achieve a level of debt/equity that maximises the value of the company. As shown in the example above, the manufacturing firm's financing is composed of 55 per cent short- and long-term debt and 45 per cent equity, therefore its assets would have to decline by more than 45 per cent before it becomes insolvent. For the bank an 8 per cent decline in its assets would make the bank insolvent.

Source: Adapted from Koch, T.W. and MacDonald, S.S. (2000), *Bank Management*, 4th edn. Orlando, FL: The Dryden Press, p. 521.

affected by changes in interest and exchange rates as well as variations in credit conditions that can affect both on- and off-balance sheet positions. In such a context banks' need for capital is much higher compared to the past.

8.2.1.4 Banks' income structure

The profitability of a bank can be derived from its income statement. Also known as its **profit and loss account**, this measures bank performance between two year-end balance sheets. The relationship between the balance sheet and income statement relates to the fact that the balance sheet reports stock values (e.g., the amount of outstanding loans), whereas the income statement represents cash flow values for a particular year (e.g., the interest received on outstanding loans). Therefore, the income statement reflects the revenue sources in banking as well as the costs.

The **costs**, derived from the liabilities side of the balance sheet, relate to the payments that banks have to undertake such as: payment of interest on deposits, dividends to shareholders, interest on debt, provision for loan losses and taxes. The **revenues**, generated by the assets, include: interest earned on loans and investments; fees and commissions (interest and non-interest revenue). Then as any other firm, banks also incur staffing and other operating costs.

> **Bank profits = Income – Costs**

In the relationship above, income is equal to interest and non-interest income; costs are the sum of interest costs, staffing costs and other operating costs. Table 8.6 shows a simplified income statement and how **profits** are calculated for a retail bank (see also Box 12.1).

The *interest income* is the income generated on all banks' assets, such as loans, securities and deposits lent out to other institutions, households and other borrowers. *Interest expense* is the sum of interest paid on all interest-bearing liabilities such as all deposit accounts, CDs, short-term borrowing and long-term debt. The difference between interest income (revenues) and interest expenses (costs) is the *Net Interest Income* (NII).

Provision for Loan Losses (PLL) is the amount charged against earnings to establish a reserve sufficient to absorb expected loan losses. It can be subtracted from net interest income in recognition that some of the reported interest income overstates what will actually be received after loan defaults. Thus *net interest income after provisions for loan losses (PLL)* is calculated as the difference between NII and PLL.

Table 8.6 A simplified bank income statement

a	Interest income
b	Interest expense
$c\ (=a-b)$	Net interest income (or 'spread')
d	Provision for loan losses (PLL)
$e\ (=c-d)$	Net interest income after PLL
f	Non-interest income
g	Non-interest expense
$h\ (=f-g)$	Net non-interest income
$i\ (=e+h)$	Pre-tax net operating profit
l	Securities gains (losses)
$m\ (=i\pm l)$	Profit before taxes
n	Taxes
o	Extraordinary items
$p\ (=m-n-o)$	Net profit
q	Cash dividends
$r\ (=p-q)$	Retained profit

Non-interest income is the income generated by fee income, commissions and trading income and has become important due to increased emphasis on this source of revenue in recent years. It includes, for example, fees and deposit service charges, such as fees paid on safe-deposit boxes; commissions (e.g., from insurance sales) and gains/losses from trading in securities; and other non-interest income sources such as gains/losses on foreign transactions and from undertaking other OBS activities (such as securities underwriting). *Non-interest expenses* include salaries and fringe benefits paid to employees, property and equipment expenses and other non-interest expenses (such as deposit insurance premiums and depreciation). *Net non-interest income* will be the difference between non-interest income and non-interest expenses.

As we move down Table 8.6 we find the item *pre-tax net operating profit*, that is the sum of interest income minus PLL plus net non-interest income. *Profit before taxes* will be equal to *Pre-tax net operating profit* ± the *securities gains (losses)* that may occur when the bank sells securities from its portfolio at prices above the initial cost to the bank. By deducting taxes and other extraordinary items (that can include for example the revenue from the sale of real assets), it is possible to obtain the *net profit* that is the profit after tax.

Finally, *retained profits* will be equal to net profit minus dividends.

A profit and loss account for Barclays is shown in Table 8.7.

Table 8.7 Barclays' profit and loss account 2000-04 (£m)

	2000	2001	2002	2003	2004
Interest income	11,788	13,458	12,044	12,427	13,665
Interest expense	6,680	7,492	5,839	5,823	6,823
Net interest income	**5,108**	**5,966**	**6,205**	**6,604**	**6,842**
Fee and commission receivable	3,676	4,202	4,454	4,896	5,672
Fee and commission payable	320	465	529	633	706
Trading income	677	1,011	833	1,054	1,493
Other operating income	353	428	364	490	644
Total non-interest income	**4,386**	**5,176**	**5,122**	**5,807**	**7,103**
Total operating income	**9,494**	**11,142**	**11,327**	**12,411**	**13,945**
Employment Costs	3,219	3,714	3,755	4,295	4,998
Other administrative expenses (e.g, property and equipment expenses)	1,967	2,303	2,312	2,404	2,758
Depreciation and amortisation	306	539	557	554	594
Total operating expenses	**5,492**	**6,556**	**6,624**	**7,253**	**8,350**
Operating profit before provisions	**4,002**	**4,588**	**4,703**	**5,158**	**5,595**
Provisions for loan losses, contingent liabilities and commitments	816	1,150	1,485	1,348	1,092
Operating profit	**3,186**	**3,438**	**3,218**	**3,812**	**4,502**
Exceptional items	206	−13	13	33	101
Profit on ordinary activity before tax	**3,392**	**3,425**	**3,205**	**3,845**	**4,603**
Tax on profit on ordinary activities	901	943	955	1,076	1,289
Profit on ordinary activity after tax	**2,491**	**2,482**	**2,250**	**2,769**	**3,314**
Payment to minority interests	46	36	20	25	46
Profit for the financial year attributable to the members of Barclays Bank PLC	**2,445**	**2,446**	**2,230**	**2,744**	**3,268**
Dividends	927	1,110	1,206	1,340	1,538
Profit retained for the financial year	1,518	1,336	1,024	1,404	1,730

Source: http://www.investorrelations.barclays.co.uk.

At year-end 2004 Barclays plc had total operating income of about £14 billion, an increase of 47 per cent from 2000. The increase had been brought about by a rise in interest income (+34 per cent) and by a significant increase (by more than 60 per cent) in non-interest income over the period. Barclays' net profits reached £3.3 billion in 2004, corresponding to a 33 per cent growth since 2000.

While the income statement gives a good indication of the profitability of a commercial bank, **bank performance** over time is usually measured in relation to ratio analysis that uses the information contained in both the balance sheet and the income statements. Section 8.4 focuses on the importance of ratio analysis and how to interpret the most common financial ratios.

Before moving on to ratio analysis, Section 8.3 illustrates the main characteristics of investment banks' financial statements and how they compare with commercial banks.

8.3 Investment banks' financial statements

We saw in Section 3.6 that large-scale wholesale financing activities are typically carried out by investment banks. Moreover, investment banks offer a range of services such as securities underwriting (including the issue of commercial paper, Eurobonds and other securities) and provide corporate advisory services on mergers and acquisition (M&As) and other types of corporate restructuring. In a nutshell, investment banks mainly deal with corporations and other large institutions and they typically do not deal with retail customers, apart from the provision of upmarket private banking services.

The different activities that investment banks perform are reflected in the structure of their financial statements. It follows that the balance sheet structure and income statement of investment banks differ substantially from those of commercial banks.

8.3.1 Investment banks' balance sheet

Table 8.8 exhibits a simplified investment bank balance sheet.

8.3.1.1 Assets side

On the asset side investment banks keep *cash and other non-earning assets*. These assets include, for example, short-term highly liquid securities along with assets set aside for regulatory purposes.

Another important item is *trading assets*. These are the banks' trading activities that consist primarily of securities brokerage, trading and underwriting, and derivatives dealing and brokerage. Generally, trading assets include cash instruments (e.g., securities) and derivatives instruments used for trading purposes to manage risk exposures. Other cash instruments can include, for instance, loans held for trading purposes (i.e., loans that can be traded in the secondary market).

Investment banks enter into secured lending in order to meet customer needs, and obtain securities for settlement. Under these transactions, they can receive collateral from resale agreements and securities borrowed transactions, customer

Table 8.8 **A simplified investment bank balance sheet**

Assets	Liabilities
Cash and other non-earning assets Trading assets Securities financing transactions (receivable) Investment securities Loans, notes and mortgages Other investments Fixed assets Other assets	Commercial paper and other short-term borrowing Trading liabilities Securities financing transactions (payable) Long-term borrowing Deposits Other payables
	Equity Other capital terms
Total assets	**Total liabilities and equity**

margin loans and other loans. *Securities financing transactions* are collaterised securities that the bank can sell or re-pledge.

Securities owned for non-trading purposes are classified as *investment securities*. They are marketable investment securities and other financial instruments the bank owns, and can include highly liquid debt securities such as those held for liquidity management purposes, equity securities and other investments such as long-term ones held for strategic purposes. Investment banks' lending and related activities such as loan originations, syndications and securitisations (see Section 9.6) are reported under *loans, notes and mortgages.*

Other investments include other receivables such as amounts due from customers on cash and margin transactions.

Fixed assets consist of equipment and facilities. Typical examples are technology hardware and software and owned facilities (e.g., premises).

Other assets consist of intangible assets and goodwill as well as assets generated from any unrealised gains on derivatives used to hedge the bank's borrowing and investing activities. It can also include prepaid expenses and real estate purchased for investment purposes.

8.3.1.2 Liabilities and equity

As shown in Table 8.8, funding of investment banks derives from various sources. The main items are:

- *Collaterised securities* – derive from the bank entering secured borrowing transactions and securities sold under agreement to repurchase; this includes payables under repurchase agreements and payables under securities loaned transactions. (This item corresponds to securities financing transactions on the asset side.)
- *Trading liabilities* – include activities that the investment bank undertakes based on future expectations such as trading securities and derivatives dealing and brokerage.
- *Commercial paper* – consists of short-term negotiable debt instruments that the bank issues to raise unsecured funding and that are traded in the money market.

The investment bank can issue *other short-term debt instruments* – that may be linked to the performance of equity or other indices – and *medium- and long-term debt instruments.* Another liability is *deposits* (savings and time deposits) that are typically high-volume corporate deposits, followed by *other liabilities* to customers, brokers and dealers, etc.; and finally, *stockholders' equity.*

8.3.2 Investment banks' income statements

Investment banks, like commercial banks, are required to publish their profit and loss accounts (or 'statement of earnings') that report all costs, revenues and net profits for the financial year. Investment banks' revenues derive from the following four sources:

- trading and principal investments;
- investment banking;
- asset management, portfolio service fees and commissions; and
- interest income.

The components of *trading and principal investments* relate to income generated from trading in: equities and equity derivatives; corporate debt; debt derivatives; mortgage and municipals; government and agency obligations; and foreign exchange. *Investment banking* generally includes underwriting and financial advisory services (e.g., M&As advice). *Asset management and portfolio services* can originate revenues in the form of commissions (e.g., agency transactions for clients on main stock and futures exchanges). More specifically, asset management is a source of fees for investment banks generated by providing investment management (e.g., managing company pension funds and other investments) and advisory services to both individuals and institutions.

Securities services can also generate fees from various activities such as brokerage, financing services and securities lending, and matched book businesses. Finally, *interest income* derives primarily from wholesale lending activity of the bank.

On the cost side, the most important item is interest expenses that can be relatively high (compared to commercial banks), while the bulk of operating expenses relates to staff costs. Other costs include, among others:

- communication and technology
- occupancy and related depreciation
- brokerage, clearing and exchange fees
- professional fees
- marketing
- other expenses.

Box 8.2 illustrates the financial statement composition of Merrill Lynch, one of the top investment banks in the world.

Box 8.2   Merrill Lynch financial statements (2004)

Founded in 1914 by Charles E. Merrill and Edmund C. Lynch, Merrill Lynch is today a global investment bank with 50,600 employees working in 36 countries and had net revenues of US$22 billion as at December 2004. Merrill Lynch provides a variety of services, from capital markets services, investment banking and advisory services, wealth management, asset management, insurance, banking and related products and services.

The pie diagrams report the assets and liabilities composition for Merrill Lynch in 2004.

On the asset side, the most relevant items are investment and collaterised securities (i.e., securities bought under agreement to resell). These constitute the bulk of total assets (41 per cent). Another relevant item is trading assets (28 per cent) that comprise securities and financial derivatives held by the bank for trading purposes.

Fixed assets – here incorporating both tangible (e.g., premises) and intangible (e.g., goodwill) assets – appear modest, at around 2 per cent; one reason could be that investment banks do not generally

▶

Figure 8.4 Merrill Lynch: sources of revenue, 2004

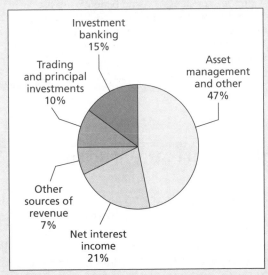

Source: Merril Lynch (2004) Fact Book and Annual Report.

Figure 8.5 Merrill Lynch: net revenues by geographic regions, 2004

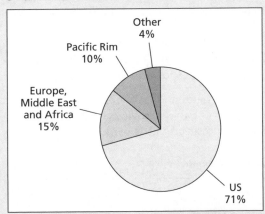

Source: Merril Lynch (2004) Fact Book and Annual Report.

need a large branch network. It is also worth noting that Merrill Lynch holds a relatively high proportion of liquid assets (around 7 per cent).

The traditional banking activity of selling loans and collecting deposits does not seem as important as other activities for the bank: wholesale loans and deposits are relatively small, amounting to 8 per cent and 12 per cent of total assets respectively. This is because unlike commercial banks, whose main activity has traditionally been to transform the maturity and size of deposits into loans, investment banks operate by reshuffling a broad range of securities

transactions. Therefore the assets and liabilities structure of investment banks usually indicates shorter maturity characteristics on the assets side of the balance sheet compared with a traditional commercial bank. Merrill Lynch's funding derives mainly from securities sold under agreement to repurchase (29 per cent), long-term borrowing (18 per cent) and trading liabilities (18 per cent).

Figure 8.6 Merrill Lynch: non-interest expenses, 2004

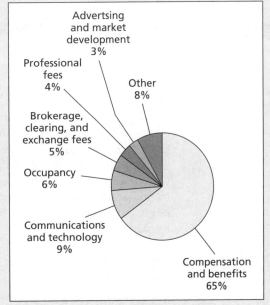

Source: Merril Lynch (2004) Fact Book and Annual Report.

Figure 8.7 Merrill Lynch breakdown of costs, 2004

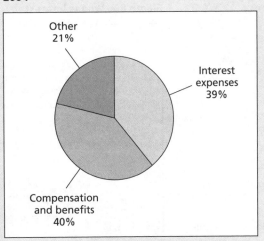

Source: Merril Lynch (2004) Fact Book and Annual Report.

The revenue sources and cost characteristics of Merrill Lynch for 2004 are illustrated in the charts above. They show that most revenues derive from asset management and commissions (47 per cent), net interest income (21 per cent) and investment banking activities (15 per cent). It is notable that Merrill Lynch earns nearly three-quarters of its net revenues in the US. Operations in Europe, the Middle East and Africa account for just 15 per cent. On the operating costs side, staff expenses (in the form of employee compensation and benefits) are prevalent (65 per cent). It is worth noting that on the cost side interest expenses can be particularly high. For Merrill Lynch the proportion of non-interest to interest expenses is about 60:40 of total costs.

Source: Merrill Lynch (2004) Fact Book and Annual Report.

8.4 Bank performance and financial ratio analysis

The significant changes that have have occurred in the financial sector industry in all advanced economies has increased the importance of performance analysis for modern banks. As discussed in Chapter 2, the new operating environment is characterised by more intense competition and a movement towards increasingly market-oriented banking systems. In many countries, the widespread privatisation process has had the effect of weakening political interference in bank management while the objective of shareholders' wealth maximisation (maximising the returns to investors holding equity shares in the bank) is now a priority restrained merely by prudential regulatory constraints. It is not surprising that the increased riskiness of the environment in which banks operate has increased the need for prudential regulation (see Chapter 7).

Performance analysis is an important tool used by various agents operating either internally to the bank (e.g., managers) or who form part of the bank's external operating environment (e.g., regulators) as shown in Figure 8.8.

● *Shareholders, bondholders*: investors in shares and in bonds issued by the bank, and bank managers and other employees have an obvious economic and strategic interest in the current and future prospects of the banking firm.

Figure 8.8 Who is interested in bank performance?

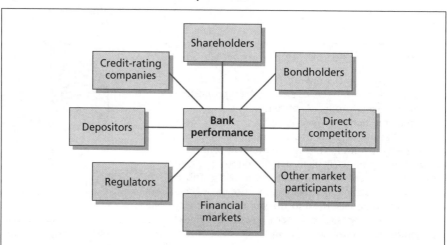

- *Direct competitors*: peer group analyses compare the profitability of similar banking institutions operating in similar operating environments; in some cases the homogeneity of the groups being analysed allows for the use of sophisticated statistical techniques.
- *Other market participants*: competitors (or other firms) that represent potential take-over or merger possibilities will rely on **financial ratio analysis** to assess the viability of potential M&A activity and to evaluate potential economic synergies.
- *Financial markets*: capital and money market participants will use ratio analysis to monitor the performance of banks. Money market participants, especially those involved with lending in the interbank market will need to assess the credit-worthiness of the banks they are lending to. A deterioration in bank performance may increase credit risk and therefore interbank lenders will require higher returns on their loans. Banks with higher capital ratios will more likely be able to achieve cheaper finance in the interbank markets (as such banks will be perceived as being less risky). Capital market participants and analysts also use ratio analysis to assess the performance of banks as a change in bank performance can alter the valuation of long-term bonds and shares issued by banks. For example, potential bondholders will rely on performance trends as a guide to their investments.
- *Regulators*: domestic and international regulatory authorities will also be concerned about the performance of banking institutions. For example, financial regulators need to evaluate the solvency, liquidity and overall performance of banking firms to gauge the likelihood of potential problems. Competition authorities also investigate bank performance indicators to analyse whether banks are making excess profits and behaving in an uncompetitive manner.
- *Depositors*: The smooth performance of banks is valuable for depositors who trust their bank will remain profitable and not expose itself to too much risk.
- Finally, *credit rating companies* – such as Moody's, Standard and Poor's and FitchIBCA – analyse performance information to compile analyses and ratings of banks operating in a certain country or group of countries.

Bank performance is calculated using ratio analysis and assessed with the aim of: (1) looking at past and current trends; and (2) determining future estimates of bank performance. Financial ratio analysis investigates different areas of bank performance, such as profitability, asset quality and solvency.

The key ratios for measuring the performance of the banking firm are discussed below. The tools that can be used to calculate performance are derived from the information revealed by periodic financial reports produced by the accounting system: the balance sheet and the income statement. Table 8.9 outlines selected indicators of 50 major EU banks' asset quality, profitability and solvency as reported recently by the European Central Bank.

8.4.1 Profitability ratios

Profitability ratios typically used in banking are ROE (Return-on-equity) ROA (Return-on-assets), NIM (**Net interest margin**) and C/I (Cost–income) ratio.

ROA is the return-on-assets calculated as net income/total assets; this ratio indicates how much net income is generated per £ of assets.

Table 8.9 **Selected indicators of 50 major EU commercial banks' asset quality, profitability and solvency (%)**

	2001	2002	2003
Profitability			
Return-on-assets (ROA) (after tax and extraordinary items)	0.48	0.39	0.44
Return-on-equity (ROE) (after tax and extraordinary items)	10.34	7.99	8.70
Net interest margin (NIM) (net interest income/total assets)	1.30	1.36	1.33
Net non-interest income/total assets	1.27	1.24	1.22
Non-interest income/total operating income	50.74	48.85	47.52
Cost–income ratio	68.27	67.90	64.47
Asset quality			
Provision for loan losses/total operating income	9.60	13.18	11.13
Provision for loan losses/total loans	0.50	0.69	0.61
Provision for loan losses/total assets	0.24	0.31	0.28
Non-Performing loans/total loans	2.45	2.84	2.30
Solvency (or capital strength)			
Basle Tier 1 ratio	6.29	6.65	6.67
Basle Tier 2 ratio	9.46	9.60	9.91

Source: Adapted from ECB (2004b) *EU Banking Sector Stability*, p. 48.

$$ROA = net\ income/total\ assets \tag{8.1}$$

ROE is probably the most important indicator of a bank's profitability and growth potential. It is the rate of return to shareholders or the percentage return on each £ of equity invested in the bank.

$$ROE = net\ income/total\ equity \tag{8.2}$$

The ROE can be decomposed into two parts: the ROA (= net income/total assets), that measures average profit generated relative to the bank's assets and the so-called Equity Multiplier (EM).

$$EM = total\ assets/total\ equity \tag{8.3}$$

so that

$$ROE = ROA \times EM \tag{8.4}$$

This decomposition[3] is important because it allows financial analysts to understand the interrelationship between the various ratios and helps banks to invest in areas where the risk-adjusted returns are greater.

NIM is net interest margin and measures the net interest income relative to the bank's total, average or earning assets.

$$NIM = [(interest\ income - interest\ expense)/total\ assets] \tag{8.5}$$

---

[3] This decomposition of the ROE uses a traditional method in corporate finance known as 'Du Pont Model', from the name of the US Corporation that first applied it in the 1920s. See for example, Sinkey (1998).

It reflects the difference between interest earned on assets minus interest costs per £ of assets. The NIM measures the bank's *spread* per £ of assets. High NIM suggests that the difference between deposit rates and loan (+ other interest earning assets) rates are high, and vice versa. As we have noted in earlier chapters, NIM has been falling in many banking markets reflecting increased competition in the deposits and loan markets – the difference between how much banks pay on deposits and how much they earn on loans is declining.

Finally, the Cost–income ratio (C/I) is a quick test of efficiency that reflects bank non-interest costs as a proportion of income.

C/I = non-interest expenses / (net interest income + non-interest income)

$$(8.6)$$

where non-interest expenses are considered as the main inputs to the production process of a bank and total operating income is the output.

As shown in Table 8.9, typically ROA ranges between 0.4 and 0.5 per cent for the 50 major EU banks over the period 2001–03 while ROE is around 10 per cent and NIM 1.30 per cent. Usually, the benchmark for ROA level is around 1 per cent while ROE is considered good when over 10 per cent. High-performing banks usually adopt a target ROE figure of 15+ per cent. Generally speaking, the higher these ratios the better from a banks' perspective, as higher NIM should feed through into greater net income thus boosting ROA and ROE. Table 8.9 illustrates the recent decline in European bank Cost–income ratios – the lower this ratio the better for the bank, because a low C/I indicates that the bank is operating in an efficient way.

Table 8.10 reports the key profitability ratios for three investment banks in 2004. It is noticeable that for all banks ROE exceeds 14 per cent while ROA ranges between 0.7 per cent and 0.9 per cent, almost twice the figure reported by commercial banks in Table 8.9. As expected, net interest margin is significantly lower than for commercial banks. We discussed the secondary role that 'traditional' banking activities have for investment banks in Box 8.2. A more suitable measure of profitability for investment banks is the **profit margin**; that is equal to earnings before income taxes to total operating income and takes into account both interest and non-interest income.

Recently investment banks have performed relatively well and this trend is expected to continue, as reported in Box 8.3.

Table 8.10 Selected ratios for three investment banks (2004)

2004	Merrrill Lynch %	Lehman Brothers %	Goldman Sachs %
Return-on-assets	0.7	0.8	0.9
Return-on-equity	14.1	15.9	18.2
Net interest margin	0.7	0.4	0.6
Cost-to-Income ratio	73.5	69.6	66.2
Profit margin	26.5	30.4	31.9

Source: Individual institutions annual reports (2004) and authors' calculations.

Box 8.3   Growth of trading: will investment banks sustain their explosive advance?

Investment banks have delivered explosive growth in trading revenue during the last five years, a performance that has helped them to weather a downturn arranging stock sales and mergers. The numbers show it. Three of the four largest US investment banks with November year-ends – Goldman Sachs, Lehman Brothers and Bear Stearns – generated record earnings in 2004 thanks, mainly, to their trading prowess.

Consider Goldman Sachs. It generated $20.55bn in total net revenue last year. Trading-related revenue made up 65 per cent of the total. In 2000, trading-related revenue accounted for 40 per cent of the $16.6bn total. The bank's biggest contributor in 2004 was the fixed income, currencies and commodities department, known as FICC. It had record net revenue last year of $7.32bn, a gain of 31 per cent from 2003, the previous record year, and about 2.5 times the $3bn reported in 2000.

Rivals have reported similar gains. The figures have impressed investors but also have generated fear that Wall Street's trading departments, especially those involved with fixed income, currencies and commodities are due for an inevitable cyclical downturn in 2005 or beyond.

The investment banks do not deny that trading is a cyclical business and do not pretend that their trading departments are immune from downturns. They do, however, argue that improvements in technology are allowing them to open new markets and manage risk more efficiently, increasing their chances of weathering downturns better than in the past. They also say another factor helping them is the rise in sophisticated clients, especially hedge funds, which adopt their new products quickly and find uses for them that go beyond that for which they were intended.

Lloyd Blankfein, president and chief operating officer of Goldman Sachs, says: 'I think that concern over the growing percentage of trading revenues at investment banks is misplaced.' Mr Blankfein has been instrumental in keeping Goldman Sachs' traders adept at managing risk and shifting resources to meet the needs of clients. Goldman Sachs reported $9.29bn in net revenue from all trading last year. If equities commissions and principal investments are included that total rises to $13.33bn, an increase of 28 per cent from 2003.

To understand further how explosive trading growth has been at Goldman Sachs, it helps to know that, in 2000, it generated net revenue from trading of $6.49bn. FICC revenue was $3bn. Lehman Brothers and Bear Stearns have also at least doubled the amount of fixed income trading revenue they generated in the five years from 2000 to 2004. Mr Blankfein says he thinks concern over the growing percentage of trading revenues at investment banks is misplaced for several reasons. 'First, client activity is the key driver of trading – it is our role and valuable franchise to be asked to price and assume risks that our clients want to shed', he says, 'and trading opportunities come from increasingly diverse businesses and sources, involving broad and often uncorrelated markets.'

Competitors echo Mr Blankfein's opinion. Morgan Stanley did not achieve record profits in 2004, but its trading divisions have generated explosive revenue growth as well, especially in fixed income.

Jim O'Brien, co-head of Morgan Stanley's corporate credit group which trades investment-grade and high-yield bonds, says: 'What has characterised the improved performance is bigger risk taking and bets in macro markets.'

Investment banks, he adds, have benefited from managing risk more dynamically and from trading more often with clients. Morgan Stanley and others, says Mr O'Brien, were taking steps to make it even easier to trade and manage risk. This includes finding ways to improve liquidity, developing more index products and promoting the development of electronic trading. 'Our view is that as the market gets bigger, we will benefit,' says Mr O'Brien. Morgan Stanley boosted its fixed income trading revenue last year to $5.56bn, up from $2.7bn in 2000.

Technology has played an enormous role in the growth of trading profits and will continue to do so this year, say traders. Advances in software have allowed investment banks to identify more efficiently the trading opportunities and to analyse the accompanying risk. Take Credit Suisse First Boston, which has an advanced execution services (AES) division that develops algorithms to help clients trade electronically. The product helps clients to protect their anonymity, provides split-second forecasts and trades throughout the day.

Source: Financial Times (2005) 'Investment Banking Survey', 27 January, by David Wells.

8.4.2 Asset quality

Lending is still one of the most important activities of banks. While it is expected that all banks will have to bear some positive levels of bad loans and loan losses (see Box 8.4), one of the key objectives of bank management is to minimise such losses. In the context of the income–expense statement, financial analysts can control the PLL to manipulate their accounting earnings. For example, more conservative bankers may understate their accounting earnings by building a large and above average loan-loss reserve; while more aggressive bankers may overstate their accounting earnings by keeping the loan-loss reserve low (Sinkey, 1998, p. 59).

As shown in Table 8.9, over the period 2001–03 the provision for loan losses/total operating income ranged between 9.60 and 13.18 per cent. Table 8.9 also indicates that the non-performing loans/total loans ratio over the same period amounted to 2.5 per cent.

8.4.3 Cost of capital and shareholder value creation in banking

While the above discussion of bank performance measures focuses on traditional indicators, one innovative indicator that is now widely used by banks (and other companies) relates to what is known as 'shareholder value creation'. The main strategic objective of a profit-oriented bank is to generate **shareholder value** for its owners (shareholders). A bank can create shareholder value by pursuing a strategy that maximises the return on capital invested relative to the (opportunity) **cost of capital** (the cost of keeping equity shareholders and bondholders happy). In other words if a bank invests in a project that generates greater returns than the cost to shareholders of financing the project then this should boost returns to holders of the banks' shares (in terms of capital appreciation of stock and higher dividends).

Box 8.4 What are non-performing loans?

Non-performing loans (NPLs) are loans on which debtors have failed to make contractual payments for a pre-determined time. It should be noted that a loan classified as non-performing does not necessarily lead to losses. If there is adequate collateral, losses might not occur. Conversely, loans may be lost even though they were never classified as non-performing. Not all countries use the same definition for NPLs, and there may even be different definitions in use within a single country depending on the sector involved (financial institutions, quoted corporations, small enterprises, government entities, and so forth). At the international level, the definition provided by paragraph 4.84 of the IMF's *Compilation Guide on Financial Soundness Indicators* reads, summarised, as follows: a loan is non-performing when payments of interest and principal are past due by 90 days or more, or at least 90 days of interest payments have been capitalised, financed or delayed by agreement, or payments are less than 90 days overdue, but there are other good reasons to doubt that payments will be made in full.

Source: IMF (2004), *The Treatment of Non-performing Loans in Macroeconomic Statistics*, An Issue Paper Prepared for the December 2004 Meeting of the Advisory Expert Group on National Accounts.

The concept can be applied to an individual project, like a bank considering making a strategic investment in another country, or for the whole banks' performance overall.

So shareholder value is created when:

> **Return on capital invested in the project > Cost of capital to the firm**

or

> **Return on capital (ROC) > Cost of capital**

In order to add shareholder value, firms must invest in projects that generate returns exceeding their cost of capital. To calculate the cost of capital we can use the Capital Asset Pricing Model (CAPM) where:

$$R_i = R_f + \beta \, (R_m - R_f) \tag{8.7}$$

where R_i is the required rate of return on an investment;
R_f is the risk-free rate;
R_m refers to the market return; and
β is a measure of the volatility of the company's equity relative to the overall market.[4]

The CAPM (see Appendix A2) states that investors require a return from holding a company's shares that exceeds the risk-free rate (R_f), to compensate them for holding equity over bonds (this is $R_m - R_f$, otherwise known as the equity risk premium) and for the riskiness of the company relative to the whole market (β).

For example, if a company has beta (β) of 1.5, and assuming a risk-free rate of 6 per cent (given by the US long-bond rate) and an equity premium of 5 per cent ($R_m - R_f$) then the cost of capital to the firm will be 13.5 per cent. In other words, to maintain shareholder value, this firm will have to invest in projects that generate returns greater than 13.5 per cent if they are to add to shareholder wealth. Investments that generate returns of less than 13.5 per cent will destroy shareholder value. The equity market premium (the difference between equity and bond returns) is usually calculated over a 20- or 25-year period and there is much debate as to how large this premium is, although the US equity market premiums are almost always found to be greater than those in the United Kingdom, and they are even lower in continental Europe. Betas (β) should also be calculated over long periods as short-term estimates may yield unreliable cost of capital estimates.

Box 8.5 explains the calculation of the cost of capital for NatWest and the Royal Bank of Scotland Group (RBSG) which was presented as evidence to the Competition Commission Report on the 'Supply of Banking Services by Clearing Banks to Small and Medium-Sized Enterprises' in 2002 (see Section 12.3.3). This shows that the equity cost of capital for the two UK banks was around 11 per cent – these banks would need to generate a return-on-equity of greater than 11 per cent if they wished to create shareholder value for their owners (equity holders).

Cost of capital calculations can be done for the whole bank or divisions/business areas within a bank in order to determine the allocation of capital within the organisation. For example, if a bank's mortgage business is generating returns

---

[4] A beta of less than one indicates lower risk than the market; a beta of more than one indicates higher risk than the market.

Box 8.5	Calculating the cost of equity capital for NatWest and the Royal Bank of Scotland Group (RBSG)

CAPM 'standard' cost of equity capital

The standard model for the cost of equity capital is the Capital Asset Pricing Model (CAPM). Despite some drawbacks this model continues to be the most widely used tool for business decision making. In correspondence to date, RBSG have been asked by the Competition Commission to provide the cost of capital that is used by the bank. However, the appropriate benchmark is not the cost of equity capital currently used, but the cost of equity capital rates that should be used for making assessments about performance in each of 1998, 1999 and 2000. This should be the cost of equity capital prevailing at the start of each year, when we can assume that decisions were made in respect of those years.

This paper therefore starts by setting out the cost of equity capital as it would have been for NatWest and RBSG (according to the CAPM) at the beginning of each of the years 1998, 1999 and 2000.

Risk-free rate

In consultation with London Business School, we have taken 31 December 1997, 1998 and 1999 six-month LIBOR as the risk-free rates applying at the start of 1998, 1999 and 2000. Six-month LIBOR is used because it avoids some of the liquidity problems that are evident with government bill rates.

Equity risk premium

A wide range of equity premiums can be quoted from the literature, ranging from 3 per cent to 9 per cent. For this analysis a rate of 4 per cent is used to reflect lower expected returns in the future.

CAPM beta figures

For a beta we have consulted the London Business School Risk Management Service to get the start of year betas for NatWest and RBS.

The cost of equity capital for NatWest and Royal Bank of Scotland Group are shown in Table 8.11:

Table 8.11 'Standard' cost of equity capital for NatWest and RBS

NatWest	1998	1999	2000
Risk free rate (six month LIBOR)	7.7%	5.9%	6.2%
Equity risk premium (%)	4.0%	4.0%	4.0%
Beta (start of year from LBS RMS)*	1.14	1.20	1.12
CAPM 'standard cost of equity capital (%)	12.3%	10.7%	10.7%
RBS			
Risk free rate (six month LIBOR)	7.7%	5.9%	6.2%
Equity risk premium (%)	4.0%	4.0%	4.0%
Beta (start of year from LBS RMS)*	1.02	1.27	1.24
CAPM 'standard' cost of equity capital (%)	11.8%	11.0%	11.2%

Note: The term 'standard' is used as the report goes on to make various adjustments to these estimates.
* LBS RMS stands for London Business School Risk Measurement Service, see http://www.london.edu/finance/riskmeasurementservice.html

Source: Competition Commission Report (2002) *Supply of Banking Services by Clearing Banks to Small and Medium-Sized Enterprises*, Appendix 13.3. Charles River Associates note on 'normal' profits and rates of return (referred to in paragraph 13.240 of the main report) pp. 148–54.

greater than the cost of capital but credit card activities are making returns less than the cost of capital the bank should consider dedicating more capital resources to the former and also should think of ways of boosting returns in (or divesting) its credit card business.

Note that this is just the equity cost of capital and we can extend the analysis to include the cost of debt to present what is known as a weighted cost of capital. Also, one should note that there is a variety of other approaches that can be used to calculate the cost of capital (including a wide range of various accounting and other adjustments) and it should be stressed that cost of capital calculations are never definitive – they vary according to the calculation method used.

8.4.4 Solvency ratios

The Basle Accord (detailed in Section 7.8) requires banks to hold a minimum overall risk-weighted capital ratio of 8 per cent of which at least 50 per cent is in the form of equity (known as Tier 1) capital. More specifically, Tier 1 capital should be at least 4 per cent. Total capital adequacy ratio measures Tier 1 capital + Tier 2 capital; this ratio should be at least 8 per cent.

The total capital adequacy ratio cannot be calculated simply by looking at the balance sheet of a bank, as the bank has to classify its assets and off-balance sheet business according to certain risk categories and varying amounts of capital have to be held according to these risks. Recalling Section 7.8, for example, cash has a 0 per cent risk weighting requiring no capital backing, whereas unsecured loans require 8 per cent capital backing. Both Tier 1 and Tier 2 ratios can only be calculated internally by the bank. Banks have the option of publishing these ratios in their annual report. Financial ratios shown in Table 8.9 illustrate that on average the 50 major banks in Europe have been able to set aside a level of Tier 1 and total capital significantly above the 4 and 8 per cent minimum requirements.

Finally, we can say that, as equity is a cushion against asset malfunction, the simple equity/assets measure (which we can calculate from bank balance sheets) indicates the amount of protection afforded to the bank by the equity they invested in it. It follows that the higher this figure the more protection there is. However, remember that this is a crude measure of a bank's financial strength because, unlike the Basle Tier 1 and Tier 2 measures, this ratio does not take into account the riskiness of banking business.

8.4.4.1 The trade-off between safety and the return to shareholders

The amount of capital affects the returns to equity holders and ROE is a good measure for shareholders to know how much profit the bank is generating on their equity investments. Indeed, ROE is related directly with ROA (a typical measure of bank profitability), as follows:

$$\text{ROA} \times \text{EM} = \text{ROE} \tag{8.8}$$

rearranging:

$$\text{EM} = \text{ROE} \times \frac{1}{\text{ROA}} \tag{8.9}$$

substituting:

$$EM = \frac{\text{Total assets}}{\text{Total equity capital}} \qquad (8.10)$$

where EM is the equity multiplier that measures the extent to which a bank's assets are funded with equity relative to debt. To understand the importance of EM, consider two banks, both having total assets (with the same risk features) equal to £50 million and earning a ROA of 1.5 per cent, as shown in Table 8.12.

Table 8.12 An illustration of the trade-off between solvency and profitability

Bank	Total assets (a)	Total capital (b)	EM = (a) / (b)	ROA	ROE = EM × ROA
Bank Alpha	£50,000,000	£5,000,000	10	1.5%	15%
Bank Beta	£50,000,000	£2,500,000	20	1.5%	30%

As illustrated in Table 8.12, there is a trade-off between total capital and ROE. In particular, Bank Alpha displays the highest level of total capital and the lowest level of EM and ROE relative to Bank Beta. However, while the shareholders of Bank Beta will be earning twice as much than those of Bank Alpha, it is not necessarily true that Bank Beta is the most desirable for shareholders as Bank Beta is more risky as it has half the amount of capital backing the same amount of risky assets. There is clearly a **trade-off between safety and returns** to shareholders.

8.4.5 Some limitations of financial ratios

Financial ratios have their own limitations. First, generally one year's figures are insufficient to evaluate the performance of banks, and financial analysts typically look at trends to evaluate the ratios and their fluctuations over a timespan of at least five years. Second, precise comparisons between similar banks may be difficult as they often compete in different markets, have varying product features and customer bases, and so on. As such, ratio analysis may be misleading as it is often difficult to compare 'like with like'. Despite these problems, financial analysts often undertake *peer analysis of* similar banks and this involves the creation of peer groups. Third, ratios do not stand in isolation: they are interrelated. For example, poor profitability may affect liquidity and capital ratios. A bank that performs poorly may have to use its liquid assets (if it has an excess of such assets) to fund future lending thus reducing its liquidity ratios. Large losses may be written out of capital thus reducing capital ratios. Another important factor is that ratios relate to a particular point in time and there are seasonal factors that can distort them. Moreover, figures in the financial statements may be 'window-dressed'; that is, made to look *better than they really are*. (As was the case mentioned earlier, referring to banks over- or under-provisioning for bad loans). Similarly, financial statements may be manipulated and may not reflect accepted accounting procedures. That is why both domestic and international regulatory authorities have pointed out the need for more transparency, disclosure as well as uniformity of bank accounts as the markets become increasingly global. For example, at the EU level all listed companies that are required to publish consolidated accounts are also required to prepare their accounts in accordance with adopted International Financial Reporting Standards (IFRS) for accounting periods beginning on or after 1 January 2005.

8.5 Conclusions

This chapter examined the main items contained in banks' financial statements and introduced the key financial ratios used by banks to compare performance. It also highlighted the role of bank capital, simply defined as the difference between assets and liabilities. Typically, banks are highly leveraged compared to non-financial firms; therefore capital management techniques are vital to ensure the solvency of banking institutions. In the chapter we also briefly discuss the concept of shareholder value creation and the cost of equity capital.

Furthermore, the analysis of the income statement (or profit and loss) account has shown the various sources of income (interest and non-interest) and cost structure for banks and how to determine the profitability. The chapter also focused on the different activities that investment banks perform and how this is reflected in the structure of their financial statements. We noted that investment banks' balance sheet structure and income statements differ substantially from those of commercial banks.

Many different agents operating either internally or externally to the banks (from managers to regulators and credit-rating companies) will be interested in their performance, thus the last part of this chapter introduces a selection of key ratios used to gauge bank performance, focusing particularly on profitability, asset quality and solvency.

Key terms

Balance sheet	Return-on-assets
Income statement (profit and loss account)	Return-on-equity
Liabilities	Cost–income ratio
Assets	Net interest margin
Capital	Profit margin
Costs	Cost of capital
Revenues	Shareholder value
Profits	Trade-off between safety and returns
Bank performance	to shareholders
Financial ratio analysis	

Key reading   Koch, T.W. and MacDonald, S.S. (2000) *Bank Management*, 4th edn. Orlando, FL: The Dryden Press.

Sinkey, J.F. Jr (1998) *Commercial Bank Financial Management*, 5th edn. London: Prentice Hall International.

Revision questions and problems

1 What is a bank balance sheet? What are the main items in a commercial bank's balance sheet?

2 What is equity capital? What are the functions of capital?

3 What is a bank income statement?

4 What are the main differences between a bank balance sheet and income statement?

5 What are the main differences between commercial and investment banks' financial statements?

6 Using the information contained in Tables 8.4, 8.5 and 8.7, calculate: Barclays' ROA, ROE, NIM and C/I.

7 Explain how to calculate the cost of equity capital for a bank. Outline the main advantages of this approach to bank performance measurement compared to using standard profitability ratios.

8 Explain the trade-off between solvency and profitability.

9 What are the main limitations of bank financial ratios?

Chapter 9

Managing banks

Learning objectives

- To understand the basics of asset–liability management
- To identify the main management concerns on the balance sheet
- To describe the features of the most common off-balance sheet (OBS) transactions
- To identify the main off-balance sheet management concerns
- To explain loan sales and the process of securitisation

9.1 Introduction

The main objective of any private firm is the maximisation of profits and shareholders' wealth. In achieving this aim, the role of financial management is threefold: (1) to make investment decisions (i.e., how to allocate finance); (2) to undertake financing decisions (i.e., how to acquire finance); and (3) to control resources (i.e., how to conserve finance). Investment and financing decisions are vital elements used in the planning process to achieve the objectives of an organisation. For a manufacturing firm, for example, these objectives are measured in sales and profit goals over a specific period supported by financial targets (e.g., stock levels). For modern banks the goal is to manage assets and liabilities in a way that maximises profits while being generally 'safe and sound'. Prudence in banking is needed due to the special role that banks have in the economy and the potential 'domino' effects that a bank's failure may cause to the financial sector as a whole (see Chapter 7). More specifically, bank managers will have the following concerns:

- **Asset management**: the bank must make sure that its portfolio of assets includes low-risk assets and is well diversified.
- **Liability management**: the bank must acquire funds at the lowest possible cost.
- **Liquidity management**: the bank must predict with the lowest possible margin of error the daily withdrawals and other payments by customers in order to keep enough cash and other liquid assets readily available.
- **Capital management**: the bank must keep an adequate level of capital to comply with regulatory requirements in order to maintain the appropriate level of solvency.
- **OBS management**: the bank must control and limit the exposures derived from off-balance sheet transactions.

The function of financial management is to monitor actual performance against planned goals and targets. In doing so, managers rely on the information revealed by periodic financial reports produced by various accounting systems. We discussed in the previous chapter that these are the balance sheet and profit and loss account. As we will see throughout this chapter, bank financial management includes all five main points described above. In recent years, the development of the financial systems in most advanced economies, together with the widespread use of technology, have meant that banks today can use a relatively large variety of negotiable financial instruments (e.g., Certificate of Deposits or CDs) and processes (e.g., securitisation, see Section 9.6) to manage their asset and liability positions. Most institutions nowadays employ a combined management on both sides of the balance sheet involving a wide range of sophisticated risk-management instruments and procedures (see Section 9.2).

Another important aspect introduced in this chapter (Section 9.5) relates to off-balance sheet (OBS) activities. Bank managers' objectives of achieving relatively high levels of profitability and safety have induced them to engage in OBS activities. These are transactions that are not recorded on a bank's balance sheet, such as, for instance, derivatives activities, loan commitments and securitisation. As we will see, OBS business may expose the bank to new risks.

9.2 Asset–liability management (ALM)

In recent years, two sets of transformations have affected the composition of banks' balance sheets: on the one hand the growing importance of the liability side and the development, for example, of the CDs markets; and on the other hand the significant expansion of the interbank markets where banks can easily buy and sell excess liquidity, even overnight.

As a result of these major changes, modern banks have become more likely to undertake a co-ordinated management of both sides of the balance sheet rather than focusing on just the asset side. The main concerns and objectives of a bank manager on the asset and liability sides are summarised in Figure 9.1.

A bank can manage its assets well when it maximises the returns on loans and securities, for example by increasing loan screening and monitoring activities and by choosing low-credit-risk/high-return customers. Moreover, the bank will aim to diversify its portfolio of assets to avoid over-investing in a single sector. Another important objective of asset management involves decisions concerning the amount of liquid assets and reserves to keep on hand, taking into account the trade-off between profitability and liquidity. (Liquid assets tend to be low return so a bank that holds a high proportion of liquid assets on its balance sheet is likely to have lower income and profits.) On the liability side, the bank manager will aim to maximise the returns when operating in the money markets while at the same time minimising the interest paid on deposits.

Figure 9.1 Forms of asset management versus liability management

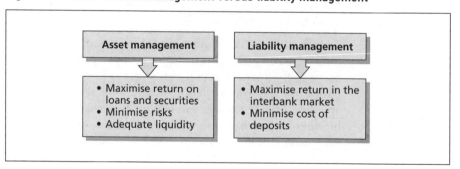

The co-ordinated and simultaneous decision on financing and investing is the essence of **asset–liability management**. Such a role is carried out by a bank's Asset and Liability Committee (ALCO). This committee can be considered the single most important management group and function in a bank. The committee should also consider the importance of the management of capital. This specific topic will be considered in more detail in Section 9.4. Box 9.1 illustrates the ALM process in practice using a useful scheme that can be found in Sinkey (1998). The next section highlights the importance of ALM in the context of liquidity management.

Box 9.1 What is asset–liability management in practice?

Sinkey (1998) defines ALM as an intermediate-term planning function (3–12 months) designed to move the bank in the direction of its long-run plan (2–5 years) while maintaining the flexibility to adapt to short-run (monthly) changes. In addition to the planning aspect of ALM, direction and control of the levels, changes (flows) and mixes of assets, liabilities and capital are integral parts of overall balance sheet management. From an accounting point of view, the key variables of ALM are NII (net interest income), ROA (return-on-assets) and ROE (return-on-equity). From an economic point of view the key variable is the MVE (market value of equity). Sinkey (1998) identifies a three-stage approach to balance-sheet co-ordinated management.

Stage I is a general approach that focuses on co-ordinated management of a bank's assets, liabilities and capital. Stage I requires co-ordination of the various specific functions that can be identified in Stage II.

Stage I: Global (or general) approach

Asset management	Liability management
	Capital management

Stage II distinguishes between the various components of a bank's balance sheet used in co-ordinating its overall portfolio management. Stage II is based on planning, directing, and controlling the levels, changes and mixes of the various balance sheet accounts, which generate the bank's income–expense statement (Stage III).

Stage II: Identification of specific components

Reserve-position management	Liability management
Liquidity management	Reserve-position liability management
Investment/securities management	Loan-position liability management
Loan management	Long-term debt management
Fixed-asset management	Capital management

Stage III illustrates a bank's profit and loss account as generated by its on- and off-balance sheet items, given prices and interest rates.

Stage III: Balance sheet generates profit and loss account

Profit = Interest revenue – interest expenses – provision for loan losses
            + non-interest revenue – non-interest expense – taxes

Policies to achieve objectives:
1. Spread management
2. Loan quality
3. Generating fee income and service charges
4. Control of non-interest operating expenses
5. Tax management
6. Capital adequacy

9.3 Liquidity management and the importance of reserves

Liquidity in banking is a key factor because a bank needs to ensure that it keeps enough cash or other liquid assets to meet its obligations to depositors and to satisfy customer loan demand. Essentially, a bank must always be able to meet both normal and abnormal shortfalls in anticipated cash-flows. Two issues are particularly important in the context of bank liquidity. First, there is a trade-off between liquidity and profitability. This means that the bank should calculate the opportunity cost of the amount kept as liquid assets because these assets are typically either non-earning or low yielding. Second, banks' reserves are an insurance against the costs associated with deposit outflows. Normally there are two types of reserves: required and excess reserves. It is obvious that if the bank has only modest excess reserves, in case of a large deposit outflow it will need changes in other parts of the balance sheet and will require a co-ordinated ALM approach. In particular, in the event of a bank having to obtain liquidity it has four options:

● borrowing from other banks;
● selling some of its securities;
● selling some of its loans; or
● borrowing from the central bank.

A bank experiencing a liquidity problem normally has to act quickly and discreetly to meet any shortfalls. If other institutions or depositors were to become aware that the bank had a liquidity shortage, it could create a run on the bank and possibly lead to insolvency. That is why selling off or calling in loans may be problematic for the troubled bank and the option of borrowing funds from the central bank may be a last resort (see Chapter 5 on the LOLR function of the central bank). It follows that liquidity and solvency are inextricably linked (see also Chapter 10).

9.4 Capital adequacy management

In Chapter 8 we illustrated a simple way to define bank capital as the value of assets minus the value of liabilities. Capital in banking is one of the major balance sheet concerns because it signals to what extent the bank is safe and sound, in other words 'solvent'. In contrast to bank liquidity, that is the ability of a bank to pay its obligations when they fall due, solvency is the ability of a bank to repay its obligations ultimately. As for bank liquidity, there is a trade-off between safety and returns because the higher the capital the lower the ROE. This is because a bank's capital resources are held in the form of very safe (and therefore low-yielding) assets such as government securities.

? Does not make sense !

However, from the point of view of the bank, capital is costly because higher capital means lower returns for equity holders; from the point of view of regulators capital is a necessary buffer to absorb possible losses before they must be charged against deposits.

The distinction between regulatory and economic capital is often made. *Regulatory capital* is the amount of capital required by regulators. (Recently the issue of how much capital is adequate has become an area of substantial discussion due to the interest that domestic and international regulators have in ensuring a safe and sound financial sector. For details on recent developments on this issue see Section 7.8). *Economic capital* is the capital that a bank believes it should hold to cover the risks it is undertaking.

Banks manage their economic capital, directing capital resources to different areas of business that aim to generate the highest risk-adjusted returns. So if a bank feels there are two business areas that carry the same risk, say unsecured lending to consumers and unsecured lending to SMEs, but the former generates higher returns – more capital should be dedicated to the former to develop this business to boost returns as the risks are the same as in SMEs lending but returns are higher (regulatory capital requirements are the same at 8 per cent). The bank should reduce capital dedicated to SMEs lending and redirect it to unsecured consumer lending. The efficient allocation of capital throughout the bank is critical if the bank wishes to maximise performance. Banks will scrutinise all areas of their business, looking at where economic capital can best be employed to generate the best risk-adjusted returns.

9.5 Off-balance sheet (OBS) business in banking

Modern banks do a considerable amount of OBS business. Typically these activities have no asset-backing and are sometimes referred to as contingent liabilities business. They generally refer to promises or commitments of the bank to undertake certain types of business in the future (by definition, *contingent* means 'dependent on something that may or may not occur'). For instance, an unused overdraft facility for a bank will be recorded as an OBS activity. Other common OBS items include derivatives transactions (such as futures, forwards, options and swaps transactions), underwriting business and various other commitments and guarantees.

For the bank, the earnings generated from OBS operations are fee-related and not shown on the balance sheet. When a contingent event occurs, the item or activity will be written in the asset (or liability) side of the balance sheet or a non-interest income item (or expense) will be generated in the income statement. Prior to the Basle Accord in 1988 no capital reserves or advancing were required for these types of operations because of their nature as OBS business for the bank. Moreover, OBS banking does not involve deposit funding (cash asset reserves are not needed).

One of the key reasons for moving assets off the balance sheet refers to the fact that bank managers' concerns about earnings and safety induce them to engage in OBS activities, securitisation and loan sales. If we recall from Chapter 8, ROE is calculated as net income/total equity and can be decomposed into two parts: the ROA (= net income/total assets), that measures average profit generated relative to the bank's assets and the Equity Multiplier (EM = assets/equity), so that *ROE = ROA × EM*. If banks wish to increase their profitability, they can engage in OBS business so that they restrain asset growth and increase fee income. These effects increase ROA and lower EM, all other things being equal, and meet the regulators' requirements of improved profitability and stronger capital positions.[1]

---

[1] The Basle Capital Accord however requires banks to convert the OBS activities into credit or asset equivalents in the calculation of risk-weighted assets. For more information, see Section 7.8.

Financial derivatives markets in particular have been growing rapidly in recent years. Derivatives are contracts involving rights or obligations relating to purchases or sales of underlying real or financial assets (e.g., gold and shares respectively), or relating to payments to be made in respect of movements in indices (e.g., the London FTSE 100)[2]. These rights and obligations are related to – or derived from – the underlying transactions, so they have been given the general name of *derivatives*. The major types of derivatives are: futures, forwards, options and swaps and these are discussed in more detail below.

The rights and obligations associated with derivatives contracts are relatively complex but these instruments often have the ability of being able to smooth out price changes in the underlying assets – on the *cash market* as it is often termed. Typically, for there to be a derivatives market, the associated cash market needs to be liquid – easy to trade in without moving the price of an asset (although prices can change for other reasons) – and volatile. 'Volatile' in this instance means 'changeable in price'. If the price cannot be moved then there is no opportunity to make a short-term profit by trading in that asset. The link between the cash market and the derivatives market is a process of buying and selling between the two, known as **arbitrage** – buying in one market and selling in another in order to exploit price differentials. If purchases are made in the lower price market and simultaneous sales are achieved in the higher price market, then as purchases will tend to raise prices and the sales will tend to lower them, the outcome will be that price differences will diminish.

Derivative products that are traded in organised exchanges are described as 'standard' contracts. However, the bank may want to strengthen customer relationships by offering products that are tailored to customers. For example, forwards contracts can only be traded over the counter (OTC) (see Box 9.2 on the differences between trading derivatives in official exchanges and OTC).

Derivative products can be used by banks to manage positions or 'hedge' for risk management purposes. **Hedging** involves reducing the risk of exposure to changes in market prices or rates that may affect bank income and value, through taking an offsetting position. For instance, a bank will be hedging risk if it engages in a financial transaction that offsets a long position (i.e., a market position in which a bank has bought an asset and thus owns it) by taking an additional short position at some future date (that is the sale of an asset that will be delivered at a future date). Alternatively, the bank can offset a short position (the bank has sold an asset that will be delivered at a future date) by taking an additional long position (that is to buy an asset) at some future date.

It is also common to distinguish between **micro-hedging** that is when a bank hedges a transaction associated with an individual asset, liability or commitment and **macro-hedging**, that is when a bank uses futures (or other derivatives) to hedge the entire balance sheet (e.g. the aggregate portfolio interest rate risk). It is obvious that the bank could also use derivatives to speculate (i.e., to take a position with the objective of making a profit) on anticipated price moves.

---

[2] The FTSE 100 is also referred to as the 'Footsie 100'.

Box 9.2   Derivative products: official exchanges and OTC markets

Derivatives can be traded either on an official exchange or OTC. In Europe the major derivative exchanges are the Euronext (since its acquisition of the LIFFE, the London International Financial Futures and Options Exchange in 2002, see http://www.liffe.com) and Eurex which is jointly operated by Deutsche Börse AG and SWX Swiss Exchange. In the United States, the major exchanges include the US Chicago Board of Trade, Chicago Board Options Exchange and Chicago Mercantile Exchange. London is currently the main centre for OTC derivatives transactions.

The first derivatives markets to be developed were the exchange-based markets and clearing houses. These are highly organised markets regulated by their owners who are usually traders. It is the exchange which decides on the:

- *Standard units* – currency, size, maturity – to be traded, and the times when trading begins and ceases each day.
- Rules of the *clearing house*, through which all deals are routed, with the result that a deal between (say) X who sells to Y becomes a deal between X selling to the clearing house which in turn sells to Y. Conversely, Y pays the clearing house who pays X (irrespective of whether Y pays the clearing house or X delivers to the clearing house). The clearing house interposes itself between all counterparties, thereby shouldering the burden of default and lessening the risk. In effect, it standardises the counterparty, just as deals are for standard products. It also facilitates delivery.
- *Margin* requirements, which all members have to deposit with the clearing house, to ensure that default is unlikely. In addition, all investors must maintain margins with their brokers who are, of course, members of the exchange. The initial margin required is usually 2–10 per cent of the value of the contract. However, if the contract involves a party making a loss that is greater than the initial margin, further deposits are required on a daily basis from the losing party. These are called 'variation margins'. So, as the price moves they (the current loser) must pay the counterparty each day a variation margin based on the day-end settlement price.
- *Marking to market* – a process by which all outstanding deals are re-valued daily, because prices may change frequently. In other words, historic pricing/costing is not used because prices may be volatile. Marking to market is done by the clearing house for all the exchange's members and, again, by members who act as brokers. The latter 'mark to market' all their transactions with their clients. As margin payments are adjusted according to the price changes in the underlying asset on a daily basis, the exposure to risk experienced by the exchange is limited.

Derivative products can also be traded OTC. These markets have no official membership, and banks, non-bank financial firms and (typically) large corporations deal with each other via telephone, fax and computer links. Regulation is undertaken by each country's regulator and co-ordinated by the Bank for International Settlements. Within these markets private contracts are established between sets of parties without any clearing house involvement.

▶

OTC markets are characterised by the existence of *quote vendors*, providing real-time price information on computer screens. Firms providing this service include: Reuters; Bloomberg News Service and Knight Ridder. Quote vendors also link into the exchange markets, thus providing a comprehensive price information service. They get their OTC prices from dealers in the markets.

To summarise, the main advantages of trading in an organised exchange versus OTC markets are:

Organised exchange	OTC market
• Guarantees every contract, meaning that counterparty risk of default is reduced • Usually requires capital base and margins (initial and variation) to be taken • Constantly monitors players and holds a clearing fund	• Investors obtain a contract which is tailored exactly to their required quantity and maturity, unlike an exchange's standard contract • The impact of deals on prices tends to be more gentle than on an exchange where liquidity is said to be more 'concentrated' • When the counterparty is a well-established commercial bank regulated by a competent regulatory body, the counterparty risk is minimal

However, trading OTC has a number of disadvantages that can be summarised as follows:

- There is no clearing house to eliminate counterparty risk, although banks are increasingly seeking security from counterparties;
- There is no daily margining, which increases the risk arising from counterparty default;
- There is a limited secondary market;
- Documentation can be more complex than on an exchange;
- Prices can be less transparent than on an exchange, although quote vendors provide as much information as possible – at a price.

9.5.1 Financial futures

Financial futures are contracts to deliver and pay for a real or financial asset on a prearranged date in the future for a specified price. Futures relate to a broad variety of financial instruments including: bonds, certificates of deposit (CD), currencies and indexes. One of the most widely traded futures contract is that on government Treasury bonds (T-bonds). For example, say that on 1 December 2005 a bank sells one £100,000 March T-bond futures contract at a price of £115,000. The buyer of the contract agrees to pay £115,000 for a £100,000 face value of long-term bonds. At the end of March 2006, if interest rates go up the price of the bond will fall to, say, £110,000 (on the inverse relationship between bond prices and interest rates, see Appendix A1). So the buyer of the contract will have lost £5,000 because the bank can now sell the bonds to the buyer for £115,000 and have to pay only £110,000 in the market.

There are various points relating to futues:

- they are traded on organised markets (e.g., Euronext) so they carry standardised terms, amounts and maturities;
- they are also highly liquid because they can be sold and bought in the secondary market;
- they are not usually intended to result in the delivery of a commodity or currency;
- they are usually offset: e.g., a purchase offset by a sale, or vice versa, before delivery;
- the clearing house requires both parties to deposit cash against the transaction and this is known as the 'initial margin';
- if the contract involves a party making a loss that is greater than the initial margin, further deposits are required on a daily basis from the losing party. These are called 'variation margins'; so, as the price moves the current loser must pay the counterparty each day a variation margin based on the day-end settlement price;[3]
- if a counterparty defaults on a futures contract, the exchange assumes the defaulting party's position and the payment obligations.

The following is an example of futures contracts employed by banks to manage positions or 'hedge' for interest rate risk management purposes. (Note that future contracts can also be used to hedge foreign exchange risk.)

Assume that a bank expects interest rates to rise in the next six months. In order to protect itself, the bank can decide today to sell interest rate future contracts, which are due for delivery in six months' time, that is, to promise to sell a set amount of Treasury bills at a specific price in the future. After six months the bank buys back the contracts from the exchange and thus agrees to take delivery of the same securities in the future at a specific price. As a result, the two contracts are closed out (i.e., cancelled out or 'reversed') by the futures exchange clearing house and if interest rates do not change the bank is clear of all commitments to buy or sell. If, as expected, interest rates rise in the first six months, this will imply that bond prices will decrease. The bank will make a profit, or at least will be able to offset all or part of the loss in value of the securities, because after six months these will be obtainable at a lower price. (More details on interest rate risk management can be found in Chapter 10.)

9.5.2 Forward contracts

In the case of **forward** contracts two parties agree to exchange a real or financial asset on a pre-arranged date in the future for a specified price. An example of a forward contract from the foreign exchange market would be for a party to agree on 30 March to sell to another party £100,000 worth of US dollars on 31 December at a rate of (say) £1 to $1.67. The forwards:

- are non-standard contracts traded OTC (over-the-counter) entered bilaterally by two negotiating partners such as two banks;
- imply private agreements between two parties so they are customised to the specific needs of the parties;
- are highly illiquid: not negotiable, there is no secondary market;

---

[3] The process of restating the value of an asset or contract to reflect the market value of the asset or the value of the underlying asset is called 'marking-to-market'.

Box 9.3   Example of 3-month Eurodollar time deposit futures

The Eurodollar time deposit future is a short-term interest rate contract traded on the International Money Market (IMM) which has been part of the Chicago Mercantile Exchange since 1981. In Europe this product was launched in March 2004 by the Euronext.liffe and soon established growing liquidity while providing trading opportunities to a wide variety of market participants. During 2004 over 4 million contracts were traded and *open interest* (i.e., the amount of outstanding contracts) exceeded 150,000 contracts, making this one of the most successful products in the derivatives industry.

The underlying asset is a Eurodollar time deposit with a 90-day maturity. 'Eurodollars' are US$ denominated bank deposits that are deposited in banks that are not subject to US banking regulations.[4] Therefore, Eurodollar Time Deposits generally pay a higher interest rate than US Bank CD's and T-Bills. The bet in such contracts concerns the changes in short-term interest rates relative to those rates at the time the contract is negotiated.

Table 9.1 reports the quotes for the 3-month Eurodollar futures contracts from the *Financial Times* (23 September 2005). In particular, it shows the following information: the delivery date; the opening and closing settlement price; and the change in settlement price from the previous day. The next two columns report the highest and lowest price reached for the contract on the day, followed by the estimated number of contracts entered into during the day; finally, the last column reports the open interest which is the number of outstanding contracts at the end of the day.

Table 9.1 Eurodollar interest rate futures*

Sep 23	(Del.) Open		Sett.	Change	High	Low	Est. vol.	Open int.
Eurodollar 3m	Dec	95.81	95.76	−0.05	95.82	95.75	136,669	1,133,636
Eurodollar 3m	Mar	95.73	95.65	−0.08	95.73	95.64	155,837	1,130,804
Eurodollar 3m	Jun	95.69	95.61	−0.09	95.70	95.60	147,315	1,062,458
Eurodollar 3m	Sep	95.67	95.59	−0.09	95.68	95.59	141,326	748,752
Eurodollar 3m	Dec	95.65	95.58	−0.08	95.66	95.57	91,077	687,994
Eurodollar 3m	Mar	95.67	95.59	−0.08	95.67	95.58	38,526	510,853
Eurodollar 3m	Jun	95.67	95.58	−0.09	95.67	95.57	20,718	403,445

* Contracts are based on volumes traded in 2004.

Source: *Financial Times*, 23 September 2005.

The contract's main characteristics are:

- each Eurodollar futures contract represents $1 million of initial face value of Eurodollar deposits maturing 90 days after contract expiration;
- contracts expire in March, June, September and December;
- they are referenced to the British Bankers' Association LIBOR (London InterBank Offered Rate) for three-month sterling deposits at 11 a.m. on the last trading day (that is the third Wednesday of the delivery month);
- they trade according to an index that equals 100 minus the rate of interest (an index of 95 for example indicates a futures interest rate of 5%);

---

[4] Originally, these deposits were held, almost exclusively, in Europe; hence their collective name: Eurodollars. However, Eurodollars are now used as a collective name for US dollars held anywhere other than in the United States.

- each basis point change in the futures rate equals a $25 change in the value of the contract (0.01% × $1 million × 90/360). Note that the change in value of the contract of $25 is known as the 'tick value'. For example a profit of 5 ticks will be equal to $25 × 5 = $125;[5]
- gains/losses are calculated by multiplying the profit/loss on the futures trade, times the number of contracts traded, times $1 million, times 90/360. For example, a buyer of 40 contracts at 94.50, offset at 96 will:
  - gain on each futures transaction = 1.5 (150 basis points)
  - gross profits = 40 × 150 × 25 = $150,000;
    alternatively the profit can be calculated as follows: 40 × (0.96–0.945) × $1,000,000 × 90/360 = $150,000;
- Eurodollar contracts are cash settled, which means that the contracts are settled with the payment of the cash difference between the future and the market price;

As a general rule,

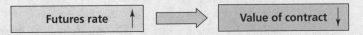

and vice versa. Specifically as a result of a Eurodollar time deposit future contract the buyer owns a commitment from the seller to pay cash if the price of the underlying asset rises; therefore the buyer expects futures rates to fall. In contrast, the seller owns a commitment from the buyer to pay cash if the asset price falls (thus the seller expect futures rates to increase). To recap:

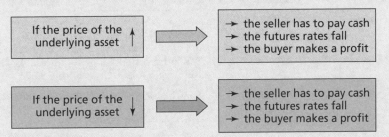

Interest rate futures can be used to hedge against current or future interest rate risk. This is done by taking a position that will generate profits to cover (or offset) losses related to an adverse movement in interest rates. Note that properly constructed futures hedges can create losses that offset beneficial interest rate movements. Moreover, participants can use futures to speculate. The trader will either buy or sell the future depending on whether the contract is perceived to be undervalued or overvalued. Typically, a borrower would sell futures to protect

---

[5] However trading can also occur for example in .0025 increments ($6.25/contract) or '$1/4$ tick' in the expiring front-month contract; and in .005 increments ($12.50/contract). This latter is the most common in the Euronext.liffe.

against a future increase in interest rates, whereas a lender would purchase futures to hedge against a fall in interest rates.

Take the following example of a long hedge:[6]

Suppose that on 30 June 2005 HSBC expects to receive a $1 million payment on 9 November 2005 and anticipates investing the funds in three-month Eurodollar time deposits. If the bank had the cash available in June it would immediately buy Eurodollar deposits; however it will not have access to the funds for five months and over this period interest rates may fall.

In order to hedge, HSBC should buy futures contracts such that if interest rates decline, futures rates will also typically fall and the long futures position will increase in value. Table 9.2 summarises the hedge results assuming that on 30 June HSBC buys one December Eurodollar futures contract (the first to expire after November 2005) at 4.24% while current interest rates are 4.15% (note the 0.09% 'basis' difference in rates). On 9 November HSBC sells the December 2005 Eurodollar futures because it receives the $1 million payment and invests in 3-month Eurodollars in the cash market. Over the period there is effectively a decrease in interest rate by 0.25% and the bank is obliged to invest at a rate of 3.90%. However the opportunity loss in the cash market ($625) is offset by a net gain in the futures market ($475) because the bank can sell the futures contract at a higher price. Overall, the bank has a cumulative income from the investment of $10,225 and its effective return is equal to 4.09%.

Table 9.2 Example of long hedge using Eurodollar futures

Date	Cash Market	Futures Market	Basis
30/06/2005 (initial futures position)	Bank anticipates investing $1 million in Eurodollars in 5 months; current cash rate = 4.15%	Bank buys one December 2005 Eurodollar futures contract at 4.24%; price = 95.76	4.24%–4.15% = 0.09%
09/11/2005 (close futures position)	Bank invests $1 million in 3-month Eurodollars at 3.90%	Bank sells one December 2005 Eurodollar futures contract at 4.05%; price = 95.95	4.05%–3.90% = 0.15%
Net effect	Opportunity loss: 4.15%–3.90% = 0.25%; 25 basis points worth $25 each = $625	Futures gain: 4.24%–4.05% = 0.19%; 19 basis points worth $25 each = $475	Basis change: 0.15%–0.09% = 0.06%

Cumulative investment income:

Interest at 3.90% = $1,000,000 (.0390) (90/360) = $9,750
Profit from futures trade= $475
Total = $10,225

Effective return = $\frac{\$10,225}{\$1,000,000} \times \frac{360}{90} = 4.09\%$

Source: Adapted from Koch and MacDonald (2000).

[6] Source: See Koch and MacDonald (2000).

- are contracts where all cash flows are required to be paid at one time (on contract maturity);
- are such that if one party cannot deliver from stock, then it must buy the commodity or currency on the spot market in order to fulfil the forward contract; and
- the clearing house does not guarantee the operation so there is a risk of default by the counterparty.

One common type of forward contract is the **forward rate agreement** (FRA) that gives the agents involved the opportunity to hedge against interest rate risk thereby 'locking in' the future price of the assets. Therefore, FRAs can be used to manage interest rate risk in a way similar to that used for financial futures. Suppose that a bank has a long position in long-term bonds currently selling at par value. In order to remove the interest rate risk from the future price of the bonds the bank can decide to enter a forward contract and sell these bonds at a future date at the current price. (The buyer must have different expectations and worry that the rate on the bonds might decline in the same period.)

Other important types of forward contracts are **currency forwards** that allow both the buyer and the seller to hedge against the risk of future fluctuations in currencies. For example, the holder of a four-months' long position in dollars can offset it by entering a forward contract that requires him to sell in four months the equivalent amount, in say Euros, at the current exchange rate. This currency forward will ensure that the transaction is protected from exchange rate fluctuations that may occur over the four months.

| Box 9.4 | **Example of forward rate agreement** |

Assume that:

- Company X expects to have to borrow £1m in three months' time for a six-month period;
- Assume short-term rates, say sixth-month LIBOR,[7] are at 6% but Company X expects this to rise over the following three months;
- To protect against this expected rise in rates, Company X buys an FRA to cover the six-month period starting three months from now – known as a '3 against – 9 month' or 3 x 9 FRA.
- A bank quotes a rate of 6.25% for such an FRA, and this would enable Company X to lock into the borrowing rate of 6.25% in three months' time for six months, so Company X buys the FRA;
- Assume six-month LIBOR increases to 7% in three months' time. Despite having the FRA, Company X is still forced to borrow in the market and pay the going 7% rate. Over a six-month period the borrower would have to pay approximately £35,000 interest in the underlying borrowing. This is the difference between 7% LIBOR borrowing minus 6.25% for the FRA divided by 2 (because the borrowing is for six months).
- Under the FRA Company X would receive approximately £3,750 to compensate for the extra 0.75% interest payable on the £1 million loan over the six-month period – this is known as the settlement sum that effectively offsets the higher borrowing costs. This is paid on the settlement date which is the date at which the contract starts.

▶

---

[7] Note there are many different LIBOR rates: overnight, one week, two weeks, 1 month, 2 month and so on.

- Note that while the FRA has not guaranteed Company X the interest rate on the specific financing, it has managed to secure its finance at the 6.25% fixed rate from the FRA.

The standard formula for calculating the payment or settlement sum can be shown as:

$$\text{Payment} = \text{notional principal} \left(\frac{(\text{reference rate} - \text{forward rate}) \ (\text{days}/360)}{\text{reference rate} \ (\text{days}/360) + 1} \right)$$

where:

notional principal = notional amount of loan

reference rate for the period of the forward rate = LIBOR, EURIBOR or another floating rate underlying the agreement

forward rate = fixed rate agreed on the FRA

days = length of the contract period

For further illustration if we take the aforementioned example, the formula is as follows:

Payment or settlement amount =	
Numerator (interest saving)	$= (0.07 - 0.0625) \times (180/360)$
	$= 0.0075 \times 0.5 = 0.00375$
Denominator (discount factor)	$= (0.07 \times (180/360)) + 1 = 1.035$
Settlement amount	$= 1{,}000{,}000 \times (0.00375 / 1.035) = £3{,}623.10$

9.5.3 Options contracts

Options give holders the right but not the obligation to buy or sell an underlying security (a financial instrument or a commodity) at a specified price known as the exercise or strike price. The purchase price of an option is called its *premium*. A contract that gives the right to buy is known as a *call option*, a contract that gives the right to sell is a *put option*. It is common to distinguish between: American options, which can be exercised at any time during their life; and European options, which can be exercised only at the end of their life; i.e., on the expiry date:

- Options can be OTC or exchange traded.
- Exchange-traded or listed options are standardised contracts with predetermined exercise prices and expiry dates.
- If the options are traded on exchanges, such as bond options, a clearing house is responsible for the settlement of debits and credits for the members (so they are virtually default risk free).
- Options may be purchased that effectively give the right to borrow or to lend (deposit funds) at a specified rate of interest (the striking rate) for an agreed period at a future date, or to purchase/sell currencies at agreed exchange rates at agreed future dates.

Box 9.5 Option contracts: payoff and profit profiles

The most common option contracts are options on individual stocks (stock options). For example, consider an April 2006 maturity call option on a share of Barclays with an exercise price of £50 per share selling on 3 January 2006 for £2. Until the expiration day (the third Friday of the expiration month, that is 21 April), the purchaser of the calls is entitled to buy shares of Barclays for £50 and thus stands to gain from a *rise* in the price of the underlying share. If at expiration Barclays stock sells for a price above the exercise price, say for example £55, then the option holder could acquire the Barclays share at £50 under the terms of the option and sell it in the spot market at £55. In this case the profit to the call holder will be equal to £3. That is, the payoff (£5) minus the premium paid to purchase the option (£2).

The relationship between market and exercise price is as follows:

- In the Money – exercise of the option would be profitable
    Call: market price>exercise price ($S_T>x$)
    Put: exercise price>market price ($x>S_T$)
- Out of the Money – exercise of the option would not be profitable
    Call: market price<exercise price ($S_T<x$)
    Put: exercise price<market price ($x<S_T$)
- At the Money – exercise price and asset price are equal ($x=S_T$)

Figure 9.2 shows the payoff and profits from the point of view of the holder of the call option. For example, if the exercise price is £50 and Barclays is now selling the shares at the market price of £60, the holder of the option will clear £10 per share. The profit will be equal to the payoff (£10) – the premium (£2) = £8. Yet if the shares sell any amount equal or below £50 the holder can sit on the option and do nothing, realising no further gain or loss. To summarise:

Payoff to call holder
$$(S_T - X) \quad \text{if } S_T >x$$
$$0 \quad \text{if } S_T \leqslant x$$
Profit to call holder
Payoff – Purchase price (premium)

Figure 9.2 Payoffs and profits on call options at expiration (from the perspective of the buyer of the option)

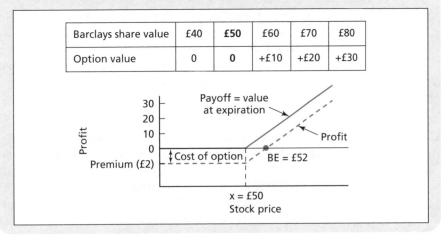

Barclays share value	£40	£50	£60	£70	£80
Option value	0	0	+£10	+£20	+£30

Figure 9.3 illustrates the payoffs and profits from the point of view of the holder of the put option. If the exercise price is £50 per share and Barclays is now selling at, say, £30, the holder of the put option will earn £20 per share (the profit will be £20–2=£18). If the shares sell any amount equal or above £50 the holder can sit on the option and do nothing, realising no further gain or loss. To recap:

Payoffs to put holder
$$0 \quad \text{if } S_T \geq x$$
$$(x - S_T) \quad \text{if } S_T < x$$
Profit to put holder
Payoff – Premium

Figure 9.3 Payoffs and profits on put options at expiration (from the perspective of the buyer of the option)

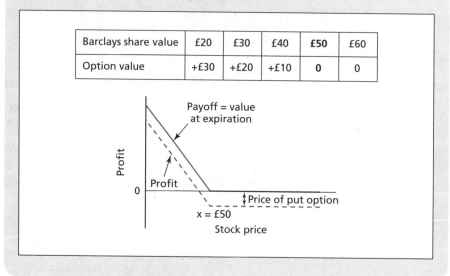

Barclays share value	£20	£30	£40	**£50**	£60
Option value	+£30	+£20	+£10	**0**	0

Options on assets other than stocks include:

- 'Index Options' that are calls or puts based on a stock market index such as the London FTSE 100;
- 'Futures Options' that give their holders the right to buy or sell a specified futures contract, using as futures price the exercise price of the option;
- 'Foreign Currency Options' that offer the right to buy or sell a quantity of foreign currency for a specified amount of domestic currency;
- 'Interest Rate Options' – options that are also traded on T-bills, bonds and CDs.

One common application of option contracts relates to the protection of banks' bond portfolios against rising interest rates. The main advantage of using options to manage interest rate risk, as opposed to futures and forwards, is that there is no delivery obligation, so the bank can decide to keep its bonds if interest rates fall and bond prices rise. For example, in order to protect itself against rising interest rates (and falling market values of bank assets, rising borrowing rates, and so on) a bank can decide to buy a put option on securities. The put option grants the bank the right to deliver the securities at a set price 'P'. If interest rates do rise, the market price of the securities will fall so the bank will be able to buy them at the current price and deliver them to the option writer at the (higher) price 'P'. The profit for the bank will be equal to P less the current price and the premium paid to exercise the option. Note that, typically, banks are buyers rather than sellers of puts and calls because of the considerable risks involved if interest rates move against the sellers.

9.5.3.1 Caps, floors and collars

Caps and **floors** are effectively types of options. They may be thought of as giving the holder a right to purchase a forward rate agreement (forward contract in interest rates) 'with hindsight'. **Collars** are hybrid products, being part forward contract and part option.

An interest rate cap may be purchased from a bank in order to protect the holder of an existing floating-rate loan from the interest rate moving upwards beyond the level specified by the cap contract. The holder (borrower) is still able to benefit if interest rates fall, but may claim any excess interest charge over the cap level from the seller of the cap.

An interest rate floor has the same characteristics as a cap, except that it protects an investor or depositor against a floating rate of interest falling below the specified floor level. The seller of the floor will pay the purchaser any interest losses below the floor rate. The purchaser is still able to benefit from increases in interest rates.

An interest rate collar is effectively a combination of a cap and a floor. A collar may be purchased by a company wishing to protect itself against the interest rate on outstanding debt going beyond a capped level, but prepared to forgo the gain from the interest rate falling below a lower specified level in exchange for a lower premium on the cap.

9.5.4 Swaps

Swaps are agreements between two parties to exchange two differing forms of payment obligations. They can be thought of as exchanges of cash flows used to manage their asset–liability structure or to reduce their cost of borrowing. The most common types of swaps are interest rate swaps and currency swaps.

9.5.4.1 Interest rate swaps

Interest rate swaps occur between borrowers and swap dealers (normally banks). The swap dealer is the counterparty to the swap transaction with the borrower. It is important to understand that only debt servicing commitments are swapped not the underlying borrowed funds. Hence, swaps are used as a risk management instrument whereby a company can change the profile of its interest rate liabilities without disturbing the underlying borrowing. In addition, swaps can be used as a basis for speculation when they are taken out without any matching exposure in the cash market.

The main features of interest rate swaps are:

- Only interest payments are swapped so there is no exchange of principal;
- Interest payments are swapped at rates and for a term agreed at the outset based on a specified notional principal;
- Transactions are usually governed by a standardised swap contract (but the amount and terms are not standardised);
- The rights and obligations under a swap contract are entirely separate from the rights or obligations associated with any underlying borrowing;
- Interest swaps normally cover initial periods of anything from 1 to 10 years or more.

Among other applications, swaps give counterparties the ability to:

- convert floating-rate debt to fixed or fixed-rate to floating-rate;
- lock in an attractive interest rate in advance of a future debt issue;
- position fixed-rate liabilities in anticipation of a decline in interest rates; and
- arbitrage or speculate on debt price differentials in the capital markets.

As stated above, swaps are normally arranged through a swap dealer, with the dealer acting as a principal rather than an agent. The dealer makes a return on this activity through the bid–ask spread.[8] Interest rate swap prices are quoted on a range of currencies for periods of up to 30 years and are published in the *Financial Times*. The quotes will, in general, move in the same direction as changes in the yields on gilt-edged securities with a similar maturity to the swap.

9.5.4.2 Currency swaps

Currency swaps transfer the obligation for payment in one currency to another party who, in turn, undertakes an obligation for payment in another currency.
  Typically a currency swap involves:

- an initial exchange of principal amounts of two currencies at the spot exchange rate;
- the exchange of a stream of fixed or floating interest rate payments in their swapped currencies for the agreed period of the swap; and
- re-exchange of the principal amount at maturity at the initial spot exchange rate. Sometimes, the initial exchange of principal is omitted and instead a net amount or 'difference' is paid.

In a currency swap, counterparties agree to exchange an equivalent amount of two different currencies for a specified time. These can be negotiated for a wide range of maturities up to at least ten years. As in the case of other foreign exchange contracts, if the cost of borrowing in one currency is higher than it would be in another then a fee may be required to compensate for the interest differential.
  The usual reason for a financial intermediary wishing to engage in a currency swap is so that it can replace cash flows in an undesired currency with flows in a desired

---

[8] Most financial instruments traded in the market have a bid–ask spread. The bid price is the price at which you can sell the instrument. The ask price is the price you would have to pay to buy the instrument. Alternatively one can view the bid price as the highest price that somebody will pay for (say) a share at a particular point in time, whereas the ask price is the lowest price at which someone is willing to sell the share. The difference between the bid and the ask price is known as the bid–ask spread. Market makers that offer to buy and sell shares create the spread so they can earn income from trading.

Box 9.6 Example of interest rate swap

Suppose a UK-based bank has recently agreed a total of £100m of mortgage loans at a rate that will remain fixed at 7% per annum for the next five years. Also, suppose that the funding is in the form of wholesale deposits with three-month maturity paying interest at LIBOR that is currently 6.6%. As long as its mortgage loans are at 7% fixed, the bank will gain if LIBOR falls and it will lose out if LIBOR rises.

A swap dealer may offer the bank the following deal:

- Swap dealer to pay the bank each year, for the next five years, a sum of money calculated on the interest that would have been paid on £100m at LIBOR.
- Bank to pay swap dealer each year, for the next five years, a sum of money calculated on the interest that would have been paid on £100m at 6.6% fixed.
- The bank may then use the swap to fix its interest rate margin between the mortgage loans and the three-month deposits for a five-year period.

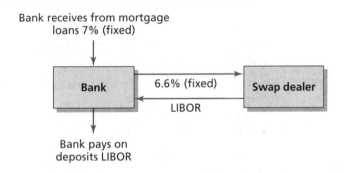

As long as the notional principal and the maturity date of the swap match the amount and maturity of the fixed-rate mortgage loans, the interest margin is fixed at 0.4%. Consequently, the bank's profit margin is insulated from the risk that LIBOR could rise. However, if LIBOR falls the margin will remain at 0.4% and the bank will not be able to benefit from this fall in market rates. The interest margin is fixed, irrespective of the level of LIBOR.

A possible problem could arise for the bank if interest rates were to fall and this created pressure for early repayment of the fixed interest mortgage loans. If the mortgage loans were to be repaid early, the bank would cease to need the wholesale deposits. However, with the swap obligations still in force, a LIBOR rate of, say, 4%, would lead to a loss for the bank of £2.6m on the transaction. That is, the bank would still have to pay the swap dealer £6.6m, but would receive only £4m from the swap dealer. To prevent this problem, the bank could incorporate early repayment penalties in mortgage loan agreements, although it would need to ensure that it did not contravene any related consumer protection legislation. This example illustrates clearly the basic rule that derivatives can reduce risk if they match a position in the underlying cash markets, but they increase risk if there is no underlying obligation in the cash market or if the underlying obligation does not come to fruition for whatever reason.

| **Box 9.7** | **Example of fixed–floating currency swap** |

Suppose that:[9]

- A US-based bank has partly financed its asset portfolio with a total of £60m three-year note issue with fixed 10% annual coupons denominated in sterling. Also, suppose that this US bank holds mostly floating-rate short-term US dollar denominated assets.
- A UK-based bank has partly financed its asset portfolio with a total of $100m short-term dollar denominated Euro CDs whose rates reflect changes in one-year LIBOR+1% premium. Also, suppose that this UK bank holds mostly fixed-rate long-term sterling denominated assets.

Both banks are faced with interest rate and foreign exchange exposure if the following situations occur:

- For the US bank if dollar short-term rates fall, and the dollar depreciates against the pound;
- For the UK bank if US interest rate rise, and the dollar appreciates against the pound.

Therefore the two banks may wish to engage in a fixed–floating currency swap whereby:

- The US bank transforms its fixed-rate sterling-denominated liabilities into variable rate dollar liabilities;
- The UK bank transforms its variable-rate short-term, dollar-denominated liabilities into fixed-rate sterling liabilities.

Each year the two banks swap payments at some prearranged dollar/sterling exchange rate, assumed to be $2/£1. The UK bank sends fixed payments in pounds to cover the cost of the US bank's pound note issue, while the US bank sends floating payments in dollars to cover the UK bank's floating-rate dollar CD costs. Table 9.3 shows that the realised cash flows from the swap result in a net nominal payment of $3 million by the US bank to the UK bank over the life of the swap.

Table 9.3 Fixed–floating rate currency swap (millions)

Year	LIBOR %	LIBOR +3%	Floating -rate payment by US bank ($ million)	Fixed-rate payment by UK bank $ million	($ million) (at $2/£1)	Net payment by US bank ($ million)
1	8	11	11	6	12	−1
2	9	12	12	6	12	0
3	10	13	130	66	132	−2
Total net payment						−3

---

[9] Adapted from Saunders (2000).

currency. Global banks and other large financial intermediaries often raise finance in the international markets and may have to service debt in a variety of currencies.

A Japanese bank, for instance, may have to service most of its debt in fixed-rate Yen, whereas a UK bank has to (say) service mainly fixed-rate British pound debt. If the Japanese bank has some fixed-rate British pound debt and the UK bank fixed-rate Yen debt this could provide an opportunity for both banks to swap principal and interest payments – so the UK bank obtains an income stream paying fixed-rate Yen and the Japanese firm fixed-rate British pounds. Put simply, both banks are swapping cash flows in different currencies.

Currency swaps come in various forms:

- fixed-for-fixed currency swaps – where the interest rate payments on the two currencies that are swapped are fixed at the start of the swap agreement;
- fixed-for-floating swaps (cross-currency swaps) – where the interest rate on one currency is floating and usually linked to the London Interbank Offered Rate (LIBOR) (the average of interest rates that major international banks charge each other to borrow US dollars in the London money market) and the other is fixed; and
- floating-for-floating currency swaps – where both interest rates are floating.

The main reasons for the development of currency swaps business is that some financial and other firms have an advantage in generating cash flows in specific currencies and it is in the interest of these firms to trade these cash flows if they desire other currency streams. As business has become more international, and financing and investment requirements more diversified, the need to have access to a wider array of cash flows in different currencies has heightened.

9.5.5 Other OBS activities offered by banks: loan commitments, guarantees and letters of credit

There are a number of other OBS activities that banks undertake to generate fee income (some of which have been briefly introduced in Chapter 4) including:

- Loan commitments (including overdrafts)
- Financial guarantees (including letters of credit)
- Securities underwriting
- Other financial services.

Loan commitments are promises to lend up to a pre-specified amount to a pre-specified customer at pre-specified terms. Many business loans are made under loan commitments. For example, a bank may avail £20mil to GlaxoSmithKline Ltd over a period of two years for building a brand new chemical plant. Over the set period the borrower may decide to use only part (or even none) of the loan commitment. The terms of the contract will also specify how the interest rate will be computed and whether the rate is fixed or variable. Typically, loan commitments involve large amounts and generate relatively low bank margins. Banks are compensated by the fees charged for making such commitments. The bank generally receives compensation for a loan commitment in a variety of ways (Greenbaum and Thakor, 1995; Buckle and Thomson, 2004) including:

- a *commitment fee*: expressed as a percentage of the total commitment and paid up front by the borrower;
- a *usage fee*: levied on the unused portion of the credit line;
- *servicing fees*: on the borrowed amount to cover the bank's transactions costs; and
- *compensating balances requirements*: deposit balances the borrower must keep at the bank during the commitment, computed as a fraction of the total commitment and on which the bank pays below market interest rates.

It is also common to distinguish between the following types of loan commitments:

- *Revolving lines of credit*: where a bank gives a line of credit and commits for several years ahead.
- *Unused overdraft facility*: an agreed amount by which a bank account can be overdrawn; the bank, however, can withdraw the agreed facility under certain circumstances. Typically, the customer will be charged a set fee for the provision of an overdraft facility. This fee is often calculated as a fairly high percentage of the total value of the overdraft.
- *Note Issuance Facilities (NIF)*: essentially the bank (or a syndicate of banks if it is a large loan) arranges and guarantees the availability of funds from the issue of a succession of short-term notes (commonly three or six months). In the case of these notes not being taken up by the market, the bank will provide the funds.

Financial guarantees are instruments used to enhance the credit standing of a borrower to help ensure a lender against default and lower the cost of borrowing. They are designed to ensure the timely repayment of the principal and interest from a loan even if the borrower goes bankrupt or cannot perform a contractual obligation. With a financial guarantee a bank underwrites the obligations for a third party, thus relieving the counterparty from having to assess the ability of the customer to meet the terms of the contract. Common examples of financial guarantees are: *commercial letters of credit* and *bankers acceptances*.

A **commercial letter of credit** (L/C) is a document issued by a bank stating its commitment to pay someone a stated amount of money on behalf of a buyer so long as the seller meets very specific terms and conditions. L/Cs are used to facilitate trade where there is uncertainty, for instance in international dealings when an exporter based (say) in Japan has limited knowledge of the European importer's ability to pay and limited ability to enforce contracts across borders. The importer arranges an L/C to be issued by its bank guaranteeing payment in exchange for a fee for bearing the risk that the importer may default. By reducing the default risk confronting the exporter, the issue of an L/C reduces the asymmetric information problems between the two parties. It should be noted that with a commercial L/C the importer's bank usually advances the payment and is repaid by its customer.

Upon presentation of the necessary documents the importers' bank will issue either an immediate payment (a 'sight draft') or a 'time draft' promising payment at some future date. In the case of the latter, the instrument becomes a **banker's acceptance**, which is marketable and usually quite liquid. If the exporter decides to hold the acceptance, it essentially extends the loan to the importer. Alternatively, if the acceptance is sold in the secondary market, the holder of the acceptance will provide funding, but the bank guarantees payment.

A **standby letter of credit** is similar to the commercial L/C in that it is a financial instrument that guarantees the performance of a party, say the importer as in the previous example, in a commercial or financial transaction. However, while a L/C always involves a funding transaction, in a standby L/C the importer's bank makes a payment only if its customer fails to fulfil their obligations (i.e., in case of default). Therefore, the standby L/Cs issued by the importer's bank obligates that bank to compensate the exporter only in the event of a performance failure. The importer will obviously pay a fee for this service and will be liable to its bank for any payments made by the bank under the standby L/C.

Securities underwriting is a type of business typically undertaken by investment banks whereby a bank agrees to buy a set amount of the securities that are not taken up in an issue. For instance, investment banks charge a compensation fee for taking IPOs (Initial Public Offerings) to market (sometimes there is an underwriting syndicate as shown in Figure 9.4); they also issue stocks and bonds for established listed companies in the secondary market. This guarantees the issuer that the whole of the issue is taken up and a fee is paid to the banks providing the underwriting service.

Other financial services that generate fee income and do not lead to a balance sheet entry can include for example the advisory services that banks give to organisations that are planning to merge with other institutions or to acquire other firms. In Europe all commercial banks have been allowed by the Second Banking Co-Ordination Directive to provide these kinds of services that in the past were undertaken only by investment banks (as have US commercial banks by the Gramm-Leach-Bliley Act of 1999 and Japanese commercial banks by Japan's Big-Bang reforms of 1999).

Another example of a financial service that generates non-interest income is the case where the bank originates a loan in exchange for a fee and then transfers it to another bank, which will provide funding and servicing for the loan (see Box 9.8 on the **process of deconstruction**). Similarly a loan sale involves a contract whereby a bank that has originated the loan removes it from the balance sheet by selling all or part of the cash streams to an outside buyer. Loan sales offer a 'primitive' option to the full securitisation of loans. An introduction to these activities is given in Section 9.6.

Figure 9.4 Securities underwriting syndicate

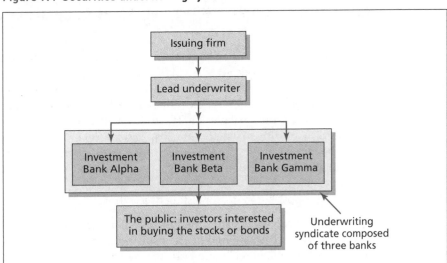

Box 9.8   The process of deconstruction of lending activity

Banks' lending activity has traditionally been composed of the following four main parts.

- Loan origination:
  - administration and processing of paperwork and documentation related to the loan application;
  - undertaking risk analysis (screening) and assessing the creditworthiness of the potential borrower;
  - design of loan contracts and loan pricing.
- Provision of funding to the borrower:
  - raising finance;
  - holding the asset on the balance sheet;
  - allocating capital to the risk.
- Servicing:
  - collecting loan payments;
  - bookkeeping.
- Undertaking monitoring activity:
  - post-lending monitoring to control for credit risk;
  - diversification to control default risk.

As a result of changes in regulation and financial innovation, modern banking institutions can specialise in providing only some of the component parts of the lending function described above. This process of 'deconstruction' of the lending function has two main effects. On the one hand it allows individual parts of the process of providing loans to be transferred to highly specialised separate financial firms (not necessarily banks) that would have not been able to enter the banking market otherwise due to high barriers to entry. Second, it encourages banks to sell individual loans or pool together a bundle of homogenous loans and securitise them for risk management and other purposes.

9.6 Loan sales and the process of securitisation

Loan sales have existed for many years. A loan sale occurs when a bank originates a loan and then decides to sell it to another legal entity, usually a financial intermediary. Where the bank is selling only part of the loan the operation is called loan participation or loan syndication. As the loan is sold or transferred, it is removed from the bank's balance sheet. However, the risk may stay with the originating bank according to whether the loan is sold *with* or *without recourse*. In the first case, the buyer can put the loan back to the selling bank if it goes bad; thus the bank retains the contingent liability; in the second case if the loan is sold without recourse then the loan buyer bears all the risk.

It is possible to distinguish between three main types of loan sales contracts:

- *Participations in loans*: the loan purchaser is not a partner to the loan contract between the bank selling the loans and the borrower so that the initial contract between loan seller and borrower remains in place after the sale. The buyer of a participation in an existing loan can exercise only partial control over changes in the loan contract's terms and bears significant risks in case of failure of either the bank or the borrower.

- *Assignments*: refers to buying a share in a loan syndication with some contractual control and rights over the borrower. The ownership of the loan is transferred to the buyer, who thereby acquires a direct claim against the borrower. The borrower in some cases has to agree to the sale of the loan before an assignment can be made.
- *Loan-strips*: a third and less common type of loan sale is a loan strip. These are short-dated pieces of a longer-term loan. The buyer of a strip is entitled to a fraction of the expected income from a loan while the bank retains the risk of borrower default.

From the point of view of a bank manager, selling loans to outside investors is an important method of funding bank operations for various reasons (Rose, 2002; Saunders and Cornett, 2003):

- they allow the replacement of lower-yielding assets with higher-yielding assets when market interest rates increase;
- they can increase the bank's liquidity if loans are replaced with more marketable assets such as government securities;
- they help in the management of credit and interest rate risk;
- they slow the growth of banks' assets which helps maintain the balance between capital and credit risk;
- they help diversify the bank's assets and lower its cost of capital (on this last issue, see Section 8.4.3).

In particular, banks trying to comply with the Basle capital regulation will find it cheaper to boost their capital-to-asset ratio by reducing assets instead of increasing capital since equity capital is more costly than debt for tax reasons.

In contrast to loan sales the process of **securitisation** is more recent and it is certainly more widespread in the United States than in Europe. The first issue in the United States took place in the 1970s, compared to 1985 in the United Kingdom. However, the United Kingdom and indeed the European securitisation market as a whole is currently growing rapidly. Figure 9.5 shows the trend over 1997–2003: issuance in the European securitisation market had reached €217.2 billion in 2003, an increase of more than 4.6 times compared to 1997. Moreover, as shown in the latest European Securitisation Forum (ESF) bulletin, in 2004 UK issuance accounted for 45.7 per cent of all the European securitised debt, followed by Spain (16.2 per cent) and Italy (12.4 per cent).

According to the ESF (1999, p. 1), the process of securitisation is defined as:

the process whereby loans, receivables and other financial assets are pooled together, with their cash flows or economic values redirected to support payments on related securities. These securities, which are generally referred to as 'asset-backed securities' or 'ABS', are issued and sold to investors – principally, institutions – in the public and private markets by or on behalf of issuers, who utilise securitisation to finance their business activities.

Often the terminology related to asset securitisation is complicated for non-practitioners; Appendix 9.1 offers a useful glossary specific to this topic.

Figure 9.5 Historical European securitisation 1997–2003

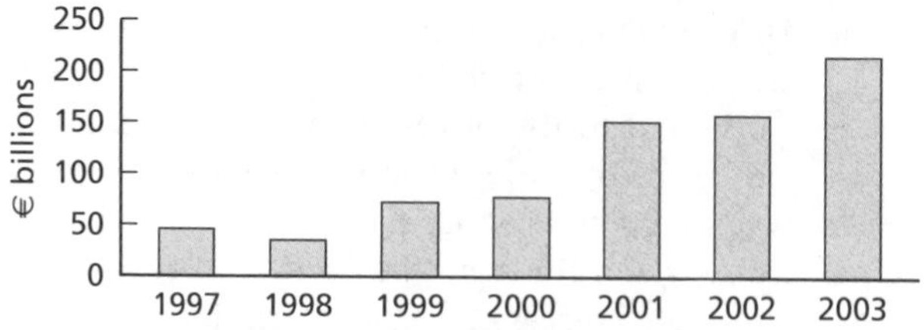

Source: http://www.europeansecuritisation.com

The ESF (1999: 1) also clarifies the types of assets that can be securitised:

> The financial assets that support payments on ABS include residential and commercial mortgage loans, as well as a wide variety of non-mortgage assets such as trade receivables, credit card balances, consumer loans, lease receivables, automobile loans, and other consumer and business receivables. Although these asset types are used in some of the more prevalent forms of ABS, the basic concept of securitisation may be applied to virtually any asset that has a reasonably ascertainable value, or that generates a reasonably predictable future stream of revenue. As a result, securitisation has been extended to a diverse array of less well-known assets, such as insurance receivables, obligations of shippers to railways, commercial bank loans, health care receivables, obligations of purchasers to natural gas producers, and future rights to entertainment royalty payments, among many others. It is a process by which assets are pooled together and sold as securities.

As shown in Figure 9.6, securitisation removes financial assets (in this example a pool of mortgage loans) from the balance sheet.

The commercial bank's long-term mortgages have been replaced on the balance sheet by the cash received in the same, which can be used to pay down liabilities. In the example below, the bank has increased its liquidity by £50 million. Therefore after securitisation the balance sheet shows fewer assets and liabilities (or at the margin does not add assets to it like in the example below), than it would if the bank originating the mortgages had used a straight debt offering as a means of raising money. This improves ROE and the capital-to-assets ratio and prevents these from declining, all other things being equal. Securitisation has also been stimulated by the new legislation implemented in many countries that has widened the type of assets that can be securitised. Other related factors that have influenced the growth of securitisation include: portfolio and risk management (see also Chapter 10). Box 9.9 highlights the most recent developments in the process of securitisation in Europe; Box 9.10 outlines the main social and economic benefits of the process of securitisation.

The assets that underlie securitisation transactions are first created when an 'originator', say a bank, makes a loan to a borrower, the 'obligor'. Typically, once the financial asset is created and funded, the bank continues to service the loan, that is it provides a collection and management function in connection to that loan. As argued by Heffernan (2005, p. 45) the bank could issue a bond with a

Figure 9.6 Simplified bank balance sheet before and after securitisation (in £ mil)

Balance sheet before securitisation

Assets		Liabilities	
Cash Reserves	£5.33	Deposits	£53.33
Long-term Mortages	£50.00	Capital	£2.00
Total	**£55.33**	**Total**	**£53.33**

Balance sheet after securitisation

Assets		Liabilities	
Cash Reserves	£5.33	Deposits	£53.33
Cash proceeds from Mortgage Securitisation	£50.00	Capital	£2.00
Total	**£55.33**	**Total**	**£55.33**

Source: Adapted from Saunders, A. and Cornett, M.M. (2003).

bundle of pooled assets acting as collateral, but the credit rating of the bank would be assigned to the new security, the proceeds of the bond would be subject to reserve requirements, and the assets would be included in the computation of the bank's capital ratio. The bank can circumvent these constraints with the process of securitisation.

Figure 9.7 shows the process of creation of an asset-backed security (ABS) as well as transaction participants and functions. The bank (originator) passes a pool of homogeneous assets on to the special purpose vehicle (SPV). The SPV, or another entity to whom the SPV conveys the assets which is often organised in the form of a trust, will issue debt securities in the financial markets.

An underwriter will serve as an intermediary between the issuer and the investors in an ABS offering. These securities are usually purchased by institutional investors, including banks, insurance companies and pension funds.

A critical element in any securitisation is the presence of credit enhancement or liquidity support. This increases the likelihood that security holders will receive timely payment on their investments. Throughout the life of the loan the borrower makes regular payments to the originator of the loan in the usual way and the intermediary passes the income to the trustee. Moreover, since investors do not originate the loan, they cannot verify the quality of the securitised loan portfolio. Rating agencies will generally issue credit ratings and often monitor the performance of the transaction throughout its life (and adjust their ratings accordingly). Moreover, in any securitisation it is important to ensure that repayment of the securities will still be made in the case of insolvency. Thus it is necessary to separate the means by which the securities are to be repaid from the risk of insolvency on the part of the originator of the assets. In cases where the credit rating of the securitised issue is higher than the originator, legal structures are set up so collection on the assets cannot be retained by the latter in the event of insolvency.

Figure 9.7 Creation of an ABS: participants and functions

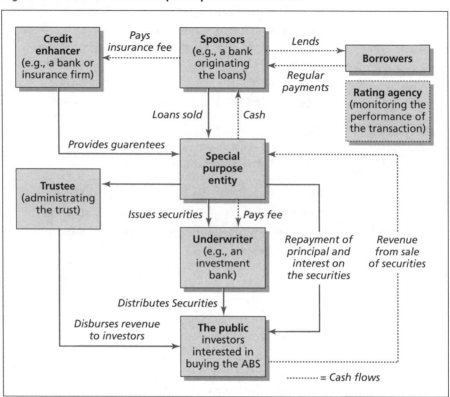

Securitisation, the issuing of bonds backed by ring-fenced cash flows, is rapidly becoming a mainstream financing method in Europe. Like many other capital market innovations, the technique – which gives the issuer an immediate lump sum in return for signing away future cash flows is long-established in the United States.

The recent European housing boom has created a prodigious appetite among mortgage banks for additional capital. They have met it by parcelling up their existing portfolios and using them as collateral to raise new funds. Recently this has helped drive double-digit annual increases in European securitisation volumes, despite the slowdown in two traditionally large markets, Germany and France. In the nine months to end-September [2004], securitisations in the United States outpaced conventional corporate bond issues for the first time. The global total of rated securitisation deals rose 35 per cent, to about $1,240bn, in the same period, according to Standard & Poor's, the credit rating agency. In

Europe, the total volume of rated securitisation deals rose 50 per cent to $250bn.

Securitisation is a low-cost way of raising additional finance and provides longer-term funds than could be obtained with bank debt. It creates a liquid security out of assets that would not be tradeable and gives immediate access to a cashflow that would otherwise only materialise over several years. 'There is still the perception of securitisation as a new science', says Kurt Sampson, European head of structured finance ratings at S&P. 'It is not an exotic technique. Increasingly, people regard it as a fundamental part of their investment strategy.'

As the technique has matured, specialised sub-sectors have developed, such as collateralised debt obligations, which package corporate debt, and whole-business securitisations, used increasingly in acquisitions and leveraged buy-outs. Securitisation has its origins in the issue of residential mortgage-backed bonds by Ginnie Mae, the US federal housing finance agency, in the 1970s. The technique survived

▶

the crisis that hit the savings and loans institutions when interest rates rose steeply at the end of that decade and by the mid-1980s was being applied to other categories of assets. It has since been extended to commercial mortgages, credit card payments, pub revenues, student loans and water bills.

The key criteria for success are a structure that ring-fences a predictable cash flow and a broad base of assets – 'granularity' – in the underlying asset pool. Because securitised cashflows are – in theory – fenced off from the operating risks that can befall any company, the bonds they support normally carry a higher rating than the company itself. If the company is unrated, the rated securitisation allows the issuer to approach investors restricted to rated offerings. 'It is becoming a much more accepted financing tool for a wide range of issuers', says Lee Rochford, head of European securitisation at CSFB [Credit Suisse First Boston].

'It has been used by banks and consumer finance companies, but the slowdown in those markets means corporates and governments will become the driving force.' 'It is moving out of the financial services sector to the mid-sized corporates and the larger unrated companies,' says Peter Jeffrey, a banking and capital markets partner at PwC. 'It will become more normal for these companies to use it as a mainstream funding tool.'

For companies experienced in the technique, the question can arise: How much of their assets should they securitise? Only a few European banks have securitised more than 5 per cent of their balance sheets yet for some it has become a core part of their business plan, S&P [Standard & Poor's] concluded in a recent study. Among the largest users were Centroleasing, an Italian company, with 49 per cent of assets securitised and Northern Rock, a UK mortgage lender, at 42 per cent.

Basle II, the revised set of rules for banks that seek to ensure that asset-backing matches risk more closely, is not due to take effect until 2007 but it will affect the securitisation market. This is because banks and financial services companies will have less of an incentive to securitise their best quality assets, which will require less asset backing, and more reason to get more lowly rated assets off their books.

Source: Financial Times (2004) 'Securitisation Survey', 29 November 2004, by Charles Batchelor.

Box 9.10 What are the social and economic benefits of securitisation?

In markets where securitisation has been employed on a broader scale, a number of public, social and economic benefits have been realised. For example, the existence of liquid and efficient secondary securitisation markets has had the effect of increasing the availability, and reducing the cost, of financing in the primary lending markets. The financing needs being serviced often relate to areas that are favoured by social or governmental policy, such as increasing the supply of funds for home ownership. Similarly, liquid and efficient secondary securitisation markets can reduce geographical and regional disparities in the availability and cost of credit throughout a particular jurisdiction by linking local credit extension activities to national, and increasingly global, capital markets systems. It has also been observed that robust securitisation markets facilitate and encourage the efficient allocation of capital by subjecting the credit-granting activities of individual financial institutions to the pricing and valuation discipline of the capital markets. In this fashion, securitisation helps to promote the allocation of scarce societal capital to its most efficient uses. From a regulatory and financial markets supervisory perspective, securitisation offers a useful mechanism by which financial institutions may shift concentrated credit, interest rate and market risks associated with their portfolio activities to investors and the more broadly dispersed capital markets, thus reducing risks to individual institutions, and systemic risks within financial systems. For all of these reasons, the widespread use and encouragement of securitisation as a matter of governmental policy can help to achieve desirable social and economic goals, such as stimulating the growth of affordable housing; increasing the availability and lowering the cost of consumer credit; promoting efficient market structures and institutions; facilitating the efficient use and rational allocation of capital; and facilitating the achievement of governmental fiscal, economic and regulatory policy goals.

Source: ESF (1999, p. 6).

9.7 Conclusions

Bank managers' role is to implement decisions that maximise the profitability of their institutions and shareholders' wealth. In order to achieve these aims, bank managers should pursue strategies in several areas, such as asset and liability management, liquidity management and capital management. This chapter describes these on-balance sheet concerns of banks and then provides a detailed account of the different types of off-balance sheet business that modern banks undertake, such as derivative activities, loan sales and securitisation.

A related area of strategic decision that carries a high potential for affecting bank profits, value and safety is risk management. The following two chapters outline the main risks that banks have to face (Chapter 10) and discuss the techniques used by banks to measure and manage these risks (Chapter 11).

Key terms

Asset management	Currency forward
Liability management	Options
Liquidity management	Caps, Floors and Collars
Capital management	Swaps
OBS management	Loan commitments
Asset–liability management	Financial guarantees
Financial derivatives	Commercial letter of credit
Arbitrage	Banker's acceptance
Micro-hedging	Standby letter of credit
Macro-hedging	Securities underwriting
Financial futures	Process of deconstruction
Forwards	Loan sales
Forward rate agreement	Securitisation

Key reading

Buckle, M. and Thomson, J. (2004) *The UK Financial System. Theory and Practice*, 3rd edn. Manchester: Manchester University Press.

ESF, European Securitisation Forum (1999), *European Securitisation: A Resource Guide*, New York. http://www.europeansecuritisation.com/pubs/ESFGuide.pdf

Koch T.W. and MacDonald, S.S. (2000) *Bank Management*, 4th edn. Orlando, FL: The Dryden Press.

Revision questions and problems

1 What is asset–liability management?
2 Why is there a trade-off between liquidity and solvency?
3 What are the main concerns in capital management?
4 Define OBS activities and explain the different implications of trading in organised exchanges versus OTC.
5 How can banks use futures and forwards for hedging an interest rate exposure?

6 What are the primary features of options contracts and how can they be used for risk management purposes?

7 What are the main differences between interest rate and currency swaps?

8 What is the process of deconstruction?

9 Explain loan sales.

10 What is the process of securitisation and what are the main reasons for its recent growth in importance?

Appendix 9.1 Securitisation glossary: a brief jargon buster

The fixed income markets have a terminology all their own, one that frequently baffles outsiders. The bankers are often too close to the subject to make a good job of explaining it to the uninitiated. One consultant recounts a stream of finance directors coming to ask him to explain what their bankers had failed to make clear when pitching an idea.

Practitioners, sceptics suggest, use jargon to confuse and make their activities appear more complex and mysterious than they are. Sometimes, terms have different meanings in different contexts. And in such a fast-developing sector, new terms are constantly being minted.

ABSs, Asset-backed security The bond or note that is issued on the back of the package of assets that have been assembled.

Collateralised debt obligations or **CDOs** Securitisations of packages of corporate bonds, loans and credit default swaps.

CDOs typically comprise between 50 and 150 underlying securities, so the spread of risk or 'granularity' is less than, for example, mortgage or credit card-backed securitisations.

Balance sheet CDOs are created by banks from assets already on their books. However, banks increasingly acquire assets in the market to create a CDO, sometimes to meet the requirements of a particular investor.

The risk of default is often insured with a specialist, monoline, insurer to achieve a higher rating for the different tranches. Depending on the underlying assets, CDOs are also known as collateralised bond or loan obligations.

CMBSs Commercial mortgage-backed security.

Conduit An arrangement that allows smaller securitisations to be pooled to cut costs and win a higher profile in the market.

Pooling also allows a larger number of bonds to be issued, making for a more liquid secondary market. They are often used to group short-term obligations such as 30- or 90-day trade receivables on the back of which commercial paper of up to 364-day maturities is issued.

They can also be used to aggregate longer-term assets such as property against which bonds are issued. Sometimes conduits handle a single underlying loan if the issuer wants to avoid the hassle of structuring its own securitisation.

Covered bonds Unlike a conventional securitisation, the underlying assets remain on the issuer's balance sheet and are not transferred to a special purpose vehicle.

Most European countries have put in place legislation that allows coupon payments and repayment of the principal of a covered bond even if the issuing bank becomes insolvent.

The UK lacks a similar law but the banks have devised a form of contract that reassures investors, and issuance has taken off. But because the UK lacks a legal framework, banks must hold more capital on their balance sheets than their continental European counterparts.

Credit default swaps Derivatives that a bank or investor buys to insure a particular credit risk. They allow a bank to avoid offending a long-standing client by buying cover rather than selling the bond or loan. If an issuer defaults, the credit purchaser is paid at par. CDSs allow investors to take a view on a credit without buying a cash security. They are now traded in their own right and the market is often more liquid than that of the underlying security.

Credit enhancement Lower quality assets can obtain a higher rating through insurance. Monoline insurance companies guarantee to make up cash flows if they fall short. Also known as 'wrapping'.

Funded/unfunded Funded deals achieve a match between the cash flow arising from the assets and the value of the bonds that are issued.

In an unfunded deal, all or most of the assets remain on the balance sheet and the issuer/originator buys credit protection, in the form of a credit default swap, against the risk of default. Unfunded deals are carried out by banks to obtain regulatory capital relief – allowing the bank to make new loans.

Granularity The degree to which a deal is backed by a wide spread of assets. Securitisations of portfolios of residential mortgages are backed by thousands of individual mortgages, thereby spreading the risk. Portfolios of commercial mortgages and collateralised debt obligations, in contrast, are backed by a smaller number of assets, so risk is more concentrated.

Monoline insurer A specialist insurer that promises to pay up if cash flows disappoint. This credit enhancement or wrapping allows the credit rating agencies to apply a higher rating than otherwise would be possible.

Over-collateralisation More assets are put into the special purpose vehicle than are thought strictly necessary. This provides additional comfort that cash flow targets will be met and bond coupons paid. The funds required are typically 60–70 per cent of the cash flow that is expected.

Pfandbrief German term meaning 'a letter of pledge'. Refers to what elsewhere is known as a covered bond. The Pfandbrief market is 235 years old.

RMBSs Residential mortgage-backed security.

Securitisation The process of taking a defined set of assets that are used to back a bond issue. The assets are put into a special purpose vehicle, separate from the original owner of the assets, which guarantees that coupons will be paid and the capital investment returned. The credit quality of the bond issue depends on the SPV, not on the financial strength of the underlying issuer. It appeals to banks and other issuers because they earn more from the assets than they pay in interest on the bonds. Banks free regulatory capital on their balance sheets and can make new loans.

Special purpose vehicle In this context, the legal owner of the underlying assets. The SPV is supposedly 'bankruptcy-remote' because it is separate from the general operating problems that may affect the company.

Structured finance Often used interchangeably with 'securitisation'. But banks frequently restrict securitisation to deals that are based on cash assets, while structured finance also refers to so-called synthetic deals that involved credit default swaps and other derivatives.

True sale initiative An attempt to create a securitisation market in Germany where assets are transferred off the issuer's balance sheet. KfW, the business development bank, has promoted the idea, but there have been lengthy delays in creating a framework. The first deal was announced this month [November 2004]; Volkswagen Bank is to issue €1.1bn of securities against car loans.

Whole business securitisation Also known as corporate securitisation. Used when a whole business is securitised rather than a discrete set of assets. Popular in sectors such as water where, if problems arise, the assets have little value when divorced from the skills of management. They started in the UK where the concept of the 'floating charge', applying to a business's assets generally, allows creditors to get control of the assets. The technique is spreading to continental Europe, but some bankers feel it will not work successfully, given the different insolvency regimes. Because the investor is exposed to corporate risk, ratings are lower than for traditional securitisations but yields are higher. They are increasingly being used by private equity houses as a means of financing acquisitions.

Source: *Financial Times* (2004) 'Securitisation Survey', November 2004, by Charles Batchelor.

Chapter 10

Banking risks

Learning objectives
- To define the most common risks in banking
- To distinguish between the various risks in banking
- To understand the importance of the interrelation among banking risks

10.1 Introduction

For any privately owned bank, management's goal is to maximise shareholders' value. If the institution is publicly listed and markets are efficient, returns are proportional to the risks taken; if the bank is small and unlisted, managers will try to maximise the value of the owner's investments by seeking the highest returns for what they deem to be acceptable levels of risk. With increased pressure on banks to improve shareholders' returns, banks have had to assume higher risks and, at the same time, manage these risks to avoid losses. Recent changes in the banking environment (deregulation, globalisation, conglomeration, etc.) have posed serious risk challenges for banks but have also offered productive opportunities. In Chapter 9 we illustrated the key return measures of banks (e.g., ROE, ROA) and their functions. In this chapter we describe the main types of risks modern banks have to face. An introduction to the prevailing risk management techniques will be provided in more detail in Chapter 11.

10.2 Credit risk

According to the Basle Committee on Banking Supervision (2000) **credit risk** is defined as 'the potential that a bank borrower or counterparty will fail to meet its obligations in accordance with agreed terms'. Generally credit risk is associated with the traditional lending activity of banks and it is simply described as the risk of a loan not being repaid in part or in full. However, credit risk can also derive from holding bonds and other securities.

Credit risk is the risk of a decline in the credit-standing of a counterparty. Such deterioration does not imply default, but means that the probability of default increases. Capital markets value the credit-standing of firms through the rate of interest charged on bonds or other debt issues, changes in the value of shares, and ratings provided by the **credit rating agencies** (such as Standard & Poor's, Moody's and FitchIBCA). However, as we will see later on in this chapter, modern banks also face credit risk in a number of other financial instruments that are typically off-balance sheet (such as for derivative products and guarantees). This particular type of credit risk is sometimes referred to as **counterparty risk**.

Bank managers should minimise credit losses by building a portfolio of assets (loans and securities) that diversifies the degree of risk. This is because very low default risk assets are associated with low credit risk and low expected return, while higher expected return assets have a higher probability of default (i.e., a higher credit risk). Focusing on loans that constitute the largest proportion of a bank's assets, in the previous chapter we mentioned that the traditional lending function involves four different components (see, for example, Greenbaum and Thakor, 1995; Sinkey, 1998):

1) originating (the application process)
2) funding (approving the loan and availing funds)
3) servicing (collecting interest and principal payments)
4) monitoring (checking on borrowers' behaviour through the life of the loan).

Banks must investigate borrowers' ability to repay their loans before and after the loan has been made (these activities are known as screening and monitoring functions of banks) because of their aim to maximise value and the responsibility they have towards their depositors and deposit insurers to be safe and sound.

To recall, banks are said to act as *delegated monitors* on behalf of lenders and to this end they use technology and innovation in the design and enforcement of contracts. These contracts are costly for the banks but they are essential for the protection of both banks' owners and lenders. However, *agency problems* may arise as a result of functions (1) and (4). As shown in Chapter 1, agency problems imply potential contractual frictions between principals (lenders) and agents (borrowers) because of asymmetric information, moral hazard and adverse selection. Banks need to account for these problems while aiming to minimise losses in lending.

While it is accepted that all banks experience some loan losses, the degree of risk aversion varies significantly across institutions. All banks have their own **credit philosophy** established in a formal written **loan policy** that must be supported and communicated with an appropriate **credit culture**. The lending philosophy could reflect an emphasis on aggressive loan growth based on flexible underwriting standards. Alternatively, it could reflect the goals of a more conservative management aiming at achieving a consistent performance of a high-quality loan portfolio. Loan policies reflect the degree of risk bank management is ready to take and may change over time. A credit culture is successful when all employees in the bank are aligned with the management's lending priorities (Hempel and Simonson, 1999).

If internal data are available, credit risk can be monitored by looking at the changes in the ratio: medium-quality loans/total assets ratio. The bank can choose to lower its credit risk by lowering this ratio. If the data on medium quality loans are not available, traditional proxies for credit risk include for instance:

- total loans/total assets
- non-performing loans/total loans
- loan losses/total loans
- loan loss reserves/total assets.

These types of ratios can be calculated for different types of loans the bank holds on its balance sheet, for example, a bank may look at its mortgage loan book and see what proportion of such loans it holds relative to total assets, the amount on non-performing mortgage loans, loan losses on mortgage loans and so on.

However, Hempel and Simonson (1999) argue that these indicators can be subject to criticism because they lag in time behind the returns gained by taking higher risk. Therefore one should look at lead indicators such as:

- loan concentration in geographic areas or sectors
- rapid loan growth
- high lending rates
- loan loss reserves/non-performing loans (NPLs).

Another important credit-risk measure is the ratio of total loans to total deposits. The higher the ratio the greater the concerns of regulatory authorities, as loans are among the riskiest of bank assets. A greater level of non-performing loans to deposits could also generate greater risk for depositors.

Since in the presence of credit risk the mean return on the banks' asset portfolio is clearly lower than if the loan portfolio say was entirely risk-free, the bank will find it necessary to minimise the probability of bad outcomes in the portfolio by using a diversification strategy. Diversification will decrease **unsystematic** or **firm-specific credit risk**. This is derived from 'micro' factors and thus is the credit risk specific to the holding of loans or bonds of a particular firm.

An interesting example of the extent of bank lending diversification was highlighted in the case of the failure of Parmalat, an Italian dairy company that was caught conducting a massive fraud in 2003. The total exposure of international banks that held loans and bonds of Parmalat was estimated at $5 billion (*The Economist*, 2004b). Nearly 30 international banks were affected and among them was Bank of America with a $274m exposure at the end of 2003 in loans and derivatives. Citigroup reported a $544m after-tax exposure in 2003 due to Parmalat-related credit and trading losses. Italian banks estimated lending exposure to Parmalat was more than €2.3bn (see Table 10.1), about half the lending exposure of all banks, the worst hit being Capitalia, the country's fourth largest bank, with €484m in exposure. While the failure had major implications for the banks concerned, the fact that a number of banks were exposed to losses – rather than just one bank – highlighted the advantages of loan diversification by international banks.

Table 10.1 **Italian banks' exposure to Parmalat and Parmatour***

Bank	Estimated exposure, €m	Potential loss, €m
Capitalia	484	290
Banca Intesa	360	216
Sanpaolo	303	182
MPS	183	110
Unicredit Banca Mobiliare	162	97
ABN Amro	160	96
Banca Popolare di Lodi	126	76
Banca Nazionale del Lavoro	120	72
BPU	105	63
Other banks (total)	263	158
Total	2,266	1,360

* Parmatour (a travel group) was a business owned and run by the family of Parmalat Group's founder.

Source: Adapted from *The Economist* (2004b).

While diversification decreases firm-specific credit risk, banks remain exposed to **systematic credit risk**. This is the risk associated with the possibility that default of all firms may increase over a given period because of economic changes or other events that have an impact on large sections of the economy/market (e.g., in an economic recession firms are less likely to be able to repay their debts).

10.3 Interest rate risk

An interest rate is a *price* that relates to *present* claims on resources relative to *future* claims on resources. An interest rate is the price that a borrower pays in order to be able to consume resources now rather than at a point in the future. Correspondingly, it is the price that a *lender* receives to forgo current consumption. Like all prices in free markets, interest rates are established by the interaction of supply and demand; in this context, it is the supply of future claims on resources interacting with the demand for future claims on resources. An interest rate may, therefore, be defined as *a price established by the interaction of the supply of, and the demand for, future claims on resources*. That price will usually be expressed as a proportion of the sum borrowed or lent over a given period.

Interest rates have a crucial role in the financial system. For example, they influence financial flows within the economy, the distribution of wealth, capital investment and the profitability of financial institutions (also see Chapter 5 for more details on the implementation of monetary policy). For banks, the exposure to interest rate risk, that is the risk associated with unexpected changes in interest rates, has grown sharply in recent years as a result of the increased volatility in market interest rates especially at the international level.[1]

However, not all banks' assets and liabilities are subject to **interest rate risk** in the same way. Important distinctions should be made between **fixed rate assets and liabilities** and **rate-sensitive assets and liabilities**:

- Fixed rate assets and liabilities carry rates that are constant throughout a certain period (e.g., 1 year) and their cash flows do not change unless there is a default, early withdrawal, or an unanticipated pre-payment.
- Rate-sensitive assets and liabilities can be re-priced within a certain period (e.g., 90 days); therefore the cash flows associated with rate-sensitive contracts vary with changes in interest rates.

Other banks' assets and liabilities can be categorised into non-earning assets (i.e., assets that generate no explicit income such as cash); and non-paying liabilities (i.e., liabilities that pay no interest, such as current accounts or, as they are known in the United States, 'checking accounts').

A rise in market interest rates has the effect of increasing banks' funding costs because the cost of variable rate deposits and other variable rate financing increases. If loans have been made at fixed interest rates this obviously reduces the net returns on such loans. On the other hand, banks will be vulnerable to falling rates if they hold an excess of fixed rate liabilities. In the case of bonds, as interest rates increase this reduces the market value of a bond investment. Typically, long-term, fixed-income securities subject their holders to the greatest amount of interest rate risk (see Appendix A1 for more details on the relation between bond prices and interest rates). In contrast, short-term securities, such as Treasury bills, are much less influenced by interest rate movements.

Traditional interest rate risk analysis compares the sensitivity of interest income to changes in asset yields with the sensitivity of interest expenses to changes in interest costs of liabilities. In particular, it is common to refer to the ratio of *rate-sensitive assets* to *rate-sensitive liabilities*: when rate-sensitive assets exceed rate-sensitive liabilities (in a particular maturity range), a bank is vulnerable to losses from falling interest rates. Conversely, when rate-sensitive liabilities exceed rate-sensitive assets, losses are likely to be incurred if market interest rates rise. Typically, if a bank has a ratio above 1.0, the bank's returns will be lower if interest rates decline and higher if they increase. However, given the difficulty in forecasting interest rates, some banks conclude that they can minimise interest rate risk with an interest sensitivity ratio close to 1.0. As pointed out by Hempel and Simonson 1999), such a ratio may be difficult for some banks to achieve and often can be reached only at the cost of lower returns on assets.

---

[1] Note that interest rate risk is faced by both borrowers (who do not want to pay higher rates on loans) and lenders who may suffer losses if rates fall.

These traditional measures of interest rate risk have a number of limitations. Bank managers today use sophisticated measures of interest rate management such as the gap buckets analysis, maturity models and duration analysis. Details of these models will be provided in Chapter 11. It is important to note that interest rate risk measurement and management will always imply an ALM approach (see Chapter 9).

Section 10.3.1 follows Saunders and Cornett's (2003) examples of the two types of interest rate risk that banks may have to face: **refinancing risk** and **reinvestment risk** and also focuses on the impact on a bank's profitability.

10.3.1 Refinancing risk and reinvestment risk

Interest rate risk is the risk arising from the mismatching of the maturity and the volume of banks' assets and liabilities as part of their asset transformation function. As we saw in Chapter 1, one of the main functions of financial intermediaries is to act as asset transformers, e.g., they transform short-term deposits into long-term loans.

Typically the maturity of banks' assets (e.g., loans) is longer than the maturity of banks' liabilities (e.g., deposits). This means that banks can be viewed as 'short-funded' and have to run the risk of refinancing their assets at a rate that maybe less advantageous than previous rates. Saunders and Cornett (2003) define refinancing risk as: 'the risk that (the) cost of rolling over or re-borrowing funds will rise above the returns being earned on asset investments'.

For example, assume the cost of funds (liabilities) for a bank is 7 per cent per annum and the interest return on an asset is 9 per cent. In year 1 by borrowing short (1 year) and lending long (2 years) the profit spread is equal to the difference between the lending and borrowing rates, i.e., 2 per cent, as in situation (a) in Figure 10.1. In year 2 profits are uncertain because if the interest rate does not change then the bank can refinance its liabilities at 7 per cent per annum and as in year 1 have a profit of 2 per cent. However, if interest rates increase as in situation (b), then the bank can borrow at 8 per cent and profits will be only 1 per cent.

Another type of mismatch could occur when the maturity of banks' liabilities is longer than the maturity of the assets. This means that banks can be viewed as

Figure 10.1 **Refinancing risk**

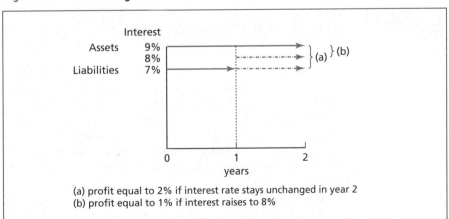

(a) profit equal to 2% if interest rate stays unchanged in year 2
(b) profit equal to 1% if interest raises to 8%

Source: Adapted from Saunders and Cornett (2003).

'long-funded', and have to run the risk of reinvesting their funds in the second period at a rate that maybe less advantageous than the previous rate, and that they were unable to forecast in advance. Such a situation can often occur in banking within specific maturity buckets (i.e., intervals of consecutive maturities, such as a three to six months' maturity bucket). Accordingly, Saunders and Cornett (2003) define reinvestment risk as: 'the risk that the returns on funds to be reinvested will fall below the cost of funds'.

For example, assume the interest return on an asset for a bank is 9 per cent per annum and the cost of funds (liabilities) is 7 per cent. In year 1 by borrowing long (2 years) and lending short (1 year) the profit spread is equal to the difference between lending rate and borrowing rate, that is 2 per cent, as in situation (c) in Figure 10.2. In year 2 profits are uncertain because if the interest rate does not change then the bank can reinvest its assets at 9 per cent per annum and as in year 1 have a profit of 2 per cent. However, if interest rates go down as in situation (d), then the bank can lend at 8 per cent and profits will be only 1%.

Figure 10.2 Reinvestment risk

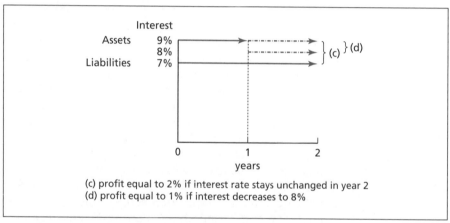

(c) profit equal to 2% if interest rate stays unchanged in year 2
(d) profit equal to 1% if interest decreases to 8%

Source: Adapted from Saunders and Cornett (2003).

10.4 Liquidity (or funding) risk

A liquid asset may be defined as an asset that can be turned into cash quickly and without capital loss or interest penalty. Most bank deposits are therefore very liquid, but investment in, for example, property is highly illiquid. The liquidity that is required by a lender will depend on a number of factors, including in particular the range of liquidity inherent in other securities held. Moreover, a bank needs liquidity to cover a possible surge in operating expenses and to satisfy loan demand. All other things being equal, lenders will wish to have a high level of liquidity in their loans.

Liquidity risk is generated in the balance sheet by a mismatch between the size and maturity of assets and liabilities. It is the risk that the bank is holding insufficient liquid assets on its balance sheet and thus is unable to meet requirements without impairment to its financial or reputational capital. Banks have to manage their liquidity to ensure that both predictable and unpredictable liquidity demands are met and taking into account that the immediate sale of assets at low or 'fire sale' prices could threaten the bank's returns.[2]

However, liquidity risk can also occur when the duration of the balance sheet is matched: consider the situation if some of the loans funded by deposits were to default. If loan defaults were so large as to leave insufficient liquidity for the bank to satisfy depositors' demands to withdraw these deposits, then the bank would need to find new deposits to fund the withdrawals. As illustrated in the example reported in Box 10.1, information asymmetries between the bank and the depositors can often originate liquidity risk.

If a bank cannot meet depositor demands there will be a bank run, as depositors lose confidence and rush to withdraw funds. This may then make it difficult for the bank to obtain funds in the interbank market and before long a **liquidity crisis** will turn into a solvency crisis and possible failure (on the distinction between liquidity and solvency see Chapter 5, Box 5.5). Hence it is common to distinguish two types of liquidity risk.

- *Day-to-day liquidity risk* relates to daily withdrawals. This is usually predictable (or 'normal') because only a small percentage of a bank's deposits will be withdrawn on a given day. Very few institutions ever actually run out of cash because it is relatively easy for the bank to cover any shortage of cash by borrowing funds from other banks in the interbank markets.

Box 10.1 Liquidity risk and information asymmetries: an example

Consider a bank that has made loans of €1 million with three-year maturity financed with uninsured demand deposits. The bank has an informational advantage compared with outsiders on the credit risk and overall quality of its loan portfolio. Suppose that one year later €500,000 of deposits are withdrawn and the bank's stock of cash assets is only 1 per cent (€100,000). The bank will need €400,000 to fund the deposit withdrawal. Two cases can occur: (1) potential new depositors have a good perception about the bank's loan portfolio and the bank will easily acquire the €400,000 in new deposits; (2) outsiders have received unfavourable information about the bank's loans despite the bank's belief that the quality is good. Here the bank will either not be able to acquire new deposits (in extreme cases it will lose all existing deposits!) or have to pay too high a price for the risk associated with the loan portfolio.

Informational asymmetries about asset quality create liquidity risk. If outsiders knew as much as the bank does about the quality of the loan portfolio, then the bank would be able to acquire deposits at the appropriate price given the risk of the loan portfolio.

Source: Adapted from Greenbaum and Thakor (1995, p. 172).

---

[2] Greenbaum and Thakor (1995) point out that the most extreme manifestation of liquidity risk is that the seller of the asset is *unable* to sell the asset at any price. This is known as *credit rationing* and occurs when a bank refuses credit to a borrower irrespective of the price that they are willing to pay.

- *A liquidity crisis* occurs when depositors demand larger withdrawals than normal. In this situation banks are forced to borrow funds at an elevated interest rate, higher than the market rate that other banks are paying for similar borrowings. This is usually unpredictable (or 'abnormal') and can be due to either a lack of confidence in the specific bank, or some unexpected need for cash. Liquidity crises can ultimately hinder the ability of a bank to repay its obligations and in the absence of central bank intervention or deposit insurance it could result in 'a run' and even the insolvency of the bank.

Typically banks can reduce their exposure to liquidity risk by increasing the proportion of funds committed to cash and readily marketable assets, such as Treasury bills (T-bills) and other government securities, or use longer-term liabilities to fund the bank's operations. The difficulty for banks, however, is that liquid assets tend to yield low returns so if a bank holds sub-optimal levels of such assets its profits will decline. This is the trade-off between liquidity and profitability: the opportunity cost of stored liquidity is high and holding low-yielding assets (and/or zero-yielding assets such as cash) on the balance sheet reduces bank profitability (this issue will be considered further in Chapter 11).

One measure banks can use to monitor liquidity risk relates short-term securities, a proxy for a bank's liquidity sources, to total deposits – this provides an approximate measure of a bank's liquidity needs. Another traditional ratio of liquidity risk is the loan/deposits ratio. This ratio tends to focus on the liquidity of assets on the balance sheet. A high ratio of short-term securities/deposits and a low loan/deposits ratio indicate that the bank is less risky but also less profitable.

There are, however, other indicators that, according to Hempel and Simonson (1999), are more suited to proxy a modern bank's need for liquidity and based on actual or potential cash flows to meet cash needs. For example, a good indication of the bank's need for liquidity may be given by the amount a bank has in purchased or volatile funds and the amount the bank has used of its potential borrowing reserve.

10.5 Foreign exchange risk

As banking markets become more global, the importance of international activities in the form of foreign direct investment and foreign portfolio investments has increased sharply. However, the actual return the bank earns on foreign investment may be altered by changes in exchange rates. Changes in the value of a country's currency relative to other currencies affect the foreign exchange rates. Like other prices, exchange rates (that essentially reflect the price of currencies) tend to vary under supply and demand pressure.

Foreign exchange relates to money denominated in the currency of another nation or group of nations. Any firm or individual that exchanges money denominated in the 'home' nation's currency for money denominated in another nation's currency can be said to be acquiring foreign exchange. This is the case whether the transaction is very small involving, say, a few pounds or whether it is a company changing a billion dollars for the purchase of a foreign company. In addition, the transaction is also viewed as acquiring foreign exchange if the type of money being acquired is in the form of foreign currency notes, foreign currency bank deposits, or any other claims that are denominated in foreign currency. Put simply, a foreign exchange transaction represents a movement of funds, or other short-term financial claims, from one country and currency to another.

Foreign exchange can take many forms. It can be in the form of cash, funds available on credit cards (credit card payments when on holiday overseas are usually made in the foreign currency, but the card is debited in home currency), bank deposits or various other short-term claims. In general, a financial claim can be regarded as foreign exchange if it is negotiable and denominated in a currency other than that in which it resides, for instance, a US dollar bank deposit in Paris. Box 10.2 provides a more formal definition and explanation of exchange rates and foreign exchange markets.

Box 10.2   What is an exchange rate? What are the features of the foreign exchange markets?

What is an exchange rate?

The exchange rate is a *price* – the number of units of one nation's currency that needs to be surrendered in order to acquire one unit of another nation's currency. There is a wide range of 'exchange rates', for example the US dollar, Japanese Yen, British pound and the Euro. In the spot market, there is an exchange rate for every other national currency traded in that market, as well as for a variety of composite currencies such as the International Monetary Fund's Special Drawing Rights 'SDRs'. There are also a variety of 'trade-weighted' or 'effective' rates designed to show a currency's movements against an average of various other currencies.

In addition to the spot rates, there is also a wide range of additional exchange rates for transactions that take place on other delivery dates, in the forward markets. While one can talk about, say, the Euro exchange rate in the market, it is important to note that there is no single, or unique Euro exchange rate in the market, as the rate depends on when the transaction is to take place, the spot rate being the current rate and forward rates being influenced by various factors most noticeably the Euro interest rate compared to the official interest rate in other currencies.

The market price is determined by supply and demand factors, namely, the interaction of buyers and sellers, and the market rate between two currencies is determined by the interaction of the official (mainly central banks) and private participants (banks, companies, investment firms, and so on) in the foreign exchange market. For a currency with an exchange rate that is set by the monetary authorities, the central bank or another official body is the key participant, standing ready to buy or sell the currency as necessary to maintain the authorised rate.

What are the features of the foreign exchange markets?

While most people are familiar with the aforementioned features of foreign exchange they are less familiar with what is known as the foreign exchange market. The foreign exchange market represents an international network of major foreign exchange dealers (central banks, commercial banks, brokers and other operators) that undertake high-volume (wholesale) trading around the world. These transactions nearly always take the form of an exchange of bank deposits of different national currency denominations. If one bank agrees to sell Euro for US dollars to another bank, there will be an exchange between the two parties of a Euro bank deposit for a US dollar bank deposit.

There is no physical location for the foreign exchange market, and transactions are carried out via computer screens based in banks, large companies and various other organisations throughout the world. The majority of foreign exchange turnover takes place in the main financial centres of London, New York and Tokyo. The main market participants include banks, non-financial firms, individuals, official bodies and other private institutions that are buying and selling foreign exchange at any particular time. Some of the buyers and sellers of foreign exchange may be involved in physical goods transactions and need foreign exchange to make purchases (such as a UK importer of car parts from Japan that needs to make a purchase in Yen). However, the proportion of foreign exchange transactions related to goods trade is generally believed to be very small – less than 5% of all foreign exchange transactions. Other participants in the market may wish to undertake foreign exchange transactions to undertake

▶

direct investment in plant and equipment, or in portfolio investment (dealing across borders in stocks and bonds and other financial assets), while others may operate in the money market (trading short-term debt instruments internationally).

Overall, the motives of participants in the foreign exchange market are wide and varied. Some participants are international investors or speculators while others may be financing foreign investments or trade. Many participants also use foreign exchange transactions for risk management purposes in order to hedge against the risks associated with adverse foreign exchange movements. Transactions may be very short-term or long-term, and can be conducted by official bodies (such as central banks) or by private institutions, the motives for conducting business can vary and the scale of activity can alter substantially over time. All these combined features make up the supply and demand characteristics of the global foreign exchange market.

Given the diverse make-up of the supply and demand features of the market, predicting the future course of exchange rates is a particularly complex and uncertain business. In addition, since exchange rates influence such an extensive array of participants and business decisions, it is a critically important price in an economy, influencing consumer prices, investment decisions, interest rates, economic growth, the location of industry, and much more. It should be clear that for a firm wishing to undertake international activity knowledge of the foreign exchange market, predictions about future exchange rates and the risks associated with foreign exchange are essential elements that senior managers must understand if they are to be successful in overseas expansion.

The foreign exchange market consists of a wholesale (or interbank) market and a retail market. Transactions in the wholesale market are dominated by bank-to-bank transactions that involve very large transactions, typically greater than $1 million. In contrast, the retail market, where clients obtain foreign exchange via their banks involves much smaller sums.

According to the 2005 Triennial Survey by the Bank for International Settlements (BIS), global foreign exchange turnover amounts to more than $1,880bn per day, over 31% of which is transacted on the London market alone. Global turnover is markedly up on the 2001 BIS survey figure of $1,200 billion (a 57% increase at current exchange rates and a 36% rise at constant exchange rates). The BIS also notes that investors became increasingly interested in foreign exchange as an asset class alternative to equity and fixed income and this helped boost foreign exchange turnover. These trends that occurred between 2001 and 2004 tended to counteract the forces that led to a decline in foreign exchange turnover between 1998 and 2001 – such as mergers in the banking and corporate sector that led to fewer banks and firms trading foreign exchange. In terms of the currencies most widely traded, the BIS reports that in April 2004 most turnover was between the US dollar and Euro, with daily turnover estimated at $501 billion accounting for 28% of market share, followed by US dollar/Yen ($296 billion).

Source: BIS (2005) 'Triennial Central Bank Survey – Foreign exchange and derivatives market activity in 2004', March, Basle.

Foreign exchange risk is the risk that exchange rate fluctuations affect the value of a bank's assets, liabilities and off-balance sheet activities denominated in foreign currency. We have seen in Chapter 8 that the UK banking sector has quite a significant amount of foreign currency assets and liabilities in its balance sheet – this is mainly from the assets and liabilities of foreign banks based in London that do predominantly wholesale foreign currency-related business (see Tables 8.2 and 8.3). A bank may be willing to take advantage of differing interest rates or margins in another country, or simply to invest abroad in a currency different from the domestic one. Clearly a bank that lends in a currency that then depreciates more quickly that its home currency will be subject to foreign exchange risk.

Suppose a Spanish bank has a net 'long' assets position in dollars (e.g., a loan in dollars) of $100 million as illustrated in Figure 10.3. (If the bank is *net long* in foreign assets it means it holds more foreign assets than liabilities. Conversely, the bank would be holding a *net short* position in foreign assets if it had more foreign liabilities than assets.) On the liability side the Spanish bank has $60 million in Spanish CDs. These CDs are denominated in Euros. The Spanish bank will suffer

Figure 10.3 **The foreign asset and liability position of a Spanish bank: a net long asset position in US$**

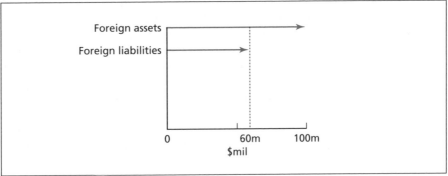

Source: Adapted from Saunders and Cornett (2003).

losses if the exchange rate for dollars falls or depreciates against the Euro over this period because the value of the US$ loan assets would decrease in value by more than the Euro CDs.

To measure foreign exchange risk banks calculate measures of net exposure by each currency. It will be equal to the difference between the assets and liabilities denominated in the same currency. In the case above the bank is exposed to the risk that its net foreign assets may have to be liquidated at an exchange rate lower than the one that existed when the bank entered into the foreign asset/liability position.

10.6 Market (or trading) risk

Market risk is the risk of losses in on- and off-balance sheet positions arising from movements in market prices. It pertains in particular to short-term trading in assets, liabilities and derivative products, and relates to changes in interest rates, exchange rates and other asset prices.

Modern conditions have led to an increase in market risk due to a decline in traditional sources of income and a greater reliance by banks on income from trading securities. This process has increased the variability in banks' earnings due to the relatively frequent changes in market conditions. International regulators have acknowledged the importance of market risk since 1996 when the Basle Capital Accord was changed to incorporate capital requirements for market risk in its capital adequacy rules (see Chapter 7).

Heffernan (2005, p. 107) distinguishes between:

● *General or systematic* market risk, caused by a movement in the prices of all market instruments due to macrofactors (e.g. a change in economic policy); and
● *Unsystematic or specific* market risk that arises in situations where the price of one instrument moves out of line with other similar instruments because of events related to the issuer of the instrument (e.g., an environmental law suit against a firm will reduce its share prices but is unlikely to cause a decline in the market index).

Market risk is the risk common to an entire class of assets or liabilities. It is the risk that the value of investments may decline over a given period simply because of economic changes or other events that affect large portions of the market. Typically, market risk relates to changes in interest rates, exchange rates and securities' prices driven by the market overall. In the case of bank lending, credit risk is the most important, but for banks lending to companies that are investing in securities (such as bank loans to hedge funds[3]) then bank assessment of credit risk will be influenced by the hedge funds' exposure to market risk. (The banks own investments and securities trading activity will also be subject to market risk.)

Bonds and shareholders' equity are especially sensitive to the movements in market interest rates and currency prices and this affects the investors' perception of a bank's risk exposure and earnings potential. Important indicators of market risk in banking are (Rose and Hudgins, 2002):

- Book value assets/estimated market value of assets
- Book value of equity capital/market value of equity capital
- Market value of bonds and other fixed-income assets/book value of bonds and other fixed-income assets
- Market value of common and preferred stock per share.

Large banks perform VaR (Value-at-Risk) analysis to assess the risk of loss on their portfolios of trading assets while small banks measure market risk by conducting sensitivity analysis. VaR is a technique that uses statistical analysis of historical market trends and volatilities to estimate the likely or expected maximum loss on a bank's portfolio or line of business over a set period, with a given probability. The aim is to get one figure that summarises the maximum loss faced by the bank within a statistical confidence interval. For instance, it can be estimated that: 'there is a 0.5% chance that a portfolio will lose £1 million in value over the next quarter'. In contrast, sensitivity analysis refers to the more traditional methods of assessing the price sensitivity of assets and liabilities to changes in interest or other rates and the corresponding impact on stockholders' equity.

10.7 Country and sovereign risk

Country risk is the risk that economic, social and political conditions of a foreign country will adversely affect a bank's commercial and financial interests. It relates to the adverse effect that deteriorating macroeconomic conditions and political and social instability may have on the returns generated from overseas investments. International lending always carries 'unusual' risks; however, it is generally accepted that a loan to a foreign government is safer than a loan to a private sector borrower (Hempel and Simonson, 1999).

Nonetheless, it is possible that even governments will default on debt owed to a bank or government agency. This is the **sovereign risk** and refers to the possibility

---

[3] Hedge funds are specialist investment vehicles (usually set up as partnerships by wealthy investors) that take positions using credit or borrowed capital. Managers often invest in liquid instruments, such as currency and interest rate derivatives, with the aim of making profits from movements in foreign exchange or bond markets. Hedge funds are increasingly large banks' borrowers and investors in the capital markets.

that governments, as sovereign powers, may enforce their authority to declare debt to external lenders void or modify the movements of profits, interest and capital. Such situations typically arise when foreign governments experience some sort of economic or political pressures and decide to divert resources to the correction of their domestic problems. Clearly the fact that governments generally benefit from a particular 'immunity' from legal process, makes international lending extremely risky for banking institutions that in case of default find it very difficult, if not impossible, to recover some of the debt by taking over some of the country's assets.

Sovereign risk can result in the re-scheduling and re-negotiation of the debt, with considerable losses for the lending banks. These types of new agreements are usually obtained with the intervention of international organisations (e.g., the International Monetary Fund and the World Bank). The extreme case for sovereign risk is *debt repudiation*, when the government simply repudiate their debts and no longer recognise their obligations to external creditors.

To help investors measure country and sovereign risks, rating company agencies provide tables of sovereign (credit risk) ratings. Table 10.2 shows the average sovereign credit ratings between 1996 and 2003 from Moody's and Standard and Poor's, for a selection of countries (Borio and Packer, 2004). It can be seen that over the period studied China (BBB) had a higher sovereign risk rating than India (BB) suggesting that in the credit rating agencies' view the Indian government was a higher credit risk than China's. The governments of Turkey, Venezuela and Pakistan with credit ratings of B were viewed as the worst credit risks (i.e., of the countries listed in the Table these are the governments most likely to default on interest and principal repayment on their bond issues).

Table 10.2 Foreign currency sovereign credit ratings

Country	Rating	Country	Rating	Country	Rating
Argentina	BB	Hong Kong SAR	A	Philippines	BB+
Australia	AA+	Hungary	BBB	Poland	BBB
Austria	AAA	Iceland	A+	Portugal	AA
Belgium	AA+	India	BB	Russia	BB–
Brazil	B+	Indonesia	BB	Singapore	AAA
Bulgaria	BB–	Ireland	AA+	Slovenia	A
Canada	AA+	Israel	A–	South Africa	BBB–
Chile	A–	Italy	AA	Spain	AA+
China	BBB	Japan	AA	Sweden	AA+
Colombia	BB+	Korea	A-	Switzerland	AAA
Croatia	BBB–	Lithuania	BBB	Taiwan, China	AA
Cyprus	A+	Malaysia	BBB+	Thailand	BBB
Czech Rep.	A–	Mexico	BB+	Turkey	B
Denmark	AAA	Netherlands	AAA	United Kingdom	AAA
Finland	AA+	New Zealand	AA+	United States	AAA
France	AAA	Norway	AAA	Venezuela	B
Germany	AAA	Pakistan	B		
Greece	A–	Peru	BB–		

Note: See Table 4.1 for a precise definition of the Standard & Poor's ratings. Remember that the best quality credits are rated AAA, followed by AA, A, BBB, BB, B and although not shown in the Table CCC, CC, and finally D for in default. The + and – signs just reflect a little fine-tuning so BB+ has a higher credit rating than BB, but not as good as BBB, etc.

Sources: Moody's Investors Service; Standard & Poor's.

10.8 Operational risk

Another important risk in banking is **operational risk**. The Risk Management Group of the Basle Committee on Banking Supervision (2001b) defines operational risk as 'the risk of loss resulting from inadequate or failed internal processes, people and systems or from external events'. In general terms, this is the risk associated with the possible failure of a bank's systems, controls or other management failure (including human error).

The definition of operational risk given above includes **technology risk**, however, there are some differences between the two that are outlined below (Saunders and Cornett, 2003, p. 146).

- Technology risk occurs when technological investments do not produce the anticipated cost savings in the form of either economies of scale or scope; this risk also refers to the risk of current delivery systems becoming inefficient because of the developments of new delivery systems.
- Operational risk occurs whenever existing technology malfunctions or back-office support systems break down.

Operational risk is one of the main innovations proposed for Basle II (see Chapter 7) requiring banks to hold capital for such risks along with credit and market risk. Table 10.3 shows a list of operational risk event types that the Basle Committee, in consultation with the industry, has identified as having the potential to result in substantial losses.

As shown in the table, operational risk includes a number of risk event types, from employee fraud to natural disaster that may damage a bank's physical assets and reduce its ability to communicate with its customers.

Table 10.3 Operational risk event types

Risk event rypes	Examples include
Internal fraud	Intentional misreporting of positions, employee theft, and insider trading on an employee's own account.
External fraud	Robbery, forgery, cheque kiting,* and damage from computer hacking.
Employment practices and workplace safety	Workers' compensation claims, violation of employee health and safety rules, organised labour activities, discrimination claims and general liability.
Clients, products and business practices	Fiduciary breaches, misuse of confidential customer information, improper trading activities on the bank's account, money laundering, and sale of unauthorised products.
Damage to physical assets	Terrorism, vandalism, earthquakes, fires and floods.
Business disruption and system failures	Hardware and software failures, telecommunication problems and utility outages.
Execution, delivery and process management	Data entry errors, collateral management failures, incomplete legal documentation, unapproved access given to client accounts, non-client counterparty mis-performance and vendor disputes.

* 'Cheque kiting' is a fraudulent method to draw against uncollected bank funds.
Source: Federal Reserve Bank of Boston (2005) http://www.bos.frb.org/bankinfo/qau/oprisk.htm.

10.9 Off-balance sheet risk

So far, we have analysed banking risks that arise through on-balance sheet activities. For example, bad loans on the asset side; and deposit withdrawals and bank runs on the liability side. But they can also derive from off-balance sheet exposures that can potentially translate into significant losses.

Off-balance sheet (OBS) risk relates to the risks incurred by a bank in dealing with non-traditional banking activities such as financial derivative products (e.g., futures and options), guarantees and letters of credit. As described in Chapter 9, such activities do not appear in the bank balance sheet and they involve the creation of contingent assets and liabilities. It is common to refer to the risks of these activities as OBS risk, but they nevertheless include all the main types of risk faced by banks including, credit risk, interest rate risk, exchange rate risk and liquidity risk.

Given the nature of OBS activities and the fact that they have become increasingly widespread, it can be difficult for investors and regulators to identify the actual level of risk a bank is taking in any given period. Paradoxically, OBS activities were introduced to reduce the amount of risk taken by a business; but recent history has shown that while OBS can provide some protection against important risks like interest rate or currency risk, excessive OBS exposures due to mismanagement or speculative use of derivative instruments can result in spectacular losses. The Barings Bank failure in 1995 is an often-quoted example of insolvency of a British investment bank due to the misuse of derivatives activities. Box 10.3 reports the Barings case as well as some other well-known examples of losses caused by 'rogue traders' in derivatives and other OBS items (foreign exchange trading and investment fund business).

Given the potential huge losses that can be derived from excessive OBS trading, the regulators' approach has been to incorporate OBS commitments (using an on-balance sheet or credit equivalent) in calculating bank capital adequacy requirements (see Section 7.8 for more details).

10.10 Other risks

There are a number of other risks that banks face. It is common to distinguish between macro- and micro-risks. Macro-risks are also known as environmental risks and some of them are common to all businesses. They can include the risk of an economic recession, a sudden change in taxation or an unexpected change in financial market conditions, due for example to war, revolution, stock market crashes or other factors. Additional examples include:

- **Inflation risk** – the probability that an increase in the price level for goods and services will unexpectedly erode the purchasing power of a bank's earnings and returns to shareholders.
- **Settlement or payment risk** – a risk typically faced in the interbank market; it refers to the situation where one party to a contract fails to pay money or deliver assets with another party at the time of settlement. It can include credit/default risk if one party fails to settle. It can also be associated with any timing differences in settlement between the two parties.

Box 10.3 Rogue traders and bank losses

In 1995 Mr Nick Leeson was the rogue trader who brought down *Barings Brothers*, a British merchant bank, by uncovered exposures in the derivatives market. He went into the red by $1.2bn by trading on Asian markets, after what he claimed was a well-intentioned attempt to cover up losses in a client's account. He was jailed for fraud. Also in 1995, Mr Toshihide Iguchi at *Daiwa Bank* in Japan lost around $1.1bn (after more than 10 years of illicit trading) while dealing in US Treasury bonds. Daiwa Bank did not fail because it sold its assets and had considerable reserves; however, it was a massive blow for its reputation. Mr Iguchi was fined $2.6m and sentenced to four years in prison.

In 2002 Mr John Rusnack caused losses of some $750m to *Allied Irish Bank*, Ireland's largest bank, in unauthorised foreign exchange dealing at its American subsidiary, Allfirst. Mr Rusnak expected the Yen to strengthen against the dollar but this did not occur. The bank thought that options contracts were purchased as the internal system showed. Instead they weren't actually bought. Therefore, there was no insurance against the loss. The bank's solvency was not threatened but the bank absorbed the losses at a price of a significant reduction in earnings and capital.

Another rogue trader, Mr Peter Young, a fund manager of investment bank *Morgan Grenfell Asset Management*, a Deutsche Bank company, lost some $380m from the funds he ran, after hiding a series of unauthorised investments. Deutsche Bank had to inject $300m in cash to replace the fund; however, they incurred huge losses after a third of the investors left the fund within a few weeks.

In 2002 central Europe had its own rogue trader in Mr Eduard Nodilo, a dealer at *Rijecka Banka*, Croatia's third-biggest bank, that accumulated $98m in foreign exchange losses, thus wiping out the bank's capital.

More recently, in January 2004, Australia's biggest bank, the *National Australian Bank*, revealed that some of its foreign currency options traders in Melbourne and London had engaged in unauthorised trading. Losses have been estimated at $445m.

- **Regulatory risk** – the risk associated with a change in regulatory policy. For example, banks may be subject to certain new risks if deregulation takes place and barriers to lending or to entry of new firms are lifted. Changing rules relating to products and dealing with customers are other examples of potential regulatory risk.
- **Competitive risk** – the risk that arises as a consequence of changes in the competitive environment, as bank products and services become available from an increasing number of new entrants including non-bank financial firms and retailers.

Microeconomic risks are generally due to factors inside the bank, rather than external factors, such as:

- **Operating risk** – the possibility that operating expenses might vary significantly from what is expected, producing a decrease in income and the bank's value.
- **Legal risk** – the risk that contracts that are not legally enforceable or documented correctly could disrupt or negatively affect the operations, profitability or solvency of the bank.

- **Reputation risk** – the risk that strategic management's mistakes may have consequences for the reputation of a bank. It is also the risk that negative publicity, either true or untrue, adversely affects a bank's customer base or brings forth costly litigation thereby affecting profitability.
- **Portfolio risk** – the risk that the initial choice of lending opportunities will prove to be poor, in that some of the alternative opportunities that were rejected will turn out to yield higher returns than those selected.
- **Call risk** – the risk that arises when a borrower has the right to pay off a loan early, thus reducing the lender's expected rate of return.

Sometimes risks may be due to both internal and exogenous factors. *Earnings risk*, for example, is the risk that earnings may decline unexpectedly and this may be due to bad management or a change in laws and regulation.

Finally, it is worth mentioning **management risk**. This is the risk that management lacks the ability to make commercially profitable and other decisions consistently. It can also include the risk of dishonesty by employees and the risk that the bank will not have an effective organisation.

10.11 Capital risk and solvency

Capital risk should not be treated as a separate risk because all risks described in this chapter can potentially affect a bank's capital. In other words, excessive credit risk, interest rate risk, operational risk, liquidity risk, OBS risk, etc. could all result in a bank having insufficient capital to cover such losses. As noted above, in the case of Barings Bank, in such an instance the bank's solvency is impaired and failure can occur.

A bank will be insolvent when it has negative net worth of stockholders' equity. We learnt in Chapter 9 that this is the difference between the market value of its assets and liabilities. Therefore, capital risk refers to the decrease in market value of assets below the market value of its liabilities. In case of liquidation the bank would not be able to pay all its creditors and would be bankrupt.

Capital risk is closely tied to financial leverage (debt/equity) and banks are typically highly leveraged firms. It also depends on the asset quality and the overall risk profile of the institution. One should realise by now that the amount of capital a bank holds is positively related to the level of risk, that is, the more risk taken, the greater the amount of capital required. Banks with high capital risk (that is, banks that have low capital to assets ratios) also normally experience greater periodic fluctuations in earnings.

Capital risk, therefore, is the same as the risk of insolvency or the risk of failure. The following are some early indicators of failure risk (Rose and Hudgins, 2002, p. 165):

- The interest rate spread between market yields on bank debt issues and market yields on government securities of the same maturity: if the spread increases then investors believe that the bank in question is becoming more risky relative to government debt – investors in the market expect a higher risk of loss from purchasing and holding the bank's debt.
- The ratio of stock price per share to annual earnings per share: the ratio will often fall if investors come to believe that a bank is undercapitalised relative to the risks it has taken on.

- The ratio of equity capital to total assets: a low level of equity relative to assets may indicate higher risk exposure for debtholders and shareholders.
- The Basle Tier 1 (equity capital to risk-weighted assets) and Basle Tier 2 (total capital to risk-weighted assets) ratios: indicate how well equity capital and total capital, respectively, relate to the minimum (4 per cent and 8 per cent) regulatory requirements. A decline in either ratio indicates that a bank has less capital to cover potential losses. Ratios that fall below the minimum levels, as was the case for certain Japanese banks between 1997 and 2005, are an indication of technically insolvent institutions (see Chapter 16 for more detail on Japanese banking crises).

10.12 Interrelation of risks

In this chapter we have presented the characteristics of the main risks that modern banks face. While we have described each risk independently, risks are often correlated. For example, an increase in interest rates may increase default risk because companies may find it more difficult to maintain the promised payments on their debt. It may also increase liquidity risk for the bank if the defaulted payments were important for liquidity management purposes. Ultimately, this will affect bank's earnings and capital.

Note that banks face a plethora of risks and these risks are not mutually exclusive. They face credit risk when lending, market risk when trading in securities, interest rate risk in their funding operations, operational risks in undertaking all activities, and so on.

10.13 Conclusions

Risks are part of any economic activity. In financial services they assume a particular relevance because the business of banking is linked to uncertain future events and the risk of a bank failure is always a possibility in a system essentially run on confidence.

We have shown in this chapter that banks have to face a number of often interrelated risks, such as interest rate risk, credit risk and liquidity risk and that banks' attempts to cope with risks have often brought about other risks. One such case is derivative products that were designed to control risk through various hedging techniques, and have demonstrated, in certain cases, to be highly risky instruments.

There are various ways for a well-managed bank to protect against risk. One way is through diversification, in all its forms (e.g., portfolio diversification and geographic diversification). In addition, a bank will have to carry out appropriate asset/liability management practices and hedging strategies. Finally, there is capital that can act as a financial buffer, thus minimising the likelihood of bank failure. The next chapter discusses these and other issues and focuses on the various approaches to managing the main risks in modern banking.

Key terms

Credit risk	Country risk
Credit rating agency	Sovereign risk
Counterparty risk	Operational risk
Credit philosophy	Technology risk
Loan policy	Off-balance sheet (OBS) risk
Credit culture	Inflation risk
Systematic/unsystematic credit risk	Settlement or payment risk
Interest rate risk	Regulatory risk
Fixed rate assets and liabilities	Competitive risk
Rate-sensitive assets and liabilities	Operating risk
Refinancing risk	Legal risk
Reinvestment risk	Reputation risk
Liquidity risk	Portfolio risk
Liquidity crisis	Call risk
Foreign exchange risk	Management risk
Market risk	Capital risk

Key reading

Hempel, G.H. and Simonson, D.G. (1999) *Bank Management: Text and Cases*, 5th edn. New York: John Wiley & Sons.

Koch, T.W. and MacDonald, S.S. (2000), Bank Management, 4th edn. Orlando, FL: The Dryden Press.

Saunders, A. and Cornett, M.M. (2003) *Financial Institutions Management: A Risk Management Approach*, 4th edn. New York: McGraw Hill/Irwin.

Sinkey, J.F. Jr (1998) *Commercial Bank Financial Management*, 5th edn. London: Prentice Hall International.

Revision questions and problems

1 What is credit risk and what is meant by credit culture?

2 Define interest rate risk and distinguish between reinvestment and refinancing risk.

3 What are rate-sensitive assets and liabilities?

4 Why is liquidity risk one of the most important concerns for bank management?

5 What is exchange rate risk? What are the main features of foreign exchange markets?

6 What types of market risk do you know?

7 What are the differences between country and sovereign risk?

8 What distinguishes operational risk from technology risk? Why is operational risk one of the main innovations of Basle II?

9 Give examples of OBS risks.

10 Explain the importance of capital risk.

Chapter 11

Banking risks management

Learning objectives

- To define risk measurement and risk management
- To understand the importance of risk management
- To identify the main risk management techniques

11.1 Introduction

This chapter focuses on risk management as a central management tool to ensure banks' soundness and profitability. Risk management is a complex and comprehensive process, which includes creating an appropriate environment, maintaining an efficient **risk measurement** structure, monitoring and mitigating risk-taking activities and establishing an adequate framework of internal controls. As we have noted in previous chapters, the management of banking risks is becoming increasingly important in the light of the new Basle Accord (Basle II), that introduced a link between minimum regulatory capital and risk. In particular, banks will be required to adopt more formal and quantitative risk measurement and risk management procedures and processes. It is not only regulators that have placed an increased emphasis on **risk management** in an attempt to foster financial stability and economic development; it is also all the more important for bankers to manage their capital more efficiently in order to maximise risk-adjusted returns from their business activities.

There are several aspects of risk management in banking and this chapter does not aim to explore them all in detail, but rather to highlight the main issues. While Section 11.2 introduces the general issues of risk management; Sections 11.3, 11.4 and 11.5 outline the main techniques used by banks to manage risks including: credit risk, interest rate risk and liquidity risk. Sections 11.6 and 11.7 illustrate the techniques that are used to manage market and operational risk, following the new Basle Accord. Finally, the management of country risk is discussed in Section 11.8.

11.2 General risk management

This section focuses on how the risk management function is handled within the banking organisation and highlights the importance given to this function by managers and the institutional environment influencing its effectiveness and efficiency. Here we aim to provide an overview of systems and practices that cut across the major types of risks faced by banks. These systems and processes include such items as the allocation of resources to risk management activities, governance issues, record-keeping, communications within the organisation and internal audit. As pointed out by Cumming and Hirtle (2001) the difference between risk measurement and risk management is that while risk measurement deals with the quantification of risk exposures, risk management deals with the overall process that a financial institution follows to define a business strategy, to identify the risks to which it is exposed, to quantify those risks and to understand and control the nature of risks. In Chapter 10 we reviewed the main risks faced by financial institutions; for each class of risk banks need to estimate the expected losses and the probability of unexpected losses, so that an appropriate amount of capital may be held.

It is important to recall that the main objective of bank risk managers is that of shareholders' wealth maximisation and in pursuit of such an objective they have to manage carefully the trade-off between risk and returns. In order to increase shareholder wealth a company has to generate returns greater than its opportunity cost of capital. The opportunity cost of capital is the perceived cost to the bank of raising equity and keeping shareholders happy (see also Section 8.4.3). For example, if a bank makes an acquisition that generates a return-on-equity of 8 per cent, but the cost of obtaining the capital funds needed to undertake the acquisition is 10 per cent then this destroys shareholder wealth. Alternatively if returns exceed 8 per cent then the acquisition creates value for shareholders. Typically, higher returns (ROE) are reflected in higher market valuations of a company's shares – or to put it another way – investors rank profitable firms more highly and this is reflected in greater equity prices. The aim of bank managers therefore is to maximise ROE relative to its cost of capital and this will maximise shareholder wealth. Note that banks can do these sorts of calculations for all parts of their business in order to identify how capital is being used within the bank and what parts are generating the best or worst returns.

Investors, on the other hand, can expect a higher rate of return only by increasing the risk they are prepared to bear. Risk measures are therefore related to profitability measures, as banks must take risks to earn adequate returns. As Sinkey (1998) points out that 'the essence of modern banking is the measuring, managing, and accepting of risk and the heart of bank financial management is risk management. The task then becomes: how to set appropriate targets for a bank's returns and the corresponding risks undertaken? Hempel and Simonson (1999), while cautioning that there is no exact answer, suggest three steps:

● assess how other similar individual banks and groups of banks have made their risk/return decisions;
● compare the bank's performance measure to those of similar banks;
● set reasonable objectives against the backdrop of a bank's historic performance, the performance of its peers and its external environment.

These steps, in turn, are essentially based on the following analysis:

● stock market expectations (if the bank is quoted);
● trend analysis of past performance;
● trend and comparative analysis of peers' performance allowing for factors such as business mix, available production technology and external environment (macroeconomic and regulatory).

One of the underlying issues in most banking systems is the fact that deregulation, globalisation and internationalisation have increased the (real or perceived) degree of competition in banking markets, requiring banks to take on more risk to achieve satisfactory returns.

Given their special role in any economy, banks should be run in a safe and sound manner. In particular, as we saw above, they should manage risks in a context of trade-off between profitability and liquidity. Regulatory authorities monitor banks' behaviour and try to ensure that they achieve a good **CAMELS** rating. Banks are rated 1 (essentially sound) to 5 (basically insolvent). Banks with ratings of 1 or 2 are considered to present few, if any, supervisory concerns, while banks with ratings of 3, 4, or 5 present moderate to extreme degrees of supervisory concern.

CAMELS summarises the following elements:

● adequate capital (C);
● good asset quality (A);
● competent management (M);
● good earnings (E);

- sufficient liquidity (L); and
- sensitivity to market risk (S)

A bank's CAMELS rating is highly confidential; it is evaluated by the bank's senior management and disclosed only to the appropriate supervisory staff. However, the public may infer such information based on subsequent bank actions or specific disclosures.

The main elements of modern risk management processes and strategies include identifying, measuring and monitoring risk exposures. The overall risk management process should be a comprehensive one, which creates risk management cultures in all departments of the financial institution. The specific Asset–Liability Management (ALM) function (its coverage and functions) varies from bank to bank. However, as detailed in Chapter 9, the ALM function takes an overall risk management view of the bank. Specifically, ALM is concerned with explicit managerial and risk functions such as: liquidity, capital management, funding and cost of funds, and managing the bank's security portfolio.

Interest rate risk management and lending and credit risk management, are key components of a bank's overall risk management function, and are also part of the ALM function, but they are usually managed specifically by separate units or divisions within a bank. For this reason, and because of the relative importance of such risks for financial institutions, we will analyse in detail their management processes. Before we move on to specific risk management techniques, let us outline the basic concepts of the risk management process.

Following the publication of the comprehensive set of '*Core Principles*' for effective banking supervision in 1997 (see BCBS, 1997a), and as part of an on-going effort to enhance sound practices in banking organisations, the Basle Committee on Banking Supervision (BCBS) has issued a number of papers to highlight the principles that should underpin the risk management process:

- 'Framework for Internal Control Systems in Banking Organisations' (September, 1998);
- 'Enhancing Corporate Governance for Banking Organisations' (September, 1999);
- 'Customer Due Diligence for Banks' (October, 2001c);
- 'Internal Audit in Banks and the Supervisor's Relationship with Auditors: A Survey' (August, 2002);
- 'Sound Practices for the Management and Supervision of Operational Risk' (February, 2003a);
- 'Risk Management Principles for Electronic Banking' (July, 2003b)
- 'International Convergence of Capital Measurement and Capital Standards – A Revised Framework' (June, 2004a);
- 'Principles for the Management and Supervision of Interest Rate Risk' (July, 2004b)
- 'Consolidated KYC (know-your-customer) Risk Management' (October, 2004c).
- 'Compliance and the Compliance Function of Banks' (April, 2005)

Basle Committee publications relating to credit risk and operational risk are also very numerous and now form part of the wider Basle II framework. The most recent publications include recommendations on:

- 'Principles for the Management of Credit Risk' (September, 2000)
- 'Sound Practices for the Management and Supervision of Operational Risk' (February, 2003a)

All of the above reports can be found at the Bank for International Settlements website at http://www.bis.org.

As mentioned in Chapter 10, the total risk a financial institution faces can be assigned to different sources. Given the general guidelines of risk management discussed above, in the next sections we detail the management process of specific risks.

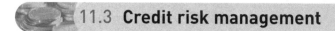

11.3 Credit risk management

Credit risk, defined as the potential that a bank borrower or counterparty will fail to meet its obligations in accordance with agreed terms, is the most familiar of banking risks (and it still remains the most difficult to quantify).

According to the BCBS, the goal of credit risk management is 'to maximise a bank's risk-adjusted rate of return by maintaining credit risk exposure within acceptable parameters'. Banks need to manage the credit risk arising both from individual creditors and individual transactions and the risk inherent in their entire portfolio. Furthermore, banks need to consider the relationships between credit risk and other risks. The effective management of credit risk is a critical component of a comprehensive approach to risk management and essential to the long-term success of any banking organisation.

While financial institutions can face difficulties for a number of reasons, loans that are not repaid (referred to as non-performing loans, or bad debts, or loan-losses) are the most frequent cause of bank losses.

For most banks, loans are the largest and most obvious source of credit risk; however, other sources of credit risk exist throughout the activities of a bank, both on and off the balance sheet. Traditionally, banks have monitored credit risk through a number of standard procedures, such as ceilings placed on the amount lent to any one customer and/or customers within a single industry and/or customers in a given country. While such procedures have long been a central feature of bank lending, credit risk measurement does raise several important issues:

- The size of the loan is not sufficient to measure the risk because risk has two dimensions – the quantity of risk, or the amount that can be lost, plus the quality of the risk, which is the likelihood of default. The quality of risk is often appraised through some form of credit ratings. These ratings may be internal to a bank or external when they come from a credit rating agency. Measuring the quality of risk ultimately leads to quantifying the default probability of customers, plus the likelihood of any recovery (how much of the loan or other debt can be recovered) in the event of default. The probability of default is obviously not easy to quantify. Historical data on defaults by credit rating class or/and by industry are available, but often they cannot be easily assigned to individual customers. The extent of recoveries is also unknown. Losses may depend upon guarantees, either from third parties or from any posted **collateral**, of recovery after bankruptcy and the liquidation of assets.
- The cumulated credit risk over a portfolio of transactions, either loans or market instruments, is difficult to quantify because of diversification effects. If the defaults of all customers tend to occur at the same time, the risk is much more important than if those default events are not related (or independent). All banks, of course, protect themselves against risk through diversification, which

makes simultaneous default very unlikely. However, the quantitative measurement of the impact of diversification still remains a modelling challenge.

Banks are increasingly facing credit risk (or counterparty risk) in various financial instruments other than loans, including acceptances, interbank transactions, trade financing, foreign exchange transactions, financial futures, swaps, bonds, equities, options, in the extension of commitments and guarantees, and the settlement of transactions.

Market transactions also generate credit risk. For instance, the inability of a company to service a swap, futures or options agreement, or make dividend repayments on bonds is also regarded as a credit risk. The loss in the event of default depends on the value of these instruments and their liquidity. If the default is totally unexpected, the loss is the market value of the instruments at the time of default. If the credit standing of the counterparty falls, e.g., Standard and Poor's reduce the credit rating of a counterparty from AAA to AA, it will still be possible to sell their instruments in the market at a discount. For financial instruments with more limited marketability such as over-the-counter (OTC) transactions, for example, as swaps and options, sale is not usually feasible. The credit risk of these types of instruments changes constantly with market movements during their lifespan. Therefore, the potential values of the transactions during the period of the contracts are at risk. Clearly, there is a relationship between credit risk and market risk during this period because values depend on market movements.

Banks are seeking ways to measure credit risk more accurately, a need which has recently been strongly driven by a variety of factors:

- the growth of the securitised loan and secondary loan trading market (see Section 9.6 and also 4.6.2);
- recent evolution of credit derivatives business;
- increased emphasis on risk-adjusted performance measurement systems (where performance for different parts of the firm/bank are assessed relative to the risk taken and capital backing) and the desire to trade credit risk;
- the desire of companies to manage the risk/return characteristics of their debt funding more effectively.

These factors have all contributed to the development of an increasingly more liquid and transparent market in tradable bank loans and other credit instruments. Such a market enables banks and large firms to trade their credit risks more effectively and therefore improve returns. It also provides banks with greater flexibility in meeting client needs as loan portfolios can be restructured in a more efficient manner, thereby releasing resources to be directed to higher-demand (and more profitable) areas. The growth in credit market instruments and the demand from banks to better assess the risks associated with their credit business has led to the development of various modelling techniques, similar in many respects to those that have previously been developed to calculate market risk[1] (such as JP Morgan's CreditMetrics™ or Credit Suisse First Boston CreditRisk+™).

The BCBS (2000) document identifies sound practices in the management of credit risk and specifically addresses the following areas:

1) establishing an appropriate credit risk environment;
2) operating under a sound credit-granting process;

---

[1] See Bessis (2002), ch. 33 for an overview of the main features of credit risk models.

3) maintaining an appropriate credit administration, measurement and monitoring process; and

4) ensuring adequate controls over credit risk.

Although specific credit risk management practices may differ among banks depending upon the nature and complexity of their credit activities, a comprehensive credit risk management programme will address these four areas. These practices should also be applied in conjunction with sound practices related to the assessment of asset quality, the adequacy of provisions and reserves, and the disclosure of credit risk.

11.4 Managing the lending function

Managing credit risk in retail banking, although based on the same broad principles, differs from wholesale banking in several ways. One first, obvious difference concerns the size of the loan commitments. Bad corporate loans can be very serious for banks because of the vast sums of money involved. Recent big corporate failures have caused more than a serious headache to banks. High-profile failures such as Enron, WorldCom and a group of other big, mainly US telecoms and energy companies have left the banks with a large amount of bad loans. The recent Argentinian financial crisis has also led to substantial write-offs. Retail lending, on the other hand, while unlikely to create serious consequences for a bank in case of individual loan defaults (although it can still create problems if a large number of retail loans default, say, as a result of a bank being overexposed to a particular sector of the economy, particularly real estate) is more difficult to assess because of the lack of information on the creditworthiness of potential borrowers.

11.4.1 Retail lending

An accurate credit decision, given a bank's credit standards, is the one that maximises the value of the loan for the bank and minimises the risk of default. Consequently, gathering, processing and analysing information on potential borrowers are key steps in credit risk management.

Prior to making a lending decision, banks need to assess the risk–return trade-off of a loan; this process involves both an assessment of the risk of the applicant and the applicant's business; an analysis of the external environment; the purpose of the loan and the particular loan structure requested by the applicant. One key step in this process is pricing the loan, where the 'price' (**loan rate**) should be:

$$R^L = \frac{1+r}{1-d} - 1 \tag{11.1}$$

where:

R^L = profitable loan rate

r = risk-free interest rate (i.e., the rate of return on a 'risk free' investment, such as government bonds)

d = expected probability of default

There are some key factors that affect a loan's expected return:

1) interest rate on the loan;
2) fees relating to the loan;
3) credit risk premium on the loan;
4) collateral backing of the loan; and
5) other non-price terms (e.g., clauses and conditions on the use of the loan).

Following a general model along the lines developed by Saunders (2000), the interest rate charged on a loan is:

$$1 + k = 1 + \frac{f + (L + M)}{1 - [b(1 - R)]} \qquad (11.2)$$

where:
k = contractually promised gross return on the loan per £ lent
f = administration fee
L = base lending rate
M = market premium
b = compensating balance requirement
R = reserve requirement

L in formula (11.2) reflects the bank's marginal cost of funds (or the so-called prime lending rate in the United States – the interest rate a bank charges its best or 'prime' customers). Compensating balances (b) is the portion of a loan that a borrower may be required to hold as deposit at the bank. They are commonly used in corporate lending business. Reserve ratios (R), are effectively a tax on deposits, and can cause the loan price to rise, as banks are not earning income for every £ of reserves. Finally, the loan price should include a market premium (M) and an administration fee (f). The administration fee should cover all the costs incurred in the origination and administration of the loan. The market premium should reflect the risk profile of the borrower: the riskier the borrower, the higher the premium.

Another factor that influences the price of the loan is the presence of any collateral (assets backing the loan that can include such things as residential property, other real estate, securities, etc.): the rate charged should be lower than in the case of no collateral. However, in times of economic trouble the price of collateral can become very volatile and banks may to have to raise either the loan price or the amount of collateral required. If collateral values fall dramatically there can be a banking sector collapse – as was the case in the Japanese banking system crises that occurred in 1997–1998 (discussed in Chapter 16). Obviously, if the value of the collateral is linked to the ability of the borrower to repay; a decrease in the value of the collateral will increase the probability of default. Box 11.1 illustrates how the fall in UK property prices in the early 1990s resulted in loan losses and negative equity.

Loans availability in retail markets may not be linked simply to the loan price, but restricted to a selected category of borrowers. This is a method for managing credit risk (**credit rationing**) that attempts to minimise the problem of adverse selection in loan markets. To reduce risk exposure, banks can limit the amount of credit available to a certain class of borrowers; for example, think of the credit limit on your credit card! Although it is illegal to discriminate against borrowers for reasons such as race, gender, religion, sexual orientation and address, there is no automatic 'right' to credit and people can be refused credit for a number of different reasons.

Box 11.1 Mortgage market, equity withdrawal and negative equity

During the late 1980s, UK house prices soared, boosting people's confidence in the housing market and prompting them to borrow against the value of their homes. Between 1980 and 1990 average mortgage debt in the UK more than doubled relative to income. A **mortgage equity withdrawal** relates to home owners borrowing against the increased value of their property (capital gains), by taking out additional housing equity loans. The Bank of England's estimate of mortgage equity withdrawal (MEW) measures the part of consumer borrowing from mortgage lenders that is not invested in the housing market. Levels of mortgage equity withdrawal reached very high levels in the late 1980s; mortgage equity loans were a major factor behind the consumer boom of 1987–88. However, the collapse in the housing market in the early 1990s led to over 1.5 million home-owners being in **negative equity** – a situation where the market value of their property was less than the outstanding mortgage loan. The slump in the UK housing market coincided with record increases in mortgage arrears and repossessions. Between 1989 and 1993, as both interest rates and unemployment rose, the number of households in mortgage arrears increased. Arrears peaked in 1993 when more than 600,000 households owed three or more months' payments. Repossessions were highest in 1991 at 75,450, falling to 58,540 by 1993.

Falling nominal house prices reduced the amount of equity in housing and, possibly, provided incentives for borrowers to accumulate arrears and for lenders to repossess property that had been used to secure loans. However, too high a level of repossession and resale was counterproductive in an already depressed market. The housing problems of the early 1990s resulted in costly losses to banks and building societies. More than ten years later, and following a period of sharp increases in housing prices, the Council of Mortgage Lenders (CML) announced that in 2005 the number of homes being repossessed had increased for the first time in seven years. However, the CML also pointed out that repossessions were 'extremely low' by historical standards, and that the UK housing market was a long way from the early 1990s experiences, as illustrated in Table 11.1 below.

Table 11.1 **Mortgages outstanding**

	Mortgages outstanding	Mortgages 3–6 months in arrears		Mortgages 6–12 month in arrears		Mortgages > 12 months in arrears	
	Number	Number	%	Number	%	Number	%
1994	10,410,000	169,080	1.62	133,700	1.28	117,110	1.12
1995	10,521,000	177,910	1.69	126,670	1.20	85,200	0.81
1996	10,637,000	139,250	1.31	100,960	0.95	67,020	0.63
1997	10,738,000	117,840	1.10	73,830	0.69	45,200	0.42
1998	10,821,000	129,090	1.19	74,040	0.68	34,880	0.32
1999	10,932,000	96,690	0.88	57,120	0.52	29,520	0.27
2000	11,173,000	95,300	0.85	47,830	0.43	20,820	0.19
2001	11,247,000	81,370	0.72	43,140	0.38	19,720	0.18
2002	11,364,000	66,580	0.59	34,040	0.30	16,490	0.15
2003	11,452,000	51,910	0.45	29.200	0.25	12,680	0.11
2004	11,512,000	53,960	0.47	26,920	0.23	11,210	0.10

Source: Council of Mortgage Lenders Research (http://www.cml.org.uk/cml/statistics).

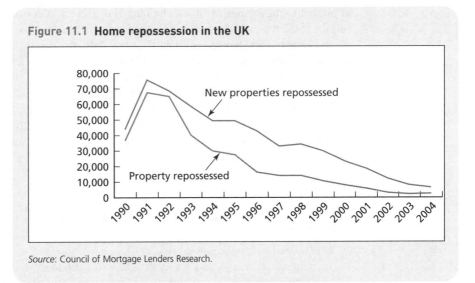

Figure 11.1 **Home repossession in the UK**

Source: Council of Mortgage Lenders Research.

As we have seen, a loan evaluation process focuses on evaluating the prospective risk and return on a loan. There are several techniques or models for assessing credit risk, but they can be broadly divided in qualitative models and quantitative models.

Qualitative models are normally used when there is limited available information on a borrower. Bank managers have to gather information from private sources and the amount of information needed will be proportional to the size of the loan. Quantitative models are to assess borrowers' creditworthiness based on the estimated probability of default.

11.4.2 Credit checking and credit scoring

Lenders want to minimise the information asymmetry problems in the retail loan market and therefore aim to ensure that potential borrowers are a good risk and do not have a history of bad debts and unpaid loans. To do this they will do two things: **Credit checking** and **Credit scoring**.

11.4.2.1 Credit checking

Lenders will check the applicant's entry on credit registers. **Credit reference agencies** in the United Kingdom such as Experian, Equifax and CallCredit PLC hold factual information on retail customers and this allows a lender to check individuals' names and address and past credit history, including any County Court Judgments or defaults recorded against the individual. This process will provide a person's so-called *credit reference*.

11.4.2.2 Credit scoring

To obtain information on a potential borrower, banks will initially adopt a quali-tative approach, which involves asking the applicant a number of questions. They will then allocate points (weights) to the answers. Questions may concern the applicant's employment history, the length of time as a customer of the bank, the number and type of accounts held, the length of time at their present address and so on. Personal judgement on behalf of loan officers based on the 'five Cs' (character, cash flow, capital, collateral and conditions)[2] is now commonly replaced by a quantitative approach based on the use of the information provided by the applicant to calculate the probability of default. Using a statistical program, creditors compare this information to the credit performance of consumers with similar profiles. A credit scoring system awards points for each factor that helps predict who is most likely to repay a debt. A total number of points – a credit score – helps predict how creditworthy the applicant is, that is, how likely it is that they will repay

---

Box 11.2 Credit scoring: how to score high

- *Have you paid your bills on time?*
  Payment history typically is a significant factor. It is likely that your score will be affected negatively if you have paid bills late, had an account referred to collections, or declared bankrupt, if that history is reflected on your credit report.

- *What is your outstanding debt?*
  Many scoring models evaluate the amount of debt you have compared to your credit limit. If the amount you owe is close to your credit limit, it is likely that it will have a negative effect on your score.

- *How long is your credit history?*
  Generally, models consider the length of your credit track record. An insufficient credit history may have an effect on your score, but that can be offset by other factors, such as timely payments and low balances.

- *Have you applied for new credit recently?*
  Many scoring models consider whether you have applied for credit recently by looking at 'inquiries' on your credit report when you apply for credit. If you have applied for too many new accounts recently, it is likely that it may negatively affect your score. However, not all inquiries are counted. Inquiries by creditors who are monitoring your account or looking at credit reports to make 'pre-screened' credit offers are not counted.

- *How many and what types of credit accounts do you have?*
  Although it is generally good to have established credit accounts, too many credit card accounts may have a negative effect on your score. In addition, many models consider the type of credit accounts you have. For example, under some scoring models, loans from finance companies may negatively affect your credit score.

Source: Adapted from the Federal Trade Commission (www.ftc.gov).

---

[2] The so-called five Cs of a credit decision can be described as follows (see for instance Sinkey, 1998): (1) *character* that refers to the willingness of the borrower to repay the loan; (2) *capacity* that refers to the borrower's cash flow and the ability of that cash flow to service the debt; (3) *capital* that refers to the strength of the borrower's balance sheet; (4) *collateral* that refers to the security backing up the loan; and finally, (5) *conditions* that refer to the borrower's sensitivity to external forces such as interest rate and business cycles and competitive pressures.

a loan and make the payments when due. Lenders will never divulge how their credit scoring works for fear of fraud and each lender will have their own system. The fact that you have been turned down by one lender will not necessarily mean that you will be declined by others.

Although such a system may seem arbitrary or impersonal, when it is properly designed it can help make decisions faster, more accurately and more impartially than individuals. In marginal cases, applicants are referred to a credit manager who decides whether the company or lender will extend credit. This may allow for discussion and negotiation between the credit manager and the consumer. Box 11.2 illustrates how a credit scoring system works in practice.

Credit scoring can be applied both to individuals and to corporations; obviously the variables used to define the scoring system will differ. Saunders (2000) and Sinkey (1998) provide detailed overviews of the main credit scoring models.

11.4.2.3 Linear probability models

Loans are divided in two groups, those that defaulted ($Z_i = 1$) and those that did not ($Z_i = 0$). These observations are then regressed on a set of j variables reflecting quantitative information about the ith borrower.

$$Z_i = \sum_{j=1}^{n} \beta_j X_{ij} + \varepsilon$$

(11.3)

Logit (and Probit) models

These constrain the cumulative probability of default on a loan between zero and one and assume the probability of default to be logistically distributed (or have a normal distribution in the Probit case).

Linear discriminant models

These models (which include the Altman Z-score model) divide borrowers according to their derived Z-scores into high or low default risk classes, contingent on their observed characteristics (X_i).

$$Z_i = \sum_{i=1}^{n} a_i X_i$$

(11.4)

11.4.3 Managing the loan portfolio

Moving from individual loans to a bank's loan portfolio, the first step in credit risk management is diversification. The principle behind portfolio diversification is the same as the one behind the old saying 'don't put all your eggs in one basket'. Bank managers should diversify their lending to different sectors of the economy, different geographical locations, different types of industry, different maturities, and so on. By diversifying their loan portfolios, i.e., by owing assets whose returns are not statistically correlated, banks can reduce the impact of any failure by diversifying away the unsystematic risk. A heavy concentration of loans in one sector of the economy can cause serious trouble for banks. For example, in the United Kingdom, building societies have historically concentrated the majority of their lending to finance residential property purchase and have therefore suffered a high number of non-performing loans when the housing market collapsed (see Box 11.1). If loans are not correlated, banks can expect to increase the expected returns on their loan portfolio by diversifying across asset classes. In other words, it is possible to apply standard portfolio theory to obtain a measure of aggregate credit risk exposure.[3]

When assessing the credit risk of the aggregate loan portfolio, bank managers need to calculate the following:[4]

- the expected loss, for each loan and for the whole portfolio, over a specific time-horizon;
- the unexpected loss for each loan and for the whole portfolio (i.e., the volatility of loss);
- the probability distribution of credit loss for the portfolio and assess the capital requirement, for a given confidence level and time-horizon (see Figure 11.2).

There are three factors that drive expected and unexpected losses on a credit portfolio:

- *customer default risk* – determined by the risk-grade profile of the portfolio;
- *exposure* – the amount that is likely to be outstanding at the time of default;
- *loss given default* – determined by the level of security cover, the effectiveness of the recovery process and the credit cycle.

The calculation of the expected loss is based on the current risk profile of the portfolio, possibly ignoring historical loss rates. Banks that rely on their average loss experience to derive expected loss are assuming that the risk profile, business mix and risk management processes remain constant over time. However, the existing profile might be considerably better than the one that created the losses in the past.

The main problem with applying portfolio theory to banks' loan portfolios is that, in the vast majority of cases, bank loans are non-tradable assets. As we noted earlier, there are several products in the market that attempt to deal with these issues. The best-known are Credit Suisse Financial Product's Credit Risk+™, CreditPortfolioView™ by McKinsey & Company and JP Morgan's CreditMetrics™. In addition, firms such as KMV[5] and KPMG[6] are actively participating in the debate

Figure 11.2 **Probability distribution of portfolio losses**

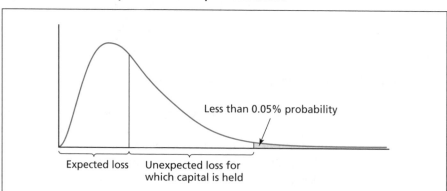

[3] For an introduction to Portfolio Theory, see Appendix A2.
[4] This discussion is modelled on Heffernan (2005) and Matten (2000).

and are openly sharing many of their analytical engines. KMV has several products on the market, including Credit Monitor™ and Portfolio Manager ™. KPMG's contribution is the Loan Analysis System™.[7]

11.5 Managing interest rate risk

Interest rate risk derives from mismatching the maturities of assets and liabilities, as part of a bank asset transformation function. Interest rate risk management is concerned with the management of the interest rate exposure of a bank. Traditionally, it is managed within the ALM function but, given the increased volatility of interest rates, together with the increased interest rate risk arising from off-balance sheet activities, it is now often managed by a dedicated department. As seen in Section 10.3, interest rate risk arises from potential variations in banks' returns that derive from unanticipated changes in interest rates. Changes in interest rates also affect a bank's underlying economic value. The value of a bank's assets, liabilities and off-balance-sheet business is affected by a change in rates because the present value of future cash flows, and in some cases the cash flows themselves, are altered. A bank interest rate risk exposure refers to market value changes in its equity position as a result of unexpected changes in market interest rates. When attempting to measure and manage interest rate risk, it is important to note that the exposure to such risk concerns *future* losses (or gains) and therefore some uncertainty will always be present. Some interest rate management techniques involve a forecast of possible interest rate scenarios and, as in every attempt to forecast the future, there is no such thing as 100 per cent accuracy. In other words, managing interest rate risk is about identifying, measuring and controlling such risk, taking uncertainty into account.

There are two broad management approaches that are used to measure interest rate risk and these are known as 'gap' and 'duration' analysis.

11.5.1 Gap analysis

Gap analysis is possibly the best-known interest rate risk management technique. The 'gap' refers to the difference between interest rate sensitive assets and interest rate sensitive liabilities over a specific time-horizon. If the interest rate sensitive liabilities are greater than the interest rate sensitive assets, then an increase in interest rates will reduce a bank's profit and vice versa. In the basic gap analysis, the focus is on the maturity of the rate-sensitive assets and liabilities.

---

[5] KMV is the acronym for Kealhofer, McQuown and Vasicek, the originators of the KMV methodology. KMV was taken over by Moody's in 2002. Nowadays Moody's KMV is the world's leading provider of quantitative credit analysis tools.
[6] One of the largest professional service firms in the world.
[7] For more information on these products, see Credit Suisse First Boston (1997), Wilson (1997a and 1997b); JP Morgan (1997).

$$\text{GAP} = \text{RSA} - \text{RSL} \qquad (11.5)$$

where:

RSA = rate-sensitive assets

RSL = rate-sensitive liabilities.

An asset or a liability is defined as rate sensitive if the cash flow from the asset or liability changes in the same direction as changes in interest rates. The gap ratio in equation (11.5) is also called the *interest-sensitivity ratio*. If this ratio is equal to one, then the rate sensitivity of assets and liabilities are perfectly matched. However, most bank have a positive gap (RSA>RSL) since they borrow short and lend long, and therefore have assets which will mature later than liabilities. The main aim of gap analysis is to evaluate the impact of a change in interest rates on the bank net interest income and net interest margin. Ideally, the gap should be managed in such a way as to expand when interest rates are rising and contract when interest rates are declining. However, it is difficult for bank managers to know what phase of the interest rate cycle they are facing. Furthermore, bank customers may be seeking opposite interest rate positions compared to the bank.

Up to now, we have defined the gap as being related to (or a function of) a specified time-horizon (for example, 90 days). However, this is rather arbitrary as it does not clearly indicate what time period is appropriate for determining the interest rate sensitivity of assets and liabilities. For instance, focusing on a short-term gap may ignore reinvestment risk (the risk that loans are repaid early). One extension of the basic gap model is the *maturity bucket* approach. Each of the bank assets and liabilities is classified according to its maturity and placed into 'maturity buckets', for example overnight, 3 months, 3–6 months, and so on. Analysts compute both incremental and cumulative gap results. An incremental gap is defined as RSA – RSL in each time bucket; the cumulative gap is the cumulative subtotal of the incremental gaps.

As illustrated in Table 11.2, as total assets equal total liabilities by definition, the incremental gaps must total to zero and therefore the last cumulative gap must be zero. The maturity bucket approach allows bank managers to concentrate on the cumulative gaps for the different time buckets.

One extension is the maturity gap (M Gap).

$$\text{M Gap} = W_A\text{RSA} - W_A\text{RSL} \qquad (11.6)$$

where:

W_ARSA = weighted average rate-sensitive assets

W_ARSL = weighted average rate-sensitive liabilities

Table 11.2 Maturity bucket gap

	Assets	Liabilities	Gap	Cumulative gap
One day	40	30	+10	−10
More than 1 day less than 3 months	50	60	−10	0
More than 3 months less than 6 months	90	110	−20	−20
More than 6 months less than 12 months	110	120	−10	−30
More than one year less than 5 years	80	70	+10	−20
Over 5 years	30	10	+20	0
	400	400		

This model better reflects the economic reality or the true value of assets and liabilities if the bank portfolio was liquidated at today's prices. If the maturity of a bank's assets is greater than the maturity of its liabilities, an increase in interest rates will cause the value of the assets to fall more than the value of the liabilities because the assets mature later. The bigger the maturity gap, the more a bank's net worth will suffer by an increase in interest rates.

Another extension is the so-called 'dynamic gap analysis' approach, that involves forecasting interest rate changes and expected changes in the bank's balance sheet for several periods in the future. Software models provide bank managers with simulation tools to inform them of the way in which gaps are expected to be structured at certain times in the future.

Gap analysis was one of the first methods developed to measure a bank's interest rate risk exposure, and continues to be widely used by banks. Despite the extensions, the gap model has been defined as 'naïve' and has been subject to a number of criticisms as the approach:

- fails to take into account the market value effect (i.e., the new value of the asset given changes in interest rates);
- suffers from over aggregation, that is, it fails to consider for intra-bucket effects;
- fails to deal with run-offs, which is the periodic cash flow of interest and principal amortisation payments on long-term assets;
- ignores banks' exposure to pre-payment risk (the risk that loans will be repaid early);
- ignores differences in spreads between interest rates that could arise as the level of market interest rates changes (basis risk);
- does not take into account any changes in the timing of payments that might occur as a result of changes in the interest rate environment;
- generally oversimplifies the complexity of a bank's ALM.

For these reasons, gap analysis provides only a rough approximation of the actual impact of changes in interest rates.

11.5.2 Duration analysis

Duration is a measure of the average life of an asset's (or liability's) cash flow. **Duration analysis** takes into account the average life of an asset (or liability) rather than its maturity. It is a technique borrowed from bond portfolio management, where duration is defined as a weighted average of the maturities of the individual coupon payments. In this context, duration may be different from maturity if, for example, an asset repayment schedule includes interest and principal. A 3-year car loan that is repaid with monthly instalments will have duration different from its maturity. Maturity and duration are only ever equal in the case of single payment assets and zero coupon bonds. Higher duration implies that a given change in the level of interest rates will have a larger impact on economic value. The duration of a coupon bond is expressed by the formula (known as Macauley duration):

$$D_1 = 1^* \frac{C_1/(1+Y)^1}{V} + 2^* \frac{C^2/(1+Y)^2}{V} + \dots + n^* \frac{C_n + P_n/(1+Y)^n}{V} \qquad (11.7)$$

where:

Y = the bond's internal yield or yield-to-maturity (YTM)
C_1 = annual coupon payment in year 1
P_n = principal payment
n = number of years to maturity
V = current market value of the bond

Box 11.3 Example of Macauley duration

Consider a bond with the following characteristics:

- £100 annual coupon
- 2 years to maturity
- YTM = 10%
- Market value £1,000

The Macaulay duration for this bond is 1.909 years.

$$1.909 = 1* \frac{£100/(1.1)}{£1000} + 2* \frac{£1100/(1.1)^2}{£1000}$$

The formula provides the weighted average payment stream, where the maturity of each payment is weighted by the fraction of the total value of the bond accounted for by the payment. As can be seen from the example, the emphasis in duration analysis is on the market value rather than on the book value, as was the case in gap analysis.

Using formula (11.7) it is possible to compute the duration of the entire asset and liability portfolios of a bank. By matching the duration of assets and liabilities, movements in interest rates should have roughly the same effect on both sides of the balance sheet. Duration gap (DG) measures the mismatch between the duration of a bank's assets and its liabilities.

$$DG = \left| D_A - \frac{L}{A} D_L \right| \tag{11.8}$$

where:

A = market value of assets
L = market value of liabilities
D_A = duration of assets
D_L = duration of liabilities
L/A = leverage or gearing ratio

The impact of a change in interest rates on the value of a bank's equity can be calculated from equation (11.9) as follows:

$$\Delta E = - DG \left(\frac{\Delta r}{(1 + r)} \right) A \tag{11.9}$$

where:

ΔE = change in the value of bank equity

DG = duration gap

Δr = change in interest rate

A = market value of assets

Box 11.4   Example of duration gap

Consider a bank with the following characteristics:

- £500 millions of assets
- £400 million of liabilities
- £100 million of own equity
- the duration of assets is five years
- the duration of liabilities is three years

Let's suppose that bank management expect an interest rate increase of 0.25 per cent to 4.5 per cent following the next meeting of the Bank of England's Monetary Policy Committee (MPC).

$$DG = [5 - (400/500)3] = 2.6$$

$$\Delta E = -2.6 [00.25/(1 + 0.0425)] 500 = -3.12 \text{ million}$$

In this case, an increase in interest rates from 4.25 to 4.5 per cent will decrease the equity value by £3.12 million.

Estimates derived from a standard duration approach may provide an acceptable approximation of a bank's exposure to changes in economic value for relatively non-complex banks. However, there are a number of problems arising from the use of the duration measure:

- Convexity – the duration formula implies a linear relationship between changes in interest rate and changes in equity; in reality the relationship is convex. Duration is a good approximation for small changes but it becomes less accurate for larger changes.
- Data requirements – the calculation of the duration gap can be data demanding.
- Duration generally focuses on just one form of interest rate risk exposure – re-pricing risk – and ignores interest rate risk arising from changes in the relationship among interest rates within a time-band (basis risk).
- The simplifying assumptions that underlie the calculation of standard duration mean that the risk from off-balance sheet activities may be underestimated.

11.5.3   Simulation approaches

Many large banks employ more sophisticated interest rate risk measurement systems than those based on simple maturity/re-pricing schedules. These simulation techniques typically involve detailed assessments of the potential effects of changes in interest rates on earnings and economic value by simulating the future path of interest rates and their impact on cash flows. Simulation approaches typically involve a more detailed breakdown of various categories of on- and off-balance sheet positions, so that specific assumptions about the interest and principal payments and non-interest income and expense arising from each type of position can be incorporated. In addition, simulation techniques can incorporate more varied and refined changes in the interest rate environment, ranging from changes in the slope and shape of the yield curve to interest rate scenarios derived from (relatively complex) statistical approaches such as Monte Carlo simulations[1].

We can distinguish between

- *static simulations*, where only the cash flows arising from the bank's current on- and off-balance sheet positions are assessed, and
- *dynamic simulations*, where the model builds in more detailed assumptions about the future course of interest rates and the expected changes in a bank's business activity over that time.

The usefulness of simulation-based interest rate risk measurement techniques depends on the validity of the underlying assumptions and the accuracy of the basic methodology. In its document 'Principles for the Management of Interest Rate Risk' (1997b), the BCBS warns that the output of sophisticated simulations must be assessed in the light of the validity of the simulation's assumptions about future interest rates and the behaviour of the bank and its customers. One of the primary concerns of BCBS is that such simulations could become '*black boxes*' that lead to false confidence in the precision of the estimates.

11.6　Managing liquidity risk

As defined in Section 10.4, a bank faces liquidity risk when, because of lack of confidence or unexpected need for cash, withdrawals are higher than normal and the bank is unable to meet its liabilities. Sound liquidity management can reduce the probability of serious problems. The importance of liquidity goes beyond the individual bank, since a liquidity shortfall at a single institution can have system-wide repercussions. Systemic risk and the problems of contagion and bank runs have been discussed already in Chapter 7 and elsewhere in this text.

If a bank experiences a temporary liquidity problem, and it is either unable or unwilling to borrow on the interbank market, the central bank can provide funds, in the form of loans and advances. However, central bank borrowing is costly not only in terms of the interest rates charged but also in terms of the bank's reputation.

Liquidity pressures can arise from both sides of the balance sheet. On the liability side, unexpectedly high cash withdrawals can cause solvent banks to have liquidity problems. On the asset side, liquidity problems can be caused by unexpectedly high loan defaults and by customers unexpectedly drawing down lines of credit. Liquidity pressures can arise from off-balance sheet activities as well as from

---

[1] A Monte Carlo simulation is a computerised technique which is the basis for probalistic risk analysis, and which replicates real-life occurrences by mathematically modeling a projected event.

problems in the payment system. Contingent liabilities, such as letters of credit and financial guarantees, represent a potentially significant drain of funds for a bank, but are usually not dependent on a bank's liquidity position. Other potential sources of cash outflows include payments relating to transactions involving swaps, over-the-counter (OTC) options, other interest rate and forward foreign exchange rate contracts, margin calls and early termination agreements.

Liquidity management is an integral part of the ALM function. Liquidity risk management aims at protecting a bank against liquidity risk, that is, to avoid a situation of negative net liquid assets.

To avoid liquidity problems, a bank can hold liquid assets. However, increased liquidity comes at a cost. There is a trade-off between liquidity and profitability, as the more liquid the asset, the lower the rate of return. Instead of holding liquid funds, a bank could make more profitable loans. Despite the costs, however, the holding of liquid assets is necessary as it:

● reassures creditors that the bank is safe and able to meet its liabilities;
● signals to the market that the bank is prudent and well managed;
● ensures that all lending commitments can be met;
● avoids forced sale of the bank's assets;
● avoids having to pay excessive borrowing costs in the interbank markets; and
● avoids central bank borrowing.

Banks can minimise withdrawal risk by diversifying funding sources (liability management). Prudent banks will also seek to minimise their *volatility ratio*:

$$VR = (VL–LA)/(TA–LA) \qquad (11.10)$$

where:
VL = volatile liabilities
LA = liquid assets
TA = total assets

Prudent banks will have a volatility ratio lower than zero.

In measuring and managing a bank's liquidity exposure, the following techniques may be used:

● cash flow projections of daily liquidity positions
● cash flow projections of daily liquidity sources
● scenario analysis and simulation models
● liquidity gap analysis

11.6.1 Liquidity gap analysis and financing gap

Liquidity gap analysis is the most widely used technique for managing a bank's liquidity position. As we have already discussed, liquidity risk is generated in the balance sheet by a mismatch between the size and maturity of assets and liabilities. It is the risk that the bank is holding insufficient liquid assets on its balance sheet to meet requirements. The liquidity gap is defined as the difference between net liquid assets and unpredictable (or volatile) liabilities. If a bank's net liquid assets are less than liabilities then the bank needs to purchase funds in the market to fill the shortfall in liquid assets. Banks typically will examine the maturity profile of their assets and liabilities to identify mismatches in liquidity that require funding.

$$L \text{ Gap} = NLA - VL \tag{11.11}$$

where:
NLA = net liquid assets
VL   = volatile liabilities

The liquidity gap analysis is similar to the *maturity bucket approach* we have discussed for interest rate risk management. In this case, balance sheet items are placed in a bucket according to the expected timing of cash flows. Net mismatched positions are accumulated over time to produce a cumulative net mismatch position. In this way, the bank can monitor the amount of cash which becomes available over time.

Another useful measure of bank liquidity is the financing gap (F Gap):

$$F \text{ Gap} = \text{Average loans} - \text{Average deposits} \tag{11.12}$$

If the F Gap is positive, the bank needs cash and will have either to sell some assets or borrow on the interbank market. The bigger the F Gap, the more a bank needs to borrow and the greater its exposure to liquidity risk. However, recent technological and financial innovations have provided banks with new ways of funding their activities and managing their liquidity. A declining ability to rely on core deposits, together with increased reliance on wholesale funds has changed the way banks view liquidity.

11.7 Managing market risk

Market risk is the risk resulting from adverse movements in the level or volatility of market prices of interest rate instruments, equities, commodities and currencies (see Section 10.6). Market risk is usually measured as the potential gain/loss in a position/portfolio that is associated with a price movement of a given probability over a specified time-horizon.

Financial institutions have always faced market risk; however, the sharp increase in asset trading since the 1980s has increased the need to ensure that these institutions have the appropriate management systems to control (and the capital to absorb) the risks posed by market-related exposures. As a risk, market risk gained a high profile when the Basle Committee on Banking Supervision published 'The Supervisory Treatment of Market Risks' in 1993, in which for the first time it was proposed that market risk, in addition to credit risk, needed to be taken into account for the calculation of bank capital requirements (this updated the 1988 Basle Capital Adequacy Accord).

The 1993 BCBS consultative document put forward a standardised measurement framework to calculate market risk for interest rates, equities and currencies which differentiates capital requirements for specific risk from those for general market risk. The 1996 BCSC document 'Amendment to the Capital Accord to Incorporate Market Risks' provides the framework for capital charges relative to market risk. It sets forth two approaches for calculating the capital charge to cover market risks: *the standardised approach* and *the internal models approach*. The methodology for banks using the standardised approach is based on a 'building blocks' approach, in which the specific risk and the general market risk arising from securities positions are measured separately. On the other hand, the focus of many internal models is on the bank's general market risk exposure, leaving specific risk (i.e., exposures to specific issuers) to be measured largely through separate credit risk measurement systems.

The central components of market risk management are the **Risk-Adjusted-Return on Capital (RAROC)** and the **Value-at-Risk (VaR)** approaches. Although VaR was originally developed to manage market risk, it has now been extended to incorporate credit risk. Other techniques used to manage market risk include scenario analysis and stress testing.

11.7.1 Risk-Adjusted-Return on Capital (RAROC)

The concept of Risk-Adjusted-Return on Capital (RAROC) was first introduced by Bankers Trust in the late 1970s as a planning and performance management tool, in the context of Risk Adjusted Performance Measurement (RAPM). Several approaches, defined as '*asset-volatility-based approaches*' as opposed to the traditional risk-based and ROE-based approaches were developed in response to the need to target shareholders' value and to allocate banks' internal resources more efficiently. The RAROC measures the risk inherent in each banking activity, and the risk factor is computed taking into account the asset price volatility, calculated on historical data. An interesting feature of RAROC is that it can be employed to estimate the relative capital allocation of all types of banking risks.

$$\text{RAROC} = \frac{\text{Revenues} - \text{Cost} - \text{Expected losses}}{\text{Total Equity Capital}} \qquad (11.13)$$

In the context of the new Basle Capital Accord (or Basle II as was explained in Section 7.8), which encourages the use of internal risk models to set banks capital requirements, the RAROC measure can help bank managers to assess in what areas they should allocate more capital.

11.7.2 Value-at-Risk (VaR)

VaR is the principal portfolio measure of market risk; it provides an estimate of the potential loss on the current portfolio from adverse market movements. It builds on modern portfolio theory and was originally developed by JP Morgan in the context of their RiskMetrics product. VaR is a statistical measure of potential trading revenue volatility, and a change in the general level of VaR would normally be expected to lead to a corresponding change in the volatility of daily trading revenues. The distinguishing feature of VaR is that it uses the volatility of assets.

The basic formula of VaR is as follows:[8]

$$\text{VaR}_x = V_x \, (dV/dP) \, \Delta P_t \qquad (11.14)$$

where:

V_x = the market value of portfolio x
dV/dP = the sensitivity to market prices movements per £ of market value
ΔP_t = the adverse price movement over a specific time horizon t (under the Basle Agreement t = 10 days)

---

[8] A general introduction to VaR can be found in Jorion (1997).

It expresses the 'maximum' amount a bank might lose, to a certain level of confidence (q), as a result of changes in risk factors (i.e., changes in interest rates, exchange rates, equity and commodity prices). The basic time period t and the confidence level q are the two major parameters that should be chosen in an appropriate way. The time-horizon can differ from a few hours for an active trading desk to a year for a pension fund. In simple terms, the VaR approach aims to answer the following question: 'How much can I lose with x% probability over a pre-set horizon?'

Suppose that a bank portfolio manager has a daily VaR equal to £1 million at a 99 per cent confidence interval. This means that there is only one chance in 100 that a daily loss bigger than £1 million occurs under normal market conditions.

The calculation of VaR specified in equation (11.14) involves several assumptions:

- prices of financial instruments are assumed to be normally distributed;
- price changes are assumed to be statistically uncorrelated;
- the volatility (standard deviation) of the price or rate changes is stable over time;
- the interrelationship between two different price movements follows a joint normal distribution.

Box 11.5 **Example of VaR**

Suppose a portfolio manager manages a portfolio which consists of a single asset. The return of the asset is normally distributed with annual mean return of 15% and annual standard deviation of 25%. The value of the portfolio today is £100 million. We want to answer various simple questions about the end-of-year distribution of the portfolio's value:

1) What is the probability of a loss of more than £20 million by year end (i.e., what is the probability that the end-of-year value is less than £95 million (£115 million minus £20 million))?
2) With 1% probability what is the maximum loss at the end of the year? This is the VaR at 1%.

To answer these questions keeping in mind the assumptions made above, we need to employ a statistical package (for example, Microsoft Excel):

1) In Excel, you need to employ the formula giving standard normal cumulative distribution. In this example:

NORMDIST (95, 115, 25, TRUE) = 0.211855

The probability of a loss of more than £20 million is 21%.

2) In Excel, you need to employ the formula giving the inverse of the normal cumulative distribution. In this example:

NORMINV (0.01, 115, 25) = 56.841325

There is 1% probability that the end of the year value will be less than £56.84 million, which means that the maximum loss is equal to

£115 million − £56.84 million = £58.16 million.

Most VaR calculations, however, are not concerned with annual value-at-risk. The main regulatory and management concern is with the loss of portfolio value over a much shorter period (typically several days). After the introduction of market risk measurement in the 1996 Amendment to the Basle I Capital Adequacy Accord, regulators have encouraged the use of VaR. The required VaR measure is for every 10 days with a confidence interval of 99 per cent. However, the 10-day VaR measure takes no account of the mitigating action that can be taken in the event of adverse market moves, nor does it express the worst result that could occur as a result of extreme, unusual or unprecedented market conditions. The absolute level of VaR should not, therefore, be interpreted as the likely range of daily trading revenues.

As there is no general consensus as to the 'best way' to carry out a VaR analysis, the approach allows various options for the choice of the underlying frequency distributions:

- parametric methods;
- non-parametric methods;
- simulation approaches (such as using Monte Carlo techniques).

Because of the different approaches that might be followed, i.e., financial institutions may use different confidence levels or holding periods, may have different sources of historical data or use longer or shorter time-series and may use approximate changes in individual risk factors following different distribution, direct comparisons between VaR numbers produced by different institutions can be misleading.

In order to determine the overall or net position, a portfolio can be divided according to its sensitivity to certain risk (the so-called Greeks):

a) Delta risk (absolute price risk): is the risk that the price of the underlying asset will change.
b) Gamma risk (convexity risk): allows for the existence of a non-linear relationship between the change in the price of the underlying asset and the change in the value of the portfolio.
c) Vega risk (volatility risk): is the risk arising from a change in the expected volatility in the price of the underlying instrument.
d) Theta risk (time-decay risk): is the risk of a change in the value of the portfolio simply connected with the passing of time.
e) Rho risk (discount risk): is the risk associated with a change in the risk-free rate.

To arrive at a VaR, the portfolio components are disaggregated according to the above risk factors, netted out and then re-aggregated.

To illustrate how VaR is reported by banks, Table 11.3 reports the figures from UBS (2004).

Some authors (Danielsonn, 2000, 2002: Taleb, 1997) have expressed the following concerns over the use of VaR:

- VaR does not give the precise amount that will be lost.
- The assumption that financial returns are normally distributed and uncorrelated may not hold.
- VaR measures are seemingly easy to manipulate.
- It does not provide an indication of the probability of a bank failure.
- If all traders are using the same approach to minimise market risk, this can result in increased liquidity risk.

Table 11.3 **Value-at-Risk at UBS**

As at 31 Dec 2004		Year ended 31 Dec 04				Year ended 31 Dec 03			
(CHF million)*	Limits	Min	Max	Avg	31 Dec	Min	Max	Avg	31 Dec
Business Groups									
Investment Bank	600	274	457	358	332	236	470	317	295
Wealth Management USA	50	12	27	17	16	8	21	14	17
Global Asset Management	30	5	16	11	7	7	16	11	8
Wealth Management & Business Banking	5	1	1	1	1	1	5	2	1
Corporate Centre	150	35	69	47	38	40	83	58	49
Reserve	170								
Diversification effect				(69)	(62)			(95)	(76)
Total	**750**	**274**	**453**	**365**	**332**	**223**	**460**	**307**	**294**

*CHF= Swiss Franc.

Source: http://www.ubs.com.

For these reasons, **back testing** (that is, an ex-post comparison of the risk measure generated by the model against actual daily changes in portfolio value) is advocated by the BCBS. Given the limitations of VaR highlighted above, most banks also employ scenario analysis and stress testing.

In simple terms, back testing compares actual revenues arising from closing positions (i.e., excluding intra-day revenues, fees and commissions) with the VaR calculated on these positions, and is used to monitor the quality of the VaR model.

Figure 11.3 shows these daily revenues and the corresponding 1-day VaR over the last 12 months for UBS. (The 10-day VaR, which is the basis of the limits and exposures in the tables above, is also reported for information.)

As illustrated in the figure, the revenue volatility over 2004 was within the range predicted by the VaR model. If we focus on the outliers, there was an increase in revenues at the beginning of the second quarter in April 2004. These have been

Figure 11.3 **Back testing VaR (UBS) 2 January 2004–31 December 2004**

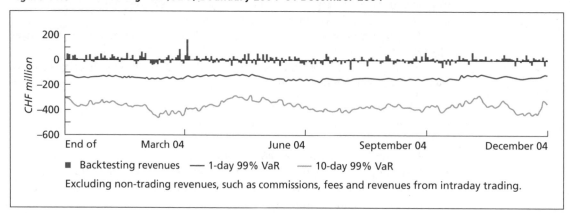

Source: http://www.ubs.com.

attributed to various international factors, including the price decline in T-bonds that caused yields to rise.

Scenario analysis and stress testing are based on simulated forecasts of plausible unfavourable scenarios to compute how much a bank would lose in the event of a 'worst-case scenario' and tests the bank's ability to withstand possible shocks.

Box 11.6 **Risk management: keeping pace with effective results** FT

If you are looking for the hot new jobs in investment banking, forget fixed-income, eliminate equities and do not bother with derivatives. Risk management . . . that's where the growth is. Banks have been ramping up their risk management operations in recent years, increasing headcount, technology investment and status.

According to the 2004 Global Risk Management Survey by Deloitte & Touche, 81 per cent of global financial services companies now have a chief risk officer. Two years ago, it was only 65 per cent. Most industry insiders believe this has resulted in a big improvement in the effectiveness of banks' risk management – in spite of the perceived increase in risk the banks are taking on, the growth of hedge funds and the ever increasing complexity of financial products. However, some regulators question whether risk management has improved quite as much as the banks like to believe. It could be they have just been lucky.

Figure 11.4 Investment banks' risk taking

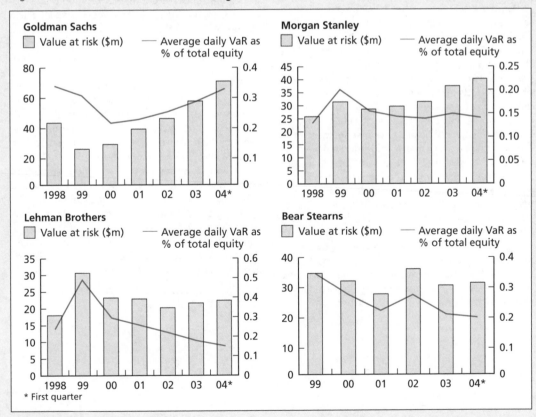

Source: Merrill Lynch (2004).

Edward Hida, head of banking risk management at Deloitte & Touche, says that, while it is difficult to prove that risk management has improved, all the evidence points that way. 'The fact that there have been fewer disasters in many of the larger markets suggests that risk management has improved.' He says there have been advances in all the main areas of risk management – credit risk, market risk and operational risk – and, in particular, in the way these all interact to create financial risk for the firm. Guy Moszkowski, investment banking analyst at Merrill Lynch in New York, agrees that the lack of 'massive blowouts' is persuasive. His analysis of the top Wall Street banks shows that the 'efficiency' of risk taking has improved, measured by the ratio of trading revenue to 'value at risk' (VAR). Value at risk is a measure of the potential loss in value of trading positions due to adverse market movements over a defined period. Mr Moszkowski disputes the widespread belief that banks have been taking on proportionately more risk. The amount of risk measured by VAR taken on by the top Wall Street investment banks as a group has not increased in relation to their growing capital in recent years, he says.

Among the European banks, Deutsche is widely seen as having been aggressive on risk recently and it recorded a sharp rise in VAR in the third quarter of last year. However, bankers say this was inflated by a statistical blip and that its risk-taking is not out of line with its US peers. The ever growing complexity of the products investment banks trade makes some outside observers nervous and risk management experts agree that they do present new challenges. Don McCree, deputy head of risk management at JP Morgan Chase, which has a huge derivatives business, says it is critical that the risk management process keeps pace with product innovation. 'We routinely move people from the business into the risk management function to ensure that we remain in step with developments', he says. However, Mr McCree says it is important to remember that, in many ways, the growth of derivatives has made risk management easier, not more difficult. In particular, the growth in credit derivatives has allowed banks, such as JPMorgan, to manage their big credit risk exposures much more efficiently. 'When we weigh credit derivatives as a risk or a benefit, we come down significantly into the benefit category.'

The other development that makes some outside observers jumpy is the growth in hedge funds. This nervousness is understandable given that the collapse of Long-Term Capital Management is still a recent memory. When the hedge fund imploded in 1998, prompting the Federal Reserve to organise a $3.6bn bail-out, its bankers had an estimated exposure of $125bn. Tim Geithner, president of the New York Federal Reserve, one of the US bank regulators, said in a recent speech that the quality of risk management of counterparties of hedge funds had 'improved substantially since 1998', but that progress had been 'uneven across the major dealers'. He also drew attention to 'signs of some erosion in standards in response to competitive pressures' as banks fought to attract increasingly lucrative hedge fund fees. Mr Geithner said that improving the overall discipline of the stress testing regime was critical. Because potential future exposure measures are based on VAR calculations, they can produce misleadingly low overall measures of counterparty credit risk, he said. This is because VAR calculations reflect recent market conditions and correlations, so do not necessarily provide an effective measure of vulnerability to loss under more severe conditions of market stress and illiquidity.

Thanks partly to the relatively benign market conditions in recent years, the biggest risks to leading investment banks, particularly in the US, have come from a completely different quarter: the wave of corporate scandals. Citigroup and JPMorgan alone have set aside billions of dollars to cover potential settlements of lawsuits related to their alleged role in scandals, such as WorldCom and Enron. Mr McCree says JPMorgan is spending an 'enormous amount of time' analysing new risks such as 'reputation risk and litigation risk created by parties we do business with'.

At the same time, banks are also facing new demands on risk management as part of their implementation of the Basle II capital adequacy rules. All of which suggests those risk management departments will keep growing for some time to come.

Source: Financial Times (2005 'Investment Banking Survey', 27 January, by David Wighton.

11.8 Managing operational risk

The Risk Management Group of the Basle Committee on Banking Supervision (2001b) broadly defines operational risk as 'the risk of loss resulting from inadequate or failed internal processes, people and systems or from external events'. In general terms, this is the risk associated with the possible failure of a bank's systems, controls or other management failure (including human error). This definition focuses on the causes of operational risk, and it is aimed at facilitating operational risk measurement and management.

Despite the increased importance of operational risk in the management of financial institutions, reflected in the fact that Basle II incorporates a new capital charge for operational risk, there is no clearly established, single way to measure operational risk on a firm-wide basis. Furthermore, the management of operational risk is still at very early stages of development.

One of the reasons behind the difficulties in quantifying operational risk lies in the fact that most risk factors usually identified by banks are typically measures of internal performance, such as internal audit ratings, volume, turnover, error rates and income volatility, rather than external factors such as market price movements or a change in a borrower's condition. As a consequence, there is uncertainty about which factors are important for measuring operational risk and the importance of different factors may vary among financial institutions. Furthermore, also unlike the cases of credit and market risk, there is a lack of a direct relationship between the risk factors usually identified and the size and frequency of losses.

In line with the management of other banking risks, a capital provision should be set aside to cover for unexpected losses due to operational risk. However, explicit pricing of the losses relating to operational risk is uncommon.

The Basle II framework proposes three methods for calculating operating risk capital charges, which present increasing sophistication and risk sensitivity:[9]

1 the *basic approach*,
2 the *standardised approach*,
3 the *internal measurement approach*.

The *basic approach* allocates capital using a single indicator (Gross Income) as a proxy for a banks' overall operational risk exposure.

In the *standardised approach*, a bank's activities are divided into a number of standardised business units and business lines. Within each business line, regulators have specified a proxy to reflect the volume of a bank's activity in this area as illustrated in Table 11.4. This proxy is then used as an indicator for the operational risk within each business line.

Within each business line, the capital charge is calculated by multiplying a bank's broad financial indicator by a 'beta' factor (which is a rough proxy for the relationship between the industry's operational risk loss experience for a given business line and the broad financial indicator for the bank's activity in that business line). The total capital charge is the sum of the capital charges in each business line.

The *internal measurement approach* allows individual banks to use internal loss data. However, the methods for calculating the capital charge would be determined by the regulators.

---

[9] BCBS (2001b) 'Consultative Document. Operational Risk'.

Table 11.4 The standardised approach to operational risk management

Business units	Business lines	Indicator
Investment banking	• Corporate finance • Trading and sales	Gross income
Banking	• Retail banking • Commercial banking • Payment and settlement	• Annual average assets • Annual average assets • Annual settlement throughput
Others	• Retail brokerage • Asset management	• Gross income • Total funds under management

Source: Adapted from BCBS (2001b).

The Basle Committee is also encouraging banks to better manage operational risk, in order to reduce the exposure, frequency and severity of losses. One mitigation technique which is growing in importance is the use of insurance to cover specific operational risk exposures.

Box 11.7   Structure of the internal measurement approach

In the internal measurement approach, a bank's activities are categorised into a number of business lines, and a broad set of operational loss types are defined and applied across business lines. Within each business line/loss type combination, the supervisor specifies an exposure indicator (EI) which is a proxy for the size (or amount of risk) of each business line's operational risk exposure.

For each business line/loss type combination, banks measure, based on their internal loss data, a parameter representing the probability of loss event (PE) as well as a parameter representing the loss given that event (LGE). The product of EI*PE*LGE is used to calculate the expected loss (EL) for each business line/loss type combination.

The supervisor supplies a factor (the 'gamma term', γ) for each business line/loss type combination, which translates the expected loss (EL) into a capital charge. The overall capital charge for a particular bank is the simple sum of all the resulting products. This can be expressed in the following formula:

$$\text{Required capital} = \Sigma i \; \Sigma j \; [\gamma \, (i,j) * EI(i,j) * PE(i,j) * LGE(I,j) \qquad (11.15)$$

where:
i = the business line, and
j = the risk type

To facilitate the process of supervisory validation, banks supply their supervisors with the individual components of the expected loss calculation (i.e., EI, PE, LGE) instead of just the product EL. Based on this information supervisors calculate EL and then adjust for unexpected loss through the gamma term to achieve the desired soundness standard.

Source: Adapted from BCBS (2001), p. 8.

11.9 International risk assessment

Banks engaged in international activities face a plethora of risks, in addition to the ones already discussed, including amongst others foreign currency risk, regulatory risk, strategic and reputation risk. These risks are not mutually exclusive and any product or service provided either domestically or internationally may expose the bank to multiple risks. For banks either contemplating an international investment or those already with substantial overseas operations the risks associated with operating in a foreign country need to be evaluated. Put simply, firms that operate internationally have to evaluate the country risk associated with their investments and/or overseas operations.

Country risk is the risk that economic, social and political conditions and events in a foreign country will adversely affect a firm's commercial/financial interests. In addition to the adverse effect that deteriorating macroeconomic conditions and political and social instability may have on the returns generated from an overseas investment, country risk also includes the possibility of nationalisation or expropriation of assets, governments revoking licences, imposition of exchange controls, and the likelihood of currency depreciation or devaluation.

Country risk can have a critical effect on a firm's international activities and therefore needs to be explicitly taken into account in the risk assessment of all overseas investments/activities. Even the risk associated with what are perceived to be the most stable (or safe) investments will increase if, for instance, the political or macroeconomic conditions change and cause the exchange rate to depreciate resulting in lower cash flows (and therefore profits) from overseas investments. Country risk is also not necessarily limited to a firm's exposure to overseas operations. A firm may have commercial relationships in its home country with a foreign firm that may be subject to such risks. For instance, country risk factors should also be taken into account, when assessing the creditworthiness of domestic trade creditors. One should also be aware that country risk factors are critically important for all types of international firms, non-financial and financial. Borrowers in higher risk countries pay higher premiums for their debt compared with those located in lower risk countries.

In banking, country risk is regarded as the exposure to a loss in cross-border lending, caused by events in a particular country that are (at least to some extent) under the control of the government but are not under the control of a private enterprise or individual. This contrasts with what is known as sovereign risk which relates to the risk associated with a government default on bond or loan repayments. A broader definition of country risk relates to any loss associated with international activity due to adverse changes in the overseas operating environment beyond the control of the firm. Transfer risk is another form of risk that is believed to be one of the most important drivers of country risk. This is simply the risk associated with the restriction of foreign payments from overseas to the home company or bank. Transfer risk refers to restrictions on payments between private agents whereas sovereign risk is associated with a government default on payments. In reality, sovereign and transfer risks are closely related as a government default on payments may lead private parties to renege on their payment obligations – especially if the government default leads to a major depreciation or crisis scenario.

11.9.1 Managing country risk

In order to effectively control the level of risk associated with their international operations, firms must have in place a procedure that systematically evaluates the country risk features of its business. This includes having in place a country risk evaluation process that has:

- effective oversight by senior managers;
- appropriate risk management policies and procedures;
- an accurate system for reporting change in country risk and potential exposures;
- an effective process for analysing country risk;
- a country risk rating system;
- regular monitoring of country conditions.

While the details and complexity of country risk assessment will vary from bank to bank, senior management must be suitably qualified to evaluate the bank's international activities.

11.9.1.1 Effective oversight by senior managers

If country risk is to be managed effectively then senior bank managers, up to board level, must oversee the process. It is likely that a team of senior project appraisers will review the bank's international operations in order to ensure that they are consistent with the company's major strategic objectives. Decisions to extend international operations and exposure to different countries' risk will ultimately be a decision for the company board, as they should have a view of the sorts of country exposure required and it is up to the board to make sure that country risk (as well as other risks) is effectively managed.

11.9.1.2 Appropriate risk management policies and procedures

It is the responsibility of senior bank management to implement policies and procedures for managing country risk. This involves:

- identifying investments and other activities exposed to country risk;
- identifying desirable and undesirable opportunities that can be used to complement or be substituted for current operations resulting in a reduction of country risk;
- establishing country risk limits if necessary;
- identifying clear lines of responsibility and accountability for country risk management decisions.

Senior management are ultimately responsible for country risk management policies, standards and practices and also need to make sure that these are communicated effectively to relevant parts of the organisation.

11.9.1.3 Systems for reporting country risk and potential exposures

In order to effectively manage country risk, banks need to have reliable systems for capturing and categorising the volume and nature of their foreign activities. Such a reporting system should cover all aspects of the company's international operations. Banks, for example, have to have country exposure reporting systems to support regulatory reporting of foreign exposures requirements.

11.9.1.4 An effective process for analysing country risk

The level of resources dedicated to the country risk analysis process will vary from bank to bank depending on the size and sophistication of the company's international activities. In order to construct an effective country risk evaluation process senior managers need to ask the following questions:

- Is there a quantitative and qualitative assessment of the risk associated with each country in which the firm is conducting or planning to undertake activities?
- Is any formal country risk analysis undertaken on a regular basis and are changes in country risk monitored in any way?
- Is the country risk analysis adequately documented, with the findings communicated to the relevant parties?
- Are adequate resources devoted to country risk evaluation procedures?
- Do the company's country risk assessments concur with the risk ratings of third-party assessors, such as rating agencies?

If the answers to these questions are in the affirmative then the bank is well placed to use the results of its country risk analysis effectively in strategic and operational decision making. In order to arrive at a conclusion about the level of country risk faced by a bank, managers need to evaluate the current (and possible future) economic, political and social characteristics of a country. For this they are likely to use some form of country risk rating system.

11.9.1.5 Country risk rating

Country risk ratings simply summarise the main findings of the country risk analysis process. While large firms and banks are likely to have teams evaluating country risk, smaller firms are more likely to rely heavily on the country risk assessments done by specialist third-party firms. Because there is a wide range of factors that can affect country risk, it is often difficult for smaller firms to dedicate the relevant resources to assess somewhat complex issues. Macroeconomic and political environments can change rapidly and it is often difficult to keep abreast of these developments, especially if one is considering or monitoring projects in a number of countries. Box 11.8 provides a broad indication of the various factors that affect country risk.

Box 11.8   Factors affecting country risk

Macroeconomic factors
- Size and structure of the country's external debt in relation to its economy
- Level of international reserves
- Potential for extreme adverse exchange rate movements and the effect on the relative price of the country's imports and exports
- GDP growth and inflation levels, current and forecast
- Role of foreign sources of capital in meeting the country's financing needs
- Country's access to international financial markets and the potential effects of a loss of market liquidity
- Country's relationships with private sector creditors
- The country's current standing with multilateral and official creditors such as the IMF

▶

- Trends in foreign investments and the country's ability to obtain foreign investment in the future
- Privatisation of government-owned entities
- The extent to which the economy of the country may be adversely affected through the contagion of problems in other countries
- The size and condition of the country's banking and financial system
- The extent to which state-directed lending or other government intervention may have adversely affected the soundness of the country's financial system and economy.

Socio-political factors
- The country's natural and human resource potential
- The willingness and ability of the government to recognise economic or budgetary problems and implement appropriate remedial action
- Extent to which political or regional factionalism or armed conflicts are adversely affecting government of the country
- Any trends toward government-imposed price, interest rate, or exchange controls
- Extent to which the legal system of the country can be relied upon to fairly protect the interests of foreign creditors and investors
- Accounting standards and the reliability and transparency of financial information
- The level of adherence to international legal and business practice standards
- Level of corruption
- Level of corporate social responsibility.

Institution-specific factors
- The bank's business strategy and its plans for investment in the country
- Types of investments, FDI or portfolio investments, joint ventures, licensing agreements, and so on
- Economic outlook for any specifically targeted business opened within the country
- Extent to which political or economic developments are likely to affect the bank's chosen lines of business
- The degree to which political or economic developments are likely to affect the credit risk of individual counterparties in the country. For instance, foreign firms with strong export markets in developed countries may have significantly less exposure to the local country's economic disruptions than do other firms operating in the country.
- The institution's ability to effectively manage its country risk through in-country or regional representation, or by some other arrangement that ensures the timely reporting of, and response to, any problems

One can see from Box 11.8 that there is a whole host of factors that affect a country's risk rating including various economic, financial and socio-political risks, as well as those risks that may be relevant to the specific bank or firm in question. In quantifying the broad economic/financial and socio-political risks companies can do their own risk evaluation but can also cross-check these with a variety of ratings calculated by third-party firms.

There are many firms that provide services that measure country risk. The main providers include:

- Control Risks Information Services (CRIS)
- Economist Intelligence Unit (EIU)
- Euromoney
- Institutional Investor
- Moody's Investor Services
- OECD
- Political risk services: International Country Risk Guide (ICRG)
- Political risk services: Coplin-O'Leary Rating System
- Standard and Poor's Rating Group

Apart from the OECD, all act as 'rating agencies' and sell their country risk ratings via the web or through other media. Each of these firms produce risk ratings using a variety of qualitative and quantitative information so as to construct a single index or country risk rating schedule. For example, Institutional Investor's credit ratings are based on a survey of leading international bankers who are asked to rate each country on a scale from zero to 100 (where 100 represents maximum credit-worthiness). Institutional Investor averages these ratings, providing greater weights to respondents with greater world-wide exposure and more sophisticated country analysis systems. International Country Risk Guide (ICRG) compiles monthly data on a variety of political, financial and economic risk factors to calculate risk indices in each of these categories as well as a composite risk index. Five financial, thirteen political and six economic factors are used. Each factor is assigned a numerical rating within a specified range. In the case of ICRG country risk weightings political risk assessment scores are based on subjective staff analysis of available information. Economic risk assessment scores are based upon objective analysis of quantitative data, and financial risk assessment scores are based upon analysis of a mix of quantitative and qualitative information.

Of the non-commercial country risk ratings, those provided on a regular basis by the OECD are widely used and often these will be cross-checked against a firm's own internal risk assessment and those of a private third-party provider. How the OECD calculates its country risk ratings is outlined in Box 11.9 and Table 11.5 reports its country risk ratings from June 2004.

Box 11.9 OECD country risk-weighting calculations

The OECD produces a regular country credit risk assessment that classifies countries into eight risk categories (0 to 7) with 7 being the most risky.

The Country Risk Classification Method measures the country credit risk, i.e., the likelihood that a country will service its external debt.

The classification of countries is achieved through the application of a methodology comprised of two basic components: (1) the Country Risk Assessment Model (CRAM), which produces a quantitative assessment of country credit risk, based on three groups of risk indicators (the payment experience of the participants, the financial situation and the economic situation) and (2) the qualitative assessment of the model results, considered country-by-country to integrate political risk and/or other risk factors not taken (fully) into account by the model. The details of the CRAM are confidential and not published.

▶

The final classification, based only on valid country risk elements, is a consensus decision of the sub-group of country risk experts that involves the country risk experts of the participating export credit agencies.

The sub-group of country risk experts meets several times a year. These meetings are organised in such a way as to guarantee that every country is reviewed whenever a fundamental change is observed and at least once a year. While the meetings are confidential and no official reports of the deliberations are made, the list of country risk classifications is published after each meeting.

Source: http://www.oecd.org.

Table 11.5 Example of OECD country risk classification of the participants to the arrangement on officially supported export credits (as of June 2005)

Country code	Country name	01 Jan 2005 28 Jan 2005	20 Jun 2005 28 Oct 2005
ALB	Albania	6	6
DZA	Algeria	4	3
AGO	Angola	7	7
ATG	Antigua and Barbuda	7	7
ARG	Argentina	7	7
ARM	Armenia	7	7
ABW	Aruba	4	4
AUS	Australia	0	0
AUT	Austria	0	0
AZE	Azerbaijan	6	6
BHS	Bahamas	3	3
BHR	Bahrain	3	3
BGD	Bangladesh	6	6
BLR	Belarus	7	7
BEL	Belgium	0	0
BLZ	Belize	6	7
BEN	Benin	7	7
BOL	Bolivia	7	7
BIH	Bosnia and Herzegovina	7	7
BWA	Botswana	2	2
BRA	Brazil	6	5
BRN	Brunei	2	2
BGR	Bulgaria	4	4
BFA	Burkina Faso	7	7
CMR	Cameroon	7	7
CAN	Canada	0	0
CPV	Cape Verde	7	7

Source: Adapted from http://www.oecd.org/dataoecd/47/29/3782900.pdf.

11.9.1.6 Regular monitoring of country conditions

While banks have a wide range of resources at their disposal to evaluate country risk they also have to ensure that this risk is monitored on an on-going basis as country circumstances can change rapidly. International banks therefore should have a system in place to monitor current conditions in each of the countries where they have significant operations and also reconcile their risk assessments with those provided by other parties (such as the rating scores provided by the firms listed in the previous section). The quantity of resources devoted to monitoring conditions within a country should, of course, be proportionate to the firm's level of overseas activity and the perceived level of risk. Information provided by senior managers in the foreign country are a valuable resource for monitoring country conditions as are regular reports by regional or country managers. There also needs to be regular contact between parent senior management and those responsible for the operations in the foreign market. All banks conducting international business should not rely solely on informal and ad hoc lines of communication, and established procedures should be in place for dealing with operations that are faced with troubled overseas environments. Also, various contingency plans should be put in place for dealing with problems associated with increases in country risk; if necessary this should include various exit strategies.

It should also be stressed that international banks also must have adequate internal controls in place so that there is a reporting mechanism ensuring the integrity of the information used by senior management to monitor country risk positions and to comply with any pre-determined country risk exposure limits.

11.10 Conclusions

This chapter reviewed various aspect of bank risk management. The basic principles of bank management, including Asset and Liability Management, were reviewed in Chapter 9, whereas Chapter 10 analysed the main banking risks. This present chapter introduced the general concepts of bank risk management in Section 11.2. It then considered the management of specific banking risks, focusing particularly on the banking risk included in the calculation of regulatory capital in the new Basle Accord (credit risk, market risk and operational risk) and the management of the 'traditional' ALM function (interest rate risk and liquidity risk). Finally, given the growing importance of international banking activities, Section 11.9.1 outlined the main features relating to the management of country risk. Risk management is a complex and comprehensive process, which includes creating an appropriate environment, maintaining an efficient risk measurement structure, monitoring and mitigating risk-taking activities and establishing an adequate framework of internal controls. Banks will increasingly need to adopt more formal and quantitative risk measurement and risk management procedures and processes.

Key terms

Risk measurement	Credit checking
Risk management	Credit scoring
CAMELS	Credit reference agencies
Collateral	Gap analysis
Loan rate	Duration analysis
Mortgage equity withdrawal	VaR
Negative equity	Back testing
Credit rationing	Risk-Adjusted Return on Capital (RAROC)

Key reading

Basle Committee on Banking Supervision (1997a), 'Core Principles for Effective Banking Supervision', September, http://www.bis.org/publ/bcbs30a.pdf.

Basle Committee on Banking Supervision (2001a) 'Overview on the New Basle Capital Accord', *Consultative Document*, http://www.bis.org/publ/bcbsca02.pdf.

Basle Committee on Banking Supervision (2003b) 'Risk Management Principles for Electronic Banking', July, http://www.bis.org/publ/bcbs98.pdf.

Basle Committee on Banking Supervision (2004a) 'International Convergence of Capital Measurement and Capital Standards – A Revised Framework', June, http://www.bis.org/publ/bcbs107.pdf.

Revision questions and problems

1 What is described as 'sound practice' in the management of credit risk?
2 Explain the process of credit scoring and describe its main applications.
3 What are the main limitations of the GAP approach?
4 Why should prudent banks seek to minimise their volatility ratio?
5 What are the main techniques used to manage a bank's liquidity exposure?
6 What is VaR? Explain the importance of VaR in the context of the new Basle Capital Adequacy Accord (Basle II).
7 What are the difficulties inherent in the measurement and management of operational risk?
8 What are the main factors affecting country risk?

Part 4

COMPARATIVE BANKING MARKETS

Chapter 12

UK banking

Learning objectives

- To understand the main structural features of the UK banking market
- To identify the main trends in the recent performance of UK banks
- To discuss the implication of increased concentration on competition in the UK banking sector
- To understand the characteristics of the UK payment system
- To describe the regulatory changes that have had an impact on the UK banking sector

12.1 Introduction

As in other countries, the UK banking market has undergone substantial change over the last 20 years, mainly driven by domestic deregulation as well as various other forces that have changed the supply and demand characteristics of the financial services industry. This chapter aims to review the structural features of the UK banking industry (Section 12.2) and the financial structure of the sector (Section 12.3), with particular focus on the **MBBGs (Major British Banking Groups)**. The impact of the increased consolidation in the sector, together with the recommendations of two major public inquires, the Cruickshank Report on bank competition and Competition Commission Report into the *Supply of Banking Services by Clearing Banks to Small and Medium-Sized Enterprises* are also assessed. Section 12.4 reviews the performance of UK banks in the past decade: they have been among Europe's best-performing financial firms, benefiting from the buoyant domestic economy and from relatively high interest margins. Section 12.5 illustrates the main characteristics of the UK payment system and Section 12.6 reviews the regulatory environment, with particular focus on the recent changes and their impact on the sector.

12.2 Structural features of UK banking

12.2.1 Numbers and types of banks

In contrast to other large European countries, the UK has a relatively small number of banks. As Figure 12.1 illustrates, the total number of authorised banking institutions had fallen from around 600 in 1985 to 346 by the end of February 2005. The figure also shows the decline in the number of mutual building societies over the same period.

The decline in the total number of banks is attributable to foreign banks, which already had UK operations, acquiring relatively small UK investment banks as well as consolidation in the domestic retail banking market. Table 12.2 shows that during the second part of the 1990s the decline in the number of foreign banks was greater than that for UK incorporated banks, although mergers and acquisitions between UK incorporated banks resulted in a fall in their number from 202 in 1999 to 171 by March 2005. During the second half of the 1990s, a decline in the number of non-European banks (particularly Japanese banks) was counteracted by the increased presence of European institutions, whose number increased from 79 to 109 between 1993 and 1999; the number of European banks had subsequently declined to 87 by 2005. Table 12.2 illustrates these trends and shows that the total number of foreign banks operating in the UK fell from 257 to 175 between 1995 and 2005.

Foreign banks typically do little sterling-denominated business, focusing mainly on wholesale foreign currency activity relating to investment banking activity. Investment banking (otherwise known as merchant banking in the United Kingdom) is a major feature of the UK financial system with most activity centred in the City of London. As we noted earlier (Section 3.6) investment banking comprises:

- corporate finance and other forms of structured finance and advice, particularly in connection with new issues of securities, mergers and takeovers;

Figure 12.1 **Number of banks and building societies 1985–2005**

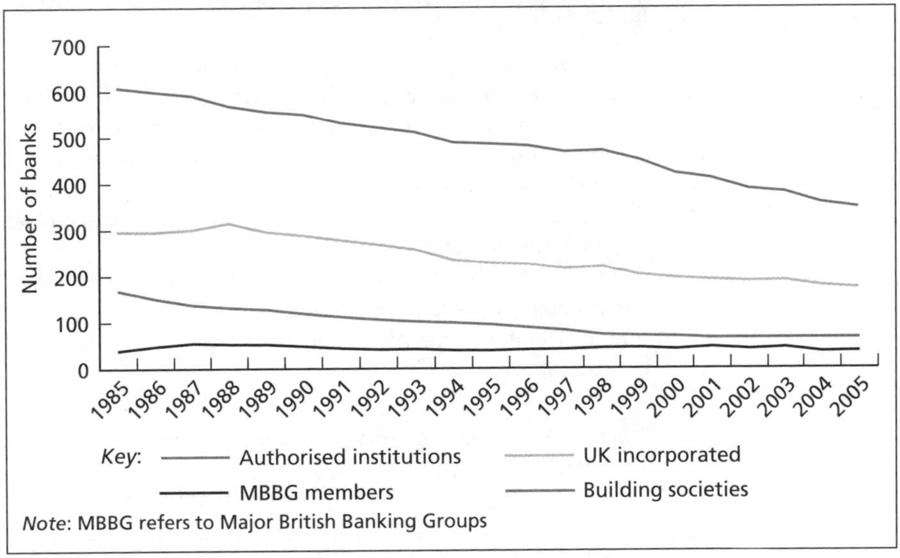

Source: Figures for end of February. Adapted from *Banking Business, An Abstract of Banking Statistics* (2004) Vol. 21, Table 1.04, p. 6, (1999) Vol. 16, Table 1.04, p. 6, and (1996) Vol. 13, Table 6.01, p. 6 (London: British Bankers Association); and *Housing Finance*, No. 44, November 1999, Table 31, p. 71 (London: Council of Mortgage Lenders), and Financial Services Authority *Building Society Statistics* (2004), http://www.fsa.gov.uk/pages/library/cooperate/annual/ar03_04_bs_statistics.shtml Table 1 Building Societies – Service Activity, July 2004. Also see the Building Societies Association at http://www.bsa.org.uk/.

- securities trading and broking in equities, bonds and derivatives;
- banking services for companies and public authorities;
- treasury dealing and financial engineering to protect corporate clients from interest rate and currency risks;
- investment management for institutions and private clients.

The investment banking industry is dominated by major US and European banks including Goldman Sachs, Morgan Stanley, Merrill Lynch, Lehman Brothers Deutsche Bank, UBS and Credit Suisse. In addition, the main UK banks also typically have investment banking subsidiaries (e.g., Barclays Capital). There are few independent UK merchant banks as most have been acquired by overseas investment and commercial banks. Box 12.1 illustrates the importance of various types of investment banking in the United Kingdom.

While the role of investment banks in the United Kingdom may be unfamiliar to many students, the role of the High Street banks in retail banking will be much more familiar. Table 12.2 illustrates the number of banks and subsidiaries of the main UK retail banks – otherwise known as the Major British Banking Groups (MBBG). These banks dominate sterling-denominated banking business in Britain. The MBBG includes Abbey National, Alliance & Leicester, Barclays, Bradford & Bingley, HBOS, HSBC Bank, Lloyds TSB, Northern Rock and the Royal Bank of Scotland (that owns NatWest). Four of these were mutual building societies that converted to bank status – Abbey National (converted in 1989), Alliance and Leicester (1997), Bradford & Bingley (2000) and Northern Rock (1997). HBOS was formed by the merger of Halifax (that converted into plc and bank status in June 1997) and the Bank of Scotland in September 2001. The MBBGs and the building societies are the major players in the retail banking market.

Box 12.1   Investment banking in the United Kingdom

Investment banking business in the United Kingdom is mainly conducted by large US investment banks, universal European banks and the investment banking subsidiaries of international (as well as UK) commercial banks. The majority of investment banking business is wholesale and corporate-related and conducted in currencies other than sterling – although the latter (obviously) predominates in the financing of UK corporate restructuring and domestic capital market issuance of bonds and equities.

Table 12.1 illustrates London's major role as an investment banking centre as banks based in the City play a dominant role in the markets in foreign equities trading, foreign exchange trading, over-the-counter derivatives and international bonds issuance.

Table 12.1 **London's share of investment banking and other international financial services (%)**

	1992	1995	1998	2000	2001	2002	2003	2004
Cross-border bank lending	16	17	20	19	19	19	19	20[i]
Foreign equities turnover	64	61	65	48	56	56	45	43[ii]
Foreign exchange dealing	27	30	33	–	31	–	–	31
Derivatives turnover								
– exchange-traded	12	12	11	8	7	6	6	–
– over-the-counter	–	27	36	–	36	–	–	43
Insurance net premium income								
– marine	29	24	19	–	–	–	–	–
– aviation	45	31	31	–	–	–	–	–
International bonds								
– primary market	60	60	60	60	60	–	60	60
– seondary market	70	70	70	70	70	70	70	70
Hedge fund assets	–	–	–	–	–	9	14	14[iii]

–   Data not available
  i March
 ii January to September
iii June

Source: International Financial Services London; Bank of England, Bank for International Settlements.

Note also the major share in other banking areas such as cross-border lending (both commercial and investment banks undertake this type of business).

Source: City of London Corporation (2005) *The City's Importance to the EU Economy 2005*, City of London Corporation, February.

Table 12.2 Number of banks in the United Kingdom

	1995	1996	1997	1998	1999	2000	2001	2002	2003	2004	2005
Number of authorised institutions of which:	481	478	466	468	449	420	409	385	380	356	346
UK incorporated	224	220	212	214	202	190	188	184	185	174	171
European authorised institutions	102	103	105	105	109	103	97	89	92	89	87
Incorporated outside the European Economic Area	155	155	149	149	138	127	124	112	103	93	88
MBBG Members and their Banking Sector subsidiaries (included above) (a)	37	40	41	44	43	41	42	41	42	35	32
BBA Member banks (included above) (b)	307	306	311	337	327	302	295	265	244	236	218

Note: Lists of authorised institutions are published by the Bank of England.

(a) Major British Banking Groups (MBBGs) in 1999 included the following: Abbey National Group, Alliance & Leicester Group, Barclays Group, Bradford and Bingley plc (from 2000), The HBOS Group, HSBC Bank Group, Lloyds TSB Group, Northern Rock Group (from 1999) and the Royal Bank of Scotland Group (that acquired NatWest in 2000).

(b) As at end-March.

Source: Adapted from *Banking Business. An Abstract of Banking Statistics* (2005) Vol. 22, Table 1.04, p. 6, (1999) Vol. 16, Table 1.04, p. 6, and (1996) Vol. 13, Table 6.01, p. 6 (London: British Bankers Association).

12.2.2 Trends in branch numbers, ATMs and employment

Over the last 20 years, the UK banks and building societies have engaged in a significant reorganisation. This is characterised by the decline in branch numbers that has occurred since the late 1980s. Figure 12.2 shows the trends in branch and ATM numbers in the United Kingdom since 1985 and illustrates that during the 1990s, while branch numbers were declining, the introduction of ATMs (at the branch and in 'remote' locations) grew significantly. Although not shown in the diagram, there was also a substantial growth in electronic funds transfer at point of sale (EFTPOS) terminals – from 4,640 in 1993 to 8,984 in 1997 – further reflecting the trend to supplement traditional with new distribution channels.[1] These are terminals placed in stores, petrol stations and so on, that process credit and debit card payments. The number of such terminals is believed to have exceeded 11,000 by 2004. The reason for the shift from branches to other means of financial service delivery relates mainly to UK retail financial service firms' desire to improve operating efficiency as well as customers increasing demands to access banking services outside traditional (rather limited) banking hours.

Together with the general decline in branch numbers, the restructuring of the system has also led to a fall in bank and building society employment as shown in Figure 12.3. The fall in staff employed is particularly noticeable for retail banks (it fell by around 75,000 between 1990 and 1996), although retail bank employment increased from then onwards by over 45,000 to reach just over 346,000 by the end of 2004. The increase in employment after 1996 is attributable to building society conversions to bank status. In addition, the figures also reveal that there has been a substantial increase in employment by foreign banks since 1996 up to 2001–02 reflecting the booming capital markets activity of foreign-owned investment banks in London.

---

[1] See European Central Bank (1999), *The Effects of Technology on EU Banking Systems*, July 1999, Table A4 for EFTPOS trends in EU banking.

Figure 12.2 **Number of branches and ATMs 1985–2004**

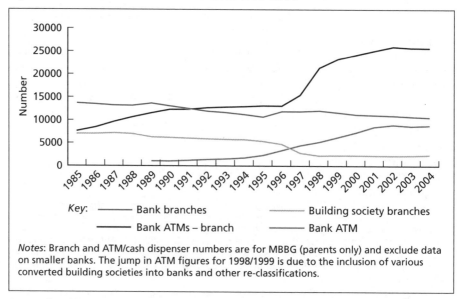

Key: —— Bank branches   —— Building society branches
—— Bank ATMs – branch   —— Bank ATM

Notes: Branch and ATM/cash dispenser numbers are for MBBG (parents only) and exclude data on smaller banks. The jump in ATM figures for 1998/1999 is due to the inclusion of various converted building societies into banks and other re-classifications.

Source: Adapted from *Banking Business. An Abstract of Banking Statistics* (2005) Vol. 22, Tables 5.02 and 5.03, pp. 54–5, (1999) Vol. 16, Tables 5.02 and 5.03, pp. 52–3 and (1996) Vol. 13, Table 5.02, pp. 52–3, (London: British Bankers Association).

Figure 12.3 **Employment in the UK banking sector 1990–2004**

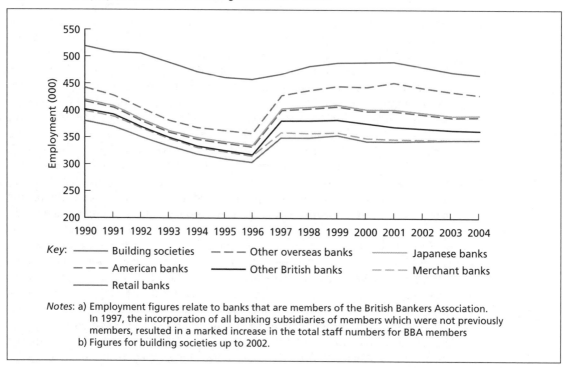

Key: —— Building societies   – – – Other overseas banks   —— Japanese banks
– – – American banks   —— Other British banks   – – – Merchant banks
—— Retail banks

Notes: a) Employment figures relate to banks that are members of the British Bankers Association. In 1997, the incorporation of all banking subsidiaries of members which were not previously members, resulted in a marked increase in the total staff numbers for BBA members
b) Figures for building societies up to 2002.

Source: Adapted from *Banking Business. An Abstract of Banking Statistics* (2005) Vol. 22, Table 5.01 p. 53, (1999) Vol. 16, Table 5.01 p. 50 and (1996) Vol. 13, Table 5.01, p. 64 (London: British Bankers Association).

Figure 12.4 **Number of staff: major banks 1998–2004**

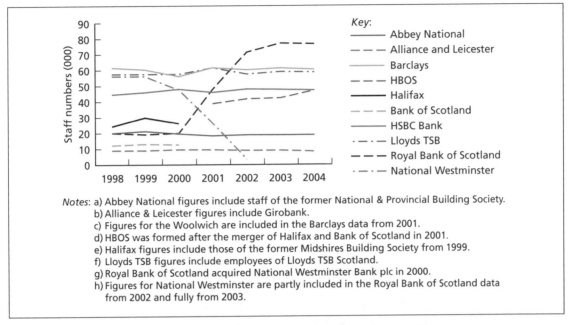

Notes: a) Abbey National figures include staff of the former National & Provincial Building Society.
b) Alliance & Leicester figures include Girobank.
c) Figures for the Woolwich are included in the Barclays data from 2001.
d) HBOS was formed after the merger of Halifax and Bank of Scotland in 2001.
e) Halifax figures include those of the former Midshires Building Society from 1999.
f) Lloyds TSB figures include employees of Lloyds TSB Scotland.
g) Royal Bank of Scotland acquired National Westminster Bank plc in 2000.
h) Figures for National Westminster are partly included in the Royal Bank of Scotland data
from 2002 and fully from 2003.

Source: Adapted from *Banking Business. An Abstract of Banking Statistics* (2005), Vol. 22, Table 5.01, p. 53.

A clearer picture of employment trends at the top UK retail banks is given in Figure 12.4. This shows that all the main banks have maintained relatively stable staff levels in recent years. It should be noted that the large decline for NatWest is mirrored by the increase at the Royal Bank of Scotland that acquired NatWest in 2000. It is also interesting to note that of the 330,700 staff employed by the Major British Banking Groups (MBBG) in 2004, around 63 per cent were female, of whom 76,300 were part-time workers (this compares with only 4,500 part-time male employees). Throughout the 1990s there has been a gradual increase in the number of part-time staff employed in the banking sector – mainly in the retail sector. Again, the general decline in total employment in the banking sector and the increase in part-time employment, are indicators of the banks' desire to improve their operating efficiency.

12.3 Financial structure of the UK banking system

The balance sheet structure of the UK banking system differs from that of many other European systems mainly because of the significant presence of foreign banks. The latter engage primarily in foreign currency-denominated business (known as Eurocurrency business) and undertake only modest sterling banking operations.[2] In contrast, the UK banks engage primarily in sterling-denominated activity. Given the important presence of foreign banks, this means that a substantial proportion of

---

[2] Eurocurrency business includes foreign currency interbank deposits as well as other debt instruments denominated in foreign currencies including commercial paper, treasury bills, certificates of deposits (CDs) and repurchase agreements (repos).

Figure 12.5 All banks in the United Kingdom: asset structure 1985–2004

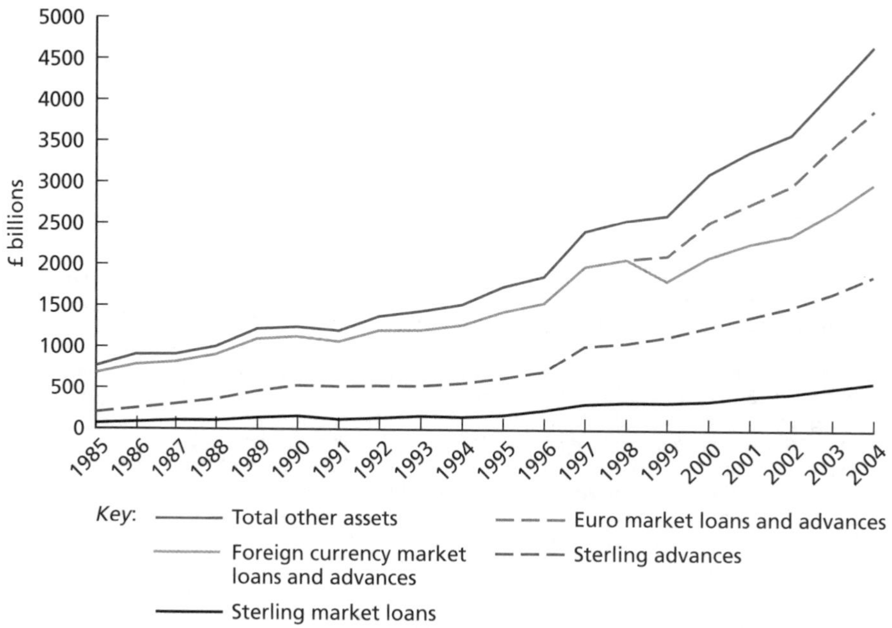

Key:
— Total other assets
– – – Euro market loans and advances

— Foreign currency market loans and advances
– – – Sterling advances

— Sterling market loans

Notes: Foreign currency market loans and advances include all types of foreign currency loans and advances up to 1998, from 1999 Euro-denominated loans and advances are reported separately, so from 1999 onwards the foreign currency segment includes all non-Euro loans and advances.

Source: Adapted from *Banking Business. An Abstract of Banking Statistics* (2005) Vol. 22, Table 1.01 p. 3, (1999) Vol. 16, Table 1.01 p. 3 (1996) Vol. 13, Table 1.01 p. 2 (London: British Bankers Association).

total balance sheet activity is foreign currency-oriented. This can be seen in Figure 12.5, which shows that foreign currency business is at least as important as sterling activity in the banking sector's balance sheet. Similarly, Figure 12.6 illustrates the importance of foreign currency deposits in the UK system.

As already mentioned, the UK banking sector's balance sheet has a high foreign currency component because of the significant presence of foreign banks mainly undertaking wholesale foreign currency money and capital markets business in London. Foreign bank presence in the domestic banking sector is minimal – the most noticeable foreign operators in the retail market are the specialist credit card providers such as MNBA and GE Capital. If one considers the assets share of the banking system in 2001, UK-owned banks account for 47 per cent of the total, followed by other European-owned banks (26 per cent assets share), US banks (9 per cent) and then Japanese banks (4 per cent).[3] The share of other European banks has increased significantly since 1990 when it stood at around 11 per cent, whereas the assets share of Japanese banks has fallen (mainly because of retrenchment related to problems in their domestic market) and US banks' share has remained relatively

---

[3] See Bank of England *Statistical Abstract* (2001) Part 1, Compiled from Tables 3.2, 3.2.1 to 3.2.4, pp. 40–53, for data on foreign bank assets share in the UK banking market. Note that the *Statistical Abstract* has been superseded by the *Monetary and Financial Statistical Interactive Database*.

Figure 12.6 All banks in the UK: liability structure 1985–2004

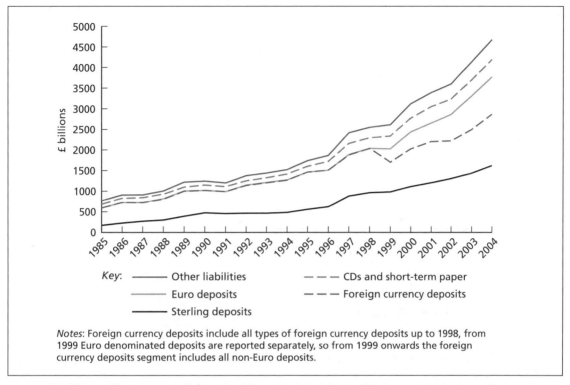

Key:
—————— Other liabilities   — — — CDs and short-term paper
—————— Euro deposits   — — — Foreign currency deposits
—————— Sterling deposits

Notes: Foreign currency deposits include all types of foreign currency deposits up to 1998, from 1999 Euro denominated deposits are reported separately, so from 1999 onwards the foreign currency deposits segment includes all non-Euro deposits.

Source: Adapted from *Banking Business. An Abstract of Banking Statistics* (2005) Vol. 22, Table 1.01 p. 3, (1999) Vol. 16, Table 1.01 p. 3 (1996) Vol. 13, Table 1.01 p. 2 (London: British Bankers Association).

constant. The large increase in the presence of continental European banks has, to a certain extent, been brought about by these banks acquiring UK merchant banks (such as Dresdner Bank's purchase of Kleinwort Benson and Swiss Bank Corporation's – now part of Union Bank of Switzerland – acquisition of Warburg's in 1995).

In addition, many large European banks have headquartered their capital markets operations, as well as built up substantial private banking and asset management businesses, in London during the latter half of the 1990s. It is difficult to say whether the increased presence of European banks in the United Kingdom has been a direct result of the EU's Single Market Programme (SMP) although there must be a presumption that it has had some effect in promoting foreign bank establishment (and growth). This is because the introduction of the single banking licence and the reduction in barriers to cross-border banking and capital markets business, brought about by the legislation, has made it easier for EU banks to conduct cross-border activity, especially in capital markets areas.[4]

---

[4] The EC (1997) Single Market Review notes that the SMP legislation had the largest impact in the capital markets and wholesale banking areas in facilitating cross-border activity. An ongoing programme of further financial system liberalisation within Europe has also been promoted by the European Unions Financial Services Action Plan (FSAP) that consists of 42 regulatory measures aimed at encouraging cross-border activity within Europe's financial system. The FSAP commenced in 1999 and ended at the end of 2005. For more information on the FSAP see: http://www.europa.eu.int/comm/internal_market/en/finances/actionplan/ index.htm.

Figure 12.7 MBBG sterling lending to UK residents 1985–2004

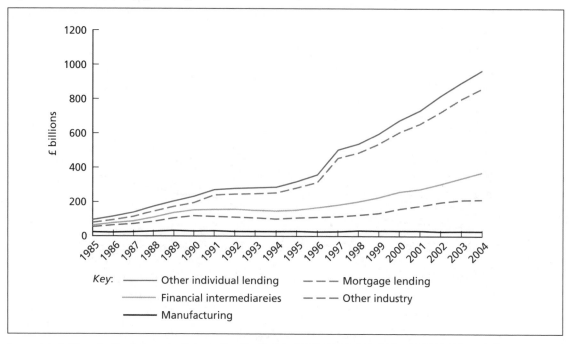

Source: Adapted from *Banking Business. An Abstract of Banking Statistics* (2005) Vol. 22, Table 2.06 p. 16 (1999) Vol. 16, Table 2.08 p. 17 and (1996) Vol. 13, Table 2.09, p. 25. (London: British Bankers Association).

The MBBGs dominate sterling business in the United Kingdom and the make-up of their lending business is shown in Figure 12.7. The diagram shows that since the mid-1990s there has been substantial growth in domestic mortgage lending relative to other types of lending. The relatively low level of lending to the manufacturing sector is also noticeable and this has raised policy concerns about inadequate bank funding available to **small and medium-sized enterprises (SMEs)**.[5] Although not shown, individual sterling deposits comprise around 55 per cent of MBBG's non-bank sterling deposits, followed by company deposits (17 per cent). Over the last decade or so the proportion of individual sterling deposits, as a percentage of total sterling deposits, has increased. This trend reflects the growing focus of UK banks on retail banking activity at the expense of corporate and investment banking business. The spectacular profits earned by UK banks between 1995 and 2000 were mainly driven by retail banking business and this has encouraged all the top banks to emphasise this business area, as well as to diversify into other retail financial services such as insurance and private pensions. The (relatively) low funding cost of retail deposits, coupled with the healthy margins generated through mortgage and other consumer lending, has encouraged the main banks to prioritise retail banking/financial services and to de-emphasise other areas (for example, Barclays Group and the former NatWest significantly reduced their investment banking operations because of poor performance at the end of 1997).

[5] Policy concerns about funding to SMEs are a central theme of the UK government's report into 'Competition in UK Banking', published in March 2000 and chaired by Don Cruickshank. The report recommended that the UK banks be referred to the Competition Commission because of the possibility of a complex monopoly existing in the provision of banking services to the SME sector. The top four UK banks account for 83 per cent of the SME market.

The main UK banks have been particularly aggressive in competing with the building societies and other specialist lenders in the consumer credit and mortgage areas. Figures 12.8 and 12.9 illustrate net lending trends in these two sectors over the last 20 years. The cyclical nature of the two areas is clearly evident – rapid

Figure 12.8 **Net lending for consumer credit 1985–2004**

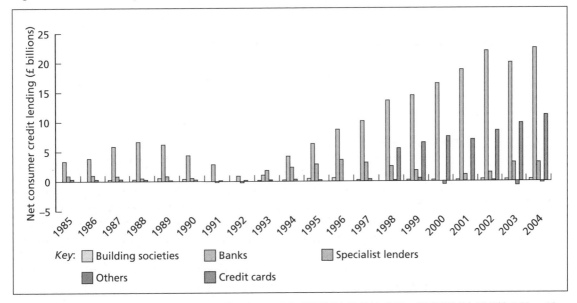

Source: Adapted from *Banking Business. An Abstract of Banking Statistics* (2005) Vol. 22, Table 4.05 p. 48, (1999) Vol. 16, Table 4.06, p. 46 and (1996) Vol. 13, Table 4.06, p. 60, (London: British Bankers Association).

Figure 12.9 **Net mortgage lending 1985–2004**

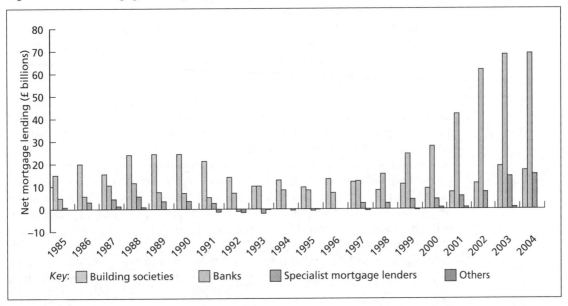

Source: Adapted from *Banking Business. An Abstract of Banking Statistics* (2005) Vol. 22, Table 4.05 p. 48, (1999), Vol. 16, Table 4.06, p. 45 and (1996) Vol. 13, Table 4.06, p. 58, (London: British Bankers Association).

growth in consumer and mortgage lending up to 1988–90 then a decline during the UK recession period and an increase thereafter. In fact, the boom in credit expansion in the late 1980s, prior to the early 1990s recession, has strong similarities with the credit trends that were experienced in the United Kingdom during the late 1990s. The two figures also show that banks dominate net lending for consumer credit from 1997 onwards (because of building society conversions) as well as being the main new lenders in the mortgage area.

12.3.1 Market concentration and competition

The UK banking market, like many other European systems, is relatively concentrated with the top four banks accounting for 37 per cent of all banking sector assets and 36 per cent of UK banking and building society assets. The level of concentration as measured by the share of the top four banks (assets) to the whole banking system, as illustrated in Figure 12.10, remained relatively stable throughout the 1980s up to 1997; this trend was contrary to concentration developments in various other European markets (see EC 1997). However, from 1997 onwards concentration increased. It can be seen that the market share of the top banks, as a proportion of UK bank and building society assets, grew rapidly from 1997 onwards due to various large-scale mergers and acquisitions, for example – Bank of Scotland merged with Halifax to form HBOS and the Royal Bank of Scotland acquired NatWest. In addition to these broad trends, concentration in specific market segments is also substantial. Logan (2004) provides an extensive analysis of concentration in the UK banking sector and finds that:

- The three largest banking groups had a combined market share of 50 per cent of non-financial private sector deposits. The five largest groups held 71 per cent and the largest nine banks (all UK-owned) held over 86 per cent of such deposits. The level of concentration in this deposit segment, however, was little different from what it had been in 1988.
- Concentration of bank lending to the non-bank financial sector was slightly higher than for the aforementioned deposits. The three biggest banking groups made 52 per cent and the top five accounted for 75 per cent of loans. Loan concentration was found to have increased since 1988.

Other concentration measures described in Bowen *et al.* (1999) find that the market share of the top three mortgage providers increased from 34 per cent in 1992 to 43 per cent in 1997 (the figures for the top four firms were 39 per cent and 50 per cent respectively). In addition, 12 mortgage providers were found to account for 80 per cent of the domestic mortgage market. The same authors also found the retail deposit market to be quite concentrated with the top four banks having 45 per cent of the market in 1997 – although this level of concentration had remained roughly the same throughout the 1990s. The area that stands out as being the most concentrated is banking services to SMEs, where the top four suppliers have 83 per cent of the market.[6]

While the above discussion may suggest that the degree of concentration in the UK banking market appears excessive, various international comparisons of broad

---

[6] This is also confirmed in Logan (2004), see Box 12.2.

Figure 12.10 **Share of top four banks' assets 1985–2004**

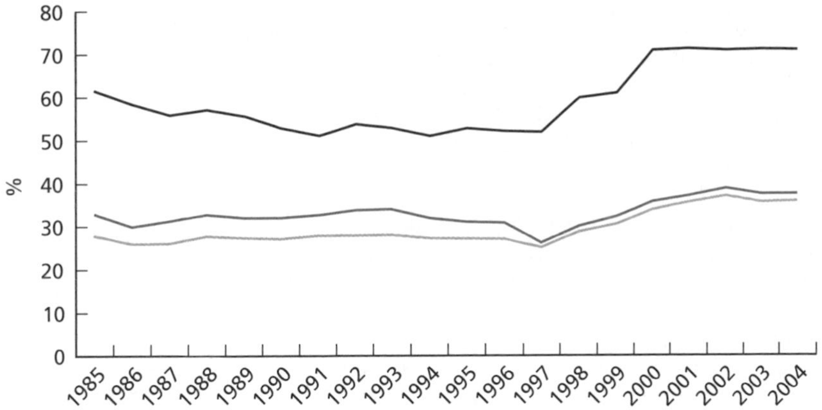

Key: ——— % of all banking sector assets ——— % of all banking and building society assets
——— % of UK banks and building society assets

Notes: The top four banks are defined as Barclays, National Westminster, Midland and Lloyds TSB up to and including 1997; Barclays, HBOS, NatWest and Lloyds TSB from 1998 to 1999 and Barclays, HBOS, Lloyds TSB and Royal Bank of Scotland from 2000 to 2003. Assets for Lloyds TSB pre-1994 are obtained by summing assets of Lloyds Bank and TSB.

Source: Adapted from *Banking Business, An Abstract of Banking Statistics* (2004) Vol. 22, Table 1.01, p. 3, Table 1.02 p. 4, Table 3.01 p. 25; (1999) Vol. 16, Tables 1.01 p. 3 and 3.01 p. 26; (1996), Vol. 13, Tables 1.01 p. 2 and 3.02 p 39; *Housing Finance*, No. 44, November 1999, Table 32, p. 71 (London: Council of Mortgage Lenders), and *Financial Services Authority Building Society Statistics* (2004) http://www.fsa.gov.uk/pages/library/cooperate/annual/ar03_04_bs_statistics.shtml Table 1 Building Societies – Service Activity, July 2004. Also see the Building Societies Association at http://www.bsa.org.uk/

concentration indicators suggest that this may not be so, as illustrated in Box 12.2, which shows that the UK banking sector is not particularly concentrated compared to other developed systems.

12.3.2 The Cruickshank Report

Growing regulatory concerns about excessive concentration, coupled with historically high UK bank profitability, led to the UK government inquiry into *Competition in UK Banking* in 2000.[7] The report (known as the **Cruickshank Report** as it was headed by Don Cruickshank) examined a broad range of issues relating to competitive conditions in the UK banking market; however, the main focus was on three areas – **money transmission services**, services to retail customers and services to small and medium-sized enterprises (SMEs). Overall, the report found that there were important limitations to competition in various key markets and that the established regulatory environment was inappropriate to deal with this.

---

[7] See 'Competition in UK Banking: A Report to the Chancellor of the Exchequer' available at the UK government's Treasury website at: http://www.hm-treasury.gov.uk/documents/financial_services/banking/bankreview/fin_bank_reviewfinal.cfm

Box 12.2 Benchmarking measures of UK banking concentration

This article does not assess whether the UK banking sector is concentrated relative to other industries or banking sectors. Such analysis is complicated by a lack of consistent data and difficulties in comparing economic activity across industries. Two potential benchmarks are:

(a) The Office of Fair Trading's (OFT) merger guidelines
The OFT use the Hirschman–Herfindahl Indexes (HHIs) as an initial indicator in deciding whether to refer a merger between two firms in the same industry to the Competition Commission. OFT (2003) states 'The OFT is likely to regard any market with a post merger HHI in excess of 1800 as highly concentrated, and any market with a post merger HHI in excess of 1000 as concentrated.' On this basis, non-financial private sector bank deposits and loans were concentrated but not highly concentrated in 2003.

(b) Other countries' banking sectors
We are unaware of any recent international study that constructs measures of concentration using 'quasi-consolidated' resident banking data. Using data constructed on a worldwide consolidated basis, Beck, Demirgüç-Kunt and Levine (2003) find the UK

The three largest banks' share of assets owned by each nationality's banks*

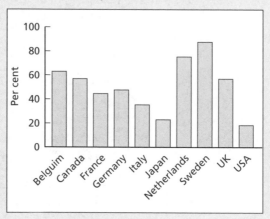

* Average for the period 1989–97.
Source: Beck, Demirgüç-Kunt and Levine (2003).

banking sector is not particularly concentrated relative to other industrialised countries (see Chart).

Source: Logan (2004), 'Banking concentration in the UK', *Financial Stability Review*, June 2004, Box 2, p. 133.

Recommendations were therefore made for a major overhaul of bank regulation in order to improve **competition** and innovation in UK banking.

One area that came in for particular criticism was the market for money transmission services (cheque payment, credit transfers and other payments media) where 'profound competition problems and inefficiencies' were found to exist. The report argued that money transmission services were dominated by a handful of major banks and the current arrangements restricted entry and resulted in high costs to retailers for accepting credit and debit cards as well as excessive charges for cash withdrawals (up to six times their cost). Money transmission services were also found to be 'cumbersome and inflexible' and slow to adapt to the new demands of e-commerce.

In the supply of retail banking services, it was found that competition had increased in the mortgage, personal loan and credit card areas, although the prices charged by new entrants so far had had only a limited impact on established bank pricing. In addition, the dominant role played by the major banks in the current account market was believed to restrict competition in many other product areas. Significant barriers to switching current accounts remained. The report voiced concerns about the inadequate representation and redress for consumers in the event of disputes. It also referred to 'significant information problems', citing the fact that consumers were rarely aware of the terms and conditions of the products they bought.

The market for small and medium-sized enterprise (SME) banking services was found to be much less competitive than the retail sector. Problems associated with switching current accounts, financial product information, representation and redress were found to be acute. The market for SME services was much more concentrated than the retail sector and entry barriers were found to be high (it is noticeable that the building societies that converted to banks have not entered the SMEs market in any significant fashion). Money transmission costs for UK SMEs was also found to be very high on an international basis and access to risk capital for high-growth firms was perceived to be limited.

Taking together the report's findings on retail and SMEs banking services, a broad range of recommendations were made including:

- strengthening the current arrangements for customer redress and representation, including the establishment of a new Financial Services Consumer Council;
- improving customer information by publishing, via the Financial Services Authority (FSA), a broad range of benchmark retail and SMEs services according to price (providing both regional and UK prices); and
- various initiatives to improve the flow of equity finance to high growth SMEs.

Other, more controversial, recommendations included:

- proposing that until UK merger law is reformed, the government should refer all mergers between financial suppliers to the **Competition Commission** if the merging firms have 'material shares of the market';
- calling for a Competition Commission inquiry into banking for SMEs.

An important theme throughout the report was the highly concentrated nature of the UK current account and SME markets as well as the structure of the domestic payments system. All these areas, the report argued, were characterised by high entry barriers as well as limited price and non-price competition. The large market shares held by a handful of banks was put as a major reason for the high profitability of UK banks during the 1990s. Market structure and adverse competitive outcomes were most pressing in the SME market. The Cruickshank Report stated that the competition problems were so significant that a change in market structure might be the only way of achieving an effectively competitive marketplace. It went on to argue that the only mechanism for delivering such a change was action following a complex monopoly reference to the Competition Commission.

Overall, the report argued that there was substantial scope for increased competition as well as the opportunity for competing banks to make adequate returns even in the provision of basic banking services. The recommendations, although unpalatable to the main UK banks at the time, were thought to go a long way towards promoting more effective competition in the UK banking market. However, in reality the report has had little actual practical effect to date.

Meanwhile, the authorities need to balance the need to promote competition against the imperatives of maintaining a safe banking system through prudential regulation. While the Cruickshank Report appears to have had little impact on bank behaviour, there is no doubt that new technologies such as the internet and other types of electronic payments systems create substantial opportunities for promoting competition in UK payments and other areas. While this may boost competition, a note of caution is that the Bank of England has noted that the growth of e-commerce and other internet developments could undermine the current role of commercial **payments systems**.

12.3.3 Competition Commission Report

The UK Competition Commission Report into the *Supply of Banking Services by Clearing Banks to Small and Medium-Sized Enterprises* followed on from the Cruickshank Report and published its findings in 2002. The report recommended a number of measures to apply to all the eight main clearing groups to reduce barriers to entry and expansion in the SME banking area. Primary among these were measures to ensure fast, error-free switching of accounts, which were regarded as crucial to a more competitive market. In addition, it was recommended that measures should be taken to limit bundling of services, improve information and transparency and examine the scope for sharing of branches. The report also concluded that the four largest clearing groups – Barclays, HSBC, Lloyds TSB and Royal Bank of Scotland Group – were charging excessive prices (including interest forgone on non-interest-bearing current accounts) and therefore making excessive profits, in England and Wales, of about £725 million a year over the last three years, with adverse effects on SMEs or their customers. For the most part, the report found no such excessive prices in Scotland or Northern Ireland. The commission recommended that the four largest clearing groups be required to pay interest on current accounts in England and Wales at Bank of England base rate less 2.5 per cent. The four largest clearing groups should be allowed alternatively to offer SMEs accounts that are free of money transmission charges, as applies in the personal sector; or to offer SMEs a choice between the two options.

The banking sector's response to the above recommendations has been to introduce a range of **banking and business banking codes**, which are voluntary codes that set standards of good banking practice for banks and building societies to follow when they are dealing with personal or business customers in the United Kingdom. As voluntary codes, it is argued that they allow competition and market forces to work to encourage higher standards for the benefit of customers. Various measures have been taken to make it much easier for retail and small business customers to switch accounts, and free banking services are now generally available to new customers, although the banks (as far as we are aware) have not adopted the recommendation that market rates be paid on current accounts, and access to payment systems still appears relatively limited. In short, there has been no noticeable improvement in competition as a result of the Competition Commission's report.

12.4 Performance of UK banks

UK banks have been among Europe's best-performing financial firms over the last decade or so. This is because UK banks have benefited from a buoyant domestic economy and have also managed to maintain relatively high interest margins (the difference between interest revenue and interest cost) although these have fallen since 1997. In addition, costs have been reduced and provisioning (the amount of funds set aside to cover loans that are not repaid) has fallen dramatically. Also the lack of foreign competition in the retail banking market has been argued by some as another reason why profitability has been substantial. Taking these factors together, this has resulted in sizable banking sector profits in recent years.

12.4.1 Sources of revenue – net interest margins and non-interest income

Table 12.3 shows the trend in domestic business net interest margins for a handful of UK banks up to 2004. One can see that some of the main banks have been able to sustain margins around the 3 per cent level. While interest income, as a proportion of total income, declined during the second half of the 1980s and the recession years of the early 1990s, it increased from 1993 onwards exceeding 60 per cent between 1996 and 1998, but has fallen gradually up to 2004. Table 12.4 shows a broader measure of interest margins – net interest income as a proportion of total assets – for banking systems overall in the United Kingdom, Europe, the United States and Japan. It can be seen that UK banks have managed to generate higher levels of margins than their counterparts in Europe and Japan, although US bank margins are substantially higher (or at least were up until 2001). This is one of the main factors explaining why US banks have been, on average, the most profitable in the Western world during recent times.

As we have seen, banks increasingly rely on non-interest income as a source of total income. This is shown for UK banks in Figure 12.11. In fact, the trends in interest and non-interest income simply reflect the cyclical characteristics of the

Table 12.3 Net interest margins – domestic business, UK retail banks 1990–2004

Bank	1990	1995	1996	1997	1998	1999	2000	2001	2002	2003	2004
Barclays	3.9	4.2	4.3	4.5	4.4	4.5	4.2	3.8	3.6	3.6	3.5
HBOS	n.a	n.a	n.a	n.a	n.a	n.a	n.a	2.0	1.9	1.8	1.7
HSBC Bank	n.a	n.a	n.a	n.a	2.5	2.7	2.7	2.8	2.3	2.2	2.1
Lloyds TSB	n.a	3.6	3.5	3.7	3.8	4.0	3.6	3.5	3.3	3.1	2.9
Royal Bank of Scotland	3.1	2.4	2.3	2.2	2.3	3.1	3.0	3.2	3.1	3.0	3.0
NatWest	4.5	4.4	4.3	4.4	4.3	4.0	n.a	n.a	n.a	n.a	n.a

Notes:
a) Net interest margins = net interest income as a percentage of average interest earning assets
b) n.a = not available
c) HSBC margins for 2002 and 2004, HBOS 2001 to 2004 and Lloyds TSB for 2004 are for the whole group, including margins on international business.

Source: Adapted from *Banking Business. An Abstract of Banking Statistics* (2005) Vol. 22, Table 3.08, p. 37; and (1999) Vol. 16, Table 3.07 p. 35 (London: British Bankers Association).

Table 12.4 Net interest income/total assets – UK, European, US and Japanese banks 1990–2001

	1990	1991	1992	1993	1994	1995	1996	1997	1998	1999	2000	2001
United Kingdom	2.88	2.91	2.39	2.37	2.30	2.20	2.07	1.99	2.01	1.96	1.66	1.68
Eurozone	1.99	2.02	1.98	1.90	1.89	1.79	1.67	1.52	1.44	1.39	1.34	1.35
European Union	2.07	2.12	2.04	1.97	1.96	1.84	1.73	1.58	1.51	1.45	1.38	1.40
United States	3.06	3.32	3.66	3.64	3.53	3.44	3.46	3.37	3.25	3.26	3.28	3.34
Japan	0.90	1.11	1.30	1.26	1.33	1.44	1.39	1.31	1.37	1.42	1.27	1.37

Notes:
a) European Union countries include: Austria, Belgium, Denmark, Finland, France, Germany, Greece, Ireland, Italy, Luxembourg, Netherlands, Portugal, Spain, Sweden and the United Kingdom. Note that the European Union consisted of these 15 countries up until 1 May 2004 but on this date membership expanded to include Cyprus, Czech Republic, Estonia, Hungary, Latvia, Lithuania, Malta, Poland, Slovakia and Slovenia.
b) Eurozone countries include: Austria, Belgium, Finland, France, Germany, Greece, Ireland, Italy, Luxembourg, Netherlands, Portugal and Spain.

Source: European Commission (2002) *The Monitoring of Structural Changes and Trends in the Internal Market for Financial Services*, Study Contract ETD/2001/B5-3001/A/63, November 2002, Annex Table 84.

Figure 12.11 Income of Major British Banking Groups 1985–2004 (% of gross income)

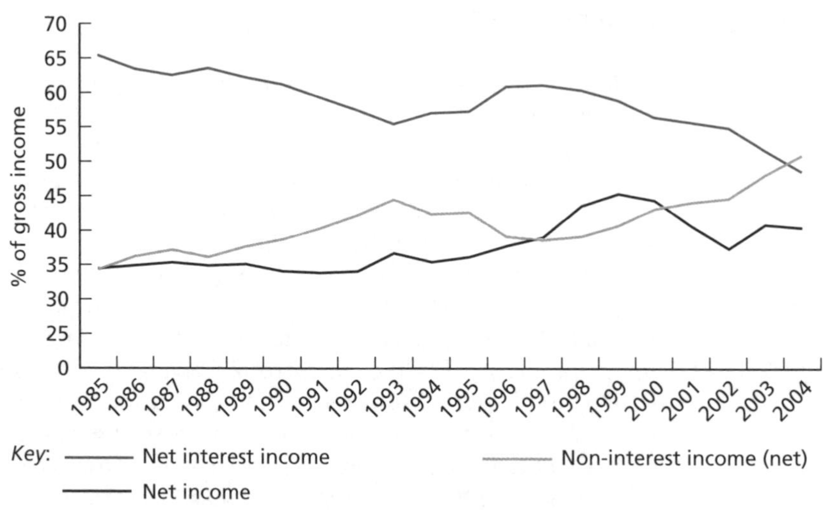

Key: ——— Net interest income   ——— Non-interest income (net)
      ——— Net income

Notes: Figures from 1996 onwards cover the expanded MBBG, including Alliance & Leicester, Halifax and Woolwich. Figures from 1999 include Bradford & Bingley.

Source: Adapted from *Banking Business. An Abstract of Banking Statistics* (2005) Vol. 22, Table 3.09, p. 38: (1999), Vol. 16, Table 3.08 p. 36; and (1996) Vol. 13, Table 3.06, p. 45 (London: British Bankers Association).

domestic economy. When in recession, demand for loan products is depressed so banks (consciously or unconsciously) depend more on non-interest income as a source of income. When the economy grows then demand for loan products increases thus helping to boost interest incomes share of total income.

12.4.2 Costs

On the cost side, the main UK banks have been, on average, successful at reducing their cost–income ratios, from around 65 per cent in 1994 to 54 per cent in 1999. However, these costs increased to around 60 per cent by 2004, presumably because of the expenditures incurred in connection with mergers and acquisitions activity and other restructuring. Staff costs as a proportion of total income have also declined to around 28 per cent of gross income by 2004. In addition, the net costs of provisioning have dramatically fallen since 1992, thus acting as a strong boost to overall profitability, although these have increased slightly from 2000 onwards. Cost trends for the MBBGs are shown in Figure 12.12.

12.4.3 Profitability

So far we have discussed income and cost trends in UK banking and as we all know

Income – Costs = Profits

Before we go on to discuss the profitability of UK banks it is important to understand how bank profits are derived. This is shown in Table 12.5 using the combined figures for the Major British Banking Groups for 2004.

Figure 12.12 Costs of Major British Banking Groups 1985–2004 (% of gross income)

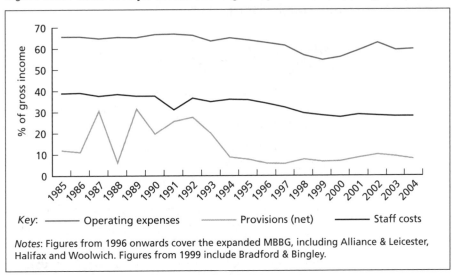

Key: ——— Operating expenses ——— Provisions (net) ——— Staff costs

Notes: Figures from 1996 onwards cover the expanded MBBG, including Alliance & Leicester, Halifax and Woolwich. Figures from 1999 include Bradford & Bingley.

Source: Adapted from *Banking Business. An Abstract of Banking Statistics* (2005) Vol. 22, Table 3.09, p. 38: (1999), Vol. 16, Table 3.08 p. 36; and (1996) Vol. 13, Table 3.06, p. 45, (London: British Bankers Association).

Table 12.5 Calculating UK bank profits

Major British Banking Group (MBBG) 2004 Income Statement	
	£ millions
Interest income	83,961
Interest expense	49,449
Net interest income	34,512
Non-interest income (net)	36,075
Gross income	70,587
Operating expenses	41,919
(of which staff costs)	(19,588)
Net income	28,668
Provisions (net)	5,278
Profit before tax	23,390
Tax	7,025
Profit after tax	16,365
Distributed profit	9,919
Retained profit	6,446

Profitability ratios	
Net income/assets (return-on-assets – ROA)	1.2%
Net income/shareholders funds (return-on-equity – ROE)	26.4%
Profit before tax/assets	1.0%
Profit before tax/gross income	33.1%
Profit before tax/net income	81.6%
Profit before tax/shareholders funds	21.3%
Profit after tax/assets	0.7%
Profit after tax/gross income	23.2%
Profit after tax/net income	57.1%
Profit after tax/shareholders funds	15.4%

Note: The average total assets of MMBG amounted to around £2,243 billion in 2004. Major British Banking Groups (MBBG) in 2004 included the following: Abbey National Group, Alliance & Leicester Group, Barclays Group, Bradford and Bingley plc, The HBOS Group, HSBC Bank Group, Lloyds TSB Group, Northern Rock Group and the Royal Bank of Scotland Group.
Source: Author's calculations and data from various tables in *Banking Business: An Abstract of Banking Statistics* (2005). London: British Bankers Association.

To calculate the profitability of UK banks we have to identify income sources and costs. This is illustrated in Box 12.3.

Box 12.3   Components of bank profits

Interest income includes interest earned on loans; on investments held by the bank that pay interest (such as bonds); interest paid to the bank on interbank deposits they hold at other banks; and other sources of interest income.

Interest expense includes interest paid to depositors; interest paid to holders of bonds that the bank has issued itself to raise debt finance; and other interest costs.

Net interest income = Interest income *minus* Interest expense.

Non-interest income includes fee and commission income (from selling insurance, share dealing, private pensions, processing various payments, sales of assets and all income unrelated to interest earnings).

Gross income = Net interest income + Non-interest income.

Operating expenses includes staff costs and other expenses associated with running branch networks and headquarters. From Table 12.5 one can see that staff costs account for just under 50 per cent of MBBG operating costs in 2004.

Net income = Gross income *minus* Operating expenses.

Provisions include funds set aside by the bank to cover losses on loans that are expected to not be repaid (as well as other types of losses). Provisions are made on a regular basis and are charged against current earnings. The total accumulated stock of provisions is known as loan-loss reserves. This is a cost to the bank and so they are deducted from net income to arrive at bank profits.

Profit before tax = Net income *minus* Provisions.

Profit after tax = Profit before tax *minus* Tax.

Retained profit = Profit after tax *minus* Distributed profit (dividends to shareholders, the owners of the bank).

As already noted, relatively high margins, lower costs and buoyant economic conditions have resulted in an increase in loan demand; this has fed through into a sustained increase in the profitability of UK banks from 1992 to 1999, with a slight downturn thereafter, as shown in Figures 12.13 and 12.14. It is interesting to note the variation in performance among the major banks. The dip in returns generated by Barclays and the former NatWest in 1996 and 1997 was mainly attributable to the poor performance of their investment banking operations. It is also interesting to note the exceptional performance of Lloyds TSB from 1995 onwards and the recent poor performance of Abbey National (that resulted in Spain's Banco Santander Central Hispano making a successful bid for the bank in July 2004). Over the last decade or so, shareholders in UK banks have increasingly benchmarked their performance against that of Lloyds TSB – one reason for NatWest (one of the poorest performers) recently losing its independence after being acquired by Royal Bank of Scotland in February 2000. Shareholders were unsatisfied with the returns that it had been generating compared with some of its major competitors.

Figure 12.13 **Profits of Major British Banking Groups 1985–2004 (% of gross income)**

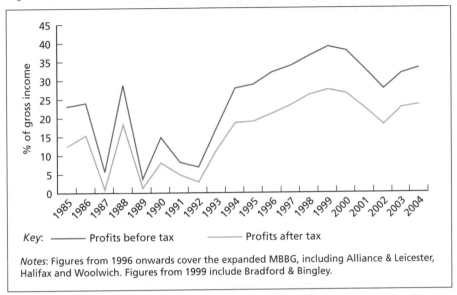

Key: ———— Profits before tax   ———— Profits after tax

Notes: Figures from 1996 onwards cover the expanded MBBG, including Alliance & Leicester, Halifax and Woolwich. Figures from 1999 include Bradford & Bingley.

Source: Adapted from *Banking Business. An Abstract of Banking Statistics* (2005) Vol. 22, Table 3.09, p. 38; (1999), Vol. 16, Table 3.08 p. 36; and (1996) Vol. 13, Table 3.06, p. 45 (London: British Bankers Association).

Figure 12.14 **Pre-tax profits of major UK banks 1985–2004**

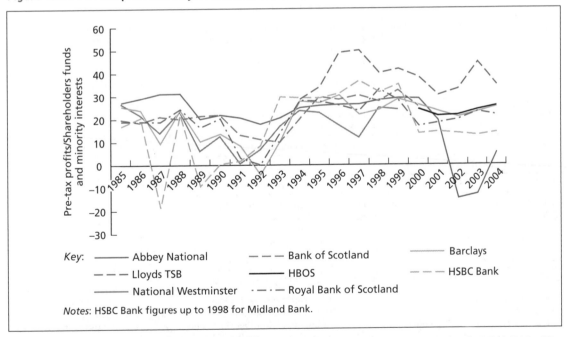

Key: ———— Abbey National   – – – Bank of Scotland   ———— Barclays
– – – Lloyds TSB   ———— HBOS   – – – HSBC Bank
———— National Westminster   – · – · Royal Bank of Scotland

Notes: HSBC Bank figures up to 1998 for Midland Bank.

Source: Adapted from *Banking Business. An Abstract of Banking Statistics* (2005) Vol. 22, Table 3.07, p. 35, (1999), Vol. 16, Table 3.06 p. 33; (1996) Vol. 13, Table 3.04, p. 41 (London: British Bankers Association).

12.5 The UK payment system

As discussed in Chapter 2, a payment system can be defined as any organised arrangement for transferring value between its participants. Some of these transactions involve high-value transfers, typically between financial institutions. However, the highest number of transactions relate to transfers between individuals and/or companies (they include the payment and receipt of wages, salaries and government benefits, direct debits, cheques, debit and credit card payments). In 2003, the value passing through UK payment systems was around £130 trillion, about 120 times UK annual gross domestic product (GDP).[8] The main UK payment systems are: **CHAPS**, CREST, CLS, LCH, Clearnet Ltd, **BACS**, Cheque and Clearing Company, Visa, MasterCard and LINK (see also Section 3.5.1.1 on payment services). Their main features are illustrated in Table 12.6. **APACS (Association for Payment Clearing Services)** is the UK Payments Association, the body responsible for promoting the UK payments industry and maximising the industry's effectiveness.

Table 12.6 UK payment systems

Payment systems	Volume[a]	Value[b]	Payment types
CHAPS[c]	137,252	359,586	• Settlement of financial markets transactions • House purchase • Other time-critical payments • CLS pay-ins and pay-outs arrangements for some other payments
BACS	18,120,354	11,352	• Salary and benefits payments • Bill payments by Direct Debit
C&CC	8,234,419	5,046	• Payments for goods and services by consumers and businesses • Bill payment and small financial transactions (e.g., payments into savings accounts) • Person-to-person payments
VISA[d]	14,909,000	806	• Payments for goods and services by consumers and businesses • Cash
MASTERCARD[d]	13,743,000	685	• Payments for goods and services by consumers and businesses • Cash
LINK	6,126,030	201	• Withdrawal of cash using an ATM not operated by the customer's own bank
Embedded payment arrangements			
CREST[e]	252,652	269,450	• Settlement of gilts, equities and money market instruments
LCH CLEARNET (PPS)[f]	707	1,664	• Payment in respect of cash margin payments • Payments for commodity deliveries • Cash settlements • Default funds contributions
Foreign Exchange Settlements			
CLS[g]	62,000	395,000	• Settlement of foreign exchange trade

[a] Daily averages, 2004.
[b] £ millions.
[c] Sterling and Euro (Sterling equivalent).
[d] Credit cards and debit cards.
[e] Sterling and US dollars and Euro (Sterling equivalent).
[f] Sterling and US dollars, Euro and other currencies (Sterling equivalent)
[g] Trades in which one leg is denominated in Sterling.

Notes: CHAPS (Clearing House Automated Payments System); CLS (Continuous Linked Settlement); C&CC (Cheque and Clearing Company); BACS (Banks Automated Clearing System).

Source: APACS; Bank of England (2005b), *Payment Systems Oversight Report 2004*.

---

[8] Bank of England (2005b) *Payment Systems Oversight Report 2004*.

Table 12.7 **Payments transactions (1993–2003)**

Total transaction volumes in the UK (millions)	1993	1994	1995	1996	1997	1998	1999	2000	2001	2002	2003
Debit card	659	808	1,004	1,270	1,503	1,736	2,062	2,337	2,696	2,994	3,364
Credit and charge card	748	815	908	1,025	1,128	1,224	1,344	1,452	1,562	1,687	1,822
Store card (estimate)	82	100	109	118	128	134	131	125	128	133	130
All plastic card purchases	**1,488**	**1,723**	**2,023**	**2,413**	**2,759**	**3,094**	**3,537**	**3,914**	**4,386**	**4,819**	**5,317**
Plastic card withdrawals at ATMs and counters	1,277	1,372	1,512	1,656	1,809	1,917	2,030	2,090	2,250	2,342	2,457
Direct debits, Standing orders, Direct credits and CHAPS	2,047	2,196	2,402	2,613	2,826	3,056	3,255	3,470	3,705	3,930	4,272
Cheques	3,559	3,430	3,283	3,203	3,083	2,986	2,854	2,699	2,565	2,393	2,251
Total non-cash (plastic card, automated and paper)	**8,371**	**8,721**	**9,220**	**9,885**	**10,477**	**11,053**	**11,672**	**12,185**	**12,907**	**13,483**	**14,297**
Cash payments (estimate)	27,273	26,179	26,270	26,318	25,540	25,309	25,596	27,910	27,684	26,622	25,859
Post Office order book payments and passbook withdrawals	1,144	1,127	1,163	1,114	1,066	1,017	962	880	791	687	690
Total transaction volumes	**36,788**	**36,026**	**36,654**	**37,318**	**37,083**	**37,379**	**38,230**	**40,963**	**41,382**	**407,92**	**40,750**

Source: APACS, Facts and Figures.

The past decade witnessed a rapid growth in the use of cards, both in the form of credit and debit cards, instead of cheques or cash transactions. Table 12.7 illustrates this trend. Cash payments have remained fairly stable whereas the use of cheques has fallen by 36 per cent between 1993 and 2003. UK businesses and consumers have switched from cheques to cards: transactions using plastic cards (credit, debit and store cards) have dramatically increased: from 1,488 million in 1993 to 5,317 million in 2003 (an increase of some 357 per cent). The total of non-cash payment increased by 170 per cent and although cash payments still remain the dominant payment method, their share of total payments has decreased steadily.

Debit cards were introduced in the United Kingdom in 1985, linking transactions directly to the holder bank or building society account and automatically debiting such account. A debit card usually functions also as an ATM and/or cheque guarantee card. By 1994, debit card volumes exceeded credit cards for the first time and more than half of all cash acquired by individuals came from withdrawals at cash machines. By 1998 there were more debit card payments than cheque payments made by personal customers. By 2001, over 6 million adults in Britain accessed their bank accounts on line (1 in 4 internet users); 2002 witnessed the largest annual decline in cheques volumes and the largest ever increase in the number of credit cards issued. By 2005 the majority of UK credit and debit card transactions were being authorised by customers keying in their personal identification number (PIN) rather than signing for the receipt of goods and services.[9]

---

[9] The source for all figures cited is APACS, 'Payment Developments and Innovations Milestones since 1985'. See APACs website, Facts and Figures, http://www.apacs.org.uk

12.6 Changing regulatory environment

The regulatory environment in the UK banking and financial services industry has changed dramatically since the mid-1980s. In general, new legislation has covered three main areas. First, a range of regulatory changes have been sought to reduce demarcation lines between different types of financial service firms (especially between banks and building societies) as well as commercial and investment banking business. Second, the UK has also implemented various pieces of EU legislation into domestic banking law facilitating the introduction of the single banking licence and harmonising prudential regulation for both commercial banks and investment firms. Finally, the most recent legislation laid down in the **Financial Services and Markets Act 2001** put in place the transfer of regulatory responsibility for the whole financial system to a 'super-regulator' – the Financial Services Authority – in the light of the Labour government's decision to make the Bank of England independent for monetary policy purposes. The major regulatory developments as well as other significant regulatory events in the United Kingdom have already been discussed in Chapter 7, Section 7.6 and detailed in Table 7.3.

Changes governing the regulatory treatment of the building society sector have probably had the biggest impact. Ironically, reforms that have been put in place to improve the competitive stance of the mutual sector vis-à-vis commercial banks have led to a systematic decline of the former. This is because most of the larger building societies, as outlined above, embraced **demutualisation** leading to a shift of assets from the mutual to commercial banking sector (see Appendix 12.1). While the mutual sector has declined in relative importance those societies that converted still mainly undertake mortgage business – their balance sheet structures have not changed dramatically. Having said this, however, the 2000 Cruickshank Report noted that the mortgage sector was one of the most competitive segments of the UK banking sector. This it attributed partially to these conversions but more importantly to new insurance company entrants (such as Standard Life Bank) that offered highly competitive mortgage products. The same report also noted that competitive conditions in the UK mortgage market compare favourably with those of North America, France and Germany.

Another area where the change in legislation has had a big impact is in the restructuring of the domestic merchant banking industry. Prior to the 1986 'Big Bang' reforms, investment banking and securities business was dominated by UK-owned banks – mainly partnerships operating in the City. Independent UK firms such as Morgan Grenfell, Kleinwort Benson, SG Warburg, and so on, dominated domestic business. The 'Big Bang' reforms allowed commercial banks to be members of the London Stock Exchange and the legal separation between stockbroking and jobbing firms (those operating on the floor of the exchange) was abandoned. This led to a frenzy of domestic and foreign commercial banks (as well as the main US investment banks) acquiring domestic securities firms. The merger and acquisition frenzy faltered, to a certain extent, after the 1987 stock market crash – although Deutsche Bank acquired Morgan Grenfell in 1989. It commenced again post-UK recession, particularly from 1995 onwards and by 2005 there were hardly any significant independent UK merchant banks. Investment banking and securities business in the United Kingdom is now dominated by the major US 'bulge bracket' firms (Goldman Sachs, Morgan Stanley, Merrill Lynch and Citigroup's Global Corporate and Investment

Banking Group) as well as by various Swiss (Credit Suisse First Boston and UBS) and German banks (Deutsche Bank).

The gradual structural deregulation relating to commercial banking, investment banking, securities business and insurance now means that financial firms have the choice of being universal operators. In the domestic banking market all of the commercial banks and building societies offer a full range of financial services to their customers. Even relatively new operators, such as Egg (the internet banking arm of the insurance company Prudential), offer banking, insurance and various investment services. The decision by the government to create a single financial services regulator (the Financial Services Authority) is another clear reflection of the ongoing universalisation of the UK banking industry.

12.7 Conclusions

The changing features of the UK banking system have mainly been a consequence of the evolving market environment and also a result of various domestic regulatory reforms. UK banks have adapted well to the changing environment and by the start of the twenty-first century were among the best-performing European financial institutions in terms of profitability. Interest margins have remained relatively high throughout the 1990s, which has helped to sustain profitability. For most of the large banks there has been little perceived threat of foreign acquisition because of the UK banks' good performance and subsequent high market valuations (although rumours abounded in the industry in mid-2005 that a large US bank was considering making a bid for a major clearing bank).[10] Profitability has been strongly driven by the retail financial services business and this is where the main banks have strategically focused (especially the retail mortgage market). The system is also becoming more concentrated as a result of more M&A activity as illustrated by Royal Bank of Scotland's acquisition of NatWest in February 2000. The deal was not referred to the competition authorities because the Scottish bank's share of the total UK domestic banking market was modest compared with that of NatWest. This deal, plus the critical Cruickshank report and subsequent Competition Commission Report appears to have ruled out any future merger or acquisition between the top banks, and has forced them to revise/reconsider potential pan-European (or at least part-European) strategies. While there still is potential for a limited number of large domestic bancassurance deals, there have been substantial market rumours about mergers between some of the main UK banks and similar institutions operating in the Eurozone. Some of the major banks are looking further afield and have made modest acquisitions in the United States. Although it has come to UK domestic banks later than in some other European countries, it seems that now the constraints imposed by both the market and regulators may force the major institutions to look overseas, whether in Europe or the United States, if they wish to make major deals. Current forces, however, suggest that irrespective of whether the United Kingdom is 'in' or 'out' of the Eurozone, the main banks are almost certainly going to have to at least consider substantial cross-border Euroland ventures within the not too distant future.

---

[10] These rumours centered around Lloyds TSB and the US-based Wells Fargo Bank.

Key terms

Major British Banking Groups (MBBGs)

Small and medium-sized enterprises (SMEs)

Cruickshank Report

Competition Policy

Competition Commission

Money transmission services

Payment System

Banking and business banking codes

Association for Payment Clearing Services (APACS)

Clearing House Automated Payments System (CHAPS)

Banks Automated Clearing System (BACS)

Financial Services and Markets Act (2001)

Demutualisation

Key reading

'Competition in UK Banking: A Report to the Chancellor of the Exchequer', available at the UK Governments Treasury website at: http://www.hm-treasury. gov.uk/documents/financial_services/banking/bankreview/fin_bank_reviewfinal.cfm

European Central Bank (1999) *The Effects of Technology on EU Banking Systems*, July 1999, http://www.ecb.int/pub/pdf/other/techbnken.pdf.

Logan, A. (2004) 'Banking concentration in the UK', *Financial Stability Review*, June 2004, http://www.bankofengland.co.uk/publications/fsr/2004/themesand issues0406.htm

Revision questions and problems

1 What are the main drivers of UK banks' profitability?

2 What are the implications of increased concentration in the UK banking market?

3 What were the main recommendations of the Cruickshank Report and how did the industry respond?

4 Are we likely to witness M&As among MBBGs in the near future?

5 What are the main features of the UK payment system?

6 Describe how changes in the regulatory structure over the past 10 years (1995–2005) have affected the UK banking industry.

Appendix 12.1 Demutualisation of the UK building society sector

Year	Building society name	Assets size	Nature of conversion or acquisition
1989	Abbey National	£38.9 billion (end 1989)	Converted to plc and bank status in July 1989
1995	Cheltenham & Gloucester	£19.4 billion (end 1994)	Acquired by Lloyds TSB in August 1995
1996	National & Provincial	£14.1 billion (end 1995)	Acquired by Abbey National in August 1996
1997	Alliance & Leicester	£22.3 billion (end 1996)	Converted to plc and bank status in April 1997
1997	Halifax	£102.1 billion (end 1996)	Halifax and Leeds Permanent Building Societies merged in 1995; the new Halifax then converted into plc and bank status in June 1997. Halifax merged with the Bank of Scotland in September 2001 to form HBOS
1997	Woolwich	£29.3 billion (end of 1996)	Converted to a bank in July 1997 and acquired by Barclays in October 2000
1997	Bristol & West	£9.4 billion (end of 1996)	Acquired by the Bank of Ireland in July 1997
1997	Northern Rock	£13.7 billion (end of 1996)	Converted to bank status in October 1997
1999	Birmingham Midshires Building Society	£8.22 billion (end of 1999)	Acquired by Halifax in April 1999. The Halifax merged with the Bank of Scotland in September 2001 to form HBOS
2000	Bradford & Bingley	£24.7 billion (end of 2000)	Converted to bank status in December 2000

Note: The year 1997 was the most significant for building society conversions into banks, when five of the eight largest societies demutualised. These five societies accounted for around 60 per cent of the total assets of the building society sector.

Chapter 13

European banking

Learning objectives

- To understand the main structural features of the European banking market
- To describe the regulatory changes that have affected the European banking sector
- To identify the recent trends in European retail, private and corporate banking
- To understand the characteristics of the European payment system
- To understand the main trends in the recent performance of European banks

13.1 Introduction

European banking markets have experienced marked changes over the last decade or so – the number of banks has fallen substantially as a result of a merger and acquisitions (M&As) wave, and industry concentration has increased. Banks have increasingly focused on generating revenue through non-interest sources of income and there has been widespread diversification into areas such as insurance, pensions, mutual funds and various securities-related areas. Technological developments are re-shaping the way in which banks distribute products and services to their customers and also re-organising back-office functions for the processing of financial transactions and information. The regulatory environment is constantly changing with the European Union progressing with legislation aimed at removing barriers for the creation of a single European financial services marketplace as well as the implementation of the new Basle II capital adequacy rules. Despite all these changes, however, on average the profitability of European banking systems has remained relatively stable since the mid-1990s and costs have declined only modestly. However, there remain substantial differences in the features and performance of banks in different countries despite a general widespread adoption of strategies aimed at boosting stock prices and generating shareholder value for bank owners.

This chapter discusses these features by first examining structural trends in European banking, as well as various regulatory developments. We then look at various developments in retail and corporate/investment banking business and also look at the impact of technology. Finally we provide an overview of the recent performance features of European banks.

13.2 Structural features and the consolidation trend

Up until the late 1980s many European financial systems were traditionally characterised by relatively high levels of controls, where regulatory authorities maintained a protected banking environment that inhibited competition. However, market conditions have undergone extensive changes over recent years. On the demand side, customer preferences have changed substantially, becoming more sophisticated and price conscious. On the supply side (as noted in Chapter 2) the globalisation of financial markets has been accompanied by governmental deregulation, financial innovation and automation. These factors imply an increasingly competitive environment. In addition, progress in technology, especially phone-based and internet banking, has enabled financial firms to extend their activities beyond local or national boundaries and to increase their market share by providing competitive products to wider markets at a lower price. Technological advances have also enabled banks to reorganise their back-office activities, making the processing of financial information faster and more efficient. New suppliers of retail financial services, such as retailers, automobile manufactures, and so on, have entered the market. As such, banks are now faced with strong competition from both banks and non-bank institutions, and this also accentuates competition within the banking and financial services sector overall.

13.2.1 Number of banks

Technological developments, **deregulation** at the EU level and the introduction of the single market for financial services, have all played their part in restructuring the features of European banking markets. This is reflected in the decline in the number of banks – mainly a consequence of increased mergers and acquisitions activity. This, in turn, has tended to increase the level of domestic market concentration where a handful of banks have a substantial share of banking sector assets. As Table 13.1 shows, a fall in the number of banks has been a shared tendency throughout Europe.

Table 13.1 Number of credit institutions in the Euro area (ranked on number of credit institutions (CIs) in 2004)

Country	Number of CIs 1995	Number of CIs 2004	Number of branches 2003	Number of M&As 1995–2004	Of which cross-border M&As (%)
DE	3,785	2,148	47,351	170	17
FR	1,469	897	25,789	157	21.3
AT	1,041	796	4,395	41	29.6
IT	970	787	30,502	275	12.2
NL	648	461	3,671	23	57.7
ES	506	346	39,762	95	31.6
FI	381	363	1,252	16	25.0
PT	233	197	5,440	38	40.0
LU	220	165	269	10	92.9
BE	145	104	4,989	34	30.1
IE	56	80	924	8	62.5
GR	53	62	3,300	34	25.7
Euroarea	9,507	6,406	167,644	901	23.2

Notes:
1) The trends are similar for the 12 countries in the Euro area shown in the table and also for the EU 15 countries (Euroarea plus UK, Sweden and Denmark). For instance, between 1997 and 2003 the number of UK banks declined from 537 to 426, Swedish banks from 237 to 222 and Danish banks from 213 to 203.
2) The estimated number of M&As in the banking sector over the period 1995–2004 may exclude a number of smaller deals that were not reported. M&A data include both minority and majority acquisitions, cross-border M&As cover both acquirers from the Euro area and third countries.

Source: Adapted from the *ECB Monthly Bulletin* (2005b) May, p. 80, Table 1.

Another indicator of the changing features of the banking sector relates to the distribution of bank branches. Table 13.2 illustrates that the number of bank branches has generally fallen since 1997.

Table 13.2 shows that in the majority of countries branch numbers have declined since 1997 although they have increased in Greece, Spain, France, Italy and Portugal. In addition, branch number per 100,000 inhabitants has also fallen, apart from the aforementioned countries. Throughout the European Union there were, on average, nearly 50 branches per 100,000 inhabitants in 2003 with Scandinavian countries, the Netherlands and the United Kingdom having the lowest branch density at around 23 branches per 100,000 inhabitants. Spanish customers have greater access to branches where there are 97 for every 100,000 of

Table 13.2 **Number of branches**

Country	1997	1998	1999	2000	2001	2002	2003
BE	7,358	7,129	6,982	6,616	6,168	5,550	4,989
DK	2,283	2,291	2,294	2,365	2,376	2,128	2,118
DE	63,186	59,929	58,546	56,936	53,931	50,867	47,351
GR	2,510	2,779	2,850	3,004	3,134	3,263	3,300
ES	38,039	39,039	39,376	39,311	39,024	39,021	39,762
FR	25,464	25,428	25,501	25,657	26,049	26,162	25,789
IE	942	1,026	977	880	970	926	924
IT	25,601	26,748	27,134	28,177	29,270	29,926	30,502
LU	318	324	345	335	274	271	269
NL	6,800	6,787	6,258	5,983	5,207	4,610	3,671
AT	4,691	4,587	4,589	4,570	4,561	4,466	4,395
PT	4,746	4,947	5,401	5,662	5,534	5,390	5,440
FI	1,289	1,254	1,193	1,202	1,257	1,267	1,252
SE	2,521	2,197	2,140	2,059	2,040	2,040	2,061
UK	16,344	15,854	15,387	14,756	14,554	14,392	14,186
MU12*	180,944	179,977	179,152	178,333	175,379	171,719	167,644
EU15	202,092	200,319	198,973	197,513	194,349	190,279	186,009

* Monetary Union.

Source: ECB (2004c) *Report on EU Banking Structure*, November 2004, Annex 1, Table 1 p. 33.

population – this high level of branch density reflects the strong savings banks sector with its substantial networks in local and regional markets.

13.2.2 Employment in the banking sector

Another factor that may be suggestive of the relative size of the banking sector is the amount of employment in the banking industry as a percentage of total employment, as shown in Figure 13.1. Here, employment in the European banking sector can be seen to be substantially larger than in the United States or Japan. Having said this, however, it should be noted that the number of employees in the banking sector has fallen slightly in recent years – EU banking sector employment stood at 2.82 million in 1999 and fell to 2.77 million by 2003 although in France, the United Kingdom and Ireland modest increases in banking sector employment were recorded over the same period.

13.2.3 M&As activity and the consolidation trend

As already mentioned, a key feature of European banking systems in recent years has been the consolidation trend that has led to a small number of banks having dominant positions in various banking systems. Overall, increases in competition appear to have forced concentration in European banking during the 1990s. Deregulation and consolidation trends within the European banking sector appear to have paralleled earlier developments in the United States. For instance, the consolidation trend in the United States resulted in the number of banking firms

Figure 13.1 Employment in banking as a percentage of total employment (2004)

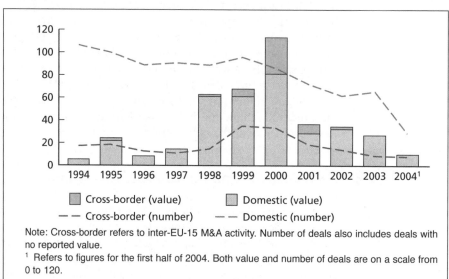

Source: Authors' own estimates.

falling from 11,500 in 1992 to just over 9,200 by 1997 (the number of banks in the United States had fallen to just under 8,000 by 2004). The US experience is illuminating because of the arguably strong parallel between financial service deregulation in Europe and in the United States. Indeed, particularly striking is the common experience with geographical restrictions, namely interstate restrictions in the case of the United States which began to fall in the early 1980s, and the cross-border deregulation brought about by the European Single Market in 1992 and the introduction of the Euro in 1999. Consequently, as shown in Figure 13.2, there has been an increase in the number of M&As of financial institutions in the European Union. The value of both domestic and cross-border M&As increased substantially between 1998 and 2000 but declined thereafter. In addition, while the number of domestic deals has gradually declined, cross-border deals increased in the latter part of the 1990s. In terms of number and value, Figure 13.2 clearly shows that domestic deals dominate, accounting for more than 70 per cent of total M&A activities in the EU banking sector.

Figure 13.2 M&As in European banking 1994–2004 (value in billion Euro and number of deals)

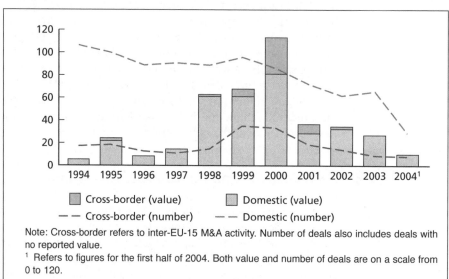

Source: ECB (2004c) *Report on EU Banking Structure*, November 2004, Chart 2 p 8.

The preference for **national consolidation** is that it offers clearer opportunities for reducing costs and fewer complications in terms of handling the merger due to a normally more homogeneous corporate culture. Besides, firms try first to establish a stronger national presence so that they could be large enough to compete in a likely cross-country consolidation phase. There are signs, however, that a greater emphasis may be placed on **cross-border mergers** in the future as domestic markets become congested and if competition authorities do not allow further mergers between major players. As we noted in Chapter 12, in the United Kingdom, for instance, the Competition Commission has made it clear that it would discourage any mergers between the top four banks (HSBC, Barclays, Lloyds TSB and Royal Bank of Scotland) due to their dominance in certain sectors – namely lending to small businesses and retail banking in general. This means that if these banks wish to do a major deal they have to look outside the UK market. In addition, the acquisition of Abbey National by the Spanish bank Banco Santander Central Hispano in November 2004 has also focused increasing attention on the possibility of large cross-border deals (see Box 13.1).

Box 13.1   Hopes of mergers revive on continent   FT

Europe's banks have just enjoyed one of their most profitable periods for some years, buoyed by higher levels of consumer borrowing and low bad debt provisions. But as the European banks have seen return on equity improve to 14 per cent from 11 per cent in 2002, talk has resumed about cross-border consolidation following Spanish bank Santander Central Hispano's £8.4bn bid for Abbey National, the UK bank.

'Thanks to the stabilisation in the operating environment, as concerns regarding the financial position of troubled institutions are alleviated, banks are more likely to consider possible transformational mergers,' says Bernard de Longevialle, analyst at Standard & Poor's rating agency.

The reason why cross-border talk has resurfaced this year amongst the European banks is that a super-league of mostly US-based global banks is forming. Some European banks are starting to look small by comparison with the likes of Bank of America which has a market capitalisation of £100bn.

This year's $58bn takeover of Bank One by JP Morgan Chase and Bank of America's $47bn takeover last year of FleetBoston Financial have created giants with vastly greater capital bases and resources than their European competitors. Moreover, some US giants are getting close to the limit of the market share in deposits they are allowed to acquire under US rules and are starting to cast their eyes across the Atlantic towards possible European acquisitions. The Santander offer for Abbey is being watched closely to see whether it could provide a blueprint for further cross-border deals.

Last month Gerrit Zalm, the Dutch finance minister whose country holds the rotating presidency of the European Union, invited three top bankers from ABN-Amro, BNP Paribas and Royal Bank of Scotland to brief him and the 24 other EU finance ministers on what is holding back cross-border retail banking mergers.

'Driving it all is fear of the US and mega US deals,' says Gerry Rawcliffe, managing director of financial institutions at Fitch Ratings. 'But I don't think some of the cross border consolidation will happen overnight in Italy and France and Germany.' John Varley, Barclays' chief executive, said the US mega-mergers had acted as a 'wake-up call to bank boards all round the world'. Sir Fred Goodwin, chief executive of Royal Bank of Scotland, now believes cross-border banking deals are beginning to look a little more likely in Europe. 'We were the first to say we didn't see any deals happening last time when there was fever around cross-border consolidation three or four years ago...(but) the climate is changing,' he said in August. 'Something has changed in the last six months.'

Ironically, however, many bankers see the takeover of the UK's Abbey National as one of a kind, rather than as part of a trend. 'We view Abbey National as a pretty unique situation', says Simon Samuels, a Citigroup analyst. 'It had a troubled past and, thanks to its size, is viewed as reasonably protected from (domestic) buyers.'

The UK is also probably the European market most tolerant of foreign bidders.

Although cross-border consolidation may happen, analysts point out that key barriers – such as different

▶

taxation and regulatory regimes – are still in place. Europe remains a highly atomised market for financial services, and different taxation and regulatory regimes, to say nothing of cultural differences, have helped create very distinct markets in each country.

Source: Financial Times (2004), 'European Banking Survey 2004', 8 October, by Jane Croft.

The reasons for banks to merge as well as the potential benefits from mergers are not clear from the literature.[1] Focusing only on the Euroarea, empirical studies tend to find that the main factors of competitive advantage are not economies of scale but rather improvements in X-efficiencies.[2] Yet, it is surprising that in reality mergers and acquisitions, on average, do not appear to offer improvements in either efficiency measures or better stock market returns.[3]

13.2.4 Banking sector concentration

The reduction in the number of banks, due to the increased number of mergers and acquisitions, has led to an increase in concentration across European banking markets in recent years. In fact, when we compare the percentage of the banking and credit sector controlled by the five largest banks, measured in terms of total assets, we observe an increase in this figure for most countries. Table 13.3 shows that EU banking markets have experienced increasing market concentration. Interestingly, activity among Europe's largest banks has accelerated recently, so that more than half of the 30 largest European banks are the result of recent mergers. The degree of concentration is particularly striking in the smaller Euroarea countries such as in Belgium, the Netherlands and Finland where a small number of banks dominate national markets.

13.2.5 Diversification

An interesting feature of the recent consolidation trend is that it was not until between 1998 and 2000 that very large deals were done between banks and also between banks and insurance companies. As was explained in Section 3.2.1, the aim of 'bancassurance' deals was to provide diversification benefits and scope economies in the provision of retail financial services. The diversification benefits are presumed to arise from the different earnings cycles of banking and insurance business whereas scope economies relate to the lower costs associated with selling

---

[1] See Dermine (2000) for a comprehensive survey of the literature.

[2] X-efficiencies are efficiencies not related either to size (scale economies) or to product mix (scope economies). They relate to the difference in best practice between banks of similar size and product mix. For example, Bank A may be the same size and have the same product mix as Bank B, but Bank A has the lowest costs for similar types of banks whereas Bank B has high costs. Bank B would be regarded as X-inefficient compared to the best practice Bank A. There is a vast number of studies evaluating the efficiency of European banking. Among others see Casu and Molyneux (2003), Girardone *et al.* (2004), Casu *et al.* (2004) and Altunbas *et al.* (2001).

[3] Although according to Cybo-Ottone and Murgia (2000), abnormal returns can be expected to be associated with the announcement of domestic bank deals.

Table 13.3 **Five-firm concentration ratio as percentage of total banking sector assets**

Country	1997	1998	1999	2000	2001	2002	2003
BE	54	63	76	75	78	82	83
DK	70	71	71	60	68	68	67
DE	17	19	19	20	20	20	22
GR	56	63	67	65	67	67	67
ES	32	35	41	46	45	44	44
FR	40	41	43	47	47	45	47
IE	41	40	41	41	43	46	44
IT	25	25	25	23	29	31	27
LU	23	25	26	26	28	30	32
NL	79	82	82	81	83	83	84
AT	44	42	41	43	45	46	44
PT	46	45	44	59	60	60	63
FI	88	86	86	87	80	79	81
SE	58	56	56	57	55	56	54
UK	24	25	28	28	29	30	33
MU12*	45	47	49	51	52	53	53
EU15	46	48	50	51	52	52	53

* Monetary Union.

Source: ECB (2004c) *Report on EU Banking Structure*, November 2004, Annex 1, Table 6, p. 35.

joint products. Banks can sell insurance products through their established branch networks whereas insurance firms can cross-sell banking services to their policy-holders. Nowadays, virtually all major European banks are part of larger financial groups and conglomerates comprising banking, insurance, pensions, asset management and investment banking operations. Diversification across the full spectrum of financial services enables banks to offer an extensive range of services to both retail and corporate clients in order to meet all their financial service needs. It is interesting to note that between 1999 and 2001 around 70 per cent of all M&A activity in the Euroarea involved domestic banks and insurance firms. Over this period most cross-border financial sector deals were initiated by insurance companies that sought to acquire banks to distribute their products. It has been suggested that the motive for cross-border bancassurance deals is driven more by product distribution factors than the geographical diversification of revenue streams.

13.3 Deregulation and the regulatory environment

13.3.1 Single European market for financial services

To assist banks in confronting challenges posed by the ever-changing economic environment, financial authorities throughout Europe have become more aware of the importance of financial deregulation to promote competition in the market, the aim being to increase concurrently both the efficiency and soundness of banking systems. In this respect EU legislation creating a **single market** and the introduction of **Economic and Monetary Union (EMU)** in 1999 (see Box 13.2 for more details) have further liberalised financial market activity.

Box 13.2 The creation of a single market for financial services in the European Union

Until the 1980s the European financial and banking sectors were mainly domestically oriented. National governments invariably acted as protectors of their banks from foreign influences and sometimes were themselves owners of major banks. Interest rate restrictions and capital controls were common, and branching restrictions existed in some countries. The objective of harmonisation of laws and practices of the Member States reflected wider changes in the domains of economic policy, internationalisation, technological advances and globalisation. The integration process embodied extensive financial liberalisation and was aimed at creating a single market for financial services.

In a recent report the Select Committee on the European Union (45th Report, 2003) clarifies the meaning of a single market in financial services for providers and consumers:

A single market in financial services means that a financial services provider authorised to provide financial services in one Member State is able to offer the same services throughout the EU competing on an equal basis within a regulatory framework that is consistent across the Union. On the other side, the consumer would have access to a wider range of more competitively priced products and would be able to shop with confidence and safety in the market place.

A milestone in the harmonisation of EU banking laws was the 1989 **Second Banking Co-ordination Directive**, which established EU-wide recognition of single banking 'passports' issued in any Member State as well as the principle of home-country supervision with minimum standards (including capital) at EU level. In addition the directive allowed banks to operate as *universal banks*: that is to engage directly in other financial activities, such as financial instruments, factoring, leasing and merchant banking. A number of other directives were enacted in an attempt to harmonise the details (e.g., setting minimum standards for deposit guarantee schemes). The single market for financial services implied also liberalisation of non-bank financial intermediaries.

Insurance companies and investment firms were granted a **single EU 'passport'** with mutual recognition as a result of directives enacted in the early 1990s. Mutual recognition is a system that allows licensed banks to set up branches across states while being subject to each state's rules and regulations.

A major barrier to the formation of a single European market for financial services was that countries still had their own national currencies and monetary policy. As part of the EU's on-going single market programme, the introduction of a single currency was viewed as a central element in the harmonisation process. A further step towards a single market in financial services was finally taken on 1 January 1999, with the launch of the third stage of the EMU. This was achieved in three stages that were detailed in the report of the committee chaired by the then President of the European Commission, Jacques Delors.

- Stage 1 of EMU began on 1 July 1990. Member States had to abolish all remaining capital controls. It required also a higher co-operation among national central banks and underlined the need for a new Treaty to permit the realisation of an economic union ('Treaty on European Union', agreed December 1991 and signed in Maastricht on 7 February 1992).
- Stage 2 of EMU began on 1 January 1994, a few months after the coming into force of the Maastricht Treaty. Member States made significant progress towards economic policy convergence. As a precursor to the European Central Bank (ECB), the EMI (European Monetary Institute) was created. Its task was to strengthen co-operation between the national central banks and to carry out the necessary preparations for the introduction of the single currency.
- Stage 3 of EMU began on 1 January 1999. Exchange rates between national currencies were fixed and a European Central Bank created. The transition to the third stage of the monetary union was made on the basis of a series of 'convergence criteria' set out in the Maastricht Treaty

▶

on European Union, the objective of which was to establish an economic environment of sustainable low inflation in all the member countries.

As noted in Chapter 6, the Euro replaced national currencies by 1 July 2002. The 11 Euroland countries originally participating in EMU are the following: Austria, Belgium, Finland, France, Germany, Ireland, Italy, Luxembourg, Netherlands, Spain and Portugal. In July 2000 the conversion rates between the Euro and the Greek drachma were set as Greece fulfilled the conditions for joining the EMU. Denmark and the UK negotiated an 'opt-out' Protocol to the EU Treaty, granting them the option of joining the Euro area or not. Sweden initially did not meet the necessary conditions for entry and in September 2003 rejected the Euro in a national referendum. The irrevocably fixed conversion rates between the Euro and the currencies of the 12 Member States adopting the Euro are shown below (OJ L 359, Vol. 41, 31/12/1998 and OJ L 167, 07/07/2000):

Austria	13.7603 ATS
Belgium	40.3399 BEF
Finland	5.94573 FIM
France	6.55957 FRF
Germany	1.95583 DEM
Greece	340.750 GRD
Ireland	0.787564 IEP
Italy	1936.27 ITL
Luxembourg	40.3399 LUF
Netherlands	2.20371 NLG
Portugal	200.482 PTE
Spain	166.386 ESP

A major aim of EU legislation has been to reduce the barriers to cross-border trade in the banking and financial services area with the ultimate aim of creating a single market in financial services. The liberalisation of structural obstacles has been accompanied by financial deregulation through the reduction of direct government control. At the same time it has been associated with upgrades of prudential regulations as witnessed by the revision of Basle II rules. Table 13.4 shows the main regulatory measures that have had (and will have) an impact on the European banking sector.

13.3.2 Financial Services Action Plan

The launch of the **Financial Services Action Plan** in 1999 provides a good example of EU policy regarding the banking and financial sectors – the ultimate aim of the FSAP was to promote a more competitive and dynamic financial services industry with better regulation and this would be expected to feed through into enhanced economic growth. Consumers of financial products should obtain lower prices, and producers of such services will benefit from lower costs. The original document put forward indicative priorities and a timetable for specific measures to achieve three strategic objectives: 1) establishing a single market in wholesale financial services; 2) making retail markets open and secure; and 3) strengthening the rules on prudential supervision. A range of other regulatory actions focus on establishing more uniform fiscal treatment of financial products and business in order to 'obtain wider conditions for an optimal single financial market'. By the start of 2005, 38 out of the original 42 measures outlined in the FSAP had been adopted and were being implemented into EU law. (See Appendix 13.1 for an indication of the timing of the introduction of some of the main measures of the FSAP.)

The FSAP has injected new urgency and momentum into the task of building a single financial market and its success is considered crucial in the integration process. Recent research [Heinemann and Jopp (2002) and London Economics (2002)] suggested that substantial potential benefits in terms of reduction of real

Table 13.4 Regulatory measures affecting the EU banking and financial sectors

Year	Regulation
1977	**First Banking Directive** – adoption of regulations, norms and procedures, which removed obstacles to the provision of services across the borders of member states and to the establishment of branches. It also harmonised the rules and conditions for issuing a licence to operate as a bank and defined the authorities that supervise banks and branches of foreign banks, as well as the procedures for co-operation among these authorities.
1988	**Basle Capital Adequacy Regulation** – established minimum capital adequacy requirements for banks – the so-called 8 per cent ratio. Established definitions of capital including Tier 1 (equity) and Tier 2 (near-equity) capital. Devised risk-weightings based on credit risk for bank business.
1988	**Deregulation of capital movements in the European Monetary System (EMS)** – enabled the free flow of capital cross-border within the EU.
1989	**Second Banking Directive** – established the rules for a single banking licence within the EU and introduced the principles of home-country control (home regulators have ultimate supervisory authority for the foreign activity of their banks) and mutual recognition (EU bank regulators recognise that their rules and regulations are equivalent). The Second Banking Directive was passed in conjunction with the Own Funds and Solvency Directives that effectively introduced capital adequacy requirements similar to those proposed by Basle into EU law.
1993	**Investment Services Directive** – set the legislative framework for investment firms and securities markets in the European Union, providing for a single passport for investment services.
1999	**Financial Services Action Plan (FSAP)** aimed at developing a legislative framework for developing the Single Market in financial services. Between its endorsement by the European Council in Lisbon in March 2000 and the end of April 2004, 38 out of the 42 FSAP measures were adopted in the EU.
2000	**Directive on e-money** was conceived and adopted at the height of the e-commerce boom, and was intended to facilitate access by non-credit institutions to the business of e-money issuance. Dealt with harmonising rules and standards relating to such things as payments by mobile telephone, payments using transport cards, as well as Basle payment facilities.
2001	**Directive on the Re-organisation and Winding-Up of Credit Institutions** – created rules to ensure that reorganisation measures or winding-up proceedings adopted by the home state of an EU credit institution are recognised and implemented throughout the Community.
2001	**Regulation on the European Company Statute** established a legal framework for a new form of company, the European Company or 'Societas Europaea (SE)', and consisted of an EU regulation (setting out the core company law framework and which has direct effect throughout the Community) and an accompanying EU Directive dealing with employee involvement in SEs. Aimed to establish standard rules for company formation in the EU.
2004	**New EU Takeover Directive** – established a common framework for cross-border takeover bids.
2006 to 2008	**Basle II – new solvency (capital adequacy) framework** – to update the original international bank capital accord (Basle I), which has been in effect since 1988. The new rules aim to improve the consistency of capital regulations internationally, make regulatory capital more risk sensitive, and promote enhanced risk-management practices among large, internationally active banking organisations.

Source: ECB *Monthly Bulletin* (2005b) May, p. 82, Table 2 and authors' own updates.

cost of capital (see Section 8.4.3) and increase in economic growth could be achieved from the full implementation of a single financial services market. Further, as illustrated in Section 7.7, a new challenge will arise with the implementation of the so-called Lamfalussy procedure, which aims to simplify and speed up the complex and lengthy EU legislative process (see Box 7.2 for details).

13.3.3 Obstacles to the creation of a single European financial market

While the creation of a single financial market is an admirable aim, it has long been recognised that this may be difficult to achieve for certain financial products – especially those that are essentially national in nature. Since the earliest assessments of conditions in European financial services there has been the recognition that retail financial services markets are segmented by national boundaries.

Table 13.5 shows an outline of the integration obstacles classified by demand and supply side factors. In general, most seem to be a result of natural or policy-induced elements. Such obstacles to further integration are apparent in a wide range of areas; some of these barriers are natural and they can only be partially influenced by policymakers, others require further regulation (e.g., new capital adequacy rules).

Moreover, various studies have identified that there remain substantial price differences of retail financial services across the EU. ECB (2004c) notes that there has been some convergence in these prices over recent years (due to the convergence of interest rates as a result of EMU) but big differences still remain. These price differences reflect a broad array of factors, not least the different institutional, legal and risk features in the various national markets. They also reflect varying degrees of competition and the lack of cross-border trade in retail products. Cross-border trade in retail financial services is marginal for unsecured loans, deposit and savings accounts, credit cards, pensions and insurance (although there is a modest amount of non-life business and retail mutual fund activity). All these factors point to a market that is far from integrated.

Table 13.5 Obstacles to full integration of EU financial retail markets

	Natural	Policy-induced
Demand side	• Language, culture • Consumer trust in national suppliers • Distance and the desire for personal contacts	• Discriminatory tax treatment of foreign services/products • Existence of national currencies (e.g., UK) • Insufficient knowledge about cross-border redress procedures
Supply side	• Information costs caused by natural factors (e.g., cultural differences) • Bias for home products in established distribution channels • Smaller national EU market commercially not attractive	• Information and adjustment costs derived rom national differences in regulation (e.g., consumer protection) • Obstacles to cross-border information flow (e.g., limited access to foreign credit registers) • Competitive privileges of domestic suppliers • Shortcomings of Internal Market rules (e.g., through slow EU legislative adjustments to new developments) • Particular costs of cross-border operations (e.g., money transfers)

Source: Adapted from Heinemann and Jopp (2002).

Regulations governing the retail financial services sector are also country-specific. It still remains problematic to undertake cross-border activity without (physical) establishment. Differences in tax treatments, consumer protection legislation, marketing rules, definition of products, investor protection, and so on, substantially hinder the cross-border provision of many retail banking and other financial services. Banks that try to sell their retail services cross-border, therefore, are likely to have a substantial competitive disadvantage. These barriers may be less onerous when banks operate in areas that have a more international dimension such as investment and international banking, although it is noticeable that even the world's largest investment banks typically have extensive physical market presence in many countries, suggesting that cross-border provision of services without establishment is also not the preferred strategy, even in wholesale business. In general, domestic regulations as well as institutional factors, culture, strength of banking relationships, the need for proximity in certain services, and so on, dictate that banks must have a physical presence in the country before they can access retail markets.

Overall, limited integration in the retail financial services in the European Union can be put down to:

- the nature of the retail banking/financial services relationship;
- limited cross-border consolidation (due to economic/business factors mainly);
- very limited cross-border provision without establishment, due to business reasons as well as obstacles such as double taxation or discriminatory taxation of financial products when sold across frontiers, consumer protection laws, data transfer issues, contract law differences, legal definitions of collateral for retail mortgages, definition of customers, difficulties in implementing 'know your customer rules', different ways of calculating prices (such as annual percentage rates or APRs) and so on.

Despite these obstacles to creating a single market in retail financial services, this area of banking business remains a key feature of many bank's operations. The following section highlights some contemporary developments in retail financial services and payments areas.

13.4 Developments in retail financial services

As in other banking markets, the retail financial services industry has become an increasingly important segment of European banking business. The offer of a wide array of retail products and services is now the norm for banks operating throughout Europe and all banks provide the usual deposits, consumer loans and credit card services. European banks now rival their US counterparts in the implementation of advanced technology for retail banking business, and automated teller machines (ATMs) and electronic funds transfer at the point of sale (EFTPOS) networks are commonplace. Many provide advanced phone- and internet-based banking services. Some of the larger banks offer sophisticated private banking and asset management services to their wealthier clients. Retail insurance and pension products are also the 'norm' in many systems.

The success of European banks' retail business depends strongly on how the banks adapt to provide products and services that meet the demands of a rapidly growing and relatively elderly population (hence the growing focus on private banking and other asset management business). It is also being influenced by the way in which banks adapt to new technology. Advances in technology will continue to influence the ways in which financial service firms do their business. Typically, technological advances contribute to reducing costs associated with the management of information (collection, storage, processing and transmission), mainly by substituting paper-based and labour-intensive activity through automation. They also change the ways in which customers have access to banks' services and products, mainly through 'new' distribution channels such as the internet, phone-based and other remote channels. There is strong evidence that a 'clicks-and-mortar' approach maximises the ability of financial institutions to capture a greater proportion of a customer's overall financial assets. This is based on the view that having a substantial physical presence strengthens brand image and provides customers with greater product confidence. In addition, extra service, advice and sales elements that come with the integrated approach encourage customers to place more of their financial services with one provider. There is also evidence that various products, such as consumer loans, mortgage products and life insurance, lend themselves more readily to different distribution channels, so by providing a multi-channel platform customers can be offered a more tailored and cost-efficient service dependent on their needs.

Just as many European banks are developing their fledgling internet activities; however, a wave of new technologies based on broadband telecommunications networks is set to transform the industry. In general, broadband networks allow for much more data to be transmitted at greater speeds – put simply it means that internet access will become much quicker allowing users to take advantage of new types of content ranging from sophisticated web pages to real-time interactivity. Three types of devices – the interactive television, the PC and the mobile handset – are able to receive broadband services that could revolutionise distribution channels. Broadband interactive television in particular could provide European banks with access to a much bigger customer base, since far more customers or potential customers own a television than a PC. Interactive television could make it attractive for banks to cater to mass segments that have proved difficult to serve profitably in the past.

In addition to interactive television, mobile financial services provided via cellular phones will also become commonplace with the evolution of broadband technology. Such services are already popular in Hong Kong and Japan where mobile balance checking, funds transfers and share trading are widely available. As identified by the EU legislation on e-money, financial firms are showing significant interest in establishing a mobile financial service presence. Some banks already provide banking and investment services via the mobile phone. For European banks the attractions of putting services on mobiles relates to the addition of an alternative distribution channel and they may also be able to earn fees from share-trading and various banking transactions. These gains, however, need to be set against the cost of developing such services.

As with the internet revolution, banks are re-appraising their technology strategies, given developments expected as a result of the introduction of broadband technology. The forces unleashed by the internet and attendant technologies are likely to be further magnified by the broadband revolution, providing great benefits to customers and major challenges to the providers of financial services. In addition to customer-facing technology, banks are also considering opportunities that allow them to reorganise their back-office.

All these forces point to an increasingly competitive European retail banking marketplace. Competition will be based on both price and product differentiation features. The focus will be on offering a wider array of financial services to an increasingly mature asset-rich (maybe pension-poor) client base.

 ## 13.5 Private banking

Another area gaining significant attention by commercial banks globally and in Europe is private banking – offering banking and investment services to high net worth individuals. The **global private banking business** is worth around $20 trillion, of which one-third is held **offshore**. Offshore assets under management have grown around 6 per cent annually since the mid-1990s and the trend is likely to continue at this rate to 2010. Demand for private banking services is very much driven by growing prosperity as illustrated by higher GDP per capita and income levels. For European countries, the demand for such services is likely to be strongly linked to inter-generational wealth transfers and pension/retirement provisions. While private banking services in various forms have long been present in most European banking markets there are prospects for opportunities in many systems as the market remains fragmented and un-concentrated. Figure 13.3 provides a snapshot of the size of the global private banking business.

Over the last few years American and European banks have rushed to develop their private banking and wealth management operations, particularly targeting the so-called mass affluent market. Typically, mass affluent clients are defined as individuals with $50,000 to $500,000 of funds to invest, whereas traditional private clients are those with more than $500,000 to invest. Typically, the very wealthy in Europe already deal with private bankers offshore in Switzerland, London and New York and this market is well established. However, banks are viewing private clients below the super-rich level as a group to target.

Figure 13.3 **Global private banking market size (US $ trillion)**

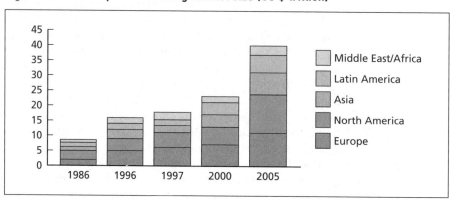

Source: Authors' own estimates.

Commercial banks are particularly attracted to private banking business due to the growth prospects and low regulatory capital requirements (low risk) related to managing third-party assets. The market is considered to be relatively large and profitable and the industry fragmented. The hallmarks of a successful private banking operation are discretion, security and confidentiality. Clients demand decent relative returns from their investments and they tend to be financially sophisticated. To meet this demand banks have to offer a multi-product capability offering a range of traditional banking services as well as a range of securities and funds services, cash management products, derivatives, mortgages and credit products, and alternative investments, to name but a few. While many banks are small compared with the largest private banks (such as the major Swiss banks UBS and Credit Suisse), they can at least provide services either in-house or obtain best-practice products by forming strategic alliances with partners (see Box 13.3).

Box 13.3 Private banking: top bankers are back on the trail of the super-rich

Once again, the world's largest banks are keen on private banking. For decades, the business of managing money for the world's rich was seen as a niche business best left to secretive institutions in Switzerland and Luxembourg.

Attitudes changed during the 1990s, when large financial institutions were seduced by the prospect of luring millions of newly wealthy investors. But when paper riches shrivelled in the bear market, most of the new ventures were scaled back.

Now the world's investment banks are, once again, showing an interest in private banking. UBS, the investment bank which has probably most successfully aligned its brand with managing money for the world's super-rich, is on an acquisition trail, snapping up smaller operators around Europe. However, others are pursuing similar strategies. Late last year Credit Suisse paid its Zurich-based rival the ultimate compliment when it announced plans to integrate more closely its investment bank, Credit Suisse First Boston, with its private banking operations.

Several trends are fuelling the vogue. To begin with, executives at UBS and elsewhere have simply spotted a growth opportunity: private banking is still a relatively fragmented business where scale can bring improved returns.

The largest players can afford to invest more in information technology and other services. As clients demand access to ever more sophisticated financial products, the private banks with the largest pools of capital can also negotiate preferred access to alternative investments, such as private equity and hedge funds.

What is more, as regulators and tax authorities crack down on offshore financial centres, much of this activity is taking place in onshore accounts. The promise of discretion and absolute secrecy – the traditional selling point for the smaller Swiss banks – no longer has the same appeal.

These factors mean the largest private banks are at an advantage. According to Goldman Sachs, the flow of capital to private banking will increase by about 7 per cent a year until 2007.

However, the private banking arms of UBS, Credit Suisse and other industry leaders should grow faster: in 2003, Goldman estimates, UBS captured 7 per cent of the industry inflows even though its market share is just 3.5 per cent.

Several large groups now argue private banking is not just a good growth opportunity, but also a business that offers substantial synergies with their investment banking arms. The benefits fall into two categories. First, there is the ability to cross-sell. Entrepreneurs who hire an investment bank to sell or float their business will also need some advice on managing their new found wealth, creating an immediate opportunity for the private banking arm. Similarly, a businessman who has developed a trusted relationship with his private banker may be willing to hire the same institution when he needs wholesale banking services.

A more compelling case for the combination of private and investment banking may be that the former is relatively stable, neatly balancing the growing risks that investment banks are taking on their own account. Under new capital adequacy rules, private banking assets can provide a stable asset base and source of steady revenues.

Source: Financial Times (2005), 'Investment Banking Survey', 27 January, by Peter Thal Larsen.

In general, European banking markets still offer substantial opportunities in the private banking area and incumbent banks are well placed to benefit from changes in the wealth management environment. Maintaining a strong domestic franchise and brand image coupled with good performance and appropriate client segmentation strategy are critical success ingredients.

13.6 Corporate and investment banking

The demand for corporate banking services has traditionally been the mainstay of European banking business and is strongly related to the business cycle. Typically, all banks provide payments, deposits and credit facilities and the larger banks provide a wider array of services for the major corporate customers. Payment services are primarily provided by means of a business current account which gives firms access to a variety of specific money transmission facilities (e.g., cash and cheque deposit facilities, cheque writing facilities, access to automated payment services that facilitate the payment of direct debits and standing orders). The main deposit facilities include standard current account and term deposit services. With larger amounts being deposited then firms may seek more sophisticated cash management and treasury services from their banks (these are core products for medium-sized and larger companies). On the credit side, companies (and especially) smaller firms typically rely on overdraft and/or term loan facilities, although overdrafts are less common in certain systems.

During the 1990s firms sought increasingly to diversify their credit services, making more use of a wider array of asset finance products such as factoring and leasing. Such products and services (otherwise known as asset finance business) have grown rapidly for various reasons, including: preferential accounting and tax treatment associated with lease finance; easier access to these products compared with overdraft finance; and the attraction associated with more certain credit flows.

As companies become larger the demand for corporate banking services becomes broader and more complex. Medium-sized companies require money transmission, deposit and credit facilities like their smaller counterparts. However, they also typically require a greater range of services relating to information about their business, risk management services, trade finance products and asset and investment management services (e.g., if they have to manage employees' pension fund assets or their own assets). Over the last decade or so the range of banking products available to mid-size European corporations has grown substantially. This is because many banks have targeted this segment with products that previously were the sole preserve of just the largest companies. In Europe, it is now estimated that large commercial banks provide around 200 products to this segment.

Commercial banks in Europe are increasingly looking to developments in the US corporate market to learn lessons on how to adapt to the changes that are expected to affect their business over the next decade or so. The reason is because the United States is the most developed in providing capital market products to its medium-sized corporate clients – and this is a business expected to grow rapidly. Large multinational companies increasingly by-pass the banking sector for their funding – by raising finance through equity and debt instrument (bond) issues. They can also raise funds in the international markets more cheaply than many banks as their credit ratings tend to be higher. As such, lending to very large companies is a low margin (profit) business, as banks have to compete on the finest terms and with capital markets. Commercial banks, therefore, are continuing to focus a significant part of their corporate banking strategy on the middle-market segment, given that this is one of the most profitable parts of the corporate lending business. Domestic banks face greater competition from capital markets and foreign banks in providing corporate banking services to the top corporations.

Another issue of which corporate bankers are aware is the growing relevance of the disintermediation trend. Larger firms now have a wider range of capital market financing options than ever before and these compete with traditional bank lending products and services. It is a force that is encouraging many large investment banks to target offering services to mid-sized firms – a market segment that was traditionally the sole preserve of commercial banks. Investment banks such as Goldman Sachs, Morgan Stanley and Merrill Lynch, which have a global expertise in capital markets, M&A and corporate advisory services are now actively competing with commercial banks to provide debt, equity and risk management services to the largest mid-market firms (mainly because this is viewed as a more profitable segment than the multinational corporation market segment on which they have traditionally focused).

Advances in technology, competition and other forces are also changing the way in which banks undertake corporate banking. The corporate credit market has changed and demarcation lines between the services offered to different sized firms are eroding. This begs the question as to what types of corporate banking operation will be successful in the future.

Given the increasing segmentation of the business it seems likely that many banks will seek to adopt some form of specialist strategy targeting a narrower market, product and/or client base. This does not mean that corporate banking will become a mono-line business with individual banks offering one-product services. Rather it means that banks will specialise in a variety of areas of corporate banking business, but will not (as has traditionally been the case) try to offer a universal corporate banking service to every type and size of firm. Commercial banks will seek to identify product or client areas in which they can specialise, and develop their business along such lines. Goldman Sachs and McKinsey (2001) suggest a variety of potentially successful business models that may inform corporate banking developments in Europe and these are shown in Table 13.6.

13.7 Technological developments affecting European banks

Technological innovations have transformed most industrial sectors, especially due to the evolution of information-based technologies. In the case of the banking industry, due to the role of banks as information-based firms and their role in gathering and analysing information, these changes have been even more acute. Information technologies offer savings in the cost and time of providing financial

Table 13.6 Eight distinct winning formulas emerging in corporate banking

Strategic focus	Winning business models
Segment focus	1) **Growth specialist** – focuses on the distinct financial needs of approximately 50,000 fast-growing companies including venture finance, IPO-related business, M&A services.
	2) **SME (direct relationship) banker** – focuses on the standard needs of the majority of European midcorps offering standard packages, self-diagnostic and advisory tools. Heavy reliance on direct channels to reduce costs on commodity products.
	3) **Midcorp (investment) banker** – targets the broader later stage financing needs of the established midcorp segment. Offering a comprehensive product mix with a strong investment banking element.
	4) **MNC bulge bracket** – is a formula that only a few banks can use as this requires the necessary skills to serve the 250 European multinational companies and eventually the remaining 2,000 large companies. Citigroup, Deutsche Bank and the top Swiss banks, United Bank of Switzerland and Credit Suisse, the 'major aspirants'.
Product focus	5) **Specialised finance provider** – some commercial banks to build up a very strong position by focusing on selected commercial credit products. Areas of specialisation presenting opportunities include: businesses with expert financial structuring skills in areas like cross-border leasing, international tax-related structures; large-scale factoring, long-term investment loans; and project finance. These types of business appeal to different clients ranging from utilities to computer manufacturers.
	6) **Credit trader** – takes a bet on the expected boom in credit trading. Majority of participants in this business are likely to outsource credit trading to a handful of 'powerhouses'. No examples of active debt traders in Europe although some US traders are trying to expand their product offering in Europe.
Functional focus	7) **Corporate financial services adviser** – corporate bank to act as an independent financial adviser to provide crafted individual financial solutions
	8) **Factory provider** – offers services further down the value chain at the production level. Offers advisory tools, scoring models, products such as asset management or asset finance. Other services may include corporate ratings or credit/securities processing services.

Source: Adapted from Goldman Sachs and McKinsey 2001, pp. 18–20.

services and increased revenues through the development of an array of new financial products, often only limited by the level of potential demand which can be created. Indeed, the rapid progress in information technology is transforming the way in which the banking industry works, through a dematerialisation of informational sources, a substantial increase of information available, and the possibility of diversification into new business areas compatible with the banks' core activities.

Two main factors can be pinpointed as consequences of technological innovation. First, the production function in banking has become more capital-intensive, given that the share of non-staff operating costs has increased in most of the European systems, at the expense of staff costs. Consequently, it has contributed to a reduction in the costs associated with the management of information (collection, storage, processing and transmission) by replacing paper-based and labour-intensive methods with automated processes. Second, diffusion of information technology is radically transforming banking delivery channels. In this respect, the competitive advantage which geographical proximity once provided by means of a large number of branches has been achieved through the installation of ATMs or alternative delivery systems and more recently through the introduction of internet banking.

Overall, progress in information technology has allowed the establishment of new delivery channels and products. It has also accelerated competition, making it easier to compare prices, lowering switching costs and diminishing barriers to entry into markets. Although these factors have intensified competition, they should also increase efficiency and, all other things been equal, reduce the amount of capital optimally held by banks. On the other hand, they may also contribute to the existence of over-capacity in terms of staffing levels in traditional or 'physical' delivery channels.

These forces are universal and European banks are well placed to take advantage of technological advances. Small banks, however, are not well positioned to develop their own innovative technology. This is a good thing. They can chose to implement best-practice systems when they have been tried and tested by their larger counterparts that have deeper pockets for investing in research and development and new innovative technologies. In fact, this is one of the reasons relatively small banks can be more efficient than larger firms, because they do not have to incur the larger development costs, can purchase bespoke best-practice systems and implement them with less disruption.

13.8 Performance in European banking

The performance features of European banking can vary considerably from country to country, not least because of the different features of the specific markets as well as the general economic climate. However, there are some features common to all systems. Probably the most noticeable is the growing emphasis of non-interest income as a source of revenue. Figure 13.4, for example, illustrates the changing income structure of European banks, highlighting the declining role of net interest income (the difference between interest income and interest costs) and the increasing amount of revenue being generated from fee and commission income. The figure shows that, on average, European banks earned around 70 per cent of

Figure 13.4 Income composition of EU banks (percentages of total income)

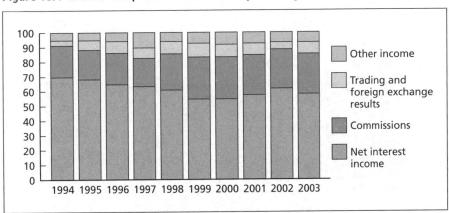

Source: ECB (2005c) *Analysing Banking Sector Conditions: How to Use Macro-Prudential Indicators*, Occasional Paper No. 26, April, Chart 1, p. 11.

their revenue from interest-related business (mainly loans) in 1994, a figure which had declined to 60 per cent by 2003. Commission income (from sales of insurance, pensions, broking and other fee-related activities) accounted for around 24 per cent of income in 2003 with the remainder coming from securities trading and other sources. The growth in non-interest income is a reflection of the growing importance of securities-based financing by firms and also the purchase of mutual funds by households. In addition, pension funds as well as hedge funds have been increasingly more active in securities purchases, much of which is organised or conducted via banks.

It is also argued that further growth in non-interest income sources of revenue is expected with an improvement in economic growth as well as the growing wealth of households and companies and an increased propensity to invest in securities via mutual funds and supplementary pension products.

Figure 13.5 illustrates recent trends in EU bank profitability and cost efficiency (as measured by the cost–income ratio). On average, bank profitability has remained fairly stable with return-on-equity (ROE) increasing from 9 to 12 per cent between 1998 and 2000, falling back to around 9 per cent in 2002 and increasing a little thereafter. In addition cost–income ratios fell modestly between 1995 and 2000, from just under 67 per cent to around 63 per cent. The ratio then increased to just over 66 per cent in 2001 but has fallen steadily since then. So overall it appears that the trend is towards improvements in bank efficiency. These figures, however, mask differences between countries and for various types and sizes of banks. For instance, typically cost–income ratios are higher for small banks compared to large banks, and are also generally greater for investment banks compared with commercial banks.

There are also substantial differences in the profitability of banks across Europe, as illustrated in Table 13.7. The low profitability of German banks stands out, as do the relatively high levels of profits generated by UK banks. Note also the losses made in various Scandinavian banking markets in the early 1990s (see also the unusually high returns for Swedish banks, an anomaly relating to a nationalisation and reorganisation of the banking sector to create a more profitable system after a banking sector collapse). Since 2001 the profitability of virtually all the European

Figure 13.5 Profitability and costs to income ratios in European banking

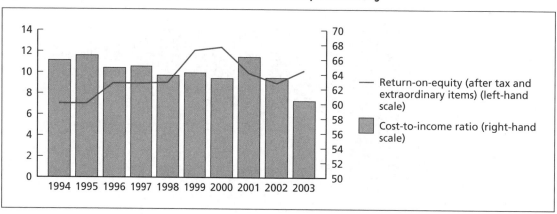

Source: ECB (2005c) *Analysing Banking Sector Conditions: How to Use Macro-Prudential Indicators*, Occasional Paper No 26, April, Chart 5, p. 14.

Table 13.7 Return-on-equity (ROE) in European, US and Japanese banking (%)

	1990	1991	1992	1993	1994	1995	1996	1997	1998	1999	2000	2001
Belgium	8.29	6.48	5.70	14.13	13.23	12.89	15.27	15.12	14.76	14.65	20.48	15.31
Denmark	−3.34	−0.14	−21.04	10.61	0.07	18.50	16.14	15.09	14.60	14.17	15.24	16.53
Germany	11.93	14.41	13.16	13.59	11.78	12.57	12.31	10.90	17.38	9.23	7.86	5.12
Greece	20.84	31.53	23.12	21.57	25.92	24.41	16.53	17.90	19.34	27.63	19.21	14.32
Spain	13.58	12.48	10.66	3.75	8.20	9.17	9.72	10.61	11.07	11.44	10.37	9.26
France	10.15	10.44	6.93	2.87	0.49	3.63	4.78	7.66	9.93	10.78	12.08	11.76
Ireland	–	–	–	–	–	20.24	20.08	19.05	21.56	18.05	17.88	12.29
Italy	16.40	13.09	9.83	12.04	4.35	5.91	7.97	5.52	13.17	13.86	17.58	14.01
Luxembourg	6.17	6.52	11.16	18.90	20.92	19.95	22.28	22.83	24.67	19.61	20.51	18.50
Netherlands	12.30	12.73	13.85	15.88	15.17	15.81	15.99	15.62	14.30	17.90	17.19	15.23
Austria	8.63	8.61	6.86	8.70	7.87	8.15	9.61	9.35	9.48	9.27	11.33	11.29
Portugal	12.54	12.36	8.83	9.25	7.35	7.65	7.72	9.08	7.56	6.91	8.84	6.31
Finland	5.61	−10.97	−48.87	−28.41	−25.21	−7.93	7.96	15.19	9.86	15.16	22.07	17.21
Sweden	3.65	54.56	5.73	2.82	18.67	22.08	25.57	11.15	17.33	15.96	19.50	19.48
United Kingdom	14.45	8.58	7.35	19.25	27.39	28.59	26.13	26.22	28.31	30.16	21.49	20.05
Eurozone	–	–	–	–	–	8.89	9.98	10.08	13.65	12.06	12.73	10.83
European Union	–	–	–	–	–	10.56	11.73	11.82	15.24	13.98	14.12	12.33
United States	6.74	9.09	15.85	19.14	19.81	19.95	19.60	20.56	19.39	22.21	20.45	18.97
Japan	11.29	9.51	7.36	4.97	3.07	−5.00	0.99	−17.70	−17.90	6.03	−0.60	−17.71

Source: Obtained from OECD Bank Profitability Database (2002).

banking systems has improved – and this is particularly the case for Spanish banks whose returns are now among the highest in Europe (averaging around 18 per cent by 2004).

One of the main puzzles that both academics and analysts have to explain is why bank performance differs so much across countries and how this is related to competition and efficiency features. Llewellyn (2003) provides an interesting insight into these issues by examining why UK banks have been more profitable than their neighbours in continental Europe. Using a dataset of the largest 150 banks across Europe between 1996 and 2001, he shows that British banks tended to have higher ROE and excess returns than other European banks. Apart from Nordic banks, UK banks had the highest levels of profitability, with Swiss and German banks being the poorest performers. British banks generated excess returns of around 7 per cent over the study period – a finding difficult to associate with a competitive banking market.

Overall, Llewellyn (2003) posits that the reason for the difference in performance between UK and European banks can be explained by six major factors:

1) the *business cycle*: its particular phase at any point in time, and its amplitude over time;
2) *structural factors* (such as the state of competition and contestability in specific product segments, the demand for banking services independent of the business

cycle, the existence of state or mutual/co-operative banks, the power of the capital market, labour laws, and so on)

3) *sectoral pressure* on the banking industry;

4) *business mix* and range of business of banks;

5) *business practice of banks* (pricing policy, how banks chose to compete, whether they exploit weak competitive conditions in sub-markets, etc.); and

6) *business strategy* of banks and most especially whether they specifically set ROE and Economic-Value-Added (EVA) (rates of return in excess of the cost of capital) targets as their central business objective. In addition, it is also important to what extent banks are prepared to follow ruthlessly the implications of pursuing shareholder wealth value-added strategies.

It is argued that British banks have performed relatively well as they have benefited from buoyant macroeconomic conditions; lack of competition and high profits in key sectors such as lending to SMEs; an aggressive financial services cross-selling product mix and pricing strategy; and most importantly (and perhaps controversially) British banks focus much more on shareholder wealth creation than many of their continental European counterparts.

An important finding from the Llewellyn (2003) study is that competition is product-specific. Some areas of banking business are highly competitive whereas in other areas market power can be exerted. The benevolent operating environment coupled with a high demand for retail financial services, aggressive pricing and cross-selling strategies and a demonic focus on shareholder value has propelled British banks to be high performers. In many respects therefore, British banks are just emulating the strategies and recent performance of US banks. One area not touched upon, however, deserves mention. While such aggressive strategy may yield high returns for shareholders it may result in banks not serving part of the economy that is not particularly profitable. Banking services in rural communities have been nearly wiped out as British banks have sought to shut unprofitable business. Parts of society are also increasingly excluded from banking services as British banks only wish to focus on profitable customer segments. Policy concerns relating to financial exclusion are growing and this is likely to persist if aggressive shareholder maximisation strategies continue to be followed. Such a strategy is clearly not a zero-sum game.

13.9 Conclusions

Major changes are impacting on the global financial system and European banks are not immune from these developments. Banking markets are becoming more concentrated, systems are becoming more liberal and the general environment is becoming more competitive. In such an environment banks continually strive to improve their performance by focusing on generating greater non-interest revenues and reducing costs. Linked to this is the need to manage capital and risks more effectively so shareholders and stakeholders obtain good returns on their investments.

Opportunities exist for European banks to develop their retail and corporate banking businesses and opportunities exist to diversify into non-traditional areas such as in insurance, pensions, mutual funds and other securities-related areas. The desire to boost non-interest income relative to margin-based revenue will undoubtedly continue. Technological advances continue to help re-shape the economics of the financial services industry and many European banks are well placed to adopt state-of-the-art technology (if needed) to broaden their delivery channels and streamline their back-office functions. Many are emulating their counterparts in the United States.

In addition to these developments, changes in the international regulatory environment are also having growing influence on European banks. Supervisory rules and regulations are being implemented to meet BIS recommendations and this is likely to lower regulatory capital across Europe. Bank performance continues to be driven by many varying factors, not least by shareholder value maximisation strategy and the state of the overall economy.

Key terms

Deregulation

National consolidation

Cross-border mergers

Single market

Economic and Monetary Union (EMU)

Second Banking Co-ordination Directive (2BCD)

Single EU passport

Financial Services Action Plan (FSAP)

Global private banking business

Offshore banking

Key reading

Cybo-Ottone, A. and Murgia, M. (2000) 'Mergers and shareholder wealth in European banking', *Journal of Banking and Finance*, **24** (6), pp. 831–58.

European Central Bank (2004c) *Report on EU Banking Structure*, http://www.ecb.int/pub/ pdf/other/reportoneubankingstructure112004en.pdf

Llewellyn, D. (2003) 'Why are British banks so profitable?'. Paper presented at the SUERF/Credit Suisse Seminar on 'Profitability of European Banking: The Challenge of Competitive Market Conditions', Zurich, 27 February.

Revision questions and problems

1 Describe the main trends that have influenced the structure of the European banking markets over the last ten years.

2 Starting from the 1977 First Banking Co-ordination Directive, what are the other important regulatory measures affecting the EU banking and financial sectors?

3 Has a single market in financial service yet been achieved in Europe?

4 To what extent, and how, has the new technology transformed European banks' retail business?

5 What strategies will European corporate banks have to adopt to be successful in the future?

6 To what extent, and why, does the performance of European banks differ across individual countries?

Appendix 13.1 The measures included in the FSAP

	2003		2004				2005			
	Q2	Q4	Q1	Q2	Q3	Q4	Q1	Q2	Q3	Q4
Measures not yet proposed										
Legal Framework for Payments		P								
Reinsurance Supervision Directive		P								
10th and 14th Company Law Directives			P							
Risk-based Capital Directive				P						
Third Money Laundering Directive						P				
Measures proposed but not yet adopted										
Takeover Bids Directive				A						
Investment Services Directive				A						
Transparency Directive				A						
Measures adopted but not yet implemented										
Life and Non-Life Insurance Directives	D									
Second Money Laundering Directive	D									
Collateral Directive		D								
UCITS Directives (amendments)			D							
Fair Value Accounting Directive			D							
Taxation of Savings Income Directive			D							
Bank Winding-Up Directive				D						
Financial Conglomerates Directive					D					
Distance Marketing Directive						D				
ECS Regulation and Employee Directive						D				
Market Abuse Directive						D				
International Accounting Standards Regulation							D			
Accounting Modernisation Directive							D			
Insurance Mediation Directive							D			
Prospectus Directive									D	
Pension Funds Directive										D

P = plan for proposal; A = plan for adoption; D = deadline for implementation

Source: The EU Financial Services Action Plan: A Guide (31 July 2003). Prepared by HM Treasury, the Financial Services Authority and the Bank of England.

Chapter 14

Banking in the new EU Member States

Learning objectives

- To offer an overview of the banking markets in the new EU Member States
- To assess the progress of new EU Member States towards the Euro
- To analyse the structure and performance of the banking sectors
- To discuss the role of foreign banks in new EU Member States
- To review the regulatory framework

14.1 Introduction

On 1 May 2004, Cyprus, the Czech Republic, Estonia, Hungary, Latvia, Lithuania, Malta, Poland, Slovenia and the Slovak Republic joined the European Union. Over the past decade, these countries faced a great degree of change and have made remarkable progress toward convergence to EU standards on a number of economic indicators. Between 1999 and 2003, for example, they recorded an average GDP growth of 3.2 per cent compared with 2.0 per cent for the EU-15 countries. Despite growth and continuing convergence, GDP levels per capita still lag behind those of the old EU Member States. The **New Member States (NMSs)** are now facing two major challenges. The first is to manage the continued and probably rapid process of further real economic convergence (i.e., convergence in terms of income and the economic cycle with EU countries). The second is to achieve the degree of nominal convergence (i.e., meeting the nominal Maastricht criteria) required to introduce the Euro. In this context, real convergence is more than the catching up in income levels; it is the adjustment of the real economies towards structures that allow the countries to participate in a monetary union without contributing to, or suffering from, significant asymmetric shocks. However, nominal convergence – the gradual fulfilment of the Maastricht criteria of exchange rate stability, price stability and controlled budget deficits – although it will only be relevant at the moment of joining the Euro, is already pursued at this stage as it is thought that it will facilitate the achievement of sustainable non-inflationary growth.

During the 1990s, the banking sectors of the NMSs have operated under favourable economic conditions, which has given rise to relatively high lending rates and boosted banks' profitability. In terms of the regulatory and supervisory environment, NMSs have also developed sound prudential frameworks. This chapter offers a review of some of the key issues relating to banking in the new Member States and discusses the structure of the various banking sectors, the most relevant recent changes and how the NMSs' banking sectors are becoming integrated with the rest of the European Union. Section 14.2 provides an overview of the macroeconomic environment; Section 14.3 focuses on the main structural features of the banking sectors in NMSs. Section 14.4 reviews the role of foreign banks in NMSs and Section 14.5 illustrates the M&As activities in these countries. Finally, Section 14.6 reviews regulatory and supervisory frameworks and the process of convergence towards EU standards.

14.2 The macroeconomic outlook

With the accession to the EU of the ten new members on 1 May 2004, the attention of the policymakers both in current member states and in the former accession countries has shifted from the political and organisational aspects of accession towards the economic challenges facing the new members. Indeed, EU membership is only the first of the many major milestones that the accession countries will be facing over the next several years.

Table 14.1 Macroeconomic outlook

Country	Total GDP[a]		Per capita GDP[b]		GDP growth rate[c]		Average annual inflation[c]		Unemployment rate[c]	
	1995	2005	1995	2005	1995	2005	1995	2005	1995	2005
CY	8.8	12.8	11,918	15,583	6.1	3.3	2.6	2.6	n.a.	n.a.
CZ	52	105.2	5,040	10,266	5.9	5.3	9.1	2.3	2.9	8.8
EE	3.6	9.4	2,415	6,921	4.3	5.5	29.0	3.4	9.7	8.4
HU	44.7	89.0	4,374	9,034	1.5	3.2	28.2	3.8	10.2	5.9
LV	4.4	11.7	1,780	5,060	-0.8	5.9	25.5	3.6	6.4	7.2
LT	6.0	20.7	1,623	5,940	3.3	5.5	39.6	4.1	6.1	9.2
MT	3.3	5.8	8,613	14,422	6.2	4.2	4.0	2.0	n.a.	n.a.
PL	127.1	262.1	3,,292	6,789	7.0	4.5	27.8	2.8	14.9	16.0
SK	19.1	39.2	3,564	7,281	6.5	5.3	9.9	3.0	13.1	15.3
SI	18.7	31.4	9,348	15,689	4.1	5.1	13.5	3.8	7.4	6.0

Note: CY= Cyprus; CZ = Czech Republic; EE = Estonia; HU = Hungary; LV = Latvia; LT = Lithuania;
MT = Malta; PL = Poland; SK = Slovakia; SI = Slovenia.
[a] Billion Current Dollars;
[b] Current Dollars;
[c] Per cent.
Source: European Forecasting Network (EFN) 2005 data forecast.

Table 14.1 summarises the main macroeconomic indicators for the 10 central and eastern and southern European countries and shows the considerable growth both in total and per capita GDP, in all countries. Indeed, growth in these countries has been higher than in the EU-15 over the same period. Further, inflation has fallen from double-digit figures to Euroarea levels. However, despite the strong economic growth, the level of unemployment increased in a number of countries to an average of 13 per cent across the region (compared to an average of 8.1 per cent in the EU-15 over the 1995–2005 period). Cross-country differences are still substantial, with the Baltic countries (Estonia, Latvia and Lithuania) displaying the lowest GDP per capita (around 50 per cent below the EU-25 average) and Cyprus and Slovenia the highest. (Note that in 2003 the GDP per capita of the Euroarea was $23,030, compared with $25,490 in the United Kingdom and $35,400 in the United States.)

Table 14.2 reports the countries' risk ratings (see Section 11.9 on country risk) on long-term foreign currency denominated debt: new Member States' ratings are still considerably lower than the EU-15, where most countries are rated AAA. In the NMSs, Poland has the lowest rating, with BBB, and only Slovenia achieves an AA rating. Most countries' domestic currency debt is rated at A to A–. If you recall Table 4.1, this is referred to as 'high to medium quality debt with strong attributes, but potentially vulnerable'.

14.2.1 Progress towards the Euro

As discussed in Chapter 6, under the Maastricht rules, a country must achieve a high degree of price stability, keep its government finances sustainable (in terms of both public deficit and public debt) and maintain a stable exchange rate and convergence

Table 14.2 Country ratings (2003)

Country	Fitch		Moody's		Standard and Poor's	
	Foreign Currency	*Domestic Currency*	*Foreign Currency*	*Domestic Currency*	*Foreign Currency*	*Domestic Currency*
CY	A+	AA	A2	A2	A	A
CZ	A–	A	A1	A1	A–	A
EE	A	A+	A1	A1	A	A
HU	A–	A+	A1	A1	A–	A
LV	A–	A	A2	A2	A–	A–
LT	A–	A	A3	A3	A–	A–
MT	A	AA–	A3	A3	A	A+
PL	BBB+	A	A2	A2	BBB+	A–
SK	A–	A+	A3	A3	A–	A–
SI	AA–	AA	Aa3	Aa3	AA–	AA

Note: CY= Cyprus; CZ = Czech Republic; EE = Estonia; HU = Hungary; LV = Latvia; LT = Lithuania; MT = Malta; PL = Poland; SK = Slovakia; SI = Slovenia.

Source: Various.

in long-term interest rates in order to qualify for Eurozone membership (see also Box 13.2). Progress towards such criteria is illustrated in Table 14.3.

In order to adopt the Euro, non-participating EU Member States have to achieve a high degree of sustainable economic and legal convergence. Compliance with the Maastricht criteria will be assessed by the Council of the EU Finance Ministers, based on reports by the Commission and the European Central Bank. If we look at the data for inflation and fiscal positions shown in Table 14.3, it seems that some of the new EU countries would already fulfil the Maastricht criteria. Fiscal policies have also been sound in the Baltic countries and in Slovenia; with government deficits below 3 per cent (Estonia even recorded a surplus). Furthermore, despite an

Table 14.3 Progress towards Maastricht (2004 data)

Country	Inflation rate	Government deficit (% of GDP)	Government debt (% of GDP)
Maastricht criteria	Not more than 1.5% above lowest three	–3.0	60.0
Cyprus	1.9	–5.2	74.9
Czech Republic	2.6	–5.2	38.6
Estonia	3.0	+0.5	4.8
Hungary	6.8	–5.5	59.9
Latvia	6.2	–2.0	14.6
Lithuania	1.1	–2.6	21.1
Malta	2.7	–5.2	73.2
Poland	3.6	–5.4	45.9
Slovakia	7.4	–3.8	43.0
Slovenia	3.6	–2.3	30.9

Source: http://www.europa.eu.int

increasing trend in recent years, the ratios of government debt/GDP are well below the 60 per cent threshold in all NMSs.

Although there is no pre-defined timetable for the adoption of the Euro, unlike Denmark and the United Kingdom, the new Member States do not have an 'opt-out' clause and eventually, they will have to adopt the common currency. Prior to the adoption of the Euro, a country must have been a member of the **Exchange Rate Mechanism (ERM II)** for a minimum of two years.

The ERM II is a new exchange-rate mechanism which succeeded the old **European Monetary System (EMS)** from 1 January 1999 – with the introduction of the Euro the EMS had become obsolete. With the creation of the new exchange rate mechanism, the EU entered Stage Three of the Economic and Monetary Union (EMU). The aims of ERM II are to maintain exchange-rate stability between the Euro and the participating national currencies and to ensure that excessive exchange-rate fluctuations do not cause problems in the internal market. Under the ERM II, a central rate against the Euro is defined for the currency of each Member State not participating in the Euroarea but participating in the exchange-rate mechanism. The mechanism allows one standard fluctuation band of 15 per cent on either side of the central rate. The original 1998 Agreement was modified in 2001 to account for the adoption of the single currency by Greece and in 2004 to take account of the enlargement of the European Union.[1] Initially, Denmark and Greece joined the ERM II. Since Greece adopted the Euro in January 2001, Denmark had been the only participant until June 2004, when Estonia, Lithuania and Slovenia joined. In May 2005 three other new Member States joined ERM II: Cyprus, Latvia and Malta. Estonia, Lithuania and Slovenia hope to start using Euro notes and coins on 1 January 2007, together with Cyprus, Malta and Latvia. The **Visegrad countries** (Poland, the Czech Republic, Slovakia and Hungary), on the other hand, have declared their commitment to join the Euro by 2009–10. Table 14.4 illustrates the fluctuation bands for the currencies currently participating in the ERM II.

Although there are no formal criteria to be met for entry into ERM II, successful participation in the mechanism requires that major policy adjustments – for

Table 14.4 The ERM II

Country (national currency)	Central rate (for 1 Euro)	Fluctuation band (%)
Cyprus (Pound)	0.585274	+/–15
Denmark (Krone)	7.46038	+/–2.25
Estonia (Kroon)	15.6466	+/–15
Latvia (Lat)	0.702804	+/–15
Lithuania (Lita)	3.45280	+/–15
Malta (Lira)	0.429300	+/–15
Slovenia (Tolar)	239.640	+/–15

Source: Adapted from http://europa.eu.int.

---

[1] ECB Agreement of 1 September 1998 (OJ C 345 of 13.11.1998); ECB Agreement of 14 September 2000 (OJ C 362 of 16.12.2000); ECB Agreement of 29 April 2004 (OJ C 135 of 13.05.2004).

example relating to fiscal policy and inflation – are undertaken before joining the mechanism. At the time of writing (2005), vulnerability to foreign exchange shocks varies considerably across countries. The Baltic States operate a full or quasi-currency board. Malta operates a basket peg regime (i.e. the country pegs its exchange rate to a basket of currency, such as the Euro, the US Dollar and the Japanese Yen), and Slovenia has a very tightly managed exchange rate regime. On the other hand, the Visegrad countries and Cyprus have more flexible exchange rates.[2]

14.3 Structural features of financial sectors in new Member States

Before we move on to describe the structural features of the banking sectors in the new Member States, we need to make a further distinction between Cyprus and Malta and the five **Central and Eastern European Countries (CEECs)** and the three Baltic States. The latter two groups are also referred to as **NIM-8** and are also former *transition countries*. The label 'transition country' is used to describe former communist countries that have been transforming their planned economies to market economies.

The NIM-8 or **transition countries** are characterised by relatively low levels of financial development, partly due to the rapid transformation of their economies from centrally planned ones, with very low levels of intermediation. CEECs and Baltic countries are however catching up rapidly with the rest of the European Union. In terms of financial structure, the new Member States are bank-oriented, thereby relying more on bank finance than on stock market financing. The largest part of their banking sectors consist of commercial banks (around 86 per cent of the whole banking sector, according to ECB statistics). In Poland and Hungary there are a number of co-operative banks and a significant number of building societies are present in the Czech Republic and Slovakia. Furthermore, there is a strong presence of foreign financial institutions particularly from neighbouring EU countries. The following sections provide a detailed analysis of the banking and financial structures of NMSs: most former accession countries have been through the same structural changes in a relatively short period of time and therefore share similar characteristics.

14.3.1 Stock markets in new Member States

In terms of financial structure, new Member States in general, and CEECs in particular, rely heavily on bank finance. According to the ECB (2005d) stock markets in these countries are relatively small as measured by a percentage of GDP. For example, the ratio of stock market capitalisation to GDP is 150 per cent in the United States and 68 per cent in the EU-15. In the NMSs it amounts to 24 per cent and only 19 per cent in the former Central and Eastern European transition countries. Table 14.5 illustrates the stock market capitalisation of NMSs compared to the

---

[2] For more information on exchange rate regimes see, among others, Ho (2002) and Winkler *et al.* (2004).

EU-15 countries, both in terms of total stock market capitalisation and as a percentage of GDP.

At the end of April 2005, the total stock market capitalisation of NMSs was 123 billion Euros, which represents 0.45 per cent of world stock capitalisation, less than 1.8 per cent of the EU market capitalisation and only 7 per cent of Euronext. The most significant market of the CEE region, the Warsaw Stock Exchange (WSE), exceeds only, among the former EU-15, the capitalisation of the Luxembourg Stock exchange. The ratio of stock capitalisation to GDP of the NMSs (at 26 per cent) appears also relatively low compared with that of the EU-15 (71 per cent). Finally, the NMSs' stock exchanges' liquidity is usually lower than in western Europe: the average turnover velocity ratio (yearly amount of trades on market capitalisation) is 35 per cent on average in the NMSs, which is the level of the smallest western European markets (Athens: 40 per cent; Vienna: 35 per cent) and three to four times lower than those of Euronext, Deutsche Börse or the LSE (between 100 and 130 per cent). The Budapest Stock Exchange presents the highest turnover in the NMSs, with a rate of 63 per cent in 2004.

Table 14.5 Stock market capitalisation of EU Member States

EU Member States	Total stock market capitalisation (billion Euros)	Ratio of stock market capitalisation to GDP (%)	Number of listed companies (including foreign firms)
Poland	44.7	23	225
Hungary	22.7	28	46
Czech Republic	24.2	27	52
Slovenia	6.8	26	138
Cyprus	4	32	148
Estonia (OMX)	4.6	52	13
Lithuania (OMX)	4.8	27	43
Slovakia	4.1	12	227
Malta	2.4	55	13
Latvia (OMX)	1.2	12	39
Total	**119.5**	**26**	**944**
LSE (London)	2,136	130	2,942
Euronext	1,764	70	983
Deutche Borse	867	40	797
Spain	694	87	3,230
Italy	595	44	278
OMX*	540	87	582
Greece	94	57	309
Ireland	79	54	62
Austria	74	32	123
Luxembourg	37	146	232
Total	**6,880**	**71**	**9,538**

Notes: Data at 1 May 2005. Euronext = France, Netherlands, Belgium, Portugal; OMX = Sweden, Finland, Denmark, Latvia, Lithuania and Estonia.
*Baltic countries not included in this figure.

Source: http://www.dree.org.

The structure of NMSs' banking sectors

Commercial banks are the dominant financial institutions in the new Member States. As illustrated in Table 14.6, commercial banks' market share of total banking sector assets stand at over 80 per cent in most countries.

Table 14.6 Banking sector structure in NMSs

	Number of banks	Number of branches	Number of employees	Total assets (million €)	Market share
CY	14	471	8,056	27,182	
Commercial banks	*11*	*459*	*7,744*	*23,765*	*87.4*
CZ	35	1,670	39,004	79,416	
Commercial banks	*20*	*1,636*	*36,392*	*63,462*	*79.9*
EE					
Commercial banks	*7*	*194*	*4,204*	*6,302*	*100*
HU	218	1,162	27,167	58,972	
Commercial banks	*31*	*1,147*	*26,549*	*50,730*	*85*
LT					
Commercial banks	*13*	*117*	*n.a.*	*6,381*	*100*
LV					
Commercial banks	*22*	*206*	*8,112*	*8,459*	*100*
MT					
Commercial banks	*16*	*103*	*3,411*	*17,800*	*100*
PL	600	4,394	151,257	103.318	
Commercial banks	*60*	*3,119*	*124,096*	*98,272*	*94.7*
SI					
Commercial banks	*20*	*1,176*	*11,397*	*21,367*	*98.7*
SK	21	553	19,797	23,751	
Commercial banks	*18*	*553*	*19,147*	*22,380*	*94.2*

Source: ECB (2005d) and authors' calculations. Data refer to the year 2003.

In terms of stability and efficiency of their banking sectors, NMSs' banks seem to be adequately capitalised and profitable. The average Tier 1 capital for NMSs, at 13.4 per cent, is higher than in the EU-15 countries. Table 14.7 shows the main financial ratios for commercial banks for the year 2003.

The overall ROE for the whole banking systems in the NMSs was 11.6 per cent in 2003; the Baltic countries outperformed the CEECs, with an average ROE of 16.5 per cent. The average cost–income ratio is 65 per cent, slightly higher than the EU-15 average (60.4 per cent). In many NMSs, domestic household lending (mortgages) is growing fast (an increase of nearly 20 per cent between 2002 and 2003). Other financial services, such as insurance, asset management and investment services are also growing rapidly. ATMs and internet banking are becoming more widespread and already play a major role in countries such as Estonia and Latvia, as illustrated in Table 14.8.

Table 14.7 **Commercial banks' financial ratios in NMSs**

Country	Tier 1 ratio	Total capital ratio	ROE	ROA	Cost–income ratio
CY	9.7	14.0	7.4	0.7	76.9
CZ	5.8	14.5	23.6	1.3	52.3
EE	9.9	14.5	12.6	1.5	54.0
HU	8.4	11.6	19.8	1.6	60.6
LT	7.8	13.2	13.4	1.26	77.7
LV	11.7	11.7	16.3	1.5	56.1
MT	19.6	19.1	11.0	1.0	66.3
PL	8.3	13.6	5.9	0.9	68.0
SI	9.8	11.5	12.6	1.03	62.5
SK	21.2	20.7	13.8	1.1	70.7

Source: ECB (2005d) and authors' calculations. Data refer to the year 2003.

Table 14.8 **Some indicators of banking capacity in NMSs**

County	Number of ATMs (per million inhabitants)		Number of EFTPOS terminals (per million inhabitants)		Number of cards with cash function (per thousand inhabitants)	
	2001	2003	2001	2003	2001	2003
CY	448	534	11,285	14,857	802	896
CZ	188	250	1,754	3,018	445	651
EE	439	476	3,848	6,773	722	883
HU	255	287	1,875	2,405	501	614
LT	198	285	2,659	3,771	233	668
LV	336	373	2,933	4,416	379	506
MT	352	370	15,287	16,185	874	980
PL	198	196	1,698	1,930	371	388
SI	516	621	13,145	16,046	922	1,437
SK	219	279	1,778	2,563	366	559

Source: ECB (2005d) and authors' calculations.

14.3.2.1 Asset quality

At the outset of their transition, CEECs banking sectors were characterised by a relatively small number of large, state-owned institutions. For various reasons – political pressures, inappropriate incentives and bad management – these banks were burdened with large volumes of non-performing loans (NPL). As Figure 14.1 shows, banks in Poland, Slovakia and Slovenia had the highest ratio of NPLs (as a percentage of total loans) with an average of 28.3 per cent in 2003; on the other hand the Baltic Countries reported the lowest share on NPLs, with an average of only 3 per cent (the EU-15 average is 3.1 per cent). It is important to note, however, that some differences in accounting standards among countries make direct comparisons problematic.

Figure 14.1 Non-performing loans (NPLs) as a percentage of total loans

Source: ECB (2005d) and authors' calculations. Data refer to the year 2003.

As a general trend, the level of non-performing loans seems to be decreasing in most countries. There might be several explanations for this: first, the favourable economic climate as described earlier in this chapter; second, structural changes that have taken place in recent years. For example, an extensive **privatisation** programme has been undertaken in the majority of transition economies, this involved restructuring the banks to make them attractive potential acquisitions – and this included the removal of bad loans from their balance sheets. The share of non-performing loans to the total loans portfolio is still high, however, compared to EU banks. However, structural and managerial reforms (for example the introduction of efficient credit scoring systems and the improved corporate performance) will further improve the NMSs banks' loan portfolio quality and help it converge with the EU average. Finally, foreign ownership is expected to have a positive impact on asset quality as foreign banks typically have introduced more sophisticated and accurate risk management skills and systems (see Section 14.4).

Box 14.1   Polish banking: retail sector gives bankers cause to cheer   FT

After a prolonged struggle with bad loans in the corporate sector, Polish bankers are plunging into retail, their confidence fuelled by record profits. Bankers who were focused on debt recovery and cost cutting 18 months ago are now concentrating on making the most of the rapid growth of retail financial services, including services for small and medium-sized businesses.

Last year's results have given them some comfort. According to the Association of Polish Banks, combined net profits soared last year from 2.3bn zloty to 7bn zloty, which took the net returns on capital from a paltry 5.5 per cent to 16.3 per cent. Interest rate and operating margins improved, bad debt provisioning dropped and banks also benefited from a sharp cut in corporate taxes and from helpful regulatory changes.

Krzysztof Pietraszkiewicz, the bank association chairman, says: 'Many banks now feel very confident and want to increase their activities.'

Following Poland's accession to the EU, banks based in other EU countries no longer need permission to start business but can simply inform the authorities of their intentions to set up shop. About 70 have done so, but few are expected to begin operations soon.

Leszek Balcerowicz, the central bank governor, says many banks would like to increase their market share by taking over rivals. But, in the good conditions now prevailing, there are few sellers.

With Poland now entering its third year of reasonably strong economic growth, banks are working through their bad debt portfolios and looking to expand corporate lending.

After prolonged stagnation, investment is growing at an annual rate of 10 per cent but from a low base. Mr Balcerowicz says that with banks still playing a relatively small role in the economy in

▶

comparison with western Europe, the banking sector should continue to grow faster than the economy as a whole.

Today, the big attraction is retail. In spite of sector growth, banking services reach less than half the Polish population. Just 45 per cent have a bank account. The number of banking transactions per head has grown quickly from 9.3 in 1999 to 24.5 last year, but is still far short of the 140 achieved in the 15 members of the 'old' EU.

The provision of consumer loans, mortgages, credit cards is expanding fast, but from low bases. Philip King, head of retail banking at Citibank Handlowy, the Polish unit of Citigroup of the US, says his bank is most interested in the middle market.

The bank estimates that some 10.6m of 24m working people earn less than 1,000 zloty monthly, 12.7m earn 1,000 zloty to 5,000 zloty, about 300,000 make 5,000 zloty to 15,000 zloty and 100,000 take home more than 15,000 zloty. Citibank Handlowy offers private banking type services at the top end of the market and basic bank accounts at the bottom.

Mr King says he sees the fastest growth in the middle, among those earning 1,500 zloty to 5,000 zloty monthly. The competition is tough, with virtually all the larger banks now focusing on retail. This includes state-controlled PKO BP, which was partly privatised last year, Pkosa, a subsidiary of Italy's Unicredit, and BPH, a unit of Bank Austria, which is in turn controlled by Germany's HVB. Overall, retail lending rose last year to 51 per cent of the the total loan book, up from 47 per cent in 2003, acording to the bankers's association.

Some banks emphasise simple low cost services. Others try to tempt richer customers into more sophisticated packages, including savings and insurance services. Mr King says: 'Competition is based on price and product quality.'

The speed of growth of retail lending raises questions about credit quality. Bankers say that having weathered the flood of bad corporate credits generated by the economic slowdown of 2000–2002, banks are in a better position to manage their risks. Credit assessment procedures, staff training and reporting systems have all been improved.

A national credit bureau, collecting information on clients from participating banks, is growing rapidly and now covers 10m customers, says the bankers' association. With companies cautiously increasing investments, bankers are also seeing the start of a recovery in corporate lending. The government hopes that banks are now better placed than in the past to lend to smaller businesses.

Mr Pietraszkiewicz says: 'We think banks will have a bigger appetite for risk now that they have more effective credit controls in place. But there is still a lack of information on smaller companies.'

Banks are also in a stronger position to recover money from defaulters following the passage last year of a bankruptcy law. Court procedures are also steadily improving. But bankers estimate that it still takes three years to secure a judgment and the average amount of money recovered is 35 per cent of the original debt.

Source: Financial Times (2005), 'Central and Eastern Europe Banking Survey', 24 June, by Stefan Wagstyl.

14.4 The role of foreign banks

As a result of the restructuring discussed earlier, by the end of 2003, the majority of the CEECs' banking sectors were in private hands and had removed a substantial proportion of bad loans from their balance sheets. As illustrated in Table 14.9, state ownership of banks (which used to be the norm before the transition period) is now very much reduced in all CEECs, with the exception of Poland (24 per cent) and Slovenia (23.8 per cent). In Estonia, Latvia and Lithuania there are no state-owned banks. On the other hand, in most new Member States foreign presence in the banking sector is very high. The ECB (2005d) reports that, on average, nearly 70 per cent of banking assets are controlled by foreign banks; the percentage increases to over 80 per cent in the Czech Republic, Slovakia, Hungary, Estonia and Lithuania (see Figure 14.2).

Table 14.9 Ownership structure (market share by total assets, %)

Country	Domestic Public Banks		Domestic Private Banks		Foreign Banks (branches and subsidiaries)	
	2001	2003	2001	2003	2001	2003
CY	4.2	4.6	83.0	83.1	12.8	12.3
CZ	4	3	1	1	95	96
EE	–	–	2.4	2.5	97.6	97.5
HU	4.2	2.3	30.6	15.7	65.2	83.3
LT	12.2	–	2.8	4.4	85.0	95.6
LV	3.2	4.1	54.7	49.5	42.2	46.3
MT	–	–	38.4	32.4	61.1	67.6
PL	23.5	24.4	7.8	7.8	68.7	67.8
SI	41.6	23.8	42.0	40.2	16.4	36.0
SK	26.5	3.7	–	–	73.5	96.3

Source: ECB (2005d) and authors' calculations.

Figure 14.2 Banks' market share (by total assets)

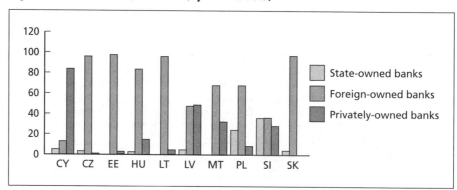

Source: ECB (2005d) and authors' calculations. Data refer to the year 2003.

The entry of foreign banks occurred at the time when CEECs underwent their transition to market economies and have therefore had a particularly important impact in the development of the banking sectors of these countries. Indeed, a large part of foreign ownership results from the privatisation process. However, a number of foreign institutions also set up 'new banks' in a bid to avoid inheriting the non-performing loans that have plagued former state-owned banks. It is usually thought that banks operating cross-border are large banks that do most of their business at the wholesale level. In NMSs, however, foreign banks seem to have preferred to develop retail business. Table 14.10 shows the relative importance of different lines of business carried out by foreign banks. In most countries, the relatively small size of the domestic capital and money markets contribute to limiting wholesale banking activity. The Czech Republic, which has the most developed interbank money market among NMSs, is also the country where wholesale versus retail banking activities are more balanced.

Table 14.10 Relative importance of business lines in NMSs' banking sectors (% of total activity)

County	Corporate finance	Trading and sales	Retail banking	Commercial banking	Asset management	Others
CZ	10.3	20.7	31.0	31.0	3.4	3.4
EE	10.0	10.0	30.0	30.0	20.0	0.0
HU	9.5	9.5	33.3	38.1	0.0	9.5
LT	0.0	0.0	42.9	42.9	14.3	0.0
LV	0.0	0.0	42.9	42.9	14.3	0.0
PL	13.9	13.9	25.0	25.0	5.6	16.7
SK	7.7	7.7	30.8	38.5	15.4	0.0
All NMSs	9.8	11.2	32.2	33.6	7.0	6.3

Source: Adapted from 'Financial FDI to the EU accession countries' ECB (2004d) DG-I/MAW/04 78.

Foreign ownership is seen favourably in NMSs as it is thought to bring know-how in bank management, in terms of expertise and human capital, that transition and emerging economies would take a long period of time to develop. Foreign banks can also promote efficiency in the host country sector. This is because foreign banks operating in NMSs are normally the largest in their domestic markets and usually among the most efficient domestically. As a consequence, they have the potential to transmit best practice. In terms of where the foreign banks are coming from, it is mainly EU banks. Table 14.11 shows the presence of EU banking groups in NMSs in the run-up to the accession.

Table 14.11 Presence of major EU banking groups

Country	Number of branches	Number of subsidiaries	Branches total assets (billion €)	Subsidiaries total assets (billion €)	Market share (%)
CY	0	2	0	2.6	11.9
CZ	4	12	6.6	53.5	60.1
EE	1	3	0.3	4.2	100
HU	1	13	0.1	14.7	39.5
LT	1	4	0.1	2.1	50.0
LV	1	3	0.2	1.7	31.1
MT	0	6	0	3.6	39.1
PL	1	19	0.8	69.7	52.0
SI	0	1	0	1.0	5.1
SK	1	7	0.4	10.0	47.7

Source: ECB (2004d) and authors' calculations. Data refer to the year 2001.

Looking at the banks' assets figure, the predominance of subsidiaries over branches is evident. This can be explained by the following factors:

● subsidiaries were acquired in the context of the privatisation programmes;
● foreign investors aimed at reaping the benefits derived from restructuring inefficient local banks rather than establishing their presence by means of new business units that would compete with local banks (Focarelli and Pozzolo, 2000);

- foreign investors aimed to develop the retail banking business and local market knowledge could be acquired quickly through the acquisition of foreign subsidiaries; and
- the need to cope with local legal constraints and requirements was less pressing than in other transition and developing countries as the former accession countries were in the process of enforcement of the **acquis communautaire** in the areas of banking regulation and supervision.[3]

As for the EU banking groups that are more heavily involved in the NMSs, Austrian banks are very active in the CEECs. This is due to several reasons, including the strategic interest of Austria with regard to the so-called Visegrad countries (Czech Republic, Hungary, Poland and Slovakia) and other neighbouring markets (see also Box 14.2). Several German banks have been among the first participants in the privatisation of the CEECs countries' banks; this is, to a large extent, a by-product of Germany's strong trade relations with many of these economies. The largest Swedish and Finnish banks also found the Baltic countries as natural markets to expand into given historical trade links and their close proximity. Italian banks have also followed an active international strategy towards the whole of central and eastern Europe. The foreign market share in the biggest banking sectors of NMSs, namely Poland, Hungary and the Czech Republic, is more evenly distributed among EU-15 countries, with German and Belgian banks having the strongest presence. According to ECB (2005d) data, at the end of 2003 three EU countries (Germany, Belgium and Italy) accounted for nearly two-thirds of cross-border lending from the EU-15 to the NMSs. On the borrowers' side, Czech Republic, Hungary and Poland made up 74 per cent of total claims.

High foreign ownership in NMSs gives raise to some policy concerns regarding the implications for the extension of local credit, the transmission of shocks and issues relating to concentration and competition.

One problem often related to the large market share of foreign banks concerns the impact that foreign institutions might have on the financial stability of the host country. It is thought that foreign banks are more likely to 'run to exit', i.e., withdraw from the host country at the earliest sign of financial distress, therefore starting a downward spiral in the banking system. However, empirical evidence is mixed.[4] Furthermore, banking crises in EU new Member States happened in the early 1990s, as a natural consequence of the transition process and restructuring of the sector, which required the exit from the market of insolvent institutions. The restructuring and recapitalisation process preceded the entry of foreign banks at the end of the 1990s so that all the problem banks, or most of them, have been restructured, rendering the likelihood of a financial system crisis nowadays much reduced.

A related concern regards the issue of whether credit provided by foreign banks is more volatile than loans from domestic institutions, even in non-crisis periods. Again, there is no empirical evidence to confirm this view.

A final concern relates to the so called 'contagion effect'. The interconnectedness of a bank's activities across several countries might open a channel for contagion between the banking systems of any of the countries where an interna-

---

[3] The entire body of European laws is known as the *acquis communautaire*. This includes all the treaties, regulations and directives passed by the European institutions as well as judgments laid down by the Court of Justice. Candidate countries must adopt, implement and enforce all the *acquis* to be allowed to join the European Union.

[4] See de Haas and van Lelyveld (2003).

tionally active bank operates. The direction of contagion could go either way, with the crisis starting either in the transition or emerging economy and spreading to the mature economy where the bank originates, or vice versa. However, it is important to note that adverse effects resulting from ownership links could be very different for home and host country. In the case of NMSs, since the foreign presence is almost entirely from EU-15 countries (the presence of non-EU banks is rather limited), any shock in these countries would have important repercussions on the banking sectors of the NMSs. However, since foreign bank entry into the former accession countries, no major banking crises have taken place in the EU-15, and therefore this hypothesis is so far untested. Furthermore, for the many EU-15 banks, their presence in NMSs seems to have had positive effects as it has helped to boost their profitability. Box 14.2 illustrates one such case, Bank Austria, which recently reported strong profits driven mainly by eastern European subsidiaries activities. However, diversification of EU banks in NMSs, and in CEECs in particular, could also potentially be a source of increased risk taking and volatility of earnings.

Box 14.2 Bank Austria and its performance in central and eastern Europe

In the first half of 2005, Bank Austria Creditanstalt (BA-CA) significantly improved its results compared with the first six months of 2004. Net income after taxes rose by EUR 168 million or 58.9 per cent to EUR 453 million (first half of 2004: EUR 285 million). The return-on-equity after taxes (ROE) improved from 9.4 per cent to 13.4 per cent, although BA-CA's already strong equity capital base increased further, by 6.7 per cent to EUR 7.1 billion. The cost–income ratio also improved, from 64.7 per cent to 61.2 per cent.

All business segments of Bank Austria Creditanstalt contributed to the improvement in results for the first six months of 2005. Net income after taxes in the CEE business segment (central and eastern Europe) rose substantially, by 52.7 per cent to EUR 201.9 million, compared with the first half of 2004. Combined total assets of the CEE banking subsidiaries also increased strongly, by 14 per cent to EUR 33.5 billion, compared with 31 December 2004. Bank Austria Creditanstalt's entire network in the region of central and eastern Europe currently comprises over 1,000 offices in eleven countries. The bank serves over 4.7 million customers in this region. Via HVB Group, BA-CA customers also have access to markets in Russia, Ukraine, the Baltic States and all international financial centres. The Group has again become the largest bank in CEE, with total assets (including BA-CA Leasing) of EUR 35.5 billion.

'As part of the integration with HVB Group we completely reoriented the bank in 2001. We are now fully concentrating on our core markets in Austria and Central and Eastern Europe, and we are very well placed. No other bank can offer its customers in this region in the heart of Europe such an extensive network with such a full range of products,' says Erich Hampel, BA-CA's CEO. 'And this clear strategy, the course we have pursued since 2001, is also reflected in the bank's business performance. Never before has Bank Austria Creditanstalt achieved such high levels of profitability and capital strength, and never before has the bank been so valuable.'

From the first half of 2000 to the first half of 2005, key figures for BA-CA have improved significantly: its market capitalisation – the company's value – has more than

▶

> doubled from EUR 6 billion to over EUR 12 billion. Operating profit has tripled. Shareholders' equity has increased by almost 60 per cent to over EUR 7 billion. Despite this fact, the ROE is better than 5 years earlier and the cost–income ratio is considerably lower. Moreover, as an employer, Bank Austria Creditanstalt has grown substantially: today it has more than 30,000 employees, compared with 19,000 in 2000.
>
> *Source:* Adapted from http://www.ba-ca.com/en/index.html.

To summarise, most empirical evidence seems to find a positive association between foreign ownership and banking sector performance in NMSs, with foreign-owned banks outperforming domestic ones.[5] However, there are also examples of EU-15 banks retreating from NMSs, due to failed expansion strategies. Finally, despite the mostly positive experience of foreign ownership in the former accession countries, it needs pointing out that it is still a relatively recent phenomenon and the long-term implications are as yet unknown.

14.5 Mergers and Acquisition activities

As discussed earlier, foreign banks have expanded their presence in the new Member States in large part benefiting from the process of privatisation of formerly state-owned banks. Privatisation was also the main driver of M&A activity. Such activity has recently slowed down, due to the fact that most banking sectors in NMSs are now highly concentrated. Considering the period in the run-up to the EU accession in 2004, M&A activity in the banking sector increased dramatically up to 2002 and then declined when the process of privatisation came to an end (see Figure 14.3).

Figure 14.3 **M&As in EU accession countries (1990–2003)**

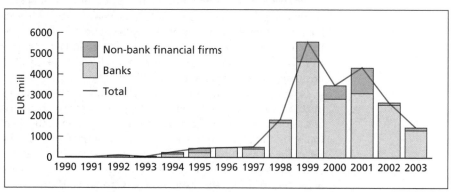

Source: Adapted from ECB (2004d).

---

[5] See, among others, Yildirim and Philppatos (2002); Weill (2003); Hasan and Marton (2003).

In the period 1991–2003 in Poland, for example, 1,695 M&A operations were carried out, for a total value of €32.6 billion and representing 35 per cent of the total M&A activity in all accession countries. A very high proportion of the total activity consisted of cross-border M&As (76 per cent). The weight of financial sector M&A in the total cross-border M&A was 34 per cent in the period under consideration (26 per cent banks and 8 per cent non-bank financial institutions).[6] The level and composition of financial cross-border M&As in Poland is shown in Figure 14.4.

Table 14.12 shows the geographical composition of the M&A activity in the three largest CEECs (Poland, Hungary and the Czech Republic) for the period 1991–2003.

Figure 14.4 Cross-border M&As in Poland (millions of €; 1991–2003)

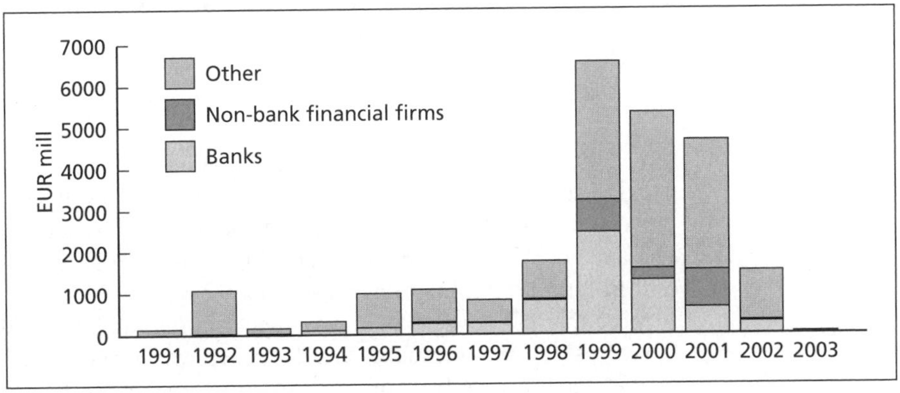

Source: Thompson SDC (adapted from ECB (2004d)).

Table 14.12 M&As in Poland, Hungary and the Czech Republic (1991–2003)

			Poland	Hungary	Czech Republic
Total M&A (EUR million)			**32,611**	**13,031**	**22,773**
Geographical composition of M&A – home country of the acquiring firm (% of total M&A)	Domestic		24	22	25
	Euro area		49	46	53
	of which:	Germany	10	20	20
		France	15	7	7
		Italy	6	5	1
		Spain	1	0	0
		The Netherlands	9	4	9
		Belguim	3	3	5
		Austria	1	5	11
		Finland	1	1	0
	Other		4	1	0
	Other EU		7	6	8
	of which: UK		2	6	6
	Other accession countries		3	1	3
	United States		14	12	7
	Other		5	14	4
Composition of cross-border M&A by sector (% of total cross-border M&A)	Banks		19	11	24
	Non-bank financial firms		6	2	2
	Other		74	87	74

Source: Adapted from ECB (2004d).

---

[6] Data quoted from ECB (2004d) *Financial FDI to the EU Accession Countries* DG-IMAW/04 78.

Figure 14.5 Market share of the five largest banks (CR-5)

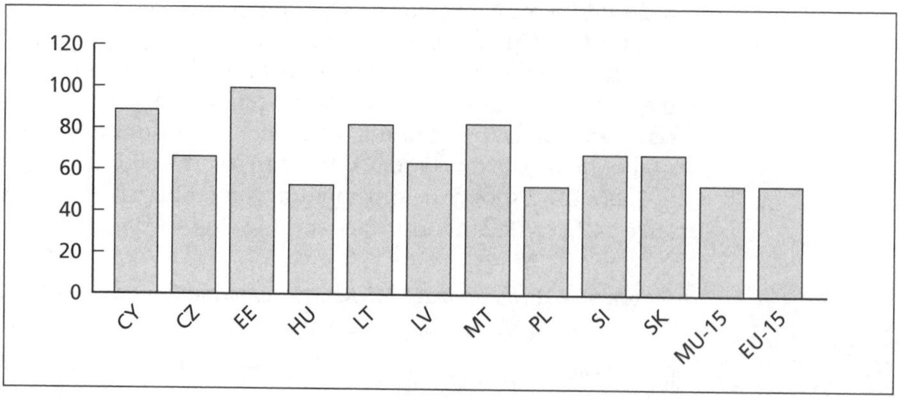

Source: ECB (2005d) and authors' calculations. Data refer to the year 2003.

After 2003 there have been very few M&As, reflecting the fact that most NMSs banking sectors are now highly concentrated, as a result of the privatisation and M&As processes. The aggregate market share of the five largest banks in 2003 averages at 72 per cent, varying between 52 per cent in Poland and Hungary and 99 per cent in Estonia (the EU-15 average is 53 per cent).

More than 80 per cent of banking sector assets are held by the five largest banks in Cyprus, Estonia, Lithuania and Malta. However, the overall size of the banking market needs also to be taken into account. Smaller banking markets in the EU-15 also have very high degrees of concentration, such as Belgium (83 per cent) and the Netherlands (84 per cent).[7]

Given the high concentration ratios in NMSs, concerns may arise regarding the level of competition in banking markets. However, competition is expected to increase, rather than decrease, owing to the increased European integration of banking and financial sectors. This may give a further impetus to the restructuring and M&A process.

14.6 The regulatory framework

As discussed earlier, NMSs in their successful bid to join the European Union had to adopt the *acquis communautaire*, which is the body of principles, practices, obligations, objectives and legal and other acts that have been agreed or have been developed over the years by the European Union. These include the EU Treaties in their entirety, as well as all existing EU legislation and Court of Justice judgments. As early as 2001, the European Bank for Reconstruction and Development (EBRD) in its 'Transition Report', was assigning very high marks to the regulatory framework of the then accession countries, many achieving a '4' which is the standard of advanced industrialised countries (see Table 14.13).

---

[7] For a comparison, see Table 13.3.

Table 14.13 Qualitative assessment of the regulatory framework in CEECs and the Baltic States

County	Extensiveness of supervision	Effectiveness of supervision	Banking reform and interest rate liberalisation	Securities markets and non-banks
Czech Rep.	3+	3	4–	3
Estonia	4–	4	4–	3
Hungary	4–	4–	4	4–
Latvia	3	3	3+	2+
Lithuania	3+	4–	3	3
Poland	4	3	3+	4–
Slovakia	3	3	3+	2+
Slovenia	4	4–	3+	3-

Source: EBRD (2001) *Transition Report* (http://www.ebrd.com/pubs/econo/series/tr.htm).

In the run-up to the 2004 accession, all countries aligned their regulatory frameworks with EU legislation to an extent that enabled them to successfully join the European Union. However, this does not automatically guarantee the implementation of the *acquis* in the domestic regulatory and supervisory framework. Whereas the most important EU Banking Directives have now been implemented in all NMSs, there are still some outstanding issues, as identified by the European Commission and illustrated in Table 14.14 below.

Table 14.14 Legislative and supervisory alignment of the NMSs (end 2003)

	CY	CZ	EE	HU	LT	LV	MT	PL	SI	SK
Legislative alignment with the *acquis communautaire* in the banking sector, except for:										
Electronic Money Institutions Directive	(*)	*	*	(*)[1]	(*)[1]		(*)	*		(*)[1]
Deposit guarantee schemes		T		T	T			*	T	*
Co-operative credit institutions	T			T				*		
Savings and loans institutions' annual accounts									*	
Capital adequacy rules		*					(*)	*		
Winding up, liquidation procedures			*				(*)	*		
Branches' and subsidiaries' annual accounts/EU Passport				*			(*)	*		
***Acquis* related tasks as a supervisory authority in the field of banking are performed satisfactorily, except for:**										
Legal protection of supervisors/enforcement powers								*		
Enhancing cross-border supervisory co-operation								*		
Strengthening co-operative banks' supervisor	*									
Improving co-operation between sectoral supervisors	(*)				*			*		(*)
Financial independence		*								
Operational and political independence				*				*		
Out-of-court redress schemes									*	

Note: T means transition agreements are in place (ending at the latest by end 2007); * certain issues need to be resolved in the field under consideration; (*) means progress has been made or the issue resolved in the mean time; blank means the issue has not been mentioned. [1] Directive transposed to national legislation in 2004.

Source: Adapted from ECB (2005d) *Banking Structures in the new EU Member States*, January.

A further challenge will arise with the implementation of the so-called Lamfalussy Procedure, which was explained in Section 7.7.

The Financial Services Action Plan (FSAP) (as briefly discussed in Section 13.3.2) also aims to reform a substantial part of the EU regulatory framework. While many areas have already been addressed in NMSs, others, such as the supervision of pension funds, still need attention.

14.6.1 Supervisory structure and safety net arrangements

In most NMSs, supervision is organised on a sectoral basis, with different regulatory authorities supervising banking, insurance, pension funds and other investments services. Estonia, Hungary, Latvia and Malta, on the other hand, have set up a single supervisory authority modelled on the FSA in the UK. As far as the oversight of the banking sector is concerned in Cyprus, the Czech Republic, Slovakia, Slovenia and Lithuania it is the responsibility of the central bank; in other NMSs, as a result of recent restructuring, it is entrusted to a newly created single supervisory authority.

Deposit protection, in most NMSs, is arranged as an explicit and compulsory scheme and in most cases deposit insurance schemes were introduced during the 1990s. These generally cover deposits both in domestic and foreign currencies, usually up to 90 per cent of the overall deposit amount. In those countries where the minimum coverage is lower than the EU standard, the EU minimum will have to be reached by 2008.[8]

14.7 Conclusions

This chapter offered an overview of the banking systems of the ten new EU Member States (NMSs). They include the former transition economies of eastern Europe (the CEECs and the Baltic States – the NIM-8) and Malta and Cyprus. Banks in new Member States have benefited from a period of favourable macroeconomic conditions in the run-up to EU accession. This has positively contributed to the development of the banking sectors and has also helped reduce the level of non-performing loans inherited from the pre-transition period. A large-scale privatisation process, that resulted in widespread foreign acquisition of banks, coupled with a more recent M&A wave, has contributed to an acceleration of the restructuring process. As a result of these processes, the number of state-owned banks (which represented the typical ownership structure before the transition period) has steadily declined, whereas the number of foreign banks has increased dramatically. Foreign banks, mainly from EU-15 countries (particularly from Austria, Germany, Belgium and Italy), have sought productive opportunities in neighbouring countries in the run-up to the EU accession. Foreign banks are credited with knowledge transfer, rationalisation and good managerial practices. Thus far, the dominant foreign presence has been positive for NMSs, even though it

[8] For more detail, see Nenovsky and Dimirova (2003).

raises concerns for possible periods of stress and economic downturns. NMSs have come a long way in the implementation of the EU regulatory and supervisory framework, even though there are still areas of concern, particularly relating to financial institutions other than banks. The next step, for most NMSs, will be the membership of the ERM II, with a view to joining the single currency, and the implementation of the Lamfalussy procedure, which aims to reform a substantial part of the EU regulatory framework.

Key terms

New Member States (NMSs)

ERM II

Visegrad countries

Central and Eastern European Countries (CEECS)

NIM-8

Transition countries

European Monetary System (EMS)

Privatisation process

Acquis Communautaire

Key reading

European Central Bank (2004d) *Financial FDI to the EU Accession Countries*, http://www.bis.org/publ/cgfs22ecb.pdf

European Central Bank (2005d) *Banking Structures in the New EU Member States*, January 2005, http://www.ecb.int/pub/pdf/other/bankingstructuresnewmembersstatesen.pdf

Hasan, I. and Marton, K. (2003) 'Development and efficiency of the banking sector in a transitional economy: Hungarian experience', *Journal of Banking and Finance*, **27** (12), pp. 2249–71.

Revision questions and problems

1 Describe the main features of the ERM II and the implications of membership for the new EU Member States.

2 Unlike Denmark and the UK, the new EU Member States do not have an 'op-out' clause and they will have, eventually, to adopt the Euro. Discuss the implications of such a decision and the potential timetable for adoption of the Euro.

3 What are the distinguishing features of the NIM-8 banking sectors compared with those of the remaining new Member States?

4 Is asset quality a problem in NMSs?

5 What are the main problems associated with the dominant foreign presence in NMSs' banking markets?

6 The process of privatisation of the banking sector, followed by a wave of M&As, has resulted in increased concentration in the banking markets of NMSs. Should we be concerned about decreased competition?

7 What is the *acquis communautaire*? How did it help shape the regulatory framework in NMSs?

8 Describe the Lamfalussy procedure and its relevance for NMSs' financial sector.

Chapter 15

Banking in the United States

Learning objectives

- To distinguish between different types of bank depository institutions and investment companies operating in the United States
- To understand the meaning of the disintermediation process
- To understand the characteristics of the US payment system
- To understand the main trends in the performance of US banks
- To understand the main tasks and organisation of the US regulatory authorities

15.1　Introduction

This chapter examines the main features of the US banking system outlining recent structural and financial developments. The first part of the chapter looks at the changing structure of the system highlighting the consolidation trend and the systematic decline in the number of banks, as well as the increase in industry concentration. We then outline the main types of banking and financial service firms operating in the United States, discussing the main deposit-taking institutions and other financial firms. Since the passing of the **Gramm-Leach-Bliley Act** of 1999, US banks can establish financial holding companies and can now engage in the full range of financial services areas. The general adoption of the universal banking model and its implications for bank balance sheet structure, performance and regulation are also covered in this chapter.

15.2　Structure of the banking and financial system

There are a wide range of financial intermediaries operating in the US system that provide a variety of banking and other financial services. A common way of distinguishing between such intermediaries is based on the main type of liabilities these institutions hold.

The main types of financial institutions operating in the United States include:

- **Depository institutions** – Commercial banks, savings institutions and credit unions. The main types of liabilities these institutions hold are deposits.
- **Contractual savings institutions** – Insurance companies and pension funds whose main liabilities are the long-term future benefits to be paid to policyholders and fund holders. These liabilities typically take the form of reserves that are listed on the company's balance sheet as part of liabilities.
- **Investment intermediaries** – Mutual funds, investment banks, securities firms and finance houses whose liabilities are usually short-term money market or capital market securities.

The following provides an overview of the main features of these types of financial intermediaries.

15.3　Depository institutions

15.3.1　Commercial banks

Commercial banks are the major financial intermediaries in the US economy. They are the main providers of credit to the household and corporate sector and operate the payments mechanism. Commercial banks are typically joint stock companies. They may either be publicly listed on the stock exchange or privately owned, and their main liabilities are deposits (of different size, currency and maturity). Often a distinction is made between *demand deposits* (deposits payable on demand) and *time deposits* (deposits that have a term, e.g., three-month deposits). Deposits are either retail (small household deposits) or wholesale (high-value deposits from companies, banks and other institutions). Deposits can be denominated in the home or foreign currency.

Figure 15.1 shows that the number of commercial banks fell from over 14,000 in 1984 to 7,501 in March 2005. According to the Federal Deposit Insurance Corporation (FDIC) Statistics on Depository Institutions these banks had $8.6 trillion in assets of which total loans amounted to $5 trillion by March 2005.

The decline in the number of banks, a trend common in many other countries, has been mainly the result of M&A activity, and recent years have witnessed deals between large banks that had the effect of increasing industry concentration. The share of banking sector industry assets controlled by the ten largest banks increased from 20 per cent in 1990 to 48 per cent by the end of 2004 and over the same period the share of the top 100 banks grew from around 50 to 77 per cent. Since the passing of the Gramm-Leach-Bliley Act of 1999 it has been possible to create financial holding companies where banks can engage in securities underwriting, insurance sales and a broad range of investment banking and other financial services business. All major banks are part of financial holding companies of which there were 636 by the end of 2004.

Another interesting feature of US banking relates to the position of foreign banks in the system as well as the growing international operations of US banks. Foreign-owned banking assets in the United States have exceeded international assets of US banks since the mid-1980s and they now account for over 18 per cent of total US banking sector assets and around 22 per cent of business lending (as noted in Chapter 4). Table 15.1 shows the major foreign banks operating in the United States at the end of 2004.

Table 15.2 illustrates the major foreign activities of US banks and shows that Citibank (the commercial banking part of the Citigroup financial holding company) has foreign assets amounting to $395 billion, 42 per cent of the total of all foreign assets of US banks. The top five banks – Citibank, JPMorganChase, Bank of America, State Street Bank and Bank of New York account for 87 per cent of foreign bank assets, and the top three account for 651 of the 777 total foreign bank branches of US banks. The majority of this foreign banking activity relates to business in Europe where around 54 per cent of foreign bank assets of US banks are located, followed by Asia (23 per cent of foreign bank assets). US bank presence in Latin America and the Caribbean has declined in recent years.

Figure 15.1 Commercial banks in the United States 1984–2005

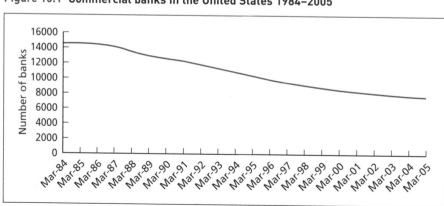

Table 15.1 Ten largest foreign-owned FDIC-insured commercial and savings institutions, 31 December 2004 ($ billions)

Name	City, State	Assets
HSBC Bank USA NA	Wilmington, DE	$138.3
LaSalle Bank NA*	Chicago, IL	63.7
Charter One Bank NA†	Cleveland, OH	50.9
Standard Federal Bank NA*	Troy, MI	39.1
Bank of the West	San Francisco, CA	38.8
Deutsche Bank Trust Co. Americas	New York, NY	33.3
Citizens Bank of Massachusetts†	Boston, MA	31.3
Citizens Bank of Pennsylvania†	Philadelphia, PA	29.8
Harris Trust & Savings Bank	Chicago, IL	21.5
RBC Centura Bank	Rocky Mount, NC	18.4
Total		**$465.1**

* Subsidiaries of ABN AMRO Holding NV
† Subsidiaries of Royal Bank of Scotland Group, Plc

Source: FDIC (2005) *Outlook: The Globalisation of the US Banking Industry*, Summer
http://www.fdic.gov/bank/analytical/regional/ro20052q/na/2005summer_03.html.

Table 15.2 FDIC-insured US bank share of foreign office assets: 1984 versus 2004 ($bn)

31 December 1984				*31 December 2004*			
Bank	Foreign office assets	Share of all US bank foreign office assets %	Cumulative share %	Bank	Foreign office assets	Share of all US bank foreign office assets %	Cumulative share %
Citibank NA	$67	17	17	Citibank NA	$395	42	42
Chase Manhattan Bank NA[a]	46	11	28	JPMorgan Chase Bank NA	326	34	76
Bank of America NT&SA	40	10	38	Bank of America NA[c]	56	6	82
Morgan Guaranty Trust Co.[a]	33	8	46	State Street Bank & Trust Co.	25	3	85
Manufacturers Hanover Trust Co.[a]	25	7	53	Bank of New York	24	3	88
Bankers Trust Co.	21	5	58	Wachovia Bank National Assn	22	2	9
Chemical Bank[a]	18	4	62	MBNA America Bank NA	18	2	9
First National Bank of Chicago[a]	13	4	66	Fleet National Bank[c]	17	2	93
Continental Illinois NB&T[b]	10	2	68	Northern Trust Co.	13	2	95
Security Pacific National Bank[b]	9	2	70	HSBC Bank USA National Assn[d]	10	1	96
Total	$281			Total	$906		

[a] Now part of JPMorgan Chase Bank NA.
[b] Now part of Bank of America NA.
[c] Subsidiaries of Bank of America Corporation.
[d] A foreign-owned bank.

Source: FDIC (2005) *Outlook: The Globalisation of the US Banking Industry*, Summer
http://www.fdic.gov/bank/analytical/regional/ro20052q/na/2005summer_03.html.

It is important to note that non-banking subsidiaries have been the most rapidly growing source of foreign assets reported by US bank holding companies over the past ten years. These subsidiaries undertake a range of activities, including securities underwriting, real estate brokerage and other commercial enterprises. The growth of these non-banking subsidiaries underscores the long-term trend toward diversification of earnings beyond traditional commercial banking products and services.

In general, the main strategic reasons for the foreign expansion of US banks relates to the desire to:

- increase profits by expanding distribution channels into new, potentially high-growth geographic markets and across demographic groups;
- provide commercial lending and capital markets products and services to complement the international expansion plans of corporate and commercial clients;
- increase revenue diversification; and
- cross-sell and leverage existing product expertise in foreign markets.

15.3.2 Savings institutions

The US financial system also hosts a variety of savings institutions that are similar in many respects to commercial banks, although their main difference (typically) relates to their ownership features – as savings institutions traditionally have mutual ownership. They are owned by their 'members' or 'shareholders', who are the depositors or borrowers. The main type of savings institutions (briefly discussed in Chapter 3) in the United States are the so-called **Savings and Loans Association (S&Ls) (or thrifts)**, which traditionally were mainly financed by household deposits and lent retail mortgages. Their business is more diversified nowadays as they offer a wider range of corporate loan, credit card and other facilities. Originally, the S&Ls were mainly mutual in ownership but now many have become listed. They compete directly with commercial banks particularly in the retail and small to medium-sized business sectors. There were 1,332 S&Ls in March 2005 with assets of $1.7 trillion – and they are the second largest deposite-taking group of financial institutions in the United States.

15.3.3 Credit unions

Credit unions are another type of mutual deposit institution that are present in the US financial system and have grown in importance over the last decade or so. These are non-profit institutions that are owned by their members. Member deposits are used to offer loans to the members. Many staff are part-time and they usually are regulated differently to banks. In the US there were 9,058 as of March 2005 with 82 million members with deposits exceeding $520 billion and loans over $355 billion.

Commercial banks and the S&Ls compete for personal and business banking services, although commercial banks focus more on larger-scale corporate banking activity. The credit unions focus almost entirely on the retail financial services segment.

Although these institutions constitute the main deposit-taking institutions in the United States it is also important to mention briefly other financial service firms that also compete and/or complement banks in the provision of financial services. This is because these firms and especially pension funds and mutual funds have become increasingly important relative to banks in the US financial system.

15.4 **Contractual savings institutions**

15.4.1 **Insurance companies**

Insurance products are an integral feature of the financial services sector and many US banks nowadays cross-sell insurance services to their banking clients. As was discussed in Chapter 3, insurance companies protect individuals and firms (or policyholders) from various adverse events. They receive premiums from policy-holders and promise compensation if the adverse event occurs. There are two main types of insurance company – life insurance and general (or property and casualty insurance). The latter is insurance that does not involve death as the main risk. It includes home, vehicle and various commercial risks such as aviation insurance. A company that undertakes both life and non-life insurance is known as a *composite insurance company*.

According to the US Insurance Information Institute[1] the assets of the life insurance sector amounted to just over £3.75 trillion and the property and causality insurance to $1.2 trillion at the end of 2003. Tables 15.3 and 15.4 illustrate the main insurance companies operating in the United States.

Table 15.3 Top 20 US property/casualty companies, by revenues, 2004 ($ millions)

Rank	Group	Revenues $	Assets $
1	American International Group	98,610	800,000
2	Berkshire Hathaway	74,382	188,874
3	State Farm Insurance Cos.	58,819	149,827
4	Allstate	33,936	149,725
5	St Paul Travelers Cos.	22,934	111,815
6	Hartford Financial Services	22,693	259,735
7	Nationwide	20,558	157,371
8	Liberty Mutual Insurance Group	19,754	72,359
9	Loews (CNA)	14,584	73,750
10	Progressive	13,782	17,184
11	Chubb	13,177	44,260
12	USAA	11,273	46,482
13	Fidelity National Financial	8,296	9,271
14	Safeco	7,336	14,586
15	First American Corp.	6,722	6,208
16	American Family Insurance Group	6,655	13,641
17	Auto-Owners Insurance	4,737	10,662
18	Erie Insurance Group	4,555	12,195
19	W.R. Berkley	4,512	11,451
20	American Financial Group	3,912	22,560

Source: http://www.iii.org/media/facts/statsbyissue/industry/.

---

[1] http://www.iii.org.

Table 15.4 Top 20 US life/health insurance groups and companies, by revenues, 2004 ($ millions)

Rank	Group	Revenues $	Assets $
1	MetLife	39,535	356,808
2	Prudential Financial	28,348	401,058
3	New York Life Insurance	27,176	144,421
4	TIAA-CREF	23,411	347,580
5	Mass. Mutual Life Ins.	23,159	124,510
6	Northwestern Mutual	17,806	123,957
7	AFLAC	13,281	59,326
8	UnumProvident	10,611	50,832
9	Guardian Life of America	8,893	35,395
10	Principal Financial	8,756	113,798
11	Assurant	7,404	23,969
12	Thrivent Financial for Lutherans	6,445	53,541
13	Lincoln National	5,371	116,219
14	Pacific Life	4,930	77,137
15	Conseco	4,330	30,756
16	Jefferson-Pilot	4,102	35,105
17	Mutual of Omaha Ins.	4,080	16,409
18	Western & Southern Financial	3,695	26,032
19	Torchmark	3,072	14,252
20	Unitrin	3,041	8,790

Source: Fortune.

15.4.2 Pension funds

Pension funds provide retirement income (in the form of annuities) to employees covered by pension plans. They obtain their income from contributions made by employees and employers and invest these in a variety of long-term securities (bonds and equity) and other investments such as property. A distinction is made between private and public pension funds:

- **Private pension funds** are pension funds that are administered by a bank, life insurance firm or pension fund manager. Contributions paid into the fund by employers and employees are invested in long-term investments with the contributing individual receiving a pension on retirement. Note, however, that many company pension plans are under-funded because they aim to meet pension obligations out of current earnings when benefits are due. If companies have sufficient earnings then this under-funding is not a problem but if they do not, then they cannot meet pension obligations. Various legislation has been put in place, particularly in the United States and the United Kingdom to try and minimise the likelihood of major under-funding – but at the time of writing (mid-2005) it is a major issue for many large private pension funds.
- **Public pension funds** are the pension provision of the government. In the United States the most important public pension plans are the Social Security Old Age and Survivors Insurance Fund.

15.5 Investment intermediaries

15.5.1 Mutual funds

A mutual fund is a company that pools the money of many investors – its share-holders – in order to invest in a range of different securities. Investments may be in stocks, bonds, money market securities or some combination of these. The mutual funds are professionally managed on behalf of the shareholders, and each investor holds a share of the portfolio and are entitled to any profits (and liable for any losses) when the securities are sold.

There are two main segments of the mutual fund industry – long-term and short-term funds. Long-term funds include bond funds, equity funds and other hybrid funds that contain a mix of bonds and equity. Short-term funds are known as money market funds and they are comprised of a range of money market instruments – in the United States (where the market for mutual funds in general is most developed) they also allow shareholders to write cheques against the value of money market funds. (These are known as *money market fund checking accounts*).

The main attraction for investors is that mutual funds provide diversification benefits as their assets are invested in many different securities. Note that there are many different types of mutual funds with different risk–return objectives. In the United States over $7.5 trillion had been invested in mutual funds by the end of the first quarter of 2005.

15.5.2 Investment banks and securities firms

As we noted in Chapter 3, the world's largest investment banks come from the United States, including such firms as Goldman Sachs, Morgan Stanley and Merrill Lynch. Their main function is to help companies and governments raise funds in the capital market. Their main business relates to issuing new debt and equity, which they arrange on behalf of clients, as well as providing corporate advisory services on mergers and acquisitions (M&As) and other types of corporate restructuring. Since 1999 and the abandonment of the Glass-Steagall Act, various US commercial banks have acquired investment banks (Citigroup now includes the investment bank Salomon Brothers and the brokerage firm Smith Barney; and the commercial bank Chase is now linked up to JP Morgan). This means that banks such as Citigroup and JPMorganChase now offer both commercial and investment banking services.

Securities firms assist in the trading of existing securities. There are two main types of securities firms: brokers (agents of investors that match buyers with sellers of securities) and dealers (agents who link buyers and sellers by buying and selling securities). In the United States there are specialist discount brokers, for instance, which undertake trading activities for clients without providing advice (like Charles Schwab) and specialist electronic trading securities firms (E*trade).

15.6 Disintermediation in the US financial system

Table 15.5 provides a snapshot of the evolution and relative size of various types of financial firms in the United States and highlights the relative decline of depository firms compared to mutual funds between 1970 and 2005. This decline is a reflection of the disintermediation trend, where customers by-pass intermediaries in order to obtain improved returns from direct financing.

Table 15.5 Shares of total financial intermediary assets, 1970–2005 (first quarter) (%)

	1970	1980	1990	2002	2005
Insurance Companies					
Life insurance	15.3	11.5	12.5	13.6	13.2
Property and casualty	3.8	4.5	4.9	3.7	3.8
Pension funds					
Private	8.4	12.5	14.9	14.7	13.6
Public (state and local government)	4.6	4.9	6.7	7.9	6.5
Finance companies	4.9	5.1	5.6	3.2	4.5
Mutual funds					
Stock and bond	3.6	1.7	5.9	10.6	17.3
Money market	0	1.9	4.6	8.8	5.8
Depository institutions					
Commercial banks	38.5	36.7	30.4	29.8	27.7
S & L and mutual savings banks	19.4	19.6	12.5	5.6	5.4
Credit unions	1.4	1.6	2	2.3	2.1
Total (%)	100	100	100	100	100.0

Note: The total of all financial intermediary assets listed in the above table summed to $31.5 trillion by the end of the first quarter of 2005.

Source: US Federal Reserve Flow of Funds Account, 9 June 2005; http://www.federalreserve.gov/releases/z1/20050609/

In formal terms, disintermediation occurs where ultimate borrowers and ultimate lenders by-pass the established financial intermediation channels and borrow/lend directly.

For large corporate borrowers possessing high credit ratings, it may simply be cheaper to raise funds directly from savers/investors than through a financial intermediary. The costs associated with the intermediary are eliminated from the transaction to the benefit of both borrowers and lenders. There are also other advantages for companies in terms of raising market profile and the diversification of sources of funds. However, these benefits of financial disintermediation must be weighed against the costs (i.e., the benefits of financial intermediation forgone). A good example of disintermediation in this context is the use of commercial paper issues by large companies as a means of raising short-term funds.

While the cost factor is the main commercial driver of disintermediation, it may also occur on account of official restrictions being placed on normal intermediation activity, perhaps with the purpose of controlling the money supply. Borrowers may be turned away from financial intermediaries and hence may seek other sources of funds, direct from savers/investors.

Whatever the cause, it is apparent from Table 15.5 that the decline in depository institutions' assets at the expense of mutual funds is a clear sign that the disintermediation process has been prevalent in the United States over the last decade or so.

15.7 US payments systems

Having a well-functioning payments system is critical for the smooth running of an economy. The challenges posed by the ever-changing demands of individuals, firms and government, and technological advances all have an impact on the evolution of the payment system. As in most developed countries, the United States has two main parts to its payments system – one that deals with wholesale large-value payments and another that deals with retail and relatively small-value payments.

15.7.1 Wholesale payments

In the United States, payment and securities settlement systems involve a large number of financial intermediaries, financial services firms and non-bank businesses that create, distribute and process large-value payments. The bulk of the dollar value of these payments are processed electronically and are generally used to purchase, sell or finance securities transactions; to make or repay loans; settle real estate transactions; and make large-value, time-critical payments, such as payments for the settlement of interbank purchases, settlement of foreign exchange transactions or other financial market transactions.

There are two main networks for interbank, or large-value, domestic, funds transfer payment orders. The first, **Fedwire**, is owned and operated by the Federal Reserve Banks, and is an important participant in providing interbank payment services as well as safekeeping and transfer services for US government and agency securities, and mortgage-backed securities. Fedwire is a real-time gross settlement (RTGS)[2] system that enables participants to make final payments in central bank money. Fedwire consists of a range of procedures and computer applications to route and settle payments orders: the system reviews payment orders and notifies participants of related credits and debits to their accounts. Fedwire is supported by the Federal Reserve's national communications network (FEDNET).

An institution that holds an account with a Federal Reserve Bank can generally become a Fedwire participant. These participants use Fedwire to instruct a Federal Reserve Bank to debit funds from the participant's own Federal Reserve account and credit the Federal Reserve account of another participant. Fedwire processes and settles payment orders individually throughout the operating day. Payment to the receiving participant over Fedwire is final and irrevocable when the amount of the payment order is credited to the receiving participant's account or when the payment order is sent to the receiving participant, whichever is earlier. Fedwire participants send payment orders electronically or by phone to a Federal Reserve Bank. Payment orders must be in the proper syntax and meet the relevant security con-

---

[2] A real-time gross settlement system is a payment system in which processing and settlement of transactions take place in real time (continuously).

trols. An institution sending payment orders to a Federal Reserve Bank is required to have sufficient funds either in the form of account balances or overdraft capacity, or a payment order may be rejected.

The value of transactions conducted via Fedwire increased from 50 times GDP in 1989 to 62 times GDP (exceeding $703 trillion in value of transactions) in 2003.

The second major wholesale payments system is known as **CHIPS**, the Clearing House Interbank Payments System, and this is the main bank-owned payments system for clearing large-value payments. CHIPS is a real-time payments system for US dollars that uses bi-lateral and multi-lateral netting (where payments are netted out between bank participants). CHIPS processes over 270,000 payments a day with a gross value of $1.4 trillion. It serves the largest banks representing 19 countries world-wide. Much of CHIPS' business relates to cross-border payments in US dollars. The number of participants using CHIPS fell from 104 in 1996 to 53 reflecting consolidation between major banks. Also the value of transactions conducted via CHIPS declined from around 40 times GDP in 1997 to under 30 times by 2003 – as a result of the fall in number of participating banks and also possibly due to the reduction in fees charged by Fedwire for wholesale payments.

The processing of large-value funds transfers involves two important elements: **clearing** and **settlement**. Clearing relates to the transfer and confirmation of information between the payer (sending financial institution) and payee (receiving financial institution). Settlement is the transfer of funds between the payer's financial institution and the payee's financial institution. Settlement discharges the obligation of the payer's financial institution to the payee's financial institution with respect to the payment order. Final settlement is irrevocable and unconditional. The finality of the payment is determined by the rules and the relevant laws that apply.

In general, payment messages may be credit transfers or debit transfers. Most large-value funds transfer systems are credit transfer systems in which both payment messages and funds move from the payer financial institution to the payee financial institution. An institution initiates a funds transfer by transmitting a payment order (a message that requests the transfer of funds to the payee). Payment order processing follows the rules and operating procedures of the large-value payment system used. Typically, large-value payment system operating procedures include identification, reconciliation and confirmation procedures necessary to process the payment orders. In some systems, financial institutions may contract directly with one or more third parties to help perform clearing and settlement activities on behalf of the institution.

15.7.2 Retail payments

In the United States, many payments traditionally made with paper instruments – cheques and cash – are now being made electronically with debit or credit cards or via the **automated clearing house (ACH)**. The ACH electronic funds transfer system provides for the clearing of electronic payments for participating banks and other depository institutions. ACH payments include such things as:

● direct deposits of payroll, Social Security and other government benefits, and tax refunds;
● direct payments of consumer bills such as mortgages, loans, utility bills and insurance premiums;

- business-to-business payments;
- e-cheques;
- e-commerce payments;
- federal, state and local tax payments.

Until recently, paper cheques accounted for the majority of non-cash payments but since the mid-1990s they have been increasingly replaced by other means of non-cash payment. Table 15.6 shows that between 2000 and 2003 the number of cheque payments in the United States fell and grew modestly for credit card transactions, while debit card payments increased rapidly. The Federal Reserve suggest that a variety of factors, such as growth in economic activity and population, have contributed to the increase in electronic payments. They also note that some of the increase is probably also due to the replacement of some cash and cheque payments with electronic payments.

Table 15.6 **Annual number of non-cash payments in 2003 and 2000 ($)**

	2000 estimate (billion)	2003 estimate (billion)	CAGR %
Non-cash payments	72.5	81.2	3.8
Cheque	41.9	36.7	–4.3
Credit Card	15.6	19.0	6.7
ACH	6.2	9.1	13.4
Offline Debit	5.3	10.3	24.9
Online Debit	3.0	5.3	21.0
EBT	0.5	0.8	15.4

Notes:
1) The cheque estimates represent cheques paid, not cheques written.
2) ACH are Automated Clearing House transactions such as direct debits, standing orders and other payments.
3) Debit card payments include online debit (PIN-based), which includes purchases at the point of sale with ATM cards, and off-line debit (signature-based).
4) CAGR is the compound annual growth rate.
5) EBT are Electronic Benefits Payments – payments of social security and such like.

Source: The 2004 Federal Reserve Payments Study. *Analysis of Non-cash Payments Trends in the United States: 2000–2003*, December, http://www.frbservices.org/Retail/pdf/2004PaymentResearchReport.pdf.

Moves to reduce paper-based processing of cheques are a major feature of the Check Clearing for the 21st Century Act (**Check 21**) that became effective on 28 October 2004. Check 21 is designed to foster innovation in the payments system and to enhance its efficiency by permitting banks greater flexibility in converting paper cheques into electronic form to speed up retail payments. Box 15.1 describes Check 21 in more detail and notes other recent developments in US retail payments.

Box 15.1   Changes in the processing of payments automation of ACH, credit card and check processing

Twenty-five years ago, all the major payment instruments in use today – cash, checks, credit cards, automated clearinghouse (ACH), and debit cards – were being used in commercial activity for some segments of the US economy.

Improvements in the processing of payments by cash, check, credit cards, and ACH over the past several decades have decreased the amount of physical processing and increased the amount of electronic processing. Because processing of payments has become more electronic generally, the rise in the share of non-cash payments made with so-called electronic instruments understates the extent of the transition of the payments industry from physical to electronic processing.

Debit card networks were originally based on automated electronic systems that linked ATMs together, and the processing of these payments did not include a significant physical processing component. However, the processing of the other two types of electronic payments – ACH and credit cards – which once included considerable physical activity, now is wholly electronic.

The ACH system has evolved from the physical exchange of computer tapes within and among regional associations of depository institutions to an integrated electronic network for clearing and settlement that connects depository institutions around the country. Similarly, credit card processing has evolved from a largely physical activity – one in which accumulated paper transaction slips were deposited into a merchant's bank and then cleared and settled in a process similar to the process for paper checks – to an activity in which the availability of funds is almost always verified in real time over an electronic network and clearing and settlement occur electronically.

Changes that increase automated, electronic processing within the check collection system have come relatively slowly. Over the past twenty-five years, technology has evolved to allow the exchange by mutual agreement of electronic information on checks between depository institutions.

Despite this capability, the collection of most checks, in the absence of an agreement between depository institutions, has involved extensive physical processing, transportation, and delivery because state laws require that the original check be presented to the paying depository institution for settlement. However, the Check Clearing for the 21st Century Act, Public Law 108–100 (Check 21), is expected to facilitate use of electronics in the processing of checks, because the original paper check is no longer necessary for settlement. Instead, when a paper check is required, a depository institution may satisfy that requirement by providing a special paper copy of the original check known as a substitute check. A substitute check that meets specified standards is the legal equivalent of the original. Thus, it is possible for depository institutions to truncate checks and collect them electronically, but also to present paper checks when necessary. As this article is written, seven months after the effective date of Check 21, the use of new electronic processing methods provided for in the act is growing only slowly. However, depository institutions are expected to increase their use of electronic check-clearing methods over time to further automate the check collection and settlement process by exchanging check images. These and other efforts will make check processing increasingly similar to the processing of other non-cash payments.

Conversion of checks

Recently, technological innovations have occurred that allow the use of information from a check to initiate an electronic payment. This process, known as check conversion, was typically initiated by merchants at point-of-sale registers and by back-office transaction processors for large billers, into payments that are processed by ACH or the debit card networks and has contributed significantly to the recent acceleration in the growth of electronic payments.

The conversion of checks began to take hold in the late 1990s, eventually resulting in changes to ACH network rules and in payments regulations that govern the practice.

Source: Federal Reserve (2005) Trends in the Use of Payment Instruments in the United States, *Federal Reserve Bulletin* (Spring), p. 182.

15.8 Balance sheet features of US commercial banks

The balance sheet structure of US commercial banks reflects the main assets and liability components of their business. An overview of the assets and liabilities of the commercial banking sector is shown in Tables 15.7 and 15.8 respectively. Table 15.7 shows the asset structure of banks and illustrates that loans constituted around 58 per cent of banking sector assets in 2004 compared with around 62 per cent in 1990 – in fact, in 2004 the proportion of loans out of total assets dropped to its lowest level since 1990. Investment securities typically comprise 18–20 per cent of total assets. In addition, the amount of liquid assets (cash and due) was at its lowest level (around 4 per cent of total assets) in 2004 compared with the previous 15 years. Other earning assets have also increased noticeably since 1999.

Table 15.8 shows the changing liability features of US commercial banks highlighting the greater reliance on purchased funds (wholesale deposits acquired through the interbank market) and the higher level of capital in recent years compared with the early 1990s.

These broad trends mask more intricate changes in the balance sheet features of US banks. The Federal Reserve publishes an annual review of profits and balance sheet developments at US commercial banks in its Federal Reserve Bulletin (see Klee and Natalucci, 2005, for the 2004 review) and this details many recent changes. A summary of recent changes to the balance sheet features of US banks can be listed as follows:

● Total assets of US commercial banks grew 10.8 per cent in 2004, the fastest growth in more than a decade;
● Liabilities increased by 9.5 per cent and there was a noticeable increase in large time deposits (wholesale deposits otherwise referred to as managed liabilities);
● Capital increased by 9.4 per cent in 2004 as a result of an increase in retained earnings and increases in goodwill resulting from merger activity;
● Small and medium-sized banks experienced rapid growth in corporate lending, whereas this activity was 'relatively flat' for the ten largest commercial banks;
● Commercial real estate lending (lending secured on commercial land and real estate development) also grew significantly;
● Residential mortgage lending increased by over 15 per cent compared with consumer loans (10 per cent growth), much of the former due to refinancing of mortgages. In fact, retail mortgage lending has grown at double digit rates in the US since 1999;
● Securities holdings also increased, reflecting the greater holding of these for bank trading activities.

It is important to remember that the above trends relate to the whole banking system and there are substantial differences in the balance sheet make-up of the largest compared to other banks. For instance, on average, the ten largest banks do less lending, hold more securities and less capital compared to smaller banks. Also, as noted above regarding commercial real estate loans, the lending structure of the banks also varies substantially with size – for example, small banks account for over 25 per cent of US commercial real estate lending, whereas the top 100 banks account for only 10 per cent. As such, it is always important to remember that bank balance sheet features vary considerably – even the Federal Reserve report noted above provides information on US commercial banks according to different asset sizes of banks (the Annex to the Federal Reserve Report gives balance sheet data for the top 10 banks, those ranked 11–100, 101–1,000 and those outside the top 1,000).

Table 15.7 Assets of US commercial banks – 1990 to 2004 ($ thousands)

Year	No. of inst.	Cash and due from investments	Investment securities	Total loans and leases	Allowance for losses, loans and leases	Net loans and leases	Other earning assets	Bank premises and equipment	Other real estate	Intangible assets	All other assets	Total assets
2004	7,630	387,534,056	1,551,261,004	4,904,781,500	73,512,822	4,831,268,678	889,290,974	86,785,796	3,845,144	274,839,734	388,018,579	8,412,843,955
2003	7,770	387,437,502	1,456,311,135	4,428,843,212	77,151,701	4,351,691,512	780,343,369	83,376,970	4,531,177	158,133,592	379,316,276	7,601,141,543
2002	7,888	383,846,730	1,334,826,345	4,156,180,940	76,999,173	4,079,181,765	708,925,611	79,236,425	4,431,010	124,840,258	361,295,397	7,076,583,550
2001	8,080	390,340,367	1,172,539,507	3,884,336,461	72,273,347	3,812,063,116	620,534,054	76,643,935	3,829,583	120,185,368	356,285,309	6,552,421,225
2000	8,315	369,930,621	1,078,984,624	3,815,497,766	64,120,431	3,751,377,337	584,102,387	75,793,540	3,209,509	103,803,239	278,358,478	6,245,559,732
1999	8,580	366,455,687	1,046,536,003	3,489,092,468	58,746,301	3,430,346,166	483,579,751	73,743,171	3,074,550	98,067,230	233,332,058	5,735,134,597
1998	8,774	356,703,083	979,867,018	3,236,641,517	57,255,228	3,179,386,287	563,907,587	71,310,530	3,655,829	80,221,532	207,552,104	5,442,603,969
1997	9,143	355,148,599	871,879,302	2,974,455,543	54,896,848	2,919,558,698	558,528,464	67,182,313	4,454,494	61,690,091	180,090,296	5,018,532,250
1996	9,527	335,987,667	800,647,095	2,811,279,465	53,457,319	2,757,822,146	404,768,013	64,610,623	5,451,359	44,719,891	164,318,259	4,578,325,044
1995	9,940	306,521,953	810,871,552	2,602,962,910	52,837,845	2,550,125,061	398,021,818	61,424,542	6,644,156	30,217,602	148,849,811	4,312,676,493
1994	10,451	303,545,899	823,024,418	2,358,212,209	52,131,832	2,306,080,378	343,050,917	58,921,793	10,176,528	24,005,662	141,711,624	4,010,517,229
1993	10,958	272,960,721	836,710,403	2,149,735,197	52,757,263	2,096,977,935	272,994,875	55,527,497	16,784,090	18,051,126	136,158,442	3,706,165,083
1992	11,462	298,077,072	772,939,104	2,031,973,704	54,476,317	1,977,497,386	238,970,157	53,102,583	26,377,354	15,550,964	123,148,759	3,505,663,368
1991	11,921	304,862,139	691,384,542	2,052,754,432	55,145,877	1,997,608,554	215,858,361	52,249,450	27,553,031	12,245,345	128,920,870	3,430,682,290
1990	12,343	318,015,934	604,622,233	2,110,170,281	55,532,472	2,054,637,808	194,601,391	51,436,835	21,607,189	10,645,512	133,922,772	3,389,489,669

Source: FDIC, *Historical Statistics on Banking, Commercial Banks*, http://www2.fdic.gov/hsob/

Table 15.8 Liabilities and equity capital of US commercial banks – 1990 to 2004 ($ thousands)

Year	No. of inst.	Liabilities					Equity capital						Total liabilities and equity capital
		Total deposits	Borrowed funds	Subordinated notes	Other liabilities	Total liabilities	Perpetual preferred stock	Common stock	Surplus	Undivided profits	Other capital	Total equity capital	
2004	7,630	5,592,824,833	1,314,426,015	110,138,206	545,386,795	7,562,775,847	6,237,011	29,760,960	492,779,825	321,473,969	−182,178	850,068,109	8,412,843,955
2003	7,770	5,029,020,293	1,266,199,148	100,759,313	513,233,058	6,909,211,809	6,496,581	30,263,456	350,461,436	304,899,133	−190,878	691,929,723	7,601,141,543
2002	7,888	4,689,852,163	1,171,038,652	94,744,141	473,500,134	6,429,135,086	5,999,585	30,005,159	320,328,385	291,287,204	−171,871	647,448,462	7,076,583,550
2001	8,080	4,377,557,731	1,071,515,172	95,313,363	414,338,729	5,958,724,997	4,377,664	30,257,687	303,722,056	255,558,344	−219,518	593,696,227	6,552,421,225
2000	8,315	4,179,567,486	1,047,273,499	87,042,965	401,319,927	5,715,203,879	3,376,563	31,244,513	260,557,296	235,177,494	n.a.	530,355,859	6,245,559,732
1999	8,580	3,831,058,463	1,000,652,778	76,449,762	347,283,638	5,255,444,641	3,128,928	32,832,719	238,903,724	204,824,582	n.a.	479,689,956	5,735,134,597
1998	8,774	3,681,390,727	853,187,665	72,784,920	373,009,623	4,980,372,948	2,698,374	34,712,537	217,730,380	207,089,728	n.a.	462,231,018	5,442,603,969
1997	9,143	3,421,663,524	774,441,095	62,014,914	342,367,401	4,600,486,933	2,406,194	34,485,024	190,992,122	190,161,982	n.a.	418,045,317	5,018,532,250
1996	9,527	3,197,135,787	678,173,675	51,167,335	276,604,462	4,203,081,260	2,001,081	35,104,428	167,459,740	170,678,526	n.a.	375,243,785	4,578,325,044
1995	9,940	3,027,574,125	627,012,684	43,535,532	264,983,621	3,963,105,969	1,834,606	35,882,641	146,780,678	165,072,597	n.a.	349,570,528	4,312,676,493
1994	10,451	2,874,438,536	562,263,460	40,755,564	220,975,328	3,698,432,891	1,504,808	34,630,280	136,046,836	139,902,423	n.a.	312,084,338	4,010,517,229
1993	10,958	2,754,329,071	497,888,857	37,371,665	120,084,256	3,409,673,859	1,522,945	32,881,296	126,498,242	135,588,721	n.a.	296,491,221	3,706,165,083
1992	11,462	2,698,681,118	406,671,354	33,730,903	103,177,314	3,242,260,678	1,609,839	32,129,729	117,352,518	112,310,611	n.a.	263,402,691	3,505,663,368
1991	11,921	2,687,663,566	379,725,913	24,961,999	106,631,664	3,198,983,160	1,524,497	31,259,152	101,522,629	97,392,850	n.a.	231,699,129	3,430,682,290
1990	12,343	2,650,149,959	385,292,446	23,920,331	111,510,762	3,170,873,491	1,672,948	30,858,127	92,382,327	93,702,771	n.a.	218,616,179	3,389,489,669

Source: FDIC *Historical Statistics on Banking, Commercial Banks*, http://www2.fdic.gov/hsob/.

15.9 Performance of US commercial banks

US commercial banks have been among the most profitable banks in the developed world over the last decade averaging return-on-equity (ROE) of around 15 per cent as shown in Figure 15.2. This is mainly a reflection of the fact that interest margins (despite falling in recent years) remain high by international standards. Net interest margins were, on average, around 3.65 per cent for commercial banks in 2004, ranging from 4.25 per cent for small banks to just over 3.2 per cent for the largest ten banks. So US banks benefit from relatively strong net interest margins and have also boosted their non-interest income in recent years – from 34 per cent of total revenue in 1990 to 43 per cent by 2004. Non-interest expenses (staff, premises and other costs) relative to total revenue have also reduced from around 68 per cent in 1990 to just under 60 per cent by 2004, reflecting the drive to greater cost efficiency. These broad trends – relatively high but declining net interest margins, growing non-interest income and lower operating costs (plus lower loan-loss provisioning) are reflected in the strong profits record of US banks. (Note that these trends are also common in many continental European banking systems although net interest margins tend to be lower and cost reduction less dramatic than in the United States so profits are, typically, not as high. One exception, perhaps is the United Kingdom as shown in Chapter 12.)

Figure 15.2 Performance of US commercial banks – Return-on-assets (ROA) and Return-on-equity (ROE)

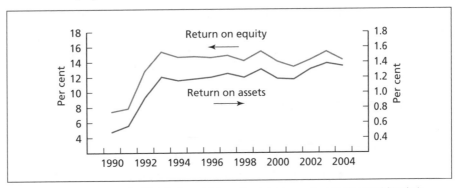

Source: Federal Reserve System (2005a) 'Profits and Balance Sheet developments at US Commercial Banks in 2004', Federal Reserve Bulletin, Spring, Chart 1, p. 143.

15.10 Regulation of the US banking system

The current system for regulating and supervising financial institutions in the United States is diverse and relatively complex. At the federal level, commercial banking organisations are regulated and supervised by three agencies which include the:

- Office of the Comptroller of the Currency (OCC);
- Federal Reserve System (Federal Reserve)
- Federal Deposit Insurance Corporation (FDIC).

15.10.1 Office of the Comptroller of the Currency (OCC)

The Office of the Comptroller of the Currency (OCC) charters, regulates and supervises all national banks. The OCC is an independent bureau of the Department of the Treasury, set up in 1863 to regulate all banks chartered by the Federal Reserve government. These banks, known as national banks, all have the word 'national' in their title or carry abbreviations 'NA' or 'NS&T'. The OCC also supervises the federal branches and agencies of foreign banks.

The OCC conducts on-site reviews of national banks and provides on-going supervision of bank operations. The agency issues rules, legal interpretations and regulatory decisions concerning banking, bank investments, bank community development activities and other aspects of bank operations.

In regulating national banks, the OCC has the power to:

- Examine the banks.
- Approve or deny applications for new licences (or charters), branches, capital, or other changes in corporate or banking structure.
- Take actions against banks that do not comply with laws and regulations or that otherwise engage in unsound banking practices. The agency can remove officers and directors, negotiate agreements to change banking practices and issue cease and desist orders as well as civil money penalties.
- Issue rules and regulations governing bank investments, lending and other practices.

By the start of 2005, the OCC was responsible for regulating more than 2,200 national banks and 56 federal branches of foreign banks in the United States that accounted for more than 55 per cent of the total assets of all US commercial banks.

15.10.2 Federal Reserve System

In addition to its (central banking) monetary policy role, the US Federal Reserve is also responsible for regulating and supervising various types of banks. These include:

- bank holding companies, including diversified financial holding companies formed under the Gramm-Leach-Bliley Act of 1999 and foreign banks with US operations;
- state-chartered banks that are members of the Federal Reserve System (state member banks);
- foreign branches of member banks;
- Edge Act and agreement corporations, through which US banking organisations may conduct international banking activities;
- US state-licensed branches, agencies and representative offices of foreign banks; and
- non-banking activities of foreign banks.

Typically, the Federal Reserve is responsible for regulating the largest and most complex US banks as it has responsibility for bank and diversified financial holding companies. It also regulates the operations of foreign banks, many of which are engaged in relatively complicated investment and corporate banking activity.

15.10.3 Federal Deposit Insurance Corporation (FDIC)

The FDIC is the main federal regulator of banks that are chartered by the states that do not join the Federal Reserve System. It can also supervise the branches and agencies of foreign banks that take deposits. As an independent agency it is funded by premiums paid by banks and thrift institutions for deposit insurance coverage, and from earnings on investments in US Treasury securities. The FDIC directly examines and supervises about 5,300 banks and Savings and Loans Associations (S&Ls or thrifts) accounting for more than half of the institutions in the banking system. At the start of 2005 it held insurance funds totalling more than $44 billion, insuring more than $3 trillion of deposits in US banks and S&Ls. In general, deposit insurance protects the deposits of retail customers in the event of a bank failure. Savings, checking and other deposit accounts, when combined, are generally insured up to $100,000 per depositor in each bank or thrift. Also deposits held in different categories of ownership – such as single or joint accounts – may be separately insured.

15.10.4 Other regulatory agencies

In addition to the three major federal regulatory agencies mentioned above there are a number of other agencies with responsibility for the other types of deposit-taking institutions in the United States. These include the Office of Thrift Supervision (OTS), established in 1989 as the main regulator of all S&Ls whether federally or state chartered. The credit union sector is supervised by the National Credit Union Administration (NCUA) which also insures credit union deposits.

Table 15.9 illustrates the regulatory responsibility of all the main bank regulatory bodies and highlights various overlaps. It can be seen that the regulatory structure is complex and apparently involves a duplication of resources. However, some have argued that this is a good thing as it allows for competition between regulators and guards against complacency. From banks' points of view, however, it has been argued that the system is burdensome and over-bureaucratic.

In general, it is important to note that the supervisor of a US domestic banking institution is generally determined by the type of institution and the governmental authority that granted it permission to undertake business.

Given that there are a number of regulatory agencies performing similar tasks, the US authorities established the Federal Financial Institutions Examination Council (FFIEC). The FFIEC is composed of the chairpersons of the FDIC and the National Credit Union Administration, the Comptroller of the Currency, the director of the OTS, and a governor of the Federal Reserve Board appointed by the board chairman. The main purpose of FFIEC is to ensure uniform federal principles and standards relating to the supervision of depository institutions and also to promote co-ordination of bank supervision among the federal agencies that regulate financial institutions. FFIEC also seeks to encourage better co-ordination of federal and state regulatory activities.

15.10.5 Regulatory issues

The US banking industry faces substantial regulatory challenges with regard to the changing structure of its banking and financial system. As various countries such as the United Kingdom adopt the single regulator approach to financial firm super-

Table 15.9 Federal supervisor and regulator of banking organisations in the United States

Component	Supervisor and regulator
Bank holding companies (including financial holding companies)	FR
Non-bank subsidiaries of bank holding companies	FR/Functional regulator[1]
National banks	OCC
State banks	
Members	FR
Non-members	FDIC
Thrift holding companies	OTS
Savings banks	OTS/FDIC/FR
Savings and loan associations	OTS
Edge and agreement corporations	FR
Foreign banks[2]	
Branches and agencies[3]	
State licensed	FR/FDIC
Federally licensed	OCC/FR/FDIC
Representative offices	FR

FR = Federal Reserve; OCC = Office of the Comptroller of the Currency; FDIC= Federal Deposit Insurance Corporation; OTS = Office of Thrift Supervision.

[1] Non-bank subsidiaries engaged in securities, commodities, or insurance activities are supervised and regulated by their appropriate functional regulators. Such functionally regulated subsidiaries include a broker, dealer, investment adviser and investment company registered with and regulated by the Securities and Exchange Commission (or, in the case of an investment adviser, registered with any state); an insurance company or insurance agent subject to supervision by a state insurance regulator; and a subsidiary engaged in commodity activities regulated by the Commodity Futures Trading Commission.

[2] Applied to direct operations in the United States. Foreign banks may also have indirect operations in the United States through their ownership of US banking organisations.

[3] The FDIC has responsibility for branches that are insured.

Source: Federal Reserve System (2005b), *Purposes and Functions*, Section 5, http://www.federalreserve.gov/pf/pf.htm.

vision (through the Financial Services Authority) this begs the question of whether US regulators should follow suit. As banks become larger and interest-based banking becomes less profitable they will continue to diversify into non-banking areas (such as insurance, investment banking, pensions, and so on) through the financial holding company route. Regulation between bank and non-bank regulators will therefore have to become increasingly co-ordinated. Also, as banks become larger and more complex, the adverse effects of failure become more pronounced and the governance issues associated with banks being 'too-big-to-fail' become a distinct possibility. Although no regulatory authority will ever state that a bank is too big to fail, with the growing consolidation and concentration in US banking markets this obviously raises concerns about large bank failure and systemic stability issues.

The increase in consolidation also raises concerns about the role of small community or local banks. These banks are seen as integral parts of local communities and as their numbers continue to fall, there is a perception at least that local areas will become de-banked and small firms may not have the same access to credit they once had or they may have to pay more for banking services provided by non-local banks that are unfamiliar with the specific features of these markets. There are also the potential adverse effects on competition that may ensue if concentration increases and the number of banks falls, although various evidence suggest that this (at least to date) has not been the case.

US banks are increasingly undertaking a wide range of securities transactions both on- and off-balance sheet. The substantial growth in derivatives activity is a clear reflection of this trend as is the growing use of various securitised instruments (such as the trading and holding of mortgage-backed securities) in business operations. As banks seek to diversify income and become more involved with securities-related business this also has implications for bank risk-taking and financial stability. Banking risks may well become more aligned to market risks driven by capital markets rather than by traditional credit risk. The substantial growth of bank lending to hedge funds and other investment firms, for instance, appears to be a growing concern for bank regulators.

The apparent decline in the liquidity of US banking (identified by the lower levels of cash and other liquid assets held on bank's balance sheets) may also be another area of regulatory concern. US banks appear to be well capitalised but have low liquidity compared with their counterparts elsewhere. They may, therefore, be more vulnerable to liquidity shocks.

Finally, the prevarication of the US regulatory authorities regarding the adoption of the new capital adequacy rules (known as Basle II) is also causing uncertainty for banks and other financial service firms. In fact, the Federal Reserve announced in April 2005 that while it was committed to the introduction of the new rules it needed further time to consider the details and even the expected 'time-line' date of implementation (from the start of 2007) could change. It is generally expected that a relatively small number of large, internationally active banks (between 10 and 20) would be required to adopt Basle II and these would implement the most advanced approaches for determining their risk-based capital requirements. Other banks could apply to be treated under the new rules. Uncertainty relating to the implementation of the new rules is, obviously, likely to affect the largest US banks.

15.11 Conclusions

This chapter examined the structural features of the US financial system with a particular focus on the banking system. The industry has experienced marked changes over recent years characterised by a decline in the number of banks, growing concentration and an increasingly international focus (both in terms of foreign bank presence in the domestic market and growing US bank presence overseas). Like many of their European counterparts, the largest banks are gradually transforming into full-service financial firms offering an increasingly diversified range of products and services to retail and corporate clients. The growth of non-interest revenue (particularly from securities-related activity) is a noticeable trend. Interest sources of income also remain favourable with relatively high net interest margins (although these are falling). Technology is also transforming banking business reflected (among other things) in the decline in paper-based payments in favour of electronic media. All these developments have implications for users and regulators of the banking and financial system. Bank customers now have a broader array of products and services on offer from their banks, although the number of banks is falling. Concentration and the emergence of very large financial service firms may also have implications for competition and systemic stability. Regulators have to face challenges in adapting to this new domestic environment and have to be increasingly aware of potential shocks that come not only from domestic credit markets but also from securities and insurance business as well as potential adverse events that emanate from outside the United States.

Key terms

Gramm-Leach-Bliley Act	Fedwire
Depository institutions	CHIPS
Contractual savings institutions	Automated Clearing House
Investment intermediaries	Check 21
Savings and Loans Association	Office of the Comptroller of the Currency (OCC)
Credit unions	Federal Reserve System (Federal Reserve)
Clearing	Federal Deposit Insurance Corporation (FDIC)
Settlement	

Key reading

Federal Deposit Insurance Corporation (2005) *FDIC Outlook: The Globalisation of the US Banking Industry*, (Summer), http://www.fdic.gov/bank/analytical/regional/ro20052q/na/2005summer_03.html.

Federal Reserve System (2005b) 'Trends in the Use of Payment Instruments in the United States', *Federal Reserve Bulletin*, www.federalreserve.gov/pubs/bulletin/2005/spring05_payment.pdf.

Klee, E.C. and Natalucci, F.M. (2005) 'Profits and Balance Sheet Developments at U.S. Commercial Banks in 2004' Federal Reserve Board, Federal Reserve Bulletin 2005 (Spring), http://www.federalreserve.gov/pubs/bulletin/2005/spring05_profit.pdf.

Revision questions and problems

1 What are the main features of the different types of depository institutions operating in the United States?
2 What are the main savings institutions operating in the United States?
3 Distinguish between different types of US investment institutions.
4 What is the disintermediation process that has characterised the US banking and financial sectors over the last decade?
5 How is the payment system organised for the wholesale and retail banking sectors?
6 What have been the most relevant changes to the United States commercial banks' balance sheet structure over the last 15 years?
7 What are the most important regulatory agencies in the United States and how are they organised?
8 What are the main regulatory challenges for the US banking sector in the near future?

Chapter 16

Banking in Japan

Learning objectives

- To distinguish between different types of financial institutions operating in Japan
- To understand the meaning of the disintermediation process
- To understand the characteristics of the Japanese payment system
- To understand the main trends in the performance of Japanese banks
- To understand the main tasks and organisation of the Japanese regulatory authorities

16.1 Introduction

This chapter outlines the main features of the Japanese banking and financial system. Japan has a bank-based financial system, where the banking system has traditionally played a more important role than the stock market. The banking system is also rather complex with a wide array of different types of private, co-operative and public banks, all undertaking a range of banking business. The main private deposit-taking institutions are the city banks and the largest public bank is the Postal Savings Bank.

The system has undergone dramatic changes over recent years, mainly as a result of the major financial crisis that occurred in 1997–98 that resulted in the failure of a number of banks and a massive build-up of **non-performing loans (NPLs)** in the banking system. The parlous state of the banking system in the late 1990s has resulted in a wide range of reforms aimed at improving banking and financial sector soundness, as well as restructuring the banking system. This chapter discusses these issues. The first part of the chapter outlines the structural features of the banking system and the various types of institution that operate in the system. We then outline the main features of the payment systems and cover the recent financial crises. The final sections look at various regulatory developments, as well as the main bank regulatory agencies.

16.2 Structure of the banking system

The Japanese banking system has experienced difficult times in recent years, mainly as a consequence of the downturn in the domestic economy that has resulted in banking sector failures and a mountain of bad debts for the banking system overall. The surge in bad debts in the 1990s resulted from a rapid increase in financial asset and property prices from the mid-1980s, which led to excessive bank lending. The subsequent collapse in asset prices during the 1990s resulted in excessive levels of bad debts contributing to a major financial crisis between 1997 and 1998, when several large financial institutions went bankrupt. In 1998, laws were enforced to stabilise the financial system and measures that included temporary government control were developed to deal with bankrupt financial institutions. At the time of writing (end of 2005), private financial institutions still have not fully recovered from this crisis.

The crisis resulted in a large number of regulatory measures aimed at restructuring the banking sector, as well as protecting depositors, and these issues will be covered in more detail later in this chapter. Given the weak operating climate, the banking system has experienced a major transformation – especially noticeable in the decline in banks and mergers between the largest institutions. While the private financial institutions have suffered in recent years, various public financial institutions, such as the Postal Savings Bank, have expanded their lending and other activities.

As already noted, the Japanese financial system consists of both public and private financial institutions. The structure of the Japanese banking system is also rather complex, with a wide range of deposit-taking institutions that perform particular functions.

The major institutions operating in the financial system can be classified according to three main groups:

- Private deposit-taking institutions;
- Private non-deposit-taking institutions; and
- Public financial institutions.

16.2.1 Private deposit-taking institutions

A variety of **private deposit-taking institutions** operate in the Japanese banking system and their main features and functions are described in Table 16.1. The main banks include:

- City banks
- Regional banks
- Second-tier regional banks
- Long-term credit banks
- Trust banks
- Foreign banks.

16.2.1.1 City banks

The **city banks** are the largest banks in the Japanese banking system and account for over 50 per cent of total banking sector assets. As Table 16.1 notes, they are commercial banks that offer the full range of banking services including retail, corporate and investment banking services. Traditionally, they have focused on providing banking services to relatively large corporations, and their retail banking activities are typically based in urban areas. The city banks had around 2,500 branches at the start of 2005.

City banks have experienced substantial restructuring in recent years – so much so that it is difficult to keep pace with all the changes. These re-organisations have been aimed at bolstering the financial strength of the country's main banks. Table 16.2 outlines the features of various city bank reorganisations – the latest of which is the merger between Bank of Tokyo-Mitsubishi and UFJ, which came into effect in October 2005. This created the world's largest bank (with assets of $1.8 trillion), a third larger than Citigroup (although the bank's market capitalisation is around one-third less).

16.2.1.2 Regional banks

Regional banks have a much larger geographical presence than the city banks, with over 7,000 branches nationwide and they tend to focus more on retail financial services and lending to small and medium-sized enterprises (SMEs) in the various regions (or prefectures). The majority of regional banks are publicly quoted and the largest offer a full range of banking and financial services although their business focuses on companies and households that operate within specific regions of Japan. Note that there are two types of regional banks – differentiated primarily by size (see Table 16.1).

Table 16.1 Private deposit-taking institutions in Japan

	Number	Features and functions
A) Banks		
City banks	7	Major commercial banks comprising: Mizuho Bank, Bank of Tokyo-Mitsubishi, UFJ Bank, Sumitomo Mitsui Banking Corporation, Resona Bank, Mizuho Corporate Bank, and Saitama Resona Bank. Note that these seven banks operated as part of 5 major financial groups until October 2005 as Mizuho Corporate Bank is part of the Mizuho Group and Saitma Resona Bank is part of the Resona Group. From October 2005 Bank of Tokyo-Mitsubishi merged with UFJ Bank to create the world's largest bank in assets terms, known as Mitsubishi UFJ Group. The city banks are Japan's largest banks and provide a full range of banking, investment and other financial services. They are the main corporate banking service providers in Japan
Regional banks	64	Regional banks focus on retail and SME (small and medium-sized enterprise) banking activity in different regions of Japan. While city banks' business has traditionally focused on urban areas the regional banks operate in various regions or 'prefectures' throughout the country. They account for around 20 per cent of retail deposit taking. Major regional banks include Bank of Yokohama, Chiba Bank and Bank of Fukuoka. As of January 2005 58 regional banks were publicly listed.
Second-tier regional banks	49	Smaller regional banks that also focus on retail and SME business. As of January 2005, 26 second-tier regional banks were publicly listed.
Trust banks	31	Trust banks provide traditional commercial banking services but focus on trust business. A trust is an investment product in which an investor (trustor) entrusts funds to a trust bank, which invests the funds in various instruments (stocks, bonds, etc.) at its own discretion and returns the investment gains to the investor (trustor) as a dividend. All the city banks have trust banking subsidiaries.
Long-term credit banks	3	These are banks established in accordance with the Long-term Credit Bank Law of 1999 that restructured/nationalised these banks. Long-term credit banks provide long- and medium-term finance to the corporate sector. They had long been a feature of high value lending at low rates to the corporate sector. Due to various factors, these banks became technically insolvent and were reorganised: Mizuho Corporate Bank was created from The Industrial Bank of Japan and others, Shinsei Bank (from the Long-Term Credit Bank of Japan) and Aozora Bank (from the former Nippon Credit Bank). Note that Mizuho Corporate Bank is part of the city bank group Mizuho.
Foreign banks	68	Foreign banks are mainly engaged in corporate and investment banking activity, although some undertake upscale retail (private banking) business.
B) Co-operative financial institutions		
Shinkin banks	299	Shinkin banks are co-operative financial institutions. Their membership is composed of local residents and small and medium-sized companies. They are non-profit organisations that operate under the principle of mutual support. Shinkin banks limit their lending, in principle, to members. However, their functions are similar to commercial banks, and they also deal with many people who are not members, accepting deposits, providing exchange services, accepting various payments including those for public utilities, and engaging in over-the-counter sales of public bonds, investment trusts, and insurance.

Table 16.1 continued

Credit co-operatives	178	A wide range of co-operative deposit-taking institutions operate in
Labour banks	17	Japan. These provide services such as deposits, lending, bill
Agricultural co-operatives	902	discounting, domestic exchange and foreign exchange. As a rule
Fishery co-operatives	357	credit associations only lend to members (deposits may be taken
		from non-members). Members have typically to be resident, working
		or owning a business in the co-operatives area. However, as a rule
		membership is not open to large businesses. The co-operative banks
		serve various sectors, agriculture, fisheries and other groups.

C) Federations of co-operative financial institutions

Shinkin Central Bank (Central institution for Shinkin banks)	1	These are the central organisations for the various co-operative banks listed above. They offer various products and services to their
Shinkumi Federation Bank (National Federation of credit co-operatives)	1	member banks, typically undertaking larger and more complex banking transactions. For instance, they provide investment and asset management services, as well as more sophisticated corporate
Rokinren Bank (National Association of Labour Banks)	1	banking services to their member banks.
Norinchukin Bank (Central Bank for the Japanese Agricultural, Forestry and Fishery Co-operatives)	1	
Shoko Chukin Bank (the Central Co-operative Bank for Commerce and Industry)	1	

Source: Compiled using information from the Bank of Japan (2005a) statistics on financial institutions http://www.boj.or.jp/en/stat/stat_f.htm and from various banking associations and individual bank accounts.

16.2.1.3 Trust banks and long-term credit banks

In addition to the city and regional banks there are also a number of **trust banks**. These perform commercial banking activity but their main function is asset management for retail and other customers. Japanese households place funds (or entrust funds) to these banks, which they invest on clients' behalf. The trust banks offer a range of such investments services as (in fact) do the city, regional and many other banks in the Japanese system. (Note that the Bank of Japan statistics for the banking sector distinguishes between banking account and trust account business when reporting features of the system – as the former relates to deposit and lending business whereas the latter relates to investment services.) In addition to these there are three **long-term credit banks** – these banks provide medium- and long-term finance to the corporate sector. The major long-term credit banks failed in 1999 and had to be reorganised as described in Table 16.1.

16.2.1.4 Co-operative banks

The mutual co-operative banking sector also plays a major role in the Japanese banking system. These are co-operative organisations and non-profit making financial institutions established for the benefit of SMEs in certain industries (such as agriculture and fisheries) and other groups including residents in various areas. They undertake mainly retail banking activity and SME services and are typically small but numerous. In March 2004 they had over 10,000 branches located throughout the country. The central organisations of the individual **credit co-operative banks** are

Table 16.2 Reorganisation of Japan's city banks

New financial groups	Major subsidiary banks	Former banks	Consolidated assets (March 2005) ¥ bn
Mitsubishi UFJ Financial Group (MUFJ) (Established in October 2005)	Bank of Tokyo-Mitsubishi (BTM), Mitsubishi Trust & Banking Corporation, UFJ Bank, UFJ Trust Bank	Mitsubishi Tokyo Financial Group and UFJ Holdings (operating as merged bank from October 2005)	¥188,000bn ($1,800bn) the world's largest bank in assets terms
Mizuho Financial Group (MHFG) (Established in January 2003)	Mizuho Bank, Mizuho Corporate Bank, Mizuho Trust & Banking	Industrial Bank of Japan, Daiichi Kangyo, Fuji, Yasuda Trust Banks	143,076
Sumitomo Mitsui Financial Group (SMFG) (Established in December 2002)	Sumitomo Mitsui Banking Corporation (SMBC)	Sumitomo Bank, Sakura Bank	99,731
Resona Holdings (Established in December 2001)	Resona, Saitama Resona, Kinki Osaka, Nara Banks, Resona Trust & Banking	Asahi Bank, Daiwa Bank	40,674
Previous major mergers			
Mitsubishi Tokyo Financial Group (MTFG) (Established in April 2001)	Bank of Tokyo-Mitsubishi (BTM), Mitsubishi Trust & Banking Corporation	Bank of Tokyo-Mitsubishi (BTM), Mitsubishi Trust Bank, Nippon Trust Bank	113,294 (September 2004)
UFJ Holdings (Established in April 2001)	UFJ Bank, UFJ Trust Bank	Sanwa Bank, Tokai Bank, Toyo Trust & Banking	82,554

Source: Compiled from individual banks' websites.

relatively large banks in their own right and these provide services direct to their member banks. The main feature of co-operative banks is that they act as strong competitors to regional banks in local banking markets.

16.2.2 Private non-deposit-taking institutions

Private non-deposit-taking financial institutions in Japan comprise a wide variety of securities, insurance and other firms. Securities firms include major broking and investment banking type operations that offer securities services to both the corporate and household sectors. Securities companies had around 2,000 offices throughout Japan in 2004 reflecting their extensive activity in retail and other investment business. Their business is solely securities-related and they do not take deposits. In addition to these, there are insurance companies that transact life and non-life business as well as a range of other firms including consumer finance, leasing, money market dealers (firms that trade short-term wholesale money market instruments) and mortgage securities firms (companies that deal in mortgage-backed securities). In many respects, the range and type of non-deposit-taking institutions is similar to those in other developed financial systems.

Public financial institutions

Unlike the United States or Britain, however, Japan has a range of *public financial institutions* that perform a significant role in the financial system. The most important (by far) is the *Post Office* that has over 24,000 branches nationwide (and nearly 10,000 more than the total for domestically licensed banks). Postal savings represents 23.1 per cent of total banking sector deposits (some ¥985.4 trillion at the start of 2005) – this compares with a market share of around 30 per cent for the major banks. The combined value of its savings and insurance businesses amounted to $3.2 trillion in April 2005.

Japan's postal savings system is the world's largest financial institution in terms of deposits. Postal savings has long been an important element in household savings and given the crises in the banking sector over the last decade or so the relative position of the Post Office in banking business has increased. Typically, the Post Office provides a variety of tax-exempt savings products with a maximum limit on how much can be deposited. All savings in the postal system have government guarantees and are therefore fully protected. However, the Japanese government has approved plans to privatise the Japan Post starting from April 2007. The holding company-owned postal savings company will then have to pay tax just like a regular private-sector company. It will split its operations into those handling new and old savings accounts. New accounts will not be covered by government guarantees, so the new entity will join the **Deposit Insurance Corporation** (which guarantees deposits up to a certain level). The Japanese parliament voted in favour of privatisation in July 2005 and also agreed that its savings and insurance arms would have to be sold by 2017.

In addition to the Post Office, there is a range of other public institutions that provide financial services to various industrial sectors and regions. These are mainly **development banks** (close to government) that direct lending (usually subsidised and medium- to long-term finance) to certain sectors of the economy. Such public institutions include:

● Development Bank of Japan (long-term financing for regional development);
● Japan Bank for International Co-operation (lending and other financial operations for the promotion of Japanese exports, imports or Japanese economic activities overseas):
● National Life Finance Corporation (lends to small businesses, students and others without access to traditional credit);
● Japan Finance for Small and Medium-Sized Enterprises (subsidised lending to SMEs);
● Agriculture, Forestry, Fisheries Finance Corporation (lending to firms involved in the respective industries and 'to maintain and develop the productivity of agriculture, forestry and fisheries, and to secure stable food supply through supporting the food industry');
● The Government Housing Loan Corporation (mortgage loans to individuals that have difficulty obtaining residential property finance through banks);
● Japan Financial Corporation for Municipal Enterprises (subsidised lending to local authorities); and
● Okinawa Development Finance Corporation (subsidised loans for business development in Okinawa).

16.3 Changing structure of the financial system

Given the turmoil in the Japanese economy and banking system it is perhaps of little surprise that financial intermediary activities have shifted from private financial intermediaries to public financial intermediaries between 1989 and 1999 although there has been a slight reversal since then. Table 16.3 illustrates that banks' share of total financial sector assets had fallen from 48.9 per cent in 1989, to 39.3 per cent by 1999, increasing to 42.9 per cent by the end of 2003. Insurance and pension funds have also increased their share of financial sector assets, although the trend towards **disintermediation** is clearly not as strong as in the United States (see Table 15.5). Box 16.1 illustrates some of the current trends in Japanese banking.

Table 16.3 Financial intermediaries' financial assets by type of institution (component ratio excluding total financial assets; %)

	FY 1979	FY 1989	FY 1999	FY 2003
Total financial assets outstanding (trillion yen)	646	2.263	2,925	2,805
Depository corporations	65.5	58.7	52.5	53.7
banks	54.0	48.9	39.3	42.9
postal savings	7.9	6.4	11.1	9.9
collectively managed trusts	3.5	3.4	2.1	0.9
Insurance and pension funds	9.3	12.0	15.1	16.0
private life and non-life insurance, mutual aid insurance	5.6	7.6	7.6	8.1
postal life insurance, etc.	2.2	2.2	4.3	4.4
pension funds	1.4	2.3	3.2	3.5
Other financial intermediaries	25.3	29.3	32.3	30.3
investment trusts	0.9	2.3	2.0	1.8
non-banks	1.7	5.7	3.4	3.7
public financial institutions	19.8	15.1	22.3	20.2
financial dealers and brokers	2.8	3.2	3.2	3.6
non-collectively managed trusts	0.1	3.1	1.4	0.9
Reclassification				
Private financial institutions	70.1	76.4	62.3	65.5
Public financial institutions, etc.	29.9	23.6	37.7	34.5

Source: Bank of Japan (2005b) *Japan's Financial Structure since the 1980s – in View of the Flow of Funds Accounts*, Research and Statistics Department,15 March, Chart 16, www.boj.or.jp/en/ronbun/05/data/ron0503a.pdf.

Box 16.1   Japanese banking – mergers are sign of return to confidence

The language used to describe Japan's leading banks has been transformed over the past 12 months. What was once a breakdown has become a revival and organisations that had been dismissed as inert have been reformed.

Even the cautious wordsmiths at the Financial Services Agency, the industry regulator, have declared that their focus has changed from one of 'financial system stability' to one of 'financial system vitality'. The message behind these linguistic devel-

opments is clear: Japan's financial services industry has entered a new and important phase.

Singular proof came late last year with the announcement of the planned merger of MTFG, Japan's third largest bank, with UFJ, the fourth largest, to create the world's largest bank with assets of ¥188,000bn.

This was followed by a proposed alliance between SMFG, the second largest bank, and Daiwa Securities, the country's largest brokerage. If they conduct a full

▶

merger the combined group could have total assets of ¥140,000bn.

These deals were high profile harbingers of the end of the country's bad loan crisis, final confirmation of which came when the main banks reported results for the year to March. The banks revealed they had halved non-performing loans since 2002, to below 5 per cent of total loans, in accordance with a directive from the FSA and in line with international standards.

But these proposed alliances are also a vision of the future, underlining a broader transformation in which the three leading banks are widening their capabilities away from corporate and retail lending to embrace the entire financial services spectrum – asset and investment management, investment banking, securities broking, syndicated lending, trust banking, insurance, consumer finance, structured products and private equity, to name a few.

A decade and a half after the economic bubble collapsed, the sector has been reduced from 13 disparate banks to three big ones. Furthermore, these three are showing tell-tale signs that they want to create huge, full-service financial services conglomerates to rival – in terms of scale, if not in terms of global reach – the world's market leaders.

The ¥188,000bn in assets of the merged MTFG/UFJ will, for example, surpass JPMorgan Chase's $1,200bn and Citigroup's $1,500bn. The stage has been set for what some in the banking industry in Japan are not just calling conglomeration, but mega-conglomeration.

Their motivation has many roots, one of which is plain fear.

'They don't want to be bought by foreign financial institutions', says Junsuke Senoguchi, banking analyst at Lehman Brothers, the investment bank. He argues that proposed changes to the Commercial Code, which will make it possible for foreign companies to use shares to buy Japanese companies, could have made some of the largest banks vulnerable to a foreign takeover. He says that, when ranked using premium over earning assets – which is the difference between the market capitalisation of the bank and the book value of its capital, over the value of its earning assets – foreign banks had a POEA [Premium Over Earning Assets) of between 15 and 20 per cent compared with 2 to 3 per cent at Japan's main banks. 'Japanese banks are very cheap', he comments.

Alongside the desire to fend off unwanted foreign interest are deeper strategic motivations, one of which is the 'Holy Grail' of Japanese financial sector reform – liberating the nation's ¥1,400,000bn in savings, which are largely in low-yielding bank deposits.

If these can be converted to investment-based assets, managed by the new conglomerates, decent returns could be generated for policyholders hoping to make up for the shortfall in their pensions, the argument goes.

'There is going to be a shift of individual assets from deposits to riskier assets such as investment trusts', says Mr Senoguchi.

This is a development that leading bankers can barely wait to embrace, as it would help solve their most pressing problem by allowing them to generate fee income from the sale of investment and other products that would compensate them for the thin margins available on loans. This would replenish and diversify their income sources and allow them to become profitable on a sustainable basis.

Source: Financial Times (2005), 'Japan Investment Banking Survey', 24 June, by David Ibison.

16.4 Payment systems

There are four major payment systems for clearing and settling interbank payments in Japan. These include three clearing systems in the private sector and a funds transfer system operated by the Bank of Japan. The clearing systems include the:

- **Zengin Data Telecommunication System** (Zengin System) – the main retail payments system in Japan and its main task is to clear retail credit transfers. Over 2,000 institutions participate in the system. The system clears transactions including remittances, direct credits such as the payment of salaries and pensions, and payments resulting from the interregional collection of bills and cheques. Small financial institutions, such as the Shinkin banks and other small co-operative and regional banks have their own interbank clearing systems. (The structure of each of these systems is similar to that of the Zengin System.) The Zengin System is owned and managed by Tokyo Bankers Association.

- **Bill and Cheque Clearing Systems** (BCCSs) – clear bills and cheques collected at regional clearing houses. The Bill and Cheque Clearing Systems (BCCSs) provide clearing services mostly for bills and cheques, which are exchanged between financial institutions located within the same geographical area. Clearing houses are established and managed by their respective regional bankers' association. Large and medium-sized financial institutions, including banks and branches of foreign banks in Japan, participate directly. Small financial institutions participate indirectly through direct participants. BCCSs predominantly handle bills and cheques used for commercial transactions between firms.

- **Foreign Exchange Yen Clearing System** (FXYCS) – clears mainly yen legs of wholesale foreign exchange transactions. The Foreign Exchange Yen Clearing System (FXYCS) was established in 1980 to facilitate clearing of yen payments for cross-border financial transactions. Clearing is undertaken through the BOJ-NET and the main participants are large banks and branches of foreign banks.

- **BOJ-NET (Bank of Japan Financial Network System) Funds Transfer System** – the central bank's funds transfer system used to settle wholesale interbank obligations including those arising from the clearing systems. The BOJ-NET Funds Transfer System undertakes most of the payment services provided by the Bank of Japan, which are: 1) funds transfers among financial institutions stemming from interbank money market and securities transactions; 2) funds transfers between different accounts of the same financial institution; 3) settlement of net positions arising from privately owned clearing systems; and 4) funds transfers between financial institutions and the Bank of Japan, including those for monetary policy operations. Most funds transfers made through the BOJ-NET Funds Transfer System are credit transfers.

(See Bank of Japan (2005c) available online at http://www.boj.or.jp/en/set/02/data/set0207a.pdf for a detailed account of the operations of these systems.)

With regards to retail payments, a key feature of the Japanese system relates to the high proportion of cash transactions compared with other developed countries. As can be seen from Figure 16.1 Japan has a much higher level of cash in circulation compared with the United States and Britain.

Figure 16.1 **Notes and coins in circulation as percentage of GDP (2001)**

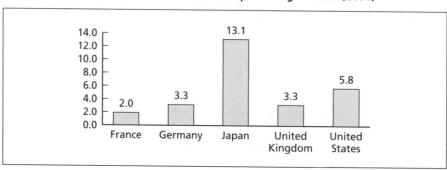

Source: Japanese Bankers Association (2003) 'Payment Systems in Japan', October, Figure 2, p. 2.
http://www.zenginkyo.or.jp/en/jbank/payment/pdf/paymentsystems2003/pdf.

Retail payments in Japan differ from other major economies because non-cash payments are dominated by credit transfers (known as giro payments) and direct debits. These account for around 35 per cent and 50 per cent, respectively, of the value of retail payments, with credit cards accounting for the bulk of the remainder. Cheque and debit card payments are negligible. This contrasts with the United States where over 70 per cent of non-cash retail payments are made by cheque. Credit transfers are widely used, for example, to pay wages, pensions, dividends and tax refunds. Direct debiting is used by individuals to pay rent, utilities, telephone bills, credit card charges, taxes, insurance policies, mortgages, automobile loans and other instalment payment plans.

One area where Japan leads the world is in the use of smart card and mobile phone technology for retail payments. By 2003 over 400 Japanese financial institutions offered banking services, including payment facilities, via mobile phone. There has been substantial growth in the use of mobile phones for a variety of services since Japan embraced 3G (third generation) mobile telephony from 2001 onwards. A wide range of smart cards are in use to make retail payments. Japanese households are the most avid users of smart cards and these have been introduced in a wide variety of applications, such as transport ticket payments, access control, electronic money and credit cards. In 2003, over 50 million smart cards were issued in Japan and the number is expected to rise to 350 million by 2010.

16.5 Balance sheet features and performance

The balance sheet and performance features of the Japanese banking system have been severely affected by the recession in the economy as well as the financial sector crises that occurred in 1997 and 1998. Between 1996 and 2005 bank lending portfolios have declined by around 30 per cent reflecting the lack of demand and the increasing number of bad loans that had to be written off. This trend appears to be on-going as bank lending continued to fall by over 3 per cent in the first quarter of 2005. Over the last decade or so there has also been a shift in lending from the private to public sector, and banks' liquid assets have grown – to around 30 per cent of total banking sector assets. The decline in lending and the increase in liquid assets is clearly an indication of the weak state of the domestic economy.

In addition to weak loan demand, the interest margins earned on bank loans is pitifully low, typically around 1 per cent, so income earned from lending business remains weak. As on the loan side, banks' share of deposits has also fallen over the last decade as households and small firms have increasingly deposited in public financial institutions such as in the postal saving system – as public financial institutions are seen as safer and also because of various tax advantages. As is the case in other systems, the Japanese banks have diversified into non-interest income areas of business – particularly insurance and various securities areas, but the increase in non-interest income has not had a significant impact on bank performance.

Table 16.4 illustrates the performance of the main banking groups in Japan between 2000 and 2003. The top part of the table shows that the major city banks as a group have on average generated losses over the period; however, these losses are exaggerated by the particularly weak performance of Resona bank that had to be restructured in 2003. The bottom half of the table reports median returns showing that the bulk of city banks returned to positive profits in 2003. In fact, during 2004 the ROE of the city banks averaged around 4–5 per cent, reflecting improved performance (mainly a consequence of reduction in bad loans and subsequent lower costs associated with provisioning).

What is noticeable, however, across all types of banks is that ROE values are very low by international standards as most major banks use a 15 per cent ROE benchmark as an acceptable level of performance. Needless to say, because Japanese banks have performed so poorly in recent years they have not been able to raise capital by issuing new shares and instead have raised funds in the capital markets through various bond issues, as well as through divesting of business and through selling parts of their loan portfolios.

Table 16.4 Japanese bank profitability (return-on-equity ROE) %

A) Mean banks' profitability

Specialisation	2000	2001	2002	2003
City Banks	0.4	−16.85	−12.04	−17.41
Regional Banks	−2.87	−6.15	−3.33	2.72
Second-tier Regional Banks	−8.6	4.54	−8.62	1.42
Central Co-operative Bank	5.59	3.73	2.94	3.5
Shinkin Banks	−0.7	−5.01	−2.91	0.57
Total	−1.73	−4.13	−3.69	0.63

B) Median banks' profitability

Specialisation	2000	2001	2002	2003
City Banks	2.15	−11.75	−11.15	3.53
Regional Banks	2.34	1.27	1.65	4.23
Second-tier Regional Banks	1.29	0.95	1.57	3.07
Central Co-operative Bank	6.12	3.52	3.2	2.88
Shinkin Banks	2.93	1.73	1.74	2.75
Total	2.63	1.51	1.66	3.07

Source: Calculated from Bankscope (a comprehensive, global database containing information on public and private banks, from Bureau van Dijk Electronic Publishing (BvDEP)).

Probably the most important factor influencing Japanese bank performance has been their enormous levels of bad loans. According to official figures from Japan's Financial Services Agency, the cumulative amount of losses by way of bad debts for all Japanese banks amounted to ¥ 100,000 billion (around $860 billion in 2005 dollar terms). In fact around 8.8 per cent of total loans were considered non-performing by 2003 although this had fallen to 5.5 per cent by September 2004 as shown in Table 16.5. The IMF's World Economic Outlook (April 2005) reports that the level of non-performing loans was expected to continue to fall and approach just over 4.4 per cent by mid-2005. The decline in loan losses has enabled city and larger regional banks to reduce the levels of provisions against bad loans and this has had the influence of increasing their profits although serious problems still remain at some of the smaller regional banks.

Table 16. 5 Japanese banks' losses on bad loans (1992–2004) (¥ billion)

Accounting year	1992	1993	1994	1995	1996	1997	1998	1999	2000	2001	2002	2003	2004 (Sept)
Losses on bad debts	1,640	3,872	5,232	13,369	7,763	13,258	13,631	6,944	6,107	9,722	6,658	5,374	1,485
Cumulated losses	1,640	5,512	10,744	24,113	31,877	45,135	58,766	65,710	71,818	81,540	88,188	83,572	85,057
Loans at risk*	12,775	13,576	12,546	28,504	21,789	29,758	29,627	30,366	32,515	42,028	34,849	26,204	23,209
% of gross loans	2.4	2.6	2.4	5.3	4.1	5.7	5.9	6.4	7.1	9.6	6.4	6.8	5.5
Provisions balance	3,698	4,647	5,538	13,293	12,334	17,615	14,797	12,230	11,655	13,353	12,685	11,430	10,209

*Strict definition of 'risk management loans' balances.
Source: Japan's Financial Services Agency, January 2005, http://www.fsa.go.jp/

Finally, major Japanese banks' capital ratios still remain below international standards, although capital positions have improved slightly over 2004/05 – and the large regional banks have higher capital ratios compared to their city bank competitors. Table 16.6 reports the capital ratios for the largest Japanese banks (in assets size) for 2004 and shows that standard capital ratios ranged between 1.29 and 6 per cent with most banks having ratios in the 4–5 per cent band. The BIS capital ratio ranged from 3.78 per cent to a high of 16.2 per cent for the Shinkin Central Bank with the majority hovering around 7–10 per cent – bear in mind that the minimum requirement is 8 per cent for the BIS ratio. To put these in context, the top US banks had capital-to-assets ratios ranging between 5 per cent and 8.2 per cent, and BIS ratios between 10.94 per cent and 13.7 per cent for 2004.

Table 16.6 Capital ratios of major Japanese banks (2004)

Banks	Capital/asset ratio	BIS capital ratio
Mizuho Financial Group	2.69	9.53
Sumitomo Mitsui Financial Group	3.21	10.10
Mitsubishi Tokyo Financial Group	3.33	10.84
UFJ Holding	3.32	9.96
Norinchukin Bank	2.91	9.87
Resona Group	1.29	3.78
Shinkin Central Bank	2.94	16.20
Sumitomo Trust & Banking	4.57	10.48
Shoko Chukin Bank	4.85	7.45
Mitsui Trust Holdings	2.83	7.50
Bank of Yokohama	4.15	10.32
Shizuoka Bank	6.00	12.42
Chiba Bank	4.02	10.40
Bank of Fukuoka	3.25	9.44

Source: Obtained from Bankscope (2005), Bureau van Dijk Electronic Publishing (BvDEP).

Since the mid-to-late 1990s there have been a number of initiatives introduced by the Japanese authorities aimed at reducing the bad loan problem and improving bank capital positions. These initiatives are on-going, with their main focus being to improve the soundness and performance of the banking system. These are discussed in the following section.

16.6 Banking crisis in Japan

Throughout this chapter we have mentioned how the banking crisis in the late 1990s has severely impacted on the financial system. The regulatory features of the system have dramatically changed as a consequence of these events and as such it is best to highlight the main features of the crisis before we look in more detail at the regulatory environment.

The banking collapse that ensued during the 1990s was mainly a consequence of three main forces:

● **Excessive lending** – bank lending, much of which was secured against land and property, grew rapidly in the late 1980s. Bank lending activity was concentrated in the wholesale and retail trade, real estate, finance and insurance and construction sectors. The fall in stock prices and reversal in the performance of the economy in the early 1990s made highly indebted firms in these sectors unable to repay their loans due to a decline in collateral values, thus creating a large pool of non-performing loans (NPLs). However, despite these problems, bank exposure to certain sectors, such as real estate and construction, continued to grow due to the low interest rate environment until the second half of the 1990s. This resulted in a further increase in bank non-performing loans and the banking system fell into a systemic crisis in 1997–98.

● **Negative impact of asset price deflation** – the rapid credit growth during the 1990s had also been accompanied by a doubling of stock prices and a rapid rise in commercial estate prices, particularly in major cities. A sharp increase in interest rates and the introduction of various credit ceilings (limits on the amounts banks could lend) to real estate-related activity led to the bursting of the asset price bubble. This created substantial losses for firms that held equities and had borrowed from banks with real estate as collateral. As a consequence this had the effect of converting a substantial portion of banks' loans into non-performing assets, and asset price deflation resulted (and has been a feature of the Japanese economy for nearly a decade).

● **Policy failure to contain problem** – various commentators have argued that the main government authorities (Bank of Japan and the Ministry of Finance) were too slow in dealing with the build-up of problem loans in the banking system. Throughout the 1990s banks were continuing to lend to the real estate sector despite signs of problems in their loan books as well as deflationary pressures in the economy overall. Interest rates had fallen to low levels and the government made various attempts to boost public spending in order to create demand in the economy, although little action was taken to deal with problems in the banking system until the crisis hit. The initial government approach was to stimulate demand by fiscal policy in the economy; this it was assumed would restore economic growth and thus return the banks to a healthy position. However, the fiscal stimulus had only a marginal impact on the economy. There was also little international pressure on the authorities to resolve their banking problem, which was viewed mainly as a domestic issue.

The gradual culmination of these forces led to the collapse of the so-called **convoy system** where the Ministry of Finance 'encouraged' healthy banks to acquire those in trouble. In addition, while the Bank of Japan (the central bank) provided liquid-

Table 16.7 Japan's banking crisis – major events

Year	Event
Mid-1995	Two large credit unions and a regional bank fail as a result of bad loans.
1995	A substantial number of housing loan companies, known as Jusen, failed and were bailed out by a group of banks and government funds. As a result of the Jusen collapse and concerns about growing levels of non-performing loans, bank stock prices declined relative to other stocks around the end of 1995, and credit rating agencies began to downgrade the credit ratings of Japanese banks – increasing their cost of funds.
November 1997	On 3 November, Sanyo Securities defaulted in the interbank loan market, delivering another shock to the market.
November 1997	Hokkaido Takushoku Bank and Yamaichi Securities (one of the four large securities houses) failed, leading to a further downgrading of bank credit ratings.
March 1998	The Japanese government sought to deal with the under-capitalisation of banks by injecting capital into the banking sector in March 1998. A newly created Financial Crisis Management Committee handled this capital injection, which was successful in calming financial markets (until May).
Mid- to late 1998	The government attempted to pass several reform bills. One of these bills was the Financial Revitalisation Act, which was designed to deal with failed financial institutions. Under this law, a failed bank could either be placed under Financial Reorganisation Administration (FRA), or could be temporarily nationalised. This law formed the basis for the government's decision in late 1998 to nationalise two major banks, the Long Term Credit Bank of Japan and Nippon Credit Bank, both teetering on the verge of bankruptcy. The establishment of the Financial Supervision Agency (FSA) in June 1998 shifted the responsibility of financial supervision of private deposit institutions from the Ministry of Finance to an independent entity. The Agency changed its name to the Financial Services Agency in 2001.

ity assistance to the banking system this was not enough to stem the crisis that ensued. Major events relating to the crisis are illustrated in Table 16.7.

Since the banking crisis a wide range of reforms have been put in place. These have aimed to stabilise the banking system and to facilitate bank restructuring. The authorities introduced a blanket deposit insurance scheme (to protect all depositors in the event of bank failure), extended emergency liquidity assistance to troubled banks, provided financial assistance to promote mergers among troubled financial institutions, injected capital into weak but viable banks and allowed for the temporary nationalisation of non-viable banks.

Various features of reforms involved with bank restructuring include:

- Public **recapitalisation** of various banks (in March 1998, March 1999 and May 2003) that amounted to around ¥9 trillion;
- More rapid recognition of non-performing loans (introduced in October 2002), with tougher loan classification and loan-loss provisioning rules which enabled the regulators to identify the size of bad loans but also encouraged faster disposals of non-performing loans (e.g., banks writing them off their balance sheets);
- Disposal of bank non-performing loans, close to ¥90 trillion since 1998 although despite these disposals, bank non-performing loans have not declined as fast as expected due to the emergence of new non-performing loans;

- Exit of a number of inefficient deposit-taking institutions;
- Establishment of various public asset management companies that deal with the sale of bank non-performing loans.

In addition to these reforms the authorities have also been active in encouraging bank mergers between the leading banks (as shown in Table 16.2), they withdrew the blanket deposit insurance guarantee in the spring of 2005 and continue to focus on measures aimed at reducing the level of non-performing loans in the system.

16.7 Regulation of Japanese banks

As should be apparent from the previous section, the regulatory environment under which Japanese banks operate has undergone substantial change in recent years. Traditionally, the Bank of Japan (the country's central bank) supervised the banking system and was instrumental in introducing various reforms known as the **'Big Bang'** that effectively introduced the universal banking model. This deregulation that occurred between 1998 and 1999:

- allowed the use of financial holding companies;
- eliminated many barriers between banking and other financial service sectors;
- liberalised stock brokerage fees;
- allowed banks to sell investment trust products.

As a result of these and other measures, financial institutions in Japan could offer a wide range of financial products and services to their customers.

From 1 April 1998, the Bank of Japan[1] was given greater independence in relation to monetary policy and on 22 June 1998, a new governmental agency called the Financial Supervisory Agency (which changed its name to the **Financial Services Agency** in 2001) was established and given supervisory and inspection functions with respect to private-sector financial institutions. (Previously, both the Bank of Japan and Ministry of Finance had supervisory responsibilities.)

The Financial Services Agency[2] is responsible for the supervision and inspection of all private banks in Japan. (Public banks remain supervised by the Bank of Japan.) The Financial Services Agency monitors the financial soundness of banks including the status and performance of their control systems for business activities. The main functions of the FSA are:

- planning and policymaking concerning the financial system;
- inspection and supervision of private-sector financial institutions including banks, securities companies, insurance companies and market participants including securities exchanges;
- establishment of rules for trading in securities markets;
- establishment of business accounting standards and others concerning corporate finance;

[1] http://www.boj.or.jp
[2] http://www.fsa.go.jp

- supervision of certified public accountants and audit firms;
- participation in activities on financial issues of international organisations and bilateral and multilateral fora to develop internationally co-ordinated financial administration;
- surveillance of compliance of rules governing securities markets.

The FSA is responsible for dealing with failed financial institutions and general oversight of the soundness of private banks in the Japanese system. There is also a Deposit Insurance Corporation[3] that protects depositor's funds in the event of a bank failure.

16.8 Conclusions

The Japanese banking sector has experienced dramatic changes over the last 20 years or so, experiencing rapid growth during the 1980s through to the mid-1990s and then a collapse between 1997 and 1998 and a subsequent clean-up thereafter. There are signs that the banking system's profitability is improving although capital levels remain low by international standards – and the level of non-performing loans (although falling) still acts as a drag on the system. There has been substantial consolidation between the largest banks, leaving four major financial services groups and the public postal savings service (to be privatised) as the dominant players. Substantial further consolidation is expected in the regional and co-operative banking sectors. Given the overall weak performance of the domestic economy, it remains to be seen how long it will take the Japanese banking system to return to strong levels of performance and financial soundness equivalent to other major systems.

Key terms

Non-Performing Loans (NPLs)
Private deposit-taking financial institutions
City banks
Regional banks
Trust banks
Long-term credit banks
Credit co-operative banks
Private non-deposit-taking financial institutions
Deposit Insurance Corporation
Development banks

Disintermediation
Zengin Data Telecommunication System
Bill and Cheque Clearing Systems
Foreign Exchange Yen Clearing System
BOJ-NET (Bank of Japan Financial Network System) Funds Transfer System
'Convoy system'
Recapitalisation
'Big Bang'
Financial Services Agency

---

[3] http://www.dic.go.jp

Key reading   International Monetary Fund (2005) *World Economic Outlook*, http://www.imf.org/external/pubs/ft/weo/2005/02/index.htm.

Ianaba N. and Kozu, T. (2005) 'A Note on the Recent Behaviour of Japanese Banks', *BIS' Working Paper*, No. 22, April 2005, http://www.bis.org/publ/bppdf/bispap22f.pdf.

Kanaya, A. and Woo, D. (2000) 'The Japanese Banking Crises of the 1990s: Sources and Lessons', *IMF Working Paper* WP/00/7 http://www.imf.org/external/pubs/ft/wp/2000/wp0007.pdf.

Revision questions and problems

1 What are the main features of the different types of financial institutions operating in Japan?

2 To what extent has the disintermediation process affected the Japanese banking and financial sectors over the last decade or so?

3 How is the payment system organised for clearing and settling interbank payments in Japan?

4 What have been the most relevant changes to the Japanese bank's balance sheet structure over the last ten years?

5 What are the most important changes to the regulatory environment under which Japanese banks operate?

6 What were the major causes of the Japanese banking crisis in the second half of the 1990s?

Chapter 17

Banking in emerging and transition economies

Learning objectives	● To provide an overview of the main structural features of banking systems in emerging markets
	● To understand the main changes that have occurred in emerging banking markets in recent years
	● To analyse the role of public sector ownership and foreign ownership in banking markets
	● To identify the main causes of banking crises
	● To identify successful bank restructuring procedure

17.1 Introduction

The world-wide banking industry has undergone dramatic changes and emerging and transition economies have not gone untouched by this transformation. This chapter aims to address some of the key issues and implications of such changes. Technological innovation, the deregulation of financial services at the national level and the opening up of most domestic sectors to foreign banks have all contributed to increasing competition and other pressures on banking institutions. In addition, recent banking crises in Central Europe, East Asia and Latin America have also transformed these sectors and fostered further transformation, through privatisation, M&A activity and other forms of industry restructuring, one common trend being a marked decrease in the number of banks. Against the background of these developments, Section 17.2 reviews the macroeconomic outlook in emerging markets and transition economies. Section 17.3 analyses the main forces of change and how these forces are affecting the structure of the banking industries in terms of privatisations, M&As and entry of foreign banks. The regulatory issues raised by recent banking crises are reviewed in Section 17.4.

17.2 The macroeconomic outlook

Before we describe the macroeconomic outlook of emerging and transition economies, it is important, in this context, to provide some terminology. The term **emerging market** was originally coined by the International Finance Corporation (IFC)[1] to describe a fairly narrow list of middle-to-higher income economies among the developing countries, with stock markets in which foreigners could buy securities. The term's meaning has since been expanded to include more or less all developing countries. **Developing countries** are those with a Gross National Income (GNI) per capita of $9,265 or less. The World Bank classifies economies as low-income (GNI $755 or less), middle-income (GNI $756–9,265) and high-income (GNI $9,266 or more). Low-income and middle-income economies are sometimes referred to as developing countries.[2] As explained in Chapter 14, the label 'transition economy' is used to describe former communist countries that have been transforming their planned economies to market economies. As a result, and for the purpose of this discussion, transition countries are considered emerging economies. In other words, the label 'emerging economies' encompasses all countries that are not included in the developed world.

Table 17.1 shows the geographical composition of countries that are included in the above definition of 'emerging and transition economies'. From the number of countries in the table it is obvious that it would be impossible to describe in detail the banking sector and associated issues of each country. For this reason, we will analyse major emerging markets regions, namely Asia, Latin America, Central Europe, the Middle East and Africa.

---

[1] The International Finance Corporation (IFC) is a member of the World Bank Group and is headquartered in Washington, DC. The IFC's aim is to promote sustainable private sector investment in developing countries as a way to reduce poverty and improve people's lives.
[2] World Bank (2002).

Table 17.1 Emerging and transition countries

Central and Eastern Europe	Southern Europe and Central Asia	South Asia	East Asia and Pacific	Latin America and the Caribbean	Middle East and North Africa	Sub-Saharan Africa
Armenia	Albania	Bangladesh	Cambodia	Argentina	Afghanistan	Angola
Belarus	Azerbaijan	Bhutan	China	Barbados	Algeria	Benin
Czech Republic	Bosnia and	India	Fiji	Belize	Arab	Botswana
Estonia	Herzegovina	Maldives	Indonesia	Bolivia	Republic	Burkina Faso
Georgia	Bulgaria	Nepal	Kiribati	Brazil	of Egypt	Burundi
Hungary	Croatia	Pakistan	Laos PDR	Chile	Bahrain	Cameroon
Latvia	Cyprus	Sri Lanka	Malaysia	Colombia	Iraq	Cape Verde
Lithuania	Federal Republic		Marshall Islands	Costa Rica	Islamic	Central
Poland	of Yugoslavia		Micronesia	Dominican	Republic	African
Russian Federation	Former Yugoslav		Mongolia	Republic	of Iran	Republic
Slovak Republic	Republic of		Myanmar	Ecuador	Jordan	Chad
Slovenia	Macedonia		Papua New	El Salvador	Kuwait	Comoros
Ukraine	Kazakhstan		Guinea	Guatemala	Lebanon	Côte
	Kyrgyz Republic		Philippines	Guyana	Libya	d'Ivoire
	Moldova		Samoa	Haiti	Morocco	Djibouti
	Romania		Solomon Islands	Honduras	Oman	Equatorial
	Tajikistan		South Korea	Jamaica	Qatar	Guinea
	Turkey		Taiwan (China)	Mexico	Republic	Eritrea
	Turkmenistan		Thailand	Nicaragua	of Yemen	Ethiopia
	Uzbekistan		Tonga	Panama	Saudi Arabia	Gabon
			Vanuatu	Paraguay	Tunisia	Gambia
			Vietnam	Peru	United Arab	Ghana
				Trinidad and	Emirates	Guinea
				Tobago	West Bank	Guinea
				Uruguay	and Gaza	Bissau
				Venezuela	Strip	Kenya
				OECS States		Lesotho
				Antigua and		Liberia
				Barbuda		Madagascar
				Dominica		Malawi
				Grenada		Mali
				Montserrat		Mauritania
				St Kitts		Mauritius
				and Nevis		Mozambique
				St Lucia		Namibia
				St Vincent		Niger
				and		Nigeria
				Grenadines		Republic
						of Congo
						Rwanda
						Sao Tome
						and Principe
						Senegal
						Seychelles
						Sierra Leone
						Somalia
						South Africa
						Sudan
						Swaziland
						Tanzania
						Togo
						Uganda
						Zambia
						Zimbabwe

Notes: OECS = Organization of Eastern Caribbean States.

In recent years, all major emerging market economies have experienced sustained growth, consumer confidence is high and inflation is relatively low. The average inflation rate in emerging economies as a whole fell from 13 per cent in the mid-1990s to 5.5 per cent in the period 2000–04. The biggest reductions have taken place in countries such as Brazil and Mexico where inflation rates have been historically high. Several factors played a role in supporting growth in these economies including: favourable global demand conditions, stronger domestic macroeconomic fundamentals which improved the credit standing of many countries, and an increase in domestic demand. Table 17.2 highlights some of these trends.

The majority of emerging economies have shared the current upturn in the global economic cycle, which started in 2001. Despite some adverse shocks such as higher oil prices, average economic growth rates are expected to remain strong. Looking at data by macro-regions, in Asia, China and India have been the leading economies. In Latin America, Mexico, Argentina and Brazil have experienced strong growth after a difficult decade in the 1990s. Private consumption recovered from the collapse suffered during recent crises. Despite some slowdown in Central and Eastern Europe, most major economies are expected to grow and economic prospects seem to be positive in many African countries.

The current economic expansion is also causing some problems: strong demand has raised inflation rates in some countries. Further, various countries have experienced a rapid growth in household credit and an increase in property prices. However, emerging markets economies seem to have become more resilient to shocks even though there are fears that a global economic slowdown could undo some of the recent progress.

Table 17.2 Output growth and inflation

	Real GDP			Inflation		
	Average 1995–2003	2004	2005[a]	Average 1995–2003	2004	2005[a]
Asia	6.6	7.8	7.2	4.2	4.4	3.9
China	8.5	9.5	8.9	3.0	3.9	3.2
India	5.9	7.1	7.1	5.2	6.7	5.6
Latin America	2.0	5.9	4.3	11.2	6.6	6.3
Argentina	0.4	9.1	6.8	4.8	6.1	10.0
Brazil	2.1	5.2	3.6	9.3	7.5	6.5
Mexico	2.5	4.4	3.9	16.6	5.2	4.0
Central Europe	3.7	4.8	4.0	10.2	3.9	2.4
Russia	2.4	7.1	5.8	49.5	10.2	11.6
Turkey	3.7	8.9	5.7	64.9	10.6	8.0
Middle East	4.1	5.5	5.0	9.2	8.3	8.6
Africa	3.7	5.1	5.0	15.6	7.7	7.7
All emerging markets[b]	5.2	7.2	6.3	9.4	5.4	5.0
G7 countries	2.4	3.2	2.3	1.9	2.0	2.0

Note:
[a] 2005 forecast are based on May consensus forecast, JP Morgan Chase and IMF, World Economic Outlook.
[b] Weighted Average.

Source: BIS 75th Annual Report.

The banking sector has contributed to the positive economic climates in most emerging markets. Bank performance has generally been good; cyclical factors, such as the strong economic growth experienced since 2003 and low global interest rates, have helped to boost banks' profitability and to improve asset quality.

17.3 Structural features and trends

This section provides an overview of recent trends that have contributed to shape the current structure of banking systems in emerging markets. First we examine some general trends as well as regulatory developments. We then look at the impact these forces of change have had on the structure and performance of selected banking systems.

The banking systems in emerging countries are heterogeneous, in terms of number and size of institutions, ownership structure, profitability and competitiveness, use of IT and other structural features. In most countries, a few large commercial banks have the majority of the market share and co-exist with a large number of small savings and co-operative banks, either family-owned, as in Asia, or state owned, as in Latin America (see Table 17.3). The foreign share of the sector also varies remarkably among countries, to the point that various restrictions to foreign ownership are in place in many emerging economies.

In this varied environment, it is important to analyse the main forces of change affecting the structure and efficiency features of banking systems.

Table 17.3 **Banking systems in selected emerging economies**

Country	Number of banks	Bank Assets (share of GDP)	CR-5 (deposits)	Share of bank's assets owned by: Government (%)	Foreigners (%)
East Asia					
Korea	17	98.0	47.5	29.7	0.0
Thailand	32	117.0	74.8	30.7	7.2
Malaysia	17	166.0	30.0	0.0	18.0
Indonesia	164	101.0	52.9	44.0	7.0
Philippines	7,612	91.0	45.6	12.1	12.8
Latin America					
Argentina	76	54.0	48.0	30.0	49.0
Brazil	140	55.0	57.6	51.5	16.7
Chile	26	97.0	59.4	11.7	32.0
Mexico	35	30.0	80.0	25.0	19.9
Peru	14	36.0	81.2	2.5	40.4
Venezuela	52	6.0	63.8	4.9	33.7
Eastern Europe					
Russia	1,243	16.0	80.0	68.0	9.0

Note: CR-5 is the five-firm concentration ratio, namely the market share of the top five banks. The figure reported in the table is the deposits market share of the top five banks.

Source: Central banks. Data refer to the most recent available year. Coppel and Davies (2003), p. 5.

17.3.1 **Deregulation and financial liberalisation**

Banking in emerging markets was traditionally characterised by high levels of government control, with restrictions on borrowing and lending rates and on domestic and foreign entry. In some countries the levels of restriction on financial activities and government intervention in financial markets were so strong (for example, during the Soviet era in the former USSR) that they could be better described as **financial repression**. The main way governments were pursuing financial repression was to maintain the monopoly of the financial sector by state banks, restricting entry of both banks and non-deposit-taking financial institutions and by strictly controlling new financial instruments which could compete with bank deposits. Financial repression could vary from mild to severe, and included:

- control over interest rates
- controls over lending
- directed lending (loans made at subsidised 'uneconomic' rates to specific politically preferred sectors)
- high reserve requirements
- restrictions on entry of new banks and other financial intermediaries
- restrictions on entry of foreign financial intermediaries
- nationalisation of financial institutions.

Traditionally, there was little incentive to change these protective banking environments and foster competition. During the 1990s, however, a combination of changes in the global financial markets, macroeconomic pressures resulting from various banking crises and fast technological developments have forced regulators to deregulate the industry at the domestic level and to open up to foreign competition.

Several changes have taken place, which have forced structural changes in the banking industries. The main changes at the domestic level, in most emerging banking markets, have been the removal of ceilings on deposit rates and the removal of the prohibition of interest payments on current accounts. These changes were very significant because they meant that banks could no longer rely on sources of cheap funding and this put pressure on their profits, thus encouraging banks to reorganise and become more market-oriented in their activities.

Other deregulation measures have included opening up to foreign competition, and opening up to competition from non-bank financial intermediaries.

The opening up of banking markets in emerging economies has led to a growing presence of global financial institutions in search of profit opportunities. As a result, most banking markets in emerging countries now depend on foreign institutions to provide capital, technology and managerial expertise. These issues will be discussed in Section 17.3.3.

Deregulation and **financial liberalisation** have long been considered a positive force as they are supposed to increase efficiency by imposing competition and removing regulations that distort economic activity. The perceived benefits of deregulation include:

- expansion of financial markets;
- increased competition;
- more choice and cheaper financial products;
- increased innovation as a result of technology developments;
- enhanced consumer welfare;
- fostering of economic growth.

However, beyond the positive aspects of deregulation, a number of economists and policymakers have been recently asking themselves whether it can cause financial crises. This debate will be analysed in Section 17.4.

Financial deregulation has certainly made it easier for intermediaries to cross industry and national boundaries. It has also fostered technological progress, which in turn has reduced costs while stimulating innovation. For example, the computer and telecommunications revolution rendered geographic branching restrictions obsolete. Financial innovation includes the development of new financial instruments, which are now extensively used by emerging countries' banks. Owing to the recent technological changes, emerging economies' banking markets are in a position to 'skip a stage of financial development', quickly moving from a rather rudimentary system to a fairly advanced one. For example, the rapid development of ATMs, debit and credit cards, telephone and internet banking has pushed developing economies from cash-based transactions to electronic based transactions, skipping the 'cheques stage'.

Emerging markets see the development of new delivery channels as an important part of the development of their retail and commercial banking activities, both because of the growing availability of IT and telecommunication technologies and the relatively lower cost of delivery compared to bank branches. One particular source of concern in emerging economies related to technological improvements is the so-called **digital divide** in the access to banking services. There is a fear that better-educated and wealthier customers will be able to obtain competitive banking services through the internet whereas the quality of services provided to poorer customers will deteriorate as bank branches are closed, particularly in rural areas.

Box 17.1   Reform of Indian banks is a priority   FT

At recent celebrations marking the 200th anniversary of the State Bank of India, the country's largest bank, Prime Minister Manmohan Singh could not resist the opportunity to boast about the country's banking system. 'If there is one aspect in which we can confidently assert that India is ahead of China, that is in the robustness and soundness of our banking system,' he said.

The banking system may not be suffering China's bad loans problem, but few economists believe its performance is a cause for celebration. There is ample evidence to show that, despite reforms launched in 1991, an inefficient financial sector remains a significant obstacle to government hopes of achieving the 8 per cent rate of economic growth it believes can lift hundreds of millions out of poverty.

India has managed to achieve an impressive rate of savings, with the World Bank estimating a share of financial assets in GDP of 173 per cent, compared with 104 per cent in Mexico, 112 per cent in Indonesia and 157 per cent in Brazil*. But this is only patchily invested in the real economy because of government funding requirements. Government inability to manage its finances is at the heart of the banking system's weakness as a financial intermediary. High deficit financing requirements – state and central budget deficits combined are 10 per cent of GDP – crowd out credit to the private sector. More than 40 per cent of the banking system's resources are invested in government securities.

'The government is absorbing such a large part of bank deposits for funding its revenue expenses and subsidies rather than long-term investments – that there's not enough left on the table for banks to explore lending opportunities beyond the large corporates,' says Chetan Ahya, an economist at JM Morgan Stanley. 'That's the whole problem with economic growth in India. It's skewed towards the people at the higher end.'

Economists are alarmed that banks hold far more in government securities than required by the statutory liquidity ratio. This has been lowered from a

▶

peak of 38.5 per cent of net demand and time liabilities in February 1992 to 25 per cent.

Large segments of the economy remain excluded from access to formal finance. The ratio of private credit to GDP remains low at less than 40 per cent, compared with more than 100 per cent for countries such as China, Malaysia and South Korea. Moneylenders have a tight grip over the 70 per cent of India's rural poor with no bank account.

'There's something going wrong here,' says Priya Basu, lead sector specialist at the World Bank. 'There's pressure on the banks to invest much more in government securities than the statutory liquidity ratio requires. Given that the banks are then obliged to lend 40 per cent of net deposits to priority sectors, there's scarcely a quarter left for bank managers to lend as they see fit.'

Poor contract enforcement, lack of credit information and weak bankruptcy laws accentuate the innate risk aversion of public sector bank managers.

For much of India's post-war history, central planners used the banking network to channel savings towards political priorities. Many banks were nationalised; credit was directed to sectors on the basis of quantitative targets and subsidised interest rates; and rural networks were built in accordance with social objectives without regard for profitability.

Over the past decade and a half, that has started to change. Interest rates have been largely liberalised, banks' required holdings of government debt reduced and obligations to lend to priority areas such as agriculture and small-scale businesses relaxed. These reforms encouraged deposit growth, the development of a credit culture and entry of private and foreign forces.

The feat of combining liberalisation and stability, overseen by the Reserve Bank of India, should not be underestimated. The RBI's conservative approach to reform was vindicated during the East Asian crises of the late 1990s. The contagious panic that spread across Thailand, Indonesia, Malaysia and South Korea left India's largely state-controlled financial sector unscathed.

'India's banking system appears to be sheltered from a crisis because [the country's] exchange rate regime is flexible, foreign exchange reserves are high, the capital account is not yet fully convertible and banks and their customers have limited, albeit growing, foreign exchange exposure,' the World Bank sector specialist argues in a recently published essay.

Despite the success of new privately owned Indian banks, such as ICICI and HFDC Bank, and the efforts of foreign banks such as Citibank, Standard Chartered and HSBC to make inroads, the country's financial landscape remains dominated by lumbering public sector institutions whose fragility and inability to liberalise has slowed reform.

The Reserve Bank of India's concern over the systemic risks involved in exposing underperforming public banks to the full blast of competition is the principal cause of the country's slow-motion liberalisation. In February, the RBI released an ultra-cautious roadmap for the sector, putting a brake on foreign takeover of banks until 2009.

'If I had to sum it up in one sentence, I'd say the banking system has traded efficiency for stability,' says Ms Basu. 'India's financial system is not about to collapse and if the government really wants the economy to grow at a faster pace, the time has come to focus on banking sector efficiency.'

The public sector banks, which control more than 52 per cent of financial assets, retain powerful positions. They have extensive branch networks and enjoy the explicit guarantee of central government, a significant confidence boost for depositors in a country whose households, according to Morgan Stanley, were in March 2005 hoarding $200bn of gold, 2.5 times their holdings in the stock market.

So far, private and foreign banks, with much smaller networks, have made little inroad into the business of mobilising savings and demand deposits from the public, a business dominated by the public banks. Their arrival has been felt most in the high grade corporate market, where spreads have come down with growing access to capital markets and offshore finance.

A second wave of reforms forcing greater efficiencies on the banking sector is long overdue. 'Many of the proposed reforms challenge the interests of privileged groups and some could involve painful adjustment, but delay will only increase the costs further,' writes Michael Carter, head of the World Bank in India. 'Financial sector reforms are critical to achieving sustained growth and prosperity.'

*For further reading, see Driya Basu (ed.) *India's Financial Sector: Recent Reforms, Future Challenges*, Macmillan India, 2005, p. 224.

Source: *Financial Times* (2005), 'Indian Banking and Finance', 27 July, by Jo Johnson.

17.3.2 Privatisations

In the 1980s and early 1990s, in most emerging economies, state-owned banks accounted for the majority of banking sector assets. The banking industry, together with utilities, telecommunications, railways and airlines was considered too important for the national economy to be left in private hands. A decade later, governments' share in the banking system has witnessed a substantial reduction both in Central Europe and in Latin America. State ownership remains high in China, India and Russia, but even these countries have recently launched privatisation programmes. Among the reasons for such a dramatic change was the poor performance of state-owned banks and frequent and costly bail-outs. Further, there was a widely held perception during the 1990s that the presence of state ownership in the banking sector could hinder financial development. Studies by Barth, Caprio and Levine (2001, 2004) established a negative and statistically significant relationship between state ownership of bank assets and several measures of financial development, including bank credit to the private sector and stock market capitalisation. On average, greater state ownership of banks tends to be associated with poorly developed banks, non-banks, and stock markets and an inefficient financial system.

In many countries, state-owned banks suffered from poor management skills and were forced to lend to under-performing, state-owned enterprises. This led to a number of bankruptcies of state-owned banks in the banking crises of the 1980s and 1990s and to vulnerable and weak banking sectors. As a response, the government of many emerging economies introduced reforms that led, among other things, to the gradual privatisation of the banking sector. This helped to restore stability, particularly in Latin America and Central Europe.

Each emerging economy had its own motives for undertaking a process of privatisation of state-owned banks; however, the aims of such programmes were to encourage competition and enhance efficiency of the sector.

Latin American countries launched bank privatisation programmes at different stages during the 1990s; these programmes were part of larger long-term pubic sector reforms, with the aim of restructuring public finances, cutting borrowing requirements and deepening the role of the stock markets. The emerging Asian economies, on the other hand, were facing the challenge of returning to private ownership the banks that were nationalised during the 1997–98 crises (see Section 17.4).

In general, policymakers do not see a useful role for state-owned banks in emerging markets, with the exception of a few special cases, as outlined by the BIS (2001) report:[3]

- in some large countries, such as Russia, Brazil and Argentina, only state-owned banks are willing to serve customers in remote areas;
- some countries, such as Thailand, Brazil and Argentina, see a continued role for state-owned banks to channel lending to farmers and small and medium-sized enterprises outside the largest cities;
- there are some indications that lending by state-owned banks is less pro-cyclical than lending by private domestic and foreign banks;
- in some cases, the restructuring of a state-owned bank (and continued, albeit temporary, public ownership) may be preferable to a quick privatisation;
- in some countries the lack of basic market and legal infrastructure may be so severe that state-owned banks are the only viable alternative.

---

[3] BIS (2001).

Despite the exceptions discussed above, policymakers in most emerging economies seem to consider state ownership of banks as a second-best solution and are subjecting the remaining public banks to market discipline, treating them in a similar manner to private banks in terms of supervision and other factors.

17.3.3 Mergers and Acquisitions

Market-driven consolidation in the form that we have witnessed both in Europe and in the NMSs (as well as in the United States and other industrialised countries) is a relatively new phenomenon in emerging economies. Most mergers have resulted from government efforts to restructure inefficient banking systems (as in many Latin American countries) or from intervention following banking crises (as in East Asian countries). However, following the deregulation and privatisation processes, competition has increased in a number of markets and the M&A trend is becoming more market driven. Cross-border activity is a major feature of M&A in emerging markets since foreign ownership is usually established through the purchase of existing enterprises, rather than 'greenfield investment' (new companies). Over the past decade (mid-1990s to early–mid-2000s), over 50 per cent of M&As in Latin America and Central and Eastern Europe was cross-border. The percentage of cross-border deals was slightly lower in East Asia, with a percentage of around 20 per cent. Africa and the Middle East witnessed a similar proportion of cross-border M&As over the period, as illustrated in Table 17.4.

In Latin America, the consolidation process that took place in recent years was a response to inefficient banking structures. In East Asia, cross-border activity has been largely through the sale of distressed private firms rather than through the privatisation process witnessed in transition countries. For example, in Thailand the finance sector registered a large number of deals in the two years following the 1997–98 crisis. However, although M&A activity has played a role in the restructuring process of East Asian economies, a number of deals have also been inspired by the desire of Western financial institutions to expand and diversify overseas. An interesting feature is the trend in cross-border deals within the East Asian economies, in line with the trend towards closer economic integration in the region.

Table 17.4 Financial sector M&As in emerging economies (world regions) 1990–2002

	Number of Transactions		Value of Transactions	
	Total	Cross Border (%)	Total	Cross Border (%)
East Asia	1,124	17.4	28.4	22.8
Rest of Asia	778	33.4	37.1	48.7
South America	394	55.3	37.1	48.7
Eastern Europe	586	52.6	13.6	85.9
Africa and Middle East	373	30.0	27.8	20.6
All emerging markets	3,436	34.7	180.3	41.8

Notes: East Asia includes Indonesia, Korea, Malaysia, the Philippines and Thailand. Eastern Europe includes also the new EU Member States (CEECs).

Source: Data from Thompson Financial Datastream, adapted from BIS (2004), p. 12.

Privatisations are likely to remain a catalyst for future M&As; however, in many emerging economies problems concerning the assessment of asset quality and the allocation of liabilities have delayed the sale of nationalised banks.

In China, where the major four state-owned banks control around 60 per cent of the banking system, strengthening the banks to cope with deregulation forced by China's entry into the World Trade Organisation (WTO) is a more immediate concern than the process of consolidation of the banking sector. The major four banks have asset quality problems with a high percentage of non-performing loans. Consolidation is more likely among the nationwide commercial banks, which have been growing rapidly during the 1990s but still lack scale when compared to the large state-owned banks. While the listing of several banks on the domestic stock exchange may provide a framework for mergers, these remain unlikely at least in the short term.

In India, in recent years, the main focus has been the restructuring of weak public sector banks. Up until March 2001, there had been limited mergers in India's banking sector and these were not significant when viewed as a proportion of the assets of the banking system. The government as a major shareholder in many banks is well placed to facilitate industry consolidation. But whether consolidation or privatisation is likely to be the dominant theme in Indian banking is unclear.

17.3.4 Foreign banks

The past decade has seen a transformation of the role of foreign banks in emerging markets; there has been a strategic shift away from pursuing internationally active corporate clients towards business opportunities in the domestic retail markets. Table 17.5 shows that foreign presence has increased significantly in many countries.

Table 17.5 Foreign ownership of banks in selected emerging economies

Country	Assets owned by banks with 50% or more foreign ownership (as % of total banking sector assets)			Assets owned by banks with more than 10% but less that 50% foreign ownership (as % of total banking sector assets)		
	1990	*2000*	*2002*	*1990*	*2000*	*2002*
Hong Kong	45.7	87.2	88.6	3.7	7.2	6.2
India	21.0	42.0	40.0	–	4.0	5.0
Korea	n.a.	32.7	32.3	n.a.	7.5	14.4
Malaysia	22.3	24.9	25.2	34.1	30.5	38.7
Singapore	89.4	75.5	76.0	n.a.	n.a.	n.a.
Thailand	–	5.9	5.8	n.a.	45.8	48.6
Argentina	17.0	48.1	41.6	n.a.	13.4	12.7
Brazil	n.a.	25.2	21.5	n.a.	7.0	6.2
Chile	18.6	33.1	44.8	5.5	16.5	3.0
Colombia	3.7	18.0	16.4	6.6	13.7	13.6
Mexico	0.3	54.6	81.9	n.a.	0.3	0.6
Peru	–	32.6	30.6	10.5	9.2	14.4
Venezuela	n.a.	49.7	37.4	n.a.	7.7	0.8
Russia	7.2	9.5	8.1	5.5	3.1	2.3
Turkey	2.9	3.6	3.3	0.8	–	–

Source: Adapted from BIS (2005), p. 14.

Table 17.6 Participation of state, private and foreign banks in selected Latin American banking systems

County	State banks	Private banks	Total	Foreign banks EU	USA	Other	Single largest foreign country
Argentina	32.5	19.1	48.4	33.6	12.1	2.7	Spain (17.9%)
Brazil	46.0	27.0	27.0	15.7	5.3	6.1	Spain (5.3%)
Bolivia	18.2	56.5	25.3	10.4	4.5	10.4	Spain (10.4%)
Chile	12.9	45.5	41.6	32.4	5.5	3.8	Spain (30.6%)
Peru	10.8	43.2	46.0	34.8	5.6	5.6	Spain (17.1%)
Mexico	–	17.7	82.3	53.7	23.7	4.8	Spain (41.5%)

Note: Participation in terms of assets in each country's banking industry. Participation is considered to be 100 per cent when a foreign bank controls a bank but owns less than 100 per cent of the capital.

Source: Bankers Almanac and National Publications. Adapted from Cárdenas *et al.* (2003).

From Table 17.5 it is possible to note that the degree of foreign penetration differs significantly across countries. Latin America has experienced a transformation similar to the one of CEECs countries described in Chapter 14, with foreign banks gaining a dominant position in the space of a few years. In the Latin American case, rather than the privatisation process experienced by the CEECs, it was the need to recapitalise the system following episodes of financial instability that drove foreign investment. Conversely, the penetration of foreign banks is much less marked in Asia, with the exception of Hong Kong and Singapore.

Table 17.6 illustrates the participation of state, private and foreign banks in the Latin American banking systems. In several countries, Spanish banks have acquired important positions, giving rise to concerns that contagion from a crisis in one country may work through investment decisions of these banks. For example, in 2002, probably influenced by their severe losses in Argentina, the Spanish bank Banco Bilbao Vizcaya (BBVA) sold the equity of its Brazilian subsidiary (BBV Brasil) to Banco Bradesco (a Brazilian bank) and Banco Santander Central Hispano sold its Peruvian subsidiary and 25 per cent of its Mexican subsidiary's shares. Note, however, that at the same time BBVA increased its participation in Mexico.

The recent wave of foreign bank expansion has developed via subsidiaries, rather than the foreign-denominated lending by head offices of international banks. This is seen as a positive development, as a deeper local presence of international banks can contribute to a greater efficiency and resilience of the financial sector, both because it implies greater borrowing in local currency (therefore minimising currency mismatches) and because foreign banks can help emerging economies recapitalise their banking systems. (See Chapter 4 for further discussion on the reason foreign banks establish or acquire subsidiaries overseas.) Foreign banks may also help enhance financial stability by enabling greater lending diversification and by improving risk management practices. A number of empirical studies suggest that foreign banks do play a stabilising role.[4] Despite the fact that the benefits that foreign banks can offer to emerging economies are now more widely accepted, there are still a number of concerns:

- a large foreign banking presence can reduce the information available to host country supervisors;
- a large foreign bank's presence can expose a country to shocks due purely to external events affecting the parent bank;

[4] Martinez Peria, Powell and Hollar (2002), Detragiache and Gupta (2004).

- the issue of foreign currency-denominated lending;
- foreign banks 'cherry pick' the best firms, leaving the domestic banking sector with a weakened lending portfolio;
- foreign banks concentrate on large and more profitable firms, leaving small and medium-sized enterprises for domestic banks.

There are also concerns that in the 2001 financial crisis in Argentina, foreign banks did not play a stabilising role but may have increased economic volatility. Some questions still remain unanswered, particularly concerning the impact of foreign banks on aggregate lending and on their responsiveness to monetary policy.

17.3.4.1 Foreign ownership and regulatory reform

The single most important driving force behind the increase in foreign activity and foreign ownership in emerging banking markets is regulatory reform.

In Latin America, most countries are completely open to international capital flows. The view taken by Latin American governments with respect to foreign banks is that their capital, expertise and prestige would help the domestic banking systems in the aftermath of the crises. However, in order to minimise the potential impact of 'sudden stops' in international capital flows (previously experienced both by Latin American and Eastern European countries) stronger prudential regulation, together with sound macroeconomic policies, are sought. Some mild forms of restrictions on portfolio capital flows are also advocated as part of a prudent financial policy.

In East Asia, the main regulatory reforms have been policies designed to strengthen competition in the service sector, particularly banking. The expansion of the trade liberalisation agenda gave additional impetus for structural reforms. Some of the earlier policy initiatives, which were designed to achieve a more open capital account and more transparent FDI policies, gained momentum following the 1997–98 crises. For example, in 1998, Korea abolished the ceiling on foreign stock investment, giving foreign investors the right to purchase all shares of a domestic company. At the same time, the Korean government also announced a policy of ending direct interference in bank management. Similarly, Indonesia lessened restrictions on foreign participation in existing banks and removed the obstacles that prevented the opening of foreign branches. In Thailand and in the Philippines the limits on the foreign shareholding of banks were lifted. In contrast, Malaysia still restricts foreign entry in the banking sector. Table 17.7 details the remaining restrictions on foreign bank presence in various East Asian economies.

An interesting case is China, given the potential size of the market. China is to open its domestic market to foreign bank competition in a phased manner under the terms of its accession to the WTO. The phasing distinguishes between products (foreign currency before domestic currency and corporate loans before household deposits), and locations (coastal cities before interior cities). Despite the Chinese government's tight controls over the ownership of Chinese banks by foreign entities, in the last few years, there has been a change in attitude and a number of transactions have taken place or are in progress (Table 17.8). Although the Chinese banking system requires improvement across a number of fronts – risk management, credit approval, product development and technology – the staged entry under the WTO opens the possibility of some of the problems in the Chinese banking system being absorbed by foreign acquirers as a price of early entry (see Box 17.2).

Table 17.7 Limitation on foreign entry in East Asian banking sectors

Country	Ownership restrictions	Operational restrictions
Indonesia	None for new licenses. For existing banks, limited to 49% of equity. Local incorporation is required.	Higher paid-up capital is required for foreign banks. Branch offices allowed only in 10 cities. Managers and technical staff granted 3 years extendable visas, but require 2 equivalent Indonesian staff for each foreigner.
Korea	Most restrictions removed in 1998. Only representative offices or branches of foreign banks are permitted. Branches may open one year after the establishment of a representative office.	Restrictions on foreign currency loans and deposits and foreign exchange services. No restrictions on expatriate staff. Since 1998 Korean banks can recruit foreign nationals as directors.
Malaysia	Foreign shareholdings in existing local commercial banks should not exceed 30% of equity. The 13 wholly foreign-owned commercial banks are permitted to remain. No new licences are allowed.	An institution owned or controlled by a foreign government is not allowed to control a commercial or merchant bank. Expatriate staff are not granted visas, except for temporary presence of senior staff and specialists.
Thailand	No restrictions on existing foreign bank branches. Foreign shareholdings in commercial banks limited to 49% of equity. Limitations on individual ownership.	Managerial, executive and specialist staff granted visa for a 1-year period, extendable for no more than 3 years. Existing banks with a branch before 1995 limited to 2 new branches.
Philippines	Local incorporation required. Foreign shareholding or acquisition in a new investment limited to 51% of equity. Foreign share of total assets limited to 30%.	Only 10 new branches were allowed between 1995 and 2000, with a limit to 6 from a single bank.

Source: Adapted from Coppel and Davis (2003), p. 32; based on Hardin and Holmes (1997), Kim (2002) and Mattoo (2003).

Table 17.8 Foreign investments in Chinese banks

Bank	Purchaser	Ownership share (%)	Year
China Everbright Bank	Asian Development Bank	3	1996
Bank of Shanghai	IFC	5	1999
Nanjing City Commercial Bank	IFC	15	2001
Minsheng Bank	IFC	2	2001
Bank of Shanghai	HSBC	8	2001
Xi'an City Commercial Bank	IFC	1	2002
Xi'an City Commercial Bank	Bank of Nova Scotia	1	2002
Shanghai Pudong Development Bank	Citigroup	5	2003
Bank of Communications	HSBC	19.9	2004
China Construction Bank	Bank of America	9	2005
Bank of China	Royal Bank of Scotland	10	2005

Note: IFC = International Finance Corporation (IFC) is a member of the World Bank Group and is headquartered in Washington, DC.

Source: Adapted from Hobson and McCauley (2003), p. 41 and authors' updates.

For example, the Citigroup investment in Shanghai Pudong has already resulted in the launch of a line of credit cards that can access 300,000 cash machines in China and 20 million worldwide, well before foreign banks are permitted to enter this line of business. Currently, foreign investors are not allowed to own more than 25 per cent of a Chinese bank, with a single investor limited to 20 per cent. In August 2004, HSBC paid US$1.75 billion for a 19.9 per cent stake in Shanghai-based Bank of Communications (the fifth biggest lender). In June 2005 Bank of America announced a definitive agreement to buy approximately 9 per cent of the stock of China Construction Bank (CCB), the second largest commercial bank in China, for $3 billion, with the option of increasing its stake in future years. Currently (August 2005) the Royal Bank of Scotland, is nearing a deal to take a 10 per cent stake in Bank of China in what would be the largest ever single foreign direct investment in China ($3.1 billion).

Box 17.2   The size of the Chinese banking market: how big is the prize?

The potential of this market is a subject of active discussion. It is usually argued in terms of the current size of the Chinese banking system, expected double-digit growth in deposits and a rise in the current low share of foreign banks in the system (2 per cent of assets, as measured by the Chinese authorities). But the potential for growth in banking in China could be overstated. Consider the forecast of one banking analyst in Hong Kong (Ramos, 1999). The foreign bank share of the Chinese market could rise to 10 per cent over ten years and yield a return on assets of 1.8 per cent; and over this same period deposits could grow by 11 per cent a year on an asset base of US dollars 1.3 trillion in 1999. On these assumptions, foreign banks could multiply their profits in China tenfold to over US dollars 6 billion per annum. The hitch in this argument, however, is the consequences of the assumed rate of growth of the Chinese banking system over 10 years. Given the starting point, this growth would carry the banking system in relation to the underlying economy to a very high level by international standards. Against this argument, however, it might be said that in fact deposit growth has in recent years been faster than the 11 per cent assumed rate. The question faced by any bank contemplating entry into China is how long China's banking system will continue to grow faster than the country's nominal output. Even if the potential size of the Chinese market is often overstated, foreign banks still could see their operations in China grow substantially in the coming years. Chinese banks, however, are not standing still. Previously subject to mandates to lend to state-owned enterprises, since 1998 lending quotas have been abolished and banks have been made responsible for their own credit decisions. Credit decisions have been brought more under central control, although priorities are still influenced by government policy. In 1999, the major Chinese banks received a capital injection of RMB 270 billion, roughly a third of the budget. The next year four asset management companies were formed to relieve the major banks of much of the legacy of directed lending to state-owned enterprises. Operational improvements have also been made: in the last six years, the big banks have closed a fifth of their 150,000 branches. This has been accompanied by an expansion of household lending. The big banks are looking to become corporations or even to be privatised. The Chinese banking system is still a big challenge for everyone.

Source: Adapted from Hobson and McCauley (2003), p. 40.

17.4 Banking crises

A common and recurring theme in the analysis of emerging economies' banking sectors is the notion of **banking crises**. Although such crises are not confined to emerging markets, the consequences tend to be more severe than in industrialised countries. This section does not aim to review all the recent financial and banking crises in detail (there would be enough material to fill a book). The objective is to provide a brief overview of the relevant issues in the context of emerging economies, focusing in particular on the resolution of the crises and **bank restructuring**.

Over the last ten years, a number of emerging market economies have suffered pronounced financial crises, with far-reaching negative economic implications. These crises resulted in substantial losses in terms of wealth, output and jobs and were often accompanied by currency and banking crises. For example, the average cumulative output losses for banking crises in Argentina (2001–02), Indonesia (1998) and Turkey (1999–2001) have been estimated in the range of 12–15 per cent of GDP. Table 17.9 summarises the most recent banking crises in emerging markets.

Banking crises in Argentina, Ecuador, Russia, Turkey and Uruguay have occurred within the context of highly dollarised economies, high levels of sovereign debt and severely limited fiscal resources. **Dollarisation** occurs when residents of a country extensively use foreign currency (in this case US dollars, but Euros are also becoming widely used particularly in Central and Eastern Europe – **Euroisation**) alongside or instead of the domestic currency. Dollarisation is widespread in emerging countries (particularly in Latin America) as it is thought to provide a hedge against inflation in the domestic currency and increase the stability of the banking system. These factors have introduced new challenges as the effectiveness of many of the typical tools for bank resolution has been affected (see Box 17.3).

Table 17.9 Recent banking crises

Country	Crisis date	Change in deposits (%)	Change in net worth (%)	Fiscal costs (%)	Net IMF disbursement ($ million)
Mexico	1994–95	−15	−64	19.3	10.67
Venezuela	1994–95	−43	−6	15.0	−0.66
South Korea	1997–2000	−6	15	31.3	6.07
Indonesia	1997–2000	13	−183	56.8	10.35
Thailand	1997–2000	−2	58	43.8	3.21
Ecuador	1998–2001	−24	−59	21.7	0.30
Turkey	2000–02	−27	97	30.5	13.42
Argentina	2002–03	−4.8	−37	11.4	−16.00

Note: Change in deposits (%) from the start of the crisis to the trough in deposits; change in net worth (%) taking into account a period of two years after the crisis.

Source: Adapted from Lacoste (2004), p. 97.

Box 17.3 Bank resolution terminology

Some terms related to bank resolution have a range of meanings. The following terminology is used in most of the IMF literature on banking crises and resolution.

Intervention or **takeover** of insolvent or nonviable institutions by the authorities refers to the assumption of control of a bank, i.e., taking over the powers of management and shareholders. The term intervened bank is used to indicate a bank where such actions have taken place. Such a bank may be closed or may stay open under the control of the authorities while its financial condition is better defined and decisions are made on an appropriate resolution strategy. Such strategies include liquidation, merger or sale, transfer to a bridge bank, recapitalisation by the government, and sales or transfers of blocks of assets or liabilities. A bank undergoing this process is termed a resolved bank.

Closure means that the bank ceases to carry on the business of banking as a legal entity. A closure may be part of a legal process of achieving the orderly exit of a weak bank through a range of resolution options, including liquidation or a complete or partial transfer of its assets and liabilities to other institutions. A bank may be left with a rump of bad assets to be worked out. Withdrawal of the banking licence typically accompanies a closure.

Liquidation is the legal process whereby the assets of an institution are sold and its liabilities are settled to the extent possible. Bank liquidation can be voluntary or forced, within or outside general bankruptcy procedures, and with or without court involvement. In liquidation, assets are sold to pay off the creditors in the order prescribed by the law. In a systemic crisis with several institutions to be liquidated simultaneously and quickly, special procedures or institutions may be needed for the liquidation because existing structures cannot carry out the job in a timely manner.

A **merger** (or **sale**) of an institution means that all the assets and liabilities of the firm are transferred to and absorbed into another institution. Mergers can be voluntary or government assisted. A key issue is to avoid mergers of weak banks that result in a much larger weak bank, or the weakening of an initially strong bank. In a purchase and assumption operation, a solvent bank purchases all or a portion of the assets of a failing bank, including its customer base and goodwill, together with all or part of its liabilities. In such a supported purchase and assumption operation, the government typically will pay with securities to the purchasing bank the difference between the value of the assets and liabilities. Purchase and assumption operations could include some form of put option, entitling the acquiring bank to return certain assets within a specified period, or a contractual profit or loss-sharing agreement related to some or all of the assets. A bridge bank involves the use of a temporary financial institution to receive and manage the good assets of one or several failed institutions. A bridge bank may be allowed to undertake some banking business, such as providing new credit and restructuring existing credits.

Source: Adapted from IMF (2003).

17.4.1 Identifying the causes of banking crises

The identification of the causes of banking difficulties is important in terms of management of the crisis and effectiveness of the proposed solutions. The nature of the underlying causes may have an important bearing in the optimal official response. The moral hazard risk associated with rescuing a bank in difficulty through little fault of its own is small and this could be a case for regulatory forbearance. However, regulatory forbearance for poorly managed banks may result in damage to the regulator's credibility and authority.

There is a vast literature on the causes of banking crises; this literature is fairly divided between advocates of microeconomic factors and supporters of macroeconomic reasons.

The often-cited *microeconomic* reasons for bank failure include:

- poor banking practices (inadequate capital, inadequate credit risk assessment resulting in non-performing loans, insufficient diversification of the lending portfolio, excessive mismatching of maturity and currency);
- principal–agent incentive problems (particularly when loan officers are rewarded on the volumes of loans granted);
- overstaffing (particularly in state-owned banks);
- restrictive labour practices (sometimes delaying the adoption of IT).

Macroeconomic reasons, although not relieving bank management of their responsibilities, are often seen as a catalyst of crises. Macroeconomic shocks, such as the oil crisis in the 1970s can strain even properly managed banks.

A third set of causes is the so-called *system-related*, in the sense that the environment is not conducive to the development of an efficient banking sector. For example:[5]

- large state-ownership in the banking sector can distort the industry. If state-owned banks enjoy special privileges, this may distort competition and limit banks' diversification possibilities;
- governments' direction of credit may prevent banks from developing credit risk management skills;
- an inadequate legal framework may limit the effectiveness of the banking system;
- an under-developed securities market may concentrate too much risk on the banking system.

Banking crises may result after rapid changes in the environment in which they operate. For example, Mexico in the early 1990s experienced a rapid privatisation process of its commercial banks, coupled with financial liberalisation measures and sudden reduction of the borrowing requirement of the public sector. The rapid expansion of credit that followed these changes, coupled with weak supervision, led to a financial sector crisis in 1994.[6]

---

[5] BIS (1999).
[6] See Gil Diaz (1998).

17.4.2 Bank restructuring

Bank restructuring has many (sometimes conflicting) aims:

- preventing bank runs;
- avoiding a credit crunch (a rapid decline in bank lending);
- improving efficiency of the financial intermediation process;
- attracting new equity into the banking system.

As a consequence, there is no universally accepted way to carry out a successful restructuring exercise. Goodhart *et al.* (1998) identify three main principles:

1) Ensure that parties that have benefited from risk taking bear a large portion of the cost.
2) Take action to prevent problem institutions from extending credit to high-risk borrowers.
3) Muster the political will to make bank restructuring a priority by allocating public funds while avoiding inflation increase.

The diversity of possible approaches is summarised in Table 17.10.

Table 17.10 Bank restructuring methods

Country	Government capital injection	Asset management corporation(s)	Domestic bank merger	Foreign bank takeover
China	●	●	●	
India	●	examined	●	allowed
Hong Kong (in 1980s)	●		●	
Indonesia	●	●	●	
Korea	●	●	●	allowed
Malaysia	●	●	●	
Philippines (in 1980s)		●	●	●
Thailand	●	●	●	●
Argentina			●	●
Brazil			●	●
Chile	●	●	●	
Colombia	●	●	●	allowed
Mexico	●	●	●	●
Venezuela	●	●		
Czech Republic		●	●	allowed
Hungary	●	●	●	
Poland	●		●	allowed
Russia	●		●	
Saudi Arabia	●		●	
Memorandum:				
Finland (early 1990s)	●	●	●	
Norway (1988–93)	●		●	
Sweden (early 1990s)	●	●		
Japan	●	●		

Source: Adapted from Hawkins and Turner (1999), p. 40.

An essential step in any bank restructuring programme is to measure correctly the amount of non-performing loans. This is a major task, due to the varying practices of loan classification and different regulatory environments. The IMF's Joint Working Group on harmonising terminology on classification and provisioning of non-performing loans is attempting this highly ambitious task given the variety of present country practices. Some use quantitative criteria, such as the number of days loan repayments are overdue, others rely on qualitative norms such as the clients' financial status, or on management judgement about future loan repayments.

Five types of loan performance categories are recommended by the IMF for external reporting purposes and these include:

1) *Standard.* Credit is sound and payments current.
2) *Watch.* Subject to conditions that if uncorrected, could raise concerns about full repayment.
3) *Substandard.* Full repayment is in doubt due to inadequate protection. Interest or principal overdue (90 days +).
4) *Doubtful.* Assets for which collection is considered improbable. Interest or principal overdue (180 days +).
5) *Loss.* Virtually uncollectible. Interest or principal overdue (1 year +).

Substandard, doubtful and loss are considered as non-performing loans (NPL) and remain so until either the loan is written off or until principal and interest payments are received.

Proper recognition and proper provisioning for NPL are essential for crises management and prevention. While there is consensus on the need for more rigorous loan classification rules, there is some controversy over the timing and tightening of rules. The fear is that markets might over-react to the full disclosure of NPLs in emerging markets. However, suspicions that the true scale of the problem is being hidden can hurt market confidence.

An area of concern during bank restructuring is the valuation of collateral. In theory, most bank loans are collateralised (typically on real estate) and this should provide means to the restructuring agency. In practice, collateral is often worth considerably less than book value and can only be recovered if bankruptcy procedures operate efficiently. As aggregate demand weakens during banking crises; collateral values (such as property prices) drop steeply. Moreover, a large number of simultaneous 'fire-sales' may force the value of collateral to drop even further. This raises the question of how long a restructuring agency should hold the assets of distressed banks. Finally, the value of the collateral depends also on the credibility of the legal process to enforce repayments. Realising assets value has taken years in Eastern Europe, Latin America and East Asia, although recent legislative changes should improve this. Table 17.11 offers an overview of bankruptcy procedures in selected emerging economies.

Governments, central banks and external agencies have dealt with banking crises in a number of ways, often according to the circumstances. Although there is no unique recipe, there are some common ingredients to successful crisis management:

● governments must be willing to recognise the scale of the problem as soon as possible;
● governments should support supervisory authorities who want to close insolvent banks;
● governments should be willing to commit substantial fiscal resources to the banking system;

Table 17.11 **Bankruptcy procedures in selected emerging economies**

Country	Typical length of time	Priority of banks' secured loans	Priority of banks' unsecured loans
China		after BF, W, T	after BF, W, T
India	a few years		
Hong Kong	4–6 months	first claim	after SC, BF, W, T
Indonesia			
Korea	6–8 months	after BF, W, T	after BF, W, T, SC
Philippines	within a year	after W, T	after T, W, SC
Singapore	under 3 years		after SC, W, T
Thailand	years		
Brazil	6–12 months	after BF, W, T	after W, T, BF, SC
Chile	2–3 years	after BF, W, T	after BF, W, T, SC
Colombia			after BF, W, T, SC
Mexico	1–7 years	after W	after W, SC, T
Peru	2–12 months	first claim	after SC, W
Venezuela	lengthy		
Czech Republic	a few years	after BF, W, T	after BF, T, W, SC
Hungary	2 years		
Poland		after BF, W	after BF, W, SC, T
Saudi Arabia	6–12 months	first claim	after SC, BF, T
South Africa	6–12 months	after BF, W, T	after BF, T, W, SC

BF = bankruptcy fees; W = wages; T = taxes; SC = secured claims.
Source: Adapted from BIS (1999), p. 29.

- transparent actions with regards to NPL should be adopted at an early stage; and
- improved regulatory and supervisory frameworks are often necessary.

The success of crisis management and bank restructuring depends, ultimately, on a favourable macroeconomic environment and the wherewithal of the authorities to make hard (often politically unpopular) decisions regarding banking system restructuring.

17.5 Conclusions

The banking systems of emerging economies are still very fragmented in terms of size, ownership structure, competitive conditions and profitability. Despite these varied characteristics, most countries have recently witnessed major changes, from deregulation and financial liberalisation, to the adoption of new information and telecommunication technologies, as well as extensive privatisation programmes. This has resulted in profound structural changes, ranging from a marked decline in the number of banks to the increasing presence of foreign financial institutions. Furthermore, the banking and financial crises suffered by many emerging markets' banking systems have resulted in a strengthening of prudential regulatory standards. However, many issues still need to be resolved, such as the strengthening of credit risk and liquidity management. In this environment, the challenges posed to policymakers by the banking systems in emerging economies depend on a wider range of factors, including the increasing degree of integration among market economies.

Key terms

Emerging markets	Dollarisation
Developing countries	Euroisation
Financial repression	Banking crises
Financial liberalisation	Intervened bank
Digital divide	Resolved bank
Bank restructuring	Bridge bank

Key reading
Beck, T., Demirgüç-Kunt, A. and Levine, R. (2003) 'Bank concentration and crises', *World Bank Policy Research Working Paper*, No. 3041.

Coppel, J. and Davies, M. (2003) *Foreign Participation in East Asia's Banking Sector*, Reserve Bank of Australia paper, in Bank for International Settlement, GCFS Publications *Foreign Direct Investment in the Financial Sector of Emerging Market Economies*, http://www.bis.org/publ/cgfs22rba.pdf.

Hobson, J. and McCauley, R.N. (2003) 'The future of banking in East Asia', *Ente Luigi Einaudi Quaderni di Ricerche*, No. 59, http://www.enteluigieinaudi.it/pdf/Pubblicazioni/Quaderni/Q_59.pdf.

Revision questions and problems

1. What are the main structural features of banking systems in emerging markets?
2. Why does state ownership of banks tends to be associated with a poorly developed financial sector?
3. In what circumstances is state ownership preferable to the privatisation of the banking sector?
4. Why is it said that technological progress has helped emerging markets' banks to 'skip a stage of financial development'?
5. What are the main concerns raised by foreign banks' presence in emerging markets?
6. What are the main causes of banking crises?
7. What are the main principles governing a successful bank restructuring exercise?

Nominal and real interest rates

Interest rates play a crucial role within the financial system. For example, they influence financial flows within the economy, the distribution of wealth, capital investment, and the profitability of financial institutions. It is important to appreciate that an interest rate is a *price*, and that the price relates to *present* claims on resources relative to *future* claims on resources. An interest rate is therefore the price that a borrower pays in order to be able to consume resources now rather than at some point in the future. Correspondingly, it is the price that a lender receives to forgo current consumption.

It is common to distinguish between nominal and real interest rates. A *nominal* interest rate is what is normally observed and quoted and represents the actual money paid by the borrower to the lender, expressed as a percentage of the sum borrowed over a stated period of time. The *real* rate of interest is the return if there is no risk and inflation is zero. In most discussions comparing real and nominal interest rates the emphasis is on short-term interest rates and so the focus is on:

$$i = r + P^e \qquad\qquad (A1.1)$$

where
i = nominal rate of interest;
r = real short-term rate of interest;
P^e = a premium based on price expectations (inflation premium).

Concept of present value

As we will discuss later on in this appendix, a precise measure of interest rate is yield to maturity. This can be measured on debt market instruments, such as loans and bonds, and requires knowledge of the concept of present value. The present value (PV) of a loan or bond is equal to the current value (i.e., the value today) of a future payment. For instance, to calculate the present value of a 1-year £1,000 loan (this is the face value, or FV, of the loan) if the interest rate (r) is 10% we will use the following formula:[1]

---

[1] Note that this formula can also be written as: $PV = FV\,(1+r)^{-1}$.

$$PV = \frac{FV}{(1+r)^t}$$ (A1.2)

PV=?   FV=£1,000
| |
t=today   t=1 year

$$PV = \frac{FV}{(1+r)^t} = \frac{£1000}{(1+0.10)^1} = £909$$

This means that given the current interest rate of 10 per cent, today the £1,000 loan is worth £909. To calculate the PV of a 2-year loan at the same interest rate:

PV=?   FV=£1,000
└──────────────┼──────────────┘
t=today   t=1 year   t=2 years

$$PV = \frac{£1000}{(1+0.10)^2} = £826$$

<h2>A1.3   Bonds and bonds pricing</h2>

The concept of PV is often used to calculate the current value of bonds and bond pricing. Bonds are instruments in which the issuer of a bond (the debtor) promises to repay the lender (the investor) the amount borrowed at some pre-determined date in the future in addition to some periodic interest payments before the due date. Because the interest payments paid by the issuer of a bond are fixed, bonds are referred to as *fixed income securities*. Bonds can be issued by governments and private companies and they pay a periodic cash flow (coupon) at set periods (once every 12 months or every six months). At maturity the issuer pays the bondholder the bond's face (or 'par') value. A *zero coupon* bond (also called discount bond) is a bond paying no coupons that sells at a discount and provides only a payment of par value at maturity.

The present value of the coupon payments will be equal to:

$$PV = \sum_{t=1}^{T} \frac{C}{(1+r)^t}$$ (A1.3)

$$= \frac{C}{(1+r)^1} + \frac{C}{(1+r)^2} + \frac{C}{(1+r)^3} + \dots + \frac{C}{(1+r)^T}$$

Consider a three-year 15 per cent coupon bond. If the bond's face value is £100 and the current interest rate is 10 per cent, the present value will be equal to $\frac{£15}{(1+0.10)^1}$ in year 1; $\frac{£15}{(1+0.10)^2}$ in year 2 and $\frac{£15}{(1+0.10)^3}$ in year 3.

PV=?   C=£15   C=£15   C=£15
└──────────┼───────────┼───────────┘
t=today   t=1   t=2   t=3

Therefore the PV of the bond coupon payment streams will be equal to the sum of the progression: 13.63+12.39+11.27= £37.29. However with bonds instruments at maturity the issuer pays the bondholder the bond's face (or 'par') value, that is usually £100 in the UK; and $1,000 in the US) so that:

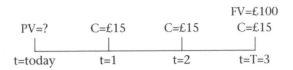

It follows that the price of the three-year bond (P_B) will be equal to the PV of the coupons plus the PV of the bond's FV:

$$P_B = \sum_{t=1}^{T} \frac{C_t}{(1+r)^t} + \frac{FV}{(1+r)^T}$$ (A1.4)

$$P_B = \frac{£15}{(1+0.10)^1} + \frac{£15}{(1+0.10)^2} + \frac{£15}{(1+0.10)^3} + \frac{£100}{(1+0.10)^3}$$

$$P_B = 37.29 + 75.13 = £112.42$$

A1.4 Bonds and yields

For an investor buying a bond, the market price (P) of the bond might be different from the bond's initial face or par value. He will therefore use the bond price (P_B), maturity date (t), and coupon payments (C) to infer the return offered by the bond over the investment period. The actual rate of return for holding a bond depends on: the price paid for the bond (P), the coupons received relative to the price paid, and changes in the price of the bond. We can define the bond's Yield to Maturity (YTM) as the interest (or more precisely 'discount') rate that makes the present value of a bond's payments equal to its price. The YTM is often viewed as a measure of the average rate of return that will be earned by the investor during the entire time span of the bond.

In the financial press, (see Table A1.1) another measure of yield is quoted. This is the current yield, which is equal to the coupon/price of the bond (C/P_B). However, the YTM is the most appropriate measure of rate of return, since it includes all aspects of the bond investment and this can be calculated using a standard discounted cash flow approach as is used to estimate net present values.

To sum up, there are three main elements that determine the annual rate of return an investor is getting on a bond investment:

- *Coupon Rate*: Annual payout as a percentage of the bond's face value.
- *Current Yield*: Annual payout as a percentage of the current market price.
- *Yield to Maturity*: Composite rate of return off *all* payouts, coupon and capital gain (or loss). The capital gain or loss is the difference between face value and the price actually paid for the bond.

Example: yield to maturity of a 4-year gilt

Consider the following example of a UK gilt bond selling for £99.15, with a coupon rate of 4 per cent. The bond matures in 4 years, and the par value is £100.

	Coupon	Maturity date	Current price/yield	Price/yield change
4-Year	4.000	03/07/2009	99.15/4.02	−0.095/0.028

The yield to maturity is calculated as follows: the coupon payment is £4 (4% of £100), substituting values into the equation A1.3 gives us:

$$£4 (1 + r)^{-1} + £4 (1 + r)^{-2} + £4 (1 + r)^{-3} + £4 (1 + r)^{-4} + £100 (1 + r)^{-4} = £99.15$$

Yield to maturity (r) = 4.24%

Note that the YTM can be relatively complicated to calculate manually and it is easier to use web-based bond yield calculators such as those found at: http://www.investinginbonds.com.

One important point to note is that yield to maturity (4.24%) is greater than the current yield (4.02%), which in turn is greater than the coupon rate (4%). (Current yield is £4/£99.15 = 4.03%.)

This will in fact always be the case for a bond selling 'at a discount'. In fact, you will always have this:

Bond selling at: …	Satisfies this condition
Discount	Coupon Rate < Current Yield < Yield to Maturity
Premium	Coupon Rate > Current Yield > Yield to Maturity
Par Value	Coupon Rate = Current Yield = Yield to Maturity

A1.5 Yield to maturity – price, maturity, coupon level and frequency of payment and tax

Calculation of the yield to maturity of a bond can obviously change depending on the current price, maturity, coupon rate, frequency of interest payments and tax (on the income from the coupon and possible capital gain if sold before maturity).

Below are some examples:

1) *Price*

Take the example of the four-year UK gilt shown above and let us assume that the bond is selling for 50 pence more at £99.65, it still has a coupon rate of 4 per cent, matures in four years, and the par value is £100. The yield to maturity is calculated as follows:

$$4 (1 + r)^{-1} + 4 (1 + r)^{-2} + 4 (1 + r)^{-3} + 4 (1 + r)^{-4} + 100 (1 + r)^{-4} = £99.65$$

Yield to maturity (r) = 4.10% (if the current price were 80 pence more at £99.85 the yield to maturity would be 4.04%)

All other things being equal, the yield to maturity declines as the market price approaches par value. In other words, bond prices and yields move in opposite directions.

2) *Maturity*

In the same example above, assume that maturity is now ten years. That is, the bond is selling for £99.15, and has a coupon rate of 4 per cent; it matures in ten years, and the par value is £100. The yield to maturity is calculated as follows

$$£4 (1 + r)^{-1} + £4 (1 + r)^{-2} + £4 (1 + r)^{-3} + £4 (1 + r)^{-4} + £4 (1 + r)^{-5}$$
$$+ £4 (1 + r)^{-6} + £4 (1 + r)^{-7} + £4 (1 + r)^{-8} + £4 (1 + r)^{-9} + £4 (1 + r)^{-10}$$
$$+ £100 (1 + r)^{-10} = £99.15$$

Yield to maturity (r) now becomes = 4.11% (if maturity was 20 years this would fall to 4.06%)

All other things being equal, the yield to maturity declines as maturity increases.

3) *Coupon*

Take the same example and now assume that the coupon is set at 5 per cent. That is, the bond is selling for £99.15, and has a coupon rate of 5 per cent; it matures in four years, and the par value is £100. The yield to maturity is calculated as follows

$$5 (1 + r)^{-1} + 5 (1 + r)^{-2} + 5 (1 + r)^{-3} + 5 (1 + r)^{-4} + 100 (1 + r)^{-4} = 99.15$$

Yield to maturity (r) = 5.24%

All other things being equal, the higher the coupon then the higher the yield to maturity.

Finally there are two other factors that may influence the YTM. One is the frequency of coupon payments and the other is taxes.

4) *The frequency of coupon payments*

This can influence the yield to maturity because if coupon payments are made semi-annually then the yield to maturity is calculated by halving the coupon payment and taking account of cash flow over eight six-monthly periods as follows:

$$2 (1 + r)^{-1} + 2 (1 + r)^{-2} + 2 (1 + r)^{-3} + 2 (1 + r)^{-4} + 2 (1 + r)^{-5} + 2$$
$$(1 + r)^{-6} + 2 (1 + r)^{-7} + 2 (1 + r)^{-8} + 100 (1 + r)^{-8} = 99.15$$

Yield to maturity (r) = 2.62%

All other things being equal the greater the frequency in coupon payments then the lower the yield to maturity.

5) *Taxes*

Finally, taxes can have a substantial impact on YTM. In the examples above we have assumed no taxes, but of course income from coupons is typically taxable (income tax) as capital gains on sale of the bond may be. Taxes can obviously reduce the size of the net coupon or potential capital gains on the bond if sold before maturity so one should be aware of potential tax implications when doing such calculations.

A1.6 The financial press

Bond prices change daily like shares prices. If you want to keep track of your bond investments, the financial press reports the previous day closing prices by types of bonds, as illustrated in Table A1.1 that is extracted from the *Financial Times*.

Table A1.1 shows that bonds issues are listed in increasing order of residual maturity: shorts, five to ten years, ten to fifteen years and over fifteen years.

- The *title* of each bond includes the type of stock, the coupon rate and redemption date (e.g., Treasury, 8.5% 2005).
- The first column of figures shows the *interest or current yield* (Int).
- The second column of figures shows the *redemption yield* (Red).
- The third column of figures shows the *current price in £s* (Price).
- The fourth column of figures shows the variation on the previous day's price (Chng).
- The last two columns show the *highest and lowest price in the previous 52 weeks* (High and Low).

Table A1.1 Reading the *Financial Times*: UK government bonds

UK GILTS - cash market

Aug 16	Notes	... Yield ... Int	Red	Price £	Chng	... 52 week ... High	Low
Shorts" (Lives up to Five Years)							
Ex 10½pc '05	✠	10.44	4.59	100.53	−.01	106.00	100.53
Tr 8½pc '05		8.40	4.34	101.24	−.01	105.52	101.24
Tr 7¾pc '06		7.48	4.25	103.59	....	105.94	103.58
Cn 9¾pc '06	✠	9.15	4.26	106.57	−.01	110.27	106.55
Tr 7½pc '06		7.20	4.23	104.10	....	106.05	104.07
Tr 4½pc '07		4.48	4.20	100.44	+.01	100.78	99.03
Tr 8½pc '07		7.89	4.22	107.78	+.01	110.10	107.71
Tr 7¼pc '07		6.80	4.22	106.59	+.02	107.90	106.12
Tr 5pc '08		4.91	4.21	101.90	+.04	102.49	100.16
Tr 5½pc '08–12		5.32	4.33	103.31	+.05	104.03	101.51
Tr 9pc '08	✠	7.92	4.31	113.70	+.05	115.75	113.27
Tr 4pc '09		4.03	4.22	99.27	+.07	99.91	96.09
Tr 8pc '09	✠	7.02	4.26	113.96	+.11	115.26	112.63
Tr 5¾pc '09		5.43	4.24	105.89	+.11	106.81	103.52
Tr 4¾pc '10		4.65	4.24	102.18	+.12	103.05	99.49

	Notes	... Yield ... Int	Red	Price £	Chng	... 52 week ... High	Low
Five to Ten Years							
Tr 6¼pc '10		5.71	4.24	109.41	+.13	110.48	106.66
Cn 9pc Ln '11		7.23	4.26	124.52	+.15	125.94	122.33
Tr 7¾pc '12–15		6.55	4.44	118.34	+.16	119.61	115.43
Tr 5pc '12		4.80	4.26	104.18	+.16	105.11	99.86
Tr 9pc '12	✠	7.03	4.31	127.98xd	+.21	129.22	125.05
Tr 8pc '13		6.39	4.28	125.26	+.23	126.66	121.54
Tr 5pc '14		4.75	4.29	105.26	+.23	106.34	99.90
Tr 4¾pc '15		4.58	4.29	103.70	+.25	104.78	97.79
Ten to Fifteen Years							
Tr 8pc '15		6.11	4.27	130.85	+.30	132.32	125.71
Tr 8¾pc '17		6.19	4.31	141.38xd	+.35	143.11	135.64
Ex 12pc '13–17	✠	7.82	4.30	153.36	+.26	155.32	150.11
Tr 4¾pc '20		4.55	4.33	104.50	+.34	105.43	103.18
Over Fifteen Years							
Tr 8pc '21		5.65	4.33	141.63	+.45	143.56	134.87
Tr 5pc '25		4.59	4.32	108.91	+.43	110.41	102.03
Tr 6pc '28		4.81	4.30	124.83	+.51	126.61	117.31
Tr 4¼pc '32		4.27	4.29	99.42	+.48	100.80	92.58
Tr 4¼pc '36		4.27	4.28	99.50	+.51	100.90	92.49
Tr 4¾pc '38		4.38	4.27	108.50	+.57	110.00	100.88
Tr 4¼pc '55		4.18	4.17	101.58	+.63	101.58	98.89

Source: *Financial Times*, 16 August 2005

The redemption yield takes into account the capital loss or gain standing on the bond. For instance, take a Treasury bond with 5 per cent coupon, and maturity 2008 currently trading at £101.9. Since on redemption you will only get back £100, and there are three years till redemption, that's an average loss of £0.63 every year for every £100 of bonds you own.

Table A1.2 shows a selection of UK government bonds with maturities ranging from 2 years to 30 years with various coupons. The data also reveal that the *yield* on these gilt-edged securities often varies quite markedly. It is this *spread of yields* paid on the same type of assets (in this case gilt-edged securities) with different terms to maturity that theories of the *term structure of interest rates* seek to explain.

A1.7   The term structure of interest rates

The 'term structure' of interest rates refers to the relationship between the term to maturity of a bond and its yield to maturity. Economists and investors believe that the shape of the yield curve reflects the market's future expectation for interest rates and the conditions for monetary policy.

Table A1.2 UK Government bond yields – 14 June 2005

	Coupon	Maturity date	Current price/yield	Price/yield change
2-Year	4.500	03/07/2007	100.32/4.3	−0.05/0.03
3-Year	5.000	03/07/2008	101.9/4.25	−0.073/0.027
4-Year	4.000	03/07/2009	99.15/4.25	−0.095/0.028
5-Year	4.750	06/07/2010	102.16/4.26	−0.116/0.026
7-Year	5.000	03/07/2012	104.16/4.28	−0.095/0.016
8-Year	8.000	09/07/2013	125.6/4.29	−0.124/0.015
10-Year	4.750	09/07/2015	103.6/4.31	−0.106/0.013
15-Year	8.000	06/07/2020	142.14/4.32	−0.086/0.006
20-Year	5.000	03/07/2025	109.17/4.3	−0.053/0.004
30-Year	4.250	03/07/2035	99.84/4.26	0.011/−0.001

Source: http://www.Bloomberg.com.

The term structure of interest rates may be defined as the spread of yields generated by the same type of assets with different terms to maturity. The concept of the term structure of interest rates is only of relevance in the case of those assets that have a fixed term to maturity and pay a fixed interest at specified points in time (bonds and other types of financial instruments, such as sterling certificates of deposit).

The term structure of interest rates on a particular type of asset may be represented diagrammatically in a yield curve. The yield that is referred to in this context is the yield to maturity. As noted above, this yield includes not only the interest income from the asset, but also any anticipated capital gain (due to the current price being less than the maturity value) or capital loss (due to the current price being greater than the maturity value).

Typically the yield curve is drawn for similar-risk securities that have different maturity dates as shown in Figure A1.1 and demonstrates that long-term bonds (30-years) give higher yields than short-term ones (5 years in the example). This can be considered a 'normal' market's expectations of future interest rates because typically longer-term instruments carry more uncertainty than shorter-term ones and thus should offer higher yields. However, if expectations on the economy are different from normal the yield curve can take different shapes (the two extremes being a flat yield curve, where short and long-term securities offer the same yield and inverted, in which short-term securities offer yields higher than the long-term ones).

Figure A1.1 Normal yield curve

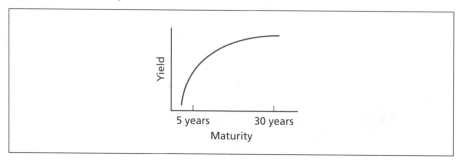

The yield curve is usually calculated on a daily basis so we can draw a different yield curve for every day. All the major central banks/monetary authorities report yield curve data for various instruments.

A1.8   Theories on the shape of the yield curve

A number of theories have been put forward to explain the various shapes of the yield curve which may be observed in practice. None of the established theories is wholly satisfactory, and many economists believe that the assumptions required by the theories undermine their practical value. Nevertheless, it is worthwhile summarising the key features of these theories as a basis for more advanced study of yield curves (not covered in this book).

Two main theories seek to explain the shapes of yield curves. These are:

- *expectations theory*, which is subdivided into:
  - pure expectations
  - liquidity-biased expectations
  - preferred habitat-biased expectations
- *market segmentation theory*, which disallows large-scale arbitrage between the various segments of the market.

A1.8.1   Pure expectations

The basis of this theory is that the shape of yield curves is determined by market expectations of future short-term interest rates. If lenders and borrowers expect short-term interest rates to rise, then lenders would wish to invest at the short end of the market, profiting when bond prices had fallen by enjoying higher yields. This would push up short-term bond prices (force down the yield curve for short maturity bonds). Borrowers would, of course, want to borrow for much longer periods, forcing up the yield for long maturity bonds. These actions will tilt the curve in an anti-clockwise direction, making it steeper (rising from left to right). However, the theory fails to consider the risks involved, as nobody knows future bond prices (price risk) or future rates of interest (reinvestment risk).

A1.8.2 Liquidity

This theory assumes that the risk associated with investment in bonds increases with their term to maturity. It is argued that this increasing risk will lead investors to require a progressively larger liquidity premium for investing in bonds with a progressively longer maturity. Investors require a premium for bonds not being liquid, e.g., buying long-dated bonds, and this urge to be compensated for holding illiquid assets may be more important than the expectations which may result in a downward-sloping curve. This premium has an upward bias on the curve. This theory fits very closely with the intuitive explanation for the shape of yield curves as discussed above.

A1.8.3 Preferred habitat

This theory argues that investors prefer to match their assets with known liabilities and borrowers will seek to raise funds for a time period that matches their needs. Also, investment institutions may try to match the maturity of their assets and liabilities.

In order to be encouraged to shift out of their preferred habitats, lenders and borrowers will require a premium on the yield to cover the risk that they feel they are being asked to accept. The premium will vary according to the extent that the investor or borrower has to shift from their preferred habitat. Therefore, as there is no reason to believe that the premium will rise uniformly with maturity, the theory is able to explain any shape of yield curve.

A1.8.4 Market segmentation

A lay person might describe this theory as 'a highly structured and inflexible version of the preferred habitat theory'. It assumes that neither investors nor borrowers are able or willing to move along the yield curve to take advantage of arbitrage opportunities.

The reason for this highly inflexible segmentation of the market might be because regulators and/or the investing institutions' own rules require them to keep certain strict percentages of their assets in each of the market's maturity sectors.

Under this theory, the yield curve is constructed from the yield curves of the various segments of the fixed-interest securities market. Some economists regard this theory as unsustainable because it presupposes that there is absolute risk aversion, whereas evidence shows that investors are willing to take risks and arbitrage along the yield curve.

A2.1 Return, risk and the concept of diversification

The return and risk characteristics associated with different types of securities vary tremendously. For example, the return on a UK Treasury bond is near certain (risk-free). By contrast, the return to be achieved on ordinary equity shares in an average company is far from certain (it carries a positive level of risk). Portfolio theory aims to show that by holding a diversified array of securities then the risk of making a loss on the investment can be reduced. Let's first see how to calculate risk and return.

In order to measure the past performance of a security or a portfolio of securities it is necessary to calculate the actual return on the security or the portfolio taking into account:

- Any change in the capital value of the security or portfolio during the relevant time period.
- The dividend or interest payments received on the security or portfolio during the relevant time period.

The single period return may be calculated using the following formula:

$$R_1 = (P_1 - P_0 + D_1) / P_0 \qquad\qquad (A2.1)$$

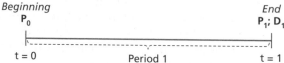

where:
R_1 = the return obtained by holding the security (portfolio) for the whole of period 1
P_0 = the market price of the security (portfolio) at the start of period 1
P_1 = the market price of the security (portfolio) at the end of period 1
D_1 = the dividend or interest income received on the security (portfolio) during period 1.

Often you will be interested in calculating the multiple period returns. One way to calculate them is by using arithmetic or geometric averages over the period.

The usual way to measure the risk associated with investment in a security is via calculation of the *probable variability of future returns*. In other words risk may be measured in terms of the variance (or standard deviation) of the expected returns.

Typically, the higher the risk the higher the variance:

The variance is the volatility or dispersion of returns. It tells us about the potential for deviation of the returns from its expected value. For example:

Table A2.1 Case 1: Overall expected return on a security

Outcome	Expected return %	Probability of expected return occurring	Expected return weighted by probability %
A	50	0.1	5
B	30	0.2	6
C	10	0.4	4
D	−10	0.2	−2
E	−30	0.1	−3
Total		1.0	10

In Case 1, it is assumed that there are five possible outcomes, A to E. The probability of each outcome occurring is specified on the basis of past experience. For example, there is a 0.1 (i.e. 10%) probability that outcome A will occur. This outcome involves the occurrence of a 50 per cent expected return on the security. If outcomes A to E cover all possible outcomes, then the combined probability must sum to 1.0 (i.e. 100%).

To calculate the overall expected return on the security, the expected return for each possible outcome is multiplied by the probability of that outcome occurring (to give the fourth column in table A2.1) and the weighted expected returns are summed. Therefore, it may be observed that whilst the security has possible expected returns ranging from 50 per cent to −30 per cent, the overall expected return is 10 per cent.

More formally we can express the expected return from a security as:

$$(E)R = p_1R_1 + p_2R_2 + p_3R_3 + \dots\dots + p_nR_n \qquad (A2.2)$$

where:
(E)R = Expected return;
R_i = Return in outcome i
p_i = probability of occurrence of the return R_i
n = number of outcomes.

Note that in practice future returns and their probabilities are not usually known so historical average returns from past historical data relating to the performance of the investment are used as indicators of future returns.

To calculate the variance of the expected return on the security: square the difference between the expected return for outcome A and the overall expected return and multiply the result by the probability that outcome A will occur.

● Repeat this step for each possible outcome.
● Sum the results generated for all possible outcomes.

Thus, for Case 1:

$$\text{Variance} = 0.1(0.5 - 0.1)^2 + 0.2(0.3 - 0.1)^2 + 0.4(0.1 - 0.1)^2$$
$$+ 0.2(-0.1 - 0.1)^2 + 0.1(-0.3 - 0.1)^2$$
$$= 0.016 + 0.008 + 0 + 0.008 + 0.016 = 0.048.$$

The standard deviation is simply the square root of the variance. For Case 1:

$$\text{Standard deviation} = \sqrt{0.048} = 0.2191$$

As a general rule, if an investor wishes to achieve a higher than average expected return then s/he should take on a higher than average level of risk.

Diversification, that is adding more securities into an existing portfolio, can reduce risk exposure (i.e. the portfolio volatility).

For a portfolio composed of n securities, the expected return will be equal to the weighted average of the expected returns on the component securities:

$$(E)R_p = w_1(E)R_1 + w_2(E)R_2 + w_3(E)R_3 + \ldots\ldots + w_n(E)R_n \tag{A2.3}$$

where:

$(E)R_p$ = weighted average of the expected return of the individual stocks composing the portfolio, where weights are the portfolio weights
w_n = portfolio weight of stock n, where $n=1,2...n$.

Example:
Assume we have a portfolio comprising 2 equities: the UK supermarket Tesco (trading at 315p on 17 June, 2005) and Barclays (trading at 536p on the same day). Also assume that 70% of the portfolio comprises Barclays shares and 30% Tesco shares. The expected return of Tesco shares is 8% and for Barclays 12%. The expected return for the portfolio is: $(0.7 \times 0.12) + (0.3 \times 0.08) = 0.084 + 0.024 = 10.8\%$.

While investors cannot escape from the inherent return–risk trade-off, they may nevertheless construct their portfolios in a manner that aims to minimise the risk assumed at any given desired rate of return. *Modern Portfolio Theory* seeks to explain this behaviour. The theory derives from the seminal work of Markowitz undertaken in the 1950s.

A2.2 Modern portfolio theory

The central principle of modern portfolio theory is that it is possible to construct a portfolio of securities that has a return that is less risky than the return on any individual security contained therein. In order to do this it is necessary that the returns on the individual component securities should not be perfectly correlated. If the performance of securities is affected in an identical way by a particular event, then it is not possible to reduce the risk of being adversely affected by the event simply by holding a portfolio of those securities. The relative variability of returns on two securities is known as their covariance.

The correlation coefficient (ρ) measures the degree to which two variables are linearly related. If there is perfect linear relationship with positive slope between the two variables, we have a correlation coefficient of 1; if there is a perfect linear relationship with negative slope between the two variables, we have a correlation coefficient of –1; a correlation coefficient of 0 means that there is no linear relationship between the variables. The correlation coefficient (ρ) comprises two elements:

- covariance (the extent to which values move together);
- standard deviations (how tightly values are clustered around the mean in a set of data).

In this context, the correlation coefficient is simply the covariance between the stocks divided by their respective standard deviations. In the case of two stocks 1 and 2, then the correlation coefficient will be calculated as follows:

$$\rho_{1,2} = \frac{Cov_{1,2}}{\sigma_1 \sigma_2} \tag{A2.4}$$

where $Cov_{1,2}$ is the covariance between the two stocks and is a measure of the extent to which the two assets covary.

To get the correlation, the covariance is divided by the standard deviation to provide a standardised measure between the movements of two different values. (Note that the correlation coefficient falls between –1 (perfect negative) and +1 (perfect positive), while zero correlation means that the returns on the two assets are unrelated to each other.)

Hence the variance of the portfolio return σ_P^2, will be equal to the sum of the contributions of the component security variances plus a term that involves the correlation coefficient between the returns of the component securities; or, in symbols:

$$\sigma_P^2 = (w_1 \sigma_1)^2 + (w_2 \sigma_2)^2 + 2(w_1 \sigma_1)(w_2 \sigma_2)\rho_{1,2} \tag{A2.5}$$

Given this information lets us run through the example relating to a portfolio consisting of Tesco and Barclays shares from above. Assume the past standard deviations of Tesco shares were 40 per cent and for Barclays shares 60 per cent. Assume the two stocks are positively correlated – they move in the same direction – but are not perfectly correlated. Assume they are correlated 0.75 ($\rho_{1,2} = 0.75$). Recall also that 70 per cent of the portfolio is held in Barclays shares and the remainder in Tesco stock.

The variance of the portfolio is therefore:

$$[(0.7)^2 \times (0.6)^2] + [(0.3)^2 \times (0.4)^2] + 2\,(0.7 \times 0.3 \times 0.6 \times 0.4 \times 0.75) =$$

$$[0.49 \times 0.36] + [0.09 \times 0.16] + 2\,(0.0378) =$$

$$0.1764 + 0.0144 + 0.0756 = 0.2664 = 26.64\%$$

So the variance of the portfolio is 26.64% and the standard deviation is

$$\sqrt{0.2664} = 0.051614 = 5.1614\%$$

Note that the variance of the portfolio return is lower than that of any individual asset, which shows that by constructing a portfolio one is able to diversify risk. Diversification increases the less correlated the stocks are in the portfolio – when stocks in the portfolio are perfectly correlated then there are no diversification benefits.

It must be emphasised that 20 or more different securities is normally thought of as being the minimum number of securities required to achieve significant risk reduction by diversification. Moreover, in order to significantly reduce risk, securities should emanate from different business sectors and ideally from different countries (i.e., international diversification).

A2.3   Efficient (mean–standard deviation) frontier

This section briefly introduces the features of the efficient frontier that can be used to demonstrate the optimal holdings of risky assets for a risk-averse investor. It is otherwise known as the mean–standard deviation frontier as it plots the mean expected return against the standard deviation of a risky asset (the risky asset is constructed by using weights of the two assets in the combined portfolio). Each point on the efficient frontier in Figure A2.1 therefore represents a risky asset.

Figure A2.1 Efficient (mean–standard deviation) frontier

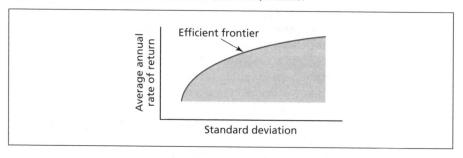

As the portfolio weights for the two assets range from zero to one, the portfolio goes from one that only combines Security 1 to a portfolio combining only Security 2. As the weights change then the new portfolios plot a curve that includes both Security 1 and 2. This can be seen in Figure A2.2.

Figure A2.2 Efficient frontier: two risky assets (Security 1 and 2)

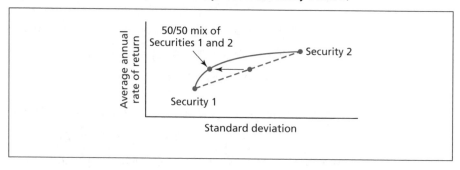

The efficient frontier shows the expected return and risk that could be achieved by constructing different portfolios of the two risky assets. Investors can use this to consider trade-offs between returns (mean returns) and risk (standard deviations) when they choose portfolio weights for their investments. It is important to note that this exposition assumes that investors are not allowed to short-sell (the selling of a security that the seller does not own).

In order to identify the optimal portfolio we have to take into account the risk return preferences of an investor – this is shown in Figure A2.2 where the investor chooses a portfolio with a 50–50 mix of both Security 1 and 2. The area inside the frontier is known as a 'feasible region' and this represents feasible but inefficient portfolios as expected return is not maximised for a given risk or standard deviation.

A2.4 Components of risk

The risk associated with the return on a security may be divided into two components:

- *Market or systematic risk* is the risk related to the macroeconomic factors or market index. Systematic risk is non-diversifiable.
- *Unsystematic risk* is the firm-specific risk, not related to the macroeconomic environment. Unsystematic risk is diversifiable.

Securities have different proportions of systematic and unsystematic risk. Diversification can reduce firm-specific risk to low levels; however, it cannot eliminate the common sources of risk that affect all firms, as shown in Figure A2.3.

Figure A2.3 Systematic and unsystematic risk: effects of diversification

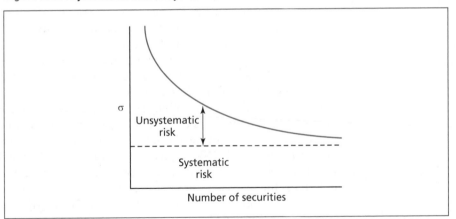

The extent to which the return on an individual equity share moves with the general trend of the average return on the market (i.e. its systematic risk component) is measured by its beta value (β). In particular, β measures the sensitivity of a security's returns to the systematic or market factor and is calculated as follows:

$$\beta_i = \frac{Cov(r_i, r_M)}{\sigma^2_M}$$

(A2.6)

where *Cov* (r_i, r_M) is the covariance with the market divided by the variance of the market.

Some shares (and portfolios) tend to respond strongly to general movements in the market. The returns on other shares (and portfolios) tend to move less markedly, and may be relatively stable in the face of major market movements.

The beta value for a company's shares is derived from the Capital Asset Pricing Model (CAPM) which is simply the reduction of Modern Portfolio Theory into a single factor model – with that single factor being called beta (β). Instead of a matrix of covariances between all securities in the market, as shown above, there is only one covariance coefficient: β, the covariance between a security and the market.

The CAPM states that the security's risk premium is proportional to both the beta and the risk premium of the market portfolio. An equity share's β is obtained from an equation that explains the expected return (or required return) from a stock that is calculated as follows:

$$E(r_i) = r_f + \beta_i \, [E(r_M) - r_f]$$ (A2.7)

where:
$E(r_i)$ is the expected return on asset i
β_i is the beta of asset i
$E(r_M)$ is the expected market rate of return
r_f is the risk-free rate of interest

From the expected return equation shown above, the expected return of a stock, $E(r_i)$, is determined by the risk-free rate (generally given by the rate on the safest investment – usually a government bond such as a UK gilt or US Treasury) plus the β of the security, multiplied by the market risk premium. This is the expected return in excess of that on risk-free securities and thus is calculated as the difference between the expected return on the market portfolio, $E(r_M)$, and the risk-free rate (r_f).

The primary determinant of the expected rate of return is the security's β. The risk-free rate and market risk premium, of course, would be the same for all securities.

If a security cannot match the required rate of return for a certain level of risk, it is considered a poor investment according to CAPM. If a security exceeds the required rate of return, it is considered a good investment according to CAPM.[1]

The interpretation of beta values is straightforward. Quite simply, a market index (such as the FTSE 100) is given a beta value of 1. If an individual equity share has a beta value greater than 1, then the return on this share is prone to fluctuate more than the average return on the market index. For example, if the average return on the market index falls by 10 per cent, the return on the share may fall by 15 per cent – this would mean that the share had a beta value of 1.5. In contrast, if an equity share had a beta value of less than 1, then the return on this share is more stable than the average return on the market. For example, a beta value of 0.3 would imply that a 10 per cent fall in the average return on the market index would be matched by a 3 per cent fall in the return on the share.

---

[1] William Sharpe published the capital asset pricing model in 1964; for this work he shared the 1990 Nobel Prize in Economics with Harry Markowitz and Merton Miller. Parallel work was also performed by Treynor (1965) and Lintner (1965). For his work on CAPM, Sharpe extended Harry Markowitz's portfolio theory to introduce the notions of systematic and specific risk.

A2.5 ## Security market line

The security market line is a graphical representation of the expected return–beta relationship of the CAPM. Its slope is the risk premium of the market portfolio. Table A.2 shows the linear relationship between expected return and beta:

Table A2.2 **Expected return and beta**

Risk-free rate (r_f)	Beta (β_i)	Market premium $E(r_i)$ minus (r_f)	Expected return $E(r_M)$
0.03	2	0.08	0.19
0.03	1.5	0.08	0.15
0.03	1	0.08	0.11
0.03	0.5	0.08	0.07
0.03	0	0.08	0.03

Using the information in Table A2, the security market line is shown in Figure A2.4 where beta is on the horizontal axis and expected return on the vertical axis. It can be seen that expected return on an asset with β of zero is 0.03 (or 3 per cent) and for a beta of 1 it is 11 per cent.

Figure A2.4 **Security market line**

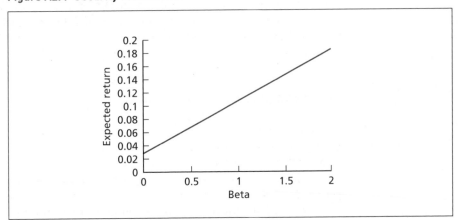

The security line is simply a straight line starting from the risk-free point passing through the market portfolio (where β = 1). Whenever the CAPM holds, all securities must lie on the security market line in market equilibrium. This is because any investor can always obtain the market risk premium β_i ($E(r_M) - r_f$) by holding a combination of the market portfolio and the risk-free rate.

The beta of a portfolio (β_p) is simply the weighted sum of the individual assets in the portfolio (β_i), where weights are the portfolio weights (w_i) so:

$$\beta_p = \Sigma w_i \beta_i \qquad\qquad (A2.8)$$

Portfolio expected returns and the capital asset pricing model

It is argued that rational risk-averse investors will:

- Require additional expected returns to compensate for taking on additional risk.
- Construct a diversified portfolio of securities.

Therefore, the return that investors require, and the return that the market is willing to pay, will be determined by that component of risk that cannot be eliminated by diversification; i.e., by systematic risk, which cannot be avoided. In other words, the CAPM suggests that:

- The *return required* on any given security (or portfolio of securities) will depend upon its *beta value*.
- The *total risk* associated with the return on any security is *irrelevant* to the determination of the required return; i.e., because it is relatively easy to eliminate unsystematic risk, investors will not receive any premium for that risk.

The operation of efficient markets in securities should ensure that diversified portfolios containing securities with the same average beta value should attract the same return, irrespective of the total risk associated with the individual securities. If this was not the case then investors holding diversified portfolios would seek to purchase the securities attracting the higher returns (presumably those with greater associated unsystematic risk) and sell securities earning the lower returns. This action would push up the price of the riskier securities and push down the price of the less risky securities. This adjustment would continue until the returns from securities with the same beta values were equalised.

Arbitrage pricing theory: a note

An alternative view on stock pricing to CAPM is known as the Arbitrage Pricing Theory (APT). This theory posits that the expected return of a financial asset can be modelled as a linear function of a variety of various macroeconomic factors, where sensitivity to changes in each factor is represented by a factor-specific beta. The model derived rate of return will then be used to price the asset correctly – the asset price should equal the expected end of period price discounted at the rate implied by model. If the price diverges, arbitrage should bring it back into line. Unlike CAPM, which specifies returns as a linear function of only systematic risk, APT may specify returns as a linear function of more than a single factor. The attraction of APT is that unlike in CAPM one does not have to identify and measure the appropriate market portfolio. However, its main drawback is that it does not specify the underlying macroeconomic factors that are to be used in estimating expected returns (although factors such as growth in real GDP, interest spreads and default probabilities are often used). CAPM, of course, assumes all these macroeconomic factors are taken into account by the market portfolio.

Glossary

A

Acquis communautaire A French term meaning 'the European Union as it is'; in other words, the rights and obligations that member states of the EU share. The 'acquis' includes all the EU's treaties and laws, declarations and resolutions, international agreements on EU affairs and the judgments given by the Court of Justice. It also includes action that EU governments take together in the area of 'justice and home affairs' and on the Common Foreign and Security Policy.

Adverse selection Refers to a market process in which bad results occur due to asymmetric information between buyers and sellers: the 'bad' products or customers are more likely to be selected.

Agencies Within an international parent bank, agencies are offices similar to branches, but with less operative tasks.

Agency capture Refers to the situation where a regulatory process can be captured by producers (banks and other financial institutions) and used in their own interest and advantage rather than in the interest of consumers.

Agency costs These are the costs that principals (typically the owners) have to incur in order to ensure that their agents (the managers) make financial decisions consistent with their best interests.

Arbitrage The simultaneous buying and selling of a commodity, or a security, in different markets to take advantage of price differentials.

Asset-backed securities Securities backed by real or financial assets (e.g., mortgage backed securities/bonds). Asset-backed securities are otherwise known as collateralised securities.

Asset-based finance A specialised method for providing capital and loans that are secured by machinery, inventory, equipment and/or real estate.

Asset-liability management The management of a business in a way that co-ordinates decisions on both sides of the balance sheet. Also known as balance sheet management.

Asset management This can either refer to the managing of an institution's asset side of the balance sheet (e.g., altering the mix of assets to increase returns or minimise risk) or to the function of managing assets on behalf of a customer.

Asset transformation The ability of financial intermediaries to transform large denomination assets into smaller units.

Assets What a firm or a person owns or is owed, such as money, securities, equipment and buildings. Assets are listed on a company's balance sheet.

Association for Payment Clearing Services (APACS) APACS was set up in 1985 as a UK-based non-statutory association of institutions delivering payment services to end customers. APACS provides the forum for institutions to discuss non-competitive issues relating to the payments industry.

Automated clearing house (ACH) An ACH transaction is an electronic method of transferring funds for the clearing and settling of payments among financial institutions. Such electronic transactions are substitutes for cheques.

Automated teller machines (ATMs) An unmanned terminal usually operated through the use of a magnetically coded card, which can dispense cash, take instructions on transfer, provide balances, etc.

B

Back testing In Value-at-Risk models, back testing is used as an ex-post comparison of the risk measure generated by the model against actual daily changes in portfolio value.

Bad loans Generally, loans that currently have not been repaid in part or in full (including those in arrears) and thus they are not currently accruing interest or on which interest is not being paid.

Balance of payments A financial statement prepared for a country which summarises the flow of goods, services and funds between the residents of that country and the residents of the rest of the world during a certain period of time.

Balance sheet A financial statement that reports a company's assets, liabilities and net worth at a point in time.

Bancassurance A French term coined to denote the combination of banking and insurance business within the same organisation. It relates to the distribution of insurance products through a bank's distribution channels.

Bank for International Settlements (BIS) An international bank set up in Basle (Switzerland) in 1930 that fosters international monetary and financial co-operation and serves as a bank for central banks. It is the world's oldest international financial organisation.

Bank performance Refers to how well a bank is doing. Two commonly used bank performance measures are return-on-assets (ROA) and return-on-equity (ROE).

Bank restructuring Usually this term refers to the change in structural features of banking markets (e.g., number of institutions operating in the market) through mergers and acquisitions. It can also refer to corporate changes internal to a bank organisation.

Bank runs Refers to the situation where a large proportion of depositors withdraw their savings because they fear that the bank is unsound and about to fail. See also banking crisis.

Banker's acceptance A short-term credit investment created by a non-financial firm and guaranteed by a bank. A bank's customer orders his/her bank to pay a sum of money at a future date, typically within six months. When the bank endorses the order for payment as 'accepted', it assumes responsibility for ultimate payment to the holder of the acceptance. At this point, the acceptance may be traded in secondary markets much like any other claim on the bank.

Banks Automated Clearing System (BACS) A UK system for sending money electronically between banks. A BACS payment allows customers to make retail payment services such as direct debits and standing orders.

Banking and business banking codes Voluntary codes which set standards of good banking practice for banks and building societies to follow when they are dealing with personal or business customers (used in the UK).

Banking crisis The situation when individuals and companies lose confidence in the banking system. For example, this may be the result of an actual (or expectations of a potential) run on the banking system. Any event, or series of events, that leads to concerns about the solvency of the banking system can be considered a banking crisis.

Base rate This is the interest rate that a bank is charged to borrow short-term funds directly from the central bank. It is the short-term interest rate set for monetary policy purposes. A profit-making bank will charge interest rate higher than the base rate. The term base rate is also used more generally to indicate the anchor interest rate used for pricing variable loans, e.g., short-term wholesale loans are typically priced at LIBOR + x% where the extra amount x% depends on the risk of the loan. In this example bankers will use LIBOR as the base rate for loan pricing.

'Big Bang' The name given to 27 October 1986, when the London Stock Exchange (LSE)'s new regulations took effect, allowing banks to own stock broking and jobbing firms and the automated price quotation system was introduced. The new rules allowed banks to undertake a broader range of securities business and resulted in many UK merchant (investment) banks being acquired by foreign institutions.

Bill and Cheque Clearing Systems (BCCS) In Japan, a system that clears bills and cheques which are exchanged between financial institutions located within the same geographical area.

Bill of Exchange A means of payment used in domestic (rarely) and international banking. Defined by the UK Bills of Exchange Act of 1882 as 'An unconditional order in writing, addressed by one person to another, signed by the person giving it, requiring the person to whom it is addressed to pay, on demand or at a fixed or determinable future time, a sum certain in money to, or to the order of, a specified person, or to bearer.'

Board of Governors The governing body of the Federal Reserve System, which is responsible for US monetary policy.

BOJ-NET (Bank of Japan Financial Network System) Funds Transfer System In Japan, it is the central bank's funds transfer system and is used to settle interbank obligations including net obligations of participants in the private sector clearing systems.

Bond A document issued by a government or company borrowing money from the public, stating the existence of a debt and the amount owing to the holder of the document (the bondholder). Bondholders use the document to obtain repayment of the loan. Bonds are usually long-term (greater than 5-year maturity) and pay fixed rates of interest.

Branch offices A branch is a key part of the distribution channel and acts as a legal and functional part of the bank, offering a full range of services.

Bridge bank In case of one or more failed institutions in a system, a bridge bank is a temporary financial institution that is established to receive and manage the good assets of the one or more failed institutions.

Broker An intermediary between market makers and investors. Brokers buy and sell securities on behalf of customers and do not take a position in securities.

Building society Mutually owned UK financial institution which issues shares (i.e., accepts deposits) and lends to borrowers mainly for home mortgages.

C

Call risk The risk that arises when a borrower or bondholder may redeem the security prior to maturity.

CAMELS A rating system used by regulatory and supervisory authorities to evaluate the safety and soundness of financial institutions. The acronym CAMELS refers to the six components of a bank's financial condition that are assessed: Capital adequacy, Asset quality, Management, Earnings, Liquidity and Sensitivity to market risk. Ratings are assigned for each component in addition to the overall rating of a bank's financial condition. The ratings are assigned on a scale from 1 to 5. Banks with ratings of 1 or 2 are considered to present few, if any, supervisory concerns, while banks with ratings of 3, 4, or 5 present moderate to extreme degrees of supervisory concern.

Capital In a balance sheet, capital is the difference between assets and liabilities. Also known as net worth or equity capital, it represents the ownership interest in a business.

Capital adequacy Refers to the level of capital a bank should hold in relation to the regulatory minimum standards, established under the Basle Accord (8%). The amount of capital a bank holds relates to the riskiness of its business activity (both on-balance sheet and off-balance sheet). The more risky a bank's assets (on-balance sheet) and its other activities not recorded as assets (off-balance sheet business including guarantees, commitments, securities underwriting, derivatives trading and so on) the more capital it needs to hold.

Capital management This term typically refers to the capital adequacy management techniques used to ensure that the bank keeps an adequate level of capital to comply with regulations.

Capital markets Markets where capital funds (debt and equity) are issued and traded. This includes private placement sources of debt and equity as well as organised markets and exchanges.

Capital risk Refers to the decrease in the market value of assets relative to the market value of liabilities. In the case of a bank it refers to the risk associated with losses that have to be borne by its capital reserves. In extreme cases a bank may not have enough capital to cover all its losses and this is when the bank becomes insolvent/bankrupt. Note that capital risk is also used as a general term that refers to losses incurred by an investor where he or she may lose all or part of the principal invested.

Caps A type of option that gives the holder a right to purchase a forward rate agreement 'with hindsight'. For example an interest rate cap may be bought in order to get protection that interest rate will not move upwards beyond the level specified by the cap contract.

Cash management and transaction services Offered by large wholesale and/or international banks, cash management and transaction services can include for instance electronic funds transfers, cheque deposit services, and electronic sending of letters of credit.

Central and Eastern European Countries (CEECs) Acronym used to indicate Central and Eastern European Countries namely the Czech Republic, Hungary, Poland, Slovakia and Slovenia.

Central bank independence This refers to the level of independence that the central bank of a country has from the government (and political interference).

Certificate of Deposit (CD) A negotiable certificate issued by a bank as evidence of an interest-bearing wholesale time deposit.

Check (US) or Cheque (UK) A form of payment used in place of cash and payable on demand that instructs a bank to pay the specified sum to the party named on the cheque from funds held on a deposit account.

Check 21 In the United States, this term is used to refer to the Check Clearing for the 21st Century Act that became effective on 28 October 2004. The legislation gives banks greater flexibility in converting paper cheques into electronic form to speed up retail payments.

CHIPS In the United States, the acronym used to indicate the Clearing House Interbank Payments System. It refers to the main bank-owned payments system for clearing large value, mainly international, payments.

City banks The largest banks in the Japanese banking system that account for over 50% of total banking sector assets.

Clearing House Automated Payments System (CHAPS) A computerised system that provides a same day guaranteed sterling electronic credit transfer service within the United Kingdom.

Collars Collars are hybrid derivative products, being part forward contract and part option. A collar (as its name suggests) puts an upper and lower bound on price movements.

Collateral Is an asset that secures repayment on a loan. The main form of collateral is real estate.

Colonial banks A term used to describe 'British overseas banks' or 'Anglo-foreign banks'. Colonial banks were institutions set up by the British in their colonies and typically only provided services outside the United Kingdom. Note that the term can also be used more generally to describe banks that operate in the colonies of any country.

Commercial bank An institution that undertakes traditional banking activities: deposit-taking, lending and payments services.

Commercial credit Loans and other forms of credit extended to financial and non-financial companies.

Commercial letter of credit (L/C) A document issued by a bank stating its commitment to pay someone a stated amount of money on behalf of a buyer so long as the seller meets very specific terms and conditions.

Commercial paper A short-term unsecured instrument that promises to repay a fixed amount representing the cost of borrowed funds (such as LIBOR) plus interest, on a certain future date at a specific time. Usually issued by companies with a high credit standing. It may be a purely financial instrument or be based on an underlying commercial transaction.

Commitment A legal commitment undertaken by a bank to lend to a customer.

Competition Commission Established by the Competition Act 1998, the Competition Commission is an independent body responsible for investigating mergers, markets and conditions and regulation of major UK industries.

Competition policy Government regulations and actions designed to promote competition and restrict monopoly practices by preventing individual firms from having excessive market power.

Competitive pressures Refers to increased rivalry between institutions for customers.

Competitive risk The risk that arises as a consequence of changes in the competitive environment.

Compliance costs The incremental costs associated with complying with regulations.

Concentration ratio Measure used to identify the proportion of total market controlled by the largest firms. In the case of banks, for example, a three-firm concentration ratio measures the proportion of total assets (or total deposits) of the banking sector held by the three largest firms.

Consumer credit Loans and other forms of credit extended to the household sector. Otherwise known as retail credit.

Contagion The tendency of a financial/banking crisis to spread or spill over from one market to another.

Contractual savings institutions Term used to refer to insurance companies and pension funds whose main funding comes from long-term regular payments (savings) made by individuals/companies. The liabilities of these firms are the long-term future benefits to be paid to policyholders and fund holders.

Convergence This term is widely used to refer to a number of features of the financial system or economy overall. It can relate to: financial regulations across countries becoming more similar as a result of the harmonisation of international regulatory standards, macroeconomic variables such as interest rates, GDP and so on across countries moving to the same level, business practices of banks becoming more similar and so on.

'Convoy system' Term used in Japan to indicate the situation where the Ministry of Finance encouraged healthy banks to acquire those in trouble.

Co-operative banks Traditionally banks that are characterised by mutual ownership; today many co-operative banks have converted into listed institutions.

Corporate banking Corporate banking relates to banking services provided to companies although typically the term refers to services provided to relatively large firms.

Correspondent banking In international banking, banks use correspondent banks to do business in markets where they have no physical presence.

Cost–income ratio A quick test of bank efficiency that can be calculated by dividing non-interest expenses by total income.

Cost of capital Relates to the costs of financing, namely, the expense of raising equity and debt. High performing banks can raise funds by issuing shares or bonds more cheaply than poor performing banks. Cost of capital arguments has been used in international banking theory to explain the rationale for overseas expansion.

Costs Derived from the liabilities side of the balance sheet, costs relate to payments that the bank has to undertake including payment of interest on deposits, staff and other operating costs.

Counterparty risk The risk that a party in a financial transaction will default. Counterparty risk is often used to indicate the credit risk on off-balance sheet products.

Countertrade Refers to a variety of commercial mechanisms for reciprocal trade, e.g., barter, switch trading, etc.

Country risk It is the risk that economic, social, and political conditions and events in a foreign country will adversely affect a firm's commercial/financial interests.

Credit checking The process of evaluating an applicant's loan request in order to determine the liklihood that the borrower will repay.

Credit co-operative banks See co-operative banks.

Credit culture Refers to the fundamental principles that drive lending activity and how management analyses risk. It is generally used in relation to an individual bank's lending and risk management procedures. For example, one may hear a banker say 'Citibank' has a different credit culture to 'Barclays' implying their loan granting procedures and risk assessments are different in some way. The term can also be used to describe the attitude to borrowing by households, for example, 'US households have a different credit culture to the Japanese', meaning that the former love to borrow whereas the latter do not.

Credit facilities Facilities available to individuals and companies such as loans, overdrafts and lines of credit.

Credit multiplier A model that illustrates how banks create money determined by the ratio of change in deposits to the change in level of reserves.

Credit philosophy Reflects a bank's management's preference for more or less conservative loan granting practices.

Credit rating agency Private agencies, such as Standard & Poor's, Moody's and FitchIBCA, that assess and rate the risk and quality of debt securities, companies, organisations and countries.

Credit rationing A technique used by banks to limit the amount of credit available to a specific segment of customers.

Credit reference agencies Banks use credit reference agencies such as Experian and Equifax, in the credit scoring process to check individuals' identity and credit history when they apply for a loan.

Credit risk The risk that a counterparty defaults on some or all of its contractual obligations. Credit risk in lending operations is the likelihood that a borrower will not be able to repay the principal or pay the interest.

Credit scoring A qualitative evaluation system employed by banks to assess the creditworthiness of an individual or firm that applies for a loan.

Credit transfers Also known as Bank Giro Credits, credit transfers are payments where the customer instructs their bank to transfer funds directly to the beneficiary's bank account.

Credit union A non-profit financial institution that is owned and operated entirely by its members. They provide financial services for their members, including savings and lending. Common in the United States, Ireland and (to a lesser extent) the United Kingdom.

Cross-border mergers Merger operations between institutions headquartered in different countries.

Cruickshank Report A report carried out by the UK government in 2000 looking into the issue of competition in UK banking and headed by Don Cruickshank.

Currency forward A derivative contract that allows both the buyer and the seller to hedge against the risk of future fluctuations in currencies.

Currency swaps A transaction in which two counterparties exchange specific amounts of two different currencies at the outset and repay over time according to a predetermined rule which reflects interest payments and possibly amortisation of principal. The payment flows in currency swaps (in which payments are based on fixed interest rates in each currency) are generally like those of spot and forward currency transactions.

D

Debentures Unsecured obligations of an issuing firm, which are claims only on the general assets of the company.

Default The inability to ultimately fulfil a contractual obligation when it falls due.

Deficit units Term used to denote the ultimate borrower in a financial transaction.

Delegated monitoring One of the theories put forward as an explanation for the existence of banking. It relates to the role of banks as 'monitors' of borrowers.

Demand deposit Current account funds that can be withdrawn at any time without notice. They can be either interest or non-interest bearing. Sometimes known as chequing (checking) accounts.

Demutualisation The process of changing from a mutual company owned by its members (e.g., in the United Kingdom the traditional building societies) to a company owned by shareholders. When the building societies demutualised, their shares became listed on the stock exchange and they converted to banks. For example, Abbey National and Alliance & Leicester, once building societies are now banks.

Deposit and lending services Personal banking services that include for instance current and savings accounts and consumers' loans and mortgages.

Deposit insurance Where bank deposits of retail customers are insured against loss in the event of bank failure. Deposit insurance schemes can be privately funded (by the banks) or by the government.

Deposit Insurance Corporation An organisation that insures retail customers' deposits. For example, Japan's Deposit Insurance Corporation is a semi-governmental organisation that was established in 1971 with the purpose of operating the country's deposit insurance system, in line with the Deposit Insurance Law.

Depository institutions/Deposit-taking institution Financial institutions that obtain their funds mainly from accepting savings and/or demand deposits from the general public and provide regular banking services such as chequing and savings accounts.

Deregulation The process of removing or reducing the rules and regulations on an industry with the objective of improving economic efficiency, competition and innovation in the market.

Derivatives Derivatives are contracts involving rights or obligations relating to purchases or sales of underlying real or financial assets (e.g., gold and shares respectively), or relating to payments to be made in respect of movements in indices (e.g., the London FTSE 100). These rights and obligations are related to – or derived from – the underlying transactions, so they have been given the general name of *derivatives*.

Developing countries Developing countries are those with a Gross National Income (GNI) per capita of $9,265 or less. The World Bank classifies economies as low-income (GNI $755 or less), middle-income (GNI $756–9,265) and high-income (GNI $9,266 or more). Low-income and middle-income economies are sometimes referred to as developing countries.

Development banks Multilateral institutions that provide financial support and professional advice for economic and social development activities in developing countries, such as the World Bank.

Digital divide Gap between those people and communities who have access to information technology (e.g., computers) and those who do not.

Direct debits Regular electronic debiting of funds from an individual's bank account to pay utility bills (electricity, gas, water bills), mortgages, etc.

Direct finance The situation where borrowers obtain funds directly from lenders in financial markets.

Discount A sum of money allowed for immediate payment of a sum due at a later date. If the sum is secured by a bill of exchange, the holder who buys the bill and receives the discount is said to discount the bill.

Discount window Monetary policy tool of central banks that allows eligible banking institutions to borrow money from the central bank, usually to meet short-term liquidity needs.

Disintermediation The process whereby borrowers and investors by-pass banks and transact business directly.

Dollarisation When a non-US country either adopts US dollars as a local currency or uses it in parallel to the domestic currency.

Duration analysis Used extensively as a risk management technique, it is a measure of the average life of an asset's (or liability's) cash flow.

E

E-banking The remote delivery of banking products and services through electronic channels.

E-money E-money includes reloadable electronic money instruments in the form of stored value cards and electronic tokens stored in computer memory.

ECOFIN Council The Economic and Financial Affairs Council is, together with the Agriculture Council and the General Affairs Council, one of the oldest configurations of the Council of the European Union. It is commonly known as the ECOFIN Council or Simply 'ECOFIN' and is composed of the Economics and Finance Ministers of the Member States, as well as Budget Ministers when budgetary issues are discussed. It meets once a month.

Economic and Monetary Union (EMU) Is the name given to the process of harmonising the economic and monetary policies of the Member States of the European Union with a view to the introduction of a single currency, the Euro.

Economies of scale Cost savings arising from decreasing unit cost of production as output increases.

Economies of scope Cost savings arising from joint production. For example, the costs of a financial institution offering banking and insurance products are lower than the costs of separate firms providing only banking and insurance services.

ECU (European Currency Unit) European Currency Unit is a composite currency made up of currencies of the members of the former European Community (EC)

Electronic Funds Transfer at Point of Sale (EFTPOS) A system which allows funds to be transferred automatically as goods are bought in a store.

Electronic Funds Transfer System (EFTS) A system which transfers funds by means of electronic communication rather than paper.

Emerging markets The term 'emerging market' was originally coined to describe a fairly narrow list of middle-to-higher income economies among the developing countries, with stock markets in which foreigners could buy securities. The term's meaning has since been expanded to include more or less all developing countries.

Equity In the context of capital markets, equity refers to an ordinary share. In accounting and legal terms, it refers to the financial interests in a firm's assets after prior claims have been made.

Euro The Euro (€) is the single currency for 12 EU countries.

Euroarea/Eurozone/Euroland Expressions used interchangeably to refer to the EU countries that have adopted the Euro.

Eurobank Banks and other financial intermediaries that bid for wholesale time deposits and make wholesale loans in a currency or currencies other than that of the country in which they are based.

Eurobond An international bond that may be issued in any currency, other than that of the issuer's home country, and subsequently traded in international markets.

Eurocommercial paper Note sold in London for same-day settlement in US dollars in New York. The maturities are more tailored to the needs of issuers and investors rather than the standard euronote terms of 1, 3 and 6 months.

Eurocurrency A currency that is held in the form of time deposits in financial institutions outside the home country of the currency, e.g., yen time deposits held in London banks.

Eurocurrency banking This involves banks undertaking wholesale (large-scale) foreign exchange transactions (loans and deposits) with both residents and non-residents.

Euroequities Equities underwritten and distributed to investors outside the country of origin of the issuer.

Euroisation Euroisation occurs when residents of a country extensively use the Euro alongside or instead of the domestic currency. For example, this is a process that is common in Central and Eastern Europe.

Euromarkets General term that refers to all the markets in which financial instruments denominated in Eurocurrencies are traded, e.g., Eurobonds, Euroequities, etc.

Euronotes A short-term note (usually 1, 3 and 6 months) issued under a note issuance facility (NIF) or Eurocommercial paper facility.

European Central Bank (ECB) The ECB is the central bank for Europe's single currency, the Euro (€).

European Community (EC) Former European Community that was superseded in 1993 by the European Union (EU).

European Monetary System (EMS) An exchange rate regime established in 1979 whose main objective was to create closer monetary policy co-operation between Community countries, leading to a zone of monetary stability in Europe. The main components of the EMS were the ECU, the exchange rate and intervention mechanism (ERM) and various credit mechanisms. It ceased to exist in 1999 at the start of Stage Three of Economic and Monetary Union (EMU), when ERM II (Exchange Rate Mechanism II) was established.

European System of Central Banks (ESCB) The European System of Central Banks includes the ECB and the National Central Banks (NCBs) of all EU member states (including those that have not yet joined the EMU).

European Union (EU) Currently an international organisation of 25 European member states established by the Treaty on European Union (i.e., Maastricht Treaty).

Eurosystem The Eurosystem comprises the ECB and the NCBs of those countries that have adopted the Euro. The Eurosystem and the ESCB will co-exist as long as there are EU Member States outside the Euroarea.

Excess managerial capacity Too many managers. Often referred to in the context of bank reorganisations after a merger. For example, when banks merge, the new organisation has two senior management teams, headquarters and a duplication of other managerial functions. A main focus of cost savings post merger is to get rid of this excess managerial capacity by removing duplication of managerial positions.

Exchange controls These are restrictions placed on the movements of funds in a particular currency (or limitations to the convertibility of a currency) imposed by central banking authorities.

Exchange Rate Mechanism (ERM and ERM II) Introduced in March 1979 by the European Community as part of the European Monetary System (EMS), the ERM was designed to reduce exchange rate variability and achieve monetary stability in Europe. In May 1999, at the start of Stage 3 of the Economic and Monetary Union (EMU), ERM II replaced the original ERM. Under ERM II, a central rate against the Euro is defined for the currency of each Member State not participating in the Euroarea but participating in the exchange-rate mechanism. The mechanism allows one standard fluctuation band of 15% on either side of the central rate. Initially, Denmark and Greece joined ERM II. Since Greece adopted the Euro in January 2001, Denmark has been the only participant until June 2004, when Estonia, Lithuania and Slovenia joined. In May 2005 Cyprus, Latvia and Malta also joined ERM II.

Exchange rate policy Relates to the control and management of a country's levels of exchange rate for its currency. Governments influence the exchange rate by using the gold and foreign currency reserves held by their central banks to buy and sell domestic currency.

F

Factoring The purchase by the factor and sale by the company of its book debts on a continuing basis, usually for immediate cash. The factor then manages the sales ledger and the collection of accounts under terms agreed by the seller.

Federal Deposit Insurance Corporation (FDIC) In the US, the FDIC is an independent agency of the federal government that preserves and promotes public confidence by insuring deposits in banks and thrifts for up to $100,000 (also see Deposit Insurance Corporation).

Federal Reserve (Fed) Established in 1913, it is the central bank of the United States of America. It comprises the Federal Reserve Board, the twelve Federal Reserve Banks, and the national and state member banks. Its primary purpose is to regulate the flow of money and credit in the country.

Fedwire A real-time gross settlement system (RTGS) that links Federal Reserve Banks to other banks and depository institutions. It is an important participant in providing interbank payment services as well as safekeeping and transfer services for US government and agency securities, and mortgage-backed securities.

Finance houses Financial institutions that accept deposits and finance leasing and hire purchase agreements.

Financial asset Term used to refer to claims held by the lender of funds against the borrower in the form of money, bank deposit accounts, bonds, shares, loans etc.

Financial claim A claim to the payment of a future sum of money and/or a periodic payment of money. It carries an obligation on the issuer to pay interest periodically or to redeem the claim at a stated value.

Financial conglomerates This term defines a group of enterprises, formed by different types of financial institutions, operating in different sectors of the financial industry.

Financial conglomeration The process relating to the creation of groups of financial institutions operating in different sectors (banking, insurance, securities and so on) of the financial industry. A financial institution that undertakes a wide range of different financial activities is known as a financial conglomerate.

Financial deregulation See deregulation.

Financial derivatives See derivatives.

Financial futures Futures contracts in an interest rate, stock index, currency or interest bearing security.

Financial guarantees See guarantees.

Financial innovation Financial innovation can be defined as the act of creating and then popularising new financial instruments as well as new financial technologies, institutions and markets. It includes institutional, product and process innovation. Institutional innovations relate to the creation of new types of financial firms (such as specialist credit card firms like MBNA, discount broking firms such as Charles Schwab, internet banks and so on). Product innovation relates to new products such as derivatives, securitised assets, foreign currency mortgages and so on. Process innovations relate to new ways of doing banking/financial business, including online banking, phone banking, new ways of implementing information technology and so on.

Financial liability The issuer of a financial claim (borrower) is said to have a financial liability.

Financial liberalisation Generally refers to the process of opening up a market and the relaxation of restrictive practices. Deregulation is required for financial liberalisation to take place.

Financial ratio analysis Refers to the use of key ratios to both measure and analyse the performance of a firm. In banking the typical performance ratios are: ROA, ROE, C/I and NIM.

Financial repression A situation where restrictions on financial activities exist and government intervention in financial markets is severe. A financially repressed system is likely to be characterised by a lack of competition in banking and financial markets, and interest rates and other financial market prices do not reflect the underlying economic fundamentals.

Financial Services Act The Financial Services Act 1986 established the regulatory framework for investor protection in the United Kingdom.

Financial Services Action Plan (FSAP) Initiated in 1999, the FSAP can be considered the European Commission response towards improving the single market in financial services in the EU.

Financial Services Agency In Japan, the governmental agency established in 1998 responsible for supervision and inspection functions of the private sector financial institutions.

Financial Services and Markets Act (2001) The UK legislation that created the Financial Services Authority.

Financial Services Authority (FSA) The Financial Services Authority was created by the Labour Government in 1997 as the regulatory body for the whole UK financial services industry. A number of separate regulatory bodies were brought together in the FSA, which also took over the responsibilities that the Bank of England had for supervising banks and other financial institutions.

Firm-specific advantages One of the theories on the rationale for international banking. For example, firms have financial, economic, business and other advantages specific to their own operations that enables them to undertake international activities.

Fiscal policy One of the five major forms of economic policy conducted by governments, fiscal policy relates to changes in the level and structure of government spending and taxation designed to influence the economy.

Fixed-rate assets and liabilities Fixed-rate assets and liabilities carry rates that are constant throughout a certain time period (e.g., 1 year) and their cash flows do not change unless there is a default, early withdrawal, or an unanticipated prepayment.

Floating-rate debt Debt instruments that pay a variable (as opposed to fixed) rate of interest.

Floating-rate note A medium-term security which carries a floating rate of interest which is reset at regular intervals, usually quarterly or half-yearly, in relation to some pre-determined reference rate, typically LIBOR.

Floors A type of option. An interest rate floor is similar to a cap except that it protects an investor or depositor against a floating rate of interest falling below a specified lower or floor level.

Forbearance Usually referred to the possibility given by the regulatory authorities to insolvent banks of staying in operation for the sake of avoiding systemic risk.

Foreign direct investment (FDI) Refers to the movement of capital across national frontiers in a way that grants the investor control over the acquired asset. Thus it is distinct from portfolio investment which may be cross-border, but does not offer such control. Firms which undertake FDI are known as multinational enterprises.

Foreign exchange risk The risk that exchange rate fluctuations affect the value of a bank's assets, liabilities and off-balance sheet activities denominated in foreign currency.

Foreign Exchange Yen Clearing System (FXYCS) In Japan, the FXYCS was established in 1980 to facilitate clearing of yen payments for cross-border financial transactions.

Forfaiting In international banking, the situation where the exporter agrees to surrender the rights to claim for payment of goods or services delivered to an importer under a contract of sale, in return for a cash payment from a forfaiting bank. The forfaiting bank takes over the exporter's debt and assumes the full risk of payment by the importer. The exporter is thereby freed from any financial risk in the transaction and is liable only for the quality and reliability of the goods and services provided.

Forward rate agreement (FRA) A common type of forward contracts that gives the agents involved the opportunity to hedge against interest rate risk thereby 'locking in' the future price of the assets.

Forwards In a forward contract, two parties agree to exchange over-the-counter (OTC) a real or financial asset on a prearranged date in the future for a specified price.

Free banking A school of thought that maintains that the financial sector would work better without regulation, supervision and central banking.

Futures contracts An exchange traded contract generally calling for the delivery of a specified amount of a particular commodity, or financial instrument, at a fixed date in the future.

G

Gap analysis Gap analysis is possibly the best known interest rate risk management technique. The 'gap' refers to the difference between interest rate sensitive assets and interest rate sensitive liabilities over a specific time horizon.

Gilt-edged securities UK government bonds.

Global onshore private banking business Refers to the business of offering banking and investment services to wealthy (high net worth) individuals in their own country (onshore). Wealthy individuals that have their personal finances managed outside their home country (e.g., UK billionaires who place their funds in Swiss banks) are said to be undertaking offshore private banking activity. The word 'global' comes from the fact that there are a number of firms that offer such services in many countries, such as Citigroup Private Bank and UBS. Note also that many banks use the term 'global' to signify that their services are available to an international clientele as well as to indicate that they have substantial international operations.

Globalisation General term used to describe the world-wide integration of both capital and money markets.

Government bonds Bonds issued on behalf of (or backed up by) the government

Government safety net Public policy regulation designed to minimise the risk of bank runs, it includes deposit insurance and the lender-of-last-resort function.

Gramm-Leach-Bliley Act Legislation passed in 1999 whereby US banks can establish financial holding companies and engage in the full range of financial services areas, such as securities underwriting, insurance sales and underwriting and investment banking business.

Guarantees These are traditional off-balance sheet exposures, where a bank has underwritten the obligations of a third party and currently stands behind the risk, e.g., standby letters of credit and acceptances.

H

Hedge fund A private investment fund that trades and invests in various assets such as securities, commodities, currency and derivatives on behalf of its clients.

Hedging Reducing risk by taking a position that offsets existing or expected exposures. Hedging is the avoidance of risk by arranging a contract at specified prices which will yield a known return.

High net worth individuals (HNWIs) Wealthy personal (retail) customers. Definitions vary but typically refer to individuals with more than $300,000 to $500,000 of investable assets.

Hire services (hire purchase) A transaction in which customers pay for the cost of the asset, together with the financing charges, over the hire period and take legal title on the equipment at the time of final payment (or there may be a nominal purchase option fee at the end of the payment period).

Home and office banking systems (HOBS) Banking facilities provided in the home or office through the means of a TV screen, personal computer or telephone.

Horizontal FDI A theory in international banking that associates the existence of multinationals in a country to trade barriers that make exporting costly.

Household information files (HIFs) Information databases containing financial files and other characteristics of households. Data is usually used for marketing purposes.

I

Indirect finance The situation where borrowers obtain funds indirectly from lenders through financial intermediaries.

Inflation risk The probability that an increase in the price level for goods and services will unexpectedly erode the purchasing power of a bank's earnings and returns to shareholders.

Information asymmetries The imperfect distribution of information among parties to a contract. They can create situations of adverse selection and moral hazard.

Innovative (or new product) stage When a good or service is produced to meet a new consumer demand or when a new technology enables the creation of innovative goods.

Inspection Term relating to when bank regulators demand to inspect the books (financial accounts) and managerial practices of a bank. Inspection is often undertaken on the bank's own premises.

Instruments of portfolio constraints Instruments that may be imposed by the authorities for the aims of monetary policy that constrain the portfolio structure of financial institutions, with the purpose of influencing credit creation and, possibly, the type of lending taking place.

Insurance services Insurance products protect policyholders from various adverse events. Policyholders pay regular premiums and the insurer promises compensation if the specific insured event occurs. There are two main types of insurance – life insurance and general (or property and casualty) insurance.

Interbank Usually refers to short-term wholesale loans traded between banks.

Interest rate risk Defined as the risk arising from the mismatching of the maturity and the volume of banks' assets and liabilities as part of their asset transformation function.

Interest rate swaps A transaction in which two counterparties exchange interest payment streams of differing character based on an underlying notional principal amount. The three main types are coupon swaps (fixed rate to floating rate in the same currency), basis swaps (one floating rate index to another floating rate index in the same currency), and cross-currency interest rate swaps (fixed rate in one currency to floating rate in another).

Interest spreads Difference between interest paid and interest owned, e.g., if interest paid on deposits averages 4 per cent and interest earned on assets equals 10 per cent then the interest spread is 6 per cent.

Intermediary An intermediary links borrowers and lenders either by acting as an agent or by bringing together potential traders, or by acting in place of a market.

Internationalisation General term used to describe the substantial increase in the presence of banks and other financial institutions doing business outside their domestic markets.

Intervened bank In bank resolution terminology, an intervened bank refers to an insolvent or non-viable institution whose control is in the hands of the authorities.

Investment bank A financial institution that deals mainly with corporate customers and specialises in securities markets activities including underwriting, trading, asset management and corporate restructuring (e.g., mergers and acquisitions) advisory activities.

Investment intermediaries In the United States, a term to designate mutual funds, investment banks, securities firms and finance houses whose liabilities are usually short-term money market or capital market securities.

Investment products Investment products offered to retail customers include various securities-related products, including mutual funds (known as unit trusts in the UK), investment in company stocks and various other securities-related products (such as bonds).

Investment services Generally speaking these are services and products offered to retail customers that include for example mutual funds (known as unit trusts in the United Kingdom), investment in company stocks and various other securities related products (such as savings bonds).

Invoice discounting services Similar to factoring, invoice discounting services involve a narrower service where the discounting company collects sales receipts but the firm still manages its ledger.

Islamic banking A type of banking particularly common in South and South-East Asia, the Gulf Co-operation Council Countries and other countries, that offers products and services that do not charge or pay interest.

J

Jobber A firm, or individual, in the Stock Exchange responsible for quoting prices to and trading securities via brokers.

L

Lamfalussy Procedure A procedure established in February 2001 by a Committee of Wise Men chaired by Alexander Lamfalussy, for improving the effectiveness of the EU's securities market regulatory process.

Leasing A financial technique for obtaining the use of an asset by contracting a series of payments over a specific period. The grantor of the lease (the lessor) remains the owner of the leased property throughout the term of the lease and receives payments from the lessee.

Legal risk The risk that contracts that are not legally enforceable or documented correctly could disrupt or negatively affect the operations, profitability or solvency of the bank.

Lender-of-last-resort (LOLR) The understanding that the central bank will always stand ready to lend money to a bank or number of banks experiencing a crisis if they cannot obtain finance from market sources.

Letter of credit A document issued by a bank stating its commitment to pay someone a stated amount of money on behalf of a buyer so long as the seller meets very specific terms and conditions.

Liabilities The debts and other financial obligations of a firm or an individual.

Liability management The process whereby banks manage liabilities and buy in (i.e. borrow) funds when needed from the markets for interbank deposits, large-sized time deposits and certificates of deposit.

LIBID (London Interbank Bid Rate) The rate at which a bank is willing to buy funds in the international interbank markets.

LIBOR (London Interbank Offered Rate) The rate at which a bank is willing to lend funds (wholesale money) in the international interbank markets.

LIMEAN The mean of LIBID and LIBOR.

Liquid asset An asset that can easily be turned into cash at short notice.

Liquidity The ability of an institution to pay its obligations when they fall due.

Liquidity crisis A situation where depositors demand larger withdrawals than normal and banks are forced to borrow funds at an elevated interest rate. A liquidity crisis is usually unpredictable and can be due to either a lack of confidence in the specific bank, or some unexpected need for cash. Liquidity crises can ultimately result in 'a run' and even the insolvency of the bank.

Liquidity management Those activities a bank should carry out to ensure that holdings of liquid assets are sufficient to meet its obligations as they fall due, including unexpected transactions.

Liquidity risk The risk that a solvent institution is temporarily unable to meet its short-term monetary obligations.

Loan commitments Promises to lend up to a pre-specified amount to a pre-specified customer at pre-specified terms.

Loan policy A fundamental part of the credit process whereby the lending guidelines that bank employees follow to conduct lending business are formalised.

Loan rate Term used in the process of loan pricing to indicate the price of the loan.

Loan sales A loan sale occurs when a bank originates a loan and then decides to sell it to another legal entity, usually a financial intermediary. Where the bank is selling only part of the loan then the operation is called loan participation or loan syndication.

Location advantages One of the theories on the rationale for international banking.

Long-term credit banks A private credit institution that provides long- and medium-term finance to the corporate sector.

M

Macro-hedging When a bank uses futures (or other derivatives) to hedge the entire balance sheet (the aggregate portfolio interest rate risk).

Major British Banking Groups (MBBGs) According to the British Bankers Association, MBBGs currently include: Abbey Group, Alliance and Leicester Group, Barclays Group, Bradford and Bingley, HBOS Group, HSBC Bank Group, Lloyds TSB Group, Northern Rock plc and The Royal Bank of Scotland Group.

Management risk The risk that management lacks the ability to make commercially profitable and other decisions consistently. It can also include the risk of dishonesty by employees and the risk that the bank will not have an effective organisation.

Market capitalisation Market value of a company's outstanding equity.

Market maker An institution that quotes bid and offer prices for a security and is ready to buy and sell at such prices.

Market risk The risk of losses in on- and off-balance sheet positions arising from movements in market prices. This type of risk pertains in particular to short-term trading in assets, liabilities and derivative products, and relates to changes in interest rates, exchange rates and other asset prices.

Market segmentation A systematic process whereby different types of groups are identified (segmented) for target marketing purposes.

Mature product stage A stage in the product life-cycle when growth has started to slow and defending market share becomes the chief concern. Additionally, more competitors have stepped forward to challenge the product at this stage, some of whom may offer a higher quality version of the product at lower price. Customers are more aware of the product's features and also are likely to become more price-sensitive (demand for the product in the home market becomes more elastic). At this stage, the producer is likely to benefit from scale economies so production costs fall. When a product or service reaches maturity, foreign expansion becomes likely.

Maturity The length of time elapsing before a debt is to be redeemed by the issuer.

Medium-term notes (MTNs) Medium-term debt securities that pay floating rates of interest.

Merchant bank A British term to indicate an investment bank, that is a financial institution that specialises in securities markets activities such as underwriting and trading and advising on such issues as mergers and acquisitions. Merchant banking is also a term used in the United States to refer to investment banks that acquire equity stakes in companies either for strategic or temporary investment purposes.

Mergers and Acquisitions (M&As) The combination of two (or more) institutions through partnering or purchase.

Micro-hedging When a bank hedges a transaction associated with an individual asset, liability or commitment.

Modern banking As opposed to traditional banking, modern banking refers to the new ways of doing banking business as a result of the forces of change. Generally used to emphasise the fact that banks have become full service financial firms operating in many different sectors of the financial industry (banking, insurance, pensions, investments, and so on) in both their home and international markets.

Modern international banking Refers to the process of expansion of banks overseas in recent years.

Monetary aggregates A series of measures for the money supply, including narrow and broad measures. Usually termed as M1, M2, M3 and M4.

Monetary policy Relates to the actions taken by central banks to influence the availability and cost of money and credit by controlling some measure (or measures) of the money supply and/or the level and structure of interest rates.

Money Money is represented by the coins and notes which we use in our daily lives; it is the commodity readily acceptable by all people wishing to undertake transactions. It is also a means of expressing a value for any kind of product or service. This, of course, is the most common and narrowest definition of money. For monetary policy purposes broader definitions of money can include coins and notes plus bank deposits and other items.

Money market Short-term financial market usually involving large-value (wholesale) assets with less than one year to maturity.

Money transmission services The activity of financial intermediation exercised for instance by the means of: the collection and transfer of funds (e.g. credit transfers); the transmission and execution of payment orders (e.g. cheque payments and other payments media); and the offsetting of debits and credits.

Monitoring Checking on borrowers' behaviour and ability to repay their loans through the life of the loan.

Moral hazard Moral hazard arises when a contract or financial arrangement creates incentives for the parties involved to behave against the interest of others.

Mortgage-backed bonds Bonds traded mainly in the United States which pay interest on a semi-annual basis and repay principal either periodically or at maturity, and where the underlying collateral is a pool of mortgages.

Mortgage equity withdrawal This relates to home owners borrowing against the increased value of their property (capital gains), by taking out additional housing equity loans.

Multinational banking Refers to banks having some element of ownership and control of banking operations outside their home market.

Mutual funds An institution that manages collectively funds obtained from different investors. In the United States they are referred to as mutual funds; in the United Kingdom, unit trusts.

N

National consolidation The reduction in the number of banks in a system generally due to mergers and/or acquisitions between domestic institutions.

National debt management policy One form of economic policy conducted by governments that is concerned with the manipulation of the outstanding stock of government debt instruments held by the domestic private sector with the objective of influencing the level and structure of interest rates and/or the availability of reserve assets to the banking system.

Negative equity This is the situation where the market value of a property is less than the outstanding mortgage loan.

Net interest margin (NIM) A common measure of bank performance that is equal to gross interest income minus gross interest expense.

New credit products Products whose importance has become particularly relevant over the last few years, such as credit derivatives.

New Member States (NMS) Refers to the ten countries that joined the EU on 1 May 2004, namely Cyprus, the Czech Republic, Estonia, Hungary, Latvia, Lithuania, Malta, Poland, Slovenia and the Slovak Republic.

NIM-8 (countries) Refers to the former transition countries. This includes the Central and Eastern European countries (CEECs) (Czech Republic, Hungary, Poland, Slovenia and the Slovak Republic) and the three Baltic States (Estonia, Latvia and Lithuania).

Non-deposit-taking institution (NDTI) A general term used to refer to financial institutions whose main activity is not to take deposits, such as insurance companies, pension funds, investment companies, finance houses and so on.

Non-performing loans (NPLs) Non-performing loans are loans on which debtors have failed to make contractual payments for a predetermined time.

Note A certificate of indebtedness like a bond, but used most frequently for short-term issues.

Note issuance facility (NIF) A medium-term arrangement enabling borrowers to issue short-term paper, typically of three or six months' maturity, in their own names. Usually a group of underwriting banks guarantees the availability of funds to the borrower by purchasing any unsold notes at each rollover date or by providing a standby credit. Facilities produced by competing banks are called, variously, revolving underwriting facilities (RUFs), note purchase facilities and Euronote facilities.

O

Off-balance sheet (OBS) activities Banks' business, often fee-based, that does not generally involve booking assets and taking deposits. Examples are swaps, options, foreign exchange futures, standby commitments and letters of credit.

Off-balance sheet (OBS) management Refers to those activities banks should carry out to control and limit their exposure derived from off-balance sheet transactions.

Off-balance sheet (OBS) risk Relates to the risks incurred by a bank in dealing with non-traditional banking activities such as financial derivative products (e.g., futures and options), guarantees and letters of credit.

Office of the Comptroller of the Currency (OCC) The OCC is an independent bureau of the US Department of the Treasury, set up in 1863 to regulate all banks chartered by the Federal Reserve government.

Offshore banking Banking activity undertaken by institutions that are located outside the country of residence of the customer, typically in a low-tax jurisdiction (e.g., Bahamas and Bermudas) and that provide financial and legal advantages.

Open market operations (OMOs) These operations are the most important tools by which central banks can influence interest rates and therefore the amount of money in the economy. The principle is that the central bank will influence the level of liquidity and the level and structure of interest rates within the financial system by purchasing or selling government debt to the non-bank private sector.

Operating risk Relates to the possibility that operating expenses might vary significantly from what is expected, producing a decrease in income and bank's value.

Operational risk Is the risk associated with the possible failure of a bank's systems, controls or other management failure (including human error).

Option The contractual right, but not the obligation, to buy or sell a specific amount of a given financial instrument at a previously fixed price or a price fixed at a designated future date. A traded option refers to a specific option traded on official markets. A call option confers on the holder the right to buy the financial instrument. A put option involves the right to sell.

Ordinary shares (see equity) Security representing the claim to the residual ownership of a company. Known as common stock in the US.

Over-the-counter (OTC) An informal dealer-based market.

Own Funds Directive EC directive adopted by Council of Ministers in April 1989. The aim was to harmonise the definition of capital for all EU credit institutions in line with the 1988 Basle I recommendations.

Ownership advantage In international banking, one of the theories for explaining overseas expansion is based on the idea that banks expand overseas to enjoy direct benefits derived from their technological expertise, marketing know-how, production efficiency, managerial expertise, innovative product capability and so on.

P

Payment system Any organised arrangement for transferring value between its participants.

Pension services Pension services offered via banks are known as private pensions. These are distinguished from public pensions that are offered by the state. Contributions paid into the pension fund are invested in long-term investments with the individual making contributions receiving a pension on retirement (a retirement income is generated by the purchase of annuities).

Plastic cards Include credit cards, debit cards, cheque guarantee cards, store cards, travel and entertainment cards and 'smart' or 'chip' cards.

Portfolio risk Is the risk that a particular combination of projects, assets, units or else in the portfolio will fail to meet the overall objectives of the portfolio due to a poor balance of risks. In the case of a bank loan portfolio, for example, it is the risk that the initial choice of lending opportunities will prove to be poor, in that some of the alternative opportunities that were rejected will turn out to yield higher returns than those selected.

Preference shares (see equity) Shares which pay a fixed dividend and rank prior to ordinary shares in liquidation. Known as preferred stock in the US.

Price elasticity of demand A measure of the degree of responsiveness of demand to a given change in price.

Price stability A situation of stability in the level of prices of goods and services that protects the purchasing power of money.

Prices and incomes policy One type of economic policy of a government intended to influence the inflation rate by means of either statutory or voluntary restrictions upon increases in wages, dividends and/or prices. Widely used in the United Kingdom during the 1960s.

Primary market Market in which securities are traded between issuers and investors, thereby raising additional funds for the issuing firm.

Prime rate One of several base interest rates used as an index to price commercial loans.

Principal–agent problems An economic theory concerning the relationship between a principal (for example, a shareholder) and an agent of the principal (for example, a company manager). It involves the costs of resolving conflicts of interest between the principals and agents (agency costs).

Private banking Specialist banking, investment, estate planning and tax services provided to wealthy (high net worth) personal customers.

Private deposit-taking financial institutions Privately owned financial intermediaries funded mainly by deposits from the public. The distinction between private and public deposit-making institutions is usually made when one describes a banking system that has both private and government owned banks, such as in Japan.

Private equity finance A type of service offered to firms that need to raise finance and that can be distinguished according to two main types: formal and informal. Formal equity finance is available from various sources including banks, special investment schemes, and private equity and venture capital firms. The informal market refers to private financing by so-called business angels – wealthy individuals that invest in small unquoted companies. Private equity finance can refer to both large and small equity stakes.

Private non-deposit-taking financial institutions Privately owned financial intermediaries that do not take deposits, including a wide variety of securities, insurance and other firms.

Privatisation process The process of conversion from a government-controlled company to a public limited company often through a sale or flotation on the stock market.

Process of deconstruction The process of deconstruction generally refers to the separation of banks' lending function into different component parts (i.e. origination, funding, servicing and monitoring) that can be provided by different financial institutions.

Product (production) diffusion This relates to the pattern of customer or firm adoption of a new product, service or production process. For example, if a new mortgage product is offered by a bank and then all other banks start offering a similar product in a short period of time then this product can be said to have fast diffusion among banks. Diffusion simply refers to the rate of take-up by potential users of the new product, process or service.

Product lifecycle The stages of development that new products go through from introduction to decline.

Profit and loss account (income statement) A document that reports data on costs and revenues and measures bank performance for a given financial year.

Profit margin A common measure of profitability that is equal to earnings before income taxes to total operating income and takes into account both interest and non-interest income.

Profits Revenues minus costs.

Prudential regulation Regulations governing the supervision of the banking system, e.g., licensing criteria, capital adequacy requirements, etc.

R

Rate-sensitive assets and liabilities Assets and liabilities that can be re-priced within a certain time period (e.g., 90 days); therefore the cash flows associated with rate-sensitive contracts vary with changes in interest rates.

Recapitalisation Term used to refer to a change in the way a firm is financed resulting from an injection of capital.

Refinancing risk It is the risk that the cost of rolling over or re-borrowing funds will rise above the returns being earned on asset investments.

Regional banks In Japan, banks with a regional focus specialised on retail and SMEs (small and medium-sized enterprises).

Regulation Refers to the setting of specific rules of behaviour that firms have to abide by – these may be set through legislation (laws) or be stipulated by the relevant regulatory agency (for instance, the Financial Services Authority in the United Kingdom). See also re-regulation.

Regulatory risk Is the risk associated with a change in regulatory policy. For example, banks may be subject to certain new risks if deregulation takes place and barriers to lending or to the entry of new firms are lifted.

Reinvestment risk The risk that the returns on funds to be reinvested will fall below the cost of funds.

Remote payments These are payment instruments that allow remote access to a customer's account.

Repos (repurchase agreements) Securities that can be sold for a finite period, but with a commitment to repurchase usually at an agreed price and at a stated time.

Representative office Representative offices can be set up by banks in risky markets abroad as the cost of running such small offices is negligible and they can easily be closed if commercial prospects are not good.

Reputation risk The risk that strategic management's mistakes may have consequences for the reputation of a bank. It is also the risk that negative publicity, either true or untrue, adversely affects a bank's customer base or brings forth costly litigation thereby affecting profitability.

Re-regulation This term describes the process of implementing new rules, restrictions and controls in response to market participants' efforts to circumvent existing regulations.

Reserve requirement The proportion of a commercial bank's total assets which it keeps in the form of liquid assets so as to comply with regulatory reserve requirements.

Resolved Bank A bank that, as a result of a crisis, has been acquired by the authorities ('intervened') and eventually is either liquidated, taken over, recapitalised or other.

Retail or personal banking Banking services provided to the household (consumer) sector.

Return-on-assets (ROA) A common measure of bank profitability that is equal to net income/total assets.

Return-on-equity (ROE) A common measure of bank profitability that is equal to net income/total equity.

Revenues The revenues, generated by the assets of a bank include: interest earned on loans and investments; fees and commissions (interest and non-interest revenue) and other revenues (e.g., from the sale of businesses).

Revolving lines of credit A commitment by a bank to lend to a customer under pre-defined terms. The commitments generally contain covenants allowing the bank to refuse to lend if there has been a material adverse change in the borrower's financial condition.

Revolving underwriting facilities (RUFs) Similar to a NIF but differs from it because issuers are guaranteed the funds by an underwriting group which buys the notes at a minimum price.

Risk-Adjusted-Return on Capital A risk-adjusted profitability measurement and management framework for measuring risk-adjusted financial performance and for providing a consistent view of profitability across businesses.

Risk–asset ratio A ratio that sets out to appraise a bank's capital adequacy on the basis of a bank's relative riskiness.

Risk management Risk management is a complex and comprehensive process, which includes creating an appropriate environment, maintaining an efficient risk measurement structure, monitoring and mitigating risk-taking activities and establishing an adequate framework of internal controls.

Risk measurement The process of quantification of risk exposure.

S

Savings and Loans Association (S&L) The most important type of savings institutions in the United States; also known as thrifts.

Savings bank A financial institution whose primary function is to offer savings facilities to retail customers. Traditionally savings banks were mutual institutions (like building societies in the United Kingdom and thrifts in the United States), i.e., they were established and controlled by groups of people for their own benefit. Today savings banks' business has become more diversified and many have become listed.

Screening The action undertaken by the less informed party to determine the information possessed by the informed party. For example the action taken by a bank before giving a loan to gather information about the creditworthiness of a potential borrower.

Second Banking Co-ordination Directive (2 BCD) A milestone in the harmonisation of EU banking laws, the 1989 Second Banking Co-ordination Directive established EU-wide recognition of single banking 'passports' issued in any Member State as well as the principle of home-country supervision with minimum standards (including capital) at the EU level. In addition the directive allowed banks to operate as universal banks.

Secondary market A market in which previously issued securities are traded.

Securities house A non-bank organisation that specialises in brokerage and dealing activities in securities.

Securities underwriting The procedure under which investment banks provide a guarantee to a company that an issue of shares (or other capital market instruments) will raise a specific amount of cash. Investment banks will agree to subscribe to any of the issue not taken up in the issue.

Securitisation The term is most often used narrowly to mean the process by which traditional bank assets, mainly loans or mortgages, are converted into negotiable securities which may be purchased either by depository institutions or by non-bank investors. More broadly, the term refers to the development of markets for a variety of new negotiable instruments, such as FRNs in the international markets and commercial paper in the United States, which replace bank loans as a means of borrowing. Used in the latter sense, the term often suggests disintermediation of the banking system, as investors and borrowers bypass banks and transact business directly.

Settlement or payment risk A risk typical of the interbank market; it refers to the situation where one party to a contract fails to pay money or deliver assets to another party at the time of settlement.

Shareholder value This refers both to the value of the firm to shareholders and to the management principle of maximising the worth of a corporation to shareholders. A bank can create shareholder value by pursuing a strategy that maximises the return on capital invested relative to the (opportunity) cost of capital (the cost of keeping equity shareholders and bondholders happy).

Signalling In an adverse selection problem, the term refers to actions of the 'informed party' and can imply, for instance, the offer of a warranty or guarantee.

Single EU passport Also known as the 'Single European Banking Licence', it ensures that EU-incorporated banks which are authorised within their own country's regulations (e.g., UK banks authorised by the Financial Services Authority) are automatically recognised as banks in any part of the European Union by virtue of their home country recognition.

Single market A single market represents the creation of one area with common policies and regulations in which there is free movement of goods, persons, services and capital.

Small and medium-sized enterprises (SMEs) In the EU SMEs are defined as companies with less than 250 employees and either an annual turnover not exceeding €50 million or a total balance sheet not exceeding €43 million. The term is also widely used to refer to small businesses in general.

Solvency The ability of an institution to repay obligations ultimately.

Solvency Ratio Directive EC directive agreed in July 1989. The aim was to harmonise the solvency ratios (capital adequacy ratios) for credit institutions (in line with Basle I 1988 proposals).

Sovereign risk Relates to the risk associated with a government default on bond or loan repayments.

Specialist banking Refers to banks specialised in the supply of specific products and services as opposed to universal banking.

Standardised products The final stage of the product lifecycle where the product is uniform and undifferentiated and competition between producers is based solely on price.

Standby letter of credit Similar to the commercial L/C. The standby L/C is issued by the importer's bank and obligates that bank to compensate the exporter in the event of a performance failure. The importer will pay a fee for this service and will be liable to its bank for any payments made by the bank under the standby L/C.

Standing orders These are instructions from the customer (account holder) to the bank to pay a fixed amount at regular intervals into the account of another individual or company.

Sterling commercial paper A collective name for sterling-denominated short-term unsecured notes issued by corporate borrowers. The majority are issued at maturities between 15 and 45 days.

Stockbrokers See brokers.

Structural deregulation This term refers to the opening up, or liberalisation, of financial markets to allow institutions to compete more freely. Specifically, this process encompasses structure and conduct rules deregulation (such as the removal of branch restrictions and credit ceilings, respectively) and not prudential rules.

Subsidiaries In international banking a subsidiary is a separate legal entity from the parent bank that has its own capital and is organised and regulated according to the laws of the host country.

Supervision A term used to refer to the general oversight of the behaviour of financial firms.

Supervisory re-regulation Defined as the process of implementing new rules, restrictions and controls in response to market participant's efforts to circumvent existing regulations (e.g., bank capital adequacy rules).

Surplus units Term used to denote the ultimate lender in a financial transaction.

Swap A financial transaction in which two bodies agree to exchange streams of payment over time according to a predetermined rule. A swap is normally used to transform interest rate or foreign exchange cash flows from one form into another. Fixed interest cash flows may be swapped for variable cash flows, or/and different currencies can be swapped. (See currency swaps and interest rate swaps).

Syndicated loans Syndicated loans are a special category of loans in which an arranger bank, or group of arrangers, forms a group of creditors on the basis of a mandate to finance the company (or government) borrower.

Systematic credit risk Is the risk associated with the possibility that default of all firms may increase over a given time period because of economic changes or other events that impact large sections of the economy.

Systemic risk The risk faced by a financial system, resulting from a systemic crisis where the failure of one institution has repercussions on others, thereby threatening the stability of financial markets.

T

Technology Term used to indicate the use of modern machines and systems, e.g., computers, internet, electronics, circuits, and so on.

Technology risk This occurs when technological investments do not produce the anticipated cost savings in the form of either economies of scale or scope; it also refers to the risk of current systems becoming inefficient because of the developments of new systems.

Thrifts See Savings and Loans Associations.

Too big to fail (TBTF) The cases of TBTF, as well as 'too important to fail', are examples of moral hazard caused by the government safety net. Because the failure of a large (or strategically important) bank poses significant risks to other financial institutions and to the financial system as a whole, policymakers may respond by protecting bank creditors from all or some of the losses they otherwise would face.

Trade-off between safety and returns to shareholders This is the trade off between total capital and ROE.

Traditional banking As opposed to modern banking, traditional banking refers to mainstream deposit and lending activity.

Traditional foreign banking In international banking, this involves transactions with non-residents in domestic currency that facilitates trade finance and other international transactions.

Transactions costs Refer to the costs associated with the buying and selling of a financial instrument (e.g., cost of searching, cost of writing contracts).

Transition economies A term used to describe former communist countries that have been transforming their planned economies to market economies.

Treasury bill (or T-bill) A financial security issued through the discount market by the government as a means of borrowing money for short periods of time (usually 3 months).

Trust banks In Japan, banks that perform commercial banking activity but their main function is asset management for retail and other customers.

U

Underwriting See securities underwriting.

Unit trust A UK institution that manages collectively funds obtained from different investors (see Mutual funds)

Universal bank An institution which combines its strictly commercial activities with operations in market segments traditionally covered by investment banks, securities houses and insurance firms and this includes such business as portfolio management, brokerage of securities, underwriting, mergers and acquisitions. A universal bank undertakes the whole range of banking activities.

Universal banking Under the universal banking model, banking business is broadly defined to include all aspects of financial service activity – including securities operations, insurance, pensions, leasing and so on.

Unlisted securities market Market for dealing in company stocks and shares that have not obtained a full stock exchange quotation.

Unsystematic credit risk Also known as firm-specific credit risk, this is derived from 'micro' factors and thus is the credit risk specific to the holding of loans or bonds of a particular firm.

V

VaR (Value at Risk) VaR is a technique that uses statistical analysis of historical market trends and volatilities to estimate the likely or expected maximum loss on a bank's portfolio or line of business over a set time period, with a given probability. The aim is to get one figure that summarises the maximum loss faced by the bank within a statistical confidence interval.

Venture capital Share capital or loans subscribed to a firm by financial specialists when these companies are considered to be high risk and would not normally attract conventional finance.

Vertical FDI A type of FDI that describes overseas investment as a consequence of differences in international factor prices (e.g., wages, raw materials).

Visegrad countries These are the following four central European states: Czech Republic, Hungary, Poland and Slovakia.

W

Wholesale banking The borrowing and lending of large amounts of money usually between banks or other financial organisations, through the interbank market.

Z

Zengin Data Telecommunication System (Zengin System) The main retail payments system in Japan that clears retail credit transfers.

References and further reading

Adalbert Winker, A., Mazzaferro, F., Nerlich, C. and Thimann, C. (2004) *Official Dollarisation/Euroisation: Motives, Features And Policy Implications Of Current Cases*, ECB Occasional Papers Series, No. 11.

Akerlof, G.A. (1970) 'The market for "Lemons": Quality uncertainty and the market Mechanism', *Quarterly Journal of Economics*, **84** (8), 488–500.

Alfon, I. and Andrews, P. (1999) 'Cost–benefit analysis in financial regulation – how to do it and how it adds value', *FSA Occasional Paper Series*, **3**, http://www.fsa.gov.uk/pubs/occpapers/OP03.pdf.

Altunbas, Y., Evans, L. and Molyneux, P. (2001) 'Ownership and efficiency in banking', *Journal of Money, Credit and Banking*, **33** (4), 926–54.

Association of British Insurers (2003) *Overview of the EU Insurance Market.* Annex to CEA Report on European Prudential Regulation and Supervisory Structure. http://www.cea.assur.org/cea/download/publ/article194.pdf.

Bank for International Settlements (2001) *The Banking Industry in the Emerging Market Economies: Competition, Consolidation and Systemic Stability: An Overview*, BIS Paper No. 4, http://www.bis.org/publ/bispap04.htm.

Bank for International Settlements (2004a) 'Statistics on payment and settlement systems in selected countries', *Committee on Payment and Settlement Systems Publication*, No. 60, Basle: BIS, http://www.bis.org/publ/cpss60.htm.

Bank for International Settlements (2004b) *74th Annual Report (1 April 2003–31 March 2004)*, Basle: BIS, http://www.bis.org/publ/ar2004e.htm.

Bank for International Settlements (2005) 'Triennial Central Bank Survey – Foreign exchange and derivatives market activity in 2004' Basle: BIS, *Regular Publication*, http://www.bis.org/publ/rpfx05.htm.

Bank of England (1999) *Fact Sheet: Monetary Policy in the United Kingdom*, March.

Bank of England (2001) *Finance for Small Firms – An Eighth Report.* March, http://www.bankofengland.co.uk/publications/financeforsmallfirms/fin4sm09.pdf.

Bank of England (2004) *Annual Report.* Main publications, http://www.bankofengland.co.uk/publications/annualreport/2004report.pdf.

Bank of England (2005a) '*Inflation Targeting in Practice: Models, Forecasts and Hunches*', speech by Rachel Lomax, Deputy Governor of The Bank of England given to the 59th International Atlantic Economic Conference in London on 12 March 2005, http://www.bankofengland.co.uk/publications/speeches/2005/speech242.pdf.

Bank of England (2005b) *Payment Systems Oversight Report 2004*, No. 1, January, http://www.bankofengland.co.uk/publications/psor/.

Bank of Japan (2005a) *Statistics on Financial Institutions*, http://www.boj.or.jp/en/stat/stat_f.htm.

Bank of Japan (2005b) *Japan's Financial Structure since the 1980s – in View of the Flow of Funds Accounts*, Research and Statistics Department, www.boj.or.jp/en/ronbun/05/data/ron0503a.pdf.

Bank of Japan (2005c) *Payment System in Japan*, http://www.boj.or.jp/en/set/02/data/set0207a.pdf.

Bankscope (2005) Bureau van Dijk Electronic Publishing.

Barclays (2004) *Annual Report*, http://www.investor.barclays.co.uk/results/2004results/annual–report/website/dowwards/index.htm.

Barth, J.R., Caprio, G. and Levine, R.E. (2001) 'Bank regulation and supervision: What works best?' *World Bank Policy Research Working Paper*, No. 2725, http://www.nber.org/papers/w9323.pdf.

Barth, J.R., Caprio, G. and Nolle, D.E. (2004) 'Comparative international characteristics of banking', *Economic and Policy Analysis Working Paper*, 2004–01, Washington DC: Office of the Comptroller of the Currency.

Basle Committee on Banking Supervision (1993) 'The supervisory treatment of market risks', April, http://www.bis.org/publ/bcbs11a.pdf.

Basle Committee on Banking Supervision (1996) 'Amendment to the capital accord to incorporate market risks', January, http://www.bis.org/publ/bcbs24.pdf.

Basle Committee on Banking Supervision (1997a) 'Core principles for effective banking supervision', September, http://www.bis.org/publ/bcbs30a.pdf.

Basle Committee on Banking Supervision (1997b) 'Principles for the management of interest rate risk', September, http://www.bis.org/publ/bcbs29a.pdf.

Basle Committee on Banking Supervision (1998) 'Framework for internal control systems in banking organisations', September, http://www.bis.org/publ/bcbs40.pdf.

Basle Committee on Banking Supervision (1999) 'Enhancing corporate governance for banking organisations', September, http://www.bis.org/publ/bcbs56.pdf.

Basle Committee on Banking Supervision (2000) 'Principles for the management of credit risk', September, http://www.bis.org/publ/bcbs75.pdf.

Basle Committee on Banking Supervision (2001a) 'Overview on the new Basle Capital Accord', *Consultative Document*, http://www.bis.org/publ/bcbsca02.pdf.

Basle Committee on Banking Supervision (2001b) 'Consultative document. Operational risk', Supporting document to the New Basle Capital Accord, January, http://www.bis.org/publ/bcbsca07.pdf.

Basle Committee on Banking Supervision (2001c) 'Customer due diligence for banks', October, http://www.bis.org/publ/bcbs85.pdf.

Basle Committee on Banking Supervision (2002) 'Internal audit in banks and the supervisor's relationship with auditors: A survey', August, http://www.bis.org/publ/bcbs92.pdf.

Basle Committee on Banking Supervision (2003a) 'Sound practices for the management and supervision of operational risk', February, http://www.bis.org/publ/bcbs96.pdf.

Basle Committee on Banking Supervision (2003b) 'Risk management principles for electronic banking', July, http://www.bis.org/publ/bcbs98.pdf.

Basle Committee on Banking Supervision (2004a) 'International convergence of capital measurement and capital standards – A revised framework', June, http://www.bis.org/publ/bcbs107.pdf.

Basle Committee on Banking Supervision (2004b) 'Principles for the management and supervision of interest rate risk', July, http://www.bis.org/publ/bcbs108.pdf.

Basle Committee on Banking Supervision (2004c) 'Consolidated KYC (know-your-customer) risk management', October, http://www.bis.org/publ/bcbs110.pdf.

Basle Committee on Banking Supervision (2005) 'Compliance and the compliance function of banks', April, http://www.bis.org/publ/bcbs113.pdf.

Batchelor, C. (2004) 'Securitisation Survey', *Financial Times*, 29 November.

Beck, T., Demirgüç-Kunt, A. and Levine, R. (2003) 'Bank concentration and crises', *World Bank Policy Research Working Paper*, No. 3041. http://www.worldbank.org/servlet/WDSContentServer/WDSP/IB/2003/05/23/000094946_03051404103446/Rendered/PDF/multipage.pdf.

Benston, G.J. and Kaufman, G.G. (1996) 'The appropriate role of bank regulation', *Economic Journal*, **106**, 688–97.

Berger, A.N. and Humphrey, D.B. (1997) 'Efficiency of financial institutions: International survey and directions for future research', *European Journal of Operational Research*, **98**, 175–212.

Berger, A.N., Dai, Q., Ongena, S. and Smith, D.C. (2003) 'To what extent will the banking industry be globalized? A study of bank nationality and reach in 20 European nations', *Journal of Banking & Finance*, **27**(3), 383–415.

Bessis, J. (2002) *Risk Management in Banking*. Chichester: John Wiley.

Boot, A.W.A. (2000) 'Relationship banking: What do we know?' *Journal of Financial Intermediation*, **9** (1), 7–25.

Boot, A.W.A. and Thakor, A.V. (2000) 'Can relationship banking survive competition?' *Journal of Finance*, **55** (2), April, 679–713.

Borio, C. and Packer, F. (2004) 'Assessing new perspectives on country risk', *BIS Quarterly Review*, http://www.bis.org/publ/qtrpdf/r_qt0412e.pdf.

Bowen, A., Hoggarth, G. and Pain, D. (1999) 'The recent evolution of the U.K. banking industry and some implications for financial stability', in *The Monetary and Regulatory Implications of Changes in the Banking Industry*. Basle: Bank for International Settlements, *BIS Conference Papers*, 7, 251–94.

British Bankers Association (1996) 'Banking Business' *An Abstract of Banking Statistics*, **13**.

British Bankers Association (1999) 'Banking Business', *An Abstract of Banking Statistics*, **16**.

British Bankers Association (2005) 'Banking Business', *An Abstract of Banking Statistics*, **22**.

Buckle, M. and Thomson, J. (2004) *The UK Financial System: Theory and Practice*, 4th edn. Manchester: Manchester University Press.

Cameron, D. (2004) 'European Banking Survey 2004', *Financial Times*, 8 October.

CapGemini Merrill Lynch (2005) *World Wealth Report*. New York: Merrill Lynch, Pierce, Fanner & Smith Incorporated, http://www.merrilllynch.com/media/48237.pdf.

Cárdenas, J., Graf, J.P. and O'Dogherty, P. (2003) 'Foreign banks entry in emerging market economies: a host country perspective', Banco de México paper, in Bank for International Settlement, GCFS Publications, *Foreign Direct Investment in the Financial Sector of Emerging Market Economies*, http://www.bis.org/publ/cgfs22mexico.pdf.

Casu, B. and Girardone, C. (2004) 'Financial conglomeration: Efficiency, productivity and strategic drive' *Applied Financial Economics*, **14**, 687–96.

Casu, B. and Molyneux, P. (2003) 'A comparative study of efficiency in European banking', *Applied Economics*, **35** (17), 1865–76.

Casu, B., Molyneux, P. and Girardone, C. (2004) 'Productivity in European banking: a comparison of parameric and non-parametric approaches', *Journal of Banking and Finance*, **28** (10), 2521–40.

Cecchini, P. (1988) *The European Challenge: 1992. The Benefits of a Single Market.* Adelshot: Wilwood House.

City of London Corporation (2005) *The City's Importance to the EU Economy 2005*, City of London Corporation, February.

Coase, R. (1937) 'The Nature of the Firm' *Economica*, **4**, 386–405.

Comité Européen des Assurances (2003) 'Annex to Project D Report: Overview of the EU Insurance Market', Brussels, 14 November.

Competition Commission Report (2002) 'The supply of banking services by clearing banks to small and medium-sized enterprises: A report on the supply of banking services by clearing banks to small and medium-sized enterprises within the UK', vols 1–4. Available at http://www.competition-commission. org.uk/rep_pub/reports/2002/462banks.htm full.

Coppel, J. and Davies, M. (2003) *Foreign Participation in East Asia's Banking Sector*, Reserve Bank of Australia paper, in Bank for International Settlement, GCFS Publications *Foreign Direct Investment in the Financial Sector of Emerging Market Economies*, http://www.bis.org/publ/cgfs22rba.pdf.

Credit Suisse First Boston (1997) *Credit Risk+ A Credit Management Framework*, Copyright ©1997, Credit Suisse First Boston International.

Croft, J. (2004) 'European Banking Survey 2004', *Financial Times*, 8 October.

Cruikshank, D. (2000) *Competition in UK Banking: A Report to the Chancellor of the Exchequer*, London: HMSO.

Cumming, C. and Hirtle, B.J. (2001) 'The challenges of risk management in diversified financial companies' *Economic Policy Review*, Federal Reserve Bank of New York, **7**, 1–17.

Cybo-Ottone, A. and Murgia, M. (2000) 'Mergers and shareholder wealth in European banking', *Journal of Banking and Finance*, **24** (6), 831–58.

Danielsson, J. (2000) 'VaR: A castle built on sand', *Financial Regulator*, **5** (2), 46–50.

Danielsson, J. (2002) 'The emperor has no clothes: Limits to risk modelling', Journal of Banking and Finance, **26** (7), 1273–96.

de Haas, R.T.A. and van Lelyveld, I.P.P. (2003) *Foreign Bank Penetration and Private Sector Credit in Central and Eastern Europe*, DNB Staff Reports 91, Amsterdam: Netherlands Central Bank.

Department of Trade and Industry (2003) White Paper 'Fair, Clean and Competitive: The Consumer Credit Market in the Twenty-first Century'. Available at http://www.dti.gov.uk/ccp/topics1/pdf1/creditwp.pdf.

Dermine, J. (2000) 'Bank mergers in Europe: The public policy issues', *Journal of Common Market Studies*, **38** (3), 409–25.

Dermine, J. (2002) 'European banking: Past present and future', *Second ECB Central Banking Conference*, http://www.ecb.int/home/conf/cbc2/dermine_comp.pdf.

Detragiache, E. and Gupta, P. (2004) *Foreign Banks in Emerging Market Crises: Evidence from Malaysia*, IMF Working Paper No. 04/129, www.imf.org/external/pubs/ft/wp/ 2004/wp04129.pdf.

Diamond, D.W. (1984) 'Financial intermediation and delegated monitoring', *Review of Economics Studies*, **51** (3), 393–414.

Diamond, D.W. and Dybvig, P.H. (1983) 'Bank runs, deposit insurance, and liquidity', *Journal of Political Economy*, **91** (3), 401–19.

Dixon, R. (1993) *Banking in Europe*. London: Routledge.

Dowd, K. (1996a) *Competition and Finance: A New Interpretation of Financial and Monetary Economics*. London: Macmillan.

Dowd, K. (1996b) *Laissez-Faire Banking*. London: Routledge.

Down, S.C. (1996) 'Why the banking system should be regulated', *Economic Journal*, **106**, 698–707.

The Economist (2003) 'Banking in China: strings attached', 6 March.

The Economist (2004a) 'Bothersome Basle', 15 April.

The Economist (2004b) 'Skimming off the cream', 22 January, pp. 65–6.

EU Second Banking Directive (1989) relating to the taking up and pursuit of the business of credit institutions in its consolidated version (including amendment 2002/87), http://www.fese.be/statistics/european_directives/dir_2000_12.pdf.

Euromoney (2005) *Private Banking Survey – UBS Tops Private Banking Poll*, January, 72–122.

European Central Bank (1999) *The Effects of Technology on the EU Banking Systems*, Report, July, http://www.ecb.int/pub/pdf/other/techbnken.pdf.

European Central Bank (2000) *Mergers and Acquisitions Involving the EU Banking Industry*, Press release, December, http://www.ecb.int/press/pr/date/2000/html/pr001220.en.html.

European Central Bank (2001) *Constitution of the ESCB History – Three Stages Towards EMU*, http://www.ecb.int/about/emu.htm.

European Central Bank (2002) *Structural Analysis of the EU Banking Sector*. Report, November, http://www.ecb.int/pub/pdf/other/eubksectorstructure2003en.pdf.

European Central Bank (2003) *EU Banking Sector Stability*. Press release, Frankfurt, November, http://www.ecb.int/press/pr/date/2003/html/pr031119.en.html.

European Central Bank (2004a) *Payment and Securities Settlement Systems in the EU*. Blue Book, April, http://www.ecb.int/pub/pdf/other/addenden.pdf.

European Central Bank (2004b) *EU Banking Sector Stability*, November, http://www.ecb.int/pub/pdf/other/eubankingsectorstability2004en.pdf.

European Central Bank (2004c) *Report on EU Banking Structure*, http:www.ecb.int/pub/ pdf/other/reportoneubankingstructure112004en.pdf.

European Central Bank (2004d) *Financial FDI to the EU Accession Countries*, http://www.bis.org/publ/cgfs22ecb.pdf.

European Central Bank (2005a) Press release, 21 March, http://www.ecb.int/press/pr/date/2005/html/pr050321.en.html.

European Central Bank (2005b) *Monthly Bulletin*, May, http://www.ecb.int/pub/mb/html/index.en.html.

European Central Bank (2005c) *Analysing Banking Sector Conditions: How to Use Macro-Prudential Indicators*, Occasional Paper No. 26, April.

European Central Bank (2005d) *Banking Structures in the New EU Member States*, January, http://www.ecb.int/pub/pdf/other/bankingstructuresnewmember statesen.pdf.

European Commission (1997) *Impact on Services, Credit Institutions and Banking, The Single Market Review*, Subseries II, vol. 4, Luxembourg: Office for the Official Publication of the European Communities/Kogan Page, Earthscan.

European Securitisation Forum (1999) *European Securitisation: A Resource Guide*. New York, http://www.europeansecuritisation.com/pubs/ESFGuide.pdf.

Federal Deposit Insurance Corporation (2005) *FDIC Outlook: The Globalisation of the US Banking Industry*, http://www.fdic.gov/bank/analytical/regional/ro20052q/na/2005summer_03.html.

Federal Reserve System (2004) *The 2004 Federal Reserve Payments Study. Analysis of Non-cash Payments Trends in the United States: 2000–2003*, http://www.frbservices.org/Retail/pdf/2004PaymentResearchReport.pdf.

Federal Reserve System (2005a) *Purpose and Functions*. Board of Governors of the Federal Reserve System, http://www.federalreserve.gov/pf/pf.htm.

Federal Reserve System (2005b) 'Trends in the use of payment instruments in the United States', *Federal Reserve Bulletin*, www.federalreserve.gov/pubs/bulletin/2005/spring05_payment.pdf.

Federal Reserve System (2005c) Profits and Balance Sheet Developments at US Commercial Banks in 2004, *Federal Reserve Bulletin*, Spring, http://www.ecb.int/pub/pdf/pdf/scpops/ecbocp26.pdf.

Ferguson, C. and McKillop, D. (1997) *The Strategic Development of Credit Unions*. Chichester: John Wiley & Sons.

Financial Services Authority (2004) *Building Society Statistics* http://www.fsa.gov.uk/pages/library/cooperate/annual/ar03_04_bs_statistics.html.

Focarelli, D. and Pozzolo, A.F. (2000) 'The determinants of cross-border bank share-holdings: an analysis with bank-level data from OECD countries', *Proceedings*, Federal Reserve Bank of Chicago, May, 199–232.

Frame, W.S. and White, L.J. (2002) *Empirical Studies of Financial Innovation: Lots of talk, Little Action?*, Federal Reserve Bank of Atlanta, Working Paper No. 12, http://www.frbatlanta.org/filelegacydocs/wp0212.pdf.

Freixas, X. and Rochet, J.C. (1997) *The Microeconomics of Banking*. Cambridge, MA: MIT Press.

Genetay, N. and Molyneux, P. (1998) *Bancassurance*. London: Macmillan.

Gil Diaz, F. (1998) 'The origins of Mexico's financial crisis', *Cato Journal*, **17** (3), http://www.cato.org/pubs/journal/g17n3_14.html.

Girardone, C., Molyneux, P. and Gardener, E.P.M. (2004) 'Analysing the determinants of bank efficiency: the case of Italian banks,' *Applied Economics*, **36**, 215–27.

Goldman Sachs (2004), Annual Report, http://www.gs.com/our_firm/investor_relations/financial_reports/articles/annual_reports_articles_050210142939.hmtl.

Goldman Sachs and McKinsey (2001) *The Future of Corporate Banking in Europe*, January, 2001. McKinsey: Frankfurt.

Goodhart, C.A.E. (1989) 'Why do banks need a central bank', ch. 8, pp. 176–93, in *Money, Information and Uncertainty*, 2nd edn. London: Macmillan.

Goodhart, C.A.E., Hartmann P., Llewellyn, D., Rojas-Suarez, L. and Weisbrod, S. (1998) *Financial Regulation. Why, How and Where Now?* London: Routledge.

Gramm-Leach-Bliley (GLB) Act in November 1999, http://banking.senate.gov/conf/.

Gray, S., Hoggarth, G. and Place, J. (2002) 'Introduction to monetary operations', *Handbooks in Central Banking*, No. 10, Centre for Central Banking Studies, Bank of England, http://www.bankofengland.co.uk/ccbs/publication/ ccbshb10 revised.pdf.

Greenbaum, S.I. and Thakor, A.V. (1995) *Contemporary Financial Intermediation*. Orlando, FL: Dryden Press.

Hardin, A. and Holmes, L. (1997) *Services Trade and Foreign Direct Investment*, Australian Industry Commission Staff Research Paper, Canberra.

Hasan, I. and Marton, K. (2003) 'Development and efficiency of the banking sector in a transitional economy: Hungarian experience', *Journal of Banking and Finance*, **27** (12), 2249–71.

Hawkins, J. and Turner, P. (1999) *Bank Restructuring in Practice: An Overview*, Bank for International Settlements Policy Papers, No. 6, August 1999.

Heffernan, S. (2005) *Modern Banking*, Chichester: John Wiley.

Heinemann, F. and Jopp, M. (2002) The Benefits of a Working European Retail Market for Financial Services, *Report to the European Financial Services Round Table*, Bonn: Europa Union Verlag.

Hempel, G.H. and Simonson, D.G. (1999) *Bank Management: Text and Cases*, 5th edn. New York: John Wiley.

HM Treasury, the Financial Services Authority and the Bank of England (2003) *The EU Financial Services Action Plan: A Guide*, 31 July 2003, http://www.hm-treasury.gov.uk/documents/financial_services/eu_financial_services/fin_euf_actionplan.cfm.

Ho, C. (2002) *A Survey of the Institutional and Operational Aspects of Modern-day Currency Boards*, BIS Working Papers, No. 110.

Hobson, J. and McCauley, R.N. (2003) 'The future of banking in East Asia', *Ente Luigi Einaudi Quaderni di Ricerche*, No. 59, http://www.enteluigieinaudi.it/pdf/Pubblicazioni/Quaderni/Q_59.pdf.

Hunter, L.W., Bernhardt, A., Hughes, K.L. and Skuratowicz, E. (2000) *It's Not Just the ATMs: Technology, Firm Strategies, Jobs, and Earnings in Retail Banking*. Wharton School Paper, No. 31, http://fic.wharton.upenn.edu/fic/papers/00/0031.pdf.

Ianaba, N. and Kozu, T. (2005) *A Note on the Recent Behaviour of Japanese Banks*, BIS Working Paper, No. 22, April 2005. http://www.bis.org/publ/bppdf/ bispap22f.pdf.

Ibson, D. (2005) 'Japan investment banking survey', *Financial Times*, 24 June.

International Monetary Fund (2003) *Managing Systemic Banking Crises*, IMF Occasional Paper, No. 224.

International Monetary Fund (2004) *The Treatment of Nonperforming Loans in Macroeconomic Statistics*. An issue paper prepared for the December 2004 Meeting of the Advisory Expert Group on National Accounts, http:www.imf.org/external/np/sta/npl/eng/discuss/.

International Monetary Fund (2005), *World Economic Outlook*, http://www.imf.org/external/pubs/ft/weo/2005/02/index.htm.

Iqbal, M. and Molyneux, P. (2005) *Thirty Years of Islamic Banking*. London: Macmillan.

Japanese Bankers Association (2003) *Payment Systems in Japan*, http://www.zenginkyo.or.jp/en/jbank/payment/pdf/paymentsystems2003.pdf.

Jensen, M.C. and Meckling, W.H. (1976) 'Theory of the firm: managerial behaviour, agency costs and ownership structure', *Journal of Financial Economics*, **3**, 303–60.

Johnson, J. (2005) 'Indian banking and finance', *Financial Times*, 27 July.

Jorion, P. (1997) *Value at Risk*, New York: Irwin.

JP Morgan (1997) 'JPM Guide to Credit Derivatives', *Risk Magazine*, March, 44–171.

Kanaya, A. and Woo, D. (2000) *The Japanese Banking Crises of the 1990s: Sources and Lessons*, IMF Working Paper WP/00/7 http://www.imf.org/external/pubs/ft/wp/2000/wp0007.pdf

Karacadag, C. and Taylor, M. (2000) *The New Capital Adequacy Framework – Institutional Constraints and Incentive Structures*, IMF Working Paper WP00/93, International Monetary Fund, http://www.suerf.org/downland/studies/study8.pdf.

Kim, Y. (2002) *Financial Opening under the WTO Agreement in Selected Asian Countries: Progress and Issues*, Asian Development Bank Economic and Research Department Working Paper, No. 24, http://www.adb.org/Documents/ERD/Working_Papers/wp024.pdf.

Klee, E.C. and Natalucci, F.M. (2005) 'Profits and Balance Sheet Developments at U.S. Commercial Banks in 2004', *Federal Reserve Bulletin* (Spring), http://www.federalreserve.gov/pubs/bulletin/2005/spring05_profit.pdf.

Koch, T.W. and MacDonald, S.S. (2000) *Bank Management*, 4th edn. Orlando, FL: Dryden Press.

Lacoste, P. (2004) *International capital flows in Argentina*, BIS Papers No. 23, http://www.bis.org/publ/bppdf/bispap23e.pdf.

Larsen, P.T. (2005) 'Investment banking survey', *Financial Times*, 27 January.

Lehman Brothers (2004), Annual Report, http://www.lehman.com/annual/2004.

Lewis, M.K. and Davis, K.T. (1987) *Domestic Versus International Banking*. London: Philip Allan.

Lintner, J. (1965) 'The valuation of risk assets and selection of risky investments in stock portfolios and capital budgets', *Review of Economics and Statistics*, **47**, 13–37.

Llewellyn, D. (1999) 'The economic rationale for financial regulation', *FSA, Occasional Papers Series*, No.1, http://www.fsa.gov.uk/pubs/occpapers/op01.pdf.

Llewellyn, D.T. (2003) 'Why are British banks so profitable?' Paper presented at the SUERF/Credit Suisse Seminar on 'Profitability of European Banking: The Challenge of Competitive Market Conditions', Zurich, 27 February.

Logan, A. (2004), 'Banking concentration in the UK', *Financial Stability Review*, June 2004.

London Economics (2002) *Quantification of the Macro-economic Impact of Integration of EU Financial Markets*, Report to the European Commission, http://www.europa.eu.int/comm/internal_market/securities/docs/studies/summary_londonecon_en.pdf.

Mahadeva, L. and Sterne, G. (eds) (2000) *Monetary Policy Frameworks in a Global Context*, New York: Routledge.

Markovitz, H. (1952) Portfolio Selection, *Journal of Finance*, **7**, 77–91.

Markovitz, H. (1959) *Portfolio Selection: Efficient Diversification of Investments*. New York: John Wiley.

Martinez Peria, M.S., Powell, A. and Hollar, I.V. (2002) *Banking on Foreigners: The Behaviour of Bank Lending to Latin America, 1985–2000,* Policy Research Working Paper Series No. 2893, http://econ.worldbank.org/files/18857_wps2893.pdf.

Matten, C. (2000) *Managing Bank Capital*. Chichester: John Wiley.

Mattoo, A. (2003) 'Shaping future rules for trade in services', in Ito, T. and Krueger, A.O. (eds) *Trade in Services in the Asia-Pacific Region*. Chicago, IL: University of Chicago Press.

Meckling, W.H. (1976) 'Values and the choice of the model of the individual in the social sciences', *Schweizerische Zeitschrift fur Volkswirtschaft*, **112** (4), 545–65.

Merrill Lynch (2004) *Fact Book and Annual Report,* http://www.ml.com/media/47195.pdf.

Mishkin, F. (2000) 'What should central banks do?', *Federal Reserve Bank of St Louis Review*, http://research.stlouisfed.org/publications/review/00/11/0011fm.pdf.

Molyneux, P. and Shamroukh, N. (1999) *Financial Innovation*. London: John Wiley.

Morgan Stanley (2001) *Private Banking in the 21st Century*, Equity Research Global Industry Report, February, 1–43.

Nenovsky, N.N. and Dimirova, K. (2003) *Deposit Insurance during EU Accession*. William Davidson Institute Working Paper No. 617, Michigan Business School, http://www.bus.umich.edu/KresgeLibrary/Collections/Workingpapers/wdi/wp617.pdf.

OECD Bank Profitability Database (2002) http://iris.sourceoecd.org/vl=4462281/cl=81/nw=1/rpsv/statistic/s2_about.htm?jnlissn=16081064.

Parks, T. (2005) *Medici Money: Banking, Metaphysics, and Art in Fifteenth-Century Florence*. New York: W.W. Norton & Co.

Peterson, J. (2001) 'Basel gives banks whip hand', *Euromoney*, March, 48–53.

Pilloff, S.J. (2004) *Bank Merger Activity in the United States 1994–2003*. Staff Study No. 176, Board of Governors of the Federal Reserve System, May, http://www.federalreserve.gov/pubs/staffstudies/2000-present/ss176.pdf.

Pollard, P.S. (2003) 'A look inside two central banks: The European Central Bank and the Federal Reserve', *Federal Reserve Bank of St Louis Review*, http://research.stlouisfed.org/publications/review/03/01/Pollard.pdf.

Ramos, R. (1999) 'The prize: WTO and the opening of China's banking market to foreign banks', *Goldman Sachs Investment Research*, **14**, December.

Rose, P.S. (2002) *Commercial Bank Management*. New York: McGraw Hill.

Rose, P.S. and Hudgins, S.C. (2002) *Bank Management and Financial Services*. New York: McGraw Hill.

Saunders, A. (2000), *Financial Institutions Management: A Modern Perspective*, 3rd edn. New York: McGraw Hill.

Saunders, A. and Cornett, M.M. (2003) *Financial Institutions Management: A Risk Management Approach*, 4th edn. New York: McGraw Hill/Irwin.

Select Committee on European Union (2003) *Towards a Single Market for Finance: The Financial Services Action Plan*. House of Lords, 45th Report, http://www.parliament.the-stationery-office.co.uk/pa/ld200203/ldselect/ldeucom/192/192.pdf.

Sharpe, W.F. (1964) 'Capital asset prices: A theory of market equilibrium under conditions of risk', *Journal of Finance*, **19**, 425–42.

Sinkey, J.F. Jr (1998) *Commercial Bank Financial Management*, 5th edn. London: Prentice Hall International.

Taleb, N. (1997) *The World According to Nassim Taleb*, Derivatives Strategy, http://www.derivativesstrategy.com.

Treynor, J.L. (1965) 'How to rate management of investment funds', *Harvard Business Review*, **43**, 63–75.

Weill, L. (2003) *Banking Efficiency in Transition Economies*, Economics of Transition, **11** (3), 569–92.

Wells, D. (2005), 'Investment Banking Survey', *Financial Times*, 27 January.

Wighton, D. (2005) 'Investment Banking Survey', *Financial Times*, 27 January.

Wilson, T. (1997a) 'Portfolio credit risk', *Risk Magazine*, September, 111–17.

Wilson, T. (1997b) 'Portfolio credit risk', *Risk Magazine*, October, 56–61.

Winkler, A., Mazzaferro, F., Nerlich, C. and Thimann, C. (2004) 'Official Dollarisation/Euroisation: Motives, Features and Policy Implications of Current Cases', ECB Occasional Papers Series, No. 11, February.

World Bank (2002) Global Economic Prospects and the Developing Countries. http://web.worldbank.org.

Yildirim, S. and Philppatos, G.C. (2002) *Efficiency of Banks: Recent Evidence from the Transitional Economies of Europe 1993–2000*, EFMA 2004 Basle Meetings Paper, http://ssrn.com/abstract=497622.

Web sites

Arab news	http://www.arabnews.com
Bank for International Settlement	http://www.bis.org
Bank of England	http://www.bankofengland.co.uk
Bank of England, Monetary and Financial Statistics Interactive Database (formerly known as 'Statistical Abstract')	http://213.225.136.206/mfsd/iadb/NewIntermed.asp
Bank of Japan	http://www.boj.or.jp
Barclays	http://www.investorrelations.barclays.co.uk
Bloomberg	http://www.bloomberg.com
The Bond Market Association	http://www.investinginbonds.com.
British Bankers' Association	http://www.bba.org.uk
British Venture Capital Association (BVCA)	http://www.bvca.co.uk
Building Societies Association	http://www.bsa.org.uk

Canadian Imperial Bank of Commerce	http://www.cibc.com/ca/ correspondent-banking
Deposit Insurance Corporation	http://www.dic.go.jp
Eur-lex Europe:	http://www.eur-lex.com
Euronext derivatives exchange	http://www.liffe.com *or* http://www.euronext.com
European Central Bank	http://www.ecb.int
European Private Equity and Venture Capital Association	http://www.evca.com
European Securitisation Forum	http://www.europeansecuritisation.com
European Union	http://europa.eu.int/index_en.htm
Federal Deposit Insurance Corporation	http://www.fdic.gov/deposit/index.html
Federal Reserve Bank of Boston	http://www.bos.frb.org
Federal Reserve Bank	http://www.federalreserve.gov
Federal Reserve Discount Window	http://www.frbdiscountwindow.org
Federal Trade Commission	http://www.ftc.gov
Financial Services Agency	http://www.fsa.go.jp
Financial Services Authority	http://www.fsa.gov.uk
Financial Services Compensation Scheme	http://www.fscs.org.uk
Financial Times	http://www.ft.com
Insurance Information Institute	http://www.iii.org
Japan's Financial Services Agency	http://www.fsa.go.jp
Organisation for Economic Co-operation and Development	http://www.oecd.org
UK's Finance and Leasing Association	http://www.fla.org.uk
Union Bank of Switzerland	http://www.ubs.com

Index

Note: page numbers in **bold** denote glossary references.